Science of Swimming Faster

Scott Riewald, PhD
Scott Rodeo, MD

Editors

Human Kinetics

Library of Congress Cataloging-in-Publication Data

Science of swimming faster / Scott Riewald, PhD, Scott Rodeo, MD, editors.
   pages cm
 Includes bibliographical references and index.
1. Swimming--Training. 2. Swimming--Physiological aspects. 3. Sports sciences--Juvenile literature.
I. Riewald, Scott A., 1970- II. Rodeo, Scott.
 GV838.67.T73S45 2015
 797.2'1071--dc23

                              2014045348

 ISBN: 978-0-7360-9571-6 (print)

The web addresses cited in this text were current as of March 2015, unless otherwise noted.

Acquisitions Editor: Tom Heine; **Developmental Editor:** Cynthia McEntire; **Managing Editor:** Elizabeth Evans; **Proofreader:** Sarah Wiseman; **Copyeditor:** Bob Replinger; **Indexer:** Nan N. Badgett; **Permissions Manager:** Martha Gullo; **Graphic Designer:** Kim McFarland; **Cover Designer:** Keith Blomberg; **Photograph (cover):** Zuma Press/Icon SMI; **Photographs (interior):** Photos provided by the authors, unless otherwise noted; chapter 20 photos © Human Kinetics; **Visual Production Assistant:** Joyce Brumfield; **Photo Production Manager:** Jason Allen; **Art Manager:** Kelly Hendren; **Associate Art Manager:** Alan L. Wilborn; **Illustrations:** © Human Kinetics; **Printer:** Sheridan Books

Human Kinetics books are available at special discounts for bulk purchase. Special editions or book excerpts can also be created to specification. For details, contact the Special Sales Manager at Human Kinetics.

Printed in the United States of America   10   9   8   7   6   5   4   3   2   1

The paper in this book is certified under a sustainable forestry program.

Human Kinetics
Website: www.HumanKinetics.com

United States: Human Kinetics
P.O. Box 5076
Champaign, IL 61825-5076
800-747-4457
e-mail: humank@hkusa.com

Canada: Human Kinetics
475 Devonshire Road Unit 100
Windsor, ON N8Y 2L5
800-465-7301 (in Canada only)
e-mail: info@hkcanada.com

Europe: Human Kinetics
107 Bradford Road
Stanningley
Leeds LS28 6AT, United Kingdom
+44 (0) 113 255 5665
e-mail: hk@hkeurope.com

Australia: Human Kinetics
57A Price Avenue
Lower Mitcham, South Australia 5062
08 8372 0999
e-mail: info@hkaustralia.com

New Zealand: Human Kinetics
P.O. Box 80, Mitcham Shopping Centre
South Australia 5062
0800 222 062
e-mail: info@hknewzealand.com

E5192

I would like to thank my wife, Suzie, and children, Maddox and Callie, for all their patience, love, and support during the process of bringing this book together. You bring me energy, and this project wouldn't have happened without you. —Scott Riewald

This book is dedicated to my wife, Christine, and children, Sarah, Scott Jr., Caitlyn, and Mark, in recognition of their unwavering love and support. They are the anchor that provides perspective about what is truly important in life. —Scott Rodeo

Contents

Part III   Applied Sport Sciences

Preface

Welcome to *Science of Swimming Faster*, a unique book that blends the theory of swimming science and medicine with practical application. How many times have you read an article or book chapter describing some aspect of sport science and swimming yet walked away asking, "How am I supposed to apply this information with the athletes I work with?" *Science of Swimming Faster* aims to break down that barrier and bridge the gap between theory and practice—providing just enough theoretical foundation to show that the authors know what they are talking about before diving in to discuss what the information means to the swimmer in the water, the coach on the pool deck, or the parent in the stands.

The world of swimming has changed considerably over the past decade. We have seen the introduction of revolutionary new suits that have had a significant effect on performance. We've watched athletes take advantage of performance-enhancing substances, sometimes legally and sometimes illegally, to achieve a competitive advantage. We've seen modifications to the ways that athletes and coaches approach training and stroke technique, leading to faster and faster times. We are seeing increasing professionalization of swimming at the elite level. No stone is left unturned to achieve peak performances, and more attention and importance are placed on such areas as performance nutrition and sport psychology. Greater consideration is given to dissecting stroke technique and analyzing race performances to milk every drop of speed out of an athlete. It is true that as athletes get to the Olympic level, *everything* affects performance. We are now seeing this increased level of interest in the sport sciences and sports medicine funnel down to collegiate, high school, and age-group swimmers as well as to masters swimmers and triathletes. All swimmers seem to want to know what they can do to swim faster and more efficiently, while staying healthy and injury free. *Science of Swimming Faster* will help athletes and coaches of all abilities gain scientific insights that will positively affect performance.

Purpose

If you perform a search of the research literature related to swimming, you would quickly find hundreds of studies on myriad topics. But what can you do with this information? Most coaches and athletes simply don't have time to read and digest every research study that is published. Couple this with the fact that scientific articles do not typically present information in a user-friendly format, and it's easy to see why staying abreast of the latest advances can become a frustrating endeavor.

But those studies contain a lot of good information—if only it could be extracted and put in a format that is easy to understand and related directly to challenges faced by coaches and athletes in the real world of swimming. Enter *Science of Swimming Faster*. The information contained here is presented in an easy-to-understand manner, using swimming terminology and examples that will be familiar to coaches, athletes, and parents. Training suggestions and sample exercises make the information real and usable right out of the box (or book). As an added benefit to those who want to delve more deeply into a specific topic, each chapter provides a comprehensive reference list that will direct you to the most current research and publications.

Whether you are coach, a swimmer who swims competitively, or a swimmer who swims just to stay fit, you will benefit from the content in this book.

Content

Science of Swimming Faster is organized into four sections. Part I overviews the technical aspects of swimming. Chapters are dedicated to understanding the mechanics of swimming—that is, how swimmers generate propulsive force while reducing drag—and looking closely at stroke-specific aspects of technique. These chapters present the latest scientific information, from in-pool studies to computer simulations of performance. Additionally, this section looks at new and emerging technologies and ways in which they can be used to dissect the intricacies of stroke technique and improve in-water performance (chapter 7).

Part II focuses on training and competition. The question has often been asked, "What is the best way to prepare for competition, and do I really have to train three hours a day to compete in a race that lasts less than two minutes?" This section of *Science of Swimming Faster* looks at how the body responds to training and what can be done to prepare the body optimally for competition. Chapters are dedicated to topics such as the physiology of swimming, planning and periodization, and tapering. Information is presented about how elite athletes swim their races and what coaches and athletes can focus on to improve performances on race day.

Part III addresses other areas of sport science that have an effect on performance—areas such as nutrition, sport psychology, and injury and illness prevention. All these areas are important to swimming performance, but they are sometimes swept under the rug in favor of focusing only on technique or training. Also included is a chapter on growth and development and ways to maximize the long-term development of swimmers. Growth and development is a theme that weaves through almost every chapter in the book because it affects how athletes should be viewed and trained. As has been stated many times, young athletes are not simply small adults. How a coach trains a 10-year-old will differ dramatically from what the same coach would do with a 20-year-old. Remember that no matter how talented a 12-year-old is, he is not a fully mature Michael Phelps, and he should not be trained in the same way.

Finally, part IV addresses special swimming populations like the female athlete. We identify specific differences between males and females that coaches should keep in mind when working with this group of athletes. Additional chapters are devoted to masters swimmers, age-group swimmers, open water swimmers, and adaptive swimmers. No other resource on the market attempts to consolidate this type of information and present it in one place, let alone share ideas on how best to work with these athletes on the pool deck.

All in all, this is a one-of-a-kind book, and we hope you enjoy it. We're confident that the information contained in *Science of Swimming Faster* will lead you, whether you are a coach or an athlete, to new levels of performance.

PART

I

Swimming Mechanics and Technique

CHAPTER 1

Fluid Dynamics, Propulsion, and Drag

—Timothy Wei, PhD, Russell Mark, and Sean Hutchison

It is fair to say that at some time in their lives, swim coaches, swimmers, and swim parents (sweating in the bleachers of hot, humid swimming-pool facilities) have contemplated and discussed what exactly the water does when someone tries to swim through it. Over the decades, a language and a perceived knowledge base have evolved across the swimming community about the fluid dynamics of swimming. Although much of this understanding is sound, some key elements are either incorrect or have been misinterpreted, resulting in inefficient or counterproductive stroke technique.

The fluid dynamics of swimming is extremely complex. Understanding the process is further complicated by the fact that seeing what the water is doing as the swimmer goes by is not possible. Even worse, every swimmer is different. What works well for one swimmer could be counterproductive for another.

The primary objective of this chapter is to provide a primer on the fundamentals of fluid dynamics in the context of swimming. First, we cover the fundamentals, discussing the physics associated with drag and thrust production in a way that is rigorous and accurate without being daunting to the nonscientist. Next, in the section "Force and Flow Measurement," we provide a brief description of two of the state-of-the-art measurement techniques that have been brought to the study of swimming. The section "Application to Swimming" contains a discussion on the fundamental physics of the arm pull. The primary purpose of this culminating section is to provide the reader with a practical example of how the fundamentals of fluid dynamics can be applied to stroke analysis to provide an accurate understanding of what constitutes good stroke production.

Ultimately, no stroke will be perfect, but we open here with the observation that every swimmer is competing with and against the same laws of fluid dynamics. Understanding those laws in a practical way is crucial to developing rational approaches to swimming fast.

The Fundamentals

To gain an understanding of the fluid dynamics of swimming, we need to start with a discussion of some of the basic physical principles. When we discuss scientific concepts, everyone in the conversation needs to understand the terms we use. Words such as *velocity, acceleration, force,* and *pressure* have distinct meanings, so they cannot be used interchangeably. In this section, we introduce the key terms and concepts that we will need to know to gain a true understanding of the fluid dynamics of swimming.

Newton's Second Law: The Critical Balance Between Thrust and Drag

A saying in the academic engineering community is that every time you show an equation, you lose half the audience. Unfortunately, mathematics is the language of physics, so talking about the fluid dynamics of swimming is virtually impossible without using equations. Fortunately, in the case of swimming, almost everything stems from a single equation: Newton's second law. In its simplest form, we know it as

$$F = Ma$$

or force is equal to mass times acceleration. That is, in order for a body of mass, M, to undergo an acceleration, a (i.e., to increase velocity with time), we need to apply a force, F.

In real life, F is often not just a single force. Rather, it is the sum of a number of forces acting on the body, sometimes simultaneously, sometimes at different times. In swimming, for example, the swimmer pulls with her arms, kicks with her legs, and possibly throws in some sort of dolphin motion. The forces created by these body motions vary with time and do not all occur at the same time, though presumably an elite swimmer has figured out how to coordinate these forces in an optimum way to go as fast as possible. These propulsive forces are counteracted by the resistance of the water to the swimmer's attempts to move through it.

We can classify the propulsive forces as thrust forces and those that oppose motion as drag forces. We can rewrite Newton's second law as

$$\text{thrust forces} - \text{drag forces} = Ma$$

or for simplicity, let's just write it as

$$T - D = Ma$$

Here, T represents all of the propulsive forces and D represents all of the forces that resist forward motion.

Note that when we write Newton's second law in this manner, we can draw the following insights. If the thrust forces are larger than the drag forces (T > D), the swimmer will speed up. If the drag is too great, the swimmer will either slow down (D > T) or will have to work a lot harder (i.e., increase T) to maintain speed. Finally, regardless of how fast the swimmer is swimming, at a constant speed the thrust exactly offsets the drag (T = D).

In the context of swimming then, Newton's second law states that a competitive swimmer needs to maximize thrust while minimizing drag. Maximizing thrust comes from building strength and improving technique, and minimizing drag is optimized primarily through adjusting body position in the water. We will return to this thought at the end of this section.

Note that noncompetitive swimmers who swim primarily for fitness do not need to worry about minimizing drag. The greater the drag is on the swimmer, the more calories the swimmer will burn. Still, using those calories to go far or fast and at less risk of injury is more satisfying.

The next step in this overall discussion is to explore in detail some of the fluid dynamic principles associated with drag and thrust. Before doing that, however, we need to throw another equation into the mix, Bernoulli's equation. This equation relates pressure with flow speed, a concept important in applications from airplane design to swimming.

Bernoulli's Equation

In 1738 Dutch-Swiss mathematician Daniel Bernoulli published the derivation of an important relation that now bears his name. At its core, it is a mechanical energy equation for fluid flows that relates the pressure and fluid speed at one location in the flow to the pressure and speed at another location.

Derivation of the Bernoulli equation involves integrating the forces experienced by a fluid particle as it travels along a streamline from one location to another. In one respect, this is a pressure equation with units of force per unit area or (mass / length / time^2). The units of the terms in the equation also can be viewed as kinetic energy per unit volume (mass $\times$ length^2 / time^2 / length^3), which becomes (mass / length / time^2). That the Bernoulli equation is a mechanical energy equation stems from the derivation and from the dimensions of the terms in the equation.

In a somewhat simplified form, the Bernoulli equation is

$$p_o = p_1 + 1/2\ \rho V_1^2 = p_2 + 1/2\ \rho V_2^2$$

Here, p, ρ, and V refer to pressure, fluid density, and flow velocity, respectively. The subscripts $_1$ and $_2$ refer to two arbitrary locations in the flow where we might be interested in comparing pressure and velocity. The first term, p_o, represents what is known as either the stagnation pressure or total pressure. It is the pressure that would result if it were possible to bring the flow to rest, that is, V = 0.

The Bernoulli equation may be thought of as a mechanical energy equation; that is, total mechanical energy in the fluid = potential energy in the fluid at some location + kinetic energy associated with the moving fluid at that same location.

To understand this better, consider a highly pressurized tank of fluid. Initially, the tank is closed. The fluid is at rest, and its pressure is as high as it will ever be. When the tank is opened, the pressure starts to drop as fluid flows out. The initial pressure in the closed tank is the total pressure, p_0. It is the maximum potential energy (per unit volume) that the fluid will ever have.

When the tank is opened, fluid starts flowing out; a conversion of energy occurs from potential energy to kinetic energy. Those familiar with physics will recognize that the term in Bernoulli's equation, $1/2 \, \rho V_1^2$, indeed looks like kinetic energy ($1/2 \, MV^2$, where M is mass and V is velocity). Because density, ρ, is mass per unit volume, then $1/2 \, \rho V_1^2$ can be understood as kinetic energy per unit volume of fluid. As such, this is probably the easiest term to recognize in terms of physical meaning. We call this the dynamic pressure.

The remaining term, that is, the pressure in the fluid, p_1 (or p_2) in Bernoulli's equation, corresponds to the potential energy of the fluid at those locations. This works out to be the difference of the total pressure and the dynamic pressure. Alternatively, this is the potential energy that remains after you convert some of the maximum possible potential energy (the pressure of the fluid at rest) into kinetic energy (hence the name, dynamic pressure). If the static pressure, p_1 or p_2, were ever to drop to zero, that would mean that all the original energy available in the flow had been converted entirely to kinetic energy; that is, this is as fast as the flow could possibly go.

So, in summary, p_0 is total energy, $1/2 \, \rho V_1^2$ is kinetic energy or dynamic pressure, and p is the potential energy or static pressure remaining in the fluid as it moves with speed, V. The Bernoulli equation provides a relationship between t e speed of the water flowing past some part of the body and the pressure of the water at that point. For a competitive swimmer in a competition swimming pool, the total pressure is constant. Thus, if the fluid slows down, the static pressure goes up. If the fluid is moving quickly, then the static pressure in the high-speed fluid will be low. Observe that if the flow speed changes by a factor of two, then the static pressure will change by a factor of four because pressure varies as velocity squared. Additionally, keep in mind that Bernoulli's equation applies under specific conditions (e.g., constant density fluids with no viscosity). For our purposes, the general physical insight provided by this equation is extremely helpful. The key point to remember is that if we are looking at two points in the flow, say, for example, on either side of the hand, if the water is flowing faster over one side than the other, then the pressure will be lower where the flow is faster. If the speeds are the same on either side of the hand, the pressure will be the same as well.

Drag

We now turn to the forces acting on or generated by a body in water. Let's define drag as any force opposing motion of a body or body part in a particular direction.

The three types of drag are pressure drag, viscous drag, and wave drag. Pressure drag is also known as bluff body drag. As the alternative name implies, this is most dominant when the body is not streamlined, or bluff. Consider for instance, how you have to lean into the wind on a windy day, shown schematically in figure 1.1. As the moving air approaches your body, it decelerates. And we know from the Bernoulli equation that decreasing speed means increasing pressure.

Remember that pressure is force divided by area, or, conversely, force caused by pressure is pressure multiplied by an appropriate area. It is incorrect, although common, to use the terms *pressure* and *force* interchangeably. This error is perhaps the greatest contributor to incorrect analysis and understanding of the fluid dynamics associated with swimming.

Pressure Drag and Viscous Drag

In an ideal fluid, figure 1.1*a*, the flow would smoothly accelerate around your body and then decelerate again as it passes around to your back. Note that in this ideal case, the flow is symmetric front to back. From the Bernoulli equation, we would then expect that the pressure on the back of your body would exactly return to the pressure on the front of your body. In this scenario, because the pressure is the same front to back, you wouldn't feel any force pushing on you. Fluid dynamicists refer to this situation as complete pressure recovery. The concept that you could somehow move through the wind without feeling any resistance is what is known as d'Alembert's paradox.

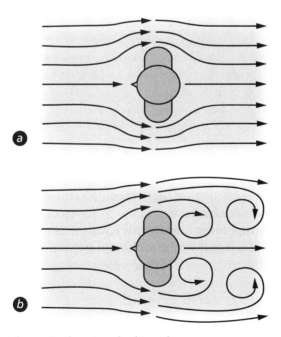

▶ **Figure 1.1** Schematic drawings looking down at a person standing facing into a steady wind. Flow is from left to right. The ideal case is shown in (*a*) on the top, and the actual case, (*b*), appears on the bottom.

In real life, of course, the harder the wind is blowing, the more you have to lean into the wind to avoid being blown over. A great deal of turbulence (lots of interacting vortices) is generated behind your body. The flow doesn't return to being nice and smooth after it passes behind your body. Rather, what is called a wake region is found behind your body, shown in figure 1.1*b*, and the pressure immediately behind you does not return to the same level as the pressure in front of you. Now a pressure difference is seen between the front and back of your body; the higher pressure is in front, and the lower pressure is in back. The net force acting against you is the pressure on the front of your body minus the pressure on the back of your body multiplied by the projected frontal area of your body, represented mathematically as

$$\text{pressure drag} = (p_{front} - p_{back})A_{front}$$

The projected frontal area is the area of the silhouette that would be formed if someone were to shine a spotlight from behind you with you standing facing a wall. That frontal area would naturally be the same whether you were standing facing the wall or standing with your back to the wall. Because p_{front} is larger than p_{back}, you feel the wind pushing you backward as you try to move forward into it.

This phenomenon is called pressure drag or bluff body drag. If the body shape does not allow the flow to travel smoothly from front to back, then pressure drag will be significant. If, however, the body shape permits smooth flow all the way around, if the body is streamlined like a wing, then pressure drag will be minimal or nonexistent. That does not mean that the drag will be zero. All real fluids are viscous, which means there is always a frictional resistance to motion through or by a fluid. To visualize this, think about a brand new deck of cards. Imagine that you set the deck on a flat horizontal table and place the palm of your hand flat on top of the deck. Now imagine sliding your hand horizontally to the right, as shown in figure 1.2. If the cards were perfectly frictionless, they would not sense the motion of your hand and the entire deck would stay put. In figure 1.2, the deck set on the table appears as dark rectangles with light edges. The deck after the application of the sliding force, *F*, is shown as grey rectangles. Clearly, if no friction were present, the before and after pictures would be identical and look like figure 1.2*a*.

In reality, some amount of friction is present between your hand and the top card, between the table and the bottom card, and between the individual adjacent cards in the deck. In that case, when your hand moves parallel to the table top, the top card moves with your hand, the bottom card sticks to the table, and all the cards in between move by varying amounts depending on how close they are to either the table or your hand. This concept is illustrated in figure 1.2*b*. The closer the cards are to your hand, the more they will move. The closer they are to the table, the less they will move. The card closest to the table is held in place by the frictional force between the table and that card. The top card experiences a frictional force imparted by the movement of your hand, which drags it forward at the same speed as your hand. Each card in between

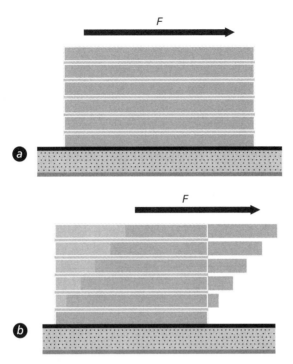

▶ **Figure 1.2** Comparison between frictionless, ideal flow (*a*) and flow with friction (*b*). The rectangles represent different layers of fluid, or laminates. The arrows labeled **F** indicate a sliding force applied to the fluid layers.

the top and bottom cards experiences a force pulling it forward from the card above and a resisting frictional force imparted by the card below. In the end, the entire deck starts to lean.

Think of viscous or frictional drag in a similar fashion. Instead of playing cards, think of the rectangles in figure 1.2 as imaginary layers or laminates of fluid. Think of the tabletop as a streamlined body, say a wing on an airplane. In this analogy, we would be sitting inside the airplane looking out the window. The wing looks as if it is stationary, and the air is flowing over the wing from left to right. If the flow were frictionless, as shown in figure 1.2*a*, the grey rectangles would all shift to the right by an equal amount like a giant cardboard box being blown along the wing. The picture for viscous, or frictional flow, figure 1.2*b*, however, would be exactly the same as it was for the deck of cards. The layer of air closest to the wing would stick to the wing and move with the wing. From our vantage point looking out the window, it would appear as if it were stationary. Far away from the wing, the air would simply blow on by. In the region referred to as the boundary layer the air speed would vary from zero at the boundary out to the speed at which the plane is flying. This boundary layer region is typically very thin. Over the wing of a large commercial airliner, it could be only a few inches (5 to 10 cm) thick before the air passed over the trailing edge of the wing.

Wave Drag

The third form of drag relevant to swimming is wave drag. Probably the simplest way to gain a conceptual understanding is to remember that as a body moves through any fluid, a bow wave forms in front of the body. For a boat or a swimmer, this wave is clearly visible. Below a certain speed, the bow wave sits in front of the swimmer and the swimmer is essentially swimming uphill, trying to get on top of the wave but never getting there. This phenomenon is known as wave drag.

For every object, there is a critical speed at which it is possible for the object to climb up on top of the bow wave. This speed is known as the hull speed. The formula for calculating the speed at which a body can overcome its own wave drag is

$$V_{hull} = 1.248 \times \sqrt{H}$$

where V_{hull} is the hull's, that is, the swimmer's, speed in meters per second and $\sqrt{H}$ is the square root of the height of the swimmer expressed in meters.

When V_{hull} is achieved or exceeded, the swimmer is in a sense surfing her own bow wave. When this happens, the wave drag drops dramatically and the speed can increase equally dramatically. To visualize this, think of a motorboat when you first try to get it to go as fast as it can and then when it later gets to high speed. When you first push the throttle forward, the hull is deep in the water. The bow rides very high, the back of the boat is very low, and the boat essentially plows through the water. When the boat speed exceeds its hull speed, the boat rises out of the water and can accelerate to high speeds by planing across the top of the water.

The reason that wave drag is so interesting is that the hull speed of a human swimmer turns out to be right around the same speed as world-class swimming speeds. As a rough estimate, suppose a swimmer is about 2 meters tall; his hull speed would be 1.76 meters per second. This speed translates to a 56.7-second time in a 100-meter race. We are, of course, neglecting the start and turn, but you will notice that only a relatively few swimmers can swim faster than this.

So the next time you are watching an elite-level race, watch how high or how low the swimmers are in the water. If you are watching the preliminary heats, you will probably notice that on average the faster swimmers ride higher in the water whereas the slower swimmers are lower in the water. Of course, other variables such as percentage and distribution of body fat will cause certain swimmers to float higher or lower. The polyurethane and neoprene body suits that were used in 2008 through 2009 were extremely helpful to many swimmers in terms of buoyancy. They automatically sat higher in the water and gained much of the benefit of overcoming wave drag without having to generate the speed necessary to overcome it.

As a quick summary up to this point, the three forms of drag experienced by a swimmer are pressure or bluff body drag, viscous or friction drag, and wave drag. Pressure drag and wave drag are the dominant forms of drag in swimming. Friction drag dominates only for very streamlined bodies such as airplanes or animals that depend on high-speed swimming or flight for survival. In those cases, friction becomes dominant not because frictional drag increases but because the pressure drag is extremely small, by virtue of body shape. Note that fish and birds typically do not move at the air or water interface like competitive swimmers do. As such, their wave drag is zero. In any event, swimmers can do little to eliminate viscous drag. Their focus needs to be on optimizing body position to reduce pressure drag and optimizing stroke production to maximize thrust. Swimmers need to be constantly winning the battle between thrust and drag by both maximizing thrust and minimizing drag.

Thrust

With this thought in mind, let's spend some time on the fluid dynamics of thrust. The underlying question in this discussion is, What must a swimmer do to make the water move in such a way as to generate as much thrust (i.e., speed) as possible?

Two thrust generation mechanisms are dominant in competitive swimming: the thrust associated with the pull of the arms and vortex-induced thrust in which body motions create an organized system of vortices that effectively pump fluid along the axis of the body. A third mechanism derived from wing theory gave rise to the S stroke popular in the 1960s and 1970s that continues at the club level today. Because of the legacy surrounding the S stroke, we will examine the underlying aerodynamic theory to provide a framework for comparing the straight pull with the S stroke.

Actually, a variety of physically accurate ways can be used to explain each of the thrust production mechanisms. For ease of comparison, the best approach is to use a single physical concept and relate each of the mechanisms to that concept. Consider the example of an ice skater standing on a smooth sheet of ice holding a ball of significant mass. At some instant in time, the skater brings the ball to his chest and throws it by pushing it away from his chest. You have likely heard of the law of equal and opposite reaction or possibly the conservation of linear momentum. In this example, when the skater throws the ball forward, he ends up being propelled backward. How much or how fast each one moves depends on their relative weights (or to be precise, their relative masses). If the ball happens to be a small balloon filled with air, the balloon will move and the skater's backward motion will be negligible. But if the ball were the same weight as the skater, each would move an equal distance in their respective directions. If the ball were as heavy as a train locomotive (let's not worry about how he manages to pick it up), it would be the skater who moves backward.

The takeaway from this example is that to propel himself forward, the swimmer must somehow take as much water as possible and throw it along the axis of his body past his feet. This action will propel him forward in the water. The trick is that water doesn't come in easily grabbed balls. Those balls of water are in fact the same stuff that the swimmer is trying to push his way through. It's slippery stuff. The swimmer must learn how to work with the water to push as much of it past his feet as quickly and effectively as possible. How he does this is through technique.

One way to propel water along the body and past the feet is to set up a system of counter-rotating vortices that pump fluid between them in a particular direction. An easy way to envision this is to think of a baseball pitching machine consisting of two rubber wheels that are very close together and spinning in opposite directions. When a baseball is dropped between the two wheels, it is squeezed through the gap and shot out by the spinning action of the wheels. The direction of the ball will be perpendicular to the line connecting the centers of the two spinning wheels.

This example illustrates the principle of vortex-induced thrust. Another example of this phenomenon is found in a swimming eel, shown in figure 1.3. As the eel undulates along, it generates vortices on either side of its body. If you think of the body undulations as a wave, the vortices form in the peaks and valleys of the waves as shown in the figure. How those vortices are created is beyond the scope of this discussion. What is important is the orientation and interaction of the system of vortices. Observe that the two vortices on the top of the figure (i.e., on the eel's left side) rotate in a clockwise direction. Conversely, the two vortices on the eel's right rotate in a counterclockwise direction. Next, note that if you were to choose a vortex on one side of the eel's body, the vortex closest to the one you've chosen is on the opposite side of the eel. Finally, if you think of the vortex you've selected and the vortex closest to it, those two vortices form a counter-rotating pair. That is, they are two vortices that rotate in opposite directions like the two spinning rubber wheels on the baseball pitching machine.

This counter-rotating vortex pair pumps fluid backward along the eel's body, which in turn propels the eel forward. The vortex pumping action is indicated by the arrows along the eel's body. The entire vortex system acts to pump water along the eel from the head to the tail. The result is a continuous pumping of

▶ **Figure 1.3** Schematic drawing of a swimming eel, the system of vortices it creates through its body motions, and the thrust generated by the pumping action of the vortices on opposite sides of the eel's body.

fluid and a continuous generation of thrust. If the eel wants to accelerate for any reason, it snaps its body to create a high-energy wave, producing a system of much stronger vortices that pump more water, faster, along the axis of its body. This mechanism is how the dolphin kick works.

The second dominant thrust production mechanism in competitive swimming comes from the arm motions in each stroke. Keeping with our concept of throwing water backward, the arms and hands push as much water as possible toward the feet. The arms must move in a manner to maximize both the amount and the speed of the water being pushed backward.

There is an alternative way to think about this. Let's return to the earlier discussion on bluff body drag. Recall that we talked about pressure differences between the front of the bluff body and the rear. We discussed that in real flows past bluff bodies, the flow separates from the body, creating a wake region; the pressure does not recover behind the body, resulting in higher pressure in front and lower pressure behind. For a body moving forward, for instance, if you stick your arm out the window of a moving car with your palm facing forward, the net action of the pressure difference multiplied by the frontal area of the arm and hand results in a drag force opposing the forward motion.

In the case of the arm stroke, however, the arm moves in the direction opposite the swimming direction. If we think of the hand and arm combination as a single bluff body with the palm of the hand typically facing toward the feet, then the pressure on the palm side of the hand and arm will be higher (we hope significantly higher) than the pressure on the back side. In this case, the drag experienced by the arm pushing backward through the water is actually a thrust for the swimmer. In this context, thrust produced by the arm is drag backward.

Wing Theory and Lift

Before closing out this section on the fundamentals of fluid dynamics, let's examine the concept of lift generated by wings. This idea is important in the context of swimming because it is the underlying phenomenon that gave rise to the S-shape pull pattern that misdirected many thoughts on ideal swimming biomechanics.

The concept is that the swimmer can generate thrust by sweeping the hand outward initially and then inward toward the centerline of the body during the front half of the pull; this is the top of the S. The swimmer then moves the hand outward again during the back half of the pull. In so doing, the hand acts like a wing, particularly in the inward sweep. We will examine this in detail in the discussion of the pull. At this point, we will focus on the underlying theory of wings.

Figure 1.4 is a sketch of a simple cambered wing. Camber means the wing is not symmetric top to bottom. In this case, the upper surface is curved whereas the bottom surface is essentially flat. The direction of the incoming wind is shown with an arrow labeled with the speed, V. Notice that the wing is at an angle of attack, α, meaning that the wing is tilted up (or down) by an angle we

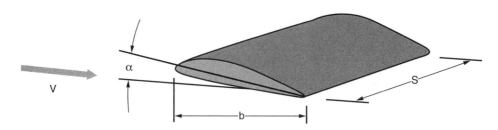

▶ **Figure 1.4** Sketch of a rectangular wing flying at angle of attack, α, in a steady wind of speed V. Key dimensions, chord and span, are indicated in the drawing.

denote with the Greek letter α. The wing is said to have a chord length, b, and a span, S. For a rectangular wing, the wing planform area is simply the product of the chord length and the span, that is, $A_{plan} = b \times S$. This is the projected area, or the area of the silhouette of the wing from a viewpoint looking straight down on the wing.

As air flows around the wing, the airspeed on top of the wing will be faster than the speed under the wing, simply because air must travel a greater distance over the top of the wing than under the bottom. If you've read the discussion of the Bernoulli equation, you will understand the consequence that the pressure on the upper surface of the wing is lower than the pressure on the lower surface. We refer to the upper and lower surfaces of the wing as the suction and pressure surfaces, respectively. Let's say those pressures are p_{upper} and p_{lower}. From our discussion of pressure drag, we know that the net lift force, L, experienced by the wing is

$$L = (p_{lower} - p_{upper})A_{plan}$$

In aerodynamics it is common to express lift in terms of a lift coefficient, C_L, defined by

$$C_L = L / (1/2\ \rho V^2 A_{plan})$$

The lift coefficient is a specific form of a more generalized force coefficient, $C_F = F / (1/2\ \rho V^2 A)$, where F can be any force of interest (typically lift or drag) and V and A are a speed and area, respectively, that are characteristically associated with the force.

The purpose for this is that it is possible to compare different wing designs by comparing plots of lift coefficient as a function of angle of attack, that is, C_L versus α. A characteristic C_L versus α curve for a simple cambered airfoil like that shown in figure 1.4 is shown in figure 1.5.

The important features of figure 1.5 are that lift, that is, C_L, increases almost linearly with angle of attack up to a limit, continues to increase albeit not at the same rate, reaches a maximum, C_{Lmax}, and then drops off dramatically. The steep drop-off in lift is because of stall, when flow no longer smoothly follows the upper wing surface but instead separates much in the manner of a bluff body.

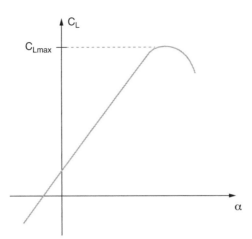

▶ **Figure 1.5** Characteristic plot of lift on a wing versus angle of attack. Observe that after lift reaches a maximum, the wing stalls and lift is dramatically lost.

For simple wings, $C_{Lmax} \approx 1$. This typically occurs at angles of attack, α, between 10 and 15 degrees. Modern commercial airliners use complex systems of flaps to increase C_{Lmax} to as high as 3.5 to 4.0 during crucial times such as takeoff and landing. These planes are also designed to fly at angles of attack much lower than maximum lift to avoid the disastrous consequences of small changes in angle of attack leading to stall.

When applied to swimming, the hand is presumably acting as the wing. The lift on the wing becomes a thrust force when the hand sweeps inward toward the centerline of the body in the S stroke. You can calculate the thrust that could be generated by such a motion in which the wing planform area, A_{plan}, would be roughly the projected area of the hand; the flight speed, V, would be roughly the speed at which the swimmer sweeps her hand across her body in the S stroke. (Note that this is distinctly different from the speed at which the swimmer is swimming or the speed at which her hand moves in the direction from head to feet.) We will use some representative numbers when we discuss the fluid dynamics of the arm pull.

Force and Flow Measurement

Up to this point, we have been discussing in a somewhat theoretical way forces that swimmers apply to the water. You have likely gained some practical insights into fluid mechanics that will be helpful with respect to swimming. In this section, we provide a description of some of the state-of-the-art measurement systems used in fluid mechanics.

Ultimately, the challenge to understanding the fluid dynamics of swimming is knowing exactly what the water is doing as the swimmer swims through it and what resulting forces the swimmer generates. Two key advances in flow and force measurement techniques have made it possible to provide time-resolved data of both flow and force.

The first of these is an adaptation of a noninvasive flow measurement technique called digital particle image velocimetry (DPIV), a term first coined by Willert and Gharib in 1991. The technique employs a high-resolution digital video camera to record flow seeded with very small reflective particles. Every individual video image in the recording is then captured and stored in a computer as raw data.

A DPIV processing program takes pairs of successive video frames in the recording (known as DPIV image pairs) and computes how much the seed particles have moved from one frame to the next. An example of how this process works appears in figure 1.6. Two successive video frames taken from flow past a cylinder are shown in figures 1.6a and 1.6b. Note that the images shown are only about 10 percent of the full frames. You can see the cylinder on the left side of both images and many little white dots that are reflections of laser light off small silver-coated glass spheres. In the lower right of figure 1.6a a white square has been drawn around a group of particles. In the second frame, figure 1.6b, the particles have moved. The previous location of the particles is shown as a square with a dotted white line. The new location of the particles is indicated by a square with a solid white line. Assuming that the particles move exactly with the flow, the flow velocity associated with the water in the square region shown is then simply the particle displacement divided by the time between images. In practice, the computer is programmed to subdivide the two frames into identical grids of small squares like the one shown in figure 1.6a. By repeating the velocity calculation for the entire video frame and for every image pair in the video record, we can generate movies of the fluid velocity everywhere in the camera field of view.

Examples of DPIV measurements of flow around swimmers are shown in figures 1.7 and 1.8. Figure 1.7 shows flow from the feet of Megan Jendrick as she is doing a breaststroke kick. This single still frame was taken from a movie in which small air bubbles were used as the seeding particles. The movie was generated by filming Megan swimming in a flume with the bubbles in the water. We calculated the velocity vectors for each pair of video frames in the video sequence and then overlaid the measured velocities on top of the original video images.

In this single frame, Megan's feet can be observed just as she is beginning the power stroke of her kick. She is swimming to the right, and her body has passed out of the field of view. Only her ankles and feet appear in this frame. Notice the long dark vectors pointing straight back from the bottoms of her feet. This particular image was used in an analysis of breaststroke kicking that led to an understanding that the thrust generated during the kick was probably best thought of as having the feet push water straight back in the thrust direction. The strength of Megan's kick greatly contributed to her winning gold in the 100 breaststroke event at the 2000 Olympics in Sydney.

Figure 1.8 is another single still frame showing an overlay of the original video frame and the corresponding flow vectors. In this example, flow associated with Ariana Kukors' freestyle pull is highlighted. In this image, Ariana's head and upper torso are visible. The key feature of figure 1.8 is the long dark vectors extending from Ariana's right hand as she engages the water early (i.e.,

▶ **Figure 1.6** Two successive video images taken of flow past a cylinder. Flow is left to right, and the downstream half of the cylinder appears on the left. The small white dots are images of small silver-coated glass seed particles illuminated by laser light. It is possible to see how the particles have moved from the first frame (*a*) to the next (*b*). For example, observe how the particles identified by the white square have moved up and to the left.

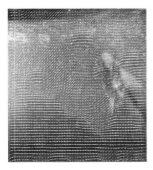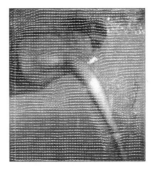

▶ **Figure 1.7** Instantaneous DPIV vector field showing the flow generated by Megan Jendrick's breaststroke kick. Note the long dark vectors pointing away from the bottom of her right foot.

▶ **Figure 1.8** Instantaneous DPIV vector field showing the flow generated by Ariana Kukors' freestyle stroke. Note the high elbow position and the long dark vectors pointing away from her right hand and arm.

uses a high elbow) and pushes water backward. Ariana's freestyle was part of a winning combination that led her to break the world record in the 200 IM twice as she took gold in that event at the 2009 World Championships.

Besides measuring flow, we can also directly measure forces generated by swimmers. This is done using a force balance shown in figure 1.9. This is essentially a much larger scale model of force measurement devices used in wind tunnels to measure forces on airplane models.

As shown in figure 1.9, the balance consists of a steel frame, shown as black lines. If the swimmer pushes on either bar A-A or bar Aρ-Aρ, a time-varying force, F(t), will be applied to the frame. In the figure, a swimmer is shown doing an underwater dolphin kick and is pushing on bar A-A. Two load cells, or force sensors, are mounted on the vertical frame elements, A-C, to measure the vertical component of the applied force. At the same time, load cells are mounted on the top two horizontal frame elements to measure the horizontal component of the force applied by the swimmer.

A single frame from a video recording of Ariana Kukors' flutter kick is shown in figure 1.10. In this video Ariana is kicking against the force balance that is

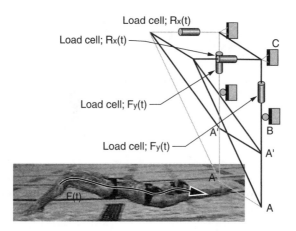

▶ **Figure 1.9** Schematic drawing of the two-component force balance used to measure forces generated by swimmers. The swimmer pushes on either bar A-A below the surface or Aρ-Aρ at the surface.

out of view to the left. The signal trace under the video image is the time trace of Ariana's force. The way the video is set up, it is possible to watch Ariana kick while the force trace sweeps across the bottom of the screen like an oscilloscope signal. Time is indicated on the horizontal axis, and the force generated is plotted on the vertical axis. The vertical line at t = 0 in the middle of the time trace corresponds to the time that the particular video frame was recorded. So the force output of 30 pounds (14 kg) at t = 0 is the force that Ariana generated while she was kicking downward with her left leg.

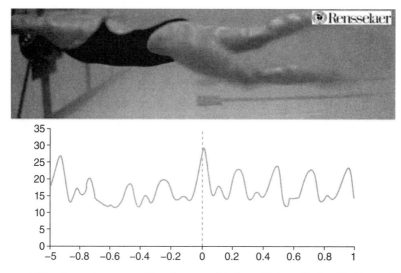

▶ **Figure 1.10** Instantaneous video image of Ariana Kukors flutter kicking with force readout below. The vertical axis is force, and the horizontal axis is time. The center of the plot, t = 0, corresponds to the video frame shown. Ariana is generating a force of about 30 pounds (14 kg) with the downward kick of her left leg.

The smaller peaks between the larger peaks on the time trace are particularly interesting. The larger peaks are spaced roughly 0.25 seconds apart, and the peak force was generally between 20 and 25 pounds (between 9 and 11 kg). Each peak corresponds to the downward kick of one of Ariana's legs. As noted, the peak at t = 0 corresponds to a left-leg kick. The peak to the right of that is a right-leg kick. The one immediately after that is another left-leg kick and so on.

Note the smaller peaks between the larger ones. These are the forces generated when Ariana kicks backward, or up toward the water surface. The ability to quantify the force generated during this reverse kick shows the power of the measurement technique. Clearly, this force is significantly less than that generated during the downward, or forward, kick. This result is not surprising; when was the last time you saw a soccer player run up to a ball backward and kick a hard shot past a diving goalie? The data create the opportunity for the coach and swimmer to discuss the relative benefits of generating this additional thrust at the cost of using energy that might be needed at the end of a race.

Application to Swimming: Optimizing the Arm Pull

We end this chapter with a discussion of how the fundamentals presented can be meaningfully and accurately brought into the analysis of a swimming stroke. Although four distinct strokes are used in competitive swimming, the arm pull for all of them share a characteristic that we will focus on in this chapter. In particular, swimmers need to catch the water as early as possible and get as much of the forearms as possible perpendicular to the swimming direction. The swimmer should get her hands and forearms pointed straight down toward the bottom of the pool as quickly as possible, especially for the free and fly. For the backstroke, the hand does not point down, but the forearm and hand should become aligned perpendicular to the swimmer's long axis as quickly as possible. This happens, of course, after the start of the pull and not before. Otherwise, the arms are a major source of drag.

When the pull is initiated in this way, we can think of the swimmer trying to move her arms backward in the direction opposite where she wants to go. While the arm is being pushed along the body toward the feet, the resulting drag force on the arm is actually toward the head in the thrust direction. This is the concept of drag backward discussed earlier. By getting the arms perpendicular to the swim direction as early as possible, the swimmer maximizes this drag backward and therefore maximizes thrust. Because this chapter is not a primer on stroke technique, the swimmer and her coach need to work out the mechanics of this concept to maximize thrust at the highest possible rate (i.e., stroke count) while maintaining good body position in the water.

At this point, we return to the discussion of the S stroke. The purpose here is to explain why elite swimmers and coaches today are emphasizing the straight-line pull as opposed to an S stroke. This approach is counter to a decades-long perception of proper swim technique.

The rationale for the S stroke can be easily understood by thinking about what happens when you stick your hand out of a moving car window with your hand slightly cupped and your palm facing down. If you twist your hand so that the thumb is slightly higher than the pinky finger, you will feel your hand being pushed up. If you twist your hand in the opposite direction so the thumb is lower than the pinky, then you will feel your hand being pushed down. In effect, you are using your hand as a small wing. If you twist your hand too far, so that the palm faces forward into the direction you are traveling, you will, of course, feel the bluff body drag discussed previously.

Developers and proponents of the S stroke believed that by pulling diagonally across the body, a swimmer combined the effects of bluff body thrust and hydro-dynamic lift. To test this reasoning, we will do a simple quantitative analysis in the following paragraphs. It is sufficient to note that the S stroke likely produces about 8 to 18 percent less thrust than the straight pull used at the top levels of swimming today.

For this comparison, we need to recall the definition of the force coefficient, $C_F = F / (1/2 \; \rho V^2 A)$, which can be written either as a drag coefficient, C_D, or a lift coefficient, C_L. We next make a number of physically justifiable approximations to simplify the analysis without unduly skewing the conclusions. The first of these approximations is that the swimmer's arm speed during the pull will essentially be the same regardless of whether he does a straight pull or an S pull. The second approximation is that $C_D \approx 1.0$ on the arm. This estimate is based on knowledge that $C_D = 1.0$ for a circular cylinder of the same diameter and speed as a typical arm.

The final assumption is not entirely correct, but we will err in favor of the S stroke. Specifically, we assume that the lift coefficient of the hand will also be unity, so $C_L \approx 1.0$. For small private planes, wing lift coefficients of 1.0 are common. To assume that the hand performs as a lifting surface as well as a Cessna wing is generous.

Figure 1.11 is a simplified schematic comparing the hand trajectories for an S stroke and a straight pull. The heavy dashed curve on the far left of the figure represents the path taken by the left hand of a swimmer when viewed from above. The straight solid black arrow on the far right of the sketch represents the trajectory of the right hand for a straight pull. The velocity of the hand in the straight pull is indicated by the shorter vertical downward arrow labeled $V_{straight}$. Recall that for a velocity vector, the length of the arrow corresponds to the speed and the orientation of the arrow indicates direction.

Immediately to the right of the S stroke hand trajectory is a triangle made of dashed velocity vectors. The vector pointing down and to the left, labeled V_S, denotes the hand velocity through about the top 60 percent of the stroke. Note that we have assumed that the magnitude of V_S is the same as the magnitude of $V_{straight}$. You will therefore find that the lengths of the V_S and $V_{straight}$ arrows are equal. The other two vectors, $V_{S\text{-}thrust}$ and $V_{S\text{-}lift}$, making up the triangle represent the two components of V_S in the thrust and lift directions (i.e., the swim and cross-body directions, respectively).

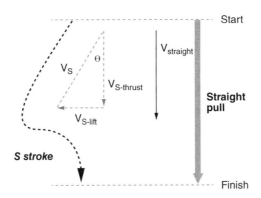

▶ **Figure 1.11** Comparison on the hand trajectories of an S stroke (left) and a straight pull (right). The vector triangle shows the velocity of the S stroke pull broken into components in the swim or thrust direction and the cross-body or lift direction. Note that the net stroke lengths are the same and that the lengths of V_S and $V_{straight}$ are the same; that is, the arm speed is the same for both strokes.

When comparing the two strokes using the corresponding velocity vector diagrams, you should immediately observe that $V_{straight}$ is longer than $V_{S\text{-thrust}}$. If we define the angle between $V_{S\text{-thrust}}$ and V_S as θ, as shown in figure 1.11, then the length of $V_{S\text{-thrust}}$ will be

$$V_{S\text{-thrust}} = V_S \cos\theta$$

But because $V_S = V_{straight}$, the ratio of $V_{S\text{-thrust}} / V_{straight}$ will be cosθ. If θ ranges between 20 and 30 degrees, then the arm speed in the direction of motion will be 6 to 13 percent slower than for a straight arm pull. Recall that the bluff body thrust is $1/2 \, \rho V^2 A_{arm} C_D$ and that the drag coefficient, C_D, is 1.0 for the arm regardless of whether it is an S or straight pull. The area of the arm, A_{arm}, presented to the flow will also not be significantly different for the two strokes. So ultimately, then, the difference in thrust between the two strokes is the difference between $V_{S\text{-thrust}}^2$ and $V_{straight}^2$. If the difference in velocity is 6 to 13 percent, then the difference in velocity squared, or thrust, is 12 to 26 percent. The straight arm pull produces significantly greater bluff body thrust.

For a swimmer doing an S stroke, the lift generated by the hand from the sideways motion across the body must make up for that lost thrust. The thrust generated by the sweeping motion of the hand is given by $1/2 \, \rho V^2 A_{hand} C_L$. Recall that we assumed $C_L \approx 1.0$. For a 20 to 30 degree inward sweep, $V_{S\text{-lift}}$ will be

$$V_{S\text{-lift}} = V_S \sin\theta = V_{straight} \sin\theta$$

or 34 to 50 percent of $V_{straight}$. But keep in mind that the hand is only a quarter to a third of the length of the arm. So if we assume that the area of the hand is a third of the area of the arm, then for a 20-degree arm sweep, the hand generates only 4 percent additional thrust for a net loss of 8 percent in comparison with a straight arm pull. The hand obviously generates more lift for the 30-degree sweep, 8.3 percent to be precise, but a 26 percent loss of bluff body thrust also occurred. So the net loss in thrust for the 30-degree S stroke is something close to 18 percent in comparison with the straight arm pull. And this assumes that the hand really does work as well as an engineered airfoil. The net result is that the S stroke produces between 8 and 18 percent less thrust than the straight arm pull. The only way to make up that difference would be for the arm to move roughly 5 to 10 percent faster than $V_{straight}$. But then the benefits of the S stroke are lost because the swimmer must work much harder to reach the same speed.

Summary

In this chapter, we have focused on the underlying physics, specifically the movement of water, associated with swimming. We have examined the principles behind thrust and drag. Presumably, the reader started the chapter already knowing that the swimmer needs to present as small a cross-section as possible to the water, that is, to streamline. You should now also have a better understanding of what needs to go into a more powerful stroke. For example, the concept of drag backward on the arm leads to the high elbow entry for the arm pull, particularly in the free and fly. And perhaps most important, we have provided an analysis of the S stroke as a practical example of how we can use fluid dynamics fundamentals to draw meaningful conclusions about the relative benefits and limitations of a particular stroke.

CHAPTER 2

Freestyle Technique

—Ross H. Sanders, PhD, and Carla B. McCabe, PhD

In competitive swimming, swimmers can use any stroke and any stroke technique in freestyle events. Because front crawl is the fastest and most efficient of the four competitive strokes, swimmers invariably use it in freestyle events. Thus, freestyle universally implies front crawl, and it is used in this chapter to mean front crawl swimming.

In this chapter we investigate freestyle technique and training. The topic is presented in three sections. In the first, freestyle technique in general is explored. The second section examines differences in technique at different paces (sprint and longer distance events) and the effect of fatigue. The third section deals with application of the general training principles to freestyle swimming.

Understanding Freestyle Technique

As in all the strokes, freestyle swimming is cyclical. So where do we start as we attempt to break down and understand the freestyle stroke technique? Strictly speaking, the stroke should really have no parts because all movements are continuous and the transition from one movement to another should be smooth. In this chapter, we refer to phases of the freestyle stroke for convenience of presentation, but you should recognize that the stroke is continuous. A major responsibility of a good teacher or coach is to ensure that the stroke is continuous and rhythmical.

In fact, rhythm is an essential element of swimming that separates efficient from less efficient swimmers (Sanders and Psycharakis 2009). The more efficient a swimmer is, the faster he can travel for a given rate of energy expenditure. Swimmers who are still developing their technique often have everything operating smoothly with good timing of the legs and arms and streamlined posture until they have to take a breath. Then the whole thing falls apart, suddenly becoming jerky and uncoordinated. The additional task, breathing, has upset the rhythm.

In contrast, skilled swimmers are able to maintain good rhythm that is not disrupted by breathing. Skilled swimmers are also able to change the frequency and amplitude of the kick readily without affecting the rhythm of the arms, body roll, or breathing. Accomplished swimmers can swim in a rhythmical and coordinated way when the swimming pace and kicking frequency change, such as when the kick changes from a two-beat kick in which each foot goes up and down once during the stroke cycle (from hand entry until the next entry of the same hand) to a six-beat kick in which each foot goes up and down three times during the stroke cycle.

How do coaches develop good rhythm among swimmers? Good rhythm is achieved by having appropriate timing of the body actions. To monitor and train rhythm, having some sort of reference to which body actions can be adjusted would be useful. In a grandfather clock, the timing is maintained by the regular oscillation of a pendulum. What could act as the rhythm generator in freestyle so that the motion of the legs, arms, and breath are sequenced in a way that maintains the rhythm?

Could the arm pull determine the timing of the swimming actions? It could, but the problem with using the arms as the rhythm generator is that their rhythm also changes in complex ways. They don't rotate about the shoulder joint in a simple regular pattern. For example, the rotation about the shoulder joint is much faster during the pull than during the entry and stretch. Unlike the flutter kick in which there is a regular alternation of the feet, the temporal relationship between the arms is constantly changing. In a catch-up technique, in which one arm stays in the extended glide position while the other recovers, this change is even greater. Similarly, skilled swimmers such as Sun Yang, the current 1,500-meter world-record holder, regularly switch between two- and six-beat kicks during a race without disrupting their rhythm and coordination.

Body Roll as a Clock Setter

The motion that sets the clock and serves as the temporal reference to coordinate all the actions is the rotation of the body about its longitudinal axis, or body roll. This rotation needs to occur all the time in a regular pattern, just like the oscillation of the pendulum in the grandfather clock, to maintain rhythm. Figure 2.1 shows that the temporal pattern of the shoulder roll (a measure of body roll) of a skilled swimmer during a stroke cycle is like a sinusoidal wave.

If, for example, the timing of breathing is set to the time when the body is rolled maximally to one side, when the pendulum has reached its most extreme position and is about to start back the other way, then breathing shouldn't disrupt the rhythm. In fact, many skilled swimmers roll the same amount whether they are breathing or not breathing, and they roll the same amount to both the

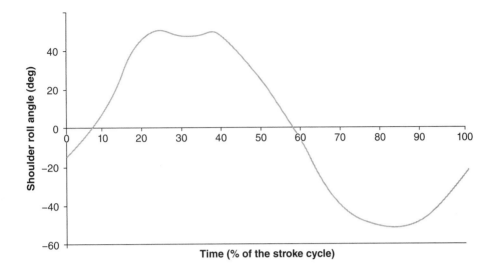

▶ **Figure 2.1**   A typical shoulder roll angle time graph of a skilled swimmer. Zero percent represents the start of a stroke cycle (e.g., right-hand entry), and 100 percent represents the completion of the cycle, in this case the subsequent right-hand entry.

breathing side and the nonbreathing side. Further, their arm actions are not changed much by breathing. In contrast, less-skilled swimmers show disruptions to this sinusoidal pattern when they take a breath.

During the development of swimming technique, teachers and coaches need to encourage breathing to both sides. Learners often have a favorite breathing side, but coaches should encourage breathing to the nonfavored side once or twice per length. Problems that arise from not practicing breathing to both sides include

- rolling more to one side and leaning on one arm,
- asymmetrical posture such as the upper body and head twisting excessively to one side,
- one side of the body contributing more to the stroke than the other, and
- different balance and timing of right-arm and left-arm actions.

Setting the body roll rhythm and then coordinating the other arm and leg actions to suit would seem to make sense. Having a simple regular rhythm as a foundation for the other actions offers obvious advantages.

Stroke Phases and Links to Body Roll

In this section we explore how the phases of the stroke are linked to the rhythm of the body roll. The elements of good technique emerge from the swimmer's attempts to ensure that her actions are tuned to the body roll with timing that promotes effective propulsion and streamlined alignment.

Recovery Phase

Coaches should emphasize a high-elbow position in recovery for several reasons. One of the main reasons is that it helps ensure that the arm does not swing out to the side. Outward swinging of the upper limbs (i.e., a wide recovery) produces a reaction in which the lower limbs naturally rotate in the opposite direction (figure 2.2). Beginning swimmers typically swing the arms out wide to the side as they recover. Consequently, the lower body swings laterally to balance the rotation of the arms. The legs then act as a brake, creating drag and making it difficult to move through the water easily. The emphasis on a high-elbow recovery helps minimize this problem so that the swimmer can maintain good alignment to minimize resistive force (drag).

A high-elbow recovery doesn't necessary mean that the elbow is flexed so that the hand is below the elbow. Many elite swimmers, including Janet Evans, who held the world record for 800-meter freestyle for many years, have been highly successful with a recovery in which the hand is higher than the elbow. But shoulder flexibility combined with body roll enables these swimmers to recover the arms close to the midline of the body rather than swing out to the side. Thus, both bent-elbow and straight-arm recovery styles can be effective if the mass of the upper limbs is not very wide of the midline during recovery. One of the advantages of rolling the body is that it enables the hand to exit easily and to recover without the arm and forearm swinging out to the side.

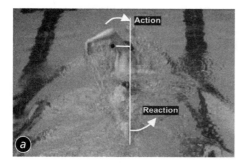 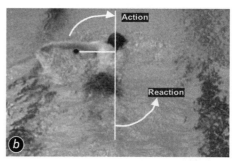

▶ **Figure 2.2**   (*a*) A skilled swimmer illustrating a high-elbow recovery and good body alignment. (*b*) An unskilled swimmer displaying a wide recovery, which causes the lower limbs to swing laterally.

Reach and Entry Phase

As the arm reaches forward, the body rolls to the other side. Let's say that the right arm is recovering and the body is rolling from having the right side out of the water to having the left side out of the water.

Depending on the amount of catch-up the swimmer is using, at some stage during the arm recovery and entry, the other arm will make its catch and start moving through its pull. The timing of that relative to the position of the recovering arm varies according to the amount of catch-up that the swimmer is using, which is influenced to some extent by whether the swimmer is swimming at a leisurely pace or sprinting (Millet et al. 2002; Lerda and Cardelli 2003; Seifert, Chollet, and Rouard 2007). The roll onto the right side (left side coming out of the water) allows the swimmer to breathe to the left if she wants to. The head rotates as part of the body roll and turns just sufficiently to enable breathing in the hollow created by the head itself. There is no need for the head to lift back or for the body to roll farther than it would if breathing wasn't required. The obvious implication is that if the swimmer's body roll rhythm is correct and the other actions are tuned to it appropriately, then breathing should not cause any disruption to the rhythm.

The body roll is important in developing a technique that is free of the common irregularities in breathing. For example, many swimmers, even swimmers at advanced stages of learning, have the unnecessary habit of raising the head back when breathing. This action increases the surface area exposed to the flow and thereby increases resistance. Second, it disrupts the rhythm and body alignment.

As the body approaches its maximum body roll, the right hand and forearm slice into the water and stretch forward. The word *stretch* can be misleading because the use of this word as a verbal cue to swimmers can cause them to try to push the hand too far forward, thus disrupting alignment and streamlining because the upper body kinks to the left. But when the body is rolled to the side, the hand can naturally reach comfortably forward without causing this misalignment. In fact, the rolled position of the body assists streamlining because the head is naturally nestled close to the upper arm. The good alignment and streamlining minimize disruption to the water flow around the body.

The rolled position minimizes form drag (resistance because of the difference in pressure between the leading and trailing boundaries of the body parts). Also, because the body has a narrower cross-section moving through the water, one shoulder is clear of the water while the other is below the surface. Disturbance at the air and water interface is minimal, thereby minimizing wave drag (resistance caused by making waves as the body moves through the water or air interface) as well as form drag.

Catch and Insweep (Pull Phase)

The body roll has helped align the arm and body to a streamlined posture. In accordance with the principle of minimizing time of resistive forces, the hand and forearm should be positioned quickly to make a strong and early catch, particularly in sprint swimming. In longer events a small glide before the catch is appropriate because it helps maintain a good rhythm at a slower stroke rate. The short glide helps optimize body alignment to reduce resistance and obtain maximum benefit from the propulsion gained by the other hand. It improves stroke length, allows some physiological recovery, and optimizes economy.

After the short glide the transition into the catch and insweep should be quick. A common fault is allowing the arm, forearm, and hand to drop lazily before making the catch. During that period the limbs are not streamlined, so they cause resistance. An elbow-up position creates a strong lever system and enables internal rotation of the shoulder to generate propulsive force. Thus, the elbow-up position should be emphasized to ensure that the catch and initial part of the pull are performed strongly.

The body roll helps to streamline the arm and body and to place the muscles in a strong position to commence the pull. The body is near its maximum roll as the catch is made. The roll, combined with shoulder internal rotation and elbow flexion, adds greatly to the speed of the hand and therefore propulsion during the insweep. The roll itself is pulling the arm, forearm, and hand, thereby creating additional hand speed.

Underwater views show that good swimmers move their hands very quickly under the water even though actions above the water appear relatively slow and relaxed. Good swimmers create fast hand speeds not only by extending the shoulder (pulling the arm back) but also by internally rotating the shoulder with the elbow somewhat flexed. This action allows the hand and forearm to move quickly at an orientation that accelerates a large mass of water using a large surface area. The larger the mass accelerated and the greater the acceleration of that mass, the larger the propulsive force.

Upsweep (Push Phase)

The hand moves from the insweep into what is commonly called the upsweep. Although these terms are used in the literature, the upsweep is not so much an upward sweep but a continuing backward push that also happens to coincide with the hand moving up to the surface. Mechanically, a transition occurs from internal rotation to a backward push in which elbow extension and shoulder extension are prominent. The body roll reverses during the transition from the insweep to the upsweep and helps to maintain the backward motion with a sort of flinging action. Just as trunk rotation contributes to a powerful throw when an athlete is throwing a ball forward, trunk rotation in swimming helps fling the hand back to apply more backward force for a longer time.

Hip and Leg Actions

Coaches need not be too concerned about teaching the body roll of the hips for several reasons. First, the hips do not roll as much as the shoulders do, as can be seen in figure 2.3. Second, the hip roll tends to occur automatically in response to the shoulder roll. Therefore, if the roll of the upper body is taught properly, then the hips and legs will roll automatically. Further, allowing the hips to roll to some extent makes it easier for the shoulders to roll through an appropriate range of motion.

The implications for the legs are that it is not necessary—in fact, it is counterproductive—to try to keep the feet kicking perfectly in the vertical plane. Allowing the hips and legs to roll so that the leg kick is oblique is beneficial in helping to offset the tendency for the lower body to swing out in reaction to

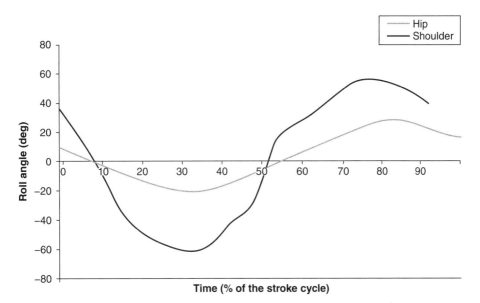

▶ **Figure 2.3** Shoulder and hip roll angles during the cycle, from entry to next entry of the same hand.

Reprinted from C.B. McCabe, 2008, "Effects of 50m and 400m race paces on three-dimensional kinematics and linear kinetics of sprint and distance front crawl swimmers," PhD dissertation thesis, University of Edinburgh.

the arm action. Oblique kicking can cancel that tendency and therefore prevent the added resistance that occurs because of the legs swinging out to the side. The legs and feet remain in a narrow channel aligned with the body, thereby minimizing resistance.

Therefore, roll of the hips and oblique kicking should be encouraged. Coaches can help swimmers understand that they are not expected to stay flat and not rotate. The analogy of the sleek yacht that is alternately tilted to one side and then the other can be useful in developing a beneficial image with regard to the rolling action of the lower and upper body.

This discussion emphasizes the value of using realistic kicking drills in which swimmers practice kicking while also rolling the body. Kickboards designed to encourage rather than discourage rotation should be used. The wider and flatter the kickboard is, the more it tends to limit the natural roll of the swimmer. Rolling is also easier if the swimmer has the hands close together rather than near the edges of the kickboard.

Reducing Drag and Increasing Economy

To reduce the effort required to maintain a certain speed, or alternatively to increase the speed for a given effort, the swimmer must reduce resistance. When that happens, an increase in stroke length and a reduction in stroke rate will occur at any given speed. It sounds simple and obvious, but reducing resistance may be more easily said than done.

A sloping body that may arise because of the tendency for the legs to sink is one of the major contributors to resistance. This problem can be partially overcome by kicking. Kicking produces a counter torque to balance the body and allow it to travel in a more level position (figure 2.4).

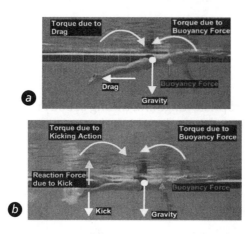

▶ **Figure 2.4** (*a*) Swimmer not using a flutter kick experiencing increased drag. (*b*) Swimmer using an effective leg kick and having better horizontal alignment.

Obviously, kicking has a physiological cost. Therefore, we need to look for mechanisms by which the rotational torque because of the buoyancy force being in front of the gravitational force can be reduced. When kicking is absent, the body's rotational equilibrium is attained at a much greater angle and the swimmer's motion is greatly affected by resistive drag. The body attains rotational equilibrium at a particular body angle and speed using torques generated by the force of water pushing against the angled body. The force tends to lift the legs but also adds to the resistive drag.

What other torques can be used to attain horizontal alignment? The catch-up technique, in which the pull is delayed until the recovering arm is about to enter the water, reduces the sinking legs effect. The catch-up technique places more mass forward of the lungs, and for a longer period, than the high-stroke-rate technique used by unskilled swimmers does. Consequently, the center of mass and center of buoyancy are more closely aligned, thereby reducing the turning effect that tends to sink the legs. Thus, we have the desirable situation whereby resistance is reduced, stroke rate is reduced, speed is maintained, and, as a consequence, stroke length is increased. Further, the rate of energy expenditure is reduced because the effort supplied by the pulling arm is applied with reduced rate because of the longer cycle time.

Another torque that tends to sink the legs is the torque produced by the upward force in reaction to the downward movement of the arm and hand during and after entry. When a swimmer is attempting to cycle the arms quickly, the hand and arm tend to be driven downward rather than stretching forward and holding a level position, as in the case of the catch-up technique. When the pull commences in the catch-up technique, the forces can be generated so that the upward component that tends to produce unwanted sinking rotation is relatively small. That is, the swimmer focuses on pulling backward rather than pushing downward. Further, at this time, the recovering arm is well forward and is above the water, thereby producing a strong torque that counters the sinking torques.

In summary, the catch-up technique reduces resistance by two main mechanisms:

1. It reduces the torques that tend to sink the legs by moving the center of mass forward so that it coincides more closely with the center of buoyancy.

2. It encourages appropriate range and timing of body roll. Thus, the swimmer can readily adopt positions that minimize resistance during some phases of the stroke, particularly during exit and recovery.

Body Roll and Resistance

In *Total Immersion*, Terry Laughlin and John Delves (1996) provide an effective analogy for reducing resistance by the swimmer being more on the side. In this analogy they compare the resistance of a flat barge with that of a leaning yacht. The leaning yacht cuts the surface with a narrower profile and thereby produces less wave and form drag. Unskilled swimmers frequently have inadequate body roll. Also common among unskilled swimmers is the tendency to roll and wobble all over the place. These unstreamlined positions do not facilitate smooth flow of water over the body.

A range of body roll whereby the cross-sectional area cutting through the water at its surface is less than when the body is flat is desirable in reducing wave drag and form drag. When the swimmer has one arm stretched forward, roll of up to 60 degrees about the long axis facilitates a streamlined position to glide through the water. In this position the water can flow readily along the body with little disruption around the submerged shoulder. Further, the body roll allows the arm to be merged nicely with the head. Meanwhile, the body roll assists the shoulder of the recovering arm to be clear of the water so that the adverse effects of its irregular shape on flow are minimized.

The slower stroke rate associated with the catch-up technique also enables a suitable range of body roll while maintaining good flow characteristics. When the stroke rate is fast, the roll associated with the pull is well underway during the recovery of the nonpulling arm. Therefore, having the resistance-reducing posture described earlier is not possible. Further, when swimming with a fast stroke rate, rolling through a large angle is difficult, in part because of a lack of time. Also, attempting a large body roll in a short period makes it difficult to maintain a smooth flow of water over the body. The rapid changes in posture tend to produce turbulence and increase drag.

Therefore, a catch-up technique can be economical. The challenge is to gain the benefits of a catch-up technique without reducing stroke rate so much that speed falls below that required to be competitive over the specific event distance.

Differences in Technique Between Sprint and Distance Swimming Pace

In the previous section, we discussed freestyle technique in terms of optimizing propulsion, minimizing resistance, and maximizing efficiency. To achieve those goals the actions of the arms and legs are tuned to the rhythm of the body roll. But when swimming at different paces, a swimmer must adapt technique to suit the changing demands of that pace. This section explores the differences in technique between sprint pace and distance pace.

Race Parameters

The main difference between swim paces is the combination of stroke frequency (also referred to as stroke rate and expressed either as stroke cycles per minute or seconds per stroke cycle) and stroke length (expressed as meters travelled per stroke cycle) used by a swimmer to optimize swimming speed. Compared with distance swimming, sprint swimming is characterized by a greater average swim velocity and stroke frequency. Because of the higher stroke frequency when sprinting, the stroke length is typically less because the swimmer has less travelling time per stroke. That is, the greater swim velocity does not compensate adequately to enable the same distance to be covered in the reduced time available.

When swimming longer distances, sprint speeds cannot be maintained because of the body's inability to supply adequate energy to the muscles. As muscles increase their speed of contraction, energy expenditure rises rapidly. In fact, energy expenditure of a muscle is proportional to the cube of the speed of the muscle's contraction. Thus, the energy required to swim at faster stroke rates goes up dramatically in sprint events and, consequently, stroke frequency needs to slow to reduce the rate of muscle contraction and therefore delay the onset of accumulating lactic acid (Maglischo 2003). The fact that sprinting is characterized by a higher stroke frequency and lower stroke length than distance swimming explains the negative relationship between these variables as reported in the literature (Keskinen and Komi, 1993; Arellano et al. 1994; Pelayo et al. 1996; Maglischo 2003). Each swimmer needs to find his optimal stroke rate to maximize performance at each event pace. This optimum varies considerably among swimmers because of differences in physiological makeup, body shape, and limb lengths (anthropometric characteristics). Specifically, stroke length is positively related to the height of the swimmer, arm span, arm length, and hand and foot cross-sectional area (Grimston and Hay 1986; Kennedy et al. 1990; dos Santos 1998). Because males are generally taller than females, males tend to have a greater stroke length compared with females when swimming at the same race pace.

Hand Pathway

McCabe, Psycharakis, and Sanders (2011) and McCabe and Sanders (2012) found that swimmers use a similar hand pathway both in terms of maximum vertical (depth) and maximum lateral (width) displacement across swim paces (approximately 0.66 and 0.39 meters, respectively). But the time when these events occur within the stroke cycle depends on the swim pace. For example, the maximum depth of the middle finger occurred approximately 10 percent later within the stroke cycle at a distance pace compared with the sprint pace (figure 2.5). McCabe (2008) reasoned that the later obtainment of maximum depth was most likely caused by the prolonged duration of the entry phase (10 percent) when distance swimming compared with sprint swimming.

Swimmers have a deeper average pull path when swimming at a distance pace than when sprinting (figure 2.6). The average range of lateral displacement of the finger also tends to be greater at distance pace than when sprinting (figure 2.6). Because upper-limb displacement has been related to the magnitude of body roll (Lui, Hay, and Andrews 1993; Hay, Lui, and Andrews 1993; Payton and Mullineaux 1996), it is reasoned that the increased magnitude of shoulder and hip roll at distance pace accounts for these differences.

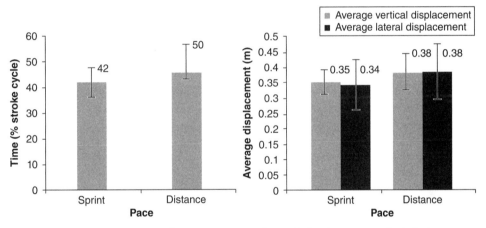

▶ **Figure 2.5** Occurrence of maximum hand depth between sprint and distance pace.

Reprinted from C.B. McCabe, 2008, "Effects of 50m and 400m race paces on three-dimensional kinematics and linear kinetics of sprint and distance front crawl swimmers," PhD dissertation thesis, University of Edinburgh.

▶ **Figure 2.6** Average vertical displacement (depth) and average lateral displacement (width or distance from the midline of the body) of the finger throughout the underwater stroke phase: sprint versus distance pace.

Reprinted from C.B. McCabe, 2008, "Effects of 50m and 400m race paces on three-dimensional kinematics and linear kinetics of sprint and distance front crawl swimmers," PhD dissertation thesis, University of Edinburgh.

Elbow Angle

The elbow angle in swimming has received attention by researchers because of its associated influence on the arm trajectory (Hay, Lui, and Andrews 1993) and links to the efficiency and power of the applied propulsive force by the arm during the underwater stroke cycle (Counsilman 1973; Colwin 1977; Deschodt, Rouard, and Monteil 1996; Cappaert 1998; Haffner and Cappaert 1998). At the instant the hand enters the water, the elbow is more extended when sprinting than when distance swimming (figure 2.7). When sprinting, swimmers enter with the arm extended to enable a quick transition from entry to catch so that they can maximize the time of applying propulsive force. When swimming at a distance pace, swimmers extend the elbow after entry to glide the hand forward so that they can adopt a streamlined gliding posture and have an economical and sustainable stroke rate.

At the catch position (the moment when the hand initiates a backward movement following hand entry), the elbow angle does not vary by swim pace. Swimmers typically have an elbow angle of 152 degrees at this position, irrespective of swim speed. As the hand continues to travel backward and becomes vertically aligned with the shoulder (transition from pull to push phase), the elbow angle does not differ between swim paces and is typically about 103 degrees (figure 2.7).

McCabe, Psycharakis, and Sanders (2011) and McCabe and Sanders (2012) revealed that the magnitude of the elbow angle at the instant when the hand stops moving backward (end of push phase) and the range of elbow angle within the push phase were greater by approximately 7 degrees when swimmers were sprinting compared with when they were swimming at a distance pace (figure 2.7). The elbow angle at the end of the push phase is a measure of elbow extension at the end of what is regarded as the most propulsive phase of the underwater stroke cycle. Therefore, the greater range of motion within the push phase when sprinting may contribute to greater generation of propulsion during the push phase compared with distance swimming.

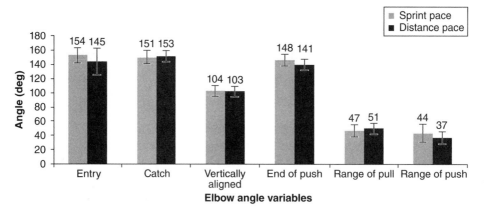

▶ **Figure 2.7**   Mean elbow angle at several instants within the stroke cycle and during the pull and push phases: sprint versus distance pace. Note: 180 degrees represents full elbow extension.

Reprinted from C.B. McCabe, 2008, "Effects of 50m and 400m race paces on three-dimensional kinematics and linear kinetics of sprint and distance front crawl swimmers," PhD dissertation thesis, University of Edinburgh.

Stroke Phase Duration

The swimming stroke cycle is typically divided into four distinct phases: entry, pull, push, and recovery. This process allows us to compare phase durations of various swim strokes and is an effective tool for coaches and teachers to assess the development of technique (Wiegand, Wuensch, and Jaehnig 1975). Phase durations are commonly expressed as a percentage of the total time of a stroke cycle.

Studies have shown that swimmers adjust the time spent in each of the stroke phases to meet the physiological and performance objectives of the event distance (Chollet, Chalies, and Chatard 2000; Millet et al. 2002; Lerda and Cardelli 2003; Seifert, Chollet, and Brady 2004; Seifert, Boulesteix, and Chollet 2004; Seifert, Chollet, and Rouard 2007). Sprint swimming is characterized by a shorter entry phase and longer pull, push, and recovery phases in comparison with distance swimming (figure 2.8). This structure of the stroke cycle results in longer application of propulsive forces (Millet et al. 2002; Lerda and Cardelli 2003; Colwin 1969; Duclos, Legreneur, and Monteil 2002; McCabe, Psycharakis, and Sanders 2011; McCabe and Sanders 2012). The longer relative time in the entry phase when swimming at distance pace supports the idea that at this pace, swimmers adopt this style to improve the hydrodynamic position of the body, reduce the stroke rate, and improve the economy of swimming (Keskinen and Komi 1993; Chollet, Chalies, and Chatard 2000; Lerda and Cardelli 2003).

Within the underwater stroke cycle, the occurrence of the catch position also occurs at different instances relative to the swim pace. Because the catch occurs at the end of the entry phase, figure 2.8 indicates that swimmers made the catch at approximately 30 percent and 40 percent of the stroke cycle for sprint and distance swimming, respectively.

Researchers have investigated the coordination between the arms throughout the stroke cycle based on the duration of the stroke phases: entry A, pull B, push C, and recovery D (figure 2.9). Chollet, Chalies, and Chatard (2000) developed the index of coordination (IdC) as a tool to quantify the relationship between the arms when swimming freestyle in a standardized manner. This index is

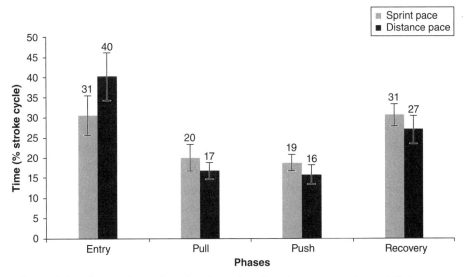

▶ **Figure 2.8** Comparison of stroke phase durations between sprint and distance pace.

Reprinted from C.B. McCabe, 2008, "Effects of 50m and 400m race paces on three-dimensional kinematics and linear kinetics of sprint and distance front crawl swimmers," PhD dissertation thesis, University of Edinburgh.

▶ **Figure 2.9** Four phases within a stroke cycle: entry A, pull B, push C, and recovery D.

From L. Seifert, D. Chollet, and B.G. Bardy, 2004, "Effect of swimming velocity on arm coordination in the front crawl: A dynamic analysis," *Journal of Sports Sciences* 22(7): 651–660. Adapted by permission of Taylor & Francis Ltd.

based on quantifying the lag time between the start of propulsion by one arm and the end of propulsion by the other.

Lag time 1 (TL1) was defined as the time between the beginning of propulsion in the first right-arm stroke and the end of propulsion in the first left-arm stroke (figure 2.10). Lag time 2 (TL2) was defined as the beginning of propulsion in the second left-arm stroke and the end of propulsion in the first right-arm stroke (figure 2.10). These lag times were then expressed as a percentage of mean duration of a stroke cycle, resulting in IdC1 and IdC2 respectively. Figure 2.10 shows that the IdC was the mean of these two indices (TL1 + TL2).

Using this measure Chollet, Chalies, and Chatard (2000) identified three modes of freestyle swimming:

1. catch-up, which is lag time between the propulsive phases of two arms (IdC < 0);

2. opposition, described as propulsive actions whereby one arm begins to pull while the other is finishing the push (IdC = 0); and,

3. superposition, described as an overlap of the propulsive phases (IdC > 0).

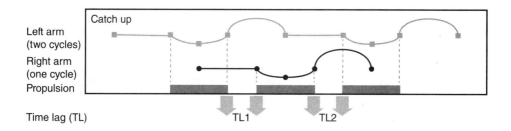

▶ **Figure 2.10** Coordination illustration. TL1 and TL2 are lag times between the beginning of propulsion of one arm and the end of propulsion of the alternate arm. Mean of these lag times provides an index of coordination.

From L. Seifert, D. Chollet, and B.G. Bardy, 2004, "Effect of swimming velocity on arm coordination in the front crawl: A dynamic analysis," *Journal of Sports Sciences* 22(7): 651–660. Adapted by permission of Taylor & Francis Ltd.

To test this new tool, Chollet, Chalies, and Chatard (2000) examined the relationship between 44 French national division swimmers, swimming at 800-meter, 100-meter, and 50-meter pace. It was found that IdC increased with swim velocity. That is, at 800-meter pace, swimmers displayed a catch-up style, whereas at 100-meter and 50-meter pace, opposition style was prevalent. The best swimmers displayed a superposition between the arms at 50-meter pace.

Other researchers have adopted this tool to examine freestyle coordination between elite swimmers and triathletes (Millet et al. 2002), with gender adaptation (Seifert, Boulesteix, and Chollet 2002; Seifert, Chollet, and Rouard 2007; Seifert et al. 2010), on the effect of swim velocity (Lerda and Cardelli 2003; McCabe 2008), during exhaustive exercise (Alberty et al. 2002), and on the effect of breathing and skill level (Lerda and Cardelli 2003; Seifert, Chollet, and Allard 2005).

These studies produced the following conclusions:

- Swimmers and triathletes adapt their stroke patterns from a catch-up style to an opposition style when changing from long-distance pace to maximum sprint pace. This change resulted in a decrease in entry phase duration and an increase in pull and push phases, thereby creating longer propulsive forces (Millet et al. 2002; Lerda and Cardelli 2003).

- Men change from catch-up to opposition spontaneously at a critical velocity and stroke frequency corresponding to 100-meter pace (1.8 meters per second) and 40 strokes per minute. Women adopt their pattern progressively (Seifert, Chollet, and Brady 2004; Seifert, Chollet, and Rouard 2007).

- A critical change of coordination occurred at the 100-meter pace relative to swimming at a distance pace. This finding was explained by the fact that the sample subjects were sprint specialists who changed to a preferred pattern at the 100-meter pace (Seifert, Chollet, and Brady 2004).

- Only the best male performers can adopt a superposition stroke pattern when maximally sprinting (Lerda and Cardelli 2003; Seifert, Boulesteix, and Chollet 2002; Seifert, Chollet, and Rouard 2007).

- Top performers demonstrate a shorter push phase during all swim paces, resulting in greater acceleration of the hand during this phase (Lerda and Cardelli 2003).

- Skilled and less-skilled swimmers illustrate changes in breathing pattern at different velocities (Lerda and Cardelli, 2003).

- Elite swimmers show no change in arm coordination when breathing. Sub-elite swimmers change arm coordination when breathing (Seifert, Chollet, and Allard 2005).

Table 2.1 presents quantitative data from previous studies with regard to the duration of each stroke phase and the coordination index. To enhance the meaningfulness of the data, only values in relation to sprint or distance swimming are presented.

Table 2.1 Presentation of Research Results of Index of Coordination and Time Spent in Each Stroke Phase, Expressed as a Percentage of the Stroke Cycle

	IdC (%)	Entry (%)	Pull (%)	Push (%)	Recovery (%)
Chollet, Chalies, and Chatard 2000 800-meter pace 100-meter pace	−6.9 ± 7.1 2.5 ± 4.4	30.3 ± 6.5 22.1 ± 3.9	21.3 ± 4.2 26.7 ± 3.7	22.9 ± 2.7 26.3 ± 2.7	25.5 ± 2.4 24.9 ± 2.6
Seifert, Chollet, and Brady 2004 400-meter pace 50-meter pace Max pace	−7.8 ± 4.5 1.1 ± 6.0 2.6 ± 6.1	31.8 ± 5.8 20.0 ± 6.7 18.5 ± 6.3	22.5 ± 3.5 28.7 ± 4.5 28.8 ± 5.1	20.0 ± 2.0 22.5 ± 3.1 23.6 ± 2.8	25.8 ± 4.0 28.8 ± 2.6 29.1 ± 3.6
Millet et al. 2002 Max pace	2.3 ± 4.8	21.5 ± 3.3	27.0 ± 2.5	26.6 ± 2.9	24.8 ± 2.1

Shoulder and Hip Roll

Distance swimming is characterized by greater rotation of the shoulders compared with sprint swimming (Castro et al. 2002; McCabe and Sanders 2012). Researchers have proposed that this action reduces the frontal surface area and consequently minimizes active drag (Cappaert, Pease, and Troup 1995; Cappaert 1998; Castro et al., 2002). Cappaert, Pease, and Troup (1995) proposed that reducing the difference in magnitudes of shoulder and hip roll would minimize active drag. Studies have shown that the difference between total shoulder and hip roll was less at distance pace (57 degrees) than in sprinting (68 degrees)—in other words, the body rolls more as a unit—confirming that swimmers adopt a more streamlined or improved hydrodynamic body position when swimming at distance pace.

Researchers have proposed that an increase in shoulder roll with increasing race distance is because of a longer entry phase (Cappaert 1998; Castro et al. 2002). Thus, the high stroke frequency associated with sprinting does not enable as great a body roll to be achieved because of the reduced time available to roll. Further, an increase in duration of the entry phase, longer stroke length, and reduced stroke frequency have been related to better economy in distance swimming in comparison with sprinting. But the reduction in economy in sprinting because of reduced body roll is offset by the advantage gained by increasing propulsive force and stroke frequency (Costill, Maglischo, and Richardson 1992; Cappaert 1998; Chollet, Chalies, and Chatard 2000; Seifert, Chollet, and Brady 2004). These priorities are higher in sprinting because of the short duration of the event.

The magnitude of the maximum hip roll is also greater when swimming at distance pace compared with sprint pace. The large difference in magnitude of hip and shoulder roll further supports the independency of the hips and shoulders in that a change in one is not necessarily reflected in a proportional change in the other. Indeed, McCabe and Sanders (2012) reported that the hip roll increased by approximately 16 degrees when swimming at distance pace compared with sprint pace, whereas the shoulder roll increased by only 5 degrees.

It has also been proposed that the magnitude of the kicking action may contribute to the change of hip rotation between paces because of the generated torques about the longitudinal axis. The suggestion was that hip rotation is dampened when sprinting because of the vigorous action of the leg kick (Yanai, 2001; Sanders and Psycharakis 2009). Although not always statistically significant, swimmers tend to kick with reduced amplitude during distance events relative to sprint events (Cappaert 1998; McCabe 2008). In distance events, swimmers may not produce torques as powerful as those they produce in sprint swimming, permitting them to increase hip rotation during this pace (Sanders and Psycharakis 2009). It is suggested that the magnitude of the kicking action may determine the degree of hip roll and consequently the degree of shoulder roll in swim paces.

This discussion raises the issue of the timing to attain maximum shoulder and hip roll. Studies have reported that swimmers reached maximum hip roll to both sides later in the stroke cycle when swimming at distance pace compared with swimming at sprint pace (figure 2.11). The longer time to reach maximum rotation of the hips at distance pace may be related to the reduced vertical kicking displacement of the feet at this pace. It is assumed that the kick is not as aggressive when distance swimming and therefore that the torques produced from the leg kick are diminished in comparison with sprinting, resulting in a longer period to obtain maximum hip rotation at distance pace.

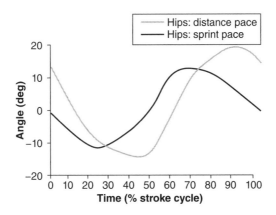

▶ **Figure 2.11** Time (percentage of stroke cycle) to maximum left (negative) and right (positive) hip roll for a sample of swimmers swimming at sprint pace and distance pace.

Reprinted from C.B. McCabe, 2008, "Effects of 50m and 400m race paces on three-dimensional kinematics and linear kinetics of sprint and distance front crawl swimmers," PhD dissertation thesis, University of Edinburgh.

Kicking Action

The magnitude of the kicking action has been linked to the change of many variables between paces, as presented previously. But the primary purpose of a greater foot vertical displacement when sprinting is to increase propulsion (Wilke 1992; Deschodt, Arsac, and Rouard 1999; Maglischo 2003). Swimmers tend to decrease the foot vertical range during periods of distance swimming, which consequently produces less propulsive force than the kicking action in sprint swimming but may be advantageous in terms of reducing the frontal surface area and minimizing active drag.

Differences Between Sprint and Distance Swimmers at the Same Pace

Although sprint and distance swimming are clearly different, it is uncertain whether sprint specialists and distance specialists need to be taught different techniques. A coach of an age-group swimmer might ask, "Do I need to teach different techniques to the sprinters and distance swimmers?" or "Given the difficulty of changing technique as the technique becomes automated through years of repetitive practice, do I need to encourage early distance specialization and fine-tune the swimmers' techniques to suit their specialist events? Or do swimmers spontaneously adjust their technique in an appropriate way when they change pace?"

These issues were addressed by analyzing both sprint and distance specialists at both sprint (McCabe, Psycharakis, and Sanders 2011) and distance paces (McCabe and Sanders 2012). The results for both groups found that swimmers adjust their technique automatically for the event distance. That is, when sprinters swim at a distance pace they swim like distance swimmers, and when distance swimmers swim at a sprint pace they swim like sprinters. The important implication for coaches is that they do not need to encourage early specialization and they do not need to coach different techniques to swimmers at an early age in anticipation of their specializing in particular event distances.

Tables 2.2 and 2.3 show that differences between sprint and distance swimmers when swimming at sprint pace and distance pace respectively were small and not significant for many variables analyzed by McCabe, Psycharakis, and Sanders (2011). Only the duration of the pull phase, which is shorter for sprinters than for distance swimmers, and the occurrence of peak shoulder roll (left and right sides), in which sprinters reach the maximal shoulder roll later within the stroke cycle compared with distance swimmers, were significantly different when both groups swam at a sprint pace. Although the explanation for the difference in shoulder roll is unclear, the difference in duration of the pull phase can be explained readily by strength differences between the groups. Sprint swimmers tend to be stronger, so they can pull against the resistance of the water at faster speeds than the distance swimmers can.

The only variable that was significantly different between sprint and distance swimmers when swimming at a distance pace was swim velocity (table 2.3). It was found that distance swimmers were able to maintain a greater swim velocity throughout the 400 meters compared with sprint swimmers.

McCabe, Psycharakis, and Sanders (2011) and McCabe and Sanders (2012) found that swimmers are not significantly different in most stroke characteristics.

Table 2.2 Data and Statistical Comparisons of the Differences Between Sprint (SG) and Distance (DG) Specialists When Swimming at a Sprint Pace

Variables	SG	DG	P-value
Swim velocity (m/s)	1.81 ± 0.07	1.80 ± 0.05	0.77
Stroke length (m)	2.0 ± 0.2	2.0 ± 0.1	0.64
Stroke frequency (cycles/min)	54.7 ± 5.1	55.4 ± 3.7	0.76
Max finger depth (m)	0.66 ± 0.05	0.66 ± 0.06	0.93
Max wrist depth (m)	0.51 ± 0.06	0.51 ± 0.05	0.97
Max elbow depth (m)	0.31 ± 0.06	0.30 ± 0.05	0.68
Max finger width (m)	0.39 ± 0.07	0.39 ± 0.07	0.90
Max wrist width (m)	0.36 ± 0.05	0.38 ± 0.04	0.35
Max elbow width (m)	0.33 ± 0.06	0.31 ± 0.04	0.49
Elbow angle: entry (degrees)	153.0 ± 10.0	154.7 ± 11.2	0.76
Elbow angle: catch (degrees)	151.1 ± 8.7	151.0 ± 9.8	0.98
Elbow angle: vertically aligned (degrees)	103.2 ± 9.3	104.2 ± 6.3	0.81
Elbow angle: end of push (degrees)	147.8 ± 7.9	147.9 ± 8.5	0.99
Elbow angle: range of pull (degrees)	48.0 ± 9.4	46.8 ± 7.4	0.80
Elbow angle: range of push (degrees)	44.7 ± 13.2	43.7 ± 11.9	0.89
Entry phase (% SC)	32.4 ± 3.8	28.7 ± 6.0	0.18
Pull phase (% SC)	14.4 ± 1.3	18.1 ± 3.5	0.02*
Push phase (% SC)	17.0 ± 1.7	17.7 ± 2.6	0.56
Recovery phase (% SC)	28.3 ± 3.4	28.8 ± 3.0	0.78
Total shoulder roll (degrees)	106.6 ± 7.3	106.1 ± 4.9	0.89
Total hip roll (degrees)	36.7 ± 9.5	40.0 ± 7.2	0.46
Time to max left shoulder roll (% SC)	34.1 ± 3.1	26.7 ± 5.1	0.01*
Time to max right shoulder roll (% SC)	82.5 ± 5.2	75.3 ± 6.0	0.03*
Time to max left hip roll (% SC)	22.5 ± 5.9	24.3 ± 6.0	0.57
Time to max right hip roll (% SC)	75.8 ± 7.7	72.7 ± 9.7	0.51
Max left foot depth (m)	0.41 ± 0.06	0.39 ± 0.05	0.48
Max right foot depth (m)	0.41 ± 0.07	0.39 ± 0.05	0.37

Data are expressed as mean ± SD.

*Significant at $p < 0.05$.

From C.B. McCabe, S. Psycharakis, and R. Sanders, 2011, "Kinematic differences between front crawl sprint and distance swimmers at sprint pace," *Journal of Sports Sciences* 29(2): 115–123. Reprinted by permission of Taylor & Francis Ltd.

These findings challenge current views with regard to freestyle sprint and distance swimmers. Coaches should be aware, however, that they do differ in terms of the duration of the pull phase, the timing of the maximum stroke width and maximum shoulder roll angle when sprinting, and the average swim speed when distance swimming. Consequently, coaches should include specific drills to develop these characteristics and emphasize them throughout the training session. Otherwise, coaches can be confident that sprint and distance swimmers are not as different in terms of technique as once suspected.

Changes in Technique Due to Fatigue

Fatigue is defined as the inability to sustain exercise at a required pace or intensity (Alberty et al. 2009). Fatigue in swimming develops during a race and can

Table 2.3 Data and Statistical Comparisons of the Differences Between Sprint (SG) and Distance (DG) Specialists When Swimming at a Distance Pace

Variable	SG	DG	P-value
Swim velocity (m/s)	1.41 ± 0.06	1.50 ± 0.05	0.01*
Stroke length (m)	2.24 ± 0.32	2.19 ± 0.18	0.73
Stroke frequency (cycles/m)	38.6 ± 6.0	41.3 ± 3.7	0.31
Max finger depth (m)	0.66 ± 0.11	0.67 ± 0.06	0.82
Max wrist depth (m)	0.52 ± 0.10	0.52 ± 0.05	0.85
Max elbow depth (m)	0.32 ± 0.10	0.33 ± 0.05	0.84
Time to max finger depth (% SC)	51.5 ± 6.7	48.8 ± 6.7	0.45
Max finger width (m)	0.39 ± 0.11	0.40 ± 0.07	0.96
Max wrist width (m)	0.37 ± 0.08	0.38 ± 0.06	0.79
Max elbow width (m)	0.34 ± 0.09	0.31 ± 0.03	0.41
Time to max finger width (% SC)	68.2 ± 11.2	66.0 ± 16.2	0.96
Elbow angle: first back (degrees)	155.2 ± 6.2	151.7 ± 8.8	0.39
Elbow angle: shoulder X (degrees)	101.4 ± 6.8	104.7 ± 7.2	0.37
Elbow angle: end back (degrees)	140.3 ± 8.2	140.8 ± 7.5	0.91
Elbow angle: hand exit (degrees)	126.6 ± 30.1	129.0 ± 22.7	0.87
Elbow angle: re-entry (degrees)	144.5 ± 13.5	146.3 ± 23.1	0.86
Elbow angle: range of pull (degrees)	53.8 ± 5.3	47.3 ± 10.2	0.14
Elbow angle: range of push (degrees)	38.9 ± 8.6	35.7 ± 9.2	0.50
Entry (% SC)	41.5 ± 5.6	39.1 ± 6.4	0.45
Pull (% SC)	14.0 ± 2.5	13.6 ± 2.5	0.72
Push (% SC)	15.1 ± 1.7	16.2 ± 1.5	0.21
Recovery (% SC)	25.4 ± 4.2	27.0 ± 3.6	0.42
Hand exit (% SC)	79.2 ± 3.8	78.0 ± 4.7	0.60
Total shoulder roll (degrees)	110.5 ± 12.9	110.6 ± 11.5	0.99
Total hip roll (degrees)	56.6 ± 27.3	51.0 ± 10.1	0.60
Max left foot depth (m)	0.30 ± 0.12	0.36 ± 0.07	0.28
Max right foot depth (m)	0.30 ± 0.14	0.35 ± 0.06	0.38

Data are expressed as mean ± SD.

*Significant at $p < 0.05$.

From C.B. McCabe, and R.H. Sanders, 2012, "Kinematic differences between front crawl sprint and distance swimmers at a distance pace," *Journal of Sports Sciences* 30(6): 601–608. Reprinted by permission of Taylor & Francis Ltd.

affect technique and coordination, particularly toward the final stages of the race. Besides reducing capacity to generate propulsive force, fatigue induces changes in technical proficiency, posture, and coordination, which can increase resistance (Alberty et al. 2009, 2011; Potts, Charlton, and Smith 2002; Seifert et al. 2010). Therefore, swimmers must learn to minimize these effects and hold form as much as possible.

Thow (2010) identified a battery of technique and coordination variables in freestyle swimming that change significantly because of fatigue. In this study, fatigue was induced by instructing 10 Scottish national-level swimmers to perform a series of repeated 100-meter max effort freestyle swims (rest 30 seconds) until their 100-meter time exceeded 125 percent of the best time relative to their personal best. The results highlighted that fatigue causes swimmers to alter their technique. In particular, swimmers do not maintain limb positions corresponding to good form in freestyle swimming when they become fatigued. This result reflects strength deficiencies of particular muscle groups. For example, increased arm recovery width reflects an inability to maintain a high elbow and may indicate deficiencies in muscles used to rotate the shoulders externally (Pollard and Fernandez 2004).

In Thow's (2010) study, changes with fatigue included increased shoulder roll and change in body angle, that is, lower-leg position. These alterations are known to increase resistance (Maglischo 2003; Sweetenham and Atkinson 2003). Given that fatigue affects technique, an additional concern is that if swimmers continually perform under a fatigued state during training, adaptations may result in incorrect muscle development, imbalances, and increased injury risk (Becker and Havriluk 2006; Brukner and Khan 2006; Grace 1985). The identification of poor or incorrect technique patterns before they become automatic in nature is imperative to maintain peak performance and prevent strength and postural imbalances that reduce performance and increase the risk of injury.

Training for Freestyle Swimming

General training principles are well established in various swimming texts, such as Maglischo's *Swimming Fastest: The Essential Reference on Technique, Training, and Program Design* (2003). In this section we look at differences resulting from event specialization with particular emphasis on event distance. We also look at how training must consider the different needs of sprint and distance swimmers.

Considering the Needs of Distance Specialists

Swimmers who are suited to longer events such as 1,500-meter freestyle are those endowed with good potential for developing the aerobic contribution to performance, that is, $\dot{V}O_2$max. A high $\dot{V}O_2$max in combination with fewer fast-twitch fibers that are producing large amounts of lactic acid means that distance swimmers can sustain fast speeds without suffering severe lactic acidosis.

Elite long-distance swimmers tend to have a high percentage of slow-twitch fibers relative to fast-twitch fibers compared with sprint swimmers and do not tend to develop great muscle bulk through training. Another characteristic common to distance swimmers is that they don't rely on a strong kick and may have a somewhat lazy kick of inconsistent rhythm that is not especially vigorous. Rather than providing propulsion, the kick is used to maintain good balance and streamlining. This is not to say that development of a strong six-beat kick is not advantageous to distance swimmers. They often use bursts of strong six-beat kicking to burn off an opponent and to bring the race home.

Because of their high aerobic capacity and preponderance of fatigue-resistant slow-twitch fibers, distance swimmers can tolerate high training volumes at relatively fast speeds (Maglischo 2003). Their lactate threshold pace tends to be faster than that of swimmers of equivalent ability in shorter events. Because slow-twitch fibers use muscle glycogen at a slower rate than fast-twitch fibers do and because slow-twitch fibers are more capable of metabolizing alternative fuels such as glucose and fat, distance swimmers can swim longer before they deplete their glycogen reserves.

Speed can be maintained over a long distance only if the metabolism is predominantly aerobic. Therefore, distance swimmers need a high $\dot{V}O_2$max and associated high anaerobic threshold pace. Thus, training is geared toward development of aerobic capacity rather than anaerobic capacity.

Lactate tolerance training is not important for distance swimmers. Overload endurance training and race-pace training should have less emphasis than in the training programs of specialists in shorter events. But distance swimmers do need to be able to maintain swimming speed and anaerobic power to bring the race home. They also need to be able to buffer the lactate buildup that occurs by swimming above threshold in a race, particularly in the final stages of the race. The ability to buffer lactate is developed through overload endurance training and race-pace endurance training.

Considering the Needs of Middle-Distance Specialists

Middle-distance events include 200-meter and 400-meter freestyle. These swimmers are all-rounders in terms of their physiological endowment. They have both good aerobic power and good anaerobic power. Thus, they have the entire physical package that allows them to swim fast for the duration of these events. They have a balance of fast-twitch and slow-twitch fibers, although possibly slightly more slow-twitch fibers than fast-twitch fibers (Maglischo 2003). Although not as explosive as sprint swimmers, they have the ability to start and finish fast across the distances in which they compete.

Middle-distance swimmers respond well to both endurance and sprint training. But because of their higher percentage of fast-twitch fibers, they are more susceptible to fatigue and depletion of glycogen. Consequently, they cannot perform the same quantity of endurance training as distance swimmers can, particularly at threshold and overload training speeds. They also require more recovery time to replace the glycogen in their muscles.

Middle-distance freestyle swimmers require a strong six-beat kick, although they may adopt a more relaxed two-beat or four-beat rhythm during the middle of the race. The training program for middle-distance freestyle swimmers emphasizes development of aerobic capacity through the first two-thirds of the season and maintenance through the remainder of the season as the focus shifts to the development of anaerobic power and buffering capacity through overload endurance training and race-pace training (Maglischo 2003).

Lactate tolerance training is not typically emphasized with this group of swimmers unless they also compete in 100-meter events. Similarly, speed is maintained primarily through technique development rather than development of muscle strength and power.

Considering the Needs of Sprint Specialists

Sprint events include 50-meter and 100-meter freestyle. The physical makeup of those who perform best at 50 meters can be quite different from those who perform best at 100 meters. Those who excel at 50 meters but drop off in the 100 meters generally do so because they have a large percentage of fast-twitch fibers. They have high levels of muscle power and anaerobic power but limited aerobic power when expressed as a percentage of body weight (Maglischo 2003). They have more muscle bulk in general and more muscle made up of fast-twitch fibers.

Those who perform well at 100 meters have a more balanced percentage of fast- and slow-twitch fibers. They have higher aerobic power and high anaerobic power, although less than that of those who excel over 50 meters. Because sprinters also tend to have more muscle bulk than middle-distance swimmers and a higher percentage of fast-twitch fibers, their aerobic capacity expressed per unit of body weight is generally less than that of middle-distance swimmers although greater than that of 50-meter sprinters.

Because of their high percentage of fast-twitch fibers, sprinters tend to improve muscle size and strength more easily than middle- and long-distance swimmers do. The kick contributes more to speed in freestyle sprint events than it does in middle- and long-distance events. Thus, sprint swimmers need to develop a powerful six-beat kick.

Because they have a large number of fast-twitch fibers, sprinters are prone to rapid accumulation of lactic acid as well as rapid depletion of glycogen stores in the muscles. Thus, they are not suited to train fast for long distances or to perform long-distance repeats with short rest intervals. This is particularly the case for those who are best at 50-meter sprints but drop off the pace in 100-meter sprints.

When doing basic endurance and threshold sets, they need to swim at a slower pace and with slower heart rates than middle-distance and distance swimmers do. They also need more recovery swimming to replace glycogen and clear the lactate. Although they can cope with paces of overload endurance training in a similar manner to middle-distance and distance swimmers, those whose best distance is 50 meters in particular tend to struggle to maintain the pace for long cumulative distances in overload sets. The overall training volume should be less for sprint swimmers than for middle-distance and distance swimmers.

Dryland Training for Freestyle Swimmers

The primary aim of land training for swimmers is to prepare the athlete physically to train and compete. The goal of land programs is to develop strength and endurance in the muscles to the levels required for optimal performance. This includes ensuring good posture for swimming and appropriate balance among the muscle groups in strength and endurance. Because athletes differ in anthropometric (body shape) and physiological makeup, the training program must be individualized to ensure optimal physical preparation for each swimmer.

Maintaining Muscle Balance and Good Posture

Because of the cyclical nature of the swim strokes and the large volumes of training, swimmers are prone to postural problems. These postures can be both a cause and effect of musculoskeletal imbalances. The imbalances and postures can lead to injury as well as limit swimming performance. An example of this issue is tight hip flexors that pull the pelvis into anterior tilt. This problem can affect the ability of the pelvis to get into full hip extension, which is important in performing correct movement patterns in starts and turns. The anterior tilt may also affect the swimmer's ability to adopt streamlined positions in the water and is likely to reduce the efficiency and effectiveness of muscles involved in swimming motions, including those of the arms, head, trunk, and lower limbs.

The upper-limb motions in freestyle involve strong internal rotation and extension of the shoulders. Specific adaptations occur in muscles such as the deltoids, pectorals, and latissimus dorsi. These muscles (agonist muscles) will adapt favorably to the volume of swim training by becoming stronger and gaining in endurance. But the muscles that provide the opposite movements (antagonist muscles) such as the trapezius, infraspinatus, and supraspinatus do not develop strength and endurance to the same level. Consequently, postural problems occur, so the athlete is unable to adopt the streamlined position that minimizes resistive drag.

Understanding Movement Patterns

Before prescribing effective land program interventions, coaches need to understand basic muscle mechanics. The actions of the shoulders are crucial in all swimming strokes. The scapula plays a pivotal role. It is the largest bone in the shoulder complex and has the greatest number of muscles attached to it. These muscles are responsible for providing stability as well as moving the arm. Any altered scapular function arising from muscular weakness or fatigue, including inability to position or stabilize the scapula properly, directly affects swimming performance and increases the risk of injury. Table 2.4 provides a basis for identifying the muscles involved in the movements in swimming and for selecting exercises in a dryland program to ensure appropriate muscle balance for swimmers. All these muscles are important in swimming and in maintaining proper shoulder function, so they should be trained appropriately.

Table 2.4 Muscles Involved in the Motions of the Scapula

Movement	Primary muscles involved
Upward rotation	Trapezius (middle and lower sections), serratus anterior
Downward rotation	Levator scapulae, rhomboids, pectoralis minor and major, latissimus dorsi
Elevation	Trapezius (upper and middle sections), serratus anterior, levator scapulae
Depression	Trapezius (lower section), latissimus dorsi, pectorals minor and major
Protraction	Serratus anterior, pectoralis minor and major, levator scapulae
Retraction	Trapezius (middle and lower sections), rhomboids, latissimus dorsi

Chapter 18, "Sports Medicine: Swimming Injuries and Prevention," and chapter 20, "Strength and Conditioning for Performance Enhancement," present some practical guidelines for preventing injury and developing swimming-specific strength. Here are some practical guidelines to help you plan your strength and conditioning program to maximize performance in freestyle swimming.

When possible, combine the individual movements listed in table 2.4 when performing strengthening exercises. An example is the bench press, in which the shoulder is internally rotated with scapular protraction and elevation during the concentric phase of the movement.

Always incorporate balance into your program. In the bench press example, include an exercise such as rowing to maintain strength balance in the rotator cuff (external rotation) and around the scapula (scapular retraction).

Selection of appropriate sets and number of repetitions for exercise balance is another key consideration. For example, doing resistance-band work for scapular retraction and shoulder external rotation is not sufficient as a stimulus to counteract the high volume of shoulder internal rotation movements in the pool. Thus, in land training, higher volumes and loading are essential. Inclusion of loaded exercises such as dumbbell rows and other loaded variations is appropriate.

During training periods in which high volumes of work are done in the pool, consider increasing the volume of dryland work that is focused on scapular retraction and shoulder external rotation while decreasing work done in exercises like the bench press and overhead press that replicate the shoulder internal rotation movements done in the pool.

Regression in certain exercises can result from weaknesses in the opposing muscle groups, which may not allow stabilization of muscle groups to exert force. An example of this occurs among athletes who struggle to perform pull-ups. The scapula may wing upward because of lack of strength in the lower trapezius to stabilize the scapula. Consequently, a reduction occurs in transmission of force through the latissimus dorsi and other musculature.

Care in performing exercises that mimic freestyle stroke patterns is essential because this work can increase the adaptation stimulus that is already dominant in pool training. The resulting strength imbalance can adversely affect posture and increase the risk of injury. A more efficient method of developing stroke-specific strength is through in-water resisted training because this work satisfies all the neurophysiological and mechanical demands for transfer in accordance with the principle of specificity.

Movements of the Hips and Lower Limbs

The musculature of the hips and lower limbs enables generation of propulsion through kicking. Understanding the muscles and the movements that they initiate is essential in designing land programs to help develop the strength of the musculature. Table 2.5 provides a basic overview of the movements of the hips and lower limbs and the muscles involved. The next stage is to identify appropriate exercises to strengthen the movements.

Table 2.5 Muscles Involved in the Motions of the Hips and Lower Limbs

Movement	Primary muscles involved
Hip flexion	Psoas major and minor, rectus femoris
Hip extension	Gluteus maximus, biceps femoris
Hip external rotation	Gluteus medius, piriformis
Hip internal rotation	Tensor fasciae latae, gluteus minimus
Hip adduction	Adductor magnus, adductor brevis, adductor longus
Hip abduction	Tensor fasciae latae, gluteus minimus
Knee flexion	Biceps femoris, semitendinosus, semimembranosus
Knee extension	Rectus femoris, vastus medialis, vastus lateralis, vastus intermedius
Ankle plantar flexion	Gastrocnemius, soleus
Ankle dorsiflexion	Tibialis anterior

As with the muscles of the upper limbs, the muscles of the lower limbs combine to perform a variety of movements working in an eccentric, concentric, and isometric fashion to provide the movement. Careful selection of training exercises can stimulate multiple muscle groups. For example, squatting variations stress all the lower-limb movements used in starts and turns, whereas squat jumps, Olympic lifts, and pull variations involve the ankle musculature and develop a power component of the leg musculature.

Ensuring balance in exercise selection and strength of muscle groups is essential to reducing risk of developing imbalances and injury.

Train movements, not muscles. Muscles work in synergy to provide movement. The hamstrings not only perform knee flexion but also work to extend the hip. Exercises that train those movements are more efficient than those that isolate muscle groups.

Core Training

The use of core musculature to transfer forces across extremities is an important factor in all sporting actions, particularly in swimming, because of the environment in which the sport is performed. Freestyle swimmers need to develop a strong trunk musculature to maintain optimal posture so that they can transfer forces and achieve a streamlined posture.

Movements of the Trunk Musculature

Traditional trunk training methods have been challenged by the findings of recent research. Previous training interventions that encouraged spinal flexion have been discouraged because of the effects on low-back health and its encouragement of a kyphotic posture. A more recent trend is to build stability through the trunk musculature in order to build endurance in specific postures and help steer forces to the extremities while encouraging mobility through the hips and shoulders. For the swimmer, this approach implies reducing the amount of movements that encourage spinal flexion and implementing exercises that encourage thoracic extension while challenging stability through the trunk musculature (table 2.6).

Table 2.6 Muscles Involved in the Motions of the Trunk

Movement	Primary muscles involved
Lumbar flexion	Rectus abdominis
Lateral flexion	External oblique, internal oblique
Lumber extension	Erector spinae
Spinal rotation	External oblique, internal oblique

Suitable exercises include static holds known as plank or bridge variations, such as plank, side plank, and back bridge. These low-level trunk exercises promote the development of stability through the trunk musculature by building endurance in an optimal posture. These exercises can be progressed by changing stance width to increase the demand on the trunk musculature.

After stability is developed, velocity-specific training can be introduced through medicine ball training to encourage higher force, high-velocity movements that increase the stimulus to trunk musculature and develop of speed and power.

Effect of Muscle Flexibility on Posture

As muscles develop strength, flexibility can be affected for two reasons. First, the increased pull of the muscle on the joint changes the resting position of the articulating components of the skeleton. That is, a change in posture occurs. Second, the muscles themselves can shorten, reducing their range of motion. Therefore, training that results in changes in strength of muscles must be accompanied by work to maintain flexibility. This point is particularly important in freestyle swimming because the shoulders, in particular, and the hips and spine must be able to move through a large range of motion with minimal internal resistance.

The muscles that commonly tend to be dominant within the swimming population are usually located within the anterior chain, that is, the muscles on the front of the body. Some of the muscles that make up the anterior chain are the anterior deltoid, pectoralis major and minor, latissimus dorsi, and hip flexors and rectus femoris. These muscles tend to be tight and strong, whereas the muscles of the posterior chain such as the gluteals, hamstrings, and calf muscles tend to be short and less strong. This situation arises from the swimming actions that favor the anterior muscles.

The identification of targeted interventions that focus on developing the flexibility of the dominant muscles while strengthening the opposing muscle groups is key to reducing musculoskeletal dysfunction and improving performance. An example of this would be doing flexibility work on the pectorals and latissimus muscle groups and doing strength work on the opposing muscle groups such as the lower trapezius and rhomboids.

When implementing flexibility interventions, keep these guidelines in mind:

- Prepool dynamic and PNF stretching (contract–relax and other variations) are appropriate interventions to change muscle length and prepare the body before performance.

- Postpool static stretching is appropriate. This stretching will have a relaxant effect on the nervous system, but it is not appropriate as a prepool exercise when an increase in nervous system activation is required.

- During periods of high-volume pool training, increase the focus on flexibility to maintain range of movement within safe ranges to reduce the risk of injury. Placing extra emphasis on pre- and postpool flexibility and mobility work as well as monitoring flexibility of individual athletes is essential.

- Each stroke has its own flexibility challenges. The breaststroke kick challenges the leg muscles, especially the adductor muscle groups, whereas backstroke and fly challenge shoulder and latissimus muscle groups. Consider the stroke and its demands and create a flexibility program specific to each swimmer and her events.

- A strength program that encourages lifting through a full range of movement is also essential to developing strength through the full range and maintaining flexibility in movements.

Summary

In this chapter we explored three facets of competitive freestyle swimming. In the first section we established the importance of rhythm and the role of body roll as the rhythm generator. The swimming actions and the elements of sound technique were linked to the goals of maintaining good rhythm and streamlined alignment to optimize swimming efficiency and minimize resistive forces.

In the second section we described differences and similarities in technique between distance and sprint swimming. These topics included comparison of sprint and distance swimming in terms of the standard race parameters of stroke length, stroke frequency, and swimming speed followed by comparison of observable technique features such as hand paths and elbow angles. Timing and coordination were considered in terms of phase durations and patterns of shoulder and hip roll. We also explored differences between distance and sprint swimmers swimming at the same pace. Surprisingly or not, these two species of swimmer display few differences when swimming at the same pace. The important implication is that coaches don't need to encourage early specialization of swimming distance and technique training. The section concluded with a discussion of how fatigue might affect technique.

The third part of the chapter provided information about the general principles of training for front crawl swimming and the different training needs of sprint, middle-distance, and distance swimmers. The section concluded with a discussion of principles of dryland training, emphasizing the importance of maintaining good muscle balance to optimize performance and minimize the risk of injury.

The authors thank Neil Donald, strength and conditioning specialist at the Sportscotland Institute, for his input on the section on dryland training.

CHAPTER 3

Backstroke Technique

—Russell Mark

Backstroke technique, as with all the competitive strokes, has seen an evolution of sorts over the past decade. We are seeing many of today's top backstrokers adopting common characteristics in their techniques. A number of the methods being used by the best in the world challenge teachings that were provided to swimmers only a generation ago.

Stroke technique analysis and instruction may be done in several ways. Each has its strong points and flaws. First, the ideal stroke can be created by using the laws of physics, our understanding of fluid dynamics, and complex modeling techniques and then teaching that ideal stroke to swimmers. Although this method may have a strong foundation in the sciences, in many cases these approaches gloss over the applied side of swimming—the way in which athletes actually execute the technique in the water. Additionally, these types of methods often present data in ways that are not intuitive to a swimmer.

Second, we can watch what the best in the world are doing and then try to explain why those swimmers are successful; we outline the kinematics of the movements and teach others to swim the same way. This is the "Michael Phelps swims this way, so you should swim this way too" approach. The best in the world are always innovative and push the envelope faster and farther than those who use a pure scientific approach. But this method overlooks the fact that all swimmers are different and that the things that work so well for one swimmer may not be best for another. This approach also runs the risk that a coach does not fully understand why certain things work to make a swimmer faster, which is certainly information required for effective coaching.

The third, and arguably best, approach to analyzing and prescribing technique is to combine the first two methods by critically analyzing the techniques used by the best in the world but interpreting those techniques through the laws of science and fluid dynamics, explaining why those methods produce faster times and reduce injury risk, and tweaking techniques to match the characteristics of the individual swimmer. This approach does not get deep into the numbers, but it matches observation with science and often presents information in a way that intuitively makes sense.

This chapter uses this third approach. The characteristics of the techniques of the best backstrokers in the world are presented and then explained using what is known about generating propulsion and reducing drag to provide guidelines for teaching the mechanics of a fast and safe backstroke. Some ideas fall in line with conventional teachings, but others challenge traditional thinking and present new ideas about backstroke mechanics and the achievement of speed.

Use of Video as a Foundation for Stroke Analysis

Underwater training and competition video of the best backstrokers has become increasingly available since the early 2000s and provides today's coaches and athletes with unique insights into how the top backstrokers swim so fast. One of the surprising insights gained after engaging in intensive video analysis is that the techniques used by elite backstrokers have many qualities in common and definitely trend toward a common, optimal technique. The development and understanding of this ideal technique and the components that contribute to it is the focus of the chapter.

The technique presented in this chapter is both derived and validated from video evidence. Real athletes, including Aaron Peirsol, Natalie Coughlin, Kirsty Coventry, Ryan Lochte, Missy Franklin, Michael Phelps, Camille LaCourt, Margaret Hoelzer, Tyler Clary, Emily Seebohm, and Elizabeth Beisel, swim with great success using the techniques described. Additionally, the technique makes sense from a scientific and theoretical standpoint. Science and the potential of the human body say that this technique will succeed.

A particular focus of this chapter is to explain why this technique leads to success because that level of understanding makes each concept more convincing and powerful. The many aspects that make up the overall stroke will be explained separately and sequentially because that is the easiest way to explain concepts in written form. In action and reality, the stroke typically isn't thought of as following from step-by-step instructions; instead, each element flows seamlessly into the next and makes for one elegant, smooth motion. Each part of the stroke is directly related to all the others. The effective backstroke coach needs to understand those relationships and the integration of all the movements as well as the mechanics of the individual pieces themselves.

As with all strokes, individual swimmers will display minor variations from the ideal technique to account for their unique characteristics, and some swimmers will succeed despite unusual aspects of their techniques. A coach must keep the ideal technique in mind and coach the majority of athletes toward that model while also being mindful that a person's physical strengths and traits could lead to unique technical aspects. These exceptions, along with common and older teachings that differ, will also be touched on because the complete picture of what the stroke should look like, what the stroke can look like, what many people think the stroke looks like, and what the stroke used to look like are all important.

Overview of the Backstroke

Swimming the backstroke can be likened to paddling a kayak or raft. The head and body represent the boat, the arms are the oars, and the legs are a propeller at the rear of the craft. To move through the water as swiftly and efficiently as possible, the body (boat) must be firm and steady. The legs (rear propeller) should be constantly motoring to assist in propulsion and stability through the core. The arms (oars) provide most of the propulsion. Like boat oars, propulsion from the arms is rather simple—push water in a straight path back toward the rear of the boat (or the feet in swimming) to move forward. Additionally, the surface area of the hand and forearm (oar) should be as large as possible to apply direct force toward the feet. This type of propulsion in swimming has been referred to in literature as drag-based or drag-dominant propulsion, as opposed to lift-based or lift-dominant propulsion. The distinction of these terms is historically significant because in the past backstroke technique was taught in a way that primarily relied on lift forces to generate propulsion.

Let's look at this in more detail because this concept is important for generating propulsion in backstroke. A swimmer always wants to generate force in the backward direction (toward the feet) to move forward. To create the backward forces, a swimmer has the option of producing drag forces or lift forces. Whether a swimmer generates propulsive lift or drag is largely determined by the orientation of the hand and the way in which it moves through the water. Propulsive drag occurs when the palm faces toward the feet and the arm moves backward to create the propulsive force. Lift-dominant propulsion is created when the palm pitches slightly downward or upward and the arm follows a curved downward or upward path to create force in the backward direction. Lift forces are an indirect way to generate backward force; drag forces are direct.

When they hear the word *drag*, many people think of resistance, something that all swimmers should avoid when it works to slow down the body. But the principles of drag can work to a swimmer's advantage when he is attempting to generate propulsion. As the hand and arm pull through the water, they experience drag, but this force helps push the body forward. The more resistance the hands and arms experience, the greater the propulsive drag will be. With all other things being equal, the swimmer will move faster through the water.

Understanding Lift Forces

In airplane flight, producing lift forces makes sense. The wing is specifically shaped so that when it moves in a forward direction, it creates an upward (lift) force perpendicular to the direction of the wing's movement, allowing the plane to leave the ground.

In swimming, lift forces do not make as much sense. A swimmer can produce lift forces, but the speed, size, and shape of the hand can never generate enough lift force to have a significant effect on forward propulsion. Upward and downward arm movements in backstroke (think of an S pull) can be observed in nearly every swimmer's stroke to some degree, but these movements are not necessarily contributing to making the swimmer go faster. These extraneous movements in backstroke can happen because of the body rotation that occurs during every stroke. They may be due to an adjustment that the swimmer makes to maintain the best backward arm movement and force generation. More likely, they happen because the swimmer changes the angle of the hand to keep the arms moving through the water as fast as possible. Although common, these indirect movements are not what make the swimmer move forward.

The backstroke arm stroke should be just like a boat oar; the face of the paddle pushes water directly back toward the feet. Propulsion from the backstroke arm movement is based on grabbing hold of as much water as possible as early in the stroke as possible and using the strongest muscles to push that water straight back so that the swimmer can move forward. To achieve that goal, let's look deeper into the stroke mechanics, particularly what goes on underwater to generate propulsion.

Underwater Phase of the Backstroke

A great catch is shallow and to the side of the body, pushes straight back through the water, and follows through to the end with a downward finish. This statement is important because as recently as the mid-2000s, a commonly accepted (and taught) pull pattern for backstroke was to press the hand down as deeply as possible during the catch, then bring the hand back up toward the surface, and then flip the hand back over with a downward finish. The hand would go down, up, and down, like the shape of a sideways letter S. The origin of this teaching is uncertain, but it was widely accepted and was based on two premises—that lift forces were important and that the initial part of the stroke needed to be deep because the deeper water was better to pull against (more on that later). What's most surprising about the wide acceptance of this idea is that so many of the best backstrokers in history, even going back to the mid-1970s and films shot by Doc Counsilman, did *not* swim like that.

Because the underwater arm stroke has the greatest effect on propulsion and speed, all other parts of the backstroke should be built to support the mechanics and strength of that perfect underwater arm movement. Body rotation, head position, body position, and kick are each important to overall performance in the water, but taken separately, none of these elements can contribute near as much to forward propulsion as the arm stroke. They can aid a swimmer in achieving the best arm stroke when used correctly; when not used correctly, they can be detrimental to the arm stroke and overall performance. With this in mind, a swimmer and coach must be careful about how each of those movements is performed and emphasized and how they each contribute to overall stroke performance. Let's look in more detail at the various components that make up the underwater stroke.

Catch

Among the pieces that make up the underwater arm stroke, the catch (figure 3.1) is arguably the most critical aspect to fast and efficient swimming. Ultimately, the catch determines how propulsive the entire arm stroke will be. The key elements to a good catch are to grab, or catch, a lot of water and to do it as early as possible. The concepts of quantity and timing are inseparable. The sooner a swimmer can grab hold of a lot of water, the better the entire arm stroke will be. If a swimmer doesn't catch water early, she won't be able to catch a lot of water. Conversely, if a swimmer does catch water early, she will also catch a lot of it, and that arm stroke will likely be highly effective.

The catch is seen as the defining characteristic of the best swimmers at every level, yet it can be the hardest and most elusive skill in backstroke to master. Every aspect of the stroke must come together to produce a solid catch, and any flaw in rotation, body position, or kick will negatively affect the stroke. At the same time, a distinct, visible catch often translates into overall backstroke success.

The catch and underwater arm stroke start after the hand is fully submerged after entry. One arm is extended above the head straight above the shoulder, the pinky finger is pointed down toward the bottom of the pool, and the palm is facing out. The body should be rotated just 30 degrees to the side of the hand entering the water. The first movement is to bend at the wrist so that the fingertips point to the side and the palm faces back. The elbow bends in immediate succession so that the entire arm moves laterally to the side. The inside of the

▶ **Figure 3.1** The backstroke catch phase.

forearm faces back as well. A rule of thumb is that the amount of elbow bend determines how good the catch is, and all good backstrokers have some degree of elbow bend. In the ideal catch position, the arm forms the shape of a hook above the head, and it can cradle and catch the water that is to the side of the body. All this happens while the arm is still well above the head.

The swimmer must achieve two prerequisite positions to initiate a good catch:

1. For the elbow to bend and for the arm to twist in the manner described, the arm has to be oriented so that the point of the elbow is facing outward or laterally. The elbow will rotate upward, away from the head, when it bends.

2. To orient the way properly and to keep the hand underwater during the entire catch, the body first needs to be rotated toward the side of hand entry and the rotation needs to be completed before the catch is made.

Without hitting these positions, the arm will physically not be able to bend to get to catch position. If a swimmer does not set up the catch well, the swimmer's arm stays straight and pushes water either downward or to the side. In either case, water is pushed in a direction that isn't optimal for producing propulsion. Regardless of whether the arm moves downward or to the side, the reason is the same—the rotation isn't completed soon enough. The swimmer usually compensates for this by pressing the arm down to help continue the body rotation onto that side. Similarly, the arm can be pressed laterally to the side if body rotation stops before reaching the recommended angle of 30 degrees relative to the surface of the water. The swimmer should attain the proper depth for the catch based on the arm entry and body rotation, not because the arm is pushing downward. Note that this way of thinking is in conflict with the instruction that many swimmers receive about the catch—to drive the hand and arm deep to assist with rotation. But using the timing and technique described here is the best way to achieve the most propulsive stroke.

In the ideal backstroke technique, the palm should never be pitched downward to face the bottom of the pool during the initial part of the stroke. The thumb should always face straight up and the palm should initially face laterally before it quickly transitions to facing backward toward the feet for the remainder of the arm stroke. The fingertips need to face directly to the side (laterally) while the palm faces rearward. Any compromise of those positions compromises the catch.

The optimal catch may be visible to an observer on deck, and anybody in the water will definitely be able to see it. Besides the body rotation and arm orientation, the proper depth and width of the hand and arm are important to achieving a proper catch.

Depth of the Stroke

The hand should travel through the water in a straight line at a constant depth for the most propulsive phase of the pull, from the start of the catch until the hand reaches the waist. The hand should be just under the surface of the water, or as shallow as a swimmer can move his hand through the water without causing disturbance on the surface. Stating an exact depth that a swimmer should aim to achieve is difficult because many of the best backstrokers vary in this to some degree, but a general depth of 4 to 12 inches (10 to 30 cm) under the surface is recommended. Swimmers often cannot think in terms of exact numbers, so the general term *shallow* should be sufficient. This depth and the straight-line pull pattern will enable the strongest and most efficient pull.

As mentioned earlier, conflicting teachings have encouraged athletes to reach as deeply as possible during the catch and then move the hand down and then up in a wave-shaped pull pattern. The rationalization that this type of a pull pattern will produce lift-based propulsion has already been discussed, but another incorrect belief behind trying to have a deep pull is that deeper water is better to pull. Some have said that deep water is still water. It is true that the hand can be too shallow if it's breaking the surface or creating waves at the surface, but if the surface is not disturbed and all the motion is directed toward pushing water in the proper direction, the shallow pull will be more effective than a deeper one. There is no compelling evidence that a deep pull will be any more beneficial or efficient than a shallow pull. In fact, a deeper pull has a number of major drawbacks that outweigh any potential insignificant benefit that we could envision. A deeper pull will

- lead to a less effective catch and initiate an S-shaped hand path that will direct water up and down, not backward toward the feet;
- increase the total time required to execute the stroke, reducing stroke rate and speed at the same time; and
- induce a weaker pull because the arm will be too far behind the plane of the body (more to come on this point later).

A pull that stays to the side of the body and keeps the hand just under the surface is definitely what we see repeatedly in video of the best backstrokers. The pull of many world-record holders and Olympic medalists is so shallow that in underwater video taken from the side just underneath the surface, the hands move through the water at a depth just underneath the laneline buoys in the pool (in other words, the pull is very shallow). Pulling in this way means that the swimmer wastes no time or movements to get deep and that the hand is constantly pushing water backward because it is not wavering up or down.

A pull that takes place just beneath the surface of the water is not only the most efficient but also the strongest because the swimmer's arm will be to the side of the body, allowing the body and arm to remain connected and work together to produce power. The concept of the kinetic chain, in which forces and power generated in one part of the body can flow to other parts of the body to augment the forces generated locally, is not new to sport, but it is not commonly discussed in swimming literature.

During the initial phase of the pull, the upper arm should be positioned in the scapular plane to achieve the strongest and most effective pull (figure 3.2).

▶ **Figure 3.2** Initial phase of the backstroke pull.

Imagine looking at a swimmer head on as she catches the water with the left arm. If the upper arm is in the scapular plane, we should be able to draw a straight line from the right shoulder to the left elbow. In this position the arm can remain connected to the body (a relatively stable base of support) so that the swimmer can engage the strongest muscles of the upper back when producing propulsion.

Although the natural range of motion for most people allows the upper arm to be slightly behind the back, the swimmer can safely aim to have the upper arm and the back form a straight line with each other. In many instances, erring on the side of having the arm too far forward is better than having the arm too far behind the scapular plane. When we see this alignment of the upper arm and back, we call it being lined up or in line. Executing a shallow pull makes it likely that the arm and back will line up and work together.

Imagine being asked to throw a ball as hard as possible toward the ground while standing up. The best, most natural arm angle for that throw would be to have it somewhere between directly in front of you and directly to the side of the body. It would definitely not be a throw that you would try to make with your arm reaching behind your body. Now make that throw while lying on your back with your upper arm also in contact with the ground. You will find that to generate the most force when throwing the ball, the arm will be to the side and in line with the back. That's how the backstroke arm pull should feel. Translate that to lying in water by rotating the body downward so that the throwing arm is completely submerged in the water. That's what the backstroke pull should be like.

Mechanics and Injury Risk

Unfortunately, backstrokers often experience shoulder pain. Most swimmers attribute shoulder pain to the repeated cyclic motion of the arm stroke, but more specifically and accurately, it should be attributed to flaws in the repeated cyclic motion of the arm stroke. This diagnosis is actually a good thing because it means that the problem can be remedied and relieved.

When the arm and back are not in line with each other, and the upper arm is behind the line of the back, the position is called humeral hyperextension. Repeated pulling motions in this position are not within the natural range of movement for most people, and the shoulder impingement can become painful over time. To diagnose the contributing factors to any pain, the swimmer must be able to locate the specific point in the stroke where the shoulder is causing pain. If the swimmer identifies the first half of the underwater arm stroke, specifically the catch, as the part that hurts, then the pain is likely arising because the arm is too far behind the back and outside the scapular plane.

A combination of two movements can fix the pathological mechanics, relieve the pain, and possibly eliminate any stroke problems. The swimmer can either bring the arm closer to the surface or increase the body rotation to that side. Most of the time, the cause of the pain is that the swimmer drives the arm too deep on the initial hand entry and catch; to remedy this problem, the swimmer just needs to bring the hand and arm closer to the surface.

Midpull Mechanics

After the catch position is established, the palm and forearm need to maintain pressure against the water and maximize propulsion. The initial hook-shape catch position of the arm becomes less of a hook as the arm moves through the water until the arm reaches shoulder level, at which point the arm should be directly out to the side of the body (figure 3.3). At this point, with the upper arm and the back lined up and the hand, elbow, and shoulder all at the same

© Human Kinetics

▶ **Figure 3.3** Backstroke midpull.

level, the elbow angle should be about 110 to 120 degrees, or slightly more than 90 degrees. Because no swimmer can determine exact arm angle when moving at full speed, this figure is just a guide to give a swimmer a goal to strive for. If the elbow angle is much larger than 110 to 120 degrees, the arm likely will be at a mechanical disadvantage because it is too straight (long moment arm from the shoulder to the hand) and it will not be possible to engage the strongest muscles in the body optimally. If the elbow angle is much smaller than 110 to 120 degrees, the arm might be too compact and too close to the body for it to be able to engage in an effective pull.

A key aspect to an effective pull is for the hand and elbow to move through the water together in the same plane. A common flaw is for the arm to collapse so that the elbow is in front of the hand as the arm moves through the water. From the moment when the swimmer initiates the catch, the goal should be to have the hand and forearm pull through the water together. If the arm collapses, the swimmer will not be able to maximize the size of the pulling surface and will likely try to rush through the pull too quickly. This often happens if a swimmer tries to swim with a higher stroke rate than her strength can handle while maintaining proper technique. With the elbow pulling in front of the hand, moving the arm through the water will definitely be easier and the arm tempo will be faster, but the position is not mechanically efficient. The swimmer should slow the motion to a speed that is appropriate for her strength to maintain the best technique. When the swimmer demonstrates the ability to maintain the proper mechanics, she can progress to faster tempos.

A similar indicator that the hand may not be holding on to water during the pull occurs when the hand slides or slices through the water, that is, when the palm is pitched downward and the thumb is leading the hand movement through the water. The palm needs to face squarely toward the feet. If this is not happening, the swimmer again might need to slow the arm speed to focus on maintaining proper mechanics.

The lats, pecs, and even the core should be involved in the pull; the goal is to pull with the entire body, not just the arm. The entire point of having the arm connected to the body is that the arm is much stronger when its motion is supported by the body. Olympic champion Aaron Peirsol went as far as describing this whole-body involvement as a side crunch. This side crunch is much more than just a feeling to this swimmer and others; it's visible to the observer in many of the top backstrokers. The upper body bends or crunches to the side during the catch, as if the nearer hip is trying to connect to the hand. Stand up and hold your right arm out to your side as if in the catch position. Now let the right side of your core tense up and cave in a little as your right hip moves outward a little. The tension of the entire right side is the body reinforcing the position of the arm. A wiggle motion in backstroke is traditionally discouraged, but this particular action, if subtle and controlled, reinforces the arm to make it stronger.

If we can agree that what's been described is a good wiggle motion, the bad wiggle that most swim coaches cringe at occurs when there is no tension in the core, which is clearly the opposite of a side crunch. It usually occurs when a young swimmer's arm enters above his head and the whole body stretches out and overextends on the side that the arm is entering. The legs of the swimmer then fishtail from side to side as each arm enters the water.

Finish

During the finish (figure 3.4), the arm should still be pushing water backward toward the feet while staying at a constant depth until the hand gets to about the waist. At that point, the hand should start to pitch downward and inward while pushing water in those directions. When the arm reaches full extension, the hand should be slightly deeper than the hip and the palm should be facing inward (pinky down, thumb up) and just wider than shoulder width.

This description of the finish contradicts the principle already discussed about pushing water backward to move forward. But the finish serves a specific role in the stroke—helping to drive body rotation and pivot the body to the other side to set up the next catch—so it's OK that water is not directed entirely toward the feet.

During each arm pull, the body (hips, torso, and shoulders) rotates toward the side that is pulling. The downward motion to the finish then provides leverage that allows that side of the body to rotate in the other direction to initiate the catch on the opposite arm. The swimmer needs to hold on to and maintain pressure on the water through the finish so that the body has a base off which to rotate. If not for the finish, the body would rely only on the kick and the opposite arm entry to rotate to the other side, and that is not sufficient. Hitting a good catch requires the body to be rotated completely before starting the catch, so the contribution from the finish is necessary.

People have conflicting views on how the finish should be performed. The most widely held view (and one that conflicts with the model described here) is that the finish should sweep upward toward the surface and straight into the

© Human Kinetics

▶ **Figure 3.4** Backstroke finish.

recovery. The thought behind this movement is derived from thinking that the swimmer can kill two birds with one stone, continuing to push water toward the feet while progressing right from the finish into the exit from the water or recovery. This technique is flawed in two ways. First, if the finish sweeps upward, that upward push opposes the rotation needed to set up the opposite arm catch. Second, sweeping upward into the recovery implies that the hand has room to move upward in the water. If the catch and pull are done at the proper depth, not much room will be available for the hand to move upward during the finish. Some successful world-class backstrokers have finished in this way, but in observing the entry, catch, and rotation of their strokes, the rotation over to the other side isn't smooth. Instead, the rotation appears to be forced by the arm entry and kick. Also, the catch isn't the sharpest.

Rotation

Body rotation in backstroke enables the body to make each arm stroke as strong and efficient as possible. An optimal body roll allows the arm to flex appropriately, hit the catch, and connect to the body. If the body stayed completely flat, the arms would pull through the water extended and straight out to the side or the arm would reach behind the scapular plane. The pull would be inefficient and weak in either case.

Another important outcome of good backstroke rotation is setting up the recovery. A good rotation raises the shoulder of the recovering arm to the surface of the water and allows the recovering arm to move freely.

In backstroke, the whole body, from the shoulders to the hips and the legs, should rotate together as a unit. The difficult element of backstroke rotation is that the body has to jump quickly from being rotated toward one side of the body to being rotated toward the other side to support the alternating arm strokes. Additionally, to optimize propulsion, each rotation needs to be completed before the catch starts. Therefore, the timing and quickness of the rotation are critically important. Luckily, rotating a large amount to each side is not necessary, so if the timing and mechanics are correct, achieving the proper body roll is manageable.

Although many swimming coaches have taught that backstrokers should rotate all the way on to the side, or alternatively that more rotation is always better, that way of executing the stroke is incorrect and counterproductive. The fastest backstroke technique takes place much more on the back than it does on the side. Using video analysis tools to measure angles of USA Olympic and national team swimmers from a head-on underwater camera view, we can say with confidence that a rotation of 30 degrees to each side is average and adequate for the world's best. For reference, the 30-degree measurement represents the separation between the horizontal surface of the water and the plane of the shoulders of the swimmer. The range of rotation seen among elite backstrokers can be as little as 20 degrees to each side and as much as 40 degrees, which is still less than halfway on to the swimmer's back.

The main benefits of rotation are that it allows the arm to be fully submerged and it sets the body up to execute the best pull possible. When those criteria are fulfilled, no more rotation is necessary. One myth in swimming is that drag (not propulsive drag, but the resistance experienced by the body as it moves through the water) will be reduced by rotating all the way on to the side. This idea is incorrect because the same amount of the body will be submerged underwater regardless of whether the body is rotated 30 degrees or 90 degrees. That is because the buoyancy of the body won't change based on the amount of body rotation. By rotating all the way on to the side, more of the body isn't floating above the surface and the frontal surface area that cuts through the oncoming water remains the same, so drag remains the same. With that being the case, a 30-degree rotation is sufficient. It allows a 110- to 120-degree elbow bend, the hand to be 4 to 12 inches (10 to 30 cm) under the surface, and the upper arm to be lined up with the back.

Regarding the timing and quickness of the rotation, the general rule is that the body should rotate quickly and at a specific time in the stroke cycle—as one arm is entering and the other arm is finishing. The rotation should happen only at the beginning and end of the arm strokes, not during the most propulsive parts of the arm stroke that occur between those times. If the rotation were to occur in the middle of the stroke, the swimmer's arm would be pushing through the water as the body would be rotating away from it. The entire pull would be weaker because the body wouldn't remain engaged with the arm throughout the pull. The arm would be positioned increasingly behind the body as the arm stroke progressed. (Note that these rotation suggestions are opposite of what is appropriate in freestyle, in which the swimmer does want to rotate during the catch and propulsive phase because the body will rotate toward the arm, essentially reinforcing and strengthening it.)

To hit the timing of the rotation correctly so that it is completed before the catch and pull are initiated, the swimmer needs to make both sides of the arm stroke—the entry of one arm and the finish of the other—work together through the core. The entire body should be turning from one side to the other while the arms provide the leverage to make that happen. As the underwater arm presses downward at the finish, the hip on that side of the body should rotate upward. As the recovering arm comes down toward the water, that side of the body should rotate downward. The body should be halfway through the rotation (flat, or at zero degrees rotation) when the hand of the recovering arm is entering the water and the underwater finish is nearly complete. The second half of the rotation (the downward rotation) should happen seamlessly as the entering hand is submerged just below the surface and is starting to move outward into the catch. At the same time, the other hand and arm will be completing the finish and preparing to exit the water.

A common question is, "Where does the body rotation originate—from the hips, the shoulders, the legs, or somewhere else?" Because the rotation is being driven by one arm entry and one arm finish, the correct answer is that the rotation comes from both the hips and shoulders. When thought of and performed in that way, the rotation will be done effectively and properly.

When it comes to errors around execution of the rotation, the part that most swimmers miss is not using the finish to drive the hips into the rotation. Late rotation is the result, which creates problems in engaging the catch with the opposite arm. In some extreme cases of late rotation, the body may not even start to rotate until the hand of the recovering arm enters the water. When swimmers use the finish of the pull as leverage for the rotation, the rotation will be on time and the catch and pull will have the best opportunity to be ideal.

Another common and noticeable mistake in backstroke occurs on the hand entry. The hand should enter the water pinky first and the palm should be facing away from the body and in line with the shoulders or just outside shoulder width so that it can move right into the catch after entry. The flaw that many swimmers have is that their hands enter too narrowly, inside the line of the shoulders and possibly even crossing over the centerline of the body behind the head. The hand may also enter with the back of the hand first instead of pinky first. This mistake is often misdiagnosed. When this crossover occurs, it becomes one of the most frustrating things to correct because most swimmers take an incorrect approach when trying to fix the stroke flaw. Most swimmers attempt to correct the entry by simply moving the arm wider, but regardless of how hard the swimmer works on it, the hand positioning at entry often never improves at all. In most cases, the narrow and back-of-the-hand entry is caused by a late rotation; when the rotation is late, the entry occurs while the body is still rotated to the wrong side. The natural point of entry for the hand is therefore too narrow because of the way that the body is angled at the time. Late rotation timing will cause the arm to swing slightly across the water instead of straight down into it. Proper rotation timing—with the body rotated flat at the time of the hand entry—will lead to the proper hand entry location.

Arm Recovery

The above-water arm recovery is the connection between the propulsive phases of the arm strokes—the finish of one arm stroke and the entry and catch of the next. The recovery itself may not directly affect propulsion, but it plays an important role in the overall execution of the stroke. The overall nature of the recovery motion can be best described as a controlled throw of the entire arm. The arm motion should be relaxed but not floppy, controlled but not tense, quick but not forced, almost like throwing a ball or swinging a golf club. After the initiation of the recovery, the momentum of the arm swinging up and around the water will help carry it through the entire above-water motion.

The recovery starts after the downward finish of the underwater arm stroke. The hand should be lifted to the surface with the thumb side up. From the end of the finish until the arm breaks the surface of the water is the only underwater phase of the stroke that is nonpropulsive, but the critical role of the downward finish in the rotation timing necessitates having this dead space.

The entire arm recovery takes place at shoulder width. Initially, the arm should rise vertically while still next to the hip, and then throughout the motion the arm stays in line with the shoulder and next to the body. Because the body is never rotated a significant amount during the recovery, the shoulders and arms remain to the side of the body. The body does not need to be rotated more than the recommended 30 degrees to lift the shoulder farther, because continued rotation will affect the underwater pull on the opposite side. From the swimmer's viewpoint, the arms will always remain to the side of the face and on the edge of the field of vision. If the shoulder touches or comes close to the chin, or if the hand or arm is in front of the face where the swimmer can easily see it, the arm recovery is too narrow or the rotation is excessive.

For more than half of the recovery, the hand should be oriented with the thumb leading the motion and the palm facing inward (medially), but the hand will enter the water with the pinky finger first and the palm facing outward to set up the best underwater catch. The rotation of the hand from a thumb-first to a pinky-first position happens after the hand is at the highest point of the recovery, as the hand and arm are on the downward approach to entering the water and in conjunction with the body's rotation to that side. The hand rotation is often taught as an independent movement at the top of the recovery, but it is functionally and technically better to execute this motion as the arm is on the downward approach to the entry and while the body is pivoting to that side.

The completion of the arm recovery and initiation of the catch happen in quick succession, as the hand and arm continue the path that has been set in motion and drive down into the water pinky first. In this phase the arm and the body move together toward the water to put the hand and arm in the perfect position together to start the next catch. This combination of simultaneous movements—the downward finish, hand rotation, body pivot, and arm entry—is critical as a swimmer prepares for the next catch, and this aspect of technique is one of the things that sets the elite backstrokers apart from everyone else.

Often coaches comment that the hand should enter the water in such a way to avoid forming air bubbles. Unfortunately, no matter how the hand enters the water, air bubbles are created and those bubbles can stay attached to the arm and trail off it throughout the catch and midpull of the underwater arm stroke. Many people believe that these air bubbles are detrimental, but further investigation is necessary to determine whether the bubbles have any effect on propulsion. The creation of bubbles is nearly inevitable as the wide, rounded edge of the human hand and arm crash straight down into the water. The fact that the arm stroke starts immediately without any time for the air bubbles to dissipate off the arm naturally also explains why the bubbles will undoubtedly trail off the arm as it moves through the water. This phenomenon exists with even the world's best backstrokers, which would lead us to believe that the existence of air bubbles in the stroke is inconsequential.

Kicking

Debate has often occurred about the contribution of kicking in freestyle and backstroke to propulsion. Some even suggest that kicking should be deemphasized because it takes up valuable energy and oxygen with disproportional gains in speed. This thinking has been contradicted by the practical evidence of the best swimmers in the United States as well as the world. Among USA national team members, an overwhelming majority are fast kickers who use a six-beat kick (i.e., six kicks per arm cycle). Kicking in backstroke serves three purposes:

1. It provides propulsion to the stroke. Certainly, when separated from the arms, kicking is much less propulsive than pulling. But kicking lightens the load on the arms and allows the arms not to pull as much or as hard to travel the same distance. Swimmers with good kicks theoretically can take fewer strokes and conserve arm strength.

2. It aids body rotation. A good kick supports good technique because it provides a stable foundation off which the body can rotate. The hips and legs rotate along with the body, and the kick helps make that happen.

3. It supports proper head and body position. A good kick allows the legs and hips to remain high in the water. Otherwise, the legs will drag and sink, bringing the hips down too.

All the best backstrokers are strong kickers, and the technique itself is generally the same for all of them.

The most propulsive part of the kick is the upkick (the kick toward the surface of the water), and the finish of the upkick is the most propulsive phase of the kick. The motion is composed of two parts: driving the knee toward the surface and snapping the lower leg upward toward the surface. The first part is driven by the hip flexors, whereas the second part is like a leg extension exercise and is driven by the quadriceps. At the completion of the leg extension, the motion should follow through the feet and toes. The upkick should finish just at the surface.

Many look for churning water at the surface as a sign of a good kick, and this will happen if the legs whip through a great upkick and the toes are at or just peek through the plane of the surface. Aiming for the feet to break the surface of the water is not recommended because this action does not increase propulsion; kicking air doesn't help a swimmer move forward. Breaking the surface of the water also throws off the body's balance in the water because one leg would be free in the air while the other is pushing on water under the surface.

Of course, every upkick is accompanied by a downkick. Some propulsion certainly results from the downkick, but because of human anatomy, the upkick (legs moving forward) is always going to be more powerful and propulsive than the downkick (legs moving backward). This doesn't mean that the downkick should be emphasized any less. The primary role of the downkick, however, should be to set up the upkick, so a quick, fast movement for the downkick just means that the upkick will be ready to fire faster and sooner. The downkick occurs by driving the leg and the heel down toward the bottom of the pool. The legs should be held straight, but without locking the knees, during this motion. The exact depth of the downkick will vary by individual (a swimmer with longer legs will finish lower than a swimmer with shorter legs), but it can definitely be said that the downkick will end (and the upkick will start) deeper than the hips. A swimmer should not be worried about kicking too deeply. As long as the swimmer is able to kick six times per arm cycle, the kick is of proper size.

A six-beat kick is the most natural and common style of kicking used in backstroke. A few elite backstrokers have been observed using a four-beat kick, and at least one swimmer kicks with an eight-beat kick (Olympic champion and world-record holder Natalie Coughlin, no less). A four- or eight-beat kick is unnatural, however, and is likely a sign that the upper body and lower body are disconnected and not working together. A four- or eight-beat kick means that an even number of kicks are occurring per arm stroke and that the right and left sides of the body will be asymmetrical. In other words, if the right arm enters when the left leg is extended in the upkick, the left arm also enters when the left leg is extended in the upkick (the opposite pattern seen with the right arm). Consideration should be given to changing a four- or eight-beat kicker into a six-beat kicker. Four beats means that there is opportunity for two more kicks per cycle. Eight beats could mean that the legs are just moving extremely fast, but it could also mean that the arms are moving too slowly in order to accommodate the extra kicks.

A few successful backstrokers cross their legs sideways on top of each other. In 2012 two elite backstrokers in the United States, national team members and Olympic Trials finalists David Plummer and Bonnie Brandon, kicked in this way. Imagining how this kick could be beneficial is difficult, but these swimmers are among the best in the country. Plummer made a concerted effort to change the kick to a more traditional, no-crossover technique. In attempting to make this change, Plummer and his coach found that the athlete's overall speed was affected because he could not maintain the same arm tempo as he had previously, and he would get tired more quickly. After college, Plummer abandoned the traditional kick, went on to achieve personal best times, and become a national champion in the 100-meter backstroke.

The national champion with the scissor kick and the Olympic champion with eight beats per cycle just go to show that occasionally someone can succeed without textbook technique. Consideration needs to be made for how a change affects other aspects of the stroke, whether it is arm tempo, physiological endurance, or something else, especially if the affected areas are strengths of the particular athlete.

Body and Head Position

The third purpose of a backstroke kick is to support good head and body position. The legs, hips, and upper body should all ride through the water as close to the surface as possible and at the same level. The reason for the legs and hips to be in the same line is to reduce resistance. If the upper body, hips, and legs are not horizontal, then more surface area of the body than necessary is pushing against the water and resisting the direction in which the swimmer wants to travel. A swimmer who is bouncing up and down in the water typically has a mechanical flaw in the stroke that pushes the swimmer upward. (The swimmer will then fall, or bounce down, in the water because the action that is pushing the swimmer upward cannot be maintained.)

The head should sit a little higher in the water than the rest of the body and poke through the surface in a slightly tilted position. In the proper position, the face and forehead will be above the surface and the line of the water will be at ear level. The head tilt is subtle, as if the head were resting on a thin pillow in bed. The head tilt will not be anywhere close to having the chin tucked and touching the chest, nor will the head be neutral so that the eyes are looking straight up at the ceiling. Thus, the neck will be slightly curved forward and the shoulders will be relaxed forward, instead of both the neck and shoulders being stiff and upright as if the person is standing at attention. This natural position of the neck and shoulders allows the shoulders to move freely to swing around and pull, and it allows the upper body to rotate and support the arms.

The hips will be in an ideal position to kick and simultaneously reduce form drag if they are at the surface of the water. But to maintain optimal position, a swimmer must avoid doing two things—arching the back and pushing the head back into the water. Arching the back may help bring the hips closer to the surface, but in doing so, it puts the legs and upper body into terribly compromised positions. With an arched back, the legs will drop lower and the shoulders will likely be pulled back too. The hips will also be tilted in such a way that the legs cannot kick freely and effectively. If the back is to be curved in any direction, being curved into flexion is much better than being arched into hyperextension. Flexing the torso slightly may lead the swimmer to sit up more than necessary and be difficult to maintain over the course of a race, but at least the arms and legs will be able to contribute maximally and not create more drag than necessary.

Summary

Coaches need to focus on a number of key elements when teaching swimmers to achieve world-class backstroke technique.

Swimmers should focus on the timing and magnitude of the body rotation. The body roll should occur within a short window as one arm finishes its pull and the other enters the water. Swimmers need to achieve between 20 and 40 degrees of rotation to each side to set up the catch and achieve proper pulling depth.

The catch sets up the entire stroke. In the catch, athletes should focus on setting the hand and arm in the proper position for the remainder of the pull. Position the upper arm in the scapular plane to link it to the body and orient the palm of the hand and the forearm to push water toward the feet throughout the stroke.

The stroke should occur between 4 and 12 inches (10 and 30 cm) below the surface of the water. Achieving a deep catch and pull is unnecessary. In fact, doing so may be counterproductive to generating propulsion.

The swimmer should push the water straight back toward the feet to generate the most propulsion. Resistive drag produces more force than the lift forces commonly generated through sweeping S motions. Directing as much force toward the feet as possible will propel the swimmer through the water.

The swimmer should maintain a flat body posture in the water with the head tilted ever so slightly forward. Lifting the head too much or arching the back increases the resistive drag experienced by the body and places the arms and legs in positions from which they cannot produce propulsion optimally.

Swimmers should strive for a six-beat kick. The kick is important for generating propulsion and maintaining body position, but more important, it sets up and drives the body rotation that is necessary for a successful stroke.

Do not be afraid to play around with things. Watch video, experiment by making small changes to mechanics, and above all ask questions. That is the way we all get better.

CHAPTER 4

Breaststroke Technique

—Russell Mark

There is a visual perception that breaststroke technique varies greatly among swimmers, even among elite breaststrokers. Therefore, a variety of explanations and teachings of the stroke exist. Many approach breaststroke technique in a timid, vague way.

But close examination and analysis of underwater video show that elite breaststrokers have a lot in common in the fundamentals of their swimming technique. Hundreds of hours of unbiased film study of the world's best breaststrokers performing in races and workouts have led to the observations detailed in this chapter. Every aspect is broken down in detail to explain the purpose and mechanics of each component. All swimmers and coaches should strive to gravitate toward these foundational traits, regardless of the above-water appearance or a swimmer's feel of the stroke.

Breaststroke Is Won in the Spaces

Bill Boomer, a renowned swimming technique expert known for his unique perspective and explanation, said that breaststroke is "won in the spaces" (personal correspondence). The significance of this phrase is profound, when it is understood and made a focus of the stroke. The "space" in breaststroke, according to Boomer, is the portion of the stroke capturing the extension of the arms and the ensuing forward glide, as in the space (or time) between the propulsive parts of the arm stroke. How the breaststroke is won in these spaces is best explained anecdotally. In a 200 or 400 individual medley race, breaststroke specialists are typically included in the field of swimmers. During the breaststroke leg of the race, dramatic lead changes can occur. When the better breaststrokers make their moves and surge ahead, we can see that the performance advantage is gained in these spaces, not during the part of the stroke in which the arms are pulling back and supposedly creating forward propulsion. Everyone would agree about this observation, yet it's still counterintuitive and important to recognize.

If the breaststroke is won in the spaces, what allows a swimmer to maximize speed in the spaces and what role does the arm pull play if the more significant part of the stroke seems to occur when the arms are recovering forward or are extended in front of the body? Several theories have been put forward to explain how performance gains are made. The predominant thought about breaststroke is that a great kick is the key to being a great breaststroker and maximizing speed in the spaces. But the kick is only part of the equation. Fast breaststroke, maximizing performance in the spaces, is all about a using the body and core to surge forward. The kick, pull, and good timing are all important components of a fast breaststroke, but they are all driven by the body and core.

Another observation can be made when comparing good and mediocre breaststrokers. Good breaststrokers do a better job of maintaining forward speed throughout the stroke. Average breaststrokers tend to adopt a stop-and-go style of stroke, stopping when the upper body is at the highest point at the peak of the breath and going when the arms are extending forward and the legs are kicking. It should be obvious why a swimmer would never want to approach a stopping point in the stroke, and the best breaststrokers minimize velocity fluctuations in the stroke cycle so that they are always moving forward. In addition, by eliminating and minimizing any dead spots in the stroke, a breaststroker will be entering the space of the stroke with more speed, which will lead to even more effective use of the space.

Body Line in Breaststroke

Every breaststroke cycle should start and finish from a highly streamlined body position, also called the body line. Even if just for a fraction of a second, a good breaststroker will achieve a good body line to maximize the speed created from the pull, kick, and body drive.

Good Body Line

An exceptional body line is similar to a tight streamlined position. This position is the fastest for traveling through the water when the arms and legs are not propelling the body forward. The position of the hands, head, hips, and feet are great indicators of a good breaststroke body line. From the fingertips to the toes, the body forms a straight horizontal line just under the surface of the water with all points aligned. The arms are outstretched above the head.

A good breaststroke body line is different from the streamlining that a swimmer achieves off a start or turn in two ways: The hands should not overlap, nor should the arms be squeezed together against the ears. A good breaststroke body line is achieved when the head is between the arms and the arms just lightly touch the sides of the head, if at all. The arms should be straight, but not forcefully extended, and the hands should be inside shoulder width. The hands should be flat, the palms should be down, and the hands should have some space between them.

Body Line Errors and Corrections

Breaks in the body line most often occur with the head position. Typically, poor positioning occurs because the head is held too high. The head needs to hide between the arms as much as possible. The eyes don't necessarily need to look straight down, and in fact many of the best breaststrokers tilt their heads slightly forward so that their eyes are looking down and slightly forward. A high head position creates additional drag and slows the swimmer by causing the hips, legs, and feet to drop in the water. This position presents more of the body to the oncoming water flow, resulting in a considerable increase in drag. If the hips and legs appear to be too low and dragging through the water, a coach should take notice of the head position first and see whether the overall body position can be corrected simply by adjusting the head position. Getting the head in line will likely raise the feet, hips, and legs.

Also, a swimmer may be forcing the head too far below the body line. This position is also not beneficial to performance. Dropping the head also creates excess drag, and it requires the swimmer to lift the head more than normal to take a breath. A swimmer's head may go below the streamline because of over-compensating for throwing the head down after the breath. The intention behind throwing the head down is a good one, but the effort typically is misdirected, resulting in increased drag. The swimmer should use this lunge to drive the body and head forward, not downward, helping to maintain the streamlined body line.

Another common contributor to a poor body line is driving the hands and arms downward and deeper into the water when extending forward during the arm recovery. Downward motion increases the overall drag experienced by the swimmer, but the consequences of these actions do not stop there. Arising from the deep position of the hands, the swimmer has to bring the hands, arms, head, and body back up to the surface of the water to get into the next stroke cycle. This effort is wasted, and the body position that results from the upper half of the body climbing back to the surface forces the lower half of the body—the hips and legs—to drop down in the water. This position is not only a poor body line but also can be deemed illegal for performing a dolphin kick.

Arm Pull

After the fundamentals of a good body line are established, the focus of the stroke should be on generating propulsion. The propulsive movements of each stroke start with the arm pull. The arm pull in breaststroke is different from that of the other three strokes in that it doesn't drive the overall propulsion of the stroke; the legs and the kick contribute as much as the arms do to the overall propulsion generated in the stroke. The general shape of the pull pattern is an oval shape that is wider to the sides and flatter and more squished in the front-to-back direction. The path of the hands never makes any sharp angles or changes of direction.

The primary role of the pull is to set up the rest of the stroke, including the all-important spaces. The focus of the pull should not be to pull water toward the feet, as in the other competitive strokes. In fact, at no point in the stroke cycle do the palms or arms push water directly backward.

Video Analysis

Abundant video evidence suggests that overall speed in breaststroke is not dictated by the arm pull. In dissecting video of four swimmers (two male and two female) who have been world champions, Olympic champions, world-record holders, or American record holders in both the 100-meter and 200-meter breaststroke, we can identify the technique differences that occur when swimmers change speeds from 200 pace to 100 pace.

What the video analysis showed was interesting. The speed and tempo of the 100-meter races, as expected, was faster than the speed and tempo of the 200-meter races. The glide time between each stroke cycle in the 100-meter races was much shorter. Also, in the 100-meter races, the feet came up and recovered toward the buttocks faster to set up the kick.

But the hand speed—the time it took from start to finish of the arm pull—remained the same despite the different speeds and tempos of the races. This same phenomenon was seen in all four swimmers, and the finding indicates that breaststroke speed may not be determined by arm speed. Instead, swimming speed is likely affected more by the glide time and the speed of the leg recovery as the breaststroke swimmer sets up the kick. The bottom line is that to swim faster, the best breaststrokers do not pull more water with the hands and arms nor do they pull faster.

Sculling Out

The first movement of the arm stroke is for the hands to scull outward (figure 4.1). With the arms remaining straight, the palms face outward and separate from each other, pressing directly out to the sides. The final width of this sculling motion varies by swimmer, but it should fall outside the athlete's shoulder width, generally with the arms at 11 o'clock and 1 o'clock position if the arms were the hands of an analog clock. Generally, male swimmers tend to scull wider than female swimmers do because men have greater strength at the wider positions than women do. The head should remain in line with the rest of the body during this beginning phase of the pull.

Of all possible movements that a swimmer can do to start the pull, this sculling action is definitely not the fastest. But it's no coincidence that all the fastest breaststrokers in the world perform a similar sculling action. Many state that

© Human Kinetics

▶ **Figure 4.1** The hands scull out.

it's a focus of their stroke. As seen in underwater video taken from a side view, the palms are clearly oriented to face toward the sides of the pool.

Isolated, the outward scull is not highly propulsive or effective, but its effect on the rest of the stroke is beneficial. The scull keeps the head and the rest of the body in line for a while longer. Most important, it sets up the round shape of the arm pull, which is crucial when the arm pull transitions from moving backward to recovering forward. So although the outward scull is not the fastest initial option of the pull, it is extremely important to proper execution of the remainder of the stroke.

The best thing that a breaststroker can do is to be patient with the initiation of the arm pull and the execution of the breath. A swimmer must trust that waiting to get propulsion out of the arms and taking a late breath are both critical to maintaining overall speed.

If a swimmer goes for immediate gratification and tries to get propulsion too early in the stroke by pointing the fingertips down toward the bottom of the pool, keeping the elbows high, and pushing water straight back with the palms and forearms, the propulsion generated by the arms in the first part of the stroke will be greater. But this approach to technique, while commonly taught, is much less efficient when looking at the big picture. It will cause the upper body to rise earlier so that the swimmer can take a breath, sinking the hips and legs lower, and force the swimmer to exert more energy because of the greater emphasis on the arms. The pull pattern will be more straight back, rather than the recommended round shape, making the transition to the recovery (and the space) more abrupt and less smooth and effective.

These negative effects make a pull in which propulsion comes from the arms a less attractive option. With that said, a swimmer may experience some success using this type of stroke in a short-course yards race because less actual swimming is done per length and the swimmer may be able to maintain this type of pull without fatiguing and slowing down. But when competing in a 25-meter or 50-meter pool, the concept of pulling straight back will not provide the best result for many athletes.

Deeper Hands

After the outward scull with straight arms, the hands continue to move wider but also start to gain some depth in the water. The fingertips pitch downward, and the forearms rotate downward as well. The elbows stay at the same level and should not drop much deeper in the water. The arms are angled so that they start to push water downward and backward. During this phase of the arm pull, the head starts to rise toward the surface and the upper body starts angling upward in preparation for the breath.

After the outward scull has been completed, the arm pull can be best described as scooping or gathering water and bringing all that water toward the hips. The motion of the arms in this phase of the stroke is actually three-dimensional; components of the pull occur front to back, side to side, and up and down. The hands and arms simultaneously move backward (toward the feet) and wider and then come closer and deeper before they return to the surface.

The widest point of the pull occurs when the arms are still in front of the shoulders. From that point, the hand path rounds out and starts moving in toward the body. The hands are pitched inward as well and press deeper at a much greater rate while also moving backward. That motion drives the shoulders and head to come out of the water.

As a rule, when the hands are moving laterally, the palms should be pitched outward or inward in the same direction that the hands are moving. The hands should never slice through the water pinky first or thumb first; rather, the palms should change their angle of attack so that they are pushing directly against the water in the direction that the hands are moving.

Taking Breath

During the inward sweep, not any earlier in the stroke, the face breaks the surface of the water. Because the upper body is rising, the elbows must remain at the same depth in the water even though the hands press deeper. Underwater video of world-class breaststrokers shows surprising depth of the hands during this phase of the stroke; in fact, some swimmers' hands are deeper than the entire rest of their bodies. Allowing some depth to the hands is necessary to support the height of the upper body during the breath. The key is that the depth of the hands occurs while the hands are moving inward and backward; they should never be oriented in such a way that they are pressing directly toward the bottom of the pool.

When the upper body is rising above the water during the arm stroke, note that the lifting of the torso occurs because of the movement of the arms, not because the swimmer is actively forcing the head up or arching the back. Additionally, the swimmer should not be thinking about lifting the upper body through the back of the neck. These movements can force the swimmer too high and cause excessive up-and-down motions that produce drag and drain energy within the stroke.

Although the body is rising, the swimmer should focus on staying forward and directing the motion of the body forward. The upper body remains at a forward angle over the surface of the water, rising up and forward through the line of the shoulders. The shoulders point diagonally forward and should never be pulled back.

Many swimmers and coaches refer to a feeling of pulling the hips forward. For many swimmers and coaches, that teaching cue helps to focus efforts on keeping the body moving forward as the torso rises up for the breath. The general concept behind pulling the hips forward draws from the inward motion of the arm stroke, during which the swimmer emphasizes anchoring the arms in the water so that the hips and body move forward toward the hands. During the inward motion, the body also rises, and by focusing on moving the hips and body forward, the upper body stays forward as well. The opposite occurs if the upper body lifts up too much; the hips and legs will angle or move downward.

Positioning the Head

The swimmer's head position also relates directly to the body position and the body line achieved during the stroke. When the head breaks the surface, and through most of the time when the head is returning under the surface, the eyes should look mostly forward with maybe a hint of looking downward. The chin and the chest need to be clearly separated, and the swimmer's chin should not be tucked.

As the head comes back down and approaches the surface of the water, the eyes can look more downward. When the head is back in line between the arms, the eyes look almost completely downward toward the bottom of the pool. Further investigation is necessary to gain complete understanding of the merit of having the eyes looking forward during the arm pull, but one USA Olympic coach who is a staunch proponent of the head-up and eyes-forward technique theorizes that the head position helps the swimmer engage the upper-body muscles in the pull more effectively.

Transitioning to Recovery

About midway through the inward motion, when the hands pitch down to the point that they are almost underneath the elbows, the critical aspect of transitioning the arms from pulling water to recovering the arms forward takes place. At this point, the arm bend at the elbows increases as the hands change directions to move forward and upward toward the surface.

One key to a good transition is that the hands should not pull back beyond the vertical plane of the shoulders. Keeping the hands in front of the body ensures that the transition to the forward recovery is smooth and efficient. Pulling any farther back might give the swimmer a little more propulsion from the arms, but doing so slows the transition, makes the space less effective, and can cause the upper body to lift too high. All of these factors contribute directly to the dreaded stop-and-go type of breaststroke discussed previously.

Although the hands should not pull back past the line of the shoulders, the elbows can go farther back than that. The elbows of most successful breaststrokers end up right next to the sides of the body, nearly touching their sides. At that point, the hands have risen to the point at which the forearms are horizontal in the water and the fingertips are pointing forward.

Being able to press the body forward and maintain forward speed throughout the arm stroke is a critical aspect to fast breaststroke, and a balance must be found between getting the most out of the pull while still being able to achieve the necessary forward body surge. A swimmer might even find that he can surge the body forward more effectively if the arms stay wider and more in front of the body. The relationship is interesting: Having the biggest or strongest pull is often not necessary to swim faster. This idea goes against the natural tendency of most swimmers, who learn in other strokes to grab as much water as possible and pull or push it backward toward the feet. The best breaststroke pull is full of subtle nuances and violations to established rules for the other strokes: Don't pull as far back as possible, scull outward initially instead of pulling straight back, and move the arms laterally more than they move toward the feet. Although different from what a swimmer would do in the butterfly, backstroke, or freestyle, these criteria set up the body to press forward faster.

Forward Lunge and Recovery

The surging and lunging forward of the body and core are the most important parts of the stroke. The ability to do this effectively sets the best swimmers apart from the rest. Basically, from the point at which the upper body is at its highest and the head is at its peak height out of the water, the head and upper body press forward dynamically to get the swimmer back into a great body line. Swimmers should experiment to find the best starting point for the body surge. The position will likely be a point at which the upper body is leaning forward over the surface of the water, as opposed to being more vertical. A vertical position may give the swimmer more time to press forward, but the swimmer likely would be starting the press when the body is at a slower velocity because the drag created in achieving the vertical position will have slowed the body considerably. By keeping the highest point of the breath more forward above the water, a swimmer will be able to press the body forward effectively while maintaining forward speed.

During the actual body press, the head should stay connected to the body, meaning that the head maintains a neutral position with respect to the spine and is not thrown down into the water. The forward movement is driven by the head but is powered by the core, like a forward crunch. On the last stroke of a breaststroke race, many swimmers lunge forward with the body and arms, and a similar type of feel and action should occur with every stroke. The breaststroke is a whole-body engagement. The body surges forward in coordination with the arm recovery to provide the most effective stroke.

Starting with the elbows beside the body and the fingertips pointing forward, the swimmer pushes the elbows and hands forward to get the most dynamic recovery. The elbows stay wide; the athlete should never try to squeeze the elbows together during the recovery because narrow elbows will just slow the body and get in the way of pressing the body forward. Instead, the swimmer should allow the elbows to follow the hands, which will come together in the middle of the arm recovery as the hands are moving forward.

Just as the elbows should not squeeze together, the hands should not clap together. For many swimmers, a key focus point is to clap the palms together right in front of the chest. Instead, the hands should just barely converge after the recovery motion has already started.

At the start of the recovery, the palms most likely will be facing upward and inward, a result of the hands moving upward and inward during the last part of the inward sweep. The palms should be oriented to face the direction of the pull. As the arms extend and reach forward, the forearms should pronate so that the palms rotate downward. With the palms down, the muscles of the arm are in a better position to extend effectively. When the arms are fully extended, the palms should be facing the bottom of the pool and the thumbs should be adjacent to each other. During the recovery, the hands should be slightly higher than the elbows, grazing just over the top of the surface of the water. The hands will continue to rise when the recovery starts to achieve this position. The elbows will rise a little too, but they should remain under the surface of the water, which is actually mandatory to remain within the technical rules of the stroke and not cause disqualification. Just as the arms are about to hit full extension, the hands come back underneath the surface in line with the elbows. When the recovery is completed, the head and upper body will be just getting back into line with the arms. The head, shoulders, elbows, and hands will be in line with each other under the surface of the water.

Breaststroke Kick

A single kick occurs during each stroke cycle. The timing of the pull and kick and their occurrence in relation to each other is an important determinant of breaststroke proficiency.

Kick Timing

Video analysis has revealed some interesting information on the timing of the pull and kick that differs from the technique taught by many coaches and from what the athletes perceive. The main findings from watching the top athletes execute the stroke is that the legs remain straight and outstretched while the arms are pulling back and the kick doesn't engage with the water and push water back until the arms are fully extended and the head is nearly in line.

This observation is contrary to traditional thought and teachings. The phrase "kick your hands forward" is commonly used to instruct athletes how to execute the breaststroke kick with proper timing. This phrase means that a swimmer is kicking while the hands are recovering forward. The rationale behind this teaching is that the power produced by the kick counteracts the forward movement of the hands, which is a nonpropulsive, drag-creating movement. Likewise, while the knees are bending and the feet are coming up toward the hips, the arms are pulling backward to counteract that nonpropulsive kick setup. Although this idea seems to make a lot of sense, what happens in reality makes more sense.

In reality, the knees do not bend and the kick does not begin to set up until the end of the inward sweep of the hands. Some elite breaststrokers do not even start to bend the knees until the arms are moving forward at the beginning of the recovery. This timing of starting the kick makes sense because in this way the swimmer can gain the maximum benefit from the arm pull without any opposition or resistance from the legs. The legs and hips remain high in the water in a great line as the arms are pulled backward.

Looking at the other end of the stroke, the kick, the feet and legs push against the water and propel the body forward just as the upper body and head are getting in line with the arms extended forward. This timing makes sense because the swimmer can gain maximum benefit from the kick when the upper body is in line. The key is for the upper body to get in line—another reason that the body press is important—and not just extend the arms forward. Video analysis shows that the kick is engaging and pushing back when the head is just getting in between the arms, regardless of when the arms are fully extended forward.

Frequently, swimmers and coaches talk about late timing. Late timing can be easy to spot. It occurs when the surge of the kick does not look coordinated with the arm recovery. The viewer sees two forward surges, one from the arms extending forward and one from the kick, instead of one single surge forward. Late timing is often easier to recognize than it is to remedy. Most people try to correct this by starting the kick sooner, thinking that an earlier start will make the kick fire backward earlier in the cycle so that it coincides with the arm recovery. This approach rarely addresses the root cause of the problem—the kick isn't engaging early enough because the head and upper body are not getting in line quickly enough. The arms may be shooting forward, but the upper body isn't lunging forward in coordination with the arms; therefore, the kick is late. To fix late timing, the coach must first make sure that the body is pressing forward dynamically with the appropriate timing.

Essentially, the best timing for fast breaststroke swimming is for the swimmer to hold the legs in line with the body for as long as possible while the arms pull and then kick when the upper body is fully extended and back in the proper body line. The mantra should be pull when the legs are streamlined and kick when the upper body is streamlined. Understanding that fast breaststroke swimming is as much about managing drag forces as it is about generating propulsion, it makes sense that all the best breaststrokers use this timing. Working within the confines of this timing means that the setup of the kick, from when the knees start to bend to when the heels are as close to the hips as possible, has to take place in a very short time—the time that it takes for the hands to recover forward. Therefore, the feet have to come up quickly. Dave Salo, PhD, one of the best breaststroke coaches, calls it "fast heels" and constantly preaches the idea to his athletes. Bringing the heels up has to be a fast and dynamic motion, one that really engages the hamstrings. A world-record holder breaststroker has said that his hamstrings are totally taxed at the end of a race. That fatigue results from the quick recovery of the feet to set up the kick.

Knee Drop

As the feet are drawn up to the hips, the knees bend and drop down. The knees must drop deeper in the water so that the feet remain under the surface of the water during the leg recovery and do not break the surface and push against air during the execution of the kick.

Some coaches and athletes are concerned about the knee drop because the deeper the knees are in the water, the more drag is created by the thighs, which are directly opposing the oncoming flow of water. Indeed, resistance does increase as the knees go deeper and the angle between the thighs and the waist becomes closer to 90 degrees. But the tradeoff needs to be weighed to determine the best body position during the leg recovery.

For most swimmers, the resistance created with the thighs will be negated by the propulsion developed from setting up the feet as high as possible, so they should choose that option. Only one or two world-class breaststrokers do not bring their heels all the way up to the buttocks when setting up the kick. Olympic medalist and national champion Eric Shanteau, whose breaststroke kick is highly regarded, has such leg anthropometry that when he brings his heels up, the angle created by the thighs is nearly 90 degrees. Another factor to consider is that the kick should occur quickly. The quicker the feet recover, the shorter the time will be that the knees will be dropped and producing drag.

Kick Width

In terms of width of the kick, the knees should generally be angled slightly out just before the propulsive phase kick is executed and should be aligned just outside the waist, around the width of the shoulder. The knees should have a gap between them throughout the duration of the kick; they should not come together. After the feet reach their highest point in the recovery and begin the push backward, they generally go slightly wider than the knees as they come around to catch water. As the legs extend rearward, the feet should come closer until the legs are fully outstretched behind the swimmer and in line with the rest of the body.

The overwhelming majority of the propulsion from the kick comes from water being pushed by the insides of the lower legs and the insides of the feet. Little propulsion comes from the two legs first separating (abducting) and then squeezing together (adducting). The general nature of the breaststroke kick is that of a leg extension that finishes downward. The emphasis should be on the extension aspect of the kick as opposed to the downward aspect because the aim should always be to push water back to move the body forward. The downward aspect of the kick is a result of the physical position of the legs from where they are set up to extend backward; the legs need to have a slightly downward push so that the insides of the legs and feet can apply direct pressure on the water. If the feet remained close to the surface throughout the extension of the legs, the legs would be sliding through the water and not pushing directly against it to create propulsion.

Foot Position

From the start of the kick, when the feet and knees start to extend backward, the feet should be rotated outward at the ankles so that the toes point toward the side of the pool and the insides of the feet face backward. This position should be referred to as the catch of the breaststroke kick because it is the position at which the feet engage in pushing water back. The more the feet can turn outward, the more water will be caught and pushed. Ankle flexibility and the ability to rotate the feet outward are important, and those who have a natural propensity for this movement are at an advantage for generating an effective kick. Those who do not have that natural flexibility can work on it with regular stretching exercises to improve.

Kick Finish

The legs extend downward to the finish of the kick. With the upper body in line throughout the propulsive part of the kick, the backward and downward extension of the kick transfers through the hips and then forward through the upper body. The feet will be slightly separated by the time the legs are straight, so the feet will finish coming together as they rise to the surface so that the legs get into a horizontal line with the rest of the body.

Underwater Pullout

Every length of breaststroke starts with one full pull and kick cycle taken completely underwater. Since 2005 a single dolphin kick is allowed during the underwater pullout, and most questions surrounding the dolphin kick have to do with when the kick should be performed.

Arm Movement

Before covering the details of the dolphin kick, we need to explain the basic arm movement of the underwater pullout. It differs from the pull in the regular swimming stroke in that the arms pull all the way back to a straight arm extension next to the sides of the body before recovering forward. The underwater pullout is more similar to the butterfly arm stroke than the breaststroke arm stroke.

From a streamline position, the hands separate, the elbows remain high, and the hands try to grab and push as much water backward as quickly as possible. Throughout the pullout, the elbows are bent and the fingertips are pointing downward. The hands and arms move straight back just wide of the body. Keeping the arms and elbows anterior to the body is important. A common flaw is for the chest to press downward and the arms to be higher than the body, which is a much weaker position to pull with. Tightening the core while initiating the arm pull can help optimize the effectiveness of the arm pull.

Body Line

As with the regular swimming stroke, the most important thing to focus on when executing the pullout with a dolphin kick is maintaining a good body line. A good body line is essential to taking advantage of any speed created off a start, turn, pulldown, or dolphin kick.

When completely submerged, a good body line consists of being flat and horizontal in the water in the same position as swimming the breaststroke at the surface, but achieving this body line can be more difficult while underwater because the swimmer doesn't have the reference of the surface of the water to help determine the horizontal plane. The legs may float upward or the upper body may press downward, so the swimmer needs to develop greater awareness to keep the entire body level. The good body line needs to be established before and after the arm pulldown and dolphin kick.

Dolphin Kick Timing

The rule for implementing the dolphin kick states that the dolphin kick can occur any time before the first breaststroke kick. Prior to 2015, the rule stated that the dolphin kick had to occur during the arm motion of the pulldown. There is now less ambiguity in regard to an official determining a rule infraction, which is a positive change for all swimmers.

For most swimmers, the proper timing when performing the dolphin kick is to initiate the kick at the beginning of the arm pull, specifically after the hands separate and before the arms start to pull down toward the feet. The kick should be compact, primarily from the knees with minimal body movement. After finishing the downward dolphin kick, the body should almost immediately be returned to a good body line. Ideally, the finish of the dolphin kick will have minimal follow-through and the swimmer will kick herself into a good line.

Many swimmers who attempt to perform the dolphin kick in the middle of the arm pull end up in a poor body line at the end of the pull and dolphin kick. When the finish of the dolphin kick is combined with the finish of the pulldown, the natural tendency of the body is to bend at the waist and end up in an upside-down V shape. Not every swimmer who performs the dolphin kick in the middle of the pulldown has this problem, but it is definitely common.

Some key points for making the dolphin kick work effectively in a pullout are to keep the kick compact (not make it as big as possible) and to make the kick come primarily from a knee bend (not a whole-body motion).

Recovery

After completing the arm pulldown, the swimmer should wait a short time before recovering the arms above the head. The swimmer needs to make a judgment call here about this length of time, waiting until just before he is about to slow down before initiating the arm recovery.

During the recovery, the hands remain close to the front of body with the palms facing upward toward the body. Some breaststrokers like to keep the elbows out to the sides of the body as they bring their arms up. Other breaststrokers prefer to bring their elbows in close to each other and close to the body as well. Either way, the idea is to keep a low profile with the arms and sneak them up above the head as quickly as possible.

Summary

Despite the perception that breaststroke is a complicated and individual technique to teach, many key elements can be taught to every swimmer to achieve the best breaststroke possible.

Each stroke starts and ends with a great body line. From fingertips to hips to toes, the body is in the same horizontal plane just underneath the surface and the head is between the arms. The head can be tilted slightly forward as long as it is in line.

All the best breaststrokers drive the body and arms forward into that great body line. The head and body, not just the arms, must press forward into the line. Making this action dynamic is important so that the arms and body do not dive downward into the water, which will compromise the body position as it arches back up to the surface.

The optimal pull shape allows the body to drive forward, which allows the great line to occur. The pull shape should be round with no sharp corners so that the hands can transition smoothly from the pull, or propulsive, phase to the dynamic recovery phase. The pull starts with an outward scull, continues with an inward motion with the hands pitching down and getting deeper, and then transitions to the recovery with the elbows staying wide and hands converging along the way. The head and upper body rise during the inward motion, allowing the breath to occur.

An important aspect of the kick is to bring the heels up quickly. This action enables the ideal timing in breaststroke—pull with the legs to streamline and then kick with the upper body in streamline. The knees bend and come forward at about hip width during the setup of the kick. When the feet push back during the propulsive part of the kick, the swimmer should focus on extending the legs and pushing water with the inside of the feet and calves.

Instinctively, swimmers try to pull harder and faster to speed up in breaststroke. Unlike in freestyle, backstroke, and butterfly, this approach isn't optimal in breaststroke. To get more speed in breaststroke, swimmers should fire the kick earlier and glide less.

Although many swimmers perceive things as black or white and view themselves as either good breaststrokers or bad breaststrokers, keeping an open mind to all these concepts can help anyone get faster. A swimmer's kick effectiveness may be limited by ankle flexibility, but many other aspects of the stroke can be easily worked on and improved.

CHAPTER 5

Butterfly Technique

—Ross H. Sanders, PhD, and Carla B. McCabe, PhD

In this chapter we describe the technique of butterfly swimming and ways to enhance swimming performance and proficiency. Specifically, the chapter looks at the importance of having a wavelike sequencing of undulations of the body segments, the phases of the stroke and their links to the undulations, and the effects of breathing and changes of pace on technique. Ultimately, by focusing on these fundamental aspects of butterfly technique, swimmers will be able to swim faster and more efficiently.

Description of Butterfly Technique

Butterfly is a symmetrical stroke in which the actions of the right upper and lower limbs are almost simultaneous with those of the left. The body undulates upward and downward rather than rolling around the longitudinal axis as in front crawl and backstroke swimming. Thus, butterfly is regarded as an undulating stroke.

In front crawl and backstroke, the timing of the arm and leg actions is linked to the timing of the rolling actions of the body. In butterfly the kick is linked to the vertical oscillations of the body parts (Sanders 2011). When watching a good butterfly swimmer, a wave appears to be travelling along the length of the body. The undulation of the body parts in a skilled butterfly swimmer mimics a moving wave of water travelling progressively from the head to the feet (Sanders, Cappaert, and Devlin 1995). In contrast, an unskilled butterfly swimmer doesn't seem to have the flow or the rhythm and often looks awkward and jerky.

Therefore, just as the body roll establishes the rhythm in front crawl and backstroke, the wave moving along the body controls the rhythm in the butterfly stroke and influences the timing of the actions of the arms and legs. Indeed, they go hand in hand. The stroking and kicking actions are set to the rhythm of the body wave, which in turn is influenced by the timing of the arm and leg actions (Sanders 2011).

Given that rhythm is crucial to well-coordinated butterfly swimming, teachers and coaches should focus on developing rhythm early in the learn-to-swim program rather than trying to establish the butterfly arm action. Experienced swimming teachers know that swimming butterfly with a smooth and economical technique is extremely difficult until swimmers have developed the ability to undulate the body in a wavelike manner. Thus, learn-to-swim classes commonly include activities designed to develop this undulating rhythm, such as by mimicking the actions of dolphins.

The rhythm is closely tied to the kicking action. In fact, the kick is highly propulsive in butterfly swimming and the stroke is not efficient without an effective kick that is the culmination of a full body wave (Sanders, Cappaert, and Devlin 1995). Because the upper-body undulations start the wave moving along the body toward the feet, learners should be told that the kick starts in the chest rather than from the hips. After the body wave and kick feel natural and well coordinated, the arm action can be superimposed.

Benefits of Undulations

Butterfly swimming is exhausting and uneconomical until the wavelike rhythm is established. The purpose of waves is to transmit energy from one place to another. A wavelike rhythm in butterfly swimming transmits energy from the upper body to the lower limbs to generate propulsion from the kick (Sanders 2011).

To enable breathing and recovery of the arms, work must be done to raise the upper body. In doing so, the upper body stores gravitational potential energy, so called because the upper body now has the potential to move downward under the influence of gravity and gain kinetic energy (the energy resulting from movement). As the upper body rotates downward into the water, much of the potential energy is changed to kinetic energy because of its rotation. The wavelike sequence of rotations of the trunk, thighs, and shanks transmits this kinetic energy to the feet to contribute to their work to propel the body forward. Therefore, some of the energy expended by the swimmer to raise the upper body is conserved in the body and simply moved from one body part to the next until it is reused to propel the body forward. Because some of the energy used in the kick comes from the movements of the upper body, the whole stroke is less exhausting than it is when the swimmer does not have the wavelike sequencing of body parts. Therefore, developing coordinated undulations of the body is essential for efficient butterfly swimming.

Phases of the Stroke and Links to Undulations

In this section we explore how the phases of the stroke are linked to the rhythm of the body wave. The elements of good technique emerge from the swimmer's attempts to ensure that his actions are timed appropriately to maximize swimming efficiency and minimize resistive forces through effective use of the body wave.

Release and Recovery

Given the link between the body undulations, energy transfer, and economical propulsion, a good place to start the description of the butterfly stroke cycle is when the hands release the water at the end of their pull and start the over-water recovery in preparation for the next pull.

At the instant of release, the body is loaded with mechanical energy. It has high kinetic energy because it is moving fast following the completion of the underwater pull combined with a downward kick. The body also has gravitational potential energy because the head and parts of the upper body have been raised (figure 5.1). A good butterfly swimmer will be able to use this potential energy to produce the next body wave that in turn contributes to the propulsion gained from the second kick.

▶ **Figure 5.1**   Butterfly stroke release as the hands exit the water and initiate recovery of the arms over the water. Notice that the head and shoulders are clear of the water without being so high that the body is steeply angled to the water, which would cause excessive drag.

Because butterfly is a symmetrical stroke, both arms recover together, so the rotational effects of one arm are cancelled by the rotation of the other arm in the opposite direction. The swimmer can therefore maintain good alignment of the body in which the body's long axis remains in line with the direction of travel. Balancing the rotational effects of the recovery of each arm means that, unlike front crawl and backstroke, butterfly does not require a high recovery in which the upper limbs are kept close to the midline of the body. This point is convenient because the height of the recovery is limited by the shoulder structure and, unlike in front crawl, cannot be assisted by a body roll about the longitudinal axis of the body.

The upper limbs and body are elevated sufficiently to clear the water but do not need to be higher than that. Indeed, the recovery of butterfly world-record holder Michael Phelps is lower than that of many butterfly swimmers. Even so, the recovery of the arms needs to be sufficiently high that the arms are not sweeping water as they move forward because this action causes unnecessary resistance. One of the problems encountered by beginning butterfly swimmers is that they cannot get the arms sufficiently clear of the water. This difficulty may be linked to either not raising the upper body sufficiently or not having sufficient shoulder flexibility. Obtaining suitable upper-body elevation is much easier after the wavelike rhythm is established because the kicking actions maintain the upward and downward oscillations of the upper body without great effort. The swimmer's efforts should be directed toward horizontal motion rather than pulling the upper body upward. With proper timing and correct actions of the arms and legs, the upper body and shoulders are above the water until the arms, forearms, and hands have recovered sufficiently far forward to avoid sweeping the water.

Entry

Approaching entry, the forward rotational motion of the body combined with the effects of the gravitational force drives the upper body downward. By this time the elbows need to be sufficiently high and the arms sufficiently forward to avoid sweeping the water. Internal rotation of the shoulders helps achieve this. The instruction to achieve the required internal rotation is simply to turn the hands so that the thumbs are pointing downward toward the bottom of the pool. The trunk is now almost level, and the head is flexing downward to enter before the arms do.

To keep the upper limbs free of the water and to bring them close to the midline for an entry that minimizes resistance, good shoulder flexibility is required. With the arms now recovered well forward, the arms and upper body can dive into the water. The downward dive is assisted by a modest downbeat of the feet that tends to rotate the body forward (figure 5.2). This downbeat does not need great effort because it takes advantage of the energy transmitted to the lower body by the pendulum-like rotation of the upper body. A body wave has transmitted the energy from hips to feet. This action is an excellent example of saving energy through transfer of motion from one body part to another.

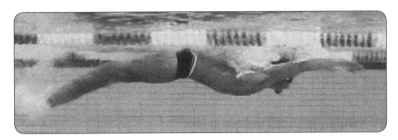

▶ **Figure 5.2** During the entry phase, the trunk and head dive downward. This forward rotation is assisted by the downbeat kick force of the legs.

Flexion of the neck before and during entry is important for two reasons. First, it creates a diving action to enter the water and continue the downward motion to penetrate the water with minimum resistance because of form and wave drag. When the head is not submerged, the body is angled to the oncoming water flow, presenting a large surface area that generates resistance. Thus, the drag is so significant that forward progress is achieved only with great effort that is not sustainable. Second, the downward rotation of the upper body continues the pendulum-like motion of the trunk and the energy exchange between potential and rotational energy. The head moves through a large range of vertical motion, and the shoulders follow as part of the wavelike sequencing from head to feet. Submerging the head commences a body wave that progresses along the body fast enough to be propulsive (Sanders, Cappaert, and Devlin 1995; Sanders 2007, 2011). Therefore, submerging the head and upper body below the surface is essential to developing proficiency in butterfly.

While the shoulders are moving down, the hips are moving up. Energy is being transmitted to the lower body by a pendulum action of the upper body about an instantaneous axis of rotation that is somewhere between the shoulders and hips. The body wave also assists in raising the hips and lower limbs to maintain good alignment and thus minimize drag effects.

Outsweep and Catch

At the beginning of the outsweep, so called because the arms sweep outward rather than backward, the arms have reached forward, the trunk is angled downward, the hips are elevated, and the legs are up near the surface (figure 5.3). The internal rotation of the shoulders has put the arms in a strong position to move the hands outward immediately after entry and encourages continuity of motion. If the swimmer has been able to complete the inward motion of the arms, forearms, and hands before entry, then the downward motion during entry can naturally round out into the outsweep.

A common fault among beginning butterfly swimmers is to continue the downward motion of the upper limbs into a backward pull rather than outward. This action disrupts the rhythm. Skilled butterfly swimmers use the outsweep

▶ **Figure 5.3** The butterfly outsweep. Note that the head and trunk have travelled downward while the lower limbs rise like a pendulum during this phase. With the shoulders internally rotated, the hands sweep outward until the catch position.

to create lift force to reverse the downward motion of the upper body, allowing the pendulum to start swinging back the other way and to continue the wave-like motion. The internal rotation of the shoulders naturally orients the hands so that the little fingers are slightly higher than the thumbs. This orientation, in combination with the outward motion, produces a lift force that starts the upper body moving upward (figure 5.4).

A second mechanism tending to reverse the downward motion of the torso is the buoyancy force. The center of buoyancy is now in front of the center of mass and tending to swing the pendulum back the other way (figure 5.5).

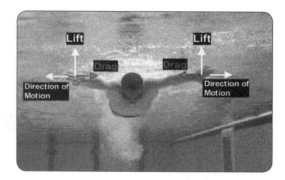

▶ **Figure 5.4** Shoulder internal rotation and hand orientation during the outsweep phase in butterfly swimming. As the hands sweep outward, a lift force is created that acts to reverse the downward motion of the upper body to maintain the undulation that creates the body wave.

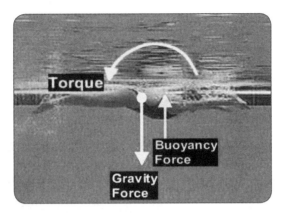

▶ **Figure 5.5** During the outsweep phase, the buoyancy force is shifted in front of the center of mass, resulting in a reverse turning effect (torque), that is, the wave action changing from a forward to backward rotation.

These mechanisms of reversing the downward rotation and producing backward rotation are then supported by the strong upbeat of the feet. Besides starting the pendulum swinging back and keeping the rhythm going, the outsweep places the hands in a strong position to make the catch, that is, to move the hands backward to generate propulsive force during the insweep.

During the transition to the insweep, the outward motion rounds out and the hands pronate to commence the insweep and make the catch.

Insweep

The insweep in butterfly is not unlike that of front crawl except that both arms are working at once and no body roll occurs about the longitudinal axis (figure 5.6). The lack of body roll means that the pull of each arm is wider with respect to the midline. But if the hands produce similar force with lines of action equidistant from the midline of the body, the torques produced by right and left arm actions cancel out and the body maintains its alignment.

▶ **Figure 5.6** Butterfly insweep is performed with both arms simultaneously.

▶ **Figure 5.7** The hourglass pattern scribed by the hands from the commencement of the (*a*) outsweep, (*b*) insweep, (*c*) upsweep, and (*d*) release.

The similarities of the butterfly insweep to the front crawl insweep include flexing the elbow and combining shoulder internal rotation, horizontal adduction, and extension to produce great hand speed and, therefore, strong propulsive forces. The hands move inward toward the midline and backward to the neck of the hourglass (figure 5.7) that is characteristic of the butterfly pull pattern.

The hourglass pattern has advantages besides enabling a strong lever system. First, the hands are moving a longer distance than they do if they are moved straight back as beginning swimmers commonly do. Second, the hands perform sweeps in terms of changing directions throughout the underwater pull, allowing them to find still water rather than pushing the same column of water and losing force (Maglischo 2003). Third, at the end of the insweep, the elbows are partly flexed and the shoulders are in a midrange position. Thus, the lever system is set to apply large forces through a combination of shoulder internal rotation, shoulder extension, and elbow extension (figure 5.7*c*). Fourth, the hands can move outward from the narrow part of the hourglass, thereby assisting the exit and a continuous rounding out into the recovery (figure 5.7*d*).

During the insweep, the trunk continues to rotate back as part of the pendulum action, transmitting energy to the lower body that contributes to the kicks. By the end of the insweep, the powerful upbeat of the feet has finished and the powerful downbeat is about to commence (figure 5.8).

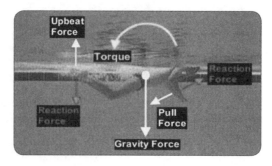

▶ **Figure 5.8** Reaction forces of the insweep pull and upbeat kick cause backward rotation of the body.

Upsweep

As in the front crawl, the insweep blends seamlessly into the upsweep. The upsweep is a strong backward push that also brings the hands toward the surface. A transition occurs from internal rotation to a backward push in which elbow extension, shoulder extension, and shoulder abduction are prominent. This action is fast and strong, and the hands accelerate progressively through the upsweep (Maglischo 2003). But unlike in the front crawl, body roll cannot assist the action.

Maintaining a high elbow throughout the upsweep to release and exit is important for pushing water backward rather than upward. The latter is a common fault that has the undesired effects of sinking the body because of the downward reaction force and making the recovery awkward and uneconomical.

During the upsweep, the downbeat of the second kick occurs. This kick, in combination with the upsweep, produces propulsion and elevates the center of mass. The hands naturally move outward and round out into the recovery. Much of the rotational motion of the upper limbs gained in the upsweep carries through into the recovery, thereby saving energy by not having to restart the forward motion of the arms from a stationary position. Swimmers should try to maintain a high elbow position as the hands exit the water to help ensure a clean exit with the hands pushing back, rather than upward, until exit.

Effects of Breathing and Changes of Pace on Technique

Butterfly swimmers, particularly in shorter events, do not breathe every stroke. Hahn and Krug (1992) found that taking a breath in butterfly swimming reduces the swimmer's velocity primarily because of increased trunk inclination angle (10 degrees), which naturally increases frontal resistance compared with breath holding. Comparing frontal and lateral breathing techniques, Alves et al. (1999) found that the latter resulted in a lower trunk inclination but also induced an unwarranted rotation of the whole body around the longitudinal axis. The authors concluded that one technique was not necessarily superior to the other.

Despite evidence to suggest that breathing in butterfly swimming negatively affects swim velocity, one question that has frequently been asked is, "Does the rhythm differ between breathing and nonbreathing strokes?" Recent research by Seifert, Chollet, and Sanders (2010) indicates that breathing causes propulsive discontinuity because of a longer glide time to facilitate catching the water to elevate the trunk and head before breathing. But Seifert, Chollet, and Sanders also reported better synchronization between hands exiting and the downbeat of the legs when breathing compared with breath holding. This finding was associated with facilitating the head's exit from the water for an inhalation without improving propulsion because of the shorter duration of the push phase. Therefore, these authors concluded that breathing significantly influences the change of coordination parameters in terms of stroke phase durations when incorporating a breath into the butterfly stroke cycle. They thus recommended that coaches monitor those changes in training.

Conversely, Sanders, Cappaert, and Devlin (1995) indicated that the wave progressed consistently along the body regardless of whether it was a breathing or a nonbreathing cycle. This finding suggests that the fundamental rhythm involving progression of a wave remains across breathing and nonbreathing cycles yet does not constrain the system from adjusting timing and duration of component parts of the stroke to adapt to the differing requirements of breathing and nonbreathing stroke cycles.

Examination of butterfly swimming across various race paces (Seifert et al. 2007; Seifert, Chollet, and Sanders 2010) revealed that the pattern of timing between kick and arm actions remained similar across race paces but became more synchronous and exhibited greater propulsive continuity with increasing pace. They reported that glide time decreased as a function of increasing race pace. These authors attributed longer duration of the glide phase with slower race paces (associated with longer swims) as a strategy to conserve oxygen by remaining in a streamlined position longer and thus obtain an instant of rest at each stroke. At higher race paces, a longer glide phase would be undesirable and should be avoided so that propulsive continuity can be maintained. Moreover, the fact that the pattern of timing remained similar across race paces suggests that adjustments such as changes in pace can be made without changing the fundamental rhythm embodied in the travelling body wave (Sanders 2011). That is, the fundamental wavelike rhythm characteristic of skilled butterfly swimmers is stable and endows the system with the capacity to adjust to changes in pace and to alternation of breathing and nonbreathing cycles.

Summary

In this chapter we described the butterfly technique, stressing the importance of obtaining an effective rhythm in which the parts of the body undulate to produce a body wave that is transmitted from head to feet. The benefits of this undulating wave were explained in terms of contributing to propulsion at minimal energy cost. The characteristics of the arm stroke and leg kick were described, and their timing was linked to the undulations. Finally, the effects of breathing and change of pace on technique were discussed.

CHAPTER 6

Techniques for Starts and Turns

—Andrew Lyttle, PhD, and Brian Blanksby, PhD

In international competitions the trend is for smaller time differentials to separate competitors. The difference between first and eighth place can hinge on how well a swimmer executes his start and turns (Newble 1982). Swimmers achieve their fastest speeds off the start, and maximizing performance in this area presents an opportunity to gain a substantial advantage over competitors. Looking more closely at the turns, pushing off the wall generates the next highest race velocities. Additionally, when the underwater phase is considered, we find that the turns make up as much as 30 percent of the distance covered in a race.

The complex interrelationship of actions required to optimize performance in these areas has led to a large variation in techniques used in competition. Research has tended to focus on discrete areas of start and turn performance, and tremendous emphasis has been placed on understanding the underwater phase. Additionally, new technologies such as computational fluid dynamics have increased our knowledge of efficiency in these skills and revealed how best to prepare elite swimmers for competition. This chapter presents the existing research and knowledge about start and turn performance and extends those findings to provide application-based recommendations for optimizing performance in the pool.

Dive Starts

The benefits of an effective start in competitive swimming cannot be underestimated. Evidence from race analyses conducted at major international competitions demonstrates significant correlations between faster start times and race times (Cossor and Mason 2001; Mason, Alcock, and Fowlie 2007). The start produces the fastest velocity that a swimmer will achieve during a race. When you consider that the start includes the first 15 meters of the race, it makes up a considerable proportion of the total event, especially in the shorter sprints over 50 to 100 meters (figure 6.1).

Consider these examples of how start performance can affect performance:

- A review of Olympic swimming results from 1972 to 2004 showed that a 0.1 second improvement in time, a difference that realistically can be achieved with a better start, would have resulted in 65 medals changing hands in sprint events (Hoof 2007). More recently at the 2008 Beijing Olympic Games, the top two competitors in the female sprint events (50 meters and 100 meters) were typically separated by less than 1 percent (Slawson 2010), again an amount that can be affected by a start.

- An analysis of the 100-meter men's butterfly final at the 1996 Olympics showed that the eventual silver medalist was 0.4 seconds slower to 15 meters than the winner, but his final time was only 0.28 seconds slower (Schnabel and Kuchler 1998); the faster swimmer placed second and essentially lost the gold medal in the first 15 meters.

The bottom line is that although less time is spent on the start than is spent swimming, starting is still a crucial skill to master at the elite level (Miller, Allen, and Pein 2003; Hay 1988).

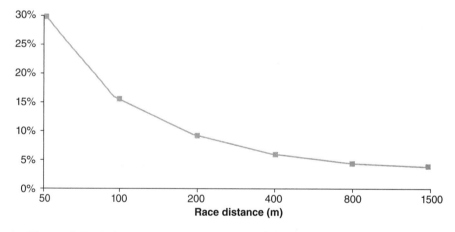

▶ **Figure 6.1** Swim starts as a percentage of the race distance (start distance is 15 meters).

Types of Dive Starts

The grab start and the track start, with variations in which body weight is positioned forward or backward, are the most commonly used start techniques. The major differences between the grab start and track start are how the feet are placed on the block and how the athlete's body weight is distributed with regard to the base of support. The technique employed by a given swimmer is selected in part based on personal preference, but the design of the starting block can also have an influence (Pearson et al. 1998). FINA, the international governing body of swimming, requires that starting blocks be constructed with a 0- to 10-degree slope and a height between 0.5 and 0.75 meters above the water (www.fina.org/rules/rules_index.htm). Thus, the swimmer can encounter considerable variability at a competition. Additionally, FINA recently approved the Omega OSB11 starting block for use in international competitions, which has the potential to alter optimal start technique considerably. This block has an inclined kick plate at the rear and side handles, which will further affect the type of start that athletes use. The addition of the FINA-approved backstroke feet wedges is likely to see further modifications in the backstroke starting technique and times.

The basic techniques for the block starts are presented in the sections that follow. The backstroke start will be addressed separately, later in the chapter.

Grab Start

The grab start is similar to a two-legged jump. To begin, the swimmer places the feet about 0.15 to 0.30 meters apart and curls the toes over the front edge of the block (figure 6.2). The hands grasp the front edge of the block, either inside or outside the feet. In this position, the swimmer's center of gravity (CG) is in a position of dynamic stability, positioned as far forward as possible within the base of support to allow for rapid movement forward. The arms are crucial in developing the initial forward momentum as they pull down and back against the block. Both arms then swing straight out toward the far end of the pool as both legs drive powerfully and simultaneously off the block (Houel et al. 2010). Kruger et al. (2003) showed that the knee and hip extensors are the main contributors to the takeoff forces generated by the legs, and the back muscles are preactivated to enable a more powerful extension of the body at the starting signal.

Courtesy of the Western Australian Institute of Sport.

▶ **Figure 6.2** Stop-action image of the grab start.

Track Start

The track start gets its name from the fact that it mimics the start used in a track sprint; the legs are staggered, and the start is performed by generating an initial drive with the rear leg followed by a front-leg drive.

The track start has two main variations: the traditional front-weighted track start, in which most of the swimmer's weight is over the front leg, and the rear-weighted track start, in which the swimmer leans back slightly so that her weight is directed more over the back leg. In both cases, one foot is placed near the rear of the block and the other is positioned with the toes curled around the front edge. Because the front leg provides more of the total propulsive force, it is logical that this should be the athlete's dominant leg (Benjanuvatra, Edmunds, and Blanksby 2007).

When performing the front-weighted track start (figure 6.3), the swimmer grasps the front edge of the block with both hands but does not lean back, keeping the CG positioned closer to the front of the block. On the starting signal, the swimmer initially pulls down and back against the block with the arms while explosively pushing back with the rear foot. When the CG passes the front edge of the block, the front leg dominates force production and continues to accelerate the body forward and upward (Benjanuvatra, Edmunds, and Blanksby 2007). Like the grab start, this type of start can be performed quickly. It potentially enables the swimmer to enter the water earlier than when using the rear-weighted track start.

This rear-weighted track start (figure 6.4) is an adapted version of the traditional track start and requires the performer to lean back as much as possible, thereby preloading the muscles of the upper back leg and the front leg. Because the swimmer leans back, the swimmer's CG is initially positioned more toward

Courtesy of the Western Australian Institute of Sport.

▶ **Figure 6.3** The front-weighted (traditional) track start. Note how the athlete's weight is positioned over the front leg.

the rear of the block. This positioning typically means that the swimmer will have a longer block time than when executing other dive starts. Advocates claim that this disadvantage is offset by the fact that the longer time allows the swimmer to generate force for a longer period and subsequently produce a greater impulse (a product of force multiplied by time). The result is that the rear-weighted track start typically produces greater takeoff velocity. In addition, the preloading or prestretch of the muscles of the arms and shoulders can increase their force production because of the length-tension properties of muscle (Welshe, Wilson, and Ettema 1998; Vilas-Boas et al. 2000). The arms are used almost exclusively to initiate horizontal propulsion. Then, after the swimmer is moving forward, the legs further accelerate the swimmer. This type of start has been suggested as being beneficial for swimmers who are able to generate a high level of upper-body power.

Courtesy of the Western Australian Institute of Sport.

▶ **Figure 6.4** The rear-weighted (slingshot) track start.

Dive Start Comparisons

Regardless of the type of dive start used, the swimmer's ultimate goals are the same: to react quickly when the starting gun sounds, leave the blocks rapidly at an appropriate takeoff angle, and achieve as much forward velocity as possible. But the inevitable tradeoffs mean that it is not possible to maximize all these factors in one start. For example, although a grab start allows a swimmer to react quickly, the longer block time in the track start allows a swimmer to generate higher takeoff velocity. Consequently, studies comparing the start techniques usually produce conflicting results about which is best. Although some have suggested that the grab start is superior to the track start (Zatsiorsky, Bulgakova, and Chaplinsky 1979; Counsilman et al. 1988; Kruger et al. 2003), other studies have found no difference between the grab and track starts (Blanksby, Nicholson, and Elliott 2002; Vilas-Boas et al. 2003; Miller, Allen, and Pein 2003; Benjanuvatra et al. 2004), and a third group has concluded that the track start is superior (Welcher, Hinrichs, and George 1999; Holthe and McLean 2001). The lack of definitive evidence makes it difficult for coaches to choose a best starting technique to teach their athletes. The contradictory findings can be attributed to a number of factors, such as the skill level of performers, length and scope of interventions, body morphology, and swimmers' familiarity and experience using specific dive techniques. Comparing techniques is inherently difficult when swimmers have their preferred starts that they have practiced almost exclusively; the adage "What one does most, one does best" often applies. Only when a new technique, despite being more complex or less practiced, yields better results can useful information be drawn. For example, athletes can perform handle start dives (Blanksby, Nicholson, and Elliott 2002) and kick start dives (Honda et al. 2010) as proficiently as their preferred starting style, despite having never tried handle or kick starts before.

The lack of consensus among the block start studies can be partially attributed to the various criteria used to define a successful start. A variety of criteria have been used in studies for evaluating starts, including takeoff velocity, velocity at 15 meters, distance travelled in a streamlined position after the start, or the time to a set distance (e.g., time to 5, 10, or 15 meters). As highlighted by Welcher, Hinrichs, and George (1999), however, few studies of start techniques have used multiple measures (e.g., both temporal and velocity characteristics). Doing this sort of analysis is crucial to capturing all the characteristics of a successful start.

In optimizing start technique, swimmers and coaches must consider the inherent tradeoff between the time on the block and the amount of velocity that can be generated at takeoff. When examining the basic physics involved, the swimmer's takeoff velocity is determined by the impulse-momentum theorem

$$F \times t = m \times \Delta v,$$

which states that the takeoff velocity is a function of the force that the swimmer can produce as well as the time over which that force is generated. To achieve a greater takeoff velocity, a swimmer needs to either create more force or generate a force over a longer time (e.g., longer block time). A dive technique with a shorter block time might be inferior to another technique that can generate a much greater takeoff velocity because the swimmer stays on the block longer. But the converse is also possible if the swimmer takes too long on the starting block and cannot make up the accrued time deficit. An ideal start would allow a swimmer to generate a greater impulse without increasing block time.

A more diligent approach to training the start often leads to greater improvements in performance. In other words, practice leads to proficiency. One group of researchers found no significant difference in 10-meter start times between the track and the grab starts before and after a training intervention for experienced competitive swimmers. But significant improvement was found in dive starts for both techniques after they were practiced, reinforcing the idea that the amount of dedicated practice, not the dive technique, is what most significantly affects start performance (Blanksby, Nicholson, and Elliott 2002). Although the dive start techniques were not specified, Hong (1999) provided auxiliary feedback to Chinese elite swimmers and found that the swimmers were able to decrease their times to 10 meters by 0.73 to 0.90 seconds.

Implications of the Recently Approved Starting Block Configurations

The recent decision by FINA to allow starting block configurations that have an adjustable slanted rear footrest or the addition of side handles has the potential to have a substantial influence on the start performance of swimmers. The adjustable footrest (commonly termed *kick plate*) on the Omega blocks can be moved forward and backward at set positions along the block to allow swimmers to use a crouch start and have the rear-positioned leg achieve a 90-degree knee angle (figure 6.5). The kick plate conceivably allows the rear leg to produce more force and generate higher horizontal velocities than can be developed with a track start on a traditional block. Further research is required to determine whether the swimmer's dominant leg would be better positioned at the front or rear of the block with this new configuration.

Several studies suggest that the new block configuration can have an effect on start performance. Honda et al. 2010 indicated that when compared with starts performed on a traditional block, starts that use the kick plate can significantly decrease block time and time to five meters, increase the force output of the rear foot, and increase horizontal takeoff velocity. In a separate study researchers found that on a custom-built instrumented block, a rear incline (at 36 degrees to horizontal) led to a less than 2 percent increase in horizontal velocity and a 3 percent decrease in the time to six meters when compared with the traditional start platform (Vint et al. 2009). This same study reported more significant

▶ **Figure 6.5** The track start with kick plate.

Courtesy of AIS Movement Science, Australian Institute of Sport.

benefits from the use of handles at the side of the block compared with the kick plate. These block modifications appear to favor the track start more than the grab start, so we may see a gradual phasing out of the grab start in international competition as these new block designs are used.

Force Development Characteristics

As a swimmer pushes off the block, force is generated and applied against the starting block, which in turn pushes back against the swimmer according to Newton's third law—for every action, there is an equal and opposite reaction. The applied force can be broken down into vertical, horizontal (antero-posterior), and lateral (side-to-side) components and produce the swimmer's takeoff velocity. Downward force application into the blocks accelerates the body vertically (increased height), and the component of the force directly backward generates propulsion in the forward direction. Any lateral force is essentially wasted and should be minimized. In the track start, however, some lateral force is unavoidable because the legs contribute to force generation at different times (Benjanuvatra et al. 2004).

The way that the three components of force are generated dictates the takeoff velocity of the swimmer and the resultant momentum that the swimmer carries through the air. The interplay of the horizontal and vertical forces also determines the angle at which the swimmer's CG leaves the block. Generating more vertical force makes the angle of takeoff steeper; if a swimmer generates more horizontal force, the angle of takeoff will be flatter. Other information that can be derived from the force profiles includes the swimmer's reaction time, defined as the time from the starting signal to the first movement. Note that electronic displays of swimmers' reaction times at various competitions actually display the swimmers' block times—the combination of both reaction time and movement time on the starting block—which can vary considerably depending on the start used.

Force Development Profiles

A number of researchers have examined how force is developed for the different start types (Arellano et al. 2000; Kruger et al. 2003; Vilas-Boas et al. 2003; Benjanuvatra et al. 2004; Honda et al. 2010). Sample force profiles for the grab and standard (forward-weighted) track starts are shown in figures 6.6 and 6.7.

Although the initial movement of swimmers pulling against the starting block with the arms is similar for both grab and track starts, subtle differences can be identified from the force-time curves. In the grab start, this effort is applied mainly in the vertical direction, reflecting the action of the arms pulling the body toward the starting block (represented by first elevation of the vertical force curves, region 1 on figure 6.6*a* and *b*). Conversely, the arm action in the track start appears to generate impulse in both the horizontal and vertical directions (region 1 on figure 6.6*c* and *d*).

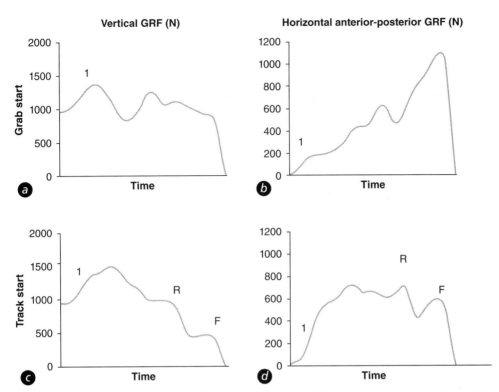

▶ **Figure 6.6** Total vertical and horizontal force profiles for the grab start (*a* and *b*) and track start (*c* and *d*). For the track start, R marks the first peak corresponding with rear-foot propulsion and F marks the peak corresponding with front-foot propulsion.

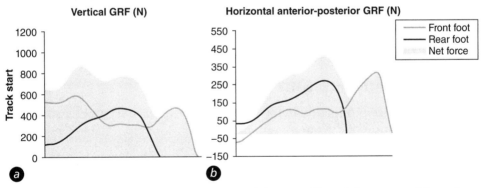

▶ **Figure 6.7** (*a*) Vertical and (*b*) horizontal force profiles of the rear and front foot for the front-weighted track start.

In the horizontal direction, the grab start is characterized by the gradual development of force, reaching a peak just before the swimmer leaves the block. In contrast, the horizontal force for the track start develops earlier and is followed by two separate peaks. The first peak corresponds to the push-off from the rear foot, and the second peak corresponds to the push-off from the front foot (figure 6.6). Aggressive arm action and a strong rear-leg drive are used to generate force and forward momentum in the early part of the dive, but the front leg typically generates the major propulsive force on a traditional starting block (figure 6.7). The greater contribution of the front leg is likely because of the forward position of the swimmer's CG at takeoff. Greater vertical force is developed by the front leg at the beginning of the start, and both legs contribute considerably during the middle and later parts of the front-weighted track start. Although Honda et al. (2010) and Vint et al. (2009) have measured the total horizontal force using a back kick plate compared with traditional starting blocks, neither group of researchers has reported on the relative contribution of the front and rear feet.

Contribution of the Upper Limbs in Force Development

Placing the fingers under the lip of the starting block before the start in all dive types helps to increase the level of pretension in muscles through the upper body and legs. Kruger et al. (2003) found that the use of the arms before the grab start mainly increases back extensor muscle activity and enables a more forceful extension of the back during the initial phase of the start. This preloading also increases the vertical force that a swimmer can generate because the swimmer can press down into the blocks to a greater degree than otherwise possible.

In the track start, swimmers show a much higher level of muscle activation (pretension) in the upper-body musculature, which aids in the forceful arm actions used to drive the body forward initially. Differences in pretension seen between start types arise from the position of the swimmer's CG for each starting technique. In general, the farther back the CG is, the greater the muscle preload is. The pretension probably reduces the reaction time required to initiate movement and increases the effectiveness of the force production because the muscles are already highly activated (Welshe, Wilson, and Ettema 1998).

Limb Dominance and Symmetry

Asymmetric force production is expected during the track start because of the asymmetric nature of the movement, but contributions from the left and right legs should be equal in the grab start in both the horizontal and vertical directions (Benjanuvatra et al. 2004). Table 6.1 provides a summary of the percentage differences found between the left and the right sides in the horizontal and vertical forces produced by 16 national-level swimmers when performing grab starts (Benjanuvatra et al. 2004). In the vertical direction, 7 of the 16 subjects recorded a greater than 10 percent difference in the average vertical force produced. An example of an asymmetric vertical force profile with the corresponding impulse plot (area under force and time curves) is illustrated in figure 6.8.

The influence of asymmetric force applied on the starting block during a grab start is unknown, but any significant asymmetry could result in suboptimum starting performance. Possible negative effects could include rotation in the body and displacement in the lateral direction away from the direct line of

Table 6.1 Percentage Difference Between Right and Left Legs in the Horizontal and Vertical Forces for the Grab Start

	Fypeak	Fzpeak	Fyavg	Fzavg
Mean	5.8%	9.6%	7.9%	10.7%
SD	5.8%	6.9%	3.3%	6.1%
N over 10%	3	6	4	7

Fy = horizontal force, Fz = vertical force.

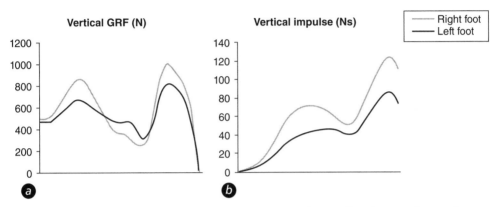

▶ **Figure 6.8** (a) Vertical force and (b) vertical impulse profiles for a grab start by an asymmetric subject.

projection. Swimmers would need to make some adjustments in the air or after entering the water.

Feedback on the force profile generated by a swimmer is increasingly being used for testing and optimizing the performance of elite swimmers. But this is only one aspect of start performance, and it should be integrated with other analysis techniques to develop a full characterization of a swimmer's starting technique. For example, a component-based system that provides force, integrated vision, and wireless three-axis acceleration data has been developed for feedback to assist British swim coaches in improving start performance (Cossor et al. 2010).

Takeoff and Water Entry Angles

Unfortunately, the optimal takeoff and entry angles needed to maximize start performance are currently unknown. The dive entry has implications for the underwater glide because it dictates the initial drag conditions that the swimmer experiences. This entry angle will be determined, at least in part, by the swimmer's takeoff angle and body movements while in flight. In general, a higher takeoff angle creates a steeper entry and reduces the distance travelled in the air. A higher takeoff angle also results in a deeper glide, which adds to the time required to return to the surface.

Conversely, a lower takeoff angle creates a flatter entry and can result in nonoptimal performance. A greater body surface area contacts the water, and the glide depth is shallow, both of which increase drag on the swimmer and reduce glide distance. Studies of elite swimmers have found that they use takeoff angles (defined as the angle that the CG travels relative to horizontal as the feet leave the block) between −5 degrees and +10 degrees (Arellano et al. 2000; Holthe and McLean 2001; Miller, Allen, and Pein 2003). These findings suggest that a relatively flat takeoff is beneficial to elite performance. Other results have demonstrated that elite swimmers tend to enter the water at angles of 30 to 40 degrees (Counsilman et al. 1988; Holthe and McLean 2001). Pike entries typically trend closer to 50 degrees and result in a steep entry and increased underwater depth. Takeda et al. 2008 simulated entry and takeoff parameters and recorded maximum flight distance (3.36 meters) at a takeoff angle of 11.8 degrees but maximum horizontal velocity (4.49 meters per second) at a takeoff angle of −18.7 degrees.

Another crucial factor in determining start performance is the body position at water entry. Variations in the swimmer's position at entry have a marked effect on the rate of deceleration experienced in the water. Despite the obvious importance of a streamlined entry, this aspect is still typically executed poorly, even at the elite level. Common technique flaws include dropping the head, separating the hands or feet, and slightly flexing the ankles or knees, any of which can dramatically increase drag on entry and rapidly decelerate the swimmer.

Backstroke Starts

The backstroke starting technique (figure 6.9) is unique, being the only swim start initiated in the water. This start has received little biomechanical research and exhibits considerable variation at the elite level. The backstroke start can be subdivided into four phases (Hohmann et al. 2006):

1. Initial reaction phase from the starting signal until movement is initiated

2. Pressure phase from first movement until the hands leave the wall

3. Jump phase from when the hands are off until the feet leave the wall

4. Flight phase from when the feet are off until the hips enter the water

Courtesy of the Western Australian Institute of Sport.

▶ **Figure 6.9** Backstroke start.

Studies of elite backstrokers have shown that during the reaction and pressure phases, swimmers tend to produce repeatable patterns of muscle activation, whereas during the jump and flight phases, they tend to show greater intra- and interindividual variability (Hohmann et al. 2006). In a study of nine elite backstrokers, the resultant force against the wall correlated significantly with the time to 7.5 meters and higher wall push-off forces led to faster start times (Kruger et al. 2003). In this study, significant positive correlations were found between the times to hands off the block and when the feet leave the wall, as well as the times to hands off the block and hip entry, although these were not related back to starting performance.

Recent rule changes in backstroke allow swimmers to start with their feet emerging from the water surface. De Jesus et al. (2010) compared backstroke starts with feet fully submerged and feet above the surface. Greater flight time, less total start time, and greater horizontal displacement of the center of mass were found when starting with feet submerged. Starting with the feet above the water, however, produced greater impulses and times of hands-off and foot takeoff. Vilas-Boas et al. 2009 also found that the submerged-feet position led to faster five-meter times and a tendency for higher forces against the wall when compared with a starting position with the feet above water.

Relay Starts (Changeovers)

Until recently, the relay start has been performed using a modified grab start with the toes curled over the end of the block and the arms used to track the incoming swimmer before being thrown forward to generate momentum. In contrast to the start of the initial relay swimmer, the subsequent swimmers have the advantage of being able to increase their forward momentum while on the blocks and therefore increase the takeoff velocity. To this end, many nonleadoff swimmers incorporate an approach, or stepping motion, on the blocks into the start. Researchers have investigated the effectiveness of these approach relay starts and have found no significant differences in start times compared with traditional relay starts (Gambrel et al. 1991; McLean et al. 2000). In a study by Takeda et al. (2008), using a one- or two-step start increased the changeover times and caused several disqualifiable dives compared with a no-step start. But because of the complex timing required to become proficient in these approach start techniques, increased practice may result in these starts becoming more effective.

Swimming Turns

When taking into account the time spent underwater and approaching the wall, turn time can account for up to one-third of total race time. Thus, minor improvements in turn performances can significantly influence race results. Figure 6.10 (Hay 1992) presents a theoretical model that outlines the myriad factors that contribute to turn performance. As with many other areas in swimming, tradeoffs within these factors must be considered when trying to optimize turn performance (Hines 1993). An increase in one variable could reverberate favorably or detrimentally on other components that also affect performance. This chapter focuses predominantly on the flip turn (or tumble turn) of freestyle and backstroke, but a number of the points made can apply to the two-handed touch and open turns (or pivot turns) for breaststroke and butterfly strokes. The latter two strokes are included in a separate section.

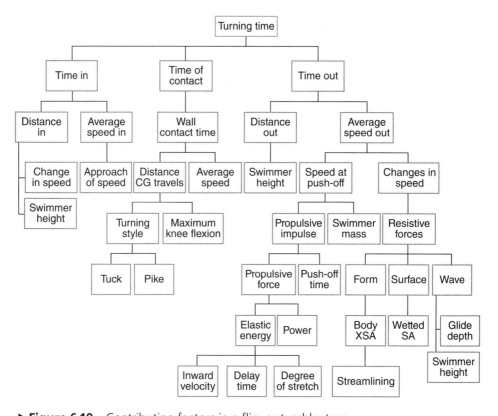

▶ **Figure 6.10** Contributing factors in a flip, or tumble, turn.

Adapted from J.G. Hay, 1985, *The biomechanics of sports techniques*, 3rd ed. (Englewood Cliffs, NJ: Prentice-Hall), 359.

Flip, or Tumble, Turn Technique

The freestyle flip turn (or tumble turn) has evolved into its current form largely because rule changes no longer require any hand touch during the turn. The rotation, wall contact, and wall push-off used in freestyle also have many similarities with the current backstroke rollover turn. Hence, research results for freestyle have some translational crossover to backstroke turns.

The freestyle flip turn includes the approach, rotation, wall contact, underwater glide, and stroke preparation phases. Note that although specific characteristics of each phase are described, successful variations by swimmers at all levels of competition have been observed within each of these phases.

Approach Phase

The approach refers to the time that the swimmer takes to prepare for the turn, and it is typically defined as starting a fixed distance from the wall (e.g., 5 or 7.5 meters) and lasting until the forward somersault begins with the arms by the swimmer's sides. The swimmer sets up the turn in this phase by coordinating breathing and timing to maintain momentum into the wall. Positioning the arms by the side in the somersault is accomplished either by stopping one arm at the end of the pull and waiting for the other arm to pull through and join it or by stopping one arm at entry and allowing the other arm to catch up with it before executing a two-handed pull back to the hips.

The distance out from the wall where the forward somersault starts varies with the skill level and anthropometric dimensions of the swimmer. Blanksby, Gathercole, and Marshall (1995, 1996) found that faster age-group swimmers tended to initiate their turns farther from the wall than less experienced swimmers did. A maximum knee flexion of around 110 to 120 degrees may be optimal at wall contact (Takahashi et al. 1983; Pereira et al. 2006) because this technique decreases the swim-in distance by about 15 centimeters and therefore starts the swimmer's push-off 15 centimeters farther from the wall, a distance saving of 0.3 meters with each turn compared with turns performed with greater knee bend. This more extended position provides less resistance because the body is already semistreamlined and therefore does not need to move as large a mass of water at push-off. Turns performed closer to the wall cause the body to be bunched up on the wall, which takes additional time and produces more drag. This knee angle of about 120 degrees suggested by Blanksby and associates is also in the range at which peak dynamic torque can be generated by the knee extensors (Thorstensson, Grimby, and Karlsson 1976).

Hitting the wall moderately hard and pushing off fast from a semistreamlined position maximizes use of elastic energy that can be stored in the leg musculature (Lyttle et al. 1999). Bending the knees or sinking into the wall after contact dissipates any stored elastic energy and increases the passive wall contact phase, both of which should be discouraged (Wilson, Elliott, and Wood 1991). Although swimmers can wind up for a big push-off using fully flexed knees and hips, they must travel closer to the wall and present a larger frontal resistance over a longer period, which inherently creates high drag forces and incurs a high energy cost (Lyttle et al. 1999).

Rotation Phase

The rotation phase of the turn, from the end of the approach until the feet hit the wall, can be initiated in various ways. The most common way is to flex the head and spine in conjunction with performing a pronounced dolphin or freestyle kick to drive the head and shoulders down and raise the hips. The increased resistance experienced by the head and shoulders as they move out of alignment with the rest of the body, together with the propulsion produced by the final kick, causes the swimmer to somersault forward. In the second common method of initiating the turn, the swimmer omits the dolphin kick but swims down the wall to commence the somersault part of the turn. The swimmer then flexes the upper body about the hips and tucks the knees close to the chest to reduce the distance from the axis of rotation and decrease the moment of inertia, which increases the speed of rotation. The swimmer then opens up the tuck position in the latter stages of the somersault to slow the rotation for an effective foot plant. This technique also prevents overrotation, whereby the feet end up deeper than the body at wall contact. A poor tuck position typically leads to a slower rotation in which the swimmer continues drifting toward the wall. This slow rotation can lead to an underrotation in which the feet are higher than the body at wall contact. This drift also increases the chance of a bunched-up turn with a large knee bend and an associated increase in wall contact time.

Elite swimmers tend to fall into two broad groups when looking at body position as the feet make contact with the wall. Many short-distance-event swimmers perform a straight somersault and initiate wall contact in a predominantly supine position (on the back) before rotating to a prone position (on the front) throughout the wall push-off and glide. In a more traditional turning style, the swimmer twists about the body's longitudinal axis approximately 150 degrees when performing the turn. The swimmer then has to rotate only a small amount after leaving the wall.

The optimal amount of long-axis rotation has not been defined and may vary based on swimmer-specific factors. Elite competitors have shown success with longitudinal rotation anywhere from 0 to 180 degrees, but these turns may not be performed optimally. Intuitively, how a swimmer pushes off on the back could potentially result in less time on the wall, but greater skill is required to ensure that the upper body remains streamlined through the push-off.

With either technique, the arms must be rapidly extended over the head as the turn is executed so that the upper body is streamlined at wall push-off. Common errors to look for are excessive arching of the back and attempts to produce the rotation throughout the push-off, which leads to suboptimal twisting force application.

Wall Contact Phase

The wall contact phase commences when the feet contact the pool wall and finishes at toe-off (Nicol and Kruger 1979). Research has shown that the swimmer's feet should hit the wall at a depth of approximately 0.3 to 0.4 meters (Lyttle et al. 1998; Prins and Patz 2006) to ensure the appropriate depth and trajectory of the subsequent push-off. Typically, It is common to see swimmers either overrotate or underrotate, which will cause foot placement to be either too low or too high, respectively. Their push-offs from the wall are then misdirected as they head toward the surface or the pool bottom. Or they may adopt other compensations such as arching the back.

The most effective use of push-off forces occurs when the ankles, hips, and shoulders are aligned (figure 6.11). Swimmers should aim for a near-horizontal torso with the arms extended overhead before starting the push-off to minimize the frontal surface area and drag and to increase streamlining during the push-off. A slight negative angle might be required to place swimmers at a preferred depth, but the forces should still be directed through the ankles, hips, and shoulders.

The degree of hip and knee flexion at wall impact varies among swimmers. Blanksby, Gathercole, and Marshall (1995) proposed a variable called the tuck index as the ratio of the smallest hip-to-wall distance to total leg length. The amount of tuck has been found to be negatively correlated with turn times. This finding suggests that the larger the tuck index is (i.e., the straighter the legs are), the faster the turn is.

As mentioned earlier, the recommended knee angle at wall contact is around 110 to 120 degrees. But the combined angles at the knees and hips are critical when optimizing the wall push-off, because collectively they determine how forcefully the major propulsive muscles in the legs, many of which cross both joints, can contract. Excessive flexion or extension at one joint will compromise how the muscles function at the other. The nature of muscle contraction suggests that an optimal level of contraction would enable both muscle groups to work in their midrange longer to provide greater force than when they operate at greater length (Blanksby, Gathercole, and Marshall 1996). Knee flexion to less than 90 degrees places the quadriceps muscles, the prime muscle group for the wall push-off, at an inefficient length, which in turn inhibits the swimmer's ability to produce force quickly.

Wall contact time can be separated into the passive and active force production phases. An optimal push-off should minimize the passive phase and maximize the active phase while keeping the total wall contact time to a minimum (Lyttle et al. 1999; Prins and Patz 2006). The passive force production phase consists of the initial wall impact and any countermovement (eccentric contraction of the

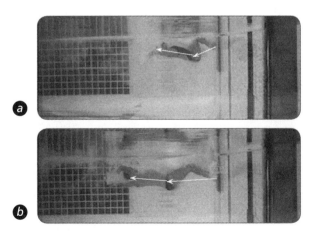

▶ **Figure 6.11**   Direction of forces during the wall push-off: (*a*) inefficient; (*b*) efficient.

quadriceps) that occurs. The active force production phase includes the forceful extension of the knees and hips as well as plantar flexion of the ankles to create velocity away from the wall.

Using a 3D force plate mounted in the wall, Puel et al. (2010) found that the best female swimmers developed maximum horizontal force early in the push-off phase and that maximum horizontal force and glide duration were related to better turn performance. Lyttle et al. (1999), on the other hand, have shown that it is not just about where the peak force occurs. Rather, optimal performance is a balance among the peak push-off force, the time spent pushing off the wall, and the resultant peak drag that is produced. This summary makes sense because large forces generated early in the push-off will cause the body to accelerate while in a nonstreamlined position, resulting in increased drag.

Figure 6.12 highlights some of these findings and displays three push-off force profiles underlying different force production strategies. In this case, the best push-off was performed by swimmer C, who, although she did not have the highest impulse, had an active pushing phase that equaled 90 percent of the total wall contact time. Combined with a low drag force, this method allowed the swimmer to achieve the highest exit velocity of the group—3.03 meters

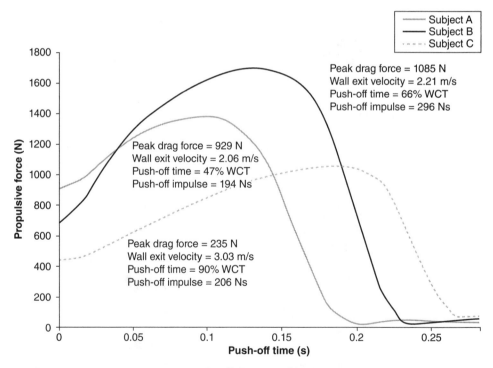

▶ **Figure 6.12** Representative push-off force profiles for subjects A, B, and C. In this case, swimmer C performed the best turn. Although she did not have the highest impulse, she had an active pushing phase that equaled 90 percent of the total wall contact time. Combined with a low drag force, this method allowed the swimmer to achieve the highest exit velocity of the group—3.03 meters per second.

per second. In short, a high final push-off velocity was achieved by an optimal combination of low peak drag force (i.e., proper depth and good streamlining), high peak propulsive force, and a wall push-off time of sufficient duration to develop this force (in other words, not as fast as possible but long enough to generate a large impulse). Of these variables, lower peak drag force was found to be the best predictor of the final push-off velocity.

In an ideal situation, any type of kinetic (force) analysis should be performed while also looking at video of the turn, because what could be considered an efficient push-off from a kinetics point of view may be offset by poor body position and streamlining. Having stated that, force curves contain a great deal of information and can yield a wealth of data about turn performance to the trained eye. Figures 6.13 to 6.16 present force traces that highlight several turning flaws, in which the solid line represents the horizontal force generated during push-off. For reference, figure 6.13 illustrates a good turn in which force is developed consistently throughout push-off. The peak force occurs closer to takeoff when the swimmer is in a streamlined position. Curves with multiple peaks usually mean that segment coordination is not optimal (figure 6.14) or that a substantial settling phase occurs on the wall (e.g., an impact phase occurs at contact when force generation is not being used to propel the swimmer off the wall; figure 6.15). Additionally, if peak force is generated too early in the push-off (figure 6.16), the swimmer will experience excessive drag, resulting in suboptimal performance.

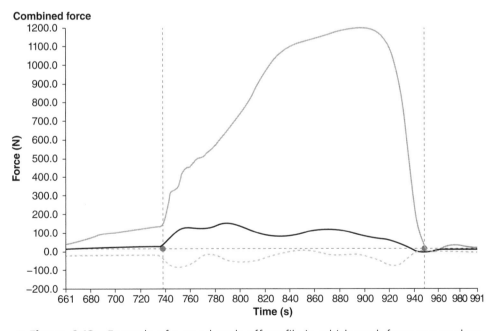

▶ **Figure 6.13** Example of a good push-off profile in which peak force occurs close to take-off and the swimmer is in a streamlined position. A more consistent increase in force initially would have been more efficient.

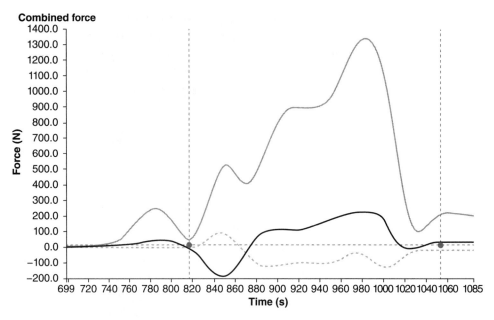

▶ **Figure 6.14** Example of poor segment coordination leading to velocity fluctuations during push-off.

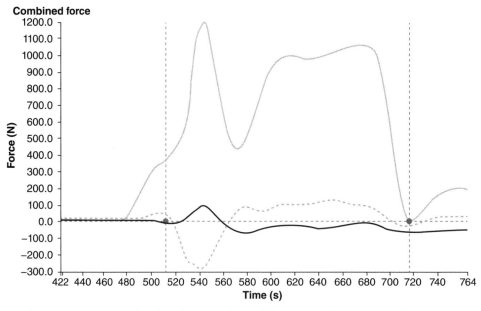

▶ **Figure 6.15** Example of settling on the wall because of high impact forces.

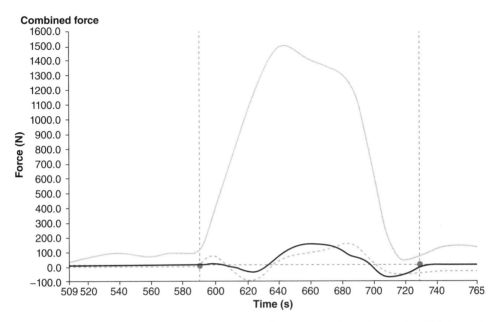

▶ **Figure 6.16** Example of developing peak force too early in the push-off followed by a drop-off in force levels. The swimmer is usually in a nonstreamlined position when peak force occurs.

Open, or Pivot, Turns

The turning motions used in breaststroke and butterfly open turn (or pivot turn) techniques are essentially the same action. The main differences occur in the underwater phase that follows the push-off. The open turn (pivot turn) is initiated in both strokes with a simultaneous two-hand touch with the shoulders parallel to the water surface, as dictated by event rules. Because breaststrokers now incorporate one dolphin kick underwater as part of the split stroke (i.e., glide, pull–push of hands to hips, dolphin kick, arm recovery to overhead with a breaststroke kick before surfacing), butterfly turns more closely resemble breaststroke turns than ever before. The same principles of body alignment, development of force, and other features of the push-off that were discussed for the flip turn (or tumble turn) can be related to the open turn (pivot turn) (Blanksby et al. 1998). Additionally, the timing of the strokes leading into an open turn (pivot turn) is important to prevent an excessively long glide into the wall and subsequent loss of momentum (Ling et al. 2004; Walker et al. 1995).

Using regression equations, Huellhorst, Ungerechts, and Willimczik (1988) found that the important criteria for fast breaststroke turns were short pivot times and high velocity at push-off. A newly proposed breaststroke and butterfly turn is the apnea turn (Kishimoto et al. 2010), which is completed underwater.

The theory is that open turns cause increased wave resistance around the water surface and that this resistance would be reduced underwater. The authors found that, except for the longer pivot time (perhaps because of insufficient practice), the apnea turn was faster overall and achieved higher wall push-off velocity in a five-meter round-trip time, including velocity of turn in and out, velocity of approach, and glide out (Kishimoto et al. 2010).

Underwater Phases

The underwater phase after a start or turn is when the swimmer travels fastest (Chatard et al. 1990). Elite swimmers typically enter the water from a dive start at between 4.50 and 5.50 meters per second (Benjanuvatra et al. 2004) and push off the wall after turning at between 2.60 and 3.20 meters per second (Lyttle et al. 1999). In contrast, free-swimming velocity, which represents the velocity at which swimmers should initiate stroking, ranges from 1.60 to 2.20 meters per second. Hence, an efficient glide and underwater kick before stroke resumption are integral to maximizing start and turn performance.

Glide Phase

Coaches and swimmers should be mindful that increased swimmer speed increases the drag experienced. Therefore, a swimmer should aim to minimize the resistive forces by holding a streamlined position and kicking at the optimal depth underwater.

Studies of drag forces when towing swimmers underwater at different speeds and depths have found that hydrodynamic drag decreases with increasing depth and decreasing velocity (Lyttle et al. 1998; Maiello et al. 1998; Marinho et al. 2010). In terms of optimizing the depth that a swimmer should be underwater, research has shown that swimmers should aim to perform their glides at a depth of approximately 0.5 meters underwater to benefit from reduced drag forces (figure 6.17). Any additional increase in glide depth did not produce any substantial reduction in drag force. Despite being a popular strategy for some elite-level swimmers, a deeper glide depth should be discouraged. With that said, the optimal glide depth following a turn will likely need to be slightly deeper so that the swimmer gets under the surface turbulence generated by the swimmer on the inbound leg of the turn. The optimum glide depth should gradually decrease the closer the swimmer gets to stroke resumption.

Form drag and wave drag are important factors in determining the total drag force experienced by the swimmer. Therefore, the swimmer must hold a good streamline throughout the glide without excess body movements. Small deviations in body positions can have a large effect on the drag characteristics (Roig 2010; Wada et al. 2010). Common faults during the glide include not having the hands together and not having the arms fully extended above the head, lifting or lowering the head, and having the feet apart (laterally or vertically) and toes dorsiflexed. An efficient glide depth and streamlined pathway increase

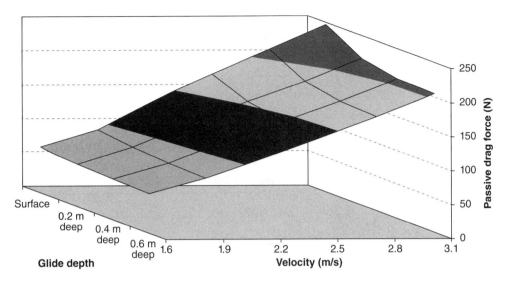

▶ **Figure 6.17**   Combined average drag force for each velocity and depth.

Adapted from A.D. Lyttle, B.A. Blanksby, B.C. Elliott, and D.G. Lloyd, 1998, "The effect of depth and velocity on drag during the streamlined glide," *Journal of Swimming Research* 13: 15–22.

the glide distance covered in the same time and improve the underwater phase performance (Prins and Patz 2006).

Traditionally, our understanding of drag and propulsive forces occurring on the streamlined body is derived from towing tests with swimmers in the water. But estimating the forces acting on the various parts of the body is now possible using high-level fluid dynamics modeling, such as computational fluid dynamics (CFD). Keys and Lyttle (2010) compared the drag forces experienced by every major body segment of a swimmer in a streamlined position when gliding at the surface and underwater. Although an overall net increase in drag force occurred at the surface (as expected), the upper-body segments (122 percent increase in drag force) were responsible for all the increase in drag force (Keys and Lyttle 2010). The lower-body segments all recorded significant reductions in drag force (104 percent reduction in drag force). The feet changed most drastically, from being an area of drag to propelling the body forward (Keys and Lyttle 2010). The authors attributed this change in drag across the body to the influence of the linear wave formation close to the water surface with concurrent areas of positive and negative acceleration across the wave formation affect the drag across the swimmer's body.

Stroke Preparation and Underwater Kicking

The stroke preparation phase consists of underwater kicking before break out for the first stroke cycle. For freestyle, butterfly, and backstroke, the dolphin kick has become the preferred underwater kicking style. Clothier et al. (2000) demonstrated that the deceleration was less during underwater dolphin kicking than during flutter kicking, and the velocity above that of free swimming was maintained longer with dolphin kicking underwater. Lyttle et al. (2000) found no significant differences in the net forces (propulsive forces minus resistive forces) between the underwater dolphin and flutter kicks when towing elite swimmers, although the dolphin kicks tended to produce better propulsion. The kicking style adopted by a given swimmer will likely depend on the streamlining position used, the stroke being swum, and swimmer and coach preferences.

Again, CFD analyses have started to provide greater insight into how drag and propulsion are generated over the body in underwater kicking patterns. Lyttle and Keys (2006) compared two patterns of underwater dolphin kicks (large, slow kicks versus small, fast kicks). Using a case-study approach on an elite swimmer, the researchers determined that, for the approximate range of velocities experienced during underwater kicking (2.40 meters per second down to 1.50 meters per second), a large, slow underwater dolphin kick showed less momentum loss at lower velocities and virtually no difference at a velocity of 2.40 meters per second. In a follow-up study, Keys and Lyttle (2010) compared these two underwater dolphin kicking techniques to the underwater flutter kick at a single velocity of 2.18 meters per second. Although the underwater dolphin kick generated greater propulsion, the total net thrust was greater for the underwater flutter kick, as evidenced by a lower total momentum loss. This resulted from more consistently applied propulsive forces in the flutter kick than the dolphin kick, which showed larger periods of deceleration.

In kicking, the relative importance of having flexible ankle joints has never been quantified, despite the fact that, anecdotally, the more effective underwater kickers tend to have better flexibility through a range of joints, particularly the ankles and knees. To illustrate the capabilities of the CFD modeling technologies, Keys and Lyttle (2010) varied an elite swimmer's ankle flexibility in the analysis to examine the effects on the swimmer's net thrust during underwater dolphin kicks. A 10-degree increase in ankle plantar flexion (the ability to point the feet down) allowed the swimmer to generate an additional 16N of propulsion from the feet during the dolphin kick downsweep, roughly a 66 percent increase in the peak force created at the feet. The effect of increased flexibility changes at different kicking velocities, but the general trend of the benefits will be the same. This research provides important information to coaches on the effects of flexibility on the generation of propulsion while kicking.

The optimum time to initiate underwater kicking presents another opportunity for improving start and turn performance. Observations of swimmers across varying levels have shown that underwater kicking can be, and often is, initiated at any stage, from immediately after the dive entry or wall push-off to after arm stroking has resumed. Intuitively, by starting the kick immediately, the drag created by deviating from a streamlined body position will likely exceed any propulsive force benefit created by kicking. Conversely, by waiting too long before initiating underwater kicking, the full benefits of the underwater kick will not be realized. These assumptions were confirmed by Lyttle et al. (2000), who used towing experiments and found that most swimmers should wait for approximately one second after the wall push-off of a turn before initiating any underwater kicking (Lyttle et al. 2000; Sanders 2003). With that said, this recommendation depends highly on the swimmer's underwater kicking proficiency. A similar rule of thumb for glide time has not been proposed for the dive start, but this period would probably be slightly longer than the one-second period recommended after wall push-off given the higher initial velocity experienced after the dive entry.

A common problem highlighted by these studies is that swimmers frequently lose time by gliding or kicking too long or too little before starting to stroke with the upper body (Blanksby, Gathercole, and Marshall 1995, 1996; Hubert et al. 2006). In the first case, swimmers decelerate to less than their free-swimming velocity and they need additional time and energy to get back up to race velocity. Conversely, when stroking is commenced too early, the swimmer's speed is still higher than the free-swimming velocity and any propulsive movements effectively slow the swimmer down unnecessarily.

Poor streamlining is another common error encountered in swimmers of all ages and abilities. Blanksby et al. (2004) found that two-thirds of male and female age-group backstrokers did not hold the streamlined position long enough to gain optimum distance from the wall and that the premature initiation of stroking resulted in increased deceleration back to the free-swimming velocity. The remaining one-third maintained the streamlined glide too long. This error was typically a result of pushing off at too great an angle. The return to stroking thus came at below free-swimming speed, and significant energy was required to regain race pace.

Breaststroke Underwater Phase

After performing a fast spin at the wall, breaststrokers prepare for the important underwater phase (Blanksby et al. 1998; Goya, Takagi, and Nomura 1999). During the underwater phase of breaststroke start and turns, swimmers choose a time to execute an extended underwater arm pull–push to the hips, followed by a single underwater breaststroke kick (split stroke). Breaststrokers then break out to the surface before the regular arm action commences. Again, little research exists on the mechanics of the breaststroke start, especially given the new rules that allow the use of the underwater dolphin kick and subsequent rules that allow the dolphin kick and underwater breaststroke actions to be separated. Towing tests have shown that the second streamline position in the breaststroke glide phase (with the arms alongside the body) leads to higher and more variable drag forces, highlighting the need to ensure that good body position is maintained in this phase (Costa et al. 2010). Likewise, although anecdotal evidence clearly shows the benefits of including the underwater dolphin kick, no research has examined the effectiveness or timing of this kick. Traditionally, swimmers have used the dolphin kick immediately following the arm pull, but an alternative technique was popularized by former 100-meter world-record holder Kosuke Kitajima of

Japan in which the dolphin kick is performed at the start of the underwater arm pull. Breaststroke starts and turns present particular challenges because there are several freely chosen moments when swimmers must streamline—arms pull–push to the hips, dolphin kick, breaststroke kick, arm recovery, and break out.

Summary

Swim starts and turns represent critical components of a swimming race. Refining these skills is integral to being competitive at the elite level. At a practical level, dedicated practice of starts and turns within a swimmer's daily training environment is likely to lead to improvement, but an understanding of the principles that lead to more efficient skill development and refinement increases the performance gains that this training can produce. Research into starts and turns is usually confounded by interactions of the numerous components that make up the performance. These interactions create tradeoffs in which overemphasizing one component can negatively affect other components. Isolating the optimal combination of the variables that affect each of the starts and turning skills is the key to providing useful, practical information to swimmers.

Despite the shortage of definitive outcomes of research into swim starts and turns, coaches and sports scientists can apply logical mechanical principles to assist with technique prescription on a case-study basis with each swimmer. The body of research can be used to support the coach's rationale for a technique change. An understanding that the swimmer's inherent technique is likely to feel more comfortable should not dissuade the coach from attempting to optimize phases of the starts and turns. A change should be attempted only if a logical thought process and basic data support the proposed change that has been tailored to the individual swimmer.

CHAPTER 7

Analyzing Strokes Using Computational Fluid Dynamics

—Matt Keys, PhD, Andrew Lyttle, PhD, Brian Blanksby, PhD, Liang Cheng, PhD, and Koji Honda

Swimming techniques used at the elite level typically arise from a mix of natural genetics, feel for the water, knowledge from experienced coaches, and some trial and error. Although these techniques are considered highly efficient, little is known from a hydrodynamics point of view about what makes any technique better or faster than another.

We know that a complex interaction of forces exists as swimmers move through the water. But to date, the exact mechanisms that create propulsion and minimize active drag during swimming are unresolved. In general, the three options for increasing swimming velocity are to increase the total propulsive forces, minimize the total resistive forces, or ideally both. For coaches and sport scientists to apply technique changes with these options, a thorough knowledge of the mechanisms that generate propulsion and drag force development is essential. Unfortunately, the ability to quantify the relative effects of flow patterns experimentally when swimming, and the resultant forces that are produced, is limited at best and provides only approximations of total-body effects.

This chapter presents a full-body analysis of a world-class freestyle sprinter using a new analysis tool called computational fluid dynamics (CFD). This type of analysis can provide considerable insight into how swimmers can effectively increase propulsion while reducing drag throughout the entire swimming stroke (Keys and Lyttle 2008).

Tools for Technique Analysis

Before embracing a new technology and learning how it can enhance the understanding of swimming technique, it is helpful to know what tools of measurement are currently used to assess swimming mechanics. For free-swimming investigations, relatively few testing methods have allowed any comprehensive, noninvasive analysis of swimming. Research has usually incorporated one or several of the following methods to estimate what is happening throughout the swimming stroke:

- Video-based kinematic analysis to quantify variations in swimming velocity and the timing of key phases throughout the stroke cycle
- Inertial sensors, such as accelerometers, to measure accelerations of body segments throughout the stroke
- Physical testing using force plates, drag lines, or towing devices to estimate the total net forces generated by or acting on the body
- Numerical modeling and analysis of recorded flow lines and vortex patterns as measured by injecting dye or using particle image velocimetry methods to visualize how fluid particles move around the body
- Computer-based numerical modeling that uses estimations of drag and inertia effects of shapes similar to those of human limbs to predict how they interact with water

Each of these systems provided valuable information and some empirical data about a few of the many questions concerning the best way to swim. But because of methodological limitations and the complex fluid flows around irregularly shaped human bodies that are always changing shape and position, no methods thus far have provided a complete picture of the influential features occurring throughout a full swimming stroke cycle. With that said, technology makes regular advances that improve the ability to analyze swimming technique.

This chapter discusses one such emerging technology available for analyzing swimming: computational fluid dynamics (CFD). Some consider CFD to be the future of swimming research. It enables athlete-specific, full-stroke analyses to explain how and where propulsive and drag forces are produced for optimal performance.

CFD can be used to model and solve complex problems of fluid flow, and it is ideally suited to analyze drag and propulsion across the body when swimming. Using known physics and fluid dynamics relationships, CFD allows complex fluid flow regimes and geometry to be simulated within a computer environment. In fact, CFD has been used successfully to optimize performance in a variety of sports. These efforts include assisting in the design of a bobsled and understanding the dynamics of how the seams on a soccer ball affect its flight characteristics. CFD can be used to visualize fluid along a swimming body and to calculate any number of performance-related variables, such as velocity, acceleration, and force.

Thus, CFD analyses can provide answers and insights into problems that have been unobtainable through traditional physical testing techniques. To date, CFD predictions of forces acting on a swimmer have been limited to studies of passive drag (Bixler, Pease, and Fairhurst 2007), hand motion through the water (Bixler and Riewald 2001; Sato and Hino 2002), and underwater kicking (Lyttle and Keys 2006; Von Loebbecke et al. 2009). These CFD studies have begun to fill a gap in testing procedures and have simplified the mathematical modeling that to date has been used primarily to determine both the passive and active drag components and frictional, pressure, wave, and inertial forces.

Besides increasing the foundational knowledge of swimming mechanics, these CFD studies have begun to provide meaningful and practical information that can be applied on the pool deck. An example of this is the underwater dolphin kicking CFD study by Lyttle and Keys (2006). The results demonstrated that when underwater dolphin kicking, a 10-degree increase in ankle plantar flexion (the ability to point the feet down) created 16N greater peak propulsive force by the feet during the dolphin kick downsweep. This represents approximately 5.5 times the average force created by the feet over the whole of the downsweep, or nearly a 17 percent increase in the total average force created by the entire body during that same period, because of the contribution of other segments in creating the propulsion. Although the relative contribution of increased ankle flexibility changes with different kicking velocities and for different swimmers, the general trend is the same—increased plantar flexion increases kicking force. This information about the potential beneficial effects of greater ankle flexibility for generating propulsion while kicking underwater is important to coaches.

A limitation of some early computerized CFD studies is that they restricted their focus to one aspect of swimming (e.g., just the arm pull) or one section of the race (e.g., immediately after the start or after pushing off the turning wall), and they do not capture the complete picture of events during a swimming race. For example, the winner of the 50-meter freestyle at the 2008 Australian Olympic Trials touched in a time of 21.28 seconds. Using race analysis techniques similar to those presented in chapter 6, it was subsequently found that he spent just over 6 percent of the race underwater after the start, either gliding or kicking in a stream-lined position (conditions often modeled in CFD analyses), and 87 percent of the total race time free swimming, a condition not yet studied using CFD. Although performance gains may still be made by optimizing start and turn performance, major competition advantages will come from improving the techniques used during the free-swimming portion of the race. Therefore, this chapter examines how technology can be used to measure full-body swimming mechanics and provides the initial steps toward calculating when the major propulsive and drag forces are created within a full freestyle stroke of an elite swimmer.

CFD Analysis of a Full Swimming Stroke

Using CFD, a case-study approach was undertaken to examine the propulsive and drag forces experienced across and around the body during full-body freestyle swimming (Keys 2010). The participant in this study, Eamon Sullivan, was the 50-meter and 100-meter freestyle world-record holder when tested. Therefore, the technique examined can be considered highly evolved and effective. Note that, as with any technique analysis, some findings will be specific to this athlete. Several common features, however, could be applied to other freestyle swimmers as coaches and scientists better understand the critical factors that affect performance.

In this chapter we cannot describe all the nuances and complexities of running a CFD analysis, but we can identify some of the main technologies and methods that render these simulations a reality. More information on general CFD theory is covered by Versteeg and Malalasekera (1995), and more in-depth information on the dynamic CFD model developed for this work can be found in Keys (2010). In general, any dynamic CFD model requires two important components.

The first is a detailed 3D mapping of the swimmer's body shape using a laser scanner (figure 7.1). In this case, the resultant scan produced a highly detailed mesh made up of approximately 100,000 triangular surface elements. The total simulation consisted of between 2 and 5 million cells. Of this vast number of cells, three to five layers of prism cells are located at the swimmer's body surface

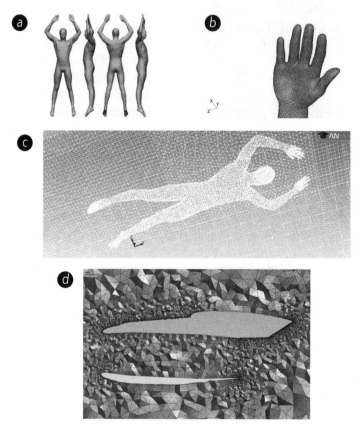

▶ **Figure 7.1** The (a) full-body and (b) hand surface meshes, respectively, developed around the swimmer; (c) the whole-body wire frame of the swimmer in the analysis volume; (d) a cross-sectional slice of the mesh around the swimmer's body.

and create a near-wall boundary layer model, which transitions to tetrahedral cells for the remaining fluid zones. The mesh was made denser in critical areas (e.g., areas of great curvature) to capture the characteristics of the fluid flow and the forces acting at each point on the swimmer. The model also has articulation points that can be placed into any position a swimmer would achieve during a stroke cycle.

The second is an accurate description of the 3D kinematics (movement patterns) of the swimmer performing the stroke (figure 7.2). The 3D kinematics were derived through manual digitizing. Although a standard method for obtaining kinematic data exists in swimming, limitations are present because of inherent inaccuracies associated with this measurement technique underwater (e.g., body shape covering visual joint location points; poor water clarity because of bubbles and light reflection near the surface; and standard camera difficulties of parallax error, distorted lenses, and setup calibration issues). Despite these potential errors, the method allows the collection of the best possible kinematic data for all body segments and provides a good basis for the developmental analyses of free-swimming stroking patterns. A subjective comparison between the animated simulation produced from the digitized data and competitive video footage taken from various angles revealed similar movement patterns throughout the stroke.

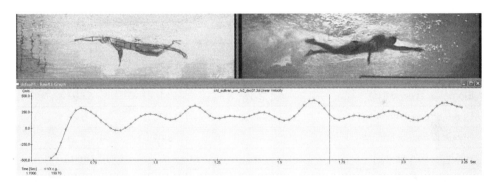

▶ **Figure 7.2** Picture of the results of the 3D kinematics output achieved from manual video digitizing.

Results of the Study

This analysis provides some new insights into the freestyle swimming stroke and the factors that affect performance. During the analysis, the pressure and viscous drag forces acting on individual body segments were calculated at each point in time throughout the full freestyle stroke cycle. When a force acts on a swimmer over time, it changes the swimmer's momentum (expressed as Newton-seconds, or Ns). Evaluating the momentum created or removed from the swimmer within each stroke cycle is the best way to assess technique effectiveness. Simply stated, if a segment contributes positive momentum, the swimmer's velocity increases. Conversely, a negative momentum change causes the swimmer to slow down.

The momentum contributions made by various body segments and joints over the course of a stroke cycle are presented in table 7.1. They represent the momentum in the direction of travel. The various segments are then displayed graphically in figure 7.3. Note that except in the first line of the table, momentum values have been normalized by the time it takes to complete a full stroke cycle (in this case 1.04 seconds), giving a per second value toward how each body part influences the swimmer's overall momentum. This normalization allows comparisons among different athletes and swimming techniques.

Figure 7.4 displays the resultant force over the entire body throughout the stroke cycle, and table 7.2 outlines the temporal points associated with critical events in the stroke cycle, along with a pictorial representation of the swimmer's animation at this time step. The velocity of the swimmer's hip (midiliac crest) ranged between 1.9 and 2.3 meters per second within the stroke cycle analyzed, and the average over this cycle was 2.08 meters per second.

Table 7.1 Momentum (Ns) Changes in the Swimmer From the Full Freestyle Stroke Simulation Over One Full Stroke Cycle

	Left side	Right side	Total
Total swimmer per cycle (Ns)			31.23
Total swimmer per second (Ns)			30.03
Hand per second (Ns)	12.21	11.59	23.80
Wrist per second (Ns)	4.65	6.47	11.12
Forearm per second (Ns)	3.89	6.03	9.92
Elbow per second (Ns)	2.35	4.21	6.56
Upper arm per second (Ns)	−0.50	0.27	−0.23
Shoulder per second (Ns)	−9.17	−8.02	−17.20
Head per second (Ns)			−10.18
Neck per second (Ns)			−0.37
Upper trunk per second (Ns)			−37.94
Mid trunk per second (Ns)			−24.74
Pelvis per second (Ns)			3.18
Hips per second (Ns)	−4.55	−2.85	−7.41
Thighs per second (Ns)	9.46	8.82	18.28
Knees per second (Ns)	4.18	5.23	9.41
Lower leg per second (Ns)	14.81	12.57	27.39
Ankles per second (Ns)	0.38	−2.29	−1.91
Feet per second (Ns)	10.67	9.67	20.34
Combined arms per second (Ns)	13.44	20.54	33.98
Combined legs per second (Ns)	34.95	31.16	66.10
Trunk and head per second (Ns)			−70.05

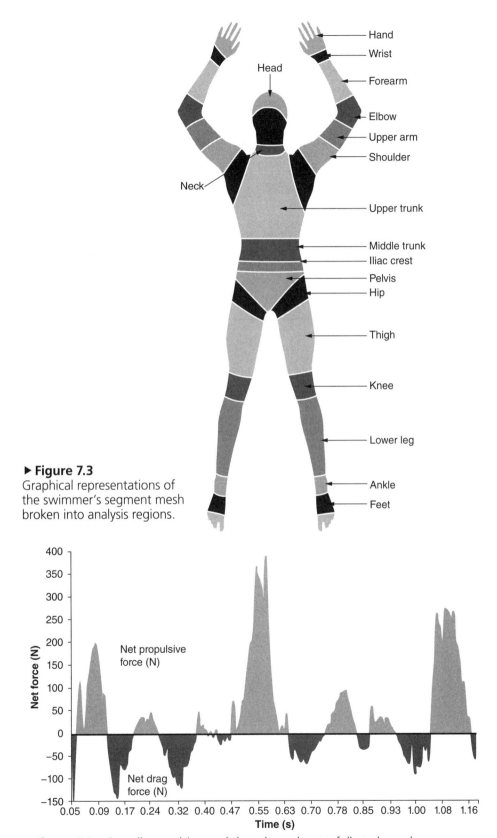

▶ **Figure 7.3**
Graphical representations of the swimmer's segment mesh broken into analysis regions.

Hand
Wrist
Head
Forearm
Elbow
Upper arm
Shoulder
Neck
Upper trunk
Middle trunk
Iliac crest
Pelvis
Hip
Thigh
Knee
Lower leg
Ankle
Feet

Net force (N)

Net propulsive force (N)

Net drag force (N)

Time (s)

▶ **Figure 7.4**   Overall propulsion and drag throughout a full stroke cycle.

Table 7.2 Critical Temporal Points Through the Total Freestyle Stroke Cycle

Point	Time (sec)	Description	Side view	Front view
1	0.19	Left foot reaches top as right foot reaches bottom of sweep.		
2	0.20	Right hand exits the water.		
3	0.37	Left foot reaches bottom as right foot reaches top of sweep.		
4	0.44	Left hand reaches the deepest point.		
5	0.56	Left foot reaches top as right foot reaches bottom of sweep.		
6	0.58	Right hand enters the water.		
7	0.64	Left forearm at closest point to vertical.		
8	0.70	Left hand exits the water.		

Point	Time (sec)	Description	Side view	Front view
9	0.73	Left foot reaches bottom as right foot reaches top of sweep.		
10	0.90	Left foot reaches top as right foot reaches bottom of sweep.		
11	0.98	Right hand at deepest point.		
12	1.04	Right forearm at closest point to vertical.		
13	1.06	Left foot reaches bottom as right foot reaches top of sweep.		
14	1.08	Left hand enters the water.		

The overall changes in force throughout the stroke (figure 7.4) were as expected in that six clear cycles occurred with four small peaks and two large peaks, representing the six-beat kick used by the swimmer. The two large peaks correlated with the peak propulsion of the left arm just after 0.56 seconds and the right arm at 1.07 seconds, and they occurred at the same time as two of the kicks in the athlete's six-beat kick cycle. The two larger propulsive peaks are validated by the overall velocity of the swimmer's hip. The two highest velocity peaks occurred just after the peak propulsive forces, at 0.64 seconds and 1.14 seconds, when the swimmer's velocity surged to around 2.3 meters per second. The smaller propulsive force peaks also had a small influence on the velocity.

Discussion and Application

So what does all this mean? Breaking down the distribution of forces shows that both the arms and the legs created large amounts of propulsion, whereas the trunk contributed most of the drag. The hands provided a total propulsive momentum of 23.8 Ns, and the combined contribution of the wrist, forearm, and elbow was 27.6 Ns. Hence, the forearm position during the underwater arm stroke was as critical as that of the hands; this topic will be covered in more depth later in the chapter. The head contributed less drag than the upper- and lower-trunk components did, possibly because the head was usually only semi-submerged or presented less volume, which could influence the potential level of wave drag encountered.

Lower-Body Propulsion and Force Profiles

A longstanding topic of debate in the swimming community concerns how much the legs and feet contribute to propulsion and whether they even contribute anything more than a stabilizing balance to the freestyle stroke. But table 7.1 clearly shows that the lower body—everything from the pelvis to the feet—contributed more to the total momentum of front crawl swimming than the upper body did, including the arm segments. Dissecting the data even further suggests that the thighs, knees, and calves provided a greater percentage of the propulsion than the feet did. These results may be misleading, however, when the mechanisms for the net propulsive force are considered in conjunction with the effects of the wave formation as the swimmer moves through the water. This topic will be discussed in detail later in the chapter.

The six cycles of the six-beat kick are relatively easy to identify when looking only at the contributions made by each leg throughout the stroke cycle (figure 7.5). Analyzing these data after correlations with the kinematics of the performance shows that the maximum propulsive peaks started as the feet began their respective downsweep phases.

Comparison of left- and right-leg actions shows some asymmetry in this athlete. Note that this athlete had greater flexibility in the left ankle (42 degrees in plantar flexion and dorsiflexion) compared with a 35-degree range of motion in the right ankle. Figure 7.5 shows that better left-ankle flexibility provided slightly more propulsion on that side (35.0 Ns) than on the right side (31.2 Ns).

Another notable difference was the variation through which the ankles moved during the execution of the stroke (the dynamic range of motion). The peak plantar flexion angle on some kicks varied by as much as 20 degrees. This peak plantar flexion angle occurred when the toes were pointed to their greatest degree, which was at the start of the feet downsweep (figure 7.6).

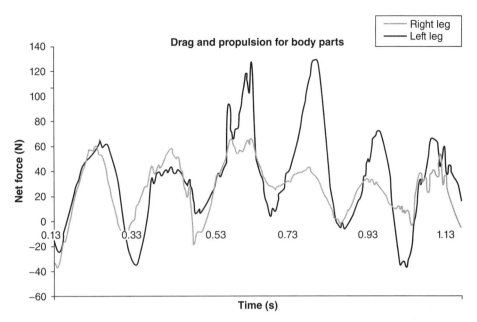

▶ **Figure 7.5** The net forces on the right and left legs throughout the freestyle stroke. Note the higher peak forces generated by the left leg in this swimmer.

These intercycle variations in ankle flexibility are of interest when considering that underwater kicking tests have demonstrated that increased ankle flexibility can lead to an increase in propulsive force, as discussed in chapter 6, "Techniques for Starts and Turns." Using the left leg as an example (because of its greater variation of maximum plantar flexion values at the start of the downsweep), it could be expected that, during the six-beat kick, the peak left foot propulsion would occur during kicks that demonstrated greater ankle plantar flexing values. Conversely, kicks in which the feet did not plantar flex effectively at the start of the downsweep could be expected to display a relative drop-off in the peak force. But the force results here suggest that the opposite occurs because the kicks displaying greater plantar flexion at the start of the downsweep produced lower net propulsive force values (figure 7.7).

To understand the difference between the underwater kicking and above-water kicking results, we need to highlight the position of the feet relative to the water surface at the top of the downsweep during each kick. For example, the maximum plantar flexion that occurred at the start of the downsweep during the first kick (at 0.26 seconds) was counteracted by this foot coming out of the water. This reduced the volume that was able to benefit from the wave water acceleration (discussed later in the chapter). In addition, the initial acceleration of the foot into the downsweep occurred when it was pushing against air rather than water. Because of the differences in fluid density between air and water, the potential propulsive force will decrease by around 800 times.

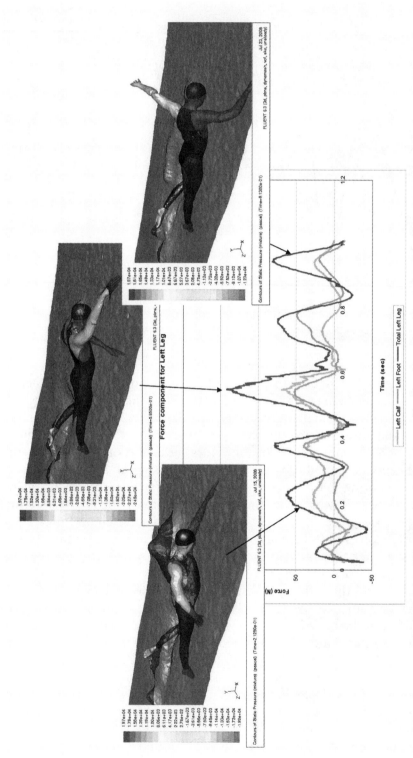

► **Figure 7.6** Image displaying the peak plantar flexion angle of the left foot at the start of the downsweep.

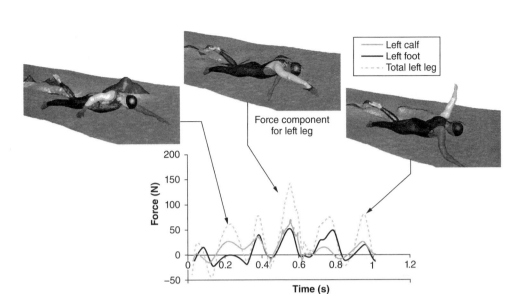

▶ **Figure 7.7** Comparison of left-limb foot positions during the start of the downsweep with the resultant net propulsion.

Using this theory of foot positioning in relation to water surface level, the comparisons of leg propulsion in each cycle have greater correlations. When comparing the foot position in figures 7.7 and 7.8, the foot was clearly out of the water at 0.22 seconds and again at 0.92 seconds. At 0.56 seconds, the foot was still mainly surrounded by water and the force peak was up to twice that of the other occurrences, even though the ankle flexibility was not nearly as effective. If the feet were lower in the water for all three kicks, we would expect an additional 60 N of propulsion to be generated for up to 0.06 seconds on each of the two out-of-water kicks. This would enable a potential difference in a kick cycle of 6.9 Ns per second for the left leg alone, which, at a swimming velocity

▶ **Figure 7.8** Example showing the left foot coming out of the water during the CFD simulations (left) and during actual filming of the swim (right).

of 2.08 meters per second, could improve overall swimming speed and time by up to 3.5 percent. This potential improvement clearly has practical significance in competition and could influence times even further if a similar reduction in magnitude occurs when the right leg stays in the water.

The concept of keeping the feet submerged at all times is not a common coaching instruction, and, as can be seen here, it does not always occur in some elite swimmers. But the concept is not new. Tom Jager, who held the world record of 21.81 seconds for the 50-meter freestyle for more than 10 years, wore only a traditional pair of Lycra briefs. One of his focus areas was ensuring that his kick was strong and that his feet were submerged at all times (Jager 1999).

Forces Experienced by the Head and Trunk

In comparison with the legs and arms, the head and trunk segments display little variation in drag because of the small ranges of movement of these body parts (figure 7.9). The largest moving component in this section of the body is the upper trunk, which also has the highest volume. Because the upper trunk twists almost 42 degrees (body roll around the longitudinal axis) from the neutral prone body position during one arm stroke cycle, it has a slight variation in force, which makes up greater than 90 percent of the variation in the force generated by the trunk. This results also from the differences in wetted surface area and frontal surface area to which the upper trunk is exposed.

The upper trunk moves through a range of about 12 degrees about the transverse axis (angle of the upper trunk relative to the water surface). The steepest

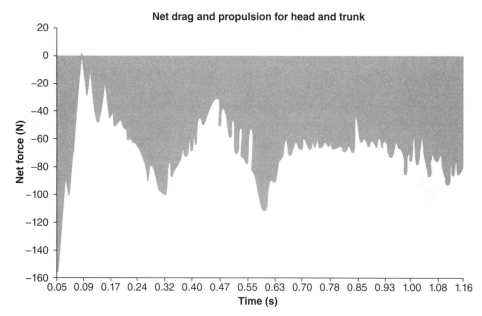

▶ **Figure 7.9** Resultant net force experienced by the head and trunk over the stroke cycle. Negative force values indicate a net drag force.

angles occur when the arms exit the water to commence recovery. The small accelerations and decelerations of the trunk can create surges in the forces experienced by the body, but most of these changes are small relative to the overall body forces experienced throughout the stroke.

Upper-Body Propulsion and Force Profiles

Reviewing the individual arm force profiles confirmed the observations detailed in the overall drag and propulsion review. Definite peaks are associated with the left and right arms as they move through the various phases of the stroke cycle. (See table 7.3 for an explanation of the stroke phases and figure 7.10 for a graphical representation of the forces generated by the right and left arms.)

Table 7.3 Timing for the Temporal Phases of the Left and Right Arms Through the Freestyle Stroke

Phase	Left hand (sec)	Right hand (sec)
1. Initial hand entry and outstretching of the arm	0.09–0.21	0.61–0.70
2. Acceleration at the start of the stroke pushing outward	0.21–0.38	0.70–0.91
3. The change of direction from pushing outward to bringing the arm back in toward the center of the body	0.38–0.45	0.92–0.98
4. The main propulsion phase along the base of the body when the forearm is close to perpendicular to the direction of travel	0.45–0.59	0.98–1.14
5. Hand exit	0.59–0.67	0.10–0.24
6. Arm recovery	0.67–1.13	0.24–0.61

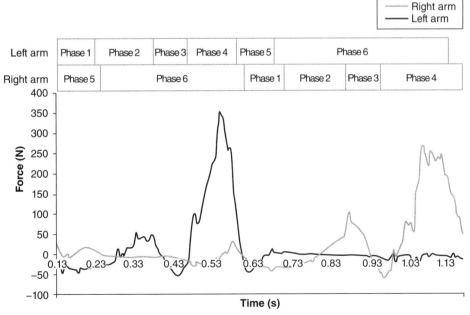

▶ **Figure 7.10** Resultant net force experienced by the left and right arms over the stroke cycle. Negative force values indicate a net drag force.

Figure 7.11 outlines the breakdown of the lower-arm components for the left arm to highlight their roles within the arm stroke force development. For both arms, we see similar things:

- Periods of almost zero force occur for about 0.4 seconds during arm recovery.
- An initial drag on the arm occurs during the downsweep after entry, followed by small and then large propulsive peaks.
- When examining total arm forces, the left arm peak occurs at 0.55 seconds and the right side peaks at 1.07 seconds near the middle of the outsweeps of the respective arm strokes.
- A secondary, lower peak occurs earlier, at 0.33 seconds for the left arm and 0.89 seconds for the right arm, which coincides with the catch positions for the arms.

The six phases of the arm pull, along with the resulting kinetic and kinematic observations, are discussed here in more detail. As you review the findings, remember that the data presented here is specific to this swimmer. But the comments and trends, along with the methods for analyzing performance, will remain relatively consistent from swimmer to swimmer.

The first phase with the arm out in front of the head appears to create an equal amount of drag for both arms of around –34 N to –38 N and lasts for between 0.09 and 0.11 seconds. The drag results from placing the arm into a zone of quickly moving water (relative to the hand and arm) and, potentially, the wave effects, which will be discussed later. The hand is the first body part to accelerate out of this extended position when it begins to move at around 0.18 seconds.

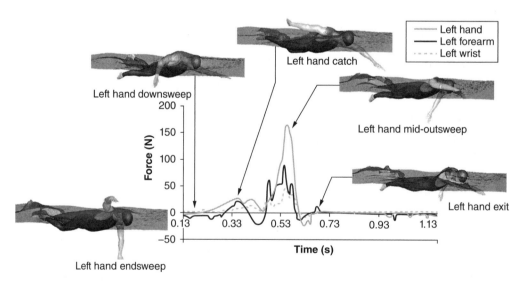

▶ **Figure 7.11** Resultant net force experienced by the left hand, wrist, and forearm over the stroke cycle. Negative force values indicate a net drag force.

The next acceleration phase occurs when the arm is pushed out laterally from the body and we see a rapid acceleration in the hands and forearms. The peak forces seen in this phase are between 50 N and 100 N. The forces are governed initially by the acceleration of the forearm and hand and then transition toward being more dependent on velocity of the body segments. For the athlete in this study, the right hand has a 15 percent greater acceleration and velocity compared with the left side, which partially explains the slightly greater forces generated at this time.

The third phase appears to be a transition between the outward part of the pull, when he is using mostly the lateral muscles, and the inward sweep, when the hand and arm move toward the midline of the body. The simulation shows considerable deceleration by the forearm and hands at this point, which may be one of the reasons for the drop in propulsion. The athlete may be slipping water by moving the hand and arm too horizontally across the body and not sufficiently along the body line (toward the feet) during this phase. The loss in propulsion might be less than these results seem to indicate, given that the acceleration drop seen in the simulation also occurs at a point where some of the kinematic data reach the outer limits of accuracy (from error analysis performed on the kinematic data). The second reason for the drop in propulsion may be that the arm is moving through the trough of the generated wave at this point (as discussed later). But the results do show that keeping this section of the pull-through at high acceleration and high velocity along the line of the body will help improve the overall stroke propulsion.

The fourth phase is the main power section of the stroke. Peak propulsive forces reach between 260 N and 340 N (figure 7.10), indicative of the need for considerable strength and power to be able to sprint effectively. The peak forces developed in the arms are quite high; 340 N is roughly equivalent to the strength needed to hold about 34 kilograms with an outstretched arm. Note that this peak force does not occur at the point of either peak acceleration or peak velocity for the hand or forearm, and it mirrors the peak hip velocity measures of the swimmer (figure 7.12). Peak force appears to occur just after the swimmer's hand and forearm are close to a vertical position and pushing directly back. It also appears to be closer to the time that the alternate hand enters the water, leading to potential benefits from the forward motion of the generated wave, which is discussed later.

The fifth phase occurs when the arm exits the water, the point at which drag is suddenly created. This may be because of arm deceleration when approaching the end of the stroke or perhaps because of some of the wave effects discussed in the following paragraphs.

The sixth phase is the recovery, when each arm, in turn, is out of the water. During this phase, the forces on the arms are almost zero because the low density of air has little effect on resistive drag forces at this speed. The forces discussed are only the fluid interaction effects on the body and do not include acceleration of the body mass.

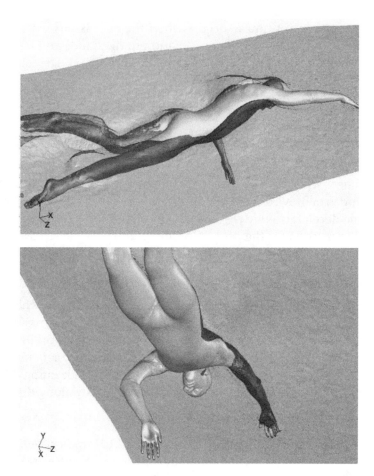

▶ **Figure 7.12** Body position at the point of the peak net force during the stroke. Note how the hands, forearms, legs, and feet are positioned to produce maximal propulsive force.

Discussion of Full-Body Propulsion

The large propulsive arm forces recorded during phase 4 in figure 7.10 are mirrored in the total-body force output (see figure 7.4). Further investigation into the mechanisms behind the development of propulsion is needed. Perhaps peak propulsive arm force results from a relatively high velocity of the hand and forearm at this point, as well as a high vertical angle of the hand and forearm pushing back against the water opposite to direction of motion. But these two factors alone do not account for the magnitude of forces registered in the analysis. To understand other possible mechanisms for this propulsion, we need to look at the ways that forces are generated by swimmers in the water.

Force in each direction on a body, with respect to time, is best described using Morrison's equation (Barltrop and Adams 1991), which combines inertial and drag terms:

$$F(t) = \underbrace{\rho C_m V \dot{U}}_{\substack{\text{Unsteady-state} \\ \text{inertial term}}} + \underbrace{\tfrac{1}{2} \rho C_d A U |U|}_{\substack{\text{Steady-state} \\ \text{drag term}}}$$

where ρ is the density of the fluid, U is the velocity of the object relative to the fluid, $\dot{U}$ is used to maintain the direction of velocity, A is the object area in the direction of the force, V is the object volume, and C_m and C_d are the inertial and drag coefficients, respectively.

Without delving too far into the math behind the fluid dynamics of swimming, this equation has two parts: the steady-state (or velocity-dependent) portion and the unsteady-state (acceleration-dependent) portion. The steady-state component is related to both the velocity and the frontal surface area of the segments. The unsteady-state component is related to the acceleration and volume of the segments. In human swimming, the inertial forces (unsteady-state) are often more important because of the relatively high acceleration of the segments during the stroke compared with relatively low velocity. These unsteady-state inertial forces are the main propulsion generators during the arm catch, and they coincide with the start of the downsweep and upsweep of the kick because of the high acceleration of the arm and feet segments at these points. This highlights the importance of accelerating these segments in these phases. The area of peak force in the mid-outsweep region of the arm stroke is not an area of high acceleration of the arm segments, although the velocity of these segments is high at this time. Hence, other phenomena must be at work in creating these large forces.

A closer look at this point of the stroke suggests that the surrounding fluid flow effects of traveling through the water may provide the answer. Part of the energy dissipated through the water can be seen to form waves on the surface of the water over the body. This wave has a crest forward of the head region, centered on the hands, and forms a trough just below the hips. This wave travels along with the swimmer and has a wavelength that is directly related to the velocity of the swimmer (using linear wave theory) (Barltrop and Adams 1991). In this wave that surrounds the swimmer, acceleration and velocity of the water vary greatly and can influence the forces generated on and by the body segments.

Under linear wave theory, a swimming speed of 2.08 meters per second implies that the wave following the swimmer travels at a similar speed as the swimmer, with a wavelength of 2.76 meters for a wave period of 1.33 seconds. The initiation of this wave starts at the point of divergence, which typically occurs close to the most forward point of the body in the direction of travel (i.e., the hands at the arm stroke entry back to the head when the arm is in the middle of the pull phase). Thus, these changes in hull length affect the position of the wave relative to the segments of the body, but not the length of the wave.

To highlight this phenomenon and show the ways in which surface waves can affect the propulsive and drag forces experienced by a swimmer, Keys et al. (2010) examined the changes in passive drag force across the various segments when the swimmer is traveling in a streamlined glide position underwater and at the water surface. Researchers have documented (Hertel 1966; Barltrop and Adams 1991) that the differences between drag below the surface and near the surface are caused primarily by related increases in wave drag. Previously, it was unclear where the drag forces change on the body. Although the overall increase in passive drag force between the submerged and near-surface trials was 18 percent, significant differences were found between the body segments where those changes occurred. The head and arms generated the largest increase in drag, making a 44 percent and 50 percent increase in contribution to the near-surface overall drag, respectively. The overall section of the body above the waist resulted in a 121.7 percent increase in drag force, but those increases were counteracted by the lower-body components. The thighs, knees, calves, and feet all recorded considerable reductions in drag, and the feet changed from an area of drag to a component that propelled the body forward. The total change for the lower-body components was a 103.5 percent reduction in drag when compared with the overall submerged segment results.

Variations in where the drag (negative acceleration) is concentrated from the wave can significantly influence understanding of the way that propulsion is generated during human swimming. The relative propulsion generated at the legs would explain the relatively high forces recorded in those regions. Conversely, most of the arm stroke occurs in regions of high negative acceleration, thus limiting the effectiveness of generating propulsion by the arm segments for most of the arm stroke. The exception to this would potentially be when the pulling arm

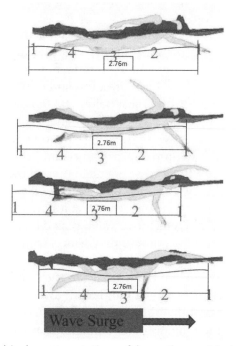

▶ **Figure 7.13** Graphical representation of how the rapid change in initial wave formation can potentially lead to a wave surge at the point of hand entry, allowing the swimmer to lever off the surge to create more force.

reaches the mid-outsweep region of the stroke when the contralateral arm starts its hand entry. The rapid change in the initial start point of the wave (moving from the vertex of the head before hand entry to the hand at entry) likely leads to a transient surge in the wave forward along the body as it changes to its new starting point at hand entry. This phenomenon is presented graphically in figure 7.13. This wave surge may provide a substantial transient forward acceleration in the form of a wall of water moving forward that the swimmer can leverage off of, providing a significant increase in the potential to generate propulsive force at this point. As mentioned, this potential forward surge of the wave is transient; traditional wave formation is restored soon after hand entry. This effect, when fully utilized, generates the greatest propulsion of any part of the swimming stroke. Keeping the hand and arm velocity high and the forearm and hand perpendicular to the direction of flow to ensure maximum volume and added mass capacity at this point can potentially produce a more effective stroke.

Summary

This case study provided insight into how propulsive and drag forces are generated throughout a full freestyle swimming stroke of an elite swimmer using CFD analysis. The resultant outcome of the analysis is greater foundational knowledge related to producing propulsive and drag forces. Some practical pointers for improving freestyle performance are listed below:

- Aim to keep the feet submerged at all times.
- Ensure that the stroke is close to symmetrical for maximum efficiency.
- Maximize the acceleration at the beginning of each arm stroke and leg kick.
- Seek the closest perpendicular angle to the direction of travel for the hands and forearm at all times. This objective is sometimes termed *getting over the stroke.*
- Prioritize keeping the vertical hand and forearm push position, especially toward the end of the stroke, to maximize the effect from any change in wave motion.
- Execute a rapid hand exit from the water as soon as any wave surge moves through.
- Limit the glide time with the arm extended at the front of the stroke.

PART

II

Physiological Aspects of Training and Competition

CHAPTER 8

Energy Systems and Physiology

—J.M. Stager, PhD, Jonathon Stickford, PhD, and Kirk Grand

In any discussion of sport science, swimming, and performance, at some time or another the conversation will probably take a turn to the area of exercise physiology, energy systems, and energy metabolism. Someone will likely comment, "When you get down to it, this topic is, well, pretty complicated, but really important in terms of how swimmers train for competition." And that statement would be true. Given the importance that exercise physiology plays in the world of swimming, specifically how energy is produced and used to fuel training and performance, coaches need to have a foundational understanding of these topics. Energy systems and overall metabolism are topics that underlie broad areas in swimming such as fatigue and recovery, optimal race pacing, pre- and postexercise nutrition, training and race recovery, overtraining, workout organization, and possibly even talent identification. An understanding of energy systems permeates virtually every aspect of swimming performance and preparation. The goal of this chapter is to provide a foundational framework and understanding of the body's energy systems and the way in which this topic relates to optimizing performance and preparing swimmers to perform at their best.

Several approaches can be taken when addressing the relatively broad topics of exercise physiology and energy systems. The first approach is to review the topic from the perspective of the metabolic pathways used to fuel athletic performance. The second is to view the topic from the perspective of the food sources that are ultimately metabolized to generate the metabolic energy to fuel muscle work. Third, the topic can be viewed from the perspective of the competitive event being performed and training characteristics needed to attain favorable performance outcomes relative to the metabolic demands. In this chapter we take all three approaches and attempt to review and intertwine them to provide a thorough, application-based discussion of how exercise physiology and energy systems affect training and swimming performance.

Swimmers Are Like Finely Tuned Race Cars

To begin our discussion of energy systems, we present an analogy. Let's consider the design and traits of various race cars and draw comparisons, albeit as imperfect analogs, to swimmers. The world of auto racing includes many types of race cars, ranging from dragsters to stock cars to open-wheeled Formula One and Indy cars. Because the events in which these race cars compete have such different characteristics (race length, course specifications, and so on), the vehicles are designed to have strengths that match the demands and requirements of the race. A dragster, for example, is designed to accelerate as quickly as possible and can achieve straight-line speeds in excess of to 500 miles per hour (800 kph) in around five seconds. They are not made to go around corners. But these dragsters have what can be described as tremendous power—an estimated 8,000 to 10,000 horsepower (6,000 to 7,500 kw) in some cases. To generate the power required to accelerate these vehicles to their top-end speeds, dragsters must run on a high-performance fuel mixture containing nitromethane and methanol. This fuel source is different from what we put into an average car, but it allows the engines to generate two to three times the power of a similar-sized engine running strictly on gasoline. Although extremely powerful, the engine in this type of race car can run at full throttle for only about 10 seconds, and within that brief period it can consume as much as 20 gallons (75 liters) of fuel. In short, the tremendous, instantaneous power accelerates these cars quickly, but it is limited to a few seconds and comes at a tremendous cost in fuel consumption.

In direct contrast to the dragster is the Indy car. Rather than using huge engines with enormous power output, Indy cars must be able to sustain high speeds in excess of 200 miles per hour (320 kph) for several hours while traveling race distances of 500 miles (800 km) or more. And these cars must be able to corner quickly and frequently. The engine of an Indy car displaces less than half of what is used in a dragster and generates much less horsepower, about 650 horsepower (500 kw) compared with 10,000 horsepower (7,500 kw). Indy cars run on different fuels as well—ethanol and gasoline—to drive performance, and they require better fuel economy because races may be won or lost based on the ability of the car to conserve fuel and minimize time spent refueling during pit stops. The contrast, then, between the dragster and the Indy car is that one is able to generate an enormous power output that lasts for a just few seconds whereas the other must maintain a more modest yet sustained power output that allows the car to race for hours on end without a drop in performance.

These race cars are purposefully designed differently, and they use different fuels based on the demands of the event in which they compete. Just like the various types of auto-racing events, the various swimming races require swimmers to tap into different physiological systems to drive performance in the pool.

Exercise physiologists frequently use race car terminology and speak of swimmers as having big engines. This term is used primarily in reference to endurance swimmers who have hearts that are able to pump large volumes of blood (cardiac output measured in liters per minute) in a relatively short amount of time (one minute). Because the blood carries oxygen, what really is being referenced when describing a big engine is the ability of the heart to deliver oxygen and other nutrients to the working muscles and the ability of the muscles to extract those nutrients to fuel performance. This cardiac capacity generally matches the aerobic properties of the peripheral tissues, most notably the voluntary skeletal muscles that the swimmer uses to drive performance in the pool. As an example, successful distance swimmers have muscles made up primarily of Type I muscle fibers that are specifically suited to aerobic metabolism. These features are well matched to the high aerobic capacity of the cardiorespiratory system. In terms of comparison with the race cars discussed earlier, a distance swimmer is more like the Indy car than the dragster, because both the swimmer and the Indy car can sustain a moderate level of power output for a relatively long time.

On the other hand, a sprint swimmer typically has a much more modest aerobic capacity, and although she may not be able to produce power to fuel moderate- to long-duration activity, she is capable of generating much greater instantaneous power for a short period, enough to finish a 50- or 100-meter race. The sprinter's engine has little resemblance to that of the distance swimmer. The sprinter's high power output is facilitated by metabolic pathways that do not require oxygen (nonaerobic, or anaerobic), and performance is not driven to the same extent by the ability of the heart to deliver oxygen and nutrients to the working muscles. The absolute capacity to generate power through the nonaerobic energy pathways is much greater than what can be produced aerobically, but similar to the dragster, the sprinter can maintain this level of power production for only a short time. Like distance swimmers, sprint athletes also have muscle fiber types and enzymatic profiles within the muscles that are appropriate for supporting the high power output needed for their short-duration events. Sprinters tend to have a greater proportion of highly fatigable fibers and place greater reliance on metabolic pathways that use carbohydrate as the fuel source. Successful sprint swimmers are the dragsters of the swimming world. Overall, the swimmer's complete underlying physiology (figure 8.1) works in concert to affect performance in the pool.

Individuality of Training

Before going further, we should state that few swimmers fall into the classification of being a 100 percent pure distance swimmer or a 100 percent pure sprinter. In reality, tremendous diversity appears within the underlying inherited genetic factors that determine performance in athletes. The examples put forward thus far identify athletes who are the far extremes of what is a continuous spectrum of physiologic makeups. Most swimmers fall somewhere between these two

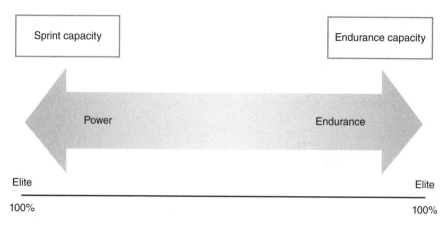

Functional continuum

▶ **Figure 8.1** The functional capacity that is defined in part by inherited traits and in part by physical training. People sit somewhere along the continuum, and the traits consistent with the ability to endure may be at odds with the ability to produce power. Coaches must be aware that focusing entirely on one side of the continuum may be detrimental to the other side. Also, any given event needs to be evaluated from the perspective of which end is paramount to elite performance in that event.

extremes (pure sprinter and pure distance athlete), expressing some combination of dragster and Indy car traits. Every person exists somewhere along a continuum for any and all traits, including the body's underlying physiology and its predisposition to produce and use energy to fuel swimming performance. Training tends to push the traits toward one end of the physiology energy system continuum or the other, and it refines inherent, inherited talent.

With that said, we need to recognize that no singular trait alone guarantees athletic success; athletic talent comes from having the appropriate combination of genetic traits necessary to be successful in a sport, the mind-set to train for that sport, and the opportunity to do so. One factor that can level the physiologic playing field in swimming is stroke technique. An athlete's cardiac capacity or muscle fiber type doesn't matter if the swimmer can't perform the appropriate motor skills and apply the appropriate muscular forces to the water.

For coaches, then, the key to optimizing performance in swimmers is to maintain constant awareness of the stimuli introduced to drive adaptation (i.e., the training regimen and the way in which training variables are provided) and to evaluate whether they are achieving the intended performance outcomes. An athlete who is physiologically set up to excel as a sprinter (with the inherited traits favoring short sprint events) can be asked to train for endurance events, and the body will subsequently adapt metabolically to handle the imposed training demands to the best of its ability. But although all athletes can definitely improve their ability to endure following an endurance-focused training plan, sprinters likely will never achieve their true athletic potential because this training does not match the demands of sprint competition nor is it aligned with the sprinters' true physiologic makeup. In contrast, by not aligning the focus of training with the athlete's physiology, the swimmer's capacity to sprint may be compromised in the short term, and potentially in the long term as well. The key is to use and apply training stimuli as a means to push and develop the inherited traits of an individual swimmer. The trick is figuring out how to do so.

Understanding the Energy Systems Used in Swimming

In the late 1700s scientists in Europe began exploring the nature of air, noting the remarkable similarities between what they observed in animal respiration and how a candle flame behaved. They noted that both activities required a yet unidentified component in the air. They postulated the existence of what we know today to be oxygen (O_2). They couldn't see it, taste it, or feel it, but they concluded that oxygen must exist in the air we breathe. The French scientist Antoine Lavoisier is credited with naming oxygen. He was the first to conclude that mammals, including humans, consume oxygen during respiration, need oxygen to react with organic substances in the body to produce heat and chemical energy, and give off water and carbon dioxide as by-products of the oxygen-based chemical reactions that occur in the body.

Lavoisier reasoned that the "fire of life" originates from within living tissues and can be directly related to the rate of metabolism taking place within that tissue. For the purpose of clarity and consistency, we need to define the term *metabolism*. Metabolism describes the myriad chemical reactions involved in maintaining the health of cells, organs, tissues, and so on in the human body. A body's overall metabolism is determined by catabolic actions, which occur to break down molecules and substrates for energy, and anabolic actions, which center on the synthesis of new structures and compounds needed to sustain life and activity. As might be expected, metabolism is closely linked to nutrition and the availability of nutrients that serve as fuel.

Digging deeper into the area of metabolism, we also need to define the term *oxidation*. Oxidation refers to a chemical reaction in which an organic compound combines with oxygen. This chemical reaction is the process by which most cells and tissues metabolize substrates to produce heat and useful chemical energy, namely adenosine triphosphate (ATP), to fuel bodily functions.

More than 200 years have passed since the connection was made between metabolism, oxidation, and the generation of heat, and it has taken the better part of that time for scientists to describe the actual biochemical pathways through which fuels (e.g., foods) are consumed by living tissues in the process of generating useful biological energy. In fact, it wasn't until the mid-1930s that we gained a more complete understanding of the pathways that support aerobic and anaerobic metabolism.

The first stage of energy metabolism within the muscle, particularly during heavy exercise, often occurs through a process called glycolysis. Glycolysis is the process by which sugars, namely glucose, are broken down within the cell cytosol to produce useful cellular energy (ATP). Figure 8.2 illustrates the pathway by which glucose is broken down to form two molecules of pyruvate and a net production of two ATP molecules and two molecules of NADH, which will be described in detail later in the chapter.

Glycolysis is the process by which sugars are metabolized as a means to provide useful physiologic energy. Glycolysis results in the net formation of two ATP but also yields compounds that can enter the electron transport chain (NADH) or the citric acid cycle of aerobic metabolism (pyruvate) to produce additional energy that can fuel muscle contraction.

Technically, glycolysis does not require the presence of oxygen nor does it consume oxygen to produce the two molecules of pyruvate from each glucose molecule. But the terms *aerobic glycolysis* and *anaerobic glycolysis* are often used to refer to what comes next in the metabolic process. This next phase is largely determined by whether glycolysis occurs in the presence or absence of oxygen, respectively. In the presence of oxygen, pyruvate is quickly converted to acetyl-CoA, a substrate that subsequently enters the cell mitochondria and undergoes aerobic metabolism through the citric acid cycle. But it can also be argued that the real key here relates to the need for energy production. When that need is

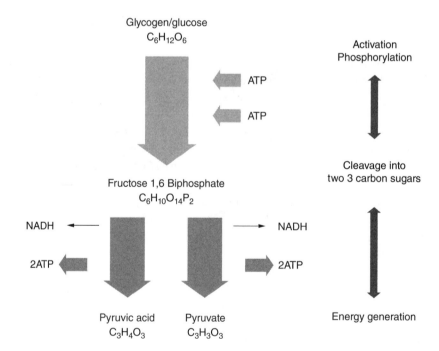

▶ **Figure 8.2** Metabolic pathway (glycolysis) by which carbohydrate is used as a fuel source. The end products are pyruvic acid, NADH, and ATP. Two common fates of pyruvic acid are oxidation through the TCA cycle or conversion to lactic acid. The outcome depends largely on the immediate energy demand, the presence of key enzymes and their affinities, and the availability of oxygen for mitochondrial respiration.

high, as it is during heavy exercise, anaerobic glycolysis is predominant. When energy needs are low, aerobic glycolysis is the predominate pathway. As a side note, acetyl-CoA can be formed through fatty acid oxidation as well as glycolysis. During fatty acid metabolism, beta oxidation splits the long carbon chains found in fat molecules into two carbon subunits, which eventually become acetyl-CoA molecules. Therefore, at this point in the pathway the remaining reactions are the same for the catabolism of both carbohydrate and fat. And, as an additional note, when oxygen is present, the NADH produced through glycolysis can enter the electron transport chain (to be described later in this section), leading to the generation of additional ATP molecules.

When oxygen is not present in sufficient amounts (or energy demand is exceedingly high) to support the energy needs through aerobic metabolism alone, pyruvate is converted to lactic acid, or lactate (figure 8.3). Lactic acid, chemically similar to lactate, is produced through a side reaction of glycolysis that allows cellular metabolism, as well as exercise, to continue by recycling a limited coenzyme called nicotinamide adenine dinucleotide (NAD^+). The recycling of this necessary coenzyme is required for glycolysis to continue producing energy through the breakdown of sugars. At this point, however, the aerobic and nonaerobic energy pathways diverge.

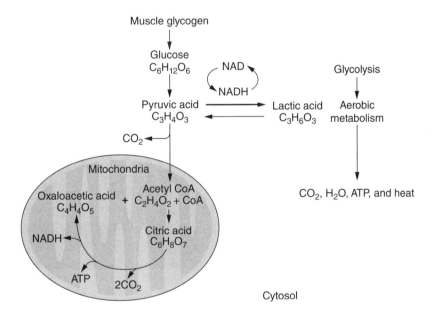

▶ **Figure 8.3** Interplay between glycolysis and aerobic metabolism. Although pyruvic acid is, in fact, generated without the use of oxygen, it is being oxidized by mitochondrial respiration within the mitochondria. If energy demands are too high to be met by mitochondrial respiration, lactic acid can be formed to sequester the hydrogen ions. The donor of these hydrogen ions is the glycolytic cofactor NADH. Because lactic acid binds these hydrogens, NAD is recycled, allowing glycolysis to continue, and as such ATP can be formed through this short pathway.

The current understanding is that glycolysis, whether it results in the formation of pyruvate or lactate, allows the generation of energy at rates that are much greater than can be provided by aerobic metabolism alone. Glycolysis occurs quickly, and therefore energy production is not limited solely by the capacity of an aerobic pathway. As a result, we have to be careful that we don't assume that the formation of lactic acid is solely a function of the availability of oxygen. Much has to do with demands for energy production that outpace the ability of aerobic metabolism to provide it. More will be said later on this topic.

Aerobic Metabolism and Swimming Performance

As mentioned, when oxygen is present the pyruvate formed as the end product of glycolysis is converted to acetyl-CoA. Although carbohydrate metabolism or glycolysis takes place in the skeletal muscle cell cytosol, the aerobic production of energy occurs only within cell organelles called mitochondria; pyruvate enters the mitochondria, where it is converted to acetyl-CoA and carbon dioxide. At that point, the acetyl-CoA enters the Krebs cycle (named after Hans Krebs, who first described the process) and the electron transport chain through which 32 additional ATP are ultimately produced to be used in support of biological functions throughout the body, including muscle contractions. The Krebs cycle is also known as the citric acid cycle and the tricarboxylic acid (TCA) cycle. For the purpose of this chapter, we will refer to the process by which energy is produced aerobically as the TCA cycle.

Although it is considered part of the aerobic pathway, oxygen is not directly used within the TCA cycle. This is because the main purpose of the TCA cycle is to produce the hydrogen ions (H+) and electrons that will reduce the vitamin-derived coenzymes NAD+ and FAD to form the energy-rich carriers NADH and $FADH_2$, respectively (refer to figure 8.2). Oxygen is used only at the tail end of the process, within what is known as the electron transport chain (ETC). Additionally, most of the ATP that is produced is a result of the ETC. The TCA cycle and ETC are tightly coupled within the mitochondria, and the energy associated with the membrane-bound transport of electrons is capable of producing a number of ATP molecules. Together, the oxidation of the coenzymes NADH and $FADH_2$ contributes to the bulk of the 32 ATP generated during aerobic metabolism. This can be compared to the two, yes, two, ATP produced for each glucose molecule during anaerobic glycolysis.

Fueling Aerobic Metabolism

In any event, the substrates required for aerobic metabolism come from the partial breakdown of basic fuel sources such as sugars, fat, and protein, which collectively contribute to the synthesis of ATP. The importance of sugars, as far as performance is concerned, is that the ability to sustain exercise, whether it is a bout of training or a competitive performance, is linked to the availability of sugars within the active muscles. Sugars are stored as glycogen in limited quantities intramuscularly and in larger amounts in the liver. As intramuscular glycogen is depleted, the body draws on food consumed during activity as well as glycogen stores in the liver to deliver glucose to the working muscles, particularly during endurance events and prolonged practice sessions. But during heavy exercise, the bulk of these substrates is intramuscular, not extramuscular. This circumstance presents a problem for the athlete because the replacement of carbohydrate, either during or after exercise, is crucial for delaying fatigue or recovering from previous exhaustive exercise bouts.

The oxidation of one glucose molecule during anaerobic glycolysis will yield the equivalent of seven ATP molecules, assuming that the NADH produced through glycolysis is shuttled to the ETC. Meanwhile, the pyruvate that is formed is converted to lactate, where it can be transported to the liver, heart, or neighboring cells for use as an aerobic substrate. Again, however, if the pyruvate enters the TCA cycle and ETC instead of being converted to lactate, 32 molecules of ATP are produced. That additional amount of energy can be produced through the aerobic metabolism for the same amount of glucose compared with anaerobic glycolytic metabolism. Thus, aerobic metabolism is economical but limited in its ability to provide power.

The energy yield from the complete oxidation of fat is much larger than that obtained from glucose. For example, the breakdown of palmitate, a 16-carbon fatty acid, yields 120 molecules of ATP. Part of the reason that fat provides more energy is that it also contains more carbon atoms than carbohydrate does. The fat molecules are simply much larger than the carbohydrate molecules because they contain more carbon molecules, more oxygen, and more hydrogen atoms. But even on a per carbon atom basis, fat can provide approximately 25 percent more energy than carbohydrate does, although the reasons behind this are not entirely understood. The energy content of one gram of fat is much greater than the energy content of one gram of carbohydrate; fat is thus a much better compound to use as an energy storage tissue.

Endurance training actually induces greater reliance on fat oxidation for a given workload and a concomitant increase in acetyl-CoA production from beta-oxidation and down regulation of glycolysis. In other words, after prolonged training, a greater percentage of the energy necessary to perform a given workload will come from fat stores as opposed to muscle carbohydrate stores. This process spares carbohydrate within the muscles, which is often cited as a major cause of fatigue and exhaustion.

As far as exercise is concerned, when examining the energy yield from the aerobic pathway, it is clear that the aerobic metabolism of a substrate is a more effective means of generating energy for sustained exercise. More sustainable energy production translates to a larger capacity for enduring work. In other words, when aerobic metabolism is the predominant pathway for producing energy, athletes are capable of exercising for a much longer duration before fatigue sets in. The caveat is that the energy is generated at a slower pace through the aerobic pathway than through the anaerobic pathways. As the exercise intensity increases, the rate of energy use increases and the rate of energy production must go up as well.

Intensity more than any other factor dictates the metabolic pathway necessary to provide the energy to train or compete. As mentioned already, as exercise intensity increases, the primary fuel sources shift from those remote to the energy stores in skeletal muscles (the liver, for example) to the skeletal muscles themselves. Thus, at higher exercise intensities (above approximately a 70 percent effort), most energy-producing substrates (glucose, glycogen, fat, protein) metabolized are from intramuscular sources. The issue of replacing these depleted intramuscular fuel sources, either during or following exercise, is therefore critical. Chapter 14 delves more deeply into the needs and strategies of postexercise nutrition as one means to replenish depleted energy stores throughout the body.

The availability of carbohydrate is especially important at these high exercise intensities, above approximately 60 percent of a swimmer's maximum oxygen consumption ($\dot{V}O_2$max). As long as the intensity remains in the low to moderate level, endurance exercise can be sustained for two hours or longer before muscle glycogen stores become depleted. Above this threshold, however, intramuscular energy stores are depleted at a much faster rate. People who deplete muscle carbohydrate stores, and subsequently have lower than desired concentrations of sugar in the blood, are likely to experience the onset of fatigue. A two-hour swim workout will undoubtedly have an effect on muscle carbohydrate stores. Carbohydrate depletion can have a dramatic effect on the ability of a swimmer to complete a two-hour workout and any subsequent workouts. The depletion of muscle carbohydrate stores will cause a shift to fat oxidation as the primary means of energy production. Fat oxidation is associated with lower rates of mitochondrial respiration and therefore reduced power output.

Energy availability and training design go hand in hand. A common practice is to plan sprint sets toward the end of a practice session, presumably to challenge the fast-twitch fibers when carbohydrate stores in the active fibers are nearly depleted. Athletes with a preponderance of fast-twitch fibers (i.e., sprinters) may be observed to have difficulty sustaining their efforts through an exhaustive practice and be unable to maximize their sprint performance at the end of a training session, regardless of their motivation to do so. When metabolic limits are reached, motivation can do little to overcome substrate exhaustion. The swimmer needs to recover and eat plenty of carbohydrate to recharge and replenish the fuel sources.

Coming back to fueling and supplying the body with the nutrients needed to produce energy, unfortunately, coaches can do only so much to influence the macronutrient quality of their swimmers' diets. Swimmers need to recognize that this aspect of performance is under their control. Because the fuel source for glycolysis is largely derived from intracellular glucose and glycogen stores, these stores must be replenished consistently as part of a recovery protocol. Athletes' diets, in general, should contain 70 percent carbohydrate. Between 1 and 1.5 grams of carbohydrate per kilogram of body weight should be consumed in the first 45 to 60 minutes following exhaustive exercise. Data now support the use of common foodstuffs such as flavored milk (chocolate milk) as a means of meeting those recommendations (Stager et al. 2014). The point to stress to swimmers who are training twice a day is that how they approach recovery nutrition can either limit or ensure success of the second daily practice. Swimmers and their parents need to use this information to the athletes' advantage.

$\dot{V}O_2$max Testing to Evaluate Aerobic Capacity

The body's maximal ability to take up, transport, and use oxygen is referred to as maximal oxygen consumption, or $\dot{V}O_2$max. $\dot{V}O_2$max is typically measured in absolute terms (e.g., liters of oxygen consumed per minute) or normalized to the athlete's size and expressed in milliliters of oxygen consumed per kilogram of body mass per minute ($ml \cdot kg^{-1} \cdot min^{-1}$). Because the consumption of oxygen is linked to the production of energy, and energy is necessary to perform the muscular contractions during exercise, $\dot{V}O_2$max is an indication of the body's upper limit to perform aerobic work. For this reason, $\dot{V}O_2$max is considered an important determinant of endurance performance. Coaches frequently target a swimmer's $\dot{V}O_2$max as a variable that they specifically want to change and improve by prescribing extended, high-yardage aerobic sets in training. But $\dot{V}O_2$max should not be viewed as *the* equivalent to athletic performance; an athlete who has a high $\dot{V}O_2$max is not guaranteed athletic success, even in endurance events. An important point to recognize is that the measurement of $\dot{V}O_2$max estimates only the capacity to generate energy aerobically and does not provide information about the capacity of nonaerobic metabolism.

The extremely high $\dot{V}O_2$max values seen in some of the top distance athletes across sports are likely driven by genetics, and many researchers postulate that aerobic capacity is more an inherited trait than it is a performance factor that can be extensively modified through an intensive training program (Stager and Tanner 2005). Interestingly, mitochondria have been shown to have their own DNA, and most of a person's mitochondrial material and subsequent ability to produce energy aerobically is believed to be inherited from the mother (Brooks, Fahey, and Baldwin 2004). With that said, aerobic capacity and $\dot{V}O_2$max are realistically affected by both genetics and training to differing degrees. The point here is that not every athlete has the capability to develop a high $\dot{V}O_2$max even if the training is developed to maximize this performance variable. Expectations are that successful middle- to long-distance swimmers (events of 800 meters and longer) will have relatively high $\dot{V}O_2$max values and sprinters will have lower values, providing an optimal match between cardiovascular supply, peripheral demand, and race demands.

The testing or measurement of $\dot{V}O_2$max is one of the oldest and most common laboratory procedures conducted in the field of exercise physiology. Beginning with the work of A.V. Hill at the Harvard Fatigue Laboratory in the early 1920s, exhaled gas was collected in large bags while athletes exercised. The gas composition was subsequently analyzed. The entire process took days to complete because all analyses were performed by hand. Today, graded exercise tests on a treadmill, swim flume, or cycle ergometer are the most common tests performed to evaluate $\dot{V}O_2$max. Researchers have instantly responding gas analyzers connected to computers that provide results immediately. The protocol used to quantify $\dot{V}O_2$max is commonly referred to as a max test. The test usually has the athlete running on a treadmill, cycling on an ergometer, or swimming in a flume at progressively faster paces until he cannot continue the test. The measurement of $\dot{V}O_2$ is made using a technique referred to as indirect calorimetry. The process requires an oxygen analyzer, a carbon dioxide (CO_2) analyzer, and a way to measure ventilatory volumes. $\dot{V}O_2$max values for mature adults range from 1 to 5 liters of oxygen per minute, in absolute terms. If these values are normalized with respect to body weight, values occur in the range of 20 to nearly 90 ml · kg^{-1} · min^{-1}. This normalization is done so that people can be compared despite being different in sizes and shape, age, gender, and so on. The low values (20 to 40 ml · kg^{-1} · min^{-1}) typically belong to sedentary and physically inactive people. The high values in the 60 to 90 ml · kg^{-1} · min^{-1} range are often observed in elite athletes or other well-trained people.

Far fewer $\dot{V}O_2$max data values are available in the literature for swimmers as compared with athletes in other sports largely because of the scarcity of flumes in which to test swimmers. The data that are available, however, show that successful swimmers score relatively high (50 to 75 ml · kg^{-1} · min^{-1}) in terms of $\dot{V}O_2$max but not as high as cross-country skiers (high 80s to low 90s ml · kg^{-1} · min^{-1}) or mid- to long-distance cyclists and runners (mid 80s ml · kg^{-1} · min^{-1}) (Capelli, Pendergast, and Termin 1998). Ventilatory threshold (the point at which ventilation increases disproportionately with an increase in exercise intensity), heart rate threshold, and the onset of blood lactate accumulation can typically be measured at the same time as $\dot{V}O_2$max is measured. All three of these indices provide an estimate of the sustainable workload that an athlete can endure. The goal for the coach is to train the athlete so that the threshold occurs at a higher percentage of $\dot{V}O_2$max. A measure of training success is represented by a shift toward a higher threshold (percentage), regardless of the index measured. The current perception is that some of these alternate measures are better predictors of the sustainable power output than $\dot{V}O_2$max (Di Prampero et al. 1974; Ivy et al. 1981; Olbrecht 2000). Even the ability to achieve and sustain a higher percentage of $\dot{V}O_2$max during training may be more important that the value of $\dot{V}O_2$max per se.

Anaerobic Energy Pathways and Swimming Performance

Anaerobic metabolism becomes the predominant energy pathway if the amount of muscular work is such that the energy requirements are greater than what can be supplied aerobically. Two anaerobic pathways assist in energy production. The first of these, glycolysis, has already been introduced. Recall that glycolysis can occur in the absence of oxygen, producing two ATP as glucose broken down into lactic acid and lactate. Although lactic acid is sometimes thought of as a waste product of metabolism, it can be argued that lactic acid production actually allows an increased capacity to do work. As it turns out, although some cells produce lactic acid at a rapid rate, other cells use it as a convenient and even preferential fuel source. The point is that without the ability to produce lactic acid, exercise capacity becomes compromised.

Anaerobic glycolysis is an effective means of energy production only during short, intense exercise; it can provide energy for 10 seconds to 2 minutes. Glycolysis produces ATP about 100 times faster than aerobic metabolism does. As such, anaerobic glycolysis is the dominant energy-producing system for maximum-effort activities performed within this time range. Because the formation of lactic acid reduces the concentration of pyruvate in the muscle, the rate of glycolysis increases (a high pyruvate concentration in muscle slows glycolysis) and provides additional NAD^+, which allows glycolysis to continue. Finally, some evidence indicates that lactic acid can move intracellularly into the mitochondria and be consumed through aerobic pathways as oxygen becomes available (Brooks and Gaesser 1980; Booth and Baldwin 1996; Brooks et al., 2004). Lactic acid easily dissociates in the body to form hydrogen ions and lactate, which can enter the bloodstream and be measured there using a simple blood test. The rate of lactate removal from the blood following an intense effort is commonly used as an index of recovery status and training state.

Note, however, that carbohydrate can be consumed aerobically. If the environment and energy balance in the cell is such that pyruvate can be oxidized by the mitochondria, little lactic acid will be produced and the available carbohydrate will be used in this manner. Insulin, the hormone produced by the pancreas, stimulates the use of glucose as a fuel source such that consuming a substance high in sugar will stimulate carbohydrate metabolism regardless of the oxygen availability or workload of the muscle. And when carbohydrate metabolism goes up, there is generally an increase in lactate production met by an increase in lactate consumption. Blood levels of lactate thus don't change (figure 8.4).

From a practical perspective, though, it has been observed that the point at which lactate begins to accumulate in the blood (onset of blood lactate accumulation, or OBLA) can be a useful marker of exercise intensity and can be used to monitor training adaptations. The OBLA represents the exercise intensity at which the lactate clearance mechanisms are outpaced by the rate at which lactic acid is being produced. Typically, this point occurs at a blood lactate concentration of around four millimoles, which is purported to be the optimal training level or intensity for building aerobic capacity. Nevertheless, a work rate at or below OBLA is thought to reflect a training intensity that an athlete can sustain for prolonged periods.

A few swim programs have the equipment, personnel, and ability to plot the relationship between swimming speed and blood lactate for each athlete. The purpose of this test is to obtain an objective measure of conditioning and progress through the season or training cycle. To determine the OBLA, a swimmer performs a series of swims, usually a set of 200s, and gets adequate rest between

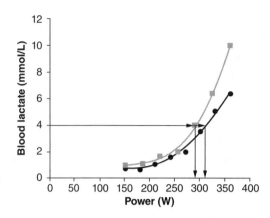

▶ **Figure 8.4** The relationship between power output and blood lactate concentrations. Swim velocity can be substituted for power and, from this, appropriate training speeds can be estimated. With this information and with heart rate as an additional measure, training bouts can be designed within the training zones that range from recovery to anaerobic, or all-out, efforts. The onset of blood lactic acid (OBLA), as well as peak lactic and the lactic acid threshold, can be estimated from this challenge. OBLA is considered one of the critical training intensities for optimal results. As training progresses, the expectation is that the blood lactate curve will shift relative to workload and that OBLA will occur at a higher swim speed.

efforts. For a two-swim test, the first 200 is typically swum at a submaximal speed and the second is swum all out. If more intervals are used, each swim is performed at a successively higher intensity, or at a faster pace, than the previous one until the swimmer is giving 100 percent effort on the final swim. After each swim, a small sample of blood is taken, typically from the ear lobe, and evaluated using a measurement device to determine blood lactate concentration. When a plot is generated with the swim speed on the x-axis and lactate concentration on the y-axis, a coach or scientist can draw inferences about the swimmer's anaerobic and aerobic capacities.

Repeated assessments of the OBLA, done over time, can assist in evaluating the success, or lack thereof, of a seasonal training schedule. Over time, a swimmer who is responding positively to the training plan would be expected to show a shift in the OBLA to higher intensities, or faster swimming paces (figure 8.5). In practical terms, the swimmer would be able to swim at a faster speed before lactic acid production outpaces the ability of the working muscles to remove it. The best description of the complexity and caveats of this assessment can be found in Olbrecht's book *The Science of Winning* (2000). Needless to say, this type of testing is beyond all but a few national programs or dedicated research laboratories.

Before leaving this topic, we need to discuss the fate of lactate after it is produced. Most of the lactic acid or lactate is ultimately metabolized through the TCA cycle, in part during exercise and in part during recovery following exercise. The rate of lactate clearance can be increased following a bout of exercise

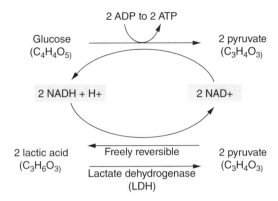

▶ Figure 8.5 The regeneration of NAD by way of the formation of lactic acid from pyruvic acid. The reaction is freely reversible and dependent on the kinetics of the enzyme lactate dehydrogenase.

by performing an active cool-down for a prescribed length of time. The aerobic metabolism during the cool-down facilitates the removal of blood lactate by using it as an aerobic fuel source. Ironically, the shorter the race is, and thus the higher the postexercise lactate blood levels are, the longer the active recovery needs to be. Conversely, the longer the race is and the more aerobically based the exercise bout is, the shorter the active recovery needs to be to clear the lactate from the system. Endurance athletes have a greater capacity to clear lactate and a smaller capacity to generate it. Generally, sprinters don't like to hear that they need a 10- to 15-minute cool-down following a 20-second, 50-meter free, but they do. Thus, sprinters need more active cool-down time and endurance athletes much less. Unfortunately, swimmers rarely cool down enough following practice. Distance swimmers may be inclined to recover adequately, but sprinters may be more inclined to cool down for less time than they need. The time needed for postevent recovery depends on the specific traits and training status of each swimmer. Research shows that at least 10 minutes of moderate exercise is necessary to begin clearing the lactate that accumulates in the body after strenuous exercise (Brooks and Gaesser 1980; Olbrecht 2000).

Phosphogens and Anaerobic Metabolism

The second anaerobic, or nonaerobic, energy pathway involves certain chemical substances found within the cells. The phosphogens—ATP (adenosine triphosphate), ADP (adenosine diphosphate), and PCr (creatine phosphate)—are found within the cytosol of the muscle cells and provide an even more immediate physiological energy source that allows muscular work to begin before engaging either anaerobic glycolysis or the aerobic metabolic pathways (figure 8.6). These high-energy compounds provide energy almost instantaneously, but the energy stores become exhausted after several seconds. The instantaneous power output of these immediately available high-energy compounds greatly exceeds the capacity of the aerobic system to generate energy. Sprinters use this immediate energy to fuel their big engines (in this case, the muscular engine rather than the cardiovascular engine) during short sprints.

In his book *The Science of Winning*, Olbrecht (2000) likens this immediate energy system to an electrical battery. The energy can be supplied nearly instantaneously, but the battery discharges at a rapid rate. The more energy that is needed, the faster the battery discharges. Some limited evidence suggests that athletes can alter this discharge rate through training or through nutritional supplements (Booth and Baldwin 1996). Only very small improvements in the energy delivery from this immediate pathway should be expected over the course of a training season, so in many ways this energy system remains constant.

The holy grail that many coaches try to achieve with their athletes represents somewhat of an oxymoron—sprint-specific endurance, or the ability to perform high-intensity efforts repeatedly. Trainability in this pathway appears to be limited, so sprinters and their coaches need to focus on other limitations as a means of getting faster in the pool. Controversy has continued over the years about whether nutritional supplements such as creatine can improve nonaerobic energy metabolism. The answer appears to be yes—supplementation can improve nonaerobic energy production at least for the glycolytic pathway, although not by nutritional supplements but through carbohydrate intake. As for increasing the available pool of phosphogens, no consensus exists about whether it is possible to boost the production of this energy pathway (Brooks, Fahey, and Baldwin 2004).

As another comment on anaerobic development, one common observation is that most outstanding swimmers begin formal training early and rarely achieve great success until they reach adult stature. This drawn-out progress may be

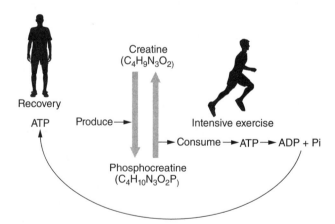

▶ **Figure 8.6** Immediate energy pathway, the phosphogens, involves the recycling of ADP and ATP when energy needs are massive. This point generally occurs at the onset of exercise but could also occur at the end of a race during the final sprint. The power output of this pathway is high but unsustainable, on the order of only a few seconds. Likewise, recovery is quick, requiring only 30 to 90 seconds, depending on the workload.

because of an inherent biological clock that prevents young swimmers from responding to some training stimuli until after adolescence. Although young swimmers can improve cardiopulmonary performance, they don't seem to be able to increase muscular power output to any great extent. Those improvements that do occur are probably a result of changes that take place in the central nervous system. Therefore, coaches must provide training that is age and developmentally appropriate. Pre- and periadolescent swimmers may not be able to respond to the training regimes used by college athletes, particularly as it applies to anaerobic development.

Anaerobic Testing

Estimating power output and anaerobic capacity of swimmers has proved to be a difficult task; no definitive markers or tests can be employed to quantify the capacity of nonaerobic pathways or an athlete's nonaerobic conditioning. Thus, most tests used to assess anaerobic capacity are performance tests during which athletes are asked to perform a task. Results are then compared with those of other athletes as well as past performances. The Wingate cycle ergometer anaerobic test is an example of this type of evaluation. The standing vertical jump test could also be described in this way. Researchers have also used modified swim benches to quantify the work capacity or power outputs of swimmers. A few have used in-water tests (e.g., tethered and semitethered swimming, or evaluation of force production against submerged force plates) to assess the power output of swimmers with varying success. The bottom line is that, in contrast to measures of aerobic capacity, the quantification of anaerobic capacity is much less routine. Currently, there is no convenient means of measuring the quantity of ATP or PCr used during a swim bout or the rate at which energy is produced nonaerobically. Coaches and scientists rely on algorithms composed primarily of performance measures as a means of comparing athletes with each other and with themselves at different times during the training regime.

Physiological Tie-Ins to Technique

One of the basic tenets of swim coaching has always been that technique trumps training. This principle is borne out not just through biomechanical analyses but also in discussions about physiology and energy systems. Improving a swimmer's ability to develop and apply forces can have a tremendous effect on how the body's energy systems are used to fuel performance. Efficiency is key because the relationship between the resistive forces in swimming and the metabolic costs to generate propulsion is not linear. In other words, as the swim speed increases, the metabolic costs increase at a faster rate, primarily because the resistive forces increase disproportionately to swim speed (resistance increases proportionally to swim velocity raised to the second power). The biomechanical reasons underlying this relationship are described in greater detail in chapter 1. Swim training is not often partitioned into two components, training and practice, but we might argue that training is directed at the cardiopulmonary aspects of performance and practice is focused on the technical and tactical aspects. The coaching emphasis is often placed on training, and much less time is spent on practice, but both should have a time and place in a well-designed periodized training plan.

Anaerobic and Aerobic Contributions to Performance

One aspect of metabolism worth mentioning at this point is the fact that the nonaerobic and aerobic pathways can be active simultaneously; they do not operate independently. Total metabolism represents the combination of aerobic and nonaerobic metabolism, and all these elements should be evaluated when structuring training for a swimmer. Coaches need to recognize that training only aerobically might be of limited benefit to some athletes and perhaps even detrimental to others, and vice versa. The role of coaches is to balance and focus the training to match the unique physical and physiological attributes of the athletes they work with.

Aerobic power output is often high when aerobic metabolism is high. As exercise intensity increases during a progressive workload, the aerobic contribution increases until it plateaus. At the same time, as the workload continues to increase, the nonaerobic contribution to the overall power output increases as well; at very high workloads, the power output of both the aerobic and nonaerobic energy systems may be near maximal. Going back to the analogy that equates swimmers to race cars, automobile manufacturers have figured out how to turn on and turn off engine cylinders depending on the need for additional power. Thus, when a driver is accelerating, the car uses all available cylinders to produce the necessary power. After cruising speed is achieved, however, the engine runs on fewer cylinders to improve fuel economy. Using all cylinders generates plenty of horsepower, but fuel economy suffers. Physiologically, though, the ability to sustain high power outputs is similarly limited because the fuel that supports anaerobic metabolism runs out relatively quickly. Athletes find it difficult to sustain maximum effort for even a minute because of this limited nonaerobic power output. Unfortunately, the only way to reduce power output while swimming a race is to slow down and turn off the cylinders. We might wonder, however, whether the limited kicking that some swimmers do during endurance events might be a way of turning off a few cylinders rather than reducing arm turnover or pace.

Finally, the fact that oxygen is not necessarily absent during nonaerobic metabolism needs to be underscored. For this reason, physiologists are beginning to favor the use of the term *nonaerobic* or *nonrobic* rather than *anaerobic*. Too often people assume that anaerobic metabolism occurs only when there is a lack of oxygen. A more accurate conception is to think of the causal factor as being a greater need for energy production than what can be met by aerobic metabolism alone. For example, at the beginning of a race, some time passes before aerobic metabolism ramps up. Research suggests that a minute and a half or two minutes might elapse before a swimmer's aerobic metabolism reaches a steady state (Di Prampero et al. 1974; Capelli, Pendergast, and Termin 1998). But the energy needs of the body during the race must be met if the required amount of muscular work is to take place. The only way to cover this energy deficit is through nonaerobic sources, so they will stay active at a high level until such a time that aerobic metabolism can meet the energetic needs of the working muscles.

At the onset of exercise, or following an increase in exercise intensity, the main sources of ATP generation are through preexisting ATP and PCr stores in the muscle along with glycolysis. Almost instantaneously, these systems quickly begin to contribute energy and ATP. Then, glycolysis represents the primary energy pathway. After roughly 30 to 90 seconds (90 to 120 seconds for a plateau) steady-state exercise is attained, and only then does aerobic metabolism become the predominant means of ATP synthesis. As indicated, the sustainable energy provided through aerobic metabolism is much greater than that provided through nonaerobic sources even though the instantaneous power output is much higher with nonaerobic metabolism. The problem is that muscles don't know beforehand that they will be doing physical work, let alone at what intensity. Thus, some time is needed to ramp up aerobic metabolism. This requirement might explain the metabolic value of a prerace warm-up. In some ways the warm-up can be thought of as an energy conservation process. By shutting down the system until needed, the necessary substrate usage (to sustain basic metabolism) drops to nearly nothing. After swimmers start training and are using large amounts of energy during practice, they need foodstuffs to supply the raw materials for the pathways. By warming up before an intensive exercise bout, the transition from immediate and available metabolism to sustainable aerobic metabolism takes place more quickly.

Training Effects and Their Effect on Performance

Different types of training induce different physical and physiological adaptations, so the training that swimmers engage in should be matched as well as possible to their physiology and the events in which they compete. The statement that James "Doc" Counsilman made famous a half-century ago remains true today: "You have to learn to treat your swimmers equally, but train them individually."

Sprint training and endurance training result in different physiologic adaptations, some of which are conflicting. Coaches have observed for years that endurance training can interfere with a swimmer's ability to develop the power needed to sustain sprint performance. Nevertheless, many coaches still attempt to improve a sprinter's ability to maintain speed by prescribing prolonged endurance sets. This approach may improve a swimmer's ability to recover, but it is not optimal for enhancing performance in the water. High-intensity exercise bouts of short duration and in surprisingly limited total weekly accumulation (6 to 12 minutes a week) have been shown to stimulate increases in glycolytic and mitochondrial enzymes within the muscle groups trained (Costill, Fink, and Pollock 1976; Booth and Baldwin 1996). Other research has shown that swim training limited to little more than swimming 1,000 meters a day (with most of the remaining physical training taking place on dry land) can result in gains in sprint performance (Hickson 1980; Stager and Tanner 2005). Although this recommendation does not apply across the board, it does demonstrate that continued evaluation of necessary training loads and optimal training distances is warranted.

For the sprinter, research suggests that power output in the water is the most critical component of performance. Of course, this statement assumes that stroke mechanics are not otherwise a limiting factor. Aerobic capacity may play a role in the sprinter's ability to recover quickly and endure a workout, but it plays just a small role in actual race performance. Coaches are cautioned to consider that the goal of optimal training should be to perform a specific event (or event distance), not simply to make it through a demanding workout of many thousands of meters a week.

Figure 8.7 illustrates what has been observed to occur during a training regime focused specifically on improving sprint performance. Peak power, the maximum

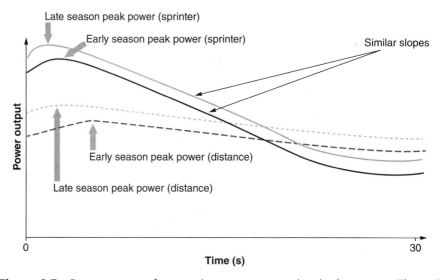

▶ **Figure 8.7** Power output of two swimmers at two points in the season. The sprint swimmer always has a high peak but fatigues rapidly and more than the distance swimmer does, regardless of the training. The opposite is true for the distance swimmer, yet the area under the curve is greater for the distance swimmer. Appropriate training appears to decrease the time from the onset of the exercise to peak power, but it does not necessarily decrease the rate of fatigue. Nevertheless, both swimmers increase their instantaneous power output at every point along the 30-second challenge.

amount of power that can be produced during this particular movement, improves, and the total power output represented by the shaded area under the curve improves with continual training. Also, the time to peak power may be shortened, which is an advantage in short swim events. But the slope of the line that reflects the ability to endure does not appear to change much over time, partly because the test lasts only 30 seconds. Nevertheless, at the end of the season the swimmers appear to fatigue at rates similar to the rates that occur preseason. The improvement in performance appears to be greater power output at each instance (allowing for greater speed), fatigue occurring at about the same rate, and earlier peak power. Not enough is known about this aspect of training to be able to provide an adequate explanation for these findings.

The reality is that all swimmers need some aerobic and some sprint, or power-focused, training. Finding the proper balance and designing the training plan to optimize an athlete's physiologic development is the key to maximizing in-water performance. This topic is part of planning and periodization, discussed in chapter 9.

Another factor to consider when incorporating physiological adaptation into a training program design is that although endurance training has been shown to result in an increase in mitochondrial mass, is does not necessarily result in an increase in mitochondrial activity or overall contractile fiber volume. In fact, physiologists have identified a simultaneous decrease in contractile myofibrils because of prolonged overdistance training. Overdistance training increases delivery of oxygen by decreasing the diffusion distance between the capillary and mitochondria, in part by increasing capillary density. But this effect can also be achieved by reducing the mass of the muscle contractile apparatus (i.e., the cross-sectional area of the muscle), which is good for gas diffusion but bad for force generation. This outcome would be positive for events primarily dependent on oxygen delivery but negative for athletic events in which muscle power or force drives performance.

A tendency in modern competitive swim training, one that is deeply rooted in the culture of swimming in the United States, is for coaches to focus on aerobic training almost exclusively as they develop an ability within their swimmers to endure and persevere through excessive yardage to achieve success in the pool. This statement is not meant to describe all swim programs, but many competitive swim programs preferentially emphasize aerobic training for all athletes. The dilemma of this type of training is that overdistance training pushes the metabolic framework of the athlete toward the aerobic end of the spectrum and can hamper the power development and power output of the athlete. Coaches need to consider the full spectrum of physiological makeups that swimmers might possess and structure the training for the sprint group to focus on power and speed, not necessarily the development of the aerobic system.

Additionally, with endurance training only slight improvements in $\dot{V}O_2$max may be observed, even with a greater than twofold increase in the amount of mitochondrial enzymes within the muscles. Although the increase in muscle mitochondria may allow a slightly greater extraction of oxygen from the blood by the working muscles, this rise contributes to only a minor increase in $\dot{V}O_2$max. Other factors besides increases in mitochondrial mass and enzyme activity contribute to a swimmer's ability to respond to and benefit from endurance training (figure 8.8). Like it or not, the very high values for $\dot{V}O_2$max observed in successful endurance performers are greatly influenced by inherited factors. We reiterate that athletic success is multifactorial and a combination of talent and training.

Still, the overall number and size of the muscle mitochondria increase with appropriate training. In addition, the enzyme activities involved in the TCA cycle, ETC, and beta-oxidation increase as a result of endurance training. The training adaptations carry the potential to increase the rate of oxidative phosphorylation within the muscle. As a result, endurance-trained muscles are able to oxidize fat at a higher rate than untrained muscles can. In other words, a larger proportion of the energy produced to fulfill the exercise demand will come from fat and less from carbohydrate (i.e., glycogen is spared). Because of less carbohydrate utilization, less lactate is produced for a given submaximal workload, and fat is increasingly used as a fuel source. Collectively, the adaptations result in less dependency on carbohydrate during exercise and prolonged endurance.

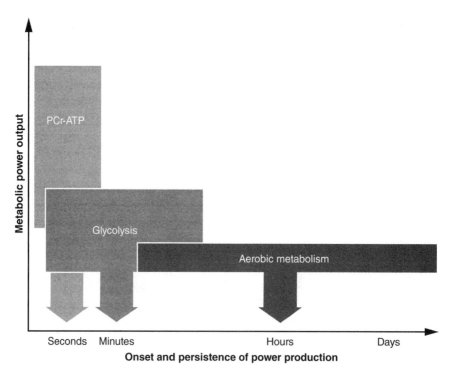

▶ **Figure 8.8** The metabolic power generation capacity of the three metabolic pathways that fuel exercise and the ability of those pathways to sustain exercise. Immediate energy is available for intense, short bursts of muscular power, whereas aerobic metabolism is almost unlimited in terms of maintenance. Most exercise, and certainly nearly all swim training, relies on all three pathways.

Summary

Energy systems are at the center of everything that athletes hope to accomplish in the pool. The ability to metabolize food or fuel rapidly is essential in terms of providing the active tissues with the energy necessary to generate muscular force and drive performance in the pool or the weight room. The rate at which usable energy can be provided to the working muscle is key to athletic success, assuming that everything else (nutrition, training, mechanics, psychology, and so forth) is already optimal. For the sprinter, it's about tapping into immediate energy sources to fuel performance. For the endurance swimmer, it really isn't about how much energy is available before the race; rather, it's about how fast energy can be generated during the race that truly matters. Energy availability before and during a prolonged practice is potentially an important performance-limiting factor.

To do physiological or mechanical work, muscle cells need energy. The energy needed to fuel swimming performance comes from three energy pathways—the immediate anaerobic phosphate-based energy system, glycolysis, and aerobic metabolism. The substrates used to provide the energy to do work are carbohydrate, fat, and protein. These nutrients are broken down to provide the substrates needed for the metabolic energy pathways.

Endurance performance largely depends on aerobic metabolism and cardiopulmonary conditioning (heart, lungs, and mitochondria). In contrast, sprint performance relies on muscular power and the nonaerobic production of intracellular energy sources (phosphogens and sugars). During workouts and many competitive events, all three energy systems are important. Coaches need to consider the underlying physiology of each athlete and design a training program that targets those features and optimizes performance results. Coaches, athletes, and parents should recognize additional performance-affecting information in the area of exercise physiology and energy systems.

Skeletal muscles can be loosely described as having two opposing traits: the ability to endure and the ability to generate high levels of force and power. Coaches need to be cognizant of the dichotomy that exists in the metabolic and muscular adaptations to swim training. Some swimmers are born dragsters, and others are Indy cars, but both need to be trained appropriately. From the perspective of metabolism and energetics, the coaching adage about the necessity of training being specific to the targeted event is as true today as it was 100 years ago.

Endurance can be enhanced by inducing metabolic (peripheral) and cardiopulmonary (central) adaptations to physical training. A robust cardiopulmonary system, one that ensures delivery of oxygen to the peripheral active tissues, is an important partner in the metabolic ability to endure. The heart and lungs must be evenly matched and capable of meeting the stress and muscular metabolic demands of intense exercise. Capillary density within the active muscles must be sufficient to provide for tissue gas exchange and nutrient delivery. Ventilatory muscles must be able to move air into the lungs for extended periods. Hemoglobin must be adequate to carry oxygen to the periphery with each heartbeat. These morphological adaptations to exercise and physical training do not occur quickly and may take many months, if not years, to be fully expressed.

As for sprinting, research has shown that increases in intramuscular phosphogens are hard to accomplish through training. Little research supports the use of supplements such as creatine as a means of improving competitive race performance. Metabolic and enzyme adaptations that are observed in response to sprint training are much more modest than what has been shown to occur in the mitochondrial enzymes as a result of endurance training. An increase in aerobic capacity may improve a swimmer's ability to tolerate training and improve recovery rates, but it does little to improve sprint performance per se. Endurance is likely a trait more easily developed than are the traits necessary for success in the shortest sprints.

Although carbohydrate stores have been shown to increase in the trained person, this expansion has a greater effect on the ability to endure workouts than the ability to generate instantaneous muscular power during a race. Much of the improvement in muscle power resulting from sprint training comes from neurological changes that favor recruitment of muscle fibers and increased muscle cross-sectional area.

Increasing the training load as a means of improving the endurance of a sprinter will likely interfere with the sprinter's ability to sprint rather than improve sprint times. Research suggests that muscle fibers contract faster after prolonged rest rather than after prolonged use. This is not to say that less training results in better performance. The point is that overdistance training for the sprinter may not improve sprinting successes.

The type of training that induces metabolic changes consistent with endurance is not the same as the training that affects muscular power. And research has shown that it is difficult, if not impossible, to improve metabolic endurance and muscular power simultaneously. We now believe that specific metabolic adaptations occur during one phase of training and specific power adaptations occur at another. This consideration should be designed into both the annual plan and the larger plan for the career of a young swimmer. The nature and characteristics of the training regime must be appropriately designed chronologically to stimulate the appropriate metabolic and muscular adaptations that will eventually favor success.

Testing, whether it is $\dot{V}O_2$max testing to evaluate aerobic performance or Wingate testing to examine anaerobic capacity, should have a consistent place in a training plan.

Coaches and athletes should be aware of the importance of postrace or posttraining recovery and take active steps to refuel the body with the intent of replenishing energy stores.

Coaches should design periodized plans to assist in the strategic development of physical and physiologic capacities over the short term and throughout a swimmer's career.

Overall, an understanding of exercise physiology, energy systems and ways to train them, and the individuality of each athlete will help coaches lead their swimmers to better performances in the pool. Coaches need to develop different training plans for sprinters and endurance athletes, offer different sets within each practice, and emphasize different aspects throughout the swim season. All coaches are encouraged to strive toward this goal. If they are able to achieve it, great things will happen with the swimmers they work with.

CHAPTER 9

Periodization and Planning

—Scott Riewald, PhD, CSCS

Throughout this book a great deal of application-focused information has been presented about how to improve the performance of swimmers. Although all the pieces of information are beneficial on their own, they can be merged to develop a focused, age-appropriate training program that will enhance performance as well as protect the health of the athlete.

This chapter addresses the concepts of planning and periodization. Although these terms are sometimes thought of as synonymous, they take on different meanings when it comes to training design. Planning incorporates elements of structure—establishing both short- and long-term training goals as well as defining the path to take to achieve those goals. Periodization, on the other hand, focuses on the methodology underlying the plan—the cyclical, or periodic, nature of manipulating training variables, including rest, to optimize performance outcomes. Proper planning and periodization are critical elements of training design; they work hand in hand. Understanding both planning and periodization will help coaches develop programs that will allow swimmers to do the following:

- Set and achieve realistic performance goals within a season as well as across longer, even multiyear, time horizons
- Achieve peak performances at specific competitions during the season
- Provide variety to a training plan to increase enjoyment while helping to prevent performance plateaus
- Engage in age-appropriate and developmentally appropriate training through all stages of development, shifting the goals and training foci as a swimmer progresses from an age-group swimmer to a senior swimmer and potentially on to the collegiate and national levels

- Achieve their true performance potential, not necessarily when they are 10, 12, or 14 years old, but when they are physically mature and can take full advantage of the strength, physiologic development, and technique that have built up as the body has matured
- Maintain health, as well as performance, while avoiding burnout and overtraining

In this chapter we look at how training can be structured to optimize performance while also discussing how the sport sciences collectively can be used to help a coach build daily, monthly, seasonal, and even quadrennial performance training plans. Where possible, the chapter draws from other sport science disciplines to create a thread that weaves throughout the book and pulls the material together in a coherent way.

Planning for Performance

A number of basic training principles underlie program design. Yet when it comes down to it, the most important thing that a coach can do is have a plan for training and development. With the end in mind, the coach must chart the proper course to get there. Every coach should know the specific goals for the program as well as for the individual swimmers being coached. Three basic principles underlie training design:

- *Know what you want to accomplish and when you want to do it.* The first part of any journey is identifying the destination. Whether working with age-group swimmers, national team members, triathletes, or masters swimmers, a coach must develop a training plan with the desired results in mind. Coaches must consider not only the seasonal and short-term goals of the athletes but also their long-term, career goals. The program should incorporate all aspects of an athlete's training and not focus only on the in-water, swimming component.

- *Design the training to achieve those goals.* A useful approach is to think of the big picture first and then focus on progressively smaller intervals of time. For example, internationally competitive athletes and coaches develop plans in four-year blocks corresponding to the four-year Olympic cycle. Age-group coaches may also develop multiyear plans, but thinking in one-year blocks or even competitive seasons within the year is usually beneficial when designing a plan. Regardless of the approach taken, the idea of planning backward should be followed. Begin by identifying the major competition or competitions that the athlete will be training to peak for and establish realistic performance goals for those competitions. From that point, build the rest of the season around achieving the specified performance goals at the specified events. Coaches must not sacrifice the goals when engaging in planning. In some instances they may need to adjust the training and competition schedule to allow the swimmer to train through a competition or get more rest during critical phases of the plan. If the work and planning has been done on the front end, the eventual results will justify the approach taken.

• *Plan, test, and then be willing to make adaptations to the plan.* Every good coach is willing to look critically at the plan and make adjustments if the results are not what were expected. To do this, coaches need to maintain accurate logs that detail training load, specific sets and exercises, and athlete performance. Conducting regular physical and physiological testing to monitor progress toward the eventual goal is also important. If the season-ending swim is the only indication of whether training is progressing along the desired path, the coach is waiting too long. Regular monitoring and adaptation of the plan based on athlete performance should be a cornerstone of any periodized training plan.

At its core, periodization and the process of varying a training program at regular intervals to bring about optimal gains in physical performance should go hand in hand with seasonal or multiyear planning. If the plan and the mechanics underlying the plan do not align, something must be adjusted; either the goals need to be refined to become more realistic, or the periodization strategy needs to be adjusted to match the performance goals. Rarely does a coach nail down a seasonal plan on the first attempt; typically, multiple iterations are required to get everything to align in such a way that performance expectations can be achieved at the desired competition.

Introduction to Periodization

Before going any further, the term *periodization* needs to be defined. The performance literature offers a number of definitions (Bompa 1999a, 1999b; Herodek, Simonovic, and Rakovic 2012; Issurin 2008; Stone et al. 1999). Although subtle differences can be identified, the best definitions contain several common themes—effective manipulation of training variables and the infusion of recovery to achieve optimal performance results. For the purpose of this text we define periodization as the systematic and cyclical manipulation of training variables, including the proper prescription of rest and recovery, across a competitive season as well as the athlete's career, to maximize performances while maintaining the athlete's long-term health (Herodek, Simonovic, and Rakovic 2012). Periodization is built on the fundamental principles of progressive overload and general adaptation (Selye 1974, 1976). These principles state that the body will adjust and adapt in response to increased performance or training demands (e.g., muscles and bone will undergo changes to become stronger and handle the increased load that comes with training). Although adaptation is described briefly in chapter 20, revisiting these principles here is useful because they underlie the theory behind strength and sport training.

The general adaptation syndrome (GAS; Selye 1974, 1976) describes three basic stages that the body goes through in response to stress (figure 9.1):

1. The body undergoes an immediate response to stress and enters an alarm stage in response to a new training stimulus, such as an increase in training load or an intense training session. In this initial phase, humans exhibit

a fight-or-flight response that prepares the body for physical activity but can also result in a short-term decrease in the effectiveness of the immune system.

2. The alarm phase is followed by the adaptation or resistance stage as the body begins the process of adapting or adjusting to the new stimuli. If the applied stress continues beyond the initial training session, the body will continue its efforts to adapt to the stressor; that is, muscles will become stronger, energy systems will become more efficient at producing ATP to support training, and so on. The body responds in this way in an attempt to reduce the effect of this prolonged stress.

3. The third phase of the GAS is the exhaustion stage. At this point, the body is unable to handle the applied stress. Either the stress has been excessive or it has been applied for too long. Consequently, the body becomes unable to adjust or repair damage caused by the stressor, typically resulting in a loss of health or performance (i.e., symptoms of overtraining).

In response to a training stimulus or block of training, the body initially enters an alarm state in which it is weakened and its ability to handle subsequent stress is reduced for a time. If given repeated exposure to the stimulus, however, the body recovers and undergoes adaptation so that it is better able to handle the stress it experienced. If the body continues to experience stress or experiences additional stress before adaptation occurs, the athlete proceeds to the exhaustion stage and may potentially face overtraining. Consider the response that muscle undergoes with strength training. The muscle experiences damage at the cellular level following a heavy weight-training session (alarm). As the muscle repairs itself, it becomes stronger and able to handle greater loads (adaptation).

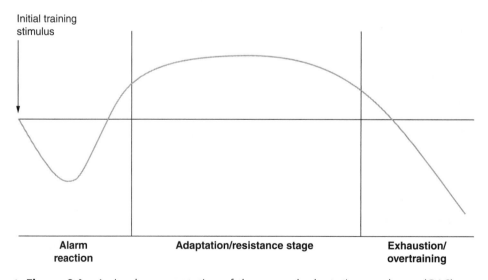

▶ **Figure 9.1** A visual representation of the general adaptation syndrome (GAS).

But if the weight or training volume is increased too quickly without allowing adaptation to occur, injury and fatigue will occur (exhaustion).

The body can experience both beneficial stress that can drive adaptation and performance improvements, termed *eustress*, and detrimental stress that can lead to injury or overtraining, termed *distress* (Selye 1976). Eustress is defined by how an athlete perceives a specific stressor (e.g., a negative threat versus a positive challenge) (Fevre, Gregory, and Matheny 2006; Rice 2012). Eustress elicits a positive physical or physiological response. In swimming, this response can take the form of increased muscular strength, increased power, or improved aerobic capacity. Distress, on the other hand, is associated with a negative response to stress such as muscle damage, injury, or overtraining.

Left unstated in the GAS model is that adequate rest must be provided as part of training to allow the body to recover appropriately from the training stimuli. By structuring training in such a way that the body is given adequate time to recover from stress before additional strenuous training is experienced, the body will go through a phase of supercompensation after which it will emerge stronger and better suited to handle subsequent stressors than it was before the initial bout of training. Figure 9.2 shows how the GAS applies to performance and how the body responds to stress. The goal of a periodization plan is to cycle the stress and rest appropriately to provide a challenging training stimulus but also give the body time to recover. By structuring training in this way, a swimmer should never enter the exhaustion stage but will experience supercompensation and get progressively stronger and faster.

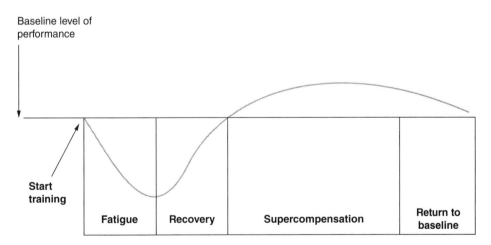

▶ **Figure 9.2** A performance-focused representation of the general adaptation syndrome (GAS). In response to a training stimulus or block of training, the body initially enters an alarmed state and performance decreases. If provided rest, however, the body recovers and even enters a phase of supercompensation, where it can perform at heightened levels. But if no further stimulus is applied to the body in this phase, it will gradually return to the baseline state that existed before the stimulus was initially applied.

The concept of general adaptation is tied directly to the principle of progressive overload. Progressive overload is the process of gradually increasing the stress placed on the body during training. It is based on the philosophy that if a training stimulus is increased gradually over time, the body will be able to adapt appropriately. But if a swimmer is asked to do too much, too soon, whether it is a dramatic increase in training volume in the pool or a large increase in resistance in a dryland program, the chance for injury increases or the body will not be able to adapt fully to the stressor.

If used correctly, the principles of general adaptation and progressive overload can work in harmony to help athletes improve performance, whether in the weight room or in the pool. Figure 9.3 illustrates how this works. A training stimulus is applied, and the body is given an opportunity to recover. Subsequently, the body enters a phase of supercompensation. In this state a subsequent and increased stimulus can be applied to improve the training response further and move the body to a new equilibrium state. This process can continue in perpetuity and forms the foundation of periodized training in swimming and sport.

A Brief History of Periodization

For as long as historical athletic records have been kept, the best athletes in the world have recognized the benefits of periodized training, starting with the ancient Greeks preparing for the Games of the ancient Olympiad. More recently, nations such as the Soviet Union have used periodized training to maximize performance in athletes across a wide range of sports. Metveyev (1966) and

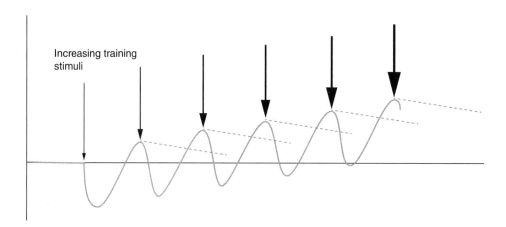

Increasing training stimuli

▶ **Figure 9.3** The principle of progressive overload. If the body is allowed to recover adequately from a training stimulus, subsequent introduction of increasingly larger stimuli can result in a continuous increase in performance. Arrows indicate the application of progressively larger training stimuli to elicit additional adaptations. Dashed lines represent the hypothetical return to baseline trajectories that would be expected if training stimuli ceased at that point.

Bompa (1999a, 1999b) are thought of as the modern-day pioneers in periodized training design because they expanded the thinking about this training method and formally organized many of the principles that underlie periodization. Building on their work, coaches and scientists have continued to advance the concept of periodization, resulting in increasingly complex, but arguably more performance-focused, periodization models. Scientific validation of periodized training methods also became more commonplace throughout the late 20th and early 21st centuries (Zatsiorsky and Kraemer 2006; Siff and Verkhoshansky 1999). As a result, periodized training principles are now being applied with positive results to a wide range of sports.

Interpreting the Periodization Literature

One of the greatest rewards of putting together a well-planned periodized training program is that a coach can design training so that swimmers will peak at specific, identified competitions. Although the point has been made that swimmers should be able to race fast at virtually any time of the year, most swimmers truly want to perform their best at one competition each season—where the physical, physiological, and mental sides of swimming all come together to achieve a peak performance. In high school, this event may be the season-ending high school championships. In college, it could be the NCAA or conference championships. A masters swimmer may want to peak for the long-course nationals at the end of the summer. One of the main tenets of periodization training is that training can be structured to allow athletes to achieve peak performances at critical times of the year.

The research conducted in the area of periodization and training is extensive and diverse. Periodization has been examined from a variety of perspectives. The data show overwhelmingly that periodization training is superior to other training methods for developing athletic performance. Rather than provide an extensive discussion of what the research shows, the following section highlights some of the key findings (and some shortcomings) as well as what this information means to coaches.

- Most research studies, regardless of the method of periodization employed by the coach, show superior performance gains compared with nonperiodized training (Stone et al. 1999; Rhea and Alderman 2004; Kiely 2012). The findings are equivocal, however, because in some rare instances, studies show that periodized training models are not superior with regard to improving athlete performance.

- Some have suggested that the improvements seen with periodized training result from the fact that athletes ultimately engage in a greater overall workload. When volume and intensity are controlled, the argument goes, periodized training produces results similar to those obtained from nonperiodized training. Thus, a causal relationship was established in which more training leads to better results. Even with that taken into account, the superiority of periodized training programs has been shown to occur when volume of training was held constant between experimental and control groups. Performance improvements were shown to be greater, however, in periodized programs in which athletes could train at higher volumes and intensities (Rhea and Alderman 2004).

- The results are equivocal as to whether periodized training is most effective in trained or untrained populations (i.e., who sees the greatest performance gains?). With that said, different forms of periodization appear to be better suited for specific athlete populations. Linear periodization is associated more with improvements in beginning athletes, whereas more complex nonlinear models of periodization training are best suited for developing performance in experienced athletes. (Note: Linear and nonlinear periodization methods are outlined in detail later in the chapter.)

- Females benefit as much from periodized training as males do. Although men tend to have greater absolute strength, women are as responsive (and in some cases more so) to periodized training as men (Kell 2011).

- Variation within a periodized program is crucial to performance (Bompa 1999a, 1999b; Stone et al. 1999; Rhea and Alderman 2004). In fact, some have postulated that the variation inherent to periodized training is what facilitates performance improvements, not the actual seasonal structure of the plan (Kiely 2012).

- Training plans, even periodized plans, need to factor in aspects of growth and development. Younger athletes who have not reached biological maturity will likely not spend the same amount of time trying to build power and maximal strength as older athletes might.

- Most important for swimming coaches, periodized training has been shown to enhance performance in swimmers (Stewart and Hopkins 2000; Thomas, Mujika, and Busso 2008; Touretski 2000; Pyne and Touretski 2003).

Note that some in the scientific community are concerned that periodization methodology has not been appropriately vetted and that coaches therefore cannot definitively say whether periodized training provides the benefits that they claim. Concern exists in some circles that periodization has been somewhat blindly accepted as a superior training method without having the data to back that claim. Along those lines, when reviewing the periodization literature, consider the following:

- Group-based observations may be misleading because the information is often too general to capture the responses of individuals. Research is inherently based on the assumption that all athletes will respond similarly to an applied training stimuli. This is known not to be the case. For any training scenario, a core group of athletes will show improvement. In addition, a smaller group will outstrip the mean. But some athletes will not improve or may even regress in performance. For this reason, even the best laid performance plans must be adapted and modified to meet the specific needs of the individual swimmer (Kiely 2012).

- Similarly, an underlying assumption is that accurate predictions can be made about how the body will adapt to training, when in fact any number of causal factors can affect how a swimmer responds. Individual athletes can respond differently when presented with identical training stimuli. Identical training sessions performed by the same person will elicit unique training responses as well, based on the context in which the workout was presented (training phase, previous training, and so forth) (Rhea and Alderman 2004; Kiely 2012).

- In the field of periodization research, most of the findings highlight short-term results and do not provide any longitudinal or long-term data or outcomes.

- Could it simply be the variation provided or the increased training load afforded the athlete that leads to the observed performance gains across athletes and sports, not the periodized programming per se? In fact, a number of studies have shown that variation alone can lead to performance gains and a reduction in overtraining.

Armed with this information about what the research says about periodization, let's dig a bit deeper into the understanding of what periodization is and how it can be used to influence swimming performance.

Training Objectives Within a Periodized Program

The basic theory behind periodization is that by rotating through various phases or training cycles, each of which focuses on developing a different training variable or set of variables, we can stress different systems more completely than if they were all trained at the same time throughout the year. Additionally, the common thought is that some fundamental building blocks should be put in place before more complex skills are developed; for example, strength should be developed before attempts are made to develop power. By approaching training design in this way and building on a foundation of skills developed over time, the swimmer can experience performance gains weekly, monthly, and yearly, in both the pool and the weight room.

Coaches and athletes need to understand the training objectives that can be incorporated into the phases of a periodized plan. A number of objectives and goals can be targeted through training, depending on things such as training phase, age, and time of the year, including the following.

Anatomical Adaptation and Injury Prevention

At specific times of the year, particularly at the start of a season, athletes should focus on building strength balance throughout the body. They should target weak muscle groups that, if not strengthened, could predispose them to injury.

Recovery and Regeneration

Following the season, swimmers need to have a period in which they can recharge their batteries and recovery both physically and mentally before the next season or training phase begins.

Maximal Strength

Maximal strength refers to the greatest amount of force that a swimmer can generate in one all-out effort. Maximal strength is commonly measured as the amount of weight that a person can lift (or force that can be generated) in a one-repetition max (1RM) test. Although swimmers may not attempt to develop maximal strength per se, at times during the training cycle they will want to develop increased strength throughout the body.

Strength Endurance

Strength endurance is the ability to produce a specified level of force repeatedly without becoming fatigued. Typically, the level of force generated in any one contraction when swimming is not maximal, but it may represent a high percentage of a swimmer's force-generating capacity in specific muscles or muscle groups. Strength endurance is critically important for swimmers because of the repetitive nature of the sport; for a swimmer to perform well and remain free from injury, many muscles need to have strength endurance. Several specific muscles or muscle groups come to mind:

- Scapular stabilizers, which control the shoulder blades and maintain proper positioning of the shoulder joint
- Core muscles, which control body posture in the water
- Muscles of the rotator cuff and upper back, which are responsible for generating upper-body propulsion
- Muscles of the hip, which drive the propulsive kick

Strategies to develop strength endurance should be incorporated into strength-training plans for these muscle groups.

Power

Power is the ability of the neuromuscular system to produce large forces in a short time. Mathematically, muscle power equals muscle force multiplied by contraction velocity. Power is an important aspect of performance in swimming, especially in certain muscle groups in which explosiveness is required to achieve optimal performance. For example, power is needed in the lower-limb extensors to drive the start or push-off from the wall following a turn. Power in the upper-body musculature is beneficial to sprint performance and to the ability to shift into another gear at the end of a longer race.

Power Endurance

Power endurance refers to the ability to perform powerful actions repeatedly while experiencing little or no fatigue.

Muscle Hypertrophy

Hypertrophy training is designed to maximize muscle size, not necessarily strength. In general, strength training designed for swimmers should not focus on gaining muscle size.

Strength Maintenance

During the competition phase of a periodized plan, strength and conditioning should be maintained at the levels that were developed over the course of the previous phases. Typically, strength gains can be maintained by engaging in at least one strength-training session per week that includes a small number of exercises involving multiple muscle groups.

General Physical Development

This approach focuses on developing physical fitness as well as foundational strength and conditioning. A training phase targeted at general physical development includes elements of flexibility training, agility, strength, coordination, balance, as well as other physical attributes associated with general athleticism.

Sport-Specific Physical Development

This aspect of training focuses on the development of the physical and physiological attributes directly related to performance. For swimmers, this work could include in-water strength and power training or dryland training targeted at improving performance in a specific stroke or race distance.

Psychological Development

At certain times of the season, it may be important to develop mental skills that contribute to swimming performance, such as resilience, determination, and confidence. Practices and training can be structured to emphasize the development of certain mental attributes.

Technical Proficiency

Swimming technique is even more important than strength in the effect on performance in the pool. As such, technique should be a critical component of training. In addition, at certain times of the year a preferential focus should be directed to developing aspects of technique.

Basic Concepts of Periodization

When discussing periodization, the words *macrocycle, mesocycle,* and *microcycle* are commonly used to describe periods of training. These words represent different phases of the periodized training plan. The following section provides more detail about each of these phases. We start with the shortest element, the microcycle, and build to the macrocycle, discussing how all three period types fit within an annual plan.

Microcycle

A microcycle is the smallest unit of planning within the periodized plan. The length of the microcycle in a training plan is typically a week, but it can last anywhere from 4 to 10 days. The microcycle can be built to focus on the development of a specific performance variable or combination of program variables. For example, microcycles can be designed to elicit high levels of fatigue, develop power, promote skill development, facilitate recovery, or reach other goals. Managing the training load during the microcycle is crucial. Within the microcycle, planned variation should occur as well. Training volume and intensity should be varied to achieve the desired level of adaptation. As far as presenting guidelines about constructing a microcycle, Bompa (1999b) provides the following advice:

- The objectives of the microcycle and the aspect of performance being targeted should be clearly identified.
- Coaches need to set the specifics of training for each day—sets, repetitions, intensity, rest—as well as plan the overall intensity of the microcycle.
- Coaches should clearly identify the methods (exercises, modalities, and so forth) to be used in developing the targeted physical or physiologic performance characteristics.
- As a rule of thumb, a microcycle should start at low to medium intensity and progress to higher intensity later in the microcycle.
- Athletes should engage in training sessions with similar objectives two or three times within a microcycle, ideally every second day, to achieve a training effect.
- Within the microcycle, swimmers should be trained to their limit in the targeted area on one or at most two days. At least one day per week should be focused on low-intensity exercise or active rest and recovery.

Figure 9.4 illustrates a moderate-intensity microcycle that includes two high-intensity (Hi) days of training, two moderate days (M), two low-intensity days (L), and one recovery day (R). Intensity can be varied as needed to achieve the desired performance objective within the microcycle.

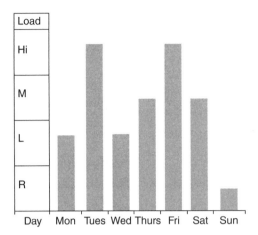

▶ **Figure 9.4** Periodization and variation of training intensity within a microcycle. This figure illustrates how a week of training could be structured to provide a balance of high (Hi), moderate (M), and low (L) intensity while also integrating a day of recovery.

Reprinted, by permission, from T.O. Bompa, 1999, *Periodization training for sports* (Champaign, IL: Human Kinetics), 77.

Mesocycle

A mesocycle represents the next longest block of training within a periodized program. It typically has a duration ranging from two to eight weeks. If each microcycle is approximately one week in length, a mesocycle typically incorporates two to eight microcycles.

More important, a mesocycle is often set up as a specific phase of a training plan that focuses on the development of certain physical attributes that will prepare the athlete for a certain aspect of competition. As discussed later in the chapter, a swimming season can be broken into preparatory, training, competition, and active rest, or transition, phases. Each of those phases corresponds to a mesocycle within the training plan and is directed toward achieving specific training or performance goals and objectives.

A mesocycle should be set up to provide a swimmer the opportunity to achieve true training adaptations. A period of six to eight weeks is typically needed to cause that change, at least when developing physical attributes such as strength or cardiovascular endurance. The full season should be considered to identify how the mesocycles can be incorporated; an appropriate amount of time is needed to provide an adequate training stimulus while also allowing the swimmer to accomplish the goals of the seasonal plan. Just as training volume and intensity should vary within a microcycle, the intensity of microcycles should be periodized within a mesocycle. Figure 9.5 shows how the intensity can be varied over a four-week period to provide a training stimulus as well as an opportunity to recover.

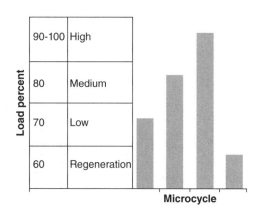

▶ **Figure 9.5**
Variation of microcycle
intensity within a mesocycle,
or training phase. Just as
training intensity can vary
within a microcycle, microcycle
intensity can be modulated
within the mesocycle.
Reprinted, by permission, from T.O. Bompa,
1999, *Periodization training for sports*
(Champaign, IL: Human Kinetics), 75.

Note that variety and variation should still be critical elements of the meso-cycle design (figure 9.6). Within an eight-week preparatory phase, a mesocycle in which the major emphasis may be on building muscular endurance and aerobic capacity, a coach will likely focus primarily on the development of those performance variables. But several one-week microcycles that emphasize power development or technique work may also be incorporated into the plan. Taking this approach will keep training fresh while still targeting a specific training goal.

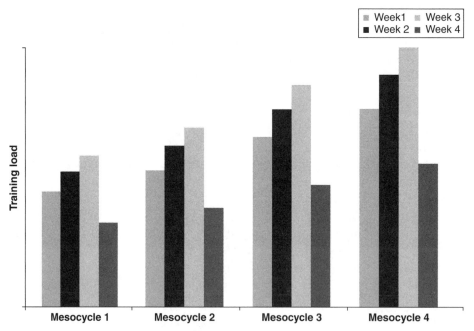

▶ **Figure 9.6** Example of a mesocycle. A mesocycle represents a phase of the training plan. In this example, four mesocycles are depicted, each made up of four microcycles. Although each mesocycle is put together in roughly the same way, with three weeks of progressive increases in volume followed by a recovery week, variability can occur in both the volume and the intensity programmed within the mesocycle.

Macrocycle

The macrocycle is the largest phase within a periodized plan. It typically refers to a full swimming season. For Olympians, the macrocycle might represent the four-year block of time between Olympic Games. For the age-group swimmer, it could represent the short-course season or the long-course competitive season within the year. The goal is for the swimmer to peak at least once during the macrocycle at an identified key competition.

No hard-and-fast rules govern what constitutes a macrocycle within a periodized plan. Many coaches develop a periodized plan in which the macrocycle constitutes the entire year of training and competition. The macrocycle is made up of a series of mesocycles, or training phases, linked together to form a comprehensive training plan. If the athlete is expected to peak once during the entire calendar year, the term *annual plan* can be used synonymously and interchangeably with macrocycle. But if two seasons occur within the calendar year (e.g., a short-course season and a long-course season), the annual plan will be made up of two macrocycles.

There is a method to the madness, and the cycles within a periodized plan build on each other:

- Days of training are grouped together to form one- to two-week microcycles.
- Microcycles are grouped together to form mesocycles, which represent phases of the training plan, each with a defined goal and training focus within the seasonal plan.
- Mesocycles are grouped together to form macrocycles, which typically represent a competitive season that culminates in a performance at the key competition identified when the seasonal plan was put together.

Types of Periodization

Since the concept of periodization was first introduced, coaches have approached this training design in a number of ways. This section illustrates some of the methods used to put together periodized programs and discusses the pros and cons associated with each.

Linear Periodization

The classical periodized model described by Matveyev (1966) is typified by a progressive transition from high-volume, moderate-intensity training to low-volume, high-intensity work over the course of the macrocycle. The linear periodized model (figure 9.7) generally follows an approach that progresses through phases or mesocycles that have the targeted goal of increasing strength and power in the lead-up to an identified key competition. Training focus begins with foundational strength development and then moves to maximal strength development, power development, and peaking for a major competition. An active rest phase follows.

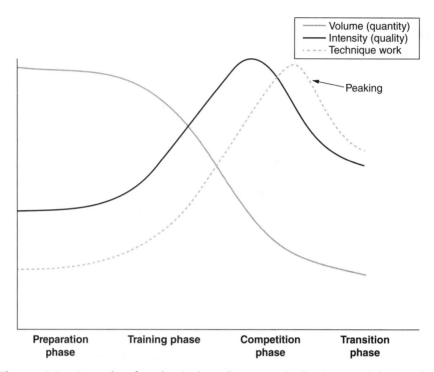

▶ **Figure 9.7** Example of a classical, or linear, periodization model. In a linear periodization model, the training volume decreases while training intensity increases over the course of a season, or macrocycle. Technique work also increases roughly in parallel with training intensity. Technique work, intensity, and volume all drop during the lead-in to the peak competition.

The linear model uses specific time intervals to develop only one training variable at a time. Athletes progress from week to week trying to improve their performance by using larger loads, more repetitions or sets, decreased rest between sets, and so on. As the athlete progresses through the season, the focus shifts to technique and sport-specific exercises as well.

Although many coaches are likely familiar with the linear model and athletes have been shown to improve performance using these methods, some important considerations must be taken into account when putting together a linear training plan (Herodek, Simonovic, and Rakovic 2012). The proper manipulation of volume is necessary, and coaches must be sure to weigh the overall training volume (in-water swimming plus dryland training plus other stressors) to ensure that athletes do not become overtrained. Additionally, when following a model in which strength is built early in the year and then neglected for the sake of developing power later in the macrocycle, the swimmer may not be able to maintain strength gains across the season.

Within the classical, or linear, periodization model, the assumption is often made that little or no variation should occur within the plan (e.g., athletes progress consistently in exercise intensity, always going upward and forward, without much rest or variety in training load). In the purest sense of the linear periodized model, that approach is in fact the case. But in truth, variation of training volume and intensity can be added to various phases of the plan to stimulate additional gains while allowing multiple performance factors to be developed, or maintained, simultaneously. This type of periodization model is more often referred to as nonlinear, or undulating, periodization, and this approach is outlined in detail later.

Generally, the linear method is thought to be a good model for beginning athletes or those who are engaging in training for the first time, either in the weight room or the pool. This method of training starts with higher volume and lower-intensity exercise, and it facilitates the development of a foundation of strength, skill, and technique. The progression through the training plan promotes slow and stable adaptation as well as performance progression. The main drawback of the classical, or linear, method is that when attention is being devoted to the development of one physical attribute, the others potentially suffer.

Reverse Linear Periodization

Like the linear periodization model, the reverse linear plan follows a consistent shift in focus over the course of a macrocycle, although the approach is opposite what is seen in the classic model. Rather than focusing ultimately on power development, the goal of a reverse linear periodization plan for swimmers would be to maximize muscle endurance (Herodek, Sinonovic, and Rakovic 2012). The research in this area supports the idea that this technique is more effective than the classic, or linear, periodization model at building muscular endurance. The reverse linear periodization plan typically includes the following elements:

- Power phase, in which intensity is high
- Strength phase
- Moderate repetition phase
- Endurance phase, in which the focus in the weight room is on executing a large number of repetitions (20 to 30) of identified exercises at moderate intensity while also engaging in in-water training to complement the dryland training
- Active rest

At the end of the macrocycle, a swimmer should have greater muscular endurance that can help with performance in distance events.

Nonlinear, or Undulating, Periodization

Undulating, or nonlinear, periodization adds an aspect of variety to a training program by adjusting training variables more frequently than the linear model does (Herodek, Simonovic, and Rakovic 2012; Issurin 2008; Zatsiorsky and Kraemer 2006; Plisk and Stone 2003; Brown 2001). With an undulating program, the intensity, volume, exercise selection, and training modality change as often as every day of training. Even with variety, a linear increase or decrease can still occur in these variables over time. But one of the hallmarks of a true nonlinear model is that a consistent, linear progression in training parameters does not occur over time.

Another benefit of adopting an undulating approach is that although a mesocycle or microcycle may have a specific training focus, multiple training goals can be addressed simultaneously within a certain phase of training. This approach is beneficial to swimmers who compete frequently. In addition, a great deal of flexibility is available to make adaptations within a training block or a season.

Although variability is the greatest strength of the undulating model, it is also the greatest concern. A coach may develop a scattered plan that tries to address the development of too many performance variables at the same time. If the focus of training is spread too thinly across too many training modalities, the result will be suboptimal performance because not enough work will have been devoted to maximizing performance in any one area. Planned reduction in variation at certain times of the year can allow an athlete to focus on the development of a specific skill or set of skills and potentially accelerate development in those areas.

Is nonlinear periodization more successful than classical training design methods at developing athletes? The jury is still out, because many periodization training models have been shown to enhance performance. But a recent meta-analysis of periodized training programs suggests that undulating periodization may be superior to traditional linear programs when it comes to building strength. These findings can be extended to describe the development of other physical or physiological parameters as well.

Conjugated Method of Periodization

As mentioned, linear models of periodization typically take a sequential approach to training design because one performance variable is developed, followed by another, and another, and so on. Conjugated, or concurrent, methods of periodization seek to develop multiple, and sometimes all, abilities simultaneously. This doesn't necessarily mean that all abilities are developed in one training session, but they are developed with the same phase of training and across the entire training plan.

One potential problem with this approach is that efforts may become spread too thinly across too many areas. Abilities that need a greater focus, or volume of work, to develop may not be maximized with this approach. A variation to this method is to touch on all training factors throughout a mesocycle but to emphasize only one or a few of them during any one phase of training. This approach allows a swimmer to concentrate on a particular ability, or set of abilities, while maintaining others, reducing the fear that untrained attributes will regress.

On the surface, this approach seems similar to the linear periodization model. However, each microcycle and each mesocycle can include tremendous variation of volume, intensity, and exercise selection. Additionally, although each microcycle or mesocycle has a focus, that does not mean that other physical attributes can't be trained as well. The key to this approach is to emphasize and develop specific attributes while maintaining all others with minimal volume. With this approach, the athlete can optimally adapt to one stimulus while maintaining others and avoiding stagnation, overtraining, and fatigue. This focused method of periodization is based on the premise that an elite athlete is unable to adapt to and recover from a large number of stimuli at the same time. These athletes benefit more from a concentrated and focused effort on a particular ability. After some time, the emphasis can be switched to developing another ability.

Taken to the extreme, the focused conjugated approach to training design can lead to the development of what is called block periodization (Fevre, Gregory, and Matheny 2006; Issurin 2010). The general idea behind block periodization is that it uses sequenced, specialized mesocycle blocks in which highly concentrated training is provided to develop a minimal number of motor and technical abilities. The structured sequencing of specialized mesocycle blocks leverages and exploits residual training effects from prior blocks to develop physical and physiologic capacities more fully. Different mesocycles focus on attributes that build on one another, ultimately to optimize performance. These methods have been shown to elicit performance improvements in elite athletes across a number of sports. In fact, conjugated periodization is thought by some to be the preferential model of training for experienced athletes. As it relates specifically to swimming, block periodization methods have been employed to train Olympic and world champions (Touretski 2000; Pyne and Touretski 2003; Vorontsov 2011).

Phases of a Periodized Model

In most sports a competitive season can be broken into phases, each of which has a primary goal and training focus. Bompa (1999a, 1999b) and others identify three phases within a periodized plan and apply this general model to all sports and athletes:

1. Preparation phase, in which the focus is on building physical and physiological capacities

2. Competition phase, in which the focus is primarily on the maintenance of strength and performance through the competitive season

3. Transition phase, which is designed to provide a period of recovery while allowing athletes to transition from one season or macrocycle into another

Issurin (2008, 2010) also defines three phases, or mesocycles, within his description of block periodization:

1. Accumulation phase, which is devoted to developing basic abilities such as aerobic capacity, foundational strength, and movement technique

2. Transformation phase, which is focused on developing sport-specific abilities such as muscular endurance or power or building anaerobic capacity

3. Realization phase, which is dedicated to competition preparation and is focused on maximal speed, recovery, and race modeling

These three mesocycles are repeated throughout the year to enhance performance and allow multiple peaks throughout the season.

Swimming is somewhat different from other sports in the way that the competitive season is structured. The phases within the periodized model can be reworked to account for this. The model proposed by Bompa has been modified slightly to include one additional mesocycle:

Phase I: preparation phase focused on building a foundation of strength and preparing the body for the demands of training and competition

Phase II: training phase during which the focus shifts to building strength, power, endurance, and the sport-specific attributes needed for a swimmer to succeed in the water

Phase III: competition phase, which includes peaking for the major competition

Phase IV: transition or active rest phase in which athletes have an opportunity to recover, both physically and mentally, after a competitive season

Each phase serves a specific purpose in preparing the athlete for the unique demands of training and competition.

Phase I: Preparation Phase

At the start of the season, the schedule should include a period during which the training is focused on anatomical adaptation and building a foundation of general strength and conditioning to prepare the body for the intense training to come. Specifically, the preparatory phase should include the following goals:

- Build strength throughout the body, targeting all muscle groups but focusing on the muscles of the core and stabilizers, such as the scapular stabilizers, shoulder girdle, and hip complex.

- Develop balance throughout the body. Swimmers are subject to strength imbalances such as trunk flexors being stronger than trunk extensors and shoulder internal rotators being stronger than external rotators. This time should be used to balance the body by preferentially targeting the weaker muscle groups.

- Build a base of aerobic conditioning and have athletes become accustomed to the regularity of training, which includes regaining a feel for the water and developing warm-up and precompetition routines.

- Work on technique and stroke consistency and efficiency.

Typically, athletes enter into the preparation phase after a transition phase or a period of active rest. Essentially, the preparation phase serves as a time for athletes to refamiliarize themselves with the water and build strength and conditioning.

Phase II: Training Phase

The focus of the training phase is to develop increased levels of strength and conditioning as well as to translate that strength into sport-specific strength and conditioning that can enhance performance. Several specific guidelines should be followed during this phase:

- Training should be structured to build high levels of strength and establish a foundation of conditioning over 4 to 12 weeks. The duration of this phase depends on the structure of the season and the overall length of the macrocycle.

- The strength achieved in the initial weeks of this phase forms the foundation for the power needed by sprinters or the muscular endurance needed by distance swimmers. Peak performances likely will be determined by the work done in this phase.

- Toward the end of this phase, the focus should shift to developing power for sprinters or muscular endurance for distance athletes. Coaches should plan to devote four or five weeks to the development of power or six to eight weeks to allow the physical and physiological adaptations to take place for muscular endurance (Bompa 1999a, 1999b).

- In some programs, the training phase is further broken down into general and specific training elements. General preparation may focus on developing generic elements of fitness, such as building an aerobic base, whereas specific training develops swimming-specific strength and power while the swimmer also learns to apply that power to the water.

Phase III: Competition Phase

The competition phase represents the main part of the competitive season, culminating in the season-ending championship meet. Much of the focus of training in this phase is on maintaining strength and power gains made during the training phase and continuing the development of sport-specific skills.

Swimmers should build on the work put in during the training phase by making in-water training more event and stroke specific. Additional emphasis should be placed on swimming fast every day and working on race-specific speed and mechanics, such as stroke rates and cycle counts.

Strength training and conditioning work becomes more swimming and event specific, focusing on developing either muscular endurance or power. In general, power development necessitates increasing training intensity, decreasing volume, and incorporating power-based exercises into the training plan. To develop muscular endurance, swimmers have to execute a large number of repetitions of swimming-specific exercises against moderate to high resistance. Research has shown that periodized training using resisted and assisted sprint training can develop strength endurance in the pool and can be seen as an option for building those swimming-specific skills (Girold et al. 2006).

Training should be done with an intensity and a work-to-rest ratio that reflect the demands of the race to be swum. Strength maintenance and development should not be neglected during this phase because detraining can occur rapidly if strength training is stopped.

The emphasis leading up the championship meet should be recovery and energy replenishment as well as fine-tuning things in preparation for competition. Strength training should be scaled back and even cease in the week before the key competition of the year.

Research shows that detraining and performance decrements can occur within a week after training ceases. The maximum time that swimmers should be expected to hold at their peak is about three weeks. After that, performance decrements occur, so swimmers need to go back to the training phase or the start of the competition phase.

Phase IV: Transition Phase

At the end of the competitive season swimmers should take a mental and physical break to recover. Although recovery is the focus of this phase, it is not supposed to be a time of physical inactivity. Activity should be reduced by 60 to 70 percent, and athletes can engage in cross-training activities to provide training variety. Athletes should try to get in the pool every couple of days to maintain a feel for the water, but they do not need to engage in intense swimming workouts.

The longer that swimmers stay in the transition phase, the more likely they are to experience detraining effects such as loss of conditioning or strength. Although the individual characteristics of the athletes should determine the length of this phase, it should last at least two weeks to allow physical and mental recovery but not more than four to six weeks to minimize detraining.

If athletes choose to cease strength training during this phase, they should still engage in training the core and the stabilizer muscles throughout the body. This work will help minimize the time they need to spend regaining lost strength in the subsequent preparatory phase.

Remember that cycles should appear in each phase. For example, even a sprinter who is in the training phase focused on power development should have days in which the primary training focus is on developing muscular endurance. Cycling periods of work and rest that include manipulation of intensity and frequency and variation of exercises are important for staying fresh and achieving peak performances.

A coach who follows the approach of breaking a season into phases and focusing training to achieve certain goals within each phase can maximize the chances of achieving peak performances at the most important competitions throughout the year. Periodization produces better results than traditional training methods do for many reasons, but one of the most important aspects is that periodization incorporates planned periods of rest and recovery.

One common observation, even when swimmers are following a periodized plan, is that athletes typically go through a period of performance decline during the training and early competition phases. This decline manifests itself in the form of decreased power output (Sharp 1986) as measured with dry-land swim bench testing and decreased pulling force in the pool (Vorontsov 2011). These findings bring into focus the importance of rest not only within the training plan but also during the taper leading into the main competition.

When applied appropriately, periodization models can result in performance improvements in both the weight room and the pool. As one example, leading into the 2000 Sydney Olympic Games, Gennadi Touretski, coach of Alexander Popov and Michael Klim, used the block periodization method to prepare his swimmers to achieve world records in their respective events. Other coaches and scientists have shown that periodized models can be used to help swimmers attain peak performances (Pyne and Touretski 2003).

Rest and Recovery as Part of the Periodization Model

If swimmers train long enough and hard enough, their bodies will eventually tell them that they need to take a break. For some, it may be an illness that forces them to stop training. For others, it may be an injury. One of the major benefits of a periodized training plan is that rest and recovery are integral elements of the plan. Periods of rest are scheduled into each training microcycle, mesocycle, and macrocycle.

Within each week swimmers need to take time to allow the body to recover from the stress that they experience over the course of a microcycle. Most programs traditionally build one off day into the microcycle for rest and recovery. Other programs may take a slightly different approach and implement a four-to-one training schedule; athletes engage in four training sessions followed by one session off. For programs that hold two training sessions a day, athletes would have double practices on days 1 and 2 in the microcycle and only one workout on the third day.

Most athletes benefit by taking at least one full day off from training during each microcycle to allow additional time for recovery. Although most coaches incorporate one full day of rest into each training microcycle, others conduct training sessions every day of the week and have good results. Nevertheless, most believe that that some time away from the pool within each training week is valuable.

Understanding the Taper

The swimming season usually culminates in a taper period, a period of reduced training volume, leading up to a major competition. The purpose of the taper is to reduce the physical, physiological, mental, and emotional stress placed on the body so that it can fully recover by the time the major competition rolls around. Tapering is built into the culture of swimming, and some tapering is necessary for swimmers to fine-tune their technique and race strategy. But many coaches and athletes place too much importance on the taper and see it as the thing that makes or breaks the season.

In several ways, placing too much emphasis on the taper goes against the general philosophy of training periodization. Consider this: The theory behind the taper is that the swimmer has stressed the body so much that he needs to take an extended period to recover leading into the main competition. In a properly designed training plan, structured rest is built into the training, so the swimmer should never get to extreme levels of fatigue. A swimmer should be prepared to swim fast at any time during the season. The taper should provide that little bit extra to allow the swimmer to achieve a best race performance. Chapter 10 provides more in-depth information on how the taper should be structured.

Building a Periodized Training Plan

When putting together a periodized plan, the best approach is to build the plan backward. Start by identifying the major competitions during the year and then fill in the rest of the plan. Building a periodized training plan, especially for the first time, is an iterative process. Even a seasoned coach cannot be expected to get everything to line up and fit into the season correctly the first time the pen is put to paper. Follow these steps to put together a periodized program:

1. Identify the most important swimming meets of the season and work backward from there. Identify those competitions as well as any taper time leading up to them and block them out first.

2. Schedule active rest phases. Block out one to two weeks after each major competition to be used to cross-train and to take a break from swimming. Waiting to plan rest until everything else is put into the plan often results in the recovery time being left out of the schedule entirely.

3. Each active rest phase should be followed by an appropriate preliminary phase that will be used to get the swimmer back into the flow of swim training, both in the water and on dry land.

4. Map out a time following each preliminary phase to build foundational strength and conditioning and then transition to swimming-specific strength (the training phase). This part of the season can last longer and be broken into multiple mesocycles if the team or specific athletes have that luxury.

5. Lay out the competition phase for the season. This phase should last at least four weeks. The program continues to transition the athlete to building swimming-specific strength and power.

6. Become even more detailed in the planning. Outline the goals for each macrocycle, mesocycle, and microcycle. Although each training phase should have major themes, include variability and work that maintains the physical and physiological attributes that are not the primary focus of the training block.

Summary

Periodization offers the potential to add variety to training while eliciting improved results. Coaches should plan training to develop the necessary skills at the right time of the season. A poorly designed or poorly executed plan will not produce the desired results. Besides identifying the primary physical and physiological attributes to be developed, coaches need to provide athletes with variation in their workouts.

Coaches need to know their athletes and monitor how they respond to training. One of the strong points of periodization is that it allows flexibility and variability. Most approaches to periodization inherently assume that physical and physiological adaptations to training follow a predicable course and therefore that it is possible to predict how training phases will interact with others and build toward a specific goal.

Variation is key, but only to a point. Variation in volume, intensity, and other training variables provides a stimulus for the body to respond and adapt. But goals and areas of focus should change as a swimmer progresses through the season. Too much variation will not allow the targeted physiological or physical systems to be trained to their fullest (Kiely 2012).

Consider all the stresses and stimuli present in an athlete's life when putting together a plan. Be willing to adapt and make course corrections if things do not seem to be going in the right direction or at the desired pace.

Build the plan but don't be concerned if it is not perfect the first time. Few coaches are able to put together a seasonal plan and have all the elements fit together properly the first time they write things out. Do not think that you have to try the most complicated periodization model first. Start simple and build in complexity over time.

Maintain accurate records and logs of performance so that you can later evaluate the success or failure of certain training approaches. Do not be afraid to tap into the expertise of other professionals. Coaches need to wear many hats. If you can bring in someone who can help with seasonal planning or at least lend some advice, take advantage of the opportunity.

Consider that in-water and dryland training need to complement each other. Both aspects are typically factored into a plan when one coach runs the entire training program (although that may not always be the case). Things can go off the rails quickly if the dryland work does not complement what is done in the pool. This point applies to scheduling rest and recovery as much as it is does to devising a plan to develop strength, power, endurance, and technique.

The information presented here provides guidelines and specific information about designing and implementing a periodized training plan. Periodized programs provide several benefits, and coaches can design a plan in many ways. Take things easy and do not expect to become a master of periodization overnight. If you are able to incorporate even some of these elements into your training plan, your swimmers will benefit in both their health and their performance.

CHAPTER 10

The Effect of Tapering on Performance

—Iñigo Mujika, PhD, and Andrew M. Stewart, PhD

Information concerning the periodization of the training cycle within and between swimming seasons was presented in chapter 9. That chapter presented evidence about the need for coaches to adjust training variables such as volume and intensity to promote performance improvements and maximize race performance. Within a typical training cycle, swimmers place the body under tremendous stress to maximize the development of the physical and physiological capacities important for swimming performance. In preparation for the main competition, athletes typically engage in a period of relative rest, called the taper, to allow for recovery while also preparing themselves physically and mentally to perform at their best.

Most agree that the taper forms an integral phase within the program of any serious athlete's preparation for competition. Where debate does exist, it can be roughly summarized in four key areas:

1. The length of the taper for the individual athlete

2. The structure, or shape, of the taper

3. The optimal combination of training load within the most appropriate taper structure

4. The best way to prepare an athlete for multiple swims over different distances and strokes within any given competition and for competition in year-round events, specifically given the relatively recent addition of a global short-course season to the historical long-course calendar

All these areas depend to some extent on the training that takes place throughout the swimming season, in particular the phase of training (overload or overreaching) just before tapering. Each of these factors is considered in this chapter.

Taper Overview

As we begin, let us set the scene to make sure that we are speaking the same language of periodization and, in particular, tapering. Over the past few decades, authors and coaches have described the taper in various ways:

- A decrease in work level that the competitive swimmer undergoes during practice to rest and prepare for a good performance (Yamamoto, Mutoh, and Miyashita 1988)
- A specialized exercise training technique that has been designed to reverse training-induced fatigue without loss of training adaptations (Neary et al. 1992)
- An incremental reduction in training volume for 7 to 21 days before a championship race (Houmard and Johns 1994)
- A progressive, nonlinear reduction of the training load during a variable amount of time that is intended to reduce the physiological and psychological stress of daily training and optimize sport performance (Mujika and Padilla 2000)
- A segment of time when the training load is reduced before a competition in an attempt to peak performance at a target time (Thomas and Busso 2005)
- A time of reduced training volume and increased intensity that occurs before a competition (McNeely and Sandler 2007)

Clearly, people respond to tapering in different ways, depending on their individual profile of fatigue dissipation and fitness gain. Several factors require consideration, although they may or may not affect taper design:

- Age and possibly gender of swimmer
- The events for which the swimmer is being prepared (distance specific or stroke specific)
- The level at which the swimmer currently performs (for example, age group, national, elite)
- Whether the swimmer will undertake a full or partial taper in preparation for the targeted competition

Part of the art of coaching consists of manipulating training loads in the weeks before competition (during overload and taper) in the optimal way for each athlete. The remainder of this chapter offers a detailed look at how to optimize the effects of tapering for a given swimmer within a seasonal, periodized model.

Tapering Models

The term *taper* is now well known by all who prepare elite athletes for competition, and people throughout the world use it in reference to the final training phase leading up to a major race or competition event. But is everyone who speaks of tapering talking about the same training concept? The scientific literature indicates that they are not. Houmard (1991) clearly differentiated between the concepts of reduced training and tapering. This author indicated that reduced training occurs when training duration, frequency, intensity, or some combination of those elements is reduced by a constant degree. During tapering, on the other hand, these variables are decreased in a systematic, nonlinear fashion.

Four training designs or tapering models have been described and used in the past in an attempt to optimize sport performance, as shown in figure 10.1. The training load during the taper is usually reduced in a progressive manner, as implied by the term *taper*. This reduction can be carried out either linearly or exponentially. As shown in figure 10.1, a linear taper usually implies a higher total training load than an exponential taper. In addition, an exponential taper can have either a slow or a fast time constant of decay; the training load is usually higher in the slow decay taper. Nonprogressive standardized reductions of the training load have also been used (figure 10.1). This reduced training procedure, which often maintains but may even improve many of the physiological and performance adaptations gained with training (Mujika and Padilla 2003), is also referred to as a step taper (Banister, Carter, and Zarkadas 1999; Mujika 1998; Zarkadas, Carter, and Banister 1995).

A study by Thomas and colleagues (2009) used a nonlinear mathematical model to determine whether a two-phase taper is more effective than a simple progressive taper. Reponses to training were simulated from the model parameters previously determined in competitive swimmers (Thomas, Mujika, and Busso 2008). For each participant, the optimal progressive taper after a simulated

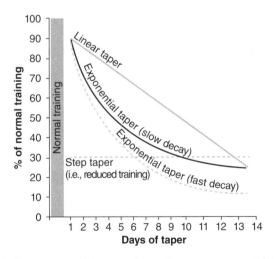

▶ **Figure 10.1** Various types of tapers: linear taper, exponential taper with slow or fast time constant of decay of the training load, and step taper (also referred to as reduced training).

Reprinted, by permission, from I. Mujika and S. Padilla, 2003, "Scientific bases for precompetition tapering strategies," *Medicine & Science in Sports & Exercise* 35(7): 1182–1187.

28-day overload training segment was compared with a two-phase taper of the same duration and the same reduction in training load, except during the last three days. In the final three days, the training load varied in a linear manner to elicit the best possible individual performance. As the authors had hypothesized, the highest performance was achieved after a moderate increase in the training load during the last three days of the taper. The optimal variation in the training load during the final three days of the two-phase taper was an increase from 35 percent (plus or minus 32 percent) to 49 percent (plus or minus 46 percent) of normal training in the swimmers (figure 10.2). Interestingly, for one of the swimmers, the optimal training load continued to decrease during the last three days of the two-phase taper, but it decreased less quickly than it did during the first phase and during the linear taper. This observation is a clear indication that not all athletes respond in the same manner to the training undertaken during the taper, which emphasizes the necessity to individualize the tapering strategies in accord with each athlete's adaptation profile. The major finding of the model study by Thomas and colleagues (2009) is that a moderate increase in training during the last few days of the taper does not appear to be detrimental to competition performance. A benefit of a two-phase taper could be expected in comparison with a simple linear taper because of additional adaptations that did not compromise the removal of fatigue. These findings should also be considered when preparing for competitions consisting of multiple rounds over several days, given that the successive qualifying rounds should increase the training load in the lead-up to the final (Thomas, Mujika, and Busso 2009).

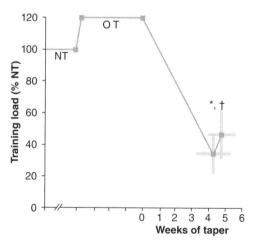

▶ **Figure 10.2** Changes in the training load during the normal training segment (NT), the overload training segment (OT), and the optimal two-phase taper in a group of elite swimmers. Values are mean plus or minus SE and are expressed in percentage of NT values.

Reprinted, by permission, from I. Mujika, 2009, *Tapering and peaking for optimal performance* (Champaign, IL: Human Kinetics), 12.

*Significantly greater than the final value of the first phase of the two-phase taper ($p < .05$).
†Significantly greater than the final value of the optimal linear taper ($p < .05$).

Performance Gains

Tapering-induced performance gains are usually in the range of 0.5 to 6.0 percent for competition performance measures (table 10.1). In an observational investigation on Olympic swimmers, Mujika, Padilla, and Pyne (2002) reported on the performance change in 99 individual swimming events during the final three weeks of training (generally coincident with the taper) in the lead-up to the Sydney 2000 Olympic Games. The overall performance change during the three weeks for all swimmers was 2.18 percent (plus or minus 1.50 percent), with a maximum loss of –1.14 percent and a maximum gain of 6.02 percent. Of the 99 performances analyzed, 91 were faster and only 8 were slower after the taper.

Table 10.1 Effects of the Taper on Performance in Trained Swimmers

Study and year	Athletes	Taper duration, days	Performance measure	Performance outcome, %
Costill et al. 1985	Swimmers	14	50- to 1,650-yard (46 to 1,509 m) competition	2.2–4.6 ↑
Cavanaugh and Musch 1989	Swimmers	28	50- to 1,650-yard (46 to 1,509 m) competition	2.0–3.8 ↑
Costill et al. 1991	Swimmers	14–21	Competition	≈3.2 ↑
D'Acquisto et al. 1992	Swimmers	14–28	100-meter, 400-meter time trial	4.0–8.0 ↑
Johns et al. 1992	Swimmers	10–14	50- to 400-yard (46 to 366 m) competition	2.0–3.7 ↑
Flynn et al. 1994	Swimmers	21	25-yard (23 m), 400-yard (366 m) time trial	≈3 ↑
Mujika et al. 1996b	Swimmers	28	100- to 200-meter competition	0.4–4.9 ↑
Raglin, Koceja, and Stager 1996	Swimmers	28–35	Competition	2.0 ↑
Taylor, Rogers, and Driver 1997	Swimmers	Not reported	Competition	1.3 ↑
Hooper, Mackinnon, and Ginn 1998	Swimmers	14	100-meter, 400-meter time trial	Unchanged
Kenitzer 1998	Swimmers	14–28	4 × 100-yard (91 m) submaximal set	≈4 ↑
Hooper, Mackinnon, and Howard 1999	Swimmers	14	100-meter time trial	Unchanged
Bonifazi, Sardella, and Luppo 2000	Swimmers	14–21	100- to 400-meter competition	1.5–2.1 ↑
Trappe, Costill, and Thomas 2001	Swimmers	21	Competition	3.0–4.7 ↑
Trinity et al. 2006	Swimmers	21	50-meter to 1,500-meter competition	4.5 ↑
Papoti et al. 2007	Swimmers	11	200-meter time trial	1.6 ↑

↑indicates improvement.
Adapted, by permission, from I. Mujika, 2009, *Tapering and peaking for optimal performance* (Champaign, IL: Human Kinetics), 90–91.

Performance improvements were not significantly different among events, and they ranged from 0.64 percent (plus or minus 1.48 percent) in 400-meter freestyle to 2.96 percent (plus or minus 1.08 percent) in 200-meter butterfly.

The 2.6 percent performance improvement attained during the taper by the male swimmers in the study by Mujika, Padilla, and Pyne (2002) was somewhat lower than some values previously published in the tapering literature. For example, Costill and colleagues (1985) reported a mean performance improvement of 3.1 percent as a result of a two-week taper in a group of 17 collegiate male swimmers. Studying a similar population of 24 college male swimmers tapering for two to three weeks, the same group of researchers observed a 3.2 percent gain in performance (Costill et al. 1991). Johns and colleagues (1992) also reported an average performance improvement of 2.8 percent (plus or minus 0.3 percent) with a 10- to 14-day taper.

Performance improvement differences between the studies mentioned in the previous paragraph and the study by Mujika, Padilla, and Pyne (2002) could be partly attributable to the higher performance level of the swimmers analyzed in the latter investigation. Indeed, some of the highest mean performance gains with taper (7.96 and 5.00 percent in 100 meters and 400 meters, respectively) have been reported in high school swimmers (D'Acquisto et al. 1992), whereas values of 2.6 percent (Cavanaugh and Musch 1989) and 2.32 percent (plus or minus 1.69 percent) (Mujika et al. 1996b) have been observed in national- and international-level male swimmers during tapers lasting four weeks. Bonifazi, Sardella, and Luppo (2000) analyzed the effects of a taper lasting two to three weeks in international-level male swimmers during two consecutive seasons. Performance improved by 1.48 percent during the first season and 2.07 percent during the second. Taken together, the results of these investigations indicate that the taper in international-level swimmers usually produces an average performance gain in the range of 1.5 to 2.5 percent. The study by Mujika, Padilla, and Pyne (2002) also evaluated performance improvement with the taper (final three weeks of training) in males and females participating in events of varying distance and showed no significant difference between any of the analyzed swimming distances, which suggests that the metabolic contribution to energy provision during competition, which varies with racing distance, does not affect the potential gain that can be obtained during a three-week taper. Similarly, the comparison between freestyle and form (backstroke, breaststroke, butterfly, and individual medley) events showed no differences in the magnitude of performance improvement, suggesting that technical and biomechanical aspects of competition do not necessarily affect the performance outcome of a taper. In addition, performance change with the taper was not significantly different among swimmers from the 14 countries represented in the sample, ranging from 0.13 percent (plus or minus 0.28 percent) for Nigerian swimmers to 3.98 percent (plus or minus 2.18 percent) for swimmers representing Swaziland.

Performance improvements regardless of the specific event have been reported by several authors. In male swimmers, Costill and colleagues (1985) observed gains ranging from 2.2 percent in 100-yard (91 m) freestyle (*n* = 2) and 200-yard (182 m) butterfly (*n* = 3), and 4.6 percent in 200-yard (182 m) individual medley (*n* = 5). Johns and colleagues (1992) reported a minimum gain of 2.0 percent in 100-yard (91 m) breaststroke (*n* = 1) and a maximum gain of 3.7 percent in 100-yard (91 m) (*n* = 5) and 200-yard (182 m) freestyle (*n* = 2). Similar values, from 2.0 percent (*n* = 6) to 3.8 percent (*n* = 4), were reported by Cavanaugh and Musch (1989) for 50-yard freestyle and 200-yard (182 m) breaststroke, respectively. All of these were similar to the 1.73 percent and 3.25 percent gains observed in 50-meter (*n* = 4) and 200-meter freestyle (*n* = 6) respectively for males in the study by Mujika, Padilla, and Pyne (2002). Again, these results support the notion that tapering elicits a relatively consistent improvement across different competitive swimming events.

Given the typical performance gains cited here, it is appropriate to look at which aspects of the training program are manipulated during the taper to derive such improvements. Of the variations in frequency, intensity, and volume (total meters swum and dryland training) that can occur during taper, the evidence is overwhelming that the key to performance gains is to maintain intensity (at least) while undergoing some reduction in other aspects of the program.

Intensity

Numerous reviews highlight the importance of training intensity during a taper (Houmard and Johns 1994; Kubukeli, Noakes, and Dennis 2002; Mujika 1998; Neufer 1989). Such a finding is not just scientific rhetoric; it is also found in best practice application by coaches. Mujika and colleagues (1996a) monitored weekly swimming distance performed at various intensity levels by 18 national- and international-caliber swimmers in the four weeks preceding the taper and during each of the three tapers performed by the athletes during a season. As shown in table 10.2, during the first taper of the season (which lasted three weeks), the swimmers reduced their weekly distance swum at moderate and maximal intensity. During the second taper (four weeks), weekly distances at all levels of intensity were reduced. During the final taper (six weeks), only moderate- and high-intensity swimming was reduced. Stewart and Hopkins (2000) provided a detailed account of the training practices of 24 swim coaches and 185 sprint (50- and 100-meter) and middle-distance (200- and 400-meter) swimmers over a summer and winter season in New Zealand. Interval training intensity and rest duration of interval workouts increased during the taper for sprinters and middle-distance specialists, whereas interval distance decreased. In this study, the authors noted that the average training program reflected principles of specificity, particularly during the taper phase.

Volume

Several studies (Mujika et al. 1995; Stewart, Hopkins, and Sanders 1997; Stewart and Hopkins 2000) have shown that the reduction in training volume during

Table 10.2 Swimming Training Before and During Each of the Three Tapers (Mean Plus or Minus Standard Deviation)

Training intensity	TAPER 1 Before (4 wk)	TAPER 1 During (3 wk)	TAPER 2 Before (4 wk)	TAPER 2 During (4 wk)	TAPER 3 Before (4 wk)	TAPER 3 During (6 wk)
I	27.28 ± 6.79	25.55 ± 5.20	25.96 ± 6.68	20.05 ± 3.96*	22.34 ± 5.24	17.76 ± 4.78
II	5.78 ± 2.62	1.12 ± 0.90**	4.95 ± 2.32	0.65 ± 0.71**	2.79 ± 1.41	1.47 ± 0.87
III	2.55 ± 1.10	0.89 ± 0.61**	2.69 ± 0.82	1.01 ± 0.52**	3.10 ± 1.09	1.55 ± 0.51**
IV	1.27 ± 0.32	1.02 ± 0.30	1.32 ± 0.42	0.92 ± 0.26*	1.43 ± 0.39	1.09 ± 0.31*
V	0.43 ± 0.11	0.29 ± 0.07*	0.38 ± 0.08	0.25 ± 0.06*	0.28 ± 0.09	0.27 ± 0.18

Intensity I = 2 mmol/L; intensity II = 4 mmol/L; intensity III = 6 mmol/L; intensity IV = 10 mmol/L; intensity V = sprint training. $^*p < .05$; $^{**}p < .001$.

Reprinted, by permission, from I. Mujika, T. Busso, L. Lacoste, et al., 1996, "Modeled responses to training and taper in competitive swimmers," *Medicine & Science in Sports & Exercise* 28(2): 251–258.

the taper was related to competition performance. Mujika et al. (1995) found a reasonably positive relationship between percentage improvement in performance during taper and percentage reduction in training volume during taper (figure 10.3). Stewart and Hopkins (2000) found a similar result with reductions in mean weekly volumes and session training volumes for sprint and middle-distance swimmers as the taper progressed. The authors noted that substantial reductions occurred in all measures of training distance (except easy swimming, which actually increased when represented as a percentage of the total workout during taper) from the start of the season (buildup phase) to the end of tapering for both sprinters and middle-distance swimmers. Similar positive effects on performance have been found in other studies of swimming, running, cycling,

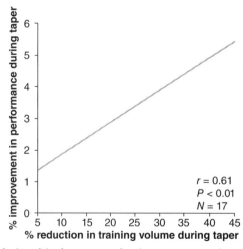

▶ **Figure 10.3** Relationship between the improvement in performance during a three-week taper and the percentage reduction in training volume during taper (mean pretaper weekly volume versus mean weekly volume of the three weeks of taper) in a group of elite swimmers.

Republished by permission of Canadian Science Publishing from I. Mujika, J.C. Chatard, T. Busso, et al., 1995, "Effects of training on performance in competitive swimming," *Canadian Journal of Applied Physiology* 20(2): 401. Permission conveyed through Copyright Clearance Center, Inc.

triathlon, and strength training (Houmard and Johns 1994; McNeely and Sandler 2007; Mujika 1998; Mujika and Padilla 2003).

Bosquet et al. (2007) conducted a meta-analysis of the influence of training volume on taper-induced changes in swimming, running, and cycling (table 10.3). Bosquet and colleagues confirmed previous research in this area of the positive performance effects of reduced training volume. With particular reference to swimming, such reductions appear to be optimized at about 41 to 60 percent of pretaper training values (figure 10.4). Such reductions appear consistent with those found by Stewart and Hopkins (2000) and those suggested by Houmard and Johns (1994) and Mujika and Padilla (2003).

Frequency

One area of prescription in which some discrepancy seems to occur between studies is frequency. Moreover, variations in reported frequency of taper workouts appear to be related to the level at which the athlete competes (e.g., age

Table 10.3 Effect of Decreasing Training Volume During the Taper on Overall Effect Size for Taper-Induced Changes in Swimming, Running, and Cycling Performance

Decrease in training volume	SWIMMING Mean (95% confidence interval)	n	RUNNING Mean (95% confidence interval)	n	CYCLING Mean (95% confidence interval)	n
≤ 20%	−0.04 (−0.36, 0.29)	72	No data available		0.03 (−0.62, 0.69)	18
21-40%	0.18 (−0.11, 0.47)	91	0.47 (−0.05, 1.00)**	30	0.84 (−0.05, 1.74)**	11
41-60%	0.81 (0.42, 1.20)*	70	0.23 (−0.52, 0.98)	14	2.14 (−1.33, 5.62)	15
≥ 60%	0.03 (−0.66, 0.73)	16	0.21 (−0.14, 0.56)	66	0.56 (−0.24, 1.35)	36

*$p \leq .01$; **$p \leq .10$

Data reprinted, by permission, from L. Bosquet, J. Monpetit, D. Arvisais, and I. Mujika, 2007, "Effects of tapering on performance: A meta-analysis," *Medicine & Science in Sports & Exercise* 39(8): 1358–1365.

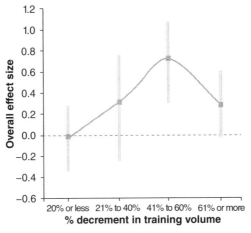

▶ **Figure 10.4** Dose-response curve for the effect of percent decrement in training volume during the taper on performance.

Reprinted, by permission, from L. Bosquet, J. Monpetit, D. Arvisais, and I. Mujika, 2007, "Effects of tapering on performance: A meta-analysis," *Medicine & Science in Sports & Exercise* 39(8): 1358–1365.

group or international level). Stewart and Hopkins (2000) reported little change in training frequency (except during postcompetition phases) throughout the season for sprint and middle-distance swimmers. Age of swimmer also played little part in the training prescription; the authors noted that most coaches simply grouped swimmers together by ability, regardless of age. The performance of swimmers in this study was approximately 80 percent of world-record pace, which is certainly not elite, but the swimmers were typically around 15 years old. Whether the effects of reducing training frequency are any different in more experienced athletes is not yet known, but after an inconclusive study of the effects of differing training frequencies on performance in middle-distance runners, Mujika et al. (2002a) concluded that athletes might have experienced a loss of feel on a restricted training regime. If so, such a situation is likely to be exacerbated in swimming given the higher degree of technicality required in that sport (McNeely and Sandler 2007; Mujika and Padilla 2003) and the difficulty in breaking a typically historical habit of double daily workouts on most days of the week for most of the season (Costill et al. 1991; Stewart and Hopkins 2000).

According to Bosquet et al. (2007), decreased training frequency has shown fairly insubstantial effects on swimming, running, and cycling performance improvements (table 10.4). The authors did highlight that the effects of decreased training frequency are partially related to training volume and intensity, which makes it difficult to isolate the precise effect of a reduction in training frequency on performance. In the study by Stewart and Hopkins (2000), the authors conducted partial correlations for most of the training effects to account for age of the swimmer. No such correlational studies have been conducted on the intricate variations of the training prescription (intensity, rest intervals, volume, frequency) on each other.

Duration

Working out the precise duration of taper for individual athletes has to be one of the biggest challenges to coaches and scientists. Part of the consideration of the optimal taper length for an individual athlete is the training status of the

Table 10.4 Effect of Decreasing or Not Decreasing Training Frequency During the Taper on Overall Effect Size for Taper-Induced Changes in Swimming, Running, and Cycling Performance

Decrease in training fre-quency	SWIMMING		RUNNING		CYCLING	
	Overall effect size, mean (95% confidence interval)	n	Overall effect size, mean (95% confidence interval)	n	Overall effect size, mean (95% confidence interval)	n
Yes	0.35 (−0.36, 1.05)	54	0.16 (−0.17, 0.49)	74	0.95 (−0.48, 2.38)	25
No	0.30 (0.10, 0.50)*	195	0.53 (0.05, 1.01)**	36	0.55 (−0.05, 1.15)***	55

*$p \leq .01$; **$p \leq .05$; ***$p \leq .10$

Data reprinted, by permission, from L. Bosquet, J. Monpetit, D. Arvisais, and I. Mujika, 2007, "Effects of tapering on performance: A meta-analysis," *Medicine & Science in Sports & Exercise* 39(8): 1358–1365.

athlete at the end of the phase just before tapering. Generally, we agree with the suggestion of Kubukeli, Noakes, and Dennis (2002) that an athlete who ends the high workload phase on the edge will require a longer taper than someone who can still make further positive adaptation to overload. This suggestion has been confirmed by a computer simulation study carried out by Thomas, Mujika, and Busso (2008), who suggested that the training performed in the lead-up to the taper greatly influences the optimal individual duration of the taper. A 20 percent increase over normal training during 28 days before the taper requires a step reduction in training of about 65 percent during three weeks, instead of two weeks when no overload training is performed. A progressive taper, however, requires a smaller reduction of training over a longer duration than a step taper does, whatever the pretaper training. The effect of the pretaper training on the duration of the optimal taper seems obvious in regard to the reduction of the accumulated fatigue.

Mujika and Padilla (2003) reported positive physical and psychological effects of tapers that lasted from 10 days up to 5 weeks for swimmers. Note that the taper is not just about preparing physically for the upcoming competition; the psychological aspect could be at least as important as the physical preparation. Most coaches can recount anecdotes of swimmers who were physically ready for the main competition but performed below expectations because they were mentally unprepared (only to perform as expected, if not better, in a minor competition when the pressure was off). On the flip side, we are sure that in plenty of instances an athlete has been ready to perform a few days before the main event but then was not be able to sustain or re-create the focus for the big day.

Stewart and Hopkins (2000) reported on the typical length of taper over consecutive summer and winter seasons for a large group of sprint-trained (50 and 100 meters) and middle-distance trained swimmers in New Zealand. The coaches of those swimmers reported typical taper durations of nearly four weeks for sprinters and about one week less for middle-distance swimmers. Detailed study by the authors of the training prescription in a specialty phase before tapering indicated a less-than-optimal program of specificity leading into the taper. As such, swimmers in that study may have derived further training adaptations before tapering, which may have then affected the duration of the taper undertaken. Without further detailed investigation, the optimum taper duration for an individual athlete is still somewhat of a mystery.

Bosquet and colleagues (2007) found a dose-response relationship between the duration of the taper and the improvement in performance (table 10.5 and figure 10.5). A taper duration of 8 to 14 days was the borderline between the positive influence of fatigue withdrawal and the negative influence of losing adaptation (detraining). Although athletes could expect improvements in performance following tapers lasting 1, 3, or 4 weeks, tapers of such duration could possibly have a negative effect. Given that individual athletes vary in physiological and psychological makeup, that such athletes respond differently to different training programs, and that an overload phase may or may not be used before tapering, several authors have concluded that the taper duration must be individually determined for each athlete to optimize performance gains (Bosquet et al. 2007; Mujika et al. 1996a).

Millet et al. (2005) used mathematical modeling to describe the relationships between training loads and anxiety and perceived fatigue as a new method for assessing the effects of training on the psychological status of the athletes. They observed that the time for self-perceived fatigue to return to its baseline level was 15 days, which was close to the time modeled by previous researchers as optimal for tapering (Busso, Candau, and Lacour 1994; Busso et al. 2002; Fitz-Clarke, Morton, and Banister 1991). The authors of this investigation and other similar studies concluded that the use of a simple questionnaire to assess anxiety and perceived fatigue could also be used to adjust the optimal duration of tapering (Chatard et al. 2003; Hooper and MacKinnon 1995; Hooper et al. 1995; Hooper, MacKinnon, and Hanrahan 1997; Millet et al. 2005).

Table 10.5 Effect of Taper Duration on Overall Effect Size of Taper-Induced Changes in Swimming, Running, and Cycling Performance

Duration of the taper	SWIMMING Mean (95% confidence interval)	n	RUNNING Mean (95% confidence interval)	n	CYCLING Mean (95% confidence interval)	n
≤7 days	−0.03 (−0.41, 0.35)	54×	0.31 (−0.08, 0.70)	52	0.29 (−0.12, 0.70)	47
8–14 days	0.45 (−0.01, 0.90)***	84	0.58 (0.12, 1.05)*	38	1.59 (−0.01, 3.19)**	33
15–21 days	0.33 (0.00, 0.65)**	75	−0.08 (−0.95, 0.80)	10	No data available	
≥22 days	0.39 (−0.08, 0.86)	36	−0.72 (−1.63, 0.19)	10	No data available	

$*p \leq .01$; $**p \leq .05$; $***p \leq .10$
Reprinted, by permission, from L. Bosquet, J. Monpetit, D. Arvisais, and I. Mujika, 2007, "Effects of tapering on performance: A meta-analysis," *Medicine & Science in Sports & Exercise* 39(8): 1358–1365.

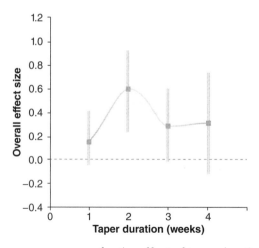

▶ **Figure 10.5** Dose-response curve for the effect of taper duration on performance.
Reprinted, by permission, from L. Bosquet, J. Monpetit, D. Arvisais, and I. Mujika, 2007, "Effects of tapering on performance: A meta-analysis," *Medicine & Science in Sports & Exercise* 39(8): 1358–1365.

Pooling all the literature regarding the intensity, volume, frequency, and duration of the taper, the consensus appears to be that tapering for approximately one to three weeks with a high-intensity, low-volume training program produces the greatest contribution to performance. During the taper, maintenance of training intensity appears to be necessary to avoid detraining, provided that reductions in other training characteristics allow sufficient recovery to optimize performance. But coaches and athletes should not use the taper as a time to increase total sprinting distance in training. As other components of training load (particularly volume) are reduced, the absolute amount of sprinting must also be reduced during the taper to allow time for recovery. The subtlety in the art of effective tapering is that the percentage of total training volume prescribed as high-intensity training may increase up to (but not beyond) some critical threshold for the individual swimmer. The optimum shape of the taper appears to be one in which overall training load is reduced in either a linear or preferably an exponential pattern.

Prior Training

Strong evidence suggests that performance improves if high training loads are prescribed for a period of one to three weeks just before the taper (Lehmann et al. 1991, 1992; Morgan et al. 1987; Morgan and Costill 1987; Morgan et al. 1988; O'Connor et al. 1989; Raglin, Koceja, and Stager 1996; Ripol 1993; Snyder et al. 1993). Although such training appears to have a positive influence (figures 10.6 through 10.9), it also engenders a state of fatigue that should such training continue for too long, it would probably lead to a deterioration in performance, longer-term fatigue, and potentially an inability to recover in time for competition (Bannister et al. 1975; Bannister and Calvert 1980; Bannister 1991; Boobis 1987; Calvert et al. 1976; Hultman et al. 1990; Karlsson et al. 1981; Morton, Fitz-Clarke, and Banister 1990; Morton 1991; Mujika et al. 1996a; Stewart, Shearman, and Hopkins 2000).

When an athlete starts to show signs of a plateau in adaptation or an adverse change occurs in the psychology of the swimmer, the taper should commence. As noted earlier, athletes respond to the taper in different ways and tapers do not work the same way for all swimmers. Coaches and scientists need to work together to determine the optimal type of taper and its duration for each swimmer. Although logistics need to be considered (many athletes training at the same time under the guidance of one or a small number of coaches), a well-designed overload and taper phase could feasibly have different athletes being prescribed different workouts at different times to account for different needs and adaptations.

A number of possible explanations may account the effect of tapering (figures 10.6 through 10.9). A high-load workout produces a greater training stimulus than a low-load workout (Bannister et al. 1975; Bannister and Calvert 1980; Bannister 1991; Calvert et al. 1976; Fitz-Clarke, Morton, and Banister 1991; Morton, Fitz-Clarke, and Banister 1990; Morton 1991; Mujika et al. 1996a), but hard training is accompanied by greater fatigue than the fatigue associated with

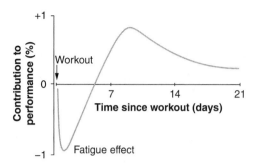

► **Figure 10.6** Contribution of a single workout to subsequent performance.

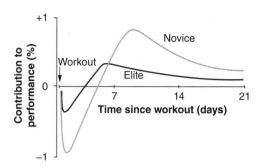

► **Figure 10.7** Contribution of a workout to performance in novice and elite athletes.

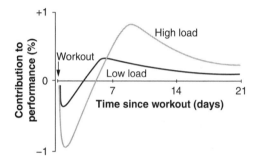

► **Figure 10.8** Contribution of a high- and low-load workout to performance.

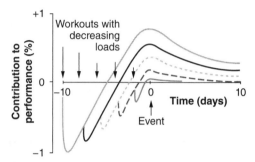

► **Figure 10.9** The way in which tapering maximizes performance for an event (for simplicity, workouts on days 9, 7, 5, and 3 are omitted).

low- or moderate-intensity training (Bannister et al. 1975; Bannister 1991; Busso et al. 1990; Calvert et al. 1976; Fry et al. 1992; Morton, Fitz-Clarke, and Banister 1990; Morton 1991). Evidence also shows that the greater fatigue associated with high-intensity training decays at a much slower rate than the fatigue that accompanies low-intensity training and that fatigue decays faster than fitness (Bannister et al. 1975; Bannister 1991; Calvert et al. 1976; Fitz-Clarke, Morton, and Banister 1991; Morton, Fitz-Clarke, and Banister 1990; Morton 1991; Mujika et al. 1996a). Thus, the various taper models that have been described previously are designed to maintain as much as possible the positive effects of training while allowing fatigue to dissipate in time for competition. Optimal performance is probably obtained when the difference between fitness and fatigue is at a maximum (figure 10.10), when swimmers feel fresh and energized and when they have mentally prepared for competition (Bannister and Calvert 1980; Colwin 1995; McNeely and Sandler 2007; Raglin, Koceja, and Stager 1996; Wittig, Houmard, and Costill 1989).

In essence, a partnership of scientist, coach, and athlete is the best approach to individualizing any given taper. The team may need to work together for years before an athlete can be prepared optimally for the exact day of competition when the peak performance is required. Over such time, some experimenta-

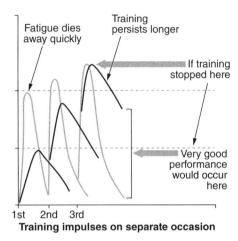

▶ **Figure 10.10** Growth and decay of fitness and fatigue in response to impulses of training on separate occasions.

Reprinted, by permission, from E.W. Banister and T.W. Calvert, 1980, "Planning for future performance: Implications for long term training," *Canadian Journal of Applied Sports Science* 5: 172.

tion involving trial-and-error approaches will likely occur. Eventually, it will be possible to work backward from the time of competition, knowing how long the taper will be and how long the overload phase will be before the taper. The combination of these two events will lead the coach–athlete–scientist team to pinpoint to the day when the overload phase should begin as the final lead-in preparation for competition.

Biological Source of Performance Gains

Now let's look at some of the biological mechanisms that underpin the effects of the taper. In this section we also present information and provide guidance about what to look for to avoid adverse effects of training, particularly during the overload and taper phases.

Cardiorespiratory System

Given the role that the cardiovascular and respiratory systems play during training, they should respond to tapered training with considerable structural and functional changes despite the relatively short duration of the taper typically performed by well-trained swimmers. The most widely used index of cardiovascular and respiratory fitness is the maximal oxygen uptake, or $\dot{V}O_2$. Research shows that $\dot{V}O_2$ can increase or remain unchanged during tapering before competition in highly trained athletes. In a study with high school swimmers who tapered for either two or four weeks, both groups improved their swimming time-trial performance by 4 to 8 percent, but $\dot{V}O_2$max was unchanged (D'Acquisto et al. 1992). Van Handel and colleagues (1988) also reported stable $\dot{V}O_2$max values (65.4 pretaper versus 66.6 ml · kg^{-1} · min^{-1} posttaper) in college-aged swimmers (including Olympic medal winners) who tapered for 20 days leading up to the U.S. National Championships. Unfortunately, performance outcomes were not reported in that investigation.

Improvements in economy of movement have also been reported in swimming, but these gains appear to be inversely related to the caliber of the athletes. High school male and female swimmers who tapered for 2 or 4 weeks showed downward shifts in their $\dot{V}O_2$–velocity curves (i.e., improved economy) of between 4.9 and 15.6 percent and between 8.5 and 16.7 percent, respectively, at a range of swimming velocities (D'Acquisto et al. 1992). The authors suggested that changes in economy were dependent on reductions in training volume, and they speculated that the taper had a beneficial effect on biomechanics, allowing the swimmers to develop better stroke mechanics (D'Acquisto et al. 1992). Johns and colleagues (1992) also reported declines of 5 to 8 percent in the oxygen cost of swimming after 10 or 14 days of taper in intercollegiate swimmers. In contrast, Van Handel and colleagues (1988) failed to observe any tapering-induced changes in the economy curves of swimmers of much higher caliber, who were described as considerably more economical than less-skilled swimmers.

Few reports are available on the effects of tapering on athletes' resting heart rate (HR), but the consensus of investigators is that resting HR does not appear to change during this phase of training. Unchanged resting HR values were observed by Flynn and colleagues (1994) before and after three weeks of taper in collegiate swimmers (54 versus 55 beats per minute). In line with these results, stable resting HRs were observed in a group of international-level swimmers who tapered for two weeks (Hooper, Mackinnon, and Howard 1999).

Results from investigations that address the effects of taper on maximal HR are not consistent, and values have variously been shown to decrease, remain constant, or increase after a taper. For instance, D'Acquisto and colleagues (1992) reported lower maximal HR in swimmers after tapers lasting two weeks (187 versus 192 beats per minute) or four weeks (185 versus 194 beats per minute). In contrast, maximal HR increased slightly after two weeks of taper in Australian swimmers (Hooper, Mackinnon, and Howard 1999).

Most of the available literature on the effects of the taper on submaximal exercise HR indicates few changes. No change in HR was observed by D'Acquisto and colleagues (1992) when swimmers were required to swim at submaximal velocities ranging from 1.0 to 1.3 meters per second before and after two or four weeks of taper. Costill and colleagues (1985) reported unchanged postexercise HR after an evenly paced 200-yard (182 m) swim at a speed representing 90 percent of an individual season's best performance after one and two weeks of taper.

Published reports on the effects of a taper on resting blood pressure (BP) failed to show any substantial effect of tapering on BP. Flynn and colleagues (1994) reported pre- and posttaper systolic BP values of 118 and 116 millimeters of mercury in five male swimmers. Diastolic pressures were 76 and 78 millimeters of mercury for the swimmers. Hooper, Mackinnon, and Howard (1999) reported modest declines of 3.4 and 2.2 percent in systolic and diastolic pressures during the taper and standard deviations of 12.5 and 12.2 percent, respectively.

Red Blood Cells

The taper can be accompanied by a positive balance between exercise-induced hemolysis and the recovery-facilitated generation of new red blood cells. Hemoglobin concentration and hematocrit increased during the taper in competitive swimmers (Burke et al. 1982a; Rushall and Busch 1980; Yamamoto, Mutoh, and Miyashita 1988). These results were attributed to decreased hemolysis and a net increase in erythrocytes, presumably facilitated by the reduced training load that characterizes tapering (Houmard 1991; Houmard and Johns 1994; Mujika et al. 1998; Neufer 1989; Shepley et al. 1992).

With respect to the possible influence of the observed hematological changes on performance, Mujika and colleagues (1998) observed a 2.3 percent mean competition performance improvement in tapered swimmers, and they found a positive correlation between posttaper red cell count and the percentage improvement in performance attained by the swimmers during taper. Red cell count, hemoglobin, and hematocrit increased by 3.5, 1.8, and 3.3 percent, respectively, in the swimmers for whom the taper was most effective, whereas decreases of 2.2, 4.3, and 2.1 percent occurred in those athletes who improved less with the taper. The authors suggested that the net increase in erythrocyte values observed in the successful swimmers during the taper could have been in part responsible for the higher performance improvement attained, given that small percentage increases in hemoglobin or hematocrit values can result in worthwhile improvements in $\dot{V}O_2$max and exercise capacity (Gledhill 1982, 1985).

Energy Metabolism

Energy metabolism underpinning exercise performance can be altered during a preevent taper. Decreases in training load in favor of rest and recovery lower an athlete's daily energy expenditure, potentially affecting energy balance and body composition. Substrate availability and utilization, blood lactate kinetics, muscle glycogen content, and other metabolic variables may also be altered during the taper.

D'Acquisto and colleagues (1992) reported the body mass and percent body fat of female swimmers before and after two- and four-week tapers. These researchers observed that neither variable changed significantly. Additional studies have reported stability in body mass in collegiate swimmers after a three-week taper consisting of a 20 to 33 percent weekly reduction in training volume (Flynn et al. 1994). Similarly, collegiate swimmers maintained their body mass during the taper preparing for the final meet of the season (Van Handel et al. 1988). This study, however, did not report the possible changes in fat mass and muscle mass of the swimmers.

Along with the previously mentioned metabolic changes, blood lactate kinetics may also be affected by a tapered training interval, during both maximal and submaximal exercise. Peak blood lactate concentration after maximal exercise can increase because of tapering. This change, which could be related to an increased posttaper muscle glycogen concentration by a mass-action effect (Houmard et al. 1994), might underpin enhanced maximal performance. Indeed, significant relationships between increases in peak postrace blood lactate levels and competition performance enhancement ($r = 0.63$) were seen in international-level swimmers during two consecutive seasons (Bonifazi, Sardella, and Luppo 2000). Competitive high school female swimmers increased their peak blood lactate concentration by 20 percent after taper programs that induced time-trial performance gains of 4 to 8 percent (D'Acquisto et al. 1992). Van Handel and colleagues (1988) also showed modest changes in peak lactate concentrations in collegiate swimmers preparing for national championships (6.9 to 7.5 mM). In contrast, Papoti and colleagues (2007) reported statistically unchanged peak blood lactate values in 16-year-old swimmers tapering for 11 days (peak blood lactate of 6.8 and 7.2 mM before and after the taper, respectively). These authors speculated that the taper promoted intramuscular creatine phosphate supercompensation (Papoti et al. 2007).

Blood lactate concentration at submaximal exercise intensity shows variable responses after the taper. Kenitzer (1998) described a decrease in blood lactate concentration at 80 percent of maximal HR during the first 2 weeks of a taper in female swimmers but a subsequent increase during weeks 3 and 4, leading to the tentative conclusion that 2 weeks was the optimum taper duration. In contrast, D'Acquisto and colleagues (1992) observed reduced blood lactate values during submaximal swimming in high school females who tapered for either 2 weeks (15 to 26 percent decline) or 4 weeks (26 to 33 percent decline). These results are consistent with those of Costill and colleagues (1985), who described a 13 percent reduction in submaximal lactate, in parallel with a mean 3.1 percent swimming performance improvement in competition after a 2-week taper. In contrast with investigators who reported higher blood lactates, Johns and colleagues (1992) failed to observe any change in blood lactate concentration in collegiate swimmers who tapered for either 10 or 14 days before a major competition (Johns et al. 1992). Van Handel and colleagues (1988) reported a subtle shift of the blood lactate–swimming velocity curve back to the left after taper. Inconsistent findings may be related to the duration and type of training performed during the taper.

Muscle glycogen concentration has been shown to increase progressively during tapering in cycling and running (Neary et al. 1992; Neary, Martin, and Quinney 2003; Shepley et al. 1992; Walker et al. 2000), but no such studies are available for swimming.

Biochemical Markers

Few biochemical parameters exhibit marked changes during the preevent taper, limiting their utility as markers of physiological recovery and increased performance capacity. One of the most widely used and studied biochemical markers of training stress is the concentration of creatine kinase (CK) in the blood. Blood levels of CK have been used as an index of training-induced physiological stress. CK is a muscle enzyme that occasionally increases in the blood following strenuous or eccentric exercise, probably because of altered permeability of tissue cell membranes. Factors that influence the degree of CK efflux into the blood include exercise duration and intensity, exercise mode, and fitness level of the individual (Millard et al. 1985). Various studies have shown decreases in CK levels during the taper. After studying 10 male and 10 female collegiate swimmers before and after a four-week taper, Millard et al. (1985) noted a 70 percent lower posttraining and a 30 percent lower resting serum CK after the taper in the males and 28 and 7 percent lower values in the females. Absolute posttaper CK values were not different between genders and fell to their lowest levels of the season during the taper. These results suggested that CK levels reflect training volume rather than intensity. Yamamoto, Mutoh, and Miyashita (1988) also observed decreased CK levels after swimming tapers correlating with the daily workout volume during the taper. Flynn and colleagues (1994) described a CK reduction of 38 percent during three weeks of taper. Mujika and colleagues (1996c) also reported a 43 percent decline in plasma CK during a four-week taper, but this decline did not relate well with swimming performance improvements, which ranged from 0.4 to 4.9 percent. Costill and colleagues (1991) measured 28 percent lower CK values after two to three weeks of taper, which resulted in an average performance improvement of 3.2 percent. Burke and colleagues (1982b) also observed a decline in CK levels after the taper in swimmers, but their values remained in the high to normal range.

In contrast to studies that showed lower CK values after the taper, a study by Hooper, Mackinnon, and Howard (1999) showed a statistically nonsignificant 17 percent increase in plasma CK during a two-week taper and large interindividual variation among swimmers. These authors argued that plasma CK is not a reliable marker of training stress and reflects an acute response to a single exercise session rather than an athlete's homeostatic status. They also suggested that the large interindividual variation could indicate large differences in athletes' physiological responses to the taper. The published literature appears to suggest that plasma CK values could be of some interest to assess recovery from acute training stress and muscle damage during the taper, but the validity of this parameter as a marker of an individual athlete's performance capabilities seems limited.

Costill and colleagues (1985) did not detect any taper-induced changes in their swimmers' blood pH, partial pressure of carbon dioxide (PCO_2), partial pressure of oxygen (PO_2), bicarbonate (HCO_3), and base excess after a 200-yard (183 m) submaximal swim at 90 percent of the season's best performance.

Hormones

Strenuous physical exercise is known to result in short- and long-term alterations of the endocrine system (Bunt 1986; Galbo 1986; Viru 1992). Because of their responsiveness to training-induced physiological stress, various hormones including testosterone, cortisol, catecholamines, growth hormone, and others are often used as markers to monitor training stress, evaluate training responses, and predict performance capacity. These hormonal markers of training stress should therefore reflect the variations in the training load that take place during different phases of a competitive season, such as during a taper, and hormonal changes should be related to changes in competition performance.

The plasma levels of testosterone (T) and cortisol (C) could represent anabolic and catabolic tissue activities, respectively. Although the T:C ratio has been suggested as a marker of training stress (Adlercreutz et al. 1986; Kuoppasalmi and Adlercreutz 1985), the available data in the literature concerning androgen and C responses to tapering in swimmers are inconclusive. In a study of collegiate swimmers, Flynn and colleagues (1994) observed that total testosterone (TT) and free testosterone (FT) returned toward baseline during the taper after showing blunted values throughout the intensive training phases of the season. No changes were noticed in the TT:C and FT:C ratios. Changes in TT and FT during training and taper, but not in TT:C or FT:C ratios, paralleled changes in performance during criterion swims (Flynn et al. 1994).

Mujika and colleagues assessed the effects of tapering on selected hormones in swimmers (Mujika et al. 1996c). Plasma TT; non-SHBG-bound testosterone (NSBT), which is the sum of FT and albumin-bound T representing the biologically active fraction of T (Cumming and Wall 1985; Manni, Partridge, and Cefalu 1985); C; TT:C; and NSBT:C remained stable during a four-week taper subsequent to eight weeks of intensive training, despite large variations in training volume (Mujika et al. 1996c). Nevertheless, the four weeks of taper resulted in a 2.3 percent improvement in competition performance, and percentage variations in swimming performance during the taper correlated with changes in the TT:C (r = 0.81) and NSBT:C (r = 0.76) ratios and with changes in NSBT concentration (r = 0.71) (Mujika et al. 1996c).

Changes in resting cortisol concentration during the taper have been proposed as a means of monitoring performance capacity in athletes. For instance, Mujika and colleagues (1996) found slight reductions in resting cortisol concentrations in swimmers who responded to a four-week taper by improving their performance by more than 2 percent but a significant increase in cortisol in swimmers less respondent to the same taper program, suggesting a relationship between resting cortisol levels and the performance response to the taper. Collegiate swimmers' resting cortisol values declined by 23 to 30 percent, their testosterone concentration increased by 22 percent during the first taper, and the athletes' competition performance improved by an average of 3.2 percent in two different two- to three-week tapers within a season (Costill et al. 1991). On the other hand, no changes in TT, C, or the TT:C ratio were observed during six weeks of progressive increase and two weeks of gradual decrease in training volume in well-trained swimmers (Tanaka et al. 1993). A follow-up investigation of elite swimmers over two seasons showed that the 1.5 to 2.1 percent performance improvements during the tapers before the major competitions of each season were positively related to the corresponding 22 to 49 percent increases in postcompetition peak lactate concentrations but negatively related ($r = -0.66$) to the 19 to 29 percent change in resting precompetition plasma cortisol concentration (Bonifazi, Sardella, and Luppo 2000). The conclusion of this study was that a low cortisol concentration was a prerequisite for improved performance in events that rely largely on the contribution of anaerobic metabolism to total energy supply (Bonifazi, Sardella, and Luppo 2000). These findings indicate that a hormonal milieu propitious to anabolic processes is necessary for optimum function of the glycolytic power system and performance in middle-distance events.

Female collegiate swimmers' salivary cortisol levels have been reported to return to baseline values after four weeks of taper consisting of a progressive 63 percent reduction in training volume (O'Connor et al. 1989). A similar finding was reported in male swimmers, whose salivary cortisol decreased marginally by 4.8 percent during the taper to attain the lowest values of the entire training season (Tharp and Barnes 1990). Other investigations, however, have reported unchanged or slightly increased cortisol concentrations because of a taper in swimmers (Mujika et al. 1996c). Plasma cortisol concentrations are subject to various kinds of physiological and psychological stressors (McCarthy and Dale 1988, Stein, Keller, and Schleifer 1985), which could explain conflicting findings. The physical stress produced by the pretaper intensive training could be replaced in the posttaper condition by the psychological stress associated with the oncoming major competition (Mujika, Chatard, and Geyssant 1996).

Plasma and urinary catecholamine concentrations have been measured as a means to monitor training stress and identify overreaching or overtraining in athletes. Hooper and colleagues (1993) reported that plasma noradrenaline was higher during the taper in swimmers who were overtrained and failed to improve their performance. In another study by the same group, a small change in time-trial swimming performance during the taper was predicted by changes in plasma noradrenaline concentration, which accounted for 82 percent of the variance. The authors concluded that the change in plasma noradrenaline concentration could be a useful marker for monitoring recovery associated with the taper, but they acknowledged that the role of catecholamines in the recovery phase after intense training is not well established and that the expense and complexity associated with catecholamine measurements preclude its use in routine screening of athletes during the taper (Hooper, Mackinnon, and Howard 1999). Other investigators have also measured plasma adrenaline, noradrenaline, and dopamine concentrations before and after taper in competitive swimmers (Mujika et al. 1996c). The only noticeable change in this study was a statistically nonsignificant 22 percent decrease in plasma noradrenaline during the taper. But in contrast with the previously mentioned investigation, this change did not correlate with the 2.3 percent gains in competition swimming performance, which ranged between 0.4 and 4.9 percent (Mujika et al. 1996c).

Insulin-like growth factor-I (IGF-I), a polypeptide that plays an important role in the regulation of somatic growth; metabolism; and cellular proliferation, differentiation, and survival, has also been measured before and after taper in athletes (Koziris et al. 1999). Nine male collegiate swimmers' total serum IGF-I increased progressively by 76 percent above baseline during four months of intensive training, and these elevated values were maintained during four weeks of tapering. The levels of free IGF-I increased by 77 to 102 percent at all training measurements, including the taper. The levels of immunoreactive IGF binding protein-3 (IGFBP-3) were 30 percent higher after intensive training and remained elevated during tapering. In contrast, IGF binding protein-1 (IGFBP-1) declined to baseline values during tapering. Performance measures were not reported, but the authors of the study suggested that the increased total and free IGF-I and total IGFBP-3 could have played a role in the observed reductions in skinfold measurements during the season (Koziris et al. 1999).

Other hormones have been suggested as markers of training stress and over-training during tapering. To date, the relevant studies have yielded inconclusive results about the usefulness of hormonal monitoring.

Neuromuscular System

The extraordinary plasticity of skeletal muscle tissue allows it to adapt to variable levels of functional demands, neuromuscular activity, and hormonal signals and reversibly change its functional characteristics and structural composition (Gordon and Pattullo 1993; Hoppeler 1986; Kannus et al. 1992; Saltin and Gollnick 1983). A precompetition taper presumably reduces the demands placed on the neuromuscular system compared with previous phases of a training program. Increased strength and power as a result of a taper have been a common observation in swimming. Costill and colleagues (1985) were among the first researchers to describe such gains. These authors described an 18 percent improvement in swim bench power and a 25 percent gain in actual swim power in a group of 17 collegiate swimmers who underwent a 2-week taper. Swim power improvement correlated with a 3.1 percent competition performance gain ($r = 0.68$). The reduced training may have allowed an increase in maximal tension development through changes in the contractile mechanisms or neural controls on fiber recruitment (Costill et al. 1985). In keeping with these results, Johns and colleagues (1992) observed a 5 percent increase in tethered swimming power and a 2.8 percent improvement in competition performance after 10 and 14 days of taper. National- and international-level swimmers' isolated mean arm and leg power has also been shown to increase during a 4-week taper, especially during the initial 5 to 24 seconds of exercise (Cavanaugh and Musch 1989). Competition performance improved by an average of 2.6 percent during the taper. Raglin, Koceja, and Stager (1996) also reported gains during a 4- to 5-week taper in swimming peak power (16 percent) and mean power (20 percent). In addition, they observed a 23 percent gain in neuromuscular function, as determined with the soleus Hoffmann reflex, an indicator of the general excitability of the α-motoneuron pool. These changes correlated with changes in power and were accompanied by a 2.0 percent improvement in competition velocity. The authors concluded that neurological adaptations may have a role in the performance gains that often follow the taper (Raglin, Koceja, and Stager 1996). Trappe, Costill, and Thomas (2001) noted a 7 to 20 percent increase in swim bench muscle power, a 13 percent increase in swim power, and a 4 percent enhancement in competition performance as a result of a 3-week taper in six male collegiate swimmers. In keeping with these results, Papoti and colleagues (2007) reported a 3.8 percent gain in swim force and a 1.6 percent gain in 200-meter time-trial performance after an 11-day taper consisting of a 48 percent reduction in weekly training volume. Swim force significantly correlated with performance both before and after the taper.

Trinity and colleagues (2006) found that elite swimmers' maximal arm power increased 10 and 12 percent during a taper. These gains in power correlated with performance gains of 4.4 and 4.7 percent. These authors observed that maximal mechanical power displayed a biphasic response during the taper, such that approximately 50, 5, and 45 percent of the total increase occurred during the first, second, and third weeks of the taper, respectively. In this study, the biphasic response was reported to be the most common response to the taper among individual swimmers, although some subjects were early responders or late responders. Prins and colleagues (1991) and Hooper, Mackinnon, and Howard (1999) reported unchanged muscular force as a result of a taper, concluding that pretaper force levels were not compromised by the training load undertaken by swimmers. Differences with studies reporting gains in force after a taper may relate to variations in the caliber of the swimmers and the training and tapering programs undertaken.

The taper appears to affect muscle fiber in various ways. In male collegiate swimmers, no changes in Type I muscle fiber diameter and cross-sectional area of deltoid muscle samples were observed after a three-week taper. On the other hand, Type IIa muscle fiber diameter increased by 11 percent and cross-sectional area increased by 24 percent. Neuromuscular adaptations also occurred at the single-fiber level after tapering; Trappe, Costill, and Thomas (2001) observed 30 percent higher peak isometric force, 67 percent faster shortening velocity, and 250 percent higher absolute fiber power in Type IIa muscle fibers. Type I fibers also increased their shortening velocity by 32 percent. On average, Type II fibers produced twice as much peak power as Type I fibers before the taper and five times as much peak power after the taper. These observations led the authors to suggest that changes in contractile properties may have been closely related to the observed improvements in whole-muscle strength and power measures after the taper (Trappe, Costill, and Thomas 2001). As concluded by a review article on single-fiber studies and exercise training, the taper has relatively little influence on the size and force characteristics of Type I muscle fibers, but Type IIa fibers seem to be more responsive, showing enhanced contraction performance, as a result of equal or increased cross-sectional area, and increased force and power. In addition, adequate adjustments in training volume and intensity seem to be necessary to elicit positive changes in single-fiber contraction velocity (Malisoux, Francaux, and Theisen 2007).

Psychology

Because competition performance is the result of a conscious effort (Noakes 2000), it would be a major oversight to ignore the paramount contribution of psychological and motivational factors to posttaper athletic performance. The optimization of an athlete's physiological status resulting from a well-designed tapering strategy is presumably accompanied by beneficial psychological changes, including mood state, perception of effort, and quality of sleep. Mood states are sensitive to variations in the training load undertaken by athletes (Morgan et al. 1987), and alterations should be expected because of a taper when the training load is markedly reduced. Numerous authors have reported mood state changes associated with a precompetition taper. Most of these reports indicate that tapering induces positive changes in the athlete's mood state, contributing to enhanced performance measures.

Morgan and colleagues (1987) and Raglin, Morgan, and O'Connor (1991) first described decreased global mood scores computed from the Profile of Mood States (POMS) questionnaire in college swimmers who tapered for four weeks. The decrease in global mood scores was associated with decreased levels of perceived fatigue, depression, anger, and confusion. These changes were also accompanied by increased levels of vigor. Morgan and colleagues also reported that decreases in mood disturbance were related to reductions in the training load. Identical effects were observed in males and females. Some athletes did not respond to the taper, however, and no declines in tension scores were observed. Values were higher in female athletes than in male athletes (Morgan et al. 1987; Raglin, Morgan, and O'Connor 1991). In fact, tension was the only mood variable that remained elevated above baseline following the taper. Elevated tension probably reflects anxiety provoked by the anticipation of the pending major championship (O'Connor et al. 1989). In contrast with the previously mentioned findings, Taylor, Rogers, and Driver (1997) reported sex differences in tapering-induced mood state alterations. Relatively small (1.3 percent) competition performance gains attained by female swimmers during taper were presumably related to a deterioration in mood state indicated by increases in tension–anxiety (56 percent), depression–dejection (218 percent), and confusion–bewilderment (86 percent) and a 20 percent decrease in vigor–activity ratings (Taylor, Rogers, and Driver 1997). Flynn and colleagues (1994) reported a 17 percent reduction in the global mood state of a group of male swimmers after a three-week taper. A similar 16 percent decline in total mood disturbance was observed by Raglin, Koceja, and Stager (1996) in 12 collegiate female swimmers who tapered for four to five weeks. This decline correlated moderately with mean swimming power ($r = .34$), which increased by 20 percent with the taper. Swimming velocity in competition also improved by 2.0 percent. Hooper, Mackinnon, and Ginn (1998) observed reduced tension, depression, and anger after one week of taper in state-level swimmers and a 10 percent lower total mood disturbance after two weeks, which resulted in marginal time-trial performance gains of 0.2 percent in 100-meter events and 0.7 percent in 400-meter events. But in a subsequent investigation of international-caliber swimmers, these authors did not detect any change in the total mood disturbance after a two-week taper (Hooper, Mackinnon, and Howard 1999). In another study, young competitive swimmers showed an acute decrease in total mood disturbance after practices that were shorter in duration than usual during a precompetition week of taper. These competitive swimmers reported short-term mood benefits including decreases in scores of depression, confusion, and tension. But these acute mood benefits during training before competition did not appear to be related to subsequent performance in competition (Berger et al. 1997).

A fatigued and overstressed athlete perceives a given training load as a heavy burden. In contrast, a fresh, well-recovered athlete may perceive a similar training load as light and easy. How athletes perceive a given training bout is their perception of effort. The perception of effort during exercise is influenced by a number of physiological and psychological variables (Borg, Hassmen, and Lagerstrom 1987; Noble and Robertson 2000; Watt and Grove 1993), some of which are presumably affected by a taper. The most widely used measure of effort perception is Borg's rating of perceived exertion (RPE) (Borg 1970, 1982), which has been shown to change as a result of tapered training. The perception of effort decreased in swimmers of both genders after a four-week taper in collegiate athletes (Morgan et al. 1987). Flynn and colleagues (1994) reported that participants' RPE while they swam at 90 percent of preseason $\dot{V}O_2$max decreased from an average value of 14 (somewhat hard to hard) after two weeks of hard training to 9 (very light) at the end of the taper.

Sleep

Sleep is a compensatory mechanism following catabolic processes of daytime activity, and sleep disturbance is often associated with excessive training loads and overtraining, defined as "an imbalance between training and recovery, exercise and exercise capacity, stress and stress tolerance" (Lehmann, Foster, and Keul 1993, p. 854). Given that tapering strategies are characterized by reduced training loads, it seems plausible that sleep quality could also be affected by the taper. The most in-depth investigation dealing with sleep patterns during tapering in athletes indicates that sleep-onset latency, time awake after sleep onset, total sleep time, and rapid eye movement sleep time were unchanged during the taper in female swimmers. On the other hand, slow-wave sleep, which represented 31 percent of total sleep time during peak training, was reduced to 16 percent following the taper, suggesting that the need for restorative slow-wave sleep declines with reduced physical demand. The number of movements during sleep fell by 37 percent after the taper, indicating less sleep disruption in comparison with previous times of higher training loads (Taylor, Rogers, and Driver 1997). Hooper, Mackinnon, and Howard (1999) reported a slightly improved quality of sleep in seven highly competitive female swimmers after two weeks of tapering for the Australian National Championships.

Compliance

One final aspect to consider in all that we have discussed and presented in this chapter is that of compliance. By compliance, we mean swimmers' compliance with training prescriptions and coaches' compliance with scientific interventions. With regard to the former, only large changes in competition performance can be predicted using physiologic monitoring and training prescription (Anderson et al. 2006, 2008; Mujika et al. 1995; Pelayo et al. 1996; Pyne, Mujika, and Reilly 2009; Stewart and Hopkins 2000). Furthermore, swimmers appear to adhere closely to all aspects of training load except the most crucial component—intensity (Stewart and Hopkins 1997). Coaches should therefore closely monitor the compliance of their swimmers to the training prescription. An example of the influence of compliance on performance outcome was found by Stewart, McGowan, and Park (2002), who followed the performances of 25 age-group swimmers (ranging from 14 to 17 years old and achieving seasonal best performances of about 80 percent of world-record pace) over several seasons. The authors concluded that there may be an additional positive effect (about 1 to 1.5 percent) of tapering for swimmers who comply strongly to the training prescription throughout the season as opposed to those who comply moderately or poorly. Although such preliminary results appear promising, coaches have yet to adopt the kind of year-round, high-intensity approach that was used in this setting, so results have yet to be rigorously verified.

Summary

The taper is a phase of reduced training that usually follows a lengthy period of progressive overload training to fine-tune the swimmer in preparation for competition. This chapter provides practitioners with current information on how to optimize the effects of tapering for a given swimmer within a seasonal, periodized model. Progressive reductions of the training load during the taper seem to be more beneficial than constant step reductions, but a final increase in training for a few days prior to the big event may allow the athlete to benefit from additional fitness adaptations.

An elite swimmer's performance usually improves by about 2 to 3 percent during the taper, provided that training intensity and frequency remain high, but volume drops by about 41 to 60 percent compared to the previous loading phase. Optimal taper duration often ranges from 8 to 21 days, depending on previous training loads and individual adaptation profiles.

The mechanisms underpinning the beneficial effects of the taper can be of a cardiovascular hematologic, metabolic, biochemical, hormonal, neuromuscular, or psychological origin. For these benefits to be obtained, it is important that swimmers comply with training prescriptions and coaches comply with scientifically proven training interventions.

CHAPTER 11

Competition-Day Strategies

—Scott Riewald, PhD, CSCS

Competition day is the day that every swimmer trains for. Although many swimmers and coaches place a tremendous amount of focus on what happens on race day, the hay is largely already in the barn, so to speak, and the meet is just where everything comes together to produce the ultimate performance. All the physical training, strength and conditioning, fueling and nutrition, and mental preparation done over the preceding months are directed at performing on this big day. Still, the swimmer and coach need to do some things on race day to make sure that everything comes together and plays out as planned.

Although what a swimmer does on race day may not make it possible to win a race, doing the wrong thing can derail a performance. The meet represents an opportunity to put the finishing touches on a swimmer's preparation and performance, yet these things do not come together by chance. Planning and developing race-day strategies are needed to provide swimmers with the greatest opportunity for success. This chapter looks at competition day and identifies strategies that swimmers can use to finish their preparation and set themselves up to achieve their peak performances.

Another important consideration is how swimmers recover, or bounce back, between events at a competition. Most swimmers compete in multiple events in a day. Even in the best scenario, when everything goes well and best times are swum, swimmers and coaches need to consider what needs to be done to get ready for the next race. When things don't go as planned, it is even more important for a swimmer to have a strategy to get back on track for the next race. Not everything goes perfectly in every race, so the swimmer needs to know how to learn from that race and move on to achieve a great performance in the next swim. Swimmers often turn in poor performances, even in the Olympic Games, only to come back and swim a best time (and in some instances win a medal) in the next race. It is all about having a practiced strategy that will prepare a swimmer to perform at her best each time she steps on the blocks.

In this chapter we draw on information presented elsewhere in the book and relate it to performance on race day. Specifically, we discuss the following:

- Warm-up and cool-down
- Race-day nutrition
- Mental preparation for competition
- Recovery
- Communication and teamwork

The number one rule for swimmers and coaches on race day is "Don't do anything new at a competition." They should stick with the strategies that they know work and lead to the best performances. The state championship is not the time to try massage if the swimmer has not had massage as part of his regular training and recovery protocol throughout the year. Nor is the big meet the time to try that new energy drink that all the other swimmers seem to be using. Without having tried it in practice or knowing how the body will react, doing anything different nutritionally at a meet is like playing with fire.

Ultimately, race-day preparation boils down to developing a series of checklists that, if followed, will set up a swimmer to achieve a peak performance. Let's go through the elements of a race day and discuss how to approach each one to enhance performance, starting with the warm-up and cool-down.

Warm-Up and Cool-Down

The warm-up and cool-down are closely related. Although separated by a considerable time at a competition, both deal with the same thing—preparation. The warm-up prepares the body to race and perform at a high level. The cool-down starts the recovery process and is essential for preparing the body for the next race. Although the warm-up and cool-down are critical components of any training or competition session, swimmers often do not do enough in these areas, nor do they typically develop the consistency and discipline needed in these areas to have a strategic effect on performance.

Warming Up

The purpose of the warm-up is literally to warm the body by increasing muscle and core body temperature. When the body is warm, the muscles are able to function more efficiently by contracting with greater force through a greater range of motion. A good warm-up also does other things to get the body physically ready for high-intensity swimming (Jeffreys 2008; Salo and Riewald 2008). Specifically, the warm-up

- primes the cardiovascular and respiratory systems, enhancing the body's ability to pump blood and deliver oxygen to the working muscles;

- develops dynamic flexibility, or flexibility with motion, actively putting muscles and joints through their range of motion, enhancing flexibility and improving stroke efficiency;
- gets the body's biochemistry working optimally—all of the body's physiological systems need to be warmed up to optimal levels to support high-intensity swimming;
- gets the mind talking to the muscles, improving coordination and efficiency of movement; and
- provides a checkpoint at which the swimmer and coach can evaluate the state of the swimmer and her performance.

Many coaches make the warm-up a designed set and use the same warm-up for every practice and competition with only slight variations. By doing the same warm-up every day, the coach has 15 to 20 minutes to assess the physical and mental state of the team. Although always doing the same warm-up may seem boring, swimmers and coaches can readily relate what they are seeing or feeling in the water and compare it with what they've experienced nearly every day in practice. By doing a consistent warm-up, swimmers also learn to prepare the body the same way before each practice and competition. Swimmers can use this time to conduct their own assessments of what and how they are feeling because they know that the training intensity will go up when the warm-up is over. The warm-up should be part of an established routine that swimmers know will prepare them to swim fast.

Data from warm-ups can be extremely valuable and powerful in the hands of a seasoned coach. Being able to draw from days, weeks, even months of warm-up performance data can provide tangible benefits on race day. If something seems off on race day, the warm-up or other aspects of the athlete's preparation can be adjusted to accommodate the observed differences. Perhaps the swimmer needs to spend more time getting loose or needs to perform a few extra higher-intensity swims to get the body ready to go. Regardless, when the swimmer is able to compare what is happening on race day with previous experiences, the chance of dialing in performance is improved.

In-Water Warm-Up

Although there is no specific recipe for what makes an effective warm-up, most warm-ups incorporate some level of moderate swimming (maybe 400 to 800 meters) that can include stroke drills and kicking as well as swimming, several higher-intensity intervals (100 or 50 seconds) in which the swimmer integrates stroke work and prepares to race, and some all-out sprints or race-specific pace work. These higher-intensity efforts are followed by several hundred meters of a lower-intensity cool-down.

Competitions present additional challenges to swimmers and coaches because athletes often have to warm up multiple times during a day, once at the start of the session and again before each swim. When facing this scenario, swimmers should do their main warm-up before the first swim and then use shorter warm-ups before subsequent swims. The duration of these secondary warm-ups can be shorter but should still follow the same general principles: start with easy swimming and then use higher-intensity swims to elevate the heart rate and warm the body.

Swimmer should follow some general preevent warm-up guidelines:

- Finish the main warm-up at least 30 minutes before the race.
- If possible, get back in the water 10 to 15 minutes before the race.
- Use mostly moderate-intensity swimming at 50 to 65 percent effort.
- Gauge the intensity of effort while warming up before an event. Swim hard enough to warm the body but not so hard that fatigue sets in before stepping on the blocks.
- Finish the preevent warm-up as close to the start of the event as possible, ideally within 5 minutes of when the race is set to begin.

Dryland Warm-Up

Everything discussed so far has centered on performing an in-water warm-up. But when pool space at a competition is limited or no warm-up pool is available, coaches and swimmers may opt for a dryland warm-up. Although a dryland warm-up is not ideal, it can help swimmers prepare physically for a race. Like the in-water warm-up, the dryland warm-up should have two main components: a general warm-up and a dynamic warm-up (Jeffreys 2008; Salo and Riewald 2008).

The general warm-up should be a moderate-intensity activity that uses many of the large-muscle groups in the body to elevate body temperature. Examples include light jogging, riding a stationary bicycle, and jumping rope. The general warm-up should last 5 to 10 minutes or until the athlete breaks into a light sweat.

Dynamic warm-up exercises involve movement and are designed to improve dynamic flexibility while keeping body temperature elevated. Exercises should target the specific muscle groups used in swimming. Each exercise should be performed for 15 to 30 seconds. The total dynamic warm-up should take 5 to 10 minutes to complete. Elastic tubing can be used to help with dynamic exercises, which can be tweaked into swimming-specific drills that enhance the entire dryland warm-up process. These drills should be planned and practiced.

This approach will help accomplish all warm-up goals and prepare the body for swimming fast. The only difference between this and a traditional swimming warm-up is that it is not done in the pool.

Mental Preparation During the Warm-Up

The warm-up helps swimmers prepare physically, but it should also help them prepare mentally. Many sport psychologists emphasize the importance of developing a prepractice or prerace routine that includes a consistent warm-up. This is another reason that swimmers should complete the same warm-up every day.

A consistent warm-up also helps to equalize the importance that a swimmer places on different competitions. Each level of competition carries a different level of anxiety. Swimmers may feel OK preparing for a local or regional meet, but what happens when they get to the pool for the state championships or nationals? Ideally, swimmers want to enter each race with the same level of focus, preparation, and comfort, knowing that they've done everything right in preparing for the race. Changing a precompetition routine and altering what the swimmer has always done to get ready for a race can add anxiety to a competition. Using a consistent warm-up tells the body, "We've been here before and we know this is what it takes to swim fast." More information on developing a precompetition routine is presented later in the chapter.

Cooling Down

Coaches agree, and exercise physiologists confirm, that the cool-down is an important component to swim training. But few coaches include enough cool-down time in training sessions and even fewer mandate adequate cool-down following a race. In fact, testing of elite swimmers by USA Swimming shows that most swimmers cool down 40 percent of what they should before they get out of the pool at a competition. The cool-down should be seen as step number one in the recovery process to get the swimmer ready for the next race or the next day of competition.

Understanding the physiological processes that occur with the cool-down may shed light on its importance. In basic terms, the cool-down brings the body back down to a normal level and begins the recovery process, setting the stage to be able to perform at a high level in the next practice or race. As discussed in chapter 8, during a race the body relies heavily on the anaerobic system to provide the energy needed to drive performance. The anaerobic energy system is capable of supplying muscles with a great deal of energy in the form of ATP very quickly, but it also produces lactic acid and lactate that should be cleared before the next high-intensity effort if peak performance is desired.

Cooling down allows the body to return to a more normal state. The amount of lactate produced following a practice or a race can be measured, although doing so is impractical in most cases. Fortunately, USA Swimming has conducted some research in the area of lactate clearance and cooling down and has provided recommendations that swimmers can follow to enhance recovery (Sokolovas 2003). Typically, lactate concentration rises over the first several minutes after a race. Then, over the next 20 to 30 minutes, this concentration declines to near baseline or prerace levels. From the research that has been conducted, four observations have been made about the rate at which lactate is produced and subsequently cleared from the body:

1. The intensity of swimming primarily determines how high the blood lactate concentration will rise. In turn, this level affects the rate at which the blood lactate concentration returns to normal resting values. Sprinters who have a

high concentration of fast-twitch, power-generating muscle fibers produce higher lactate concentrations than endurance swimmers do, and they need more time to clear lactate from their bodies.

2. With all else equal, the lactate concentration will rise higher and decline faster in a better-conditioned swimmer than in a less-conditioned swimmer.

3. Swimmers who perform a cool-down after racing increase the rate at which the blood lactate returns to normal resting values.

4. Older swimmers take longer to clear lactate and require a longer cool-down than younger swimmers. Masters swimmers, for example, could likely avoid muscular discomfort in the days following an exceptionally hard training session or intense competition by performing a longer cool-down.

Taking this information into account, additional guidelines on structuring a proper cool-down have been developed. In general, a proper cool-down should consist of at least 15 minutes of moderately paced swimming; cooling down even longer is usually better. In fact, information from USA Swimming suggests that the shorter the event is, the longer a swimmer should cool down (Sokolovas 2003):

- For 50- and 100-meter races, swimmers should cool down for 25 to 30 minutes at an intensity that keeps the heart rate at approximately 120 to 130 beats per minute (20 or 21 beats in 10 seconds).

- For 200- and 400-meter races, swimmers should cool down for 15 to 20 minutes, maintaining a heart rate of 130 to 140 beats per minute (21 to 23 beats in 10 seconds).

- For races longer than 400 meters, swimmers should cool down for 10 to 15 minutes, maintaining a heart rate of 140 to 150 beats per minute (23 to 25 beats in 10 seconds).

These guidelines are useful in shaping a cool-down. Remember that all swimmers are different and that their experiences may differ from what an average swimmer experiences, so these recommendations may need to be adjusted accordingly.

The cool-down guidelines presented encourage an active cool-down, or performing an actual activity to cool down. In general, the body removes lactate most efficiently when the swimmer cools down by swimming at 55 to 65 percent of maximum velocity. Recovery will occur even if a swimmer is not able to do anything after the race. This is termed passive recovery, meaning that the swimmer doesn't need to do anything for it to occur. Knowing that the body will be recovering as the swimmer rides home after the meet is reassuring, but passive recovery occurs much more slowly than active recovery does. The rate of recovery may not be important for swimmers who only swim one event per day, but many swimmers compete in multiple events per session and repeat that routine for several days in a row. For those swimmers in particular, an active cool-down is critically important.

Again, swim meets present some potentially complicating circumstances relating to a cool-down. What happens when an athlete swims multiple events per day or does not have access to a cool-down pool? If possible, swimmers should cool down after every race if they want to swim their best the next time they step on the blocks. Even if only a short time is scheduled between swims, getting in the pool immediately after a race will help with recovery. Unlike the warm-up when swimmers can get by with doing less after they have gone through the main warm-up at the start of the day, the cool-down may need to be longer with each event that swimmers compete in.

If a cool-down pool is not available, the swimmer should engage in some type of moderate-intensity active cool-down such as light jogging or riding a stationary bike. Maintaining an intensity of 55 to 65 percent of the swimmer's maximal effort should adequately facilitate the recovery process without causing undue fatigue. Stretching has even been shown to be an acceptable form of cooling down if the swimmer does not have access to a pool or other activity. The take-home message is that the body recovers more quickly if the athlete engages in some sort of moderate-intensity activity rather than passively sitting and waiting for the recovery process to happen.

Mental Preparation and the Prerace Routine

Competition provides athletes the opportunity to demonstrate their abilities and to challenge themselves as to how fast and how well they can swim. The opportunity to compete is one of the reasons that swimmers train hard every day. When standing on the blocks waiting for the gun to go off, it all boils down to what the swimmer's body can do, right?

Although physical ability is one factor that contributes to performance, mental strength and conditioning are important as well. How athletes train mentally and what they do to prepare for the specific race has a lot to do with the eventual outcome. Swimmers need to be purposeful about preparing both their minds and their bodies for competition.

Just as scientists have identified physical, physiological, and technical profiles of elite athletes, similar work has been done to identify psychological profiles and characteristics. This research has identified a number of psychological attributes related to success. One of the key characteristics of top performers is having a well-developed precompetition routine. Combined with high levels of motivation and commitment, coping skills, self-confidence, and arousal management skills, having a precompetition routine helps athletes achieve higher levels of performance.

After the 1996 Olympics, researchers identified factors that had positive and negative effects on performance at the Games. One of the findings that distinguished athletes who performed well from those who didn't was the development of and adherence to physical and mental preparation plans. Successful athletes had a precompetition routine that they developed, practiced, and stuck to even at the biggest competitions (Gould and Dieffenbach 2002).

In 1998, 10 athletes from the U.S. World Championships swim team were interviewed to uncover how they approached and dealt with the mental aspect of swimming. In particular, the athletes were asked to describe how they got ready to race. Although they prepared for their races differently, all the athletes had a routine or plan to get mentally ready to race (Riewald 2002).

Although the benefits of mental training and the development of a toolbox of mental skills is discussed in detail in chapter 16, it is helpful here to highlight the reasons why and how a prerace routine can influence performance. Following a consistent and practiced routine will help athletes achieve the following goals.

Attain an Ideal State or Zone

The primary benefit or purpose of a mental preparation plan is to get the athlete in a mental state that seems to relate to successful performance. The process that the swimmer goes through to get there will be unique to the individual.

Achieve Greater Self-Confidence

Success breeds confidence. When athletes are able to see and feel past and future successes as part of their mental preparation, confidence is not far behind. Imaging a successful upcoming race is the dress rehearsal to the real deal. Visualizing a great performance enhances the athlete's belief that he can really do it.

Gain Greater Control of Mental Energy

Swimmers need to manage mental energy so that they are neither too flat nor too amped up before racing. The goal is to get into that ideal state. During preparation, athletes may listen to certain songs to increase energy and put them into the proper racing state. Alternatively, they may visualize a relaxing scene to slow their hurrying thoughts. Such strategies can be a purposeful part of a mental routine to manage mental energy.

Give More Effective Focus

A mental preparation routine can help swimmers focus on important aspects of their performance. Technical cues ("explode off the blocks" or "hold your streamline") or images ("torpedo") can be integrated into preparation to direct attention where it needs to be as opposed to having the focus on unproductive or negative things.

Provide Comfort in Structure

A mental routine can be a security blanket, something to turn to in the stressful moments leading up to the competition. Swimmers can use their mental routine to bring consistency to their preparation and performance, whether they are swimming in a dual meet or at Olympic Trials. To some degree, a mental preparation routine can take the environment out of the performance.

Engage the Mind

The mind is a valuable commodity. When purposefully recruited and engaged, the athlete has the additional support of positive emotions, feelings, and thoughts. Athletes should make wise use of all the resources at their disposal as they prepare for competition.

Coaches can do certain things to help their swimmers develop and strengthen effective prerace routines. Coaches should talk to their swimmers about what mental preparation is and why they should have a mental plan. Coaches need to define some of the key components that make up a mental plan, such as imagery, goal setting, self-talk, concentration, and energy management, and explain that there is no right or wrong way to create a mental plan. Each swimmer will have a personal, unique mental plan.

Next, the coach should have the swimmers reflect on past performances to begin to understand how they feel when they perform well and what they need to do to ensure good performances. Additionally, they should examine how they feel when they do not perform well and identify what they need to do to get out of that state.

Coaches should have the athletes create a mental plan, write the plan down, and refer to it throughout the season. Coaches must provide opportunities and encouragement to practice the plans. For example, a coach might set up a swim practice before a big meet and have the swimmers run through their prerace routines, giving them a chance to do their own premeet warm-up. This approach allows the athletes to take ownership of their prerace readiness routines and make changes if needed.

Although these things may seem insignificant when taken individually, consider what it is that distinguishes the gold medal winner from the athlete who won the silver, the third-place finisher from those who did not win a medal. It often boils down to how the athletes prepared for the competition. The best athletes in the world have strategies that help them perform to their utmost ability, and they think about those points as they prepare for competition. Swimmers who do the same will see their athletic performances improve.

Race-Day Nutrition

Nutrition for performance does not end when the competition starts. The swimmer can do a number of things to improve performance by planning nutrition on race day.

Again, the key word is *planning*. Even the most nutritionally focused swimmers find challenges at competitions, particularly if they are traveling to attend the meet. But by thinking through nutritional obstacles before stepping on the pool deck, swimmers can make decisions that will enhance performance rather than detract from it.

Swimmers should never enter a swim meet with the expectation that the competition snack bar will provide them with the fuel they need to perform at their best. Athletes need to bring any foods they need to stay fueled and hydrated throughout the competition. They need to think about how long the meet will last, how much time will be scheduled between events, what foods they will need to keep energy levels up during a long day of swimming, and so on. Swimmers can develop nutritional checklists to make sure they have thought through all their nutritional needs for race day. The bottom line is that swimmers should plan to bring their own food to swim meets. An example of a nutrition checklist is presented in table 11.1.

Swimmers should follow some general guidelines on competition days about when they should consume meals and what should make up those meals, starting with the precompetition meal. The focus of this meal should be to top off carbohydrate and glycogen stores and hydrate the body. At the meet, the goal should be to maintain energy and hydration levels by consuming small amounts of nutrients, primarily carbohydrate and fluids, throughout the day (Burke 2000).

Athletes should consume a low-fat, high-carbohydrate meal composed mainly of low to moderate glycemic index (GI) carbohydrate several hours before the first race. Athletes should consume foods they are comfortable with. If nervousness interferes with an athlete's ability to consume solid food, liquid meal supplements or smoothies are a suitable alternative.

An athlete who has two or more hours between races should consume a small meal made up of high glycemic index carbohydrate to replenish glycogen stores rapidly. An athlete who has less than two hours between races should be encouraged to eat a small snack made up of low GI food choices to avoid a sugar high and the subsequent crash.

Athletes should continue to drink fluids regularly throughout the day to avoid dehydration. They should replace lost fluids with water or sports drinks and stay away from things like sodas and energy drinks.

Athletes should not try any new foods at a competition. Swimmers should stick with foods that they have trialed at previous competitions or in practices and go with what they know works. The body can respond in unexpected ways when foods are tested for the first time on race day.

Just as a cool-down sets the stage for the next race, the same applies to nutrition; what happens nutritionally after a race or competition session is just as

Table 11.1 Swim Meet Nutrition Checklist

Nutritional item	What and how much?	Packed in swim bag (P)?
Water	1 liter	P
Fruit juice or sports drink	2 × 500 ml	P
Fruit	Banana and grapes	P
Low-fat fruit yogurt	One container	P
Precooked pasta with tomato-based sauce	250 g in a sealed container	P
Recovery snacks for between races	Two cereal bars or two sports gels	P
Carbohydrate-based recovery meal for after the competition	600 ml of chocolate milk or turkey sandwich	P

important as what happened during or before it. Recovery is key, and the sooner that swimmers start the recovery process, the better off they will be entering the next race. Chapter 14 provides detailed information about recovery nutrition. Swimmers need to get carbohydrate and some protein into the body as soon as possible after a training or competition session ends. Additionally, fluid losses should be replenished immediately. Ideally, everything during competition should be an extension of what is done every day in training. Competition fueling should be part of the routine, not a new experiment! If done properly, race-day nutritional strategies can provide swimmers with a competitive advantage over their competitors.

Communication Plan With Parents, Coaches, and Teammates

The idea may sound silly, but one aspect of race day that can negatively influence a swimmer's performance is not having predefined communication strategies that outline how that athlete will interact with parents, coaches, and even other athletes during and after competition. Both sides in each of these relationships need to have a clear understanding of the expectations for talking after a race and the topics that are off limits.

Coach and Athlete

Athletes need to meet with the coach shortly after a race is completed so that the two parties can discuss what went well and what the swimmer can work on in the next race. If this debriefing is part of the team's culture, the coach should clearly communicate that she expects to speak with each athlete within a set time after a race is completed. The coach should outline the topics to be discussed during this review period, such as splits, race strategy, and strengths or weaknesses.

With that said, some flexibility should be allowed given the unique attributes of each athlete. If an athlete prefers to reflect on the race for a while before speaking with the coach and that postponement in turn leads to more productive discussions and the athlete's taking increasing accountability for his swims, the coach should probably think about letting things play out that way. The coach also needs to know the personality of each athlete on the team and tailor feedback appropriately to elicit a positive response that will lead to improved performances in the next swim.

Athlete and Parent

All parents want to talk with their sons or daughters immediately after races and tell them all the good and bad things they saw from the stands. Although this practice may be OK following a good swim, these immediate discussions may spiral out of control if the athlete's performance was disappointing. Athletes need to define some ground rules with their parents about when they will talk about races and what they will talk about. If the parent and athlete agree that no discussion of the race will occur until the car ride home, then the parent should honor that agreement. The swimmer also needs to respect the predefined agreement, even if he does not want to talk about a given race. The coach may need to help define these boundaries, and parents and swimmers should be expected to honor them. This approach of setting guidelines and expectations can facilitate constructive communication and minimize unwanted distractions that could otherwise come up on the competition pool deck.

Athlete and Athlete

Athlete-to-athlete communication can take various forms during a competition. Although specific guidelines may need to be established between certain sets of athletes (similar to the rules for parents and athletes), in general the coach should strive to create a culture in which teamwork, sportsmanship, and positive support are expected among teammates.

Race Strategy

One important facet of racing is for swimmers to know how they want to swim a specific race and then to go out and swim that race. But the exhortation to "Go out there and swim your race!" is often easier said than done. Swimmers may find it difficult not to react to the other swimmers in the pool, and they can be drawn away from the planned race strategy. A few things can be done to assist in developing and sticking to a strategy come race day.

Develop a race strategy in advance of the big competition and practice it. All of a swimmer's training is designed for one thing—to prepare the athlete to swim fast in competition. Part of that training should focus on developing strategies and tactics for swimming the race (splits and pacing, number of kicks underwater off the wall, breathing patterns, and so on), and these need to be practiced. As with many of the items discussed so far, most of this preparation occurs before the day of the meet, and it should be so ingrained into the swimmer that he enters the competition with the confidence to swim the race as planned.

Drive the race strategy with data. As discussed in chapter 12, there are many more ways to look at a race than simply analyzing splits. How does an athlete swim a race most effectively? Is she a swimmer who needs to go out hard and try to hold on, or is she more effective by negatively splitting a race? Should she kick the full 15 meters underwater off each turn, or is she better off coming up at 10 meters? Collect data from races throughout the season and use those pieces of information to narrow in on the strategies that work for each athlete. Build the race plan to maximize a swimmer's strengths and minimize the weaknesses.

Emphasize routine. Again, nothing should change on race day, and the swimmers should follow the practiced prerace routines that have been shown to lead to competitive success. For many athletes, visualization of the race unfolding exactly as planned is a part of the prerace preparation and routine that leads to success in the pool.

Know the tendencies of the competitors. Swimmers are often told to ignore the competitors in the pool and to focus just on themselves. That approach is fine until the swimmer in the adjacent lane takes off on the first 100 of the 1,500-meter freestyle. Now what does your swimmer do? The best plan is to scout opponents and understand their tendencies. Use the same race analysis data to understand what the opponent is likely to do in the water so that your swimmer is prepared for what unfolds in the pool and can react accordingly. A swimmer will react much differently if, rather than coming into the race blind, he knows that the rabbit who takes off at the start of the race has shown that he will eventually fade and come back to the field. Use information to your advantage, both to understand your own swimmers' tendencies and to scout opponents.

Taking these relatively simple steps to develop and maintain a race strategy will go a long way to achieving peak performances in the pool.

Maintain a Performance Diary

Many of the best athletes in the world keep a performance diary that contains objective and subjective information about training and performance. This diary would contain not only the sets performed in practice and the races and times achieved in a meet but also information about how the swimmer slept the night before the race; what she ate during the day; what she did to warm up; how things felt before, during, and after the race; and so on. Athletes should be encouraged to keep training and performance logs because they serve as useful resources for identifying the strategies and factors that should be in place to achieve peak performances. Being able to look back at a year of training data, along with the athlete's comments, can help a coach and swimmer develop athlete-specific training and preparation strategies that will help drive success in the pool.

An example of a performance diary for a swimmer is presented in table 11.2. The specifics of the information contained in the diary presented here are not as important as the concepts conveyed. Tracking this information and reviewing it periodically will help identify patterns and trends of things that support fast swimming performance and things that may detract from performance.

Table 11.2 Sample Meet Performance Diary

Action	Time	Comments and notes
Ate breakfast	Around 7:00 am	Was nervous and didn't really feel like eating. Ate cereal with milk and some orange juice.
Arrived at the pool and warmed up	8:00 to 8:35	Did my standard prerace warm-up: 800 swim, 200 kick, 200 drill, 4 × 50 descend pace, 3 × dive 25s. Felt good.
First race: 200 free	9:20	Felt flat; had no legs in the second 100.
Recovery	9:30	No cool-down pool. Drank 200 ml Gatorade.
Prepare for second race: 100 butterfly	10:30	Did dynamic warm-up because there was no pool.
100 butterfly	10:47	Best time. Felt full of energy.

This performance diary shows detailed information about foods consumed at a competition and the athlete's feeling about the food consumed.

Injury Management and Recovery

What happens immediately after the race is critical to how a swimmer will perform in subsequent races. Recovery has been a theme of much of the information presented thus far—cooling down to clear lactate, fueling the body to replenish energy stores, and so on—but athletes must also learn to take care of any injuries. Competition pushes the body to limits that it does not attain in practice, and the physical demands imposed by racing can aggravate, or in some instances even cause, injury.

Athletes need to address injuries appropriately and follow the advice of medical providers, even in competition. The treatment for a soft-tissue injury such as a strain, sprain, or tendonitis should typically be to follow the PRICE principle. Each letter stands for one aspect of treatment the swimmer should follow:

Protection: Immediately following a session (or a race if there is enough time between events), protect the area from excessive movement to encourage healing and to minimize any additional damage that could occur.

Rest: Avoid performing any activity that causes pain in the injured area.

Ice: Apply ice to the injured areas for approximately 15 to 20 minutes. Ice helps control inflammation within the injured structures. Athletes should not apply heat to a soft-tissue injury unless directed to do so by a health care professional. In many instances, heat will only induce more swelling and is counterproductive during the initial phase of healing.

Compression: Compression, even when not applying ice, will help to minimize inflammation and swelling. Use an ACE bandage to wrap the injured area firmly but not so tightly that blood flow is restricted. Start by wrapping at the point farthest from the heart and move toward the torso. Loosen the bandage if you feel any numbness or tingling.

Elevation: To reduce swelling, elevate the injured area above the level of the heart when possible.

Again, these are general guidelines. The best advice is for swimmers to follow the recommendations of their medical provider to achieve the best results.

Develop a Checklist

As we have seen in this chapter, at every competition each swimmer needs to do a list of things, from remembering to put the goggles in the swim bag to making sure to bring an extra suit in case one splits. Most swimmers carry around a mental checklist of what needs to be done, but the better method is to write down the checklist on paper or enter the checklist into a tablet or smart phone and then actually go through the entire list before each competition or race. The world of sport offers some fantastic examples of athletes who forgot something in their preparation for a key competition, even though they had done the same thing hundreds of times before. We all should learn from their mistakes and make sure that those deterrents do not sabotage the swimmers on race day.

What should the checklist consist of? It should be a combination of general points, the things that all swimmers need to do such as pack suit, goggles, towel, and cap, and athlete-specific items such as prerace music and nutritional snacks. The coach should encourage each swimmer to develop a personal checklist and then go through that checklist with the athlete. The checklist should contain things that the swimmer needs to do the night before the competition, the morning of the competition before leaving for the pool, during the meet and before each race, and after the session has ended. As boring as it may sound, before each meet and even before each race within a meet, the swimmer should walk physically through the checklist to make sure that all the steps have been taken and that nothing the swimmer can control is being left to chance. A swimmer might have the following items, among others, on the checklist:

- Set the alarm the night before the meet to prevent oversleeping.
- Eat breakfast before leaving for the pool.
- Pack two pairs of goggles in case the goggle strap breaks.
- Make sure that the racing suit and other identified equipment is in the swim bag.
- Bring nutritional snacks and enough of them to consume throughout the day.
- Pack the iPod with the prerace psych-up music.
- Bring the diary to write down thoughts about the race.
- Refuel appropriately after each race or session.

Following these simple steps can help reduce stress and anxiety while putting the athlete in a better position to succeed on race day.

Summary

The first take-home message from this chapter is that competition should be fun. It should be the reward for all the hard work put in over months and sometimes years of training. Squandering all that hard work simply by forgetting something on race day would be a shame.

Swimmers should never do anything new or try anything new on race day. They need to use tried-and-true strategies that have proved successful before and have positively affected performance. Trying something new just because it is available or because other top athletes are using it is a mistake.

Coaches and athletes must plan tirelessly and think about the scenarios that can play out at a competition. They should develop solutions for challenges such as the lack of a cool-down pool or limited nutritional options and practice them before getting to the meet.

Every athlete should have a codified prerace or precompetition routine that can help prepare the body for competition while also focusing the swimmer on attaining the right energy state for competing. This precompetition strategy should include a warm-up and cool-down strategy, appropriate music to play before a race, visualization, and so on.

Swimmers need to plan for the nutritional challenges that are likely to occur at a meet. In short, all athletes should be encouraged to bring their own food and not rely on the venue-provided foods.

Athletes should develop checklists and follow them to avoid forgetting things important to being ready to compete. Communication plans for interactions between athlete and coach and between athlete and parents during a competition should be developed and practiced. Overall, coaches should strive to create an atmosphere of fun!

Following these basic principles will go a long way to enhancing the performance of swimmers on race day, whether it is a local competition or the Olympic Games.

CHAPTER 12

Analyzing Elite Swimming Performances

—Jodi Cossor, PhD

As the science of swimming has developed, the need to analyze competitions and the myriad factors that contribute to peak performances has evolved. Every aspect of an athlete's race, whether it is the start, a turn, or race strategy, offers an opportunity to improve and gain an advantage over competitors. Coaches have always used a stopwatch to record times and take splits within a race, but this information typically tells only part of the story about a race. Some coaches go an additional step and monitor the stroke rate in either strokes per minute (SPM) or seconds per stroke (SPS), and this information starts to paint a more detailed picture of what an athlete is doing in the water. Now technology has advanced to the point that it is possible to get even more detailed information about swimming performances that go far beyond split times and stroke rates. Tapping into this information and digging deep into the race factors to understand where races are won and lost is the emerging field of race analysis. By assessing what happens within a race, coaches and athletes are able to adapt their race models to maximize their potential and take advantage of their competitors' weaknesses. Even small insights gained through race analysis can enable an athlete to make technical or tactical changes during a competition and, more important, capitalize on opportunities and strengthen weaknesses over the following training cycle.

By using the race analysis support systems found as a part of many swimming programs, these days it is possible to capture more accurate and detailed information than coaches have previously been able to generate on their own. In theory, because the analysis is typically automated or performed with the assistance of a technical team, the coach is free to concentrate on the race and provide useful feedback to the swimmer soon after the event rather than simply focusing on capturing splits. This approach provides a powerful combination that is being used all over the world.

History of Race Analysis and Evaluation of Swimming Performances

The foundation of a race analysis system is the automatic capture of data from athletes as they swim or from video of the race to pull out the pertinent performance data. The development of race analysis systems has been an evolution of sorts. The first Olympic Games to be analyzed by swimming researchers was the 1988 Games held in Seoul, Korea (Kennedy et al. 1990). The analysis relied on the technology available at the time. Early race analysis systems required scientists to trawl manually through recorded video of a race and physically draw lines on transparent sheets placed over the video monitor to indicate the various distances in the pool. The scientists recorded the times required for each swimmer to execute various aspects of the race and manually input the information into a database to assist with further calculations, such as computing the swimmer's velocity. Stroke rates were measured directly using a stopwatch to record the time needed by the swimmer to execute a specified number of strokes (e.g., from right-hand entry to hand entry three strokes later), giving a stroke rate in either stroke cycles per minute (SPM) or seconds per stroke (SPS). By knowing swimming velocity and stroke rate, it was then possible to calculate stroke length, or the distance travelled during a stroke cycle, for various points in the race. This process was time consuming and labor intensive.

As technology improved, the analysis process became more automated and at the same time more accurate, to the point that results could be provided within minutes of the end of the race rather than the months it took to analyze races in a major competition using earlier methods. Even so, multiple sport scientists from various nations often filmed the races to conduct independent analyses for their own teams. Continued technological developments such as machine vision, which has the potential to track defined objects such as a swimmer's cap to measure real-time velocity and race segment times, aim to automate the process further so that less equipment and fewer staff are required to analyze more swims simultaneously and with greater accuracy.

Today's race analysis systems typically come in one of several flavors, depending on the scope of the analyses to be performed. Larger analysis systems tend to use multiple fixed cameras that have specific views of the pool, but none are able to follow a swimmer through a complete race, so they cannot be used effectively for feedback between swimmers and coaches. The separate images do allow a better field of view that permits accurate analyses, because the various cameras and the spaces they are filming can be calibrated to provide more accurate velocities and segment times. This approach uses similar processes to the original race analysis systems but includes better technology and software packages. Tracking of swimmers would be much easier if specific colored caps were used or computer chips could be placed on the cap or suit of the swimmer. Current FINA rules do not refer specifically to the use of colored caps or computer chips, although reference is made to prohibiting devices that may aid performance. The color of the cap normally is related to the team that the swimmer competes for, and the chip may change the profile of the swimmer and potentially increase drag as the swimmer moves through the water. For now, advances in camera technology still enable programmers to remove the noise of light and water around swimmers to track them in the pool. Researchers in Australia (Bruce Mason), Europe (Rein Haljand), France, Spain (Raul Arellano), and the United States have the capability to run these large systems, but they still generally require a large staff to operate them.

More portable and user-friendly systems have been developed in Great Britain, Australia, Japan, the Netherlands, and Switzerland. Generally, these systems are made up of a small video camera mounted on a tripod that is connected to a laptop to capture the race footage directly to a computer in electronic format. The race analysis is completed after the race is finished, usually as soon as a gap in the schedule allows. Feedback to coaches and athletes is usually multifaceted, combining video of the swim shared through computers or iPads and numerical data provided by reports generated from the quantifiable data recorded by the system. Feedback is typically provided to the coaches and athletes both at the pool and at team accommodations to satisfy their needs based on the competition and rest schedules.

Data Collection

As mentioned earlier, a typical race analysis aims to provide detailed information to coaches so that they can find small areas of improvement that can be used to enhance athlete performance either in the next race or at subsequent competitions. The data that is collected contains both temporal and performance data. Time is relatively easy to measure. In most instances, information about the actual split times is taken directly from the official timing system at the competition. To provide more detailed analysis within a specific length of the pool, the pool is often divided into sections for further analysis.

Besides providing lap split times, many race analysis systems record and track additional temporal variables such as the following:

• **Start time.** The start time is the time from the gun until the swimmer's head passes through a set distance, usually 15 meters. Within this parameter, information can be provided on the time that the swimmer spends on the block as well as when the swimmer enters the water after the flight phase and surfaces after the underwater phase. Because most swimmers surface before the 15-meter mark, a free-swimming component is included in this time.

• **Turn time.** Turn times tend to have the greatest variation in measurements when comparing systems among countries, but most measure the time it takes the athlete to swim from a predefined distance out from the wall when entering the turn until the swimmer passes a second predefined point when exiting the turn. Early turn information measured the time it took for the swimmer's head to travel from 7.5 meters in to the wall and back out to the same distance.

Other systems use 5 meters in and out (the distance from the backstroke flags to the wall) to compute turn times, because this distance is easy to measure in both competition and training. Some systems use 5 meters in to the wall and 10 meters out, whereas others use 5 meters in to the wall and back out to 15 meters. In every case, the scientists aim to use distances that most closely relate to the turn component and rely on swimmers' maximizing their speed when traveling underwater such that they should be aiming to surface as close to 15 meters as possible after each wall. Like the start time, turn time includes some information on the actual swimming (not just the turn), but the use of set distances allows comparisons to be made among different swimmers.

- **Finish time.** As the swimmer finishes a race, the finish time is measured from the time the head passes the 5-meter mark until the hand is on the wall. An allowance is made for the swimmer's outstretched hand during this phase because all other time measures taken during the race are based on the position of the head when it crosses specified landmarks. The main advantage of recording the finish time is to determine whether any decrease in velocity occurs during the final few strokes of the race.

- **Lap segment times.** Within each lap a swimmer is highly unlikely to travel at exactly the same speed through each 50-meter segment of a race. So to provide more detailed analysis and give a better picture of how speed may change within a lap, the pool length may be divided into several segments. The most traditional division occurs at the 25-meter mark (for long-course competitions), giving two segments per lap, but other systems divide the lap into three to five segments. This method allows a more accurate representation of what is occurring at each stage of the race, but it can also been seen as providing too much information, particularly in longer events.

- **Velocity.** Using the time and distance data generated from the free-swimming components of the race analysis, velocity can be calculated using the formula $V = d / t$, where velocity (V) is expressed in meters per second (m / s), distance (d) is the traveled distance measured in meters, and time (t) is the time in seconds it took to cover the set distance. Velocity can be computed as an average for the entire length of the pool or for smaller predefined segments within a lap. A swimmer's velocity is also influenced by stroke rate and stroke length, and the mathematical relationship is shown in the formula $V = SL \times SR$, where velocity (V) is measured in meters per second, stroke length (SL) in meters per stroke cycle, and stroke rate (SR) in stroke cycles per second.

- **Stroke rate (SR).** Stroke rates are not always used by coaches, but they can help increase the understanding of how efficient a swimmer is throughout the various free-swimming segments of a race. This measurement can be taken relatively easily using a stopwatch as the time needed to complete a set number of stroke cycles. Stroke rates for all four strokes are typically expressed as stroke cycles per minute (or second) and do not look specifically at individual strokes (e.g., a single arm pull in freestyle or backstroke). This number represents the number of strokes that a swimmer would take in each unit of time if he maintained the same stroke rate for an entire minute (or second). To measure stroke rates accurately in freestyle and backstroke, the time must be recorded between consistent points within a stroke cycle, such as from one right-hand entry through to the following right-hand entry. Each complete stroke in breaststroke and butterfly is also classified as a stroke cycle because both arms are pulling at the same time. If calculating the stroke rate using the SR function available on many stopwatches these days, the coach would time how long it takes the swimmer to complete three full stroke cycles. Note that some coaches and race analysis programs may express SR in a slightly different way, as seconds per stroke cycle. When using this convention, SR is computed by again measuring the time taken by the swimmer to complete a set number of stroke cycles (usually 10) and dividing this time by the number of stroke cycles completed.

- **Stroke length (SL).** Stroke length, the distance that a swimmer travels in each stroke cycle, is a bit more complicated to measure than stroke rate. Some coaches like to count the number of strokes per lap and divide this by the distance travelled, typically incorporating some form of allowance for the underwater phase. A more accurate measure, however, is to use the equation that swimming velocity = stroke rate × stroke length, where stroke rate is expressed in cycles per second ($V = SR \times SL$). If velocity and stroke rate are known, it is possible to solve for stroke length ($SL = V / SR$). The general trend is that an increase in stroke rate results in a decrease in stroke length, resulting in a similar velocity. In many races, swimmers increase their stroke rate in the final 15 meters. Stroke length usually decreases when stroke rate increases, and this decrease in stroke length may offset any gains from increased stroke rate, resulting in decreased swimming velocity and an increase in energy use.

- **Stroke count.** Counting strokes is simple to do, and it is measured as a count of individual arm strokes rather than cycles for all strokes. Most swimmers cover a set distance (e.g., 50 meters) using a consistent number of strokes for a given pace. Coaches are able to monitor changes in stroke efficiency by noting any changes in stroke count for a given pace. Additionally, they can note changes throughout a race and gain a feeling for how technique changes. In general, swimmers tend to have a lower stroke count on the first lap of a race, but they should be fairly consistent for every lap thereafter if the race is made up of only one stroke. A change in stroke count could result from a change in the underwater distance, stroke length, and kick rate.

- **Efficiency index.** Some race analysis systems include information on the efficiency of the swimmer through the calculation of an efficiency index. An efficiency index is computed as the product of swimming velocity and stroke length (efficiency index = $V \times SL$) and is measured in m^2 / s (i.e., a high efficiency rating means fast and long swimming). This measure allows comparisons to be made within a swimmer, but not between swimmers. An ideal race would be one in which a swimmer has a minimal decrease in the efficiency index between the first and last free-swimming segments of the race.

Race Analysis Feedback

People tend to prefer receiving information and data feedback in one of three main formats: video, graphical, or numerical. Therefore, most of the reports generated from the race analysis provide information in both graphical and numerical formats to facilitate interpretation. A video is also provided to accompany the data so that coaches and swimmers are able to see what the numbers mean and relate that to what the athlete is doing in the pool. The video is usually the first form of feedback that an athlete receives, and the coach can use it as reinforcement to confirm or deny what was seen during the actual race. Some coaches use the information right away, but others do not look at the race statistics until they are planning the next training cycle and can account for the strengths and weaknesses of the previous race to train for an improvement in the next race.

With more scientists and swimming federations providing race analysis during competitions, further improvements to race evaluation and data interpretation are being discussed. For example, let's consider at the start. As highlighted earlier, a number of factors can influence the final start time, including the time on the block, the flight time while the athlete is in the air, the time underwater, and the free-swimming phase. A wide range of parameters could be measured within each of these phases, but doing this with the current analysis software packages and hardware is not possible. But some countries have developed technologies that can record force data from the blocks and integrate that with video to gain a clearer picture of how start technique, specifically the forces that are generated, affects overall start performance. Likewise, the turn should also be divided into further components within the in phase, rotation phase, underwater phase, and out phase of the skill, and these components should be monitored throughout the race. The point where the weakness occurs is currently not always clear, although it is easy to see whether one swimmer is better than another. Access to underwater images for all lanes will further increase understanding of the mechanics of the stroke, particularly at the point where efficiency drops off.

A fine line will always separate providing enough data to help improve performance and delivering so much information that the coach and athlete become overwhelmed and subject to paralysis by analysis. Race analysis will continue to evolve as technology develops and we gain new understanding about the factors that truly influence performance. Some areas currently included in race analysis will remain; others may be discarded if people find that they are no longer relevant to the outcome. Coaches can always work with their team scientists after the competition to delve further into the race to measure something specific to their swimmers.

Competition Data Examples

Now that we have established a theoretical framework about race analysis, let's look at some of the ways in which a coach can use race analysis to dissect a race and make decisions that can affect athlete performance. A number of researchers provide race analysis to coaches from all nations during selected competitions. One of these is Rein Haljand of Estonia, who is responsible for the analysis of LEN competitions held in Europe. The information provided by his analysis group can be invaluable both during the competition and afterward because it allows detailed analysis of all swimmers in the semifinals and finals, whereas other systems may focus on individual athletes.

The website http://swim.ee/competition/index.html contains information from competitions that Mr. Haljand and his team analyzed and the way in which they conduct the race analysis. Mr. Haljand has developed and adapted a software and analysis package over the years to work with the latest technology as well as to provide information quickly. Fixed cameras set up along the length of the pool require only one operator and one person to analyze the videos, which makes it portable and efficient. The current version provides information on stroke rates at various stages of the race, depending on the length and type of race. Turn in and out times are provided, and this data can be used with information on race splits such as those found at www.omegatiming.com to generate substantially more information about the race.

An example of the data output from this analysis system is outlined in table 12.1. The table shows race data from the women's 400-meter IM final at the 2010 European Long Course (ELC) Championships held in Budapest. Here are some pieces of information to consider as you review the data:

- Block time, an estimate of reaction time, measures the time from when the race starts to when the athlete actually leaves the block.
- Start time is the time to 15 meters.
- Within each length, two stroke rates are taken, one in the first 25-meter segment of the pool and the other in the second 25-meter segment.
- Split times taken at various points as the athlete approaches and leaves the wall give an idea of turn times and where speed is being gained or lost.

Using this information, it is relatively easy to make direct comparisons among the swimmers in the race in both their splits and stroke rates for each of the four strokes. As evident from the data presented, most swimmers have quite even stroke rates for the two laps of butterfly except Hosszu, who shows a difference of 10 SPM, suggesting a lack of efficiency in one of the two laps. By looking at more of her individual races, her coach would be able to determine the rate at which she is the most efficient and work on this during training. The rest of the race appears to be similar for all swimmers between the first and second stroke rates calculated in each stroke. Although comparing one swimmer to another is often helpful in understanding what the best are doing and how they swim their races, the true power of race analysis comes in looking at data from an individual swimmer and seeing how those numbers change within a race or over time.

Coaches can use this information to enhance the skill components of the race, which have been shown to be important to the result of many races (Arellano

Table 12.1 Race Statistics for the Women's 400-Meter IM Final at the 2010 ELC

	Nordenstam	Murphy	Hosszu	Miley	Klinar	Martynova	Jakabos	Zavadova
	1	2	3	4	5	6	7	8
Block	0.79	0.85	0.84	0.78	0.87	0.86	0.87	0.93
Start	7.50	7.54	7.04	7.42	7.36	7.48	7.42	7.76
SR 1	50	57	52	56	54	54	47	47
SR 2	47	55	42	55	51	49	42	45
45 m	26.96	27.18	26.12	26.84	27.22	26.86	26.74	27.10
50 m	30.03	30.12	29.07	30.04	30.27	29.91	29.67	30.30
65 m	39.89	40.06	38.74	39.70	39.96	39.46	39.54	40.42
95 m	01:00.60	01:01.00	00:58.86	01:00.22	01:00.38	01:00.10	00:59.80	01:01.40
100 m	01:03.92	01:04.27	01:01.97	01:03.50	01:03.38	01:03.29	01:02.83	01:04.70
115 m	01:14.78	01:14.96	01:12.18	01:13.68	01:13.86	01:13.66	01:13.16	01:15.14
SR 3	34	41	40	43	41	37	34	36
SR 4	33	39	37	42	38	37	34	33
145 m	01:38.00	01:37.70	01:33.54	01:35.04	01:35.96	01:36.18	01:34.56	01:37.26
150 m	01:42.11	01:41.30	01:37.32	01:38.65	01:39.67	01:39.93	01:38.12	01:41.06
165 m	01:52.00	01:51.22	01:46.42	01:48.06	01:49.36	01:49.38	01:47.48	01:50.66
195 m	02:15.24	02:14.32	02:08.36	02:09.84	02:12.14	02:12.20	02:09.60	02:12.98
200 m	02:18.61	02:17.55	02:11.69	02:13.05	02:15.62	02:15.56	02:12.31	02:16.38
215m	02:29.72	02:29.18	02:22.68	02:23.96	02:27.06	02:26.96	02:24.10	02:28.20
SR 5	37	39	36	37	37	40	36	34
SR 6	36	38	37	40	39	41	35	37
245 m	02:53.02	02:54.02	02:47.66	02:47.86	02:51.94	02:52.02	02:49.42	02:53.84
250 m	02:56.80	02:57.98	02:51.32	02:51.50	02:55.80	02:55.74	02:53.69	02:57.71
265 m	03:08.08	03:09.52	03:02.92	03:02.60	03:06.92	03:07.18	03:05.04	03:09.58
295 m	03:32.36	03:34.96	03:28.48	03:26.74	03:32.30	03:33.10	03:30.26	03:35.26
300 m	03:36.14	03:39.02	03:32.21	03:30.42	03:36.00	03:37.08	03:34.03	03:39.29
315 m	03:46.02	03:48.62	03:41.52	03:39.70	03:45.40	03:46.64	03:43.90	03:49.08
SR 7	42	50	40	44	48	47	41	45
SR 8	42	48	38	45	47	46	41	43
345 m	04:06.92	04:08.98	04:00.84	03:59.04	04:04.64	04:06.66	04:03.56	04:09.10
350 m	04:10.62	04:11.88	04:04.30	04:02.33	04:07.94	04:10.16	04:06.97	04:12.67
365 m	04:19.50	04:20.86	04:13.10	04:10.94	04:16.52	04:18.94	04:15.66	04:21.68
395 m	04:40.02	04:40.68	04:33.36	04:30.28	04:35.44	04:39.60	04:35.10	04:42.24
400 m	04:43.00	04:43.45	04:36.43	04:33.09	04:38.13	04:42.50	04:37.92	04:45.24

LEN competition analyses by swim.ee, Rein Haljand.

et al. 2000; Blanksby, Nicholson, and Elliott 2002; Burkett, Mellifont, and Mason 2010; Mason 1997). For example, the reaction and start times to 15 meters show that Hosszu was on average 0.5 seconds faster to 15 meters than the other swimmers in the race although her block time (the total time on the block from when the gun is fired until the toes leave the block) was not the fastest in this race. In shorter events, the start time can make up more than 20 percent of the overall race time (Mason and Cossor 2001), but it is less important to the outcome of longer races.

Taking the information presented in table 12.1, turn times were calculated for each swimmer, and those times are presented in table 12.2. Turn time was computed as the time needed to cover the 5 meters in to and 15 meters out of the wall. Because the event was an individual medley, each turn time was expected to be different, but the fastest (bold) and slowest (italics) swimmer could still be identified for each turn.

In the example, Zavadova showed the slowest turn times in five of the seven turns, and Miley had the fastest turn times for three of the seven turns. Coaches can use this information to identify strengths as well as areas where swimmers can improve relative to the competition. Although the information presented in table 12.1 may seem like a jumble of numbers at first glance, after coaches have had time to become familiar with the data and understand what it means, they are quickly able to identify areas of strength and areas in need of improvement.

A second example of how the race analysis can be used to evaluate performance is illustrated using data from the men's 100-meter backstroke final at the European Championships (table 12.3).

Note that more information is included in this table because of the shorter duration of the event. More changes are expected to take place in shorter events like this, so this analysis shows split information for a greater number of segments in each lap. The assumption is that stroke rates would not vary much in this event, so only one parameter is calculated for each lap.

The time turned in by Camille Lacourt was a European record at the time. We can see how he achieved this by looking closely at the free-swimming and skill components of the race. Table 12.3 shows that Lacourt did not have the fastest

Table 12.2 Total Turn Times for the Women's 400-Meter IM Final at the 2010 ELC

	Nordenstam	Murphy	Hosszu	Miley	Klinar	Martynova	Jakabos	Zavadova
Turn 1	00:12.93	00:12.88	00:12.62	00:12.86	00:12.74	**00:12.60**	00:12.80	*00:13.32*
Turn 2	*00:14.18*	00:13.96	**00:13.32**	00:13.46	00:13.48	00:13.56	00:13.36	00:13.74
Turn 3	*00:14.00*	00:13.52	**00:12.88**	00:13.02	00:13.40	00:13.20	00:12.92	00:13.40
Turn 4	00:14.48	00:14.86	00:14.32	**00:14.12**	00:14.92	00:14.76	00:14.50	*00:15.22*
Turn 5	00:15.06	00:15.50	00:15.26	**00:14.74**	00:14.98	00:15.16	00:15.62	*00:15.74*
Turn 6	00:13.66	00:13.66	00:13.04	**00:12.96**	00:13.10	00:13.54	00:13.64	*00:13.82*
Turn 7	*00:12.58*	**00:11.88**	00:12.26	00:11.90	**00:11.88**	00:12.28	00:12.10	*00:12.58*

Table 12.3 Race Statistics for the Men's 100-Meter Backstroke Final at the 2010 ELC

	Donets	Driebergen	Borisov	Lacourt	Stravius	Grigoriadis	Wildeboer	Tancock
	1	2	3	4	5	6	7	8
Block	0.70	0.63	0.57	0.68	0.65	0.65	0.62	0.59
Start	6.18	6.54	6.48	6.34	6.20	6.62	6.38	6.26
SR 1	47	48	50	48	48	53	50	55
25 m	11.74	12.16	11.98	11.72	11.72	12.00	11.84	11.68
35 m	17.18	17.58	17.52	16.98	17.24	17.36	17.28	17.16
45 m	23.12	23.26	23.42	22.70	23.04	23.20	23.14	23.02
50 m	26.00	26.23	26.24	25.43	25.86	26.20	25.99	25.80
65 m	32.84	33.56	33.46	32.24	32.76	33.70	33.40	33.10
75 m	38.76	39.28	39.38	37.80	38.60	39.44	39.20	38.84
85 m	44.92	45.22	45.30	43.46	44.52	45.32	45.20	44.82
95 m	51.34	51.44	51.60	49.46	50.76	51.58	51.56	51.18
SR 2	46	50	51	49	46	47	46	54
100 m	54.10	54.40	54.34	52.11	53.44	54.27	54.38	53.86

LEN competition analyses by Swim.ee, Rein Haljand.

start time to 15 meters (Donets did at 6.18 seconds), but table 12.4, generated from information on www.swim.ee and www.omegatiming.com, shows that his total turn time was 0.18 seconds faster than Donets' time. The outbound turn time (time from feet touching the wall until the head passed the 65-meter mark) was similar for the two swimmers, so Lacourt gained the advantage during the inward turn phase (the time from the head passing the 45-meter mark until the feet touched the wall).

Table 12.3 shows that Lacourt increased his stroke rate slightly between the first lap and the second, whereas Tancock and Stravius decreased theirs slightly. It is unlikely that this would account for the differences in velocity among the swimmers. Based on this information, the assumption is that Lacourt was able to maintain a greater stroke length (longer stroke) throughout the race compared with the other medalists. Consequently, this aspect would be something that Lacourt's competitors could work on in the future to improve race performance.

Table 12.4 Skill Information in the Men's 100-Meter Backstroke Final at the 2010 ELC

	Donets	Driebergen	Borisov	Lacourt	Stravius	Grigoriadis	Wildeboer	Tancock
Turn in	2.88	2.97	2.82	**2.73**	2.82	*3.00*	2.85	2.78
Turn out	6.84	7.33	7.22	**6.81**	6.90	*7.50*	7.41	7.30
Turn total	9.72	10.30	10.04	**9.54**	9.72	*10.50*	10.26	10.08
Start	**6.18**	6.54	6.48	6.34	6.20	*6.62*	6.38	6.26

Attention can then be focused on the free-swimming segment data for further information about the race. Figure 12.1 is a graph generated from the race analysis; it tracks the free-swimming velocities for the medalists Lacourt, Stravius, and Tancock. The graph shows that for every segment, Lacourt was the fastest swimmer in the pool, and he appeared to increase his velocity from the first to the second segment, something that the other two medalists did not do.

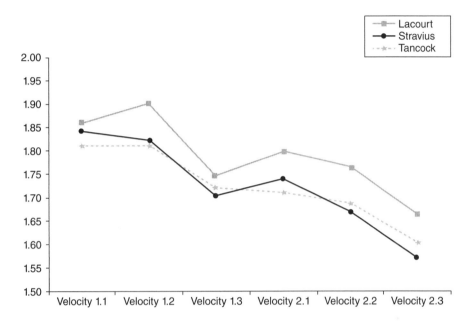

▶ **Figure 12.1** Free-swimming velocity in the men's 100-meter backstroke final at the 2010 ELC.

Race analysis data is valuable not only for comparing one swimmer with another but also, when used regularly over time, for charting improvements within a given swimmer. Figure 12.2, produced from the website www.swim-rankings.net, highlights the dramatic improvement in performance for Camille Lacourt in the 100-meter backstroke over an 18-month period. The graph illustrates that his performance improved steadily and continued to improve even after the changes to the swimsuit rules. Further analysis of his race statistics will give greater understanding of where the dramatic improvements came from and how others in the same event can maximize their performances.

As these examples have shown, coaches and swimmers can gain a great deal of information from race statistics that are available freely on the Internet from a number of websites. What they choose to do with this information is generally limited only by imagination. The more that people play with the numbers, the more questions they will likely come up with.

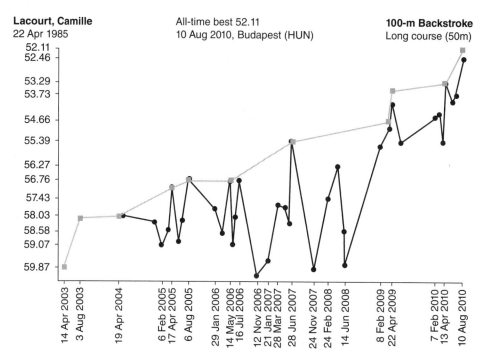

▶ **Figure 12.2** Personal best times for Camille Lacourt in the 100-meter backstroke (50 meters).

Improving Performance

Each swimmer has an optimal stroke rate and stroke length, depending on factors such as athlete physiology, anthropometric variables, and event distance, but coaches and swimmers should know that it is possible to alter both stroke rate and stroke length during different phases of the training cycle to maximize swimming velocity throughout the race. After the free-swimming phases of the race have been optimized, individual skill components of the event can be improved. As discussed earlier, the start and turn can be broken down into a number of phases, but finding accurate information on how swimmers perform in those areas during competitions is generally not possible. The easiest area to improve is the underwater phase of both starts and turns, because the velocity underwater is faster than the free-swimming velocity in many events. Swimmers have some choices to make about how to optimize underwater performance; they can choose to use large-amplitude, small-frequency kicks or a small-amplitude, large-frequency technique to generate propulsion. No general recommendations apply to all swimmers when it comes to identifying the best kick, so swimmers should experiment with various techniques to find the one that works best for them.

Kicking is a trainable skill, and all swimmers should practice various techniques off every wall to see the benefits. Depending on the athlete, several limiting factors, such as range of movement in the hip region, can affect performance. Most of these areas can be improved easily through specific interventions such as stretching techniques. As a rule, coaches should train athletes to maximize both the distance off the wall in the underwater phase and the kicking speed.

Evolution of Competition Analysis Research and Findings

With information having been collected at major competitions for more than 40 years, a number of research groups have attempted to make sense of the reams of data and information that has been collected. Generally, this analysis has relied on a large group of people to collect and then analyze the video footage to provide race statistics, but as technology improves, so does the processing speed.

As mentioned earlier, the first race analysis of an Olympic Games was performed in 1988; nearly all 400 swimmers who competed in the heats of the 100-meter events, across all four strokes, were filmed and analyzed. Stroke length and stroke rate were computed from the video footage and then combined with age, height, and race time. The main findings of this research were the following:

- The men were faster, taller, and older and had longer stroke lengths than the women.
- Each stroke (FR, BA, BR, FL) appeared to differ from the others in the relationships between stroke rate, stroke length, and final time and velocity.

An international team then analyzed the swimming events at the 1992 Olympics in Barcelona. One of the papers written by Arellano et al. (1994) focused on the 50-meter, 100-meter, and 200-meter freestyle races. More than 300 swimmers who competed in these events were analyzed so that trends could be highlighted. All swimmers who competed in both the heats and finals had their fastest swim time used for statistical purposes. Races were analyzed to determine the start time (time to cover the first 10 meters), turn time (from 7.5 meters in to the wall and back to the same point), and finish time (the final 10 meters of the event). Information on the free-swimming component of the race included the time for set distances (varying from 30 to 35 meters, depending on the lap) and stroke rates over five stroke cycles. The distance and time were then used to calculate the velocity in the midsection of the pool. Stroke length was derived from the velocity and stroke rate information. Swimmers reported their own age and height. Because of the close relationship between height and weight, weight was not included in the research. The research produced the following results:

- Males were approximately 9 percent faster, older, and taller than the female swimmers competing in the same events. For example, the males had between 9.0 and 9.4 percent longer strokes than females and were 9.1 percent faster for the event time in the 100-meter freestyle.

- A strong correlation was found between stroke length and event time. Swimmers who were more successful (based on time) had a longer stroke length compared with their competitors. As expected, height was a major contributor to having a longer stroke length.

- Surprisingly, stroke rate was significantly correlated only to height in the women's 50-meter freestyle and to the start time in the women's 200-meter freestyle.

- As the race distance increased from 50 meters to 200 meters, the swimmers tended to be younger and the stroke rates decreased.

In a more detailed analysis, Cappaert, Pease, and Troup (1995) conducted a three-dimensional analysis of the swimmers in the center lane for the heats and finals of the men's 100-meter freestyle. They found the following results:

- Elite swimmers (those in the cyclically seeded heats and finals) had a lower hip roll angle compared with the shoulder roll angle, but they both occurred in the same direction.

- The subelite swimmers (those in the unseeded heats) had greater lateral hip movement and less body symmetry compared with the elite group.

- The calculated propulsive forces were more effective throughout the stroke rather than demonstrating larger forces within the elite group.

- The elite athletes were more streamlined, which aided in their superior performance compared with the subelite group.

A team led by Dr. Bruce Mason of the Australian Institute of Sport was responsible for analyzing the swimming races at the Sydney 2000 Olympic Games. Fixed cameras were placed in the overhead gantry and were then cabled back to a central analysis room. More than 40 staff and volunteers worked around the clock to provide feedback to all swimmers qualifying for the semifinals and finals before the next round of competition. As in previous research, each race was divided into the free-swimming and skill components for analysis. Starts were defined as the time from the starting signal until the swimmer passed the 15-meter mark, and turns were measured for the 7.5 meters in to the wall and back out to the same point. Finishes were the final 5 meters of the race, but 0.5 meter was allowed for the outstretched arm during velocity calculations. Stroke rate, stroke length, and velocity were calculated for each of the free-swimming sections. All this information was provided as a table and graph. Individual reports and a summary of eight swimmers in the semifinals and finals were generated.

Researchers wrote numerous papers using this data, including information on the different strokes (Chatard et al. 2001a, 2001b, 2001c, 2001d, 2001e), medalists versus nonmedalists (Girold et al. 2001), swimming efficiency (Riewald 2001; Wilson et al. 2001), and distances (Arellano et al. 2001). Mason and Cossor (2001) looked specifically at the turns, and Cossor and Mason (2001) focused on the starts. Ikuta, Mason, and Cossor (2001) then compared the Japanese finalists with other finalists in the 100-meter events. All research was supported by FINA. The research initiatives produced several key findings:

- Chatard et al. (2001d) and Girold et al. (2001) found that the fastest backstroke swimmers had a higher stroke rate and lower stroke length than the nonmedalists.
- In the breaststroke events, a long stroke length was important for the female swimmers, whereas for the men performance in the third 50-meter lap was most highly correlated with race time.
- Turns and the breaststroke leg were seen to be important and distinguishing factors in the women's individual medley results.
- The first lap was important to overall placing in the women's freestyle event, whereas turns were important for the men's freestyle.
- Although previous research had suggested the relevance of stroke length to overall performance, Riewald (2001) found no significant differences between the finalists and semifinalists when looking at normalized stroke length and normalized efficiency (both normalized to athlete height).
- Mason and Cossor (2001) found significant relationships between the turn in and out times in the short-axis strokes (butterfly and breaststroke) as well as the underwater phase of the turn.
- The fastest turns were those in which the swimmer spent more time and travelled farther under the water.
- The start analysis showed that the underwater phase was significantly correlated to good start times to 15 meters (Cossor and Mason 2001).
- Ikuta, Mason, and Cossor (2001) showed that skill performance is important to overall race results. They speculated that inferior skills by the Japanese swimmers resulted in poor swims compared with those of the other competitors.
- Arellano et al. (2001) noted the lack of trends in race strategies of elite swimmers.

A French team was contracted by FINA to analyze the swimming events during the Athens Olympic Games. Cameras were set up perpendicular to the swimming pool and recorded at a central station. Analysis of the race variables was then provided to the national teams for all finalists and semifinalists on the day after the event had been swum. Hellard et al. 2008 compared the 200-meter race analysis of female French swimmers from their Olympic Trials with their performances in Athens. The start was the time needed to reach 15 meters, turns were 7.5 meters in to the wall and back out again, and the finish was defined as the final 7.5 meters of the race. Stroke rate was calculated from one stroke cycle, and one rate was used for each 100-meter race segment. The changes in variables over the course of the race were measured, and they showed that less difference occurred in the stroke rate variability for elite swimmers compared with national-level swimmers. The velocity drop-off between the first segment and the last segment was least in freestyle and greatest in breaststroke.

Additional research by Pyne, Trewin, and Hopkins (2004); Trewin, Hopkins, and Pyne (2004); and Costa et al. (2010) looked at performance progressions over time and found that approximately 1 percent improvement is seen each year in top-ranked swimmers.

Practical Applications: Competition

What can coaches do in their home environment with this wealth of swimming competition information? The first step is to collect as much race-specific information on the athlete as possible, looking specifically at the free-swimming and skill components of a race. As discussed earlier in the chapter, figure 12.3 presents graphically the factors that contribute to swimming performance. The second step is to use this information within the training environment to improve performances at the next major competition. During less important competitions, coaches may be able to focus on one particular skill (i.e., fast turns, negative splitting, or lower stroke count) rather than the entire race strategy.

Where can coaches get their data? Generally, split times are provided by the official timing systems used at each competition, so coaches should be free to step back and watch the race or collect additional information. Dividing each lap into different segments and measuring times needed to cover each segment provides an estimate of the velocity throughout the lap. The first 25-meter section in each length is usually faster than the second because of the push-off from the wall in a start or turn.

To obtain additional data, the most accurate way to analyze performances is by using video-recording equipment. But if this is not available, coaches can enlist the services of a parent or another swimmer to collect stroke data. Stroke counts are simple to measure, and stroke rate can be determined using most stopwatches. The greater the number of stroke cycles used to calculate the stroke

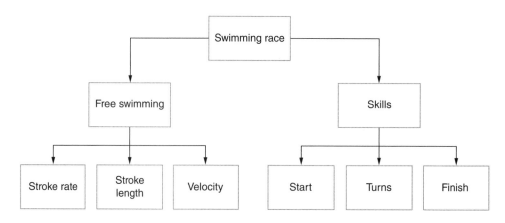

► **Figure 12.3** Broad-level race components.

rate, the more accurate it will be, but this can be difficult when observing more than one swimmer in a race. Aim to time at least three complete stroke cycles when possible. Stroke rate can be measured in either SPM or SPS, as mentioned earlier. Coaches will have a personal preference about calculating and referring to stroke rate when working with their swimmers.

A crude method of calculating stroke length is to divide the number of stroke cycles by the distance traveled. Maglischo (2003) suggested using the 40-meter section between the flags to limit the influence of the turn in the calculation. If a butterfly swimmer takes 18 strokes to cover 40 meters with a stroke rate of 46 strokes per minute using the stroke rate feature on a stopwatch, the following information can be computed:

$$\text{Stroke length} = \text{distance} / \text{stroke count}$$
$$= 40 / 18$$
$$= 2.22 \text{ meters}$$

$$\text{Stroke rate} = 46 \text{ strokes per minute}$$
$$= 46 \text{ (strokes)} / 60 \text{ (seconds)}$$
$$= 0.77 \text{ stroke cycles per second}$$

$$\text{Velocity} = \text{stroke length (in meters per stroke cycle)} \times$$
$$\text{stroke rate (in stroke cycles per second)}$$
$$= 2.22 \text{ meters per stroke cycle} \times$$
$$0.77 \text{ cycles per second}$$
$$= 1.71 \text{ meters per second}$$

Race Analysis Equipment

Some new technologies, and some not so new, can help coaches break down races. Stopwatches such as the NK (www.nkhome.com) can store splits and stroke rate information that can then be downloaded to a computer using their software. Therefore, one skilled operator is all that is required. Most coaches will find taking splits and stroke rates throughout a race easier than what they do in most training sessions.

The video performance monitor produced and sold by YSDI (ysdi.jp) is a slightly larger tool that is able to monitor the stroke rate, stroke length, and velocity of a swimmer throughout a race. A video signal can be input into the system so that the data is saved onto the race footage, and the printout produces both numerical and graphical formats of the race variables.

Although many countries have developed and use their own race analysis software, one is available for purchase (www.natrisoft.nl/sportswatch/en/products.html) and is used by a number of European teams. A pocket version is available as well as the more detailed software for laptop use when the races are filmed and analyzed after the event. In some instances, the database of earlier competitions can be purchased so that comparisons can be made with other swimmers.

Practical Applications: Training

Research has been mixed on the benefits of analyzing stroke rate and stroke length in practice to find optimal values for each. Improving either of these variables, however, is likely to improve swimming velocity. In general, as stroke length increases, stroke rate decreases. The net result is relatively little change to swimming velocity. This phenomenon can be seen particularly during the last segment of a race when swimmers tend to increase their stroke rate but do not increase their swimming velocity. As a general recommendation, stroke length can be improved by minimizing the number of strokes taken per lap while maintaining set times. When this has become automatic, swimmers can work on increasing their stroke rate. Although an increased stroke rate is likely to be more beneficial in the shorter events, this trend has not always been seen in the literature. Sprinters need to be able to hold the water to generate power from each stroke and may have adopted a flatter sprinting technique. Coupled with a longer stroke length and lower stroke rate, this approach can lead to improved performances in some swimmers. Keep in mind, however, that all swimmers have an optimal stroke rate that is influenced by the swimmer's physiology and anthropometry. Remember that more is not always better (i.e., higher SR does not always translate to faster swimming) because any deviation from the optimal SR leads to wasted energy.

An additional area of focus for the coach and athlete should be the underwater portion of a race. Swimmers should work on this skill every day in training. Not everyone is good underwater after starts and turns, but nearly all swimmers can develop this skill. Underwater distance can be maximized early in the season, and speed can be improved later. Watching athletes such as Michael Phelps, who excels in the underwater portion of a race, highlights the advantages that can be achieved in this phase, even at the end of a 400-meter IM. The goal for elite swimmers should be to travel with a velocity of approximately 2 meters per second when under the water, because this is faster than most free-swimming velocities and is simple to measure during training. Start and turn times can be measured over set distances and monitored throughout a training season, but for consistency the same person should be used.

Coaches can also incorporate test sets into training that factor in a combination of pacing, stroke count, and stroke rate to produce a score that, in turn, can be used to evaluate performance and progress toward developing more efficient strokes.

- Pacing sets: Pacing is required in most training sets, and the more effective the swimmer can become at achieving the set times, the more effective the set can become.
- Stroke count sets: Swimmers can count their strokes and provide feedback to the coach in training. This method does rely on honesty, but stroke count is a simple marker that all swimmers in the training group can use.

- Stroke rate sets: Measuring stroke rate does become a little more complicated in the training environment, so in this instance some people find it easier to use one stroke cycle rather than three.

After swimmers have done these sets more than once, they quickly identify ways in which to improve their scores. But because these performance indices are related to the key race components, any improvements in the test sets have the potential to improve race performance.

Summary

The monitoring of swims in competitions and training can provide valuable insight into performance and identify ways in which swimmers can improve their performances. Although systems are available to generate a wide array of data, race analysis does not need to be user intensive or require expensive equipment to provide the swimmer and coach with insightful information. Combining the data with video footage appears to be the most effective form of feedback during competitions. A number of teams around the world use this approach. In using race analysis data, race strategies should be designed with the swimmer's strengths and weaknesses in mind. The ideal performance model should include information on desired splits, stroke rates, and stroke counts. Start and turn times are also easy to record and can provide feedback that can lead to improved performance. The bottom line is that coaches and athletes alike can benefit from this type of analysis and should use it as a regular part of training.

CHAPTER 13

Overtraining and Recovery

—Randall L. Wilber, PhD, FACSM

U nfortunately, when training does not go as planned, an athlete may reach a point of overtraining. Many Olympic athletes experience overtraining at some point in their careers. A survey conducted by the U.S. Olympic Committee (USOC) sport psychology staff after the 1996 Atlanta Olympics revealed that an astonishing 28 percent of Team USA athletes indicated that they had overtrained for the Games and that this overtraining had a negative effect on their performance. These U.S. Olympians also identified tapering, resting, traveling less, and staying healthy as changes they would make if they could prepare again for the Olympics. Overtraining is not limited to elite athletes. In fact, it may be just as prevalent among subelite and recreational athletes, especially endurance athletes.

This chapter provides athletes and coaches with scientifically based information on overtraining. Specific sections include the following:

- Terminology: overreaching versus overtraining
- Symptoms of overtraining
- Causes of overtraining
- Prevention of overtraining

The information provided in this chapter will help athletes and coaches better understand overtraining and therefore be better equipped to avoid it.

Terminology: Overreaching Versus Overtraining

Many terms are used in reference to overtraining, including overtraining, under-recovery, unexplained underperformance, and chronic fatigue syndrome. For the purpose of this chapter, we will use the two basic terms—overreaching and overtraining—to describe the various aspects of the overall phenomenon known as overtraining.

Distinguishing between overreaching and overtraining is important. Whereas overreaching is positive training and necessary for an athlete to improve performance, overtraining is negative training that results in a decrement in performance. In general, overreaching and overtraining can be distinguished by the following characteristics:

Overreaching

- Short-term effects, lasting on the order of days
- Reversible with recovery
- Positive training adaptation, necessary to improve performance

Overtraining

- Long-term effects, lasting on the order of weeks or months
- Irreversible with recovery
- Negative training adaptation, causes chronic poor performance

Perhaps the best way to think of overtraining is as the extreme point on a continuum. As shown in figure 13.1, a single training session produces an acute physiological stimulus and accompanying fatigue. A series of several high-intensity workouts may result in overreaching. For example, a four-week training macrocycle composed of three progressively harder weeks followed by a week of

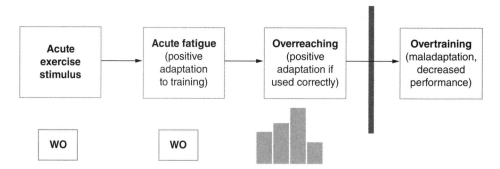

▶ **Figure 13.1** The overtraining continuum showing the difference between overreaching and overtraining. WO: workout.

Adapted, by permission, from A.C. Fry and W.J. Kraemer, 1997, "Resistance exercise overtraining and overreaching: Neuroendocrine responses," *Sports Medicine* 23(2): 106–129, with kind permission from Springer Science and Business Media.

recovery is commonly classified as overreaching; the initial three weeks of hard training provide a progressive overload and produce abnormal fatigue, but the fourth week provides time for the athlete to recover and regenerate. This rest allows positive physiological and psychological adaptations to take place and performance to improve. Without the recovery week, however, an athlete who follows essentially the same program of high-intensity training may become overtrained. Of course, the challenge lies in being able to walk that line, knowing how to overreach without overtraining.

Symptoms of Overtraining

More than 100 documented symptoms of overtraining appear in the scientific literature. Therefore, identifying an overtrained athlete using only one or two telltale signs is not possible. Perhaps a better way to think of the symptoms of overtraining is as a picture puzzle containing hundreds of individual pieces. The individual pieces can be compared to the many symptoms of overtraining; the more pieces of the puzzle you have lined up and pieced together, the better you are able to make an accurate assessment of overtraining.

A number of the physiological, biochemical, immunological, and psychological symptoms that have been used to describe the overtrained athlete are shown in table 13.1. Some of these symptoms are synergistic to one another (i.e., they occur together), whereas others are more isolated in nature. Collectively, this large and varied number of symptoms provides an appreciation of the complex nature of overtraining.

Again, it is naive to think that we can identify and diagnose overtraining in athletes based on one or two symptoms, such as an abnormal elevation in morning heart rate or an increased level of the skeletal muscle enzyme creatine kinase (CK). Coaches thus need to be familiar with the full spectrum of overtraining symptoms so that they can be on the lookout for potential clusters and patterns with athletes. Continue to think in terms of the picture puzzle analogy. The more pieces you have lined up and fit together, the clearer the overtraining picture will be. Let's look at some of the symptoms of an overtrained athlete in a bit more detail.

Physical and Physiological Symptoms of Overtraining

The most obvious symptom of overtraining is a consistent decrease in performance. This decrease in performance may be in comparison with what a swimmer achieved earlier in the season or with a performance achieved in a similar training phase from a previous season, when performance was relatively good and at a level expected by the coach and athlete based on the prescribed training. The overtrained athlete has reduced tolerance to the required training load, which may be seen in the inability to complete training sessions.

Table 13.1 Symptoms of Overtraining

Performance	Consistent decrease in performance compared with earlier in the current season or at the same point in the previous season
	Prolonged recovery after workouts and competition
	Reduced toleration of training load; inability to complete workouts
	Decreased muscular strength
	Loss of coordination
	Deterioration of technical skills
Physiological	Increased heart rate at rest, during submaximal exercise, and during recovery
	Increased oxygen consumption during exercise
	Reduced maximal exercise capacity
	Decreased blood lactate level during submaximal and maximal exercise
	Decrease in normal or healthy total body weight and body fat
	Poor sleep and chronic fatigue
	Loss of appetite and gastrointestinal disturbances
	Chronic muscle soreness
	Increased muscle and joint injury
Immunological	Increased susceptibility to colds, flu, and allergies
	Swelling of the lymph glands
	Bacterial infection
	Slow healing of minor cuts
	Abnormal white blood cell (WBC) profile on blood test
Biochemical	Reduced muscle glycogen level
	Elevated serum cortisol
	Decreased serum ferritin (iron deficiency)
	Mineral depletion
	Menstrual dysfunction such as oligomenorrhea (irregular menstrual periods) or amenorrhea (lack of menstrual periods)
	Decreased bone mineral density
Psychological	General apathy and lethargy
	Lack of concentration
	Mood changes
	Decreased self-esteem
	Fear of competition

The overtrained athlete typically needs significantly more recovery after workouts and competitions and may present excuses for not wanting to practice or train as scheduled. Loss of strength and coordination are evident, and technical skills are negatively affected.

Overtraining has a number of physiological symptoms as well. These include perturbations to normal cardiac response, as evidenced by abnormal elevations in overnight resting heart rate, as well as higher submaximal and recovery heart rates. Maximal exercise capacity (e.g., maximal oxygen uptake, or $\dot{V}O_2$max; maximal swimming velocity) is commonly reduced in the overtrained state, and physiological economy and efficiency are poorer because of overtraining. Overtrained athletes typically have a significant reduction in total body mass, including both lean mass and fat mass. Poor sleep and ongoing fatigue are also major physiological symptoms of overtraining. Contributing to chronic fatigue and poor performance is a reduced appetite and potential gastrointestinal disturbances. Overtrained athletes often complain of skeletal muscle soreness and appear to be more prone to muscle and joint injury.

Immunological and Biochemical Symptoms of Overtraining

Overtrained athletes typically present with certain immunological disturbances and symptoms. In general, overtraining has a compromising effect on the immune system, leading to greater susceptibility to colds, flu, and allergies. In addition, overtrained athletes may be more prone to bacterial infection. Signs of a disturbed immune system are swollen lymph glands, slow healing of cuts and bruises, and an abnormal white blood cell differential (neutrophils, lymphocytes, monocytes) as documented by a standard blood test.

Several biochemical indicators show that an athlete may be overtrained. Muscle glycogen levels are often reduced because of the inability of the athlete to replace carbohydrate stores adequately following training sessions. Additionally, overtrained athletes typically have an abnormally elevated level of the stress hormone cortisol because of the accumulated physical or psychological stress that comes from both training and nontraining activities. Abnormally low levels of serum ferritin are often seen in overtrained athletes, suggesting potential iron depletion or iron deficiency. In overtrained female athletes, menstrual dysfunction such as oligomenorrhea (irregular menstrual flow) or amenorrhea (absence of menstrual flow) may be seen. A decrease in bone mineral density may be present in overtrained athletes, both male and female.

Psychological Symptoms of Overtraining

Finally, a number of psychological symptoms are present in overtrained athletes. Overtrained athletes exhibit a general sense of apathy and lethargy for both sport and nonsport activities. Lack of concentration will likely be evident when an athlete is overtrained, especially during technical training sessions and team-based drills. Overtrained athletes often display mood swings, and their overall self-confidence suffers. An obvious symptom of overtraining, especially among elite athletes, is hesitancy to engage in formal competition. This reluctance is a telltale sign of overtraining for top-level athletes because, after all, competition is a fundamental part of their overall being and essentially their means of making a living.

In summary, coaches should be aware of numerous documented and anecdotal symptoms of overtraining. Remember that overtraining cannot be identified by using only one or two markers. Rather, overtraining is a condition that involves a relatively complex interaction of human physiology, biochemistry, immunology, and psychology that ultimately has a negative effect on athletic performance. Having a working knowledge of these various symptoms can help coaches identify and prevent overtraining in their athletes.

Causes of Overtraining

Athletes and coaches often ask, "What causes overtraining?" This question is difficult to answer, and neither sport scientists nor coaches have a precise explanation for how an athlete becomes overtrained. Several working hypotheses have been proposed to help define the causes of overtraining. These working hypotheses are described here and are based on the symptoms of overtraining—performance, physiological, immunological, biochemical, and psychological— outlined in the previous section of this chapter.

Chronic Glycogen Depletion

Chronic glycogen depletion has been proposed as a potential cause of overtraining. Heavy training loads—relatively high volume or intensity—combined with inadequate glycogen replacement following workouts and competition are thought to lead to chronically low muscle glycogen stores. Glycogen is stored in the muscles and liver and is broken down by the body to produce glucose, which in turn fuels muscle contraction as well as many other functions throughout the body. Adequate carbohydrate ingestion before, during, and after practice is essential to ensure that glycogen levels are replenished to levels that can maintain high-level athletic performance. If chronically low muscle glycogen stores persist over several days, the athlete may become overtrained. Let's look in more detail about why this might occur.

Recall that three metabolic pathways produce the biochemical energy, known technically as adenosine trisphosphate (ATP), to fuel muscle performance during swim training and competition. The first metabolic pathway is known as the adenosine trisphosphate (ATP)–creatine phosphate (CP) energy system. It relies on endogenously stored phosphagens to produce the ATP used in dynamic, explosive sporting events of relatively short duration such as diving and weightlifting.

The second metabolic pathway is known as the anaerobic glycolytic energy system. It relies on the breakdown of the stored form of carbohydrate—muscle glycogen—to blood glucose, which is then metabolized to produce a limited amount of ATP for sustained sprint events such as a 100- or 200-meter swim or a 400-meter run. In addition, the anaerobic glycolytic energy system produces lactic acid, which contributes in part to fatigue along with other metabolic, neuromuscular, and psychological factors.

The third metabolic pathway is known as the oxidative phosphorylation energy system. Like the anaerobic glycolytic energy system, the oxidative phosphorylation energy system begins by breaking down liver and muscle glycogen stores into glucose that can be used within the muscle itself or, in the case of glycogen, stored in the liver. The glucose enters the bloodstream, where it can be transported to the working muscles. Blood glucose is ultimately metabolized in the mitochondria of the muscle cell. A single molecule of glucose produces a relatively large amount of ATP for sustained aerobic events such as a 10-kilometer open-water swim or a marathon. In addition, the oxidative phosphorylation system produces no lactic acid.

In the sport of swimming, Olympic events range from the 50-meter freestyle sprint (2014 world records are 20.91 seconds for males and 23.73 seconds for females) to the 10-kilometer open-water swim (about 1 hour 52 minutes for males and about 2 hours for females). Regardless of which events swimmers compete in across this wide range, they have to train all three energy systems to some degree. Obviously, the 50-meter sprint athlete will train the ATP–PC and anaerobic glycolytic systems to a greater degree than the oxidative phosphorylation system. At the other end of the spectrum, the open-water 10-kilometer swimmer will train the oxidative phosphorylation system to a large degree, put secondary emphasis on the anaerobic glycolytic system, and put minimal emphasis on the ATP–CP system. The important point here is that all swimmers, regardless of event, spend significant time training either one or both of the energy systems (anaerobic glycolysis, oxidative phosphorylation) that rely on glycogen or glucose as their primary source of energy. Thus, to avoid overtraining, swimmers need to focus on replenishing muscle glycogen stores on a workout-by-workout basis. Recommendations for replacing glycogen in a timely, practical, and scientifically based manner are given later in this chapter in the section "Prevention of Overtraining."

In summary, chronic glycogen depletion has been proposed as a potential cause of overtraining. Heavy training loads combined with inadequate glycogen replacement following workouts and competition are believed to lead to chronically low muscle glycogen stores. This, in turn, contributes to overtraining as evident by symptoms of persistent muscular fatigue, inability to complete workouts as expected, deterioration of technical skills and swimming mechanics, and loss of strength and power.

Immunosuppression

Training-induced suppression of the body's natural immune system has been proposed as a possible cause of overtraining. Heavy training loads (relatively high volume or intensity) and the accompanying physiological and psychological stress are believed to produce chronically elevated levels of cortisol. Cortisol is a stress hormone secreted by the zona fasiculata region of the adrenal cortex. Physical or psychological stress serves as a potent trigger for the release of cortisol into the blood. Abnormally elevated serum cortisol levels are often seen in athletes, especially elite athletes. This makes sense, given the high physiological and psychological stress that accompanies training for elite-level sport. Thus, athletes are prone to be right on the edge of overtraining during periods when the training load results in relatively high physiological and psychological stress. But abnormally high serum cortisol levels can produce several physiological responses, including suppression of the effectiveness of the body's natural immune system. Cortisol-induced suppression of the immune system can provide an open door through which an athlete may become predisposed to illness or injury. This circumstance, in turn, can lead to overtraining, as evident by chronic illness, an injury that fails to heal with proper treatment, and abnormal white blood cell counts.

Research has shown that proper overnight sleep can have a positive effect on attenuating abnormal increases in serum cortisol. Similarly, a commercial carbohydrate electrolyte drink such as Powerade or Gatorade can have a beneficial effect on reducing serum cortisol levels. We discuss these strategies in detail in the next section, "Prevention of Overtraining."

In summary, heavy training loads and the accompanying physiological and psychological stress are thought to produce chronically elevated levels of the stress hormone cortisol. Significantly elevated serum cortisol levels may lead to overtraining by suppressing the body's natural immune system, causing the athlete to become chronically fatigued, sick, or injured.

Autonomic Nervous System Imbalance

An imbalance of the autonomic nervous system (ANS) may be a cause of overtraining. Heavy training loads and psychological stress are believed to lead to impaired brain function, which ultimately results in overtraining. The ANS is composed of the sympathetic (SNS) and parasympathetic (PSNS) nervous systems. The SNS is often referred to as the fight-or-flight system. Its activity is dominant during times of excitement, danger, emergency, and, of course, exercise. Characteristics of an activated SNS include a significant increase in heart rate, respiratory rate, systolic blood pressure, and sweat rate, all of which are positive effects during exercise. The PSNS is sometimes called the resting and digesting system. It is dominant during quiet, nonstressful situations such as lying on the couch watching TV. When the PSNS is activated, blood pressure, heart rate, and respiratory rate are relatively low and are considered to be at baseline levels.

The ANS imbalance model of overtraining suggests that extensive training loads (relatively high volume or intensity) and accompanying psychological stress lead to impaired function of the hypothalamus, which is located in the brain and controls the ANS. The result is an imbalance of the ANS, affecting either the SNS or the PSNS, depending on the athlete's specific sport or event. Impairment of the SNS (sympathetic overtraining) is typically seen in team sports and sprint or power athletes, whereas impairment of the PSNS (parasympathetic overtraining) is more common among endurance athletes. So, depending on the athlete and his events, either system could contribute to overtraining in swimming. In addition, sympathetic overtraining is considered an early and less debilitating form of overtraining, whereas parasympathetic overtraining is viewed as an advanced and more serious form of overtraining. A few of the symptoms of sympathetic and parasympathetic overtraining are similar, but most of them are different or even opposite in nature, as shown in table 13.2.

In summary, autonomic nervous system imbalance may be a cause of overtraining. Heavy training loads and psychological stress are thought to lead to

Table 13.2 Symptoms of Sympathetic Overtraining and Parasympathetic Overtraining

Sympathetic overtraining	Parasympathetic overtraining
Impaired performance	Impaired performance
Lack of supercompensation	Lack of supercompensation
Restlessness, irritability	Fatigue, depression, apathy
Disturbed sleep	Normal sleep
Weight loss	Normal weight
Increased resting heart rate	Decreased resting heart rate
Increased resting blood pressure	Decreased resting blood pressure
Impaired recovery	Suppressed submax and max heart rate
	Suppressed submax and max lactate
	Suppressed submax and max glucose
	Suppressed epinephrine and norepinephrine sensitivity
	Altered hypothalmic–pituitary–adrenal (HPA) function
	Altered hypothalmic–pituitary–gonadal (HPG) function

impairment of the hypothalamus, which in turn results in either sympathetic overtraining or parasympathetic overtraining. Sympathetic overtraining is believed to be more common in team sports and sprint or power sports or events, and it is considered an early form of overtraining. In contrast, parasympathetic overtraining is believed to be more prevalent in endurance sports or events, and it is considered an advanced form of overtraining.

Central Fatigue

The word *central* in central fatigue refers to the central nervous system, that is, the brain. Training- and dietary-induced changes in brain neurochemistry may be a cause of overtraining. Heavy training loads (relatively high volume or intensity) in combination with inadequate postworkout or postcompetition carbohydrate replacement are believed to result in chronically low muscle glycogen stores. As a result of low muscle glycogen, there is a greater reliance on branched-chain amino acids (BCAAs) for energy, mostly during endurance exercise. This greater utilization of BCAAs increases the amount of free tryptophan (fTRP) that crosses the blood–brain barrier and enters the brain. fTRP is a biochemical precursor for 5-hydroxytryptamine (5-HT), more commonly known as the neurotransmitter serotonin. The result of this process is a significant increase in serotonin, a powerful chemical neurotransmitter that produces lethargy, sleepiness, moodiness, and depression. Thus, the psychological symptoms evident in an overtrained athlete may be because of changes in brain neurochemistry that can be traced back to a significant increase in training load combined with inadequate glycogen replenishment.

Elevated Proinflammatory Cytokines

Within the human immune system, specific chemicals called proinflammatory cytokines are produced. As the name suggests, they promote inflammation in various parts of the body. An abnormally high level of these proinflammatory cytokines may be a cause of overtraining. Excessive training-induced musculo-skeletal stress (relatively high volume or intensity) in combination with insufficient recovery can result in chronic skeletal muscle inflammation or joint trauma. In turn, this chronic skeletal muscle inflammation triggers the release of several proinflammatory cytokines, including interleukin-1 beta (IL-1β), interleukin-6 (IL-6), and tumor necrosis factor-alpha (TNF-α). As shown in figure 13.2, these proinflammatory cytokines

- affect the central nervous system, resulting in loss of appetite, sleep disturbances, and negative mood changes;
- affect the hypothalamic–pituitary–adrenal (HPA) axis, resulting in increased levels of the stress hormones (cortisol, epinephrine, norepinephrine), leading to immunosuppression; and
- affect the hypothalamic–pituitary–gonadal (HPG) axis, resulting in decreased levels of testosterone and luteinizing-hormone-releasing hormone, decreased skeletal muscle anabolism, and impaired reproductive function.

Thus, according to this model, overtraining may be caused by excessive amounts of circulating proinflammatory cytokines, which in turn produce negative psychological and physiological effects through the brain and endocrine system that ultimately prevent the athlete from training and competing effectively.

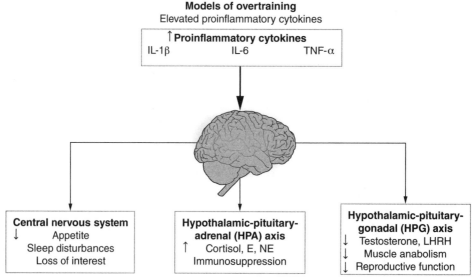

▶ **Figure 13.2** Elevated proinflammatory cytokines as a potential cause of overtraining. E: epinephrine; NE: norepinephrine; LHRH: luteinizing-hormone-releasing hormone.

Prevention of Overtraining

As previously mentioned, athletes and coaches face a challenge in knowing when they have crossed the boundary between overreaching and overtraining. Whereas overreaching is considered positive training that is necessary for an athlete to improve performance, overtraining is negative training and can result in loss of training time and a significant decrease in performance. The following practical strategies are offered as potential tools to prevent overtraining.

Recognition of Overtraining Risk Factors

In general, overtraining risk factors can be organized into three categories based on athlete, sport, and training. Table 13.3 outlines several risk factors for overtraining.

Athlete Personality

Coaches need to be on the lookout for potential overtraining risk factors within the athlete's inherent personality.

• **Perfectionism.** Athletes who possess a perfectionist or obsessive-compulsive personality and who are highly motivated toward success may be more prone to overtraining than those who have moderate goals and are less motivated to reach them. Working with a highly motivated and perfectionist athlete is like wielding a double-edge sword. Perfectionism and exceptional motivation will probably lead to outstanding performances and attainment of high goals but may ultimately lead the athlete across that fine line from overreaching into overtraining.

Table 13.3   Risk Factors for Overtraining

Athlete	Perfectionist or obsessive-compulsive personality Excessive level of motivation "More is better" training approach, based on either good or bad performance Resistance to taking time off from training, whether because of injury or illness or not Sport specialization at an early age Eating disorders or disordered eating Competitive schedule designed to chase points or money External stressors such as home, school, work, relationships, money
Sport	Ultrasports such as Ironman events, multiday cycling events Multisports such as triathlon or pentathlon Endurance sports such as marathon Sport that allows little or no individualized training "Meat grinder" sports such as distance running in Kenya or soccer in Brazil
Training	Overloading adolescent athletes during growth spurts Transition from junior or developmental level to senior level and accompanying increase in training load Lack of scientifically based periodization leading to imbalance of stress and recovery and overtraining Knee-jerk response to underperformance leading to an excessive increase in training load Training individually with minimal or no face-to-face coaching and objective monitoring Training with significantly more skilled or fit athletes Poor monitoring of recovery workouts Olympic or world championship season Lack of scientifically based taper Coaching by a former successful elite athlete Change in training environment (e.g., heat, humidity, altitude)

- **"More is better" approach to training.** This personality trait is another one that athletes and coaches should be aware of in regard to overtraining. It may become a factor leading to overtraining coming out of a good performance or, more likely, after a subpar performance when the athlete is looking to do whatever is necessary to get back on track. Often the athlete and coach will decide to work harder in an effort to get back to performing as expected. Instead of working harder, however, a better approach may be to work smarter and include more, not less, rest and recovery. This decision to work smarter by adding more rest and recovery instead of blindly working harder is difficult for athletes and coaches to make, particularly coming off a poor performance. Thus, coaches and athletes need to communicate openly and consider all the factors involved in a subpar performance before deciding to do additional and harder training.

- **Resistance to taking time off when needed.** Other personality-based overtraining risk factors for coaches to be aware of are situations when the athlete is resistant to taking time off from training, even when injured or ill. This counterproductive behavior overlaps with an obsessive-compulsive type of personality.

- **Disordered eating.** Other dangerous behaviors that can contribute to overtraining are eating disorders and disordered eating. Professional help should be sought if an athlete demonstrates these types of behaviors.

- **High levels of external (nontraining) stress.** Finally, external stressors such as the home environment, family or personal relationships, school or job demands, and financial burdens can contribute to an athlete's inability to train effectively. These circumstances should be on the coach's radar as potential overtraining risk factors.

Sport

The sport that the athlete participates in may also be a risk factor for overtraining. Athletes who participate in ultrasport events such as the Ironman event or multiday cycling races are relatively prone to overtraining because of the high training volume required to be successful in those events. The same can be said for multisport events such as triathlon and traditional endurance sport events such as the marathon or distance swimming.

In addition, sports that allow little or no individualized training can cause an athlete to get lost in the training progression and ultimately reach an overtrained state. This issue may surface in individual sports such as club-based swimming, in which a relatively large number of athletes and a limited number of coaches prevent adequate one-on-one interaction and the development of individualized training programs. The same may apply to team sports such as soccer, in which team play and strategy take precedence over individualized training.

Finally "meat grinder" sports are notorious for producing overtrained athletes. A meat grinder sport is one in which a relatively large number of athletes, usually at a young age, enter the sport at the top of the meat grinder, so to speak. Ultimately, a relatively small number of elite-level athletes emerge from the bottom of the meat grinder at the expense of several of their fellow athletes, who are ground up or overtrained in the process. Examples of meat grinder sports include gymnastics in China, distance running in Kenya and Ethiopia, and soccer in Brazil. Some have argued that swimming is a meat grinder sport in the United States.

Training

The training program carried out by athletes and their coaches may include several overtraining risk factors that should be evaluated.

• **Inappropriate training load.** Overloading adolescent athletes during growth spurts may lead to overtraining. Similarly, junior or developmental athletes who are making the transition to the senior level may become overtrained because of the accompanying increase in training load. For all athletes, a training program that lacks a scientifically based periodization structure, including a well-designed taper, can lead to chronic imbalances between stress and recovery and, in turn, overtraining.

• **Poor monitoring of recovery.** Another training-based overtraining risk factor is poor monitoring of recovery workouts. In this scenario, athletes are assigned a moderate-intensity workout but instead feel good and end up doing a high-intensity workout, thereby throwing the entire training week out of balance and stacking several hard workouts on top of one another.

• **Little interaction between coach and athlete.** Other training-based risk factors include training individually with minimal or no face-to-face coaching or objective monitoring, training with significantly more skilled or fit athletes, and sudden changes in the training environment, such as a sudden move to a hot and humid environment or to a different altitude.

• **Ramping up for the big meet.** Finally, one training-based risk factor is more prevalent in elite athletes than in nonelite athletes. Elite athletes often formally or informally ramp up their training during the Olympic or world championship season to a level that takes them across the fine line from overreaching to overtraining. The thinking becomes, "I need to do more, something special, something harder than I have ever done before, so that I can be ready to compete successfully in the Olympics." Again, this attitude becomes a double-edge sword for the Olympic-caliber athlete. On the one hand, the increase in training load may be a key factor to success at the Olympic Games, but it may also take the athlete into the realm of overtraining. Recall from the first section of this chapter that 28 percent of U.S. Olympic team athletes said that they had overtrained in preparation for the 1996 Atlanta Olympics.

In summary, if overtraining is to be avoided, coaches must have a good working knowledge of the risk factors of overtraining. We have discussed in this section three general categories of overtraining risk factors: athlete, sport, and training. For example, athletes who exhibit a perfectionist personality along with an excessive level of motivation may be prime candidates for overtraining. Sports that require a relatively high training load (volume or intensity) may produce a greater number of overtrained athletes than technically based sports do. Training programs that are not scientifically based or are poorly monitored are prone to produce overtrained athletes. Coaches who are able to detect these overtraining risk factors in their athletes and act effectively to keep them under control will likely be successful in preventing overtraining from taking place.

Scientifically Based Training Program

The best way to prevent overtraining is to use a scientifically based training plan that includes periods of progressive overload in combination with adequate recovery and regeneration. This type of training program will result in optimal performance at the peak of the competitive season. The training program should be organized and periodized to ensure a logical and systematic progression in the training load based on the four physiological principles of training:

1. Sport specificity: The program should be designed to train the body for a specific sport or activity.
2. Progressive overload: The stress or overload applied to the human body must be progressive and gradual, avoiding the alteration of too many training variables such as volume, duration, intensity, and recovery at the same time.
3. Individualization: The program should be designed to meet the physical capabilities, limitations, and goals of each athlete.
4. Tapering and peaking: The final days of training before a major athletic event should have a lower training load to allow increased recovery and peak physical performance.

Dr. Iñigo Mujika of Spain has conducted extensive research on tapering in elite athletes. Much of his research is summarized in chapter 10. Although the details about tapering appear there, a summary of the recommendations for tapering is included here because of its importance for maximizing rest and recovery and optimizing performance:

- Training intensity should be either maintained or increased during the taper period to prevent detraining.
- Training volume should be reduced by 40 to 60 percent.
- Training frequency should be maintained to prevent detraining.
- Positive physiological and performance adaptations can be expected as a result of a taper that lasts about two weeks.
- Progressive, nonlinear tapers seem to produce better performances than step-wise or linear tapers.

Detailed Monitoring of Training Response

Systematic and detailed monitoring of the athlete's response to training is critical to the prevention of overtraining. This checking can be done through open communication between the athlete and coach or by having the athlete keep a detailed training diary. The training diary should include physical and psychological responses to training such as heart rate, weight, length and quality of sleep, tiredness sensation, training willingness, appetite, competitive willingness, and muscle soreness. These training responses should be tracked daily. The coach should be looking for any patterns that might suggest that the athlete is moving from the overreaching stage to the overtraining stage.

In addition, laboratory or field tests can provide valuable information regarding the athlete's response to training and the potential for overtraining. Several laboratory tests can be used to monitor training response:

- Maximal oxygen consumption ($\dot{V}O_2$max)
- Lactate threshold velocity (swim, run)
- Lactate threshold power output (bike)
- Economy (doing the same work with less effort)
- Maximal velocity (swim, run)
- Maximal power output (bike)

The following field tests can be used to monitor training response:

- Time trials (whole or partial competition distance)
- Any workout designed to mimic the protocol of a laboratory test
- Benchmark workouts or standardized test sets that can be performed periodically as part of training and used to evaluate progress

Nutritional Intervention

As stated in a previous section, "Causes of Overtraining," proper nutrition, particularly carbohydrate consumption, is important for long-term training progression, regardless of the swimming event. Muscle and liver glycogen stores can be depleted during daily workouts. Inattention to glycogen replacement could result in overtraining, as suggested in the chronic glycogen depletion and central fatigue models of overtraining. In addition, research has shown that commercial carbohydrate drinks such as Gatorade and Powerade help reduce abnormally high levels of the stress hormone cortisol, which can impair normal function of the immune system (see the immunosuppression model of overtraining). Taken together, we can see that proper carbohydrate intake is a crucial nutritional strategy for the prevention of overtraining.

Chapter 14 deals exclusively with swimming nutrition, but some key concepts are presented here about proper nutrition and its role in preventing overtraining. An effective carbohydrate supplementation regimen requires the athlete to consume the proper type of food or drink before, during, and after a workout or competition:

- The athlete should consume a high glycemic index (GI) drink or food, such as a commercial carbohydrate drink, bagel, or baked potato, three to four hours before a workout or competition or a low GI food, such as an apple, banana, or flavored yogurt, 30 to 60 minutes before a workout or competition.

- The athlete should consume a moderate to high GI drink or food, such as a sports drink or power bar, during the workout or competition.
- The athlete should consume a high GI drink or food, such as a sports drink, bagel, baked potato, or watermelon, immediately and for up to two hours after the workout or competition.

Use of a protein additive containing essential amino acids may also be beneficial in the postworkout or postcompetition period because it may stimulate the insulin response and ultimately enhance glycogen replacement. It may also aid in the repair of skeletal muscle breakdown incurred during the workout or competition.

Although most athletes are probably attentive to replenishing carbohydrate stores during and after a competition, they tend to neglect carbohydrate supplementation before, during, and after daily training sessions. Athletes in training should be aware of this tendency and make sure that carbohydrate supplementation and replacement are as much a part of the daily workout as the warm-up and cool-down are.

In terms of vitamin and mineral intake, swimmers in training may want to consider the following to reduce the risk of overtraining:

- Beta-carotene, vitamin C, and vitamin E for their antioxidant properties
- Folate, vitamin B_6, and vitamin B_{12} for their positive effects on the immune system
- Zinc, selenium, and copper for their positive effects on the immune system
- Iron for its positive effect on red blood cell production and cytochrome-c oxidase

These vitamins and minerals be obtained through a well-balanced diet and a good multivitamin. Additional supplements containing these vitamins and minerals may not be necessary. In fact, oversupplementation may be unhealthy.

Blood Chemistry

To help reduce the tendency toward overtraining, blood chemistry tests should be conducted periodically throughout the training season. Three to five blood tests during the season can provide a strong database from which the coach can make good decisions about how to proceed with training. Although some coaches prefer to do blood testing using a chronological schedule such as every three or four months regardless of the training phase, we recommend that blood testing be done at times related to specific training and competition scenarios. This testing schedule can help the coach make better decisions about the athlete's subsequent training plan. For example, blood testing can be beneficial in evaluating the athlete's current state in response to a hard training block to determine how much rest and recovery is needed. Or blood testing could be done after a recovery period to see whether the athlete is ready to begin another hard training block.

Another recommendation regarding blood testing is for coaches and athletes to work with someone who is knowledgeable in interpreting blood chemistry results in the context of a well-trained swimmer. Most likely, this person will be a sports medicine physician, exercise physiologist, athletic trainer, or other certified health professional. For example, to the untrained eye, an abnormally high creatine kinase (CK) level may cause concern. But a health professional who is used to evaluating blood chemistry results of athletes will have minimal concern because skeletal muscle microtrauma (and thus elevated CK) is a normal and expected response in well-trained athletes.

Blood chemistry tests need not be extremely expensive. A relatively comprehensive test that can be repeated three to five times a season can be done for less than $50 (U.S.). Although limited budgets will prohibit coaches from having all their swimmers tested regularly, we believe that blood testing for top-end athletes, particularly those prone to overtraining, is a good investment of funds and an item that should be built into the seasonal budget. Table 13.4 lists several blood chemistry parameters and the accompanying physiological and performance-based rationale for each panel of parameters. Again, the budget of a typical team will not realistically allow regular evaluation of all these parameters. We suggest that the coach communicate with a local hospital or laboratory to identify a reliable place to perform blood testing.

Training During Illness

Athletes may become sick during the season. How an illness is handled relative to training and competition can be the difference between becoming overtrained and returning to normal health. A commonly asked question among athletes is, "Can I train or compete when I'm sick?" In general, if the sickness is in the throat or below, the answer is no. If the sickness is above the throat, however, the answer is yes, if the athlete wants to train or compete. Here are some guidelines for training or competing during illness:

If the illness is in the throat or below, the athlete should take time off from training and competition to recover. In this case, the athlete is experiencing symptoms of systemic involvement such as fever, extreme fatigue, muscle aches, or swollen lymph glands. Submaximal and maximal exercise should not be attempted. The athlete should allow two to four weeks of recovery before gradually resuming training.

If the illness is above the throat, the athlete can train and compete. In this case, the athlete is experiencing symptoms of a common cold and has no systemic involvement or fever. Submaximal exercise and short-duration maximal exercise are OK. The athlete should attempt to get additional sleep and pay more attention to proper hydration and nutrition.

Table 13.4 Blood Chemistry Parameters

Skeletal muscle inflammation or microtrauma	Amino acid profile Alanine transaminase (ALT) Aspartate transaminase (AST) Bilirubin Blood or serum urea nitrogen (BUN) Creatine kinase (CK) C-reactive protein (CRP) Homocysteine Lactate dehydrogenase (LDH) Sedimentation rate Uric acid WBC differential: neutrophils, lymphocytes, monocytes
Catabolic versus anabolic trend	Cortisol Dehydroepiandrosterone (DHEA) Insulin growth factor-1 (IGF-1) Sex-hormone-binding globulin (SHBG) Testosterone, free Testosterone, total Thyroid panel: thyroid stimulating hormone (TSH), T3, rT3, T4
Abnormal or negative training response	Adrenocorticotropic hormone (ACTH) Cortisol Luteinizing hormone (LH) Prolactin Testosterone, free Testosterone, total Thyroid panel: thyroid stimulating hormone (TSH), T3, rT3, T4 WBC differential: neutrophils, lymphocytes, monocytes
Cellular oxidative stress	Serum lipid hydroperoxides (LOOH) Serum reduced glutathione (GSH) Urinary malondialdehyde (MDA) Urinary 8-hydroxydeoxyguanosine (8-OHdG)
Red blood cell status	RBC Hemoglobin Hematocrit Mean corpuscular volume (MCV) Mean corpuscular hemoglobin (MCH) Mean corpuscular hemoglobin concentration (MCHC) Red cell distribution width (RDW) Reticulocyte count Platelet count Mean platelet volume (MPV) Urine specific gravity (USG) to determine hemoconcentration
Iron status	Serum ferritin Serum iron Total iron binding capacity (TIBC) Saturation percentage Folate Vitamin B_{12}
Bone health (prevention of stress fractures)	Calcium Vitamin D, 25 OH
Euhydration, thermoregulation, and kidney function	Albumin Electrolytes: sodium, potassium, chloride, magnesium Blood or serum urea nitrogen (BUN) Creatinine BUN or creatinine Urine specific gravity (USG)
Sleep and recovery abnormality	Adrenocorticotropic hormone (ACTH) Cortisol Melatonin

Table 13.4, *continued*

Asthma, exercise-induced bronchoconstriction, or allergies	Eosinophils
General health	Glucose Lipid panel: total cholesterol, LDL cholesterol, HDL cholesterol Lipoprotein (a), cardiac risk ratio, triglycerides Blood type and Rh factor Hemoglobin A1C (type 1 or type 2 diabetes) Mononucleosis (monospot test, heterophile antibody) Epstein Barr virus

Recovery Techniques

Athletes can use several recovery techniques to reduce the risk of overtraining. Some of these techniques are relatively simple and inexpensive, whereas others require special equipment.

One recovery technique that is easy to do but often overlooked or compromised is passive recovery, or sleep. Athletes engaged in daily training should get a minimum of seven to nine hours of sleep per night. Athletes plant the seeds of improved fitness during the daily workout, but it is at night when they are sound asleep that the garden grows. In other words, during the time of sound sleep the body adapts to the physiological stress of the daily workout. The skeletal muscles, cardiopulmonary system, enzymatic profile, and so on grow, thereby enhancing the athlete's ability to perform physically. These positive adaptations occur because of increased levels of human growth hormone and decreased levels of cortisol that occur during deep, uninterrupted sleep. The stress hormone cortisol is at a very low level during the period of deep sleep from about midnight to 3:00 am, indicating that little catabolic effect is taking place in the body. In contrast, during the same period of deep sleep, a dramatic increase occurs in human growth hormone, indicating a significant anabolic effect (the garden is growing). Collectively, this combined effect of depressed cortisol and elevated human growth hormone is beneficial for athletes who are attempting to recover from hard training and ultimately improve their performance.

The critical factor driving this beneficial hormonal flux is deep sleep. We cannot expect the same positive effects to occur if deep sleep is minimal, interrupted, or compromised in any other way. Again, a good night's sleep on a consistent basis is one of the simplest, cheapest, and most effective ways to prevent overtraining. Finally, afternoon cat naps (30 to 60 minutes) may also be beneficial, but some athletes may be unable to nap during the day because of school, job, and family commitments.

Another recovery technique that may reduce the chance of overtraining is hydrotherapy, which can take the form of sauna, cold-water immersion, and contrast baths. Low-intensity swimming and water running are effective hydrotherapy techniques for nonswimmers. A poor man's contrast bath can be done by simply standing in the shower and alternating cold and hot water every few minutes for approximately 20 minutes.

An effective neuromuscular recovery technique is massage, which can be done following workouts or competitions. Another simple but effective recovery technique is monitoring hydration status, which can be accomplished by checking total body mass, or scale weight, using the same accurate scale each time and weighing in at the same time each day. Fluid replacement should make up for the body weight lost.

Other effective and practical recovery techniques include pneumatic massage (e.g., Normatec) and low-frequency vibration of specific muscle groups. These recovery techniques require special equipment that can be purchased commercially.

Recommendations for Further Reading

Hausswirth, C., and I. Mujika. 2013. *Recovery for performance in sport*. Champaign, IL: Human Kinetics.

Kellman, M. 2002. *Enhancing recovery: Preventing underperformance in athletes*. Champaign, IL: Human Kinetics.

Kellman, M., and K.W. Kallus. 2001. *Recovery-stress questionnaire for athletes*. Champaign, IL: Human Kinetics.

Kreider, R.B., A.C. Fry, and M.L. O'Toole, eds. 1998. *Overtraining in sport*. Champaign, IL: Human Kinetics.

Meeusen, R., M. Duclos, C. Foster, A. Fry, M. Gleeson, D. Nieman, J. Raglin, G. Rietjens, J. Steinacker, and A. Urhausen. 2013. Prevention, diagnosis, and treatment of the overtraining syndrome: Joint consensus statement of the European College of Sport Science and the American College of Sports Medicine. *Medicine & Science in Sports & Exercise* 45(1): 186–205.

Mujika, I. 2009. *Tapering and peaking for optimal performance*. Champaign, IL: Human Kinetics.

Richardson, S.O., M.B. Andersen, and T. Morris. 2008. *Overtraining athletes: Personal journeys in sport*. Champaign, IL: Human Kinetics.

Summary

Overtraining is common among athletes engaged in regular high-volume, high-intensity training, and it is particularly prevalent in Olympic athletes. Distinguishing between overreaching and overtraining is often difficult. Because overtraining appears to be caused by a complex combination of physiological, immunological, and psychological factors, no single marker can quickly and clearly identify overtraining.

Recommendations to prevent overtraining include the following:

- Recognition of overtraining risk factors
- Adherence to a scientifically based training program that includes strategically placed recovery phases and a well-designed taper
- Detailed monitoring and documentation of the training response
- Nutritional intervention emphasizing carbohydrate replacement
- Periodic blood testing
- Wise decisions about training or competing when sick
- Daily use of recovery techniques, including passive rest

In closing, it would be wise to remember the words of coach Bobby McGee, who has coached several athletes to World Championship or Olympic medals including 1996 Olympic marathon champion, Josiah Thugwane of South Africa: "More performances are spoiled by slight overtraining than by slight lack of fitness. An athlete who is 90 percent conditioned for an event will do better than an athlete who is 0.5 percent overtrained."

PART
III

Applied
Sport Sciences

Nutrition: Fueling for Performance

—Charlene Boudreau

The primary training goal of most competitive swimmers is to swim faster and improve times. This type of training outcome can be achieved through thoughtfully prescribed work that promotes a training response and adaptation. Such a training program typically includes elements that target

- the development of the aerobic and anaerobic energy systems,
- the development of effective and efficient stroke mechanics,
- strength and conditioning and muscle development,
- the development of neuromuscular control and the neural processes related to swimming performance, and
- solid nutritional practices that focus on fueling efficiency and recovery.

This last item is the focus of this chapter. After all, whether it's breathing, standing, warming up, or swimming through a demanding practice, every single movement and muscular contraction requires energy from inside the body. The foods and beverages that we consume help build and maintain those energy stores and thereby affect performance in the pool. Call it training or call it work—food provides the energy that we need to train, recover, and then train again. And swimmers have more control over their nutrition and the way that the body performs than they may think!

The mechanism through which nutrition affects swimming performance is, at its core, a collection of intricately linked biochemical reactions. Although the term *biochemistry* may strike fear into the heart of many swimmers, some relatively simple explanations and examples show how this all works to influence performance and how athletes can control the ways in which they approach nutrition to swim better. This chapter integrates research and experience to provide a practical approach to answering the two most common and fundamentally important questions asked by swimmers and their support teams:

1. What exactly is fueling for performance?
2. What should I eat or drink, how much, and when?

What Exactly Is Fueling for Performance?

The mechanism by which nutrition affects performance is a collection of intricately linked chemical reactions. The body's overall performance is closely tied to nutrition. The brain, which ultimately controls all body movements and functions, relies primarily on blood sugar for fuel. The immune system relies primarily on glutamine to function properly, sufficient stores of which rely on sufficient dietary intake of carbohydrate. Explosive movements rely heavily on glycogen, the storage form of carbohydrate, and fatigue is directly linked to glycogen depletion. Additionally, carbohydrate has been the topic of many debates related to nutrition and dieting, including the athlete's diet.

Notice the repeated mention of glucose or glycogen, which highlights the important role played by carbohydrate in how the body performs. Different, but equally important, statements could be developed to draw attention to the role that protein and fat play in supporting overall body function and athletic performance. These statements offer just a taste of the complexity and reach of nutrition in supporting athletes in terms of energy, fuel, and optimal health. Staying well nourished helps swimmers maintain physical and mental performance both in and out of the pool.

Food Is Fuel

Food and water are basic needs of the body, and both play critical roles in proper and efficient muscle, organ, and energy system function. Food provides the body with the six basic (and required) nutrients:

1. Carbohydrate: Carbohydrate is broken down by the body into sugar such as glucose, and it is critical to swimming performance.
2. Protein: Although it provides little energy to the body, protein is essential for building muscle and repairing damage that can occur during training.
3. Fat: Contrary to popular belief, dietary fat is essential to athletes. It provides a dense source of energy, contributes essential fatty acids, allows fat-soluble vitamins (vitamins A, D, E, and K) to be absorbed in the digestive tract, and supports many physiological functions.
4. Vitamins: Vitamins are organic compounds that allow the body to produce energy during exercise while also supporting a variety of other physiological functions.
5. Minerals: Minerals are inorganic substances such as iron, calcium, and sodium that assist in the breakdown of food and support many bodily

functions. Like vitamins, minerals are not produced by the body and must be consumed in the foods that people eat. The body needs more than 20 minerals to function properly, and these minerals must be available in sufficient amounts to ensure health and athletic performance.

6. Water: Water makes up as much as 60 percent of total body weight (75 percent in lean tissues like muscle), and adequate intake of water is critical in the function of many physiological systems. Dehydration, a loss of body water, can quickly lead to impaired performance.

These nutrients can be used immediately or stored in the body to be used later. Consider the following examples of how the body works to use food to support immediate and long-term energy needs.

To be stored or used as fuel, all dietary carbohydrate must ultimately be converted to glucose. This simple sugar can be taken up by muscles or the liver for storage as muscle or liver glycogen. Muscle glycogen is used in the formation of adenosine triphosphate (ATP), an immediately available source of energy for most body functions and all explosive sport movements. Liver glycogen can be converted back to glucose and transported by blood (i.e., blood sugar) to organs such as the brain that need to use it as a fuel source. Every gram of carbohydrate provides the body with approximately four kilocalories.

Dietary fat is stored as triglycerides in subcutaneous, visceral, and intramuscular locations, and it must be converted to free fatty acids to travel in the blood and be used for fuel during, for example, low- or moderate-intensity sets or events of 200 meters or longer. Every gram of fat provides the body with approximately nine kilocalories. A healthy, well-nourished body can store 30 to 40 times as much energy as fat than as carbohydrate (see table 14.1).

Dietary protein is stored as a structural element of the body, including muscle tissue and cells. Body protein can be converted to glucose or free fatty acids if necessary, but the body's preferred use of protein is in its basic units, amino acids. Protein rarely contributes significantly to the energy needs of exercise (usually it accounts for only 5 to 10 percent). Every gram of protein provides the body with approximately four kilocalories.

Table 14.1 Body Stores of Fuels and Energy

		g	kcal
Carbohydrate	Liver glycogen	110	451
	Muscle glycogen	500	2,050
	Glucose in body fluids	15	62
Fat	Subcutaneous and visceral	7,800	73,320
	Intramuscular	161	1,513
Total		8,586	77,396

Estimates based on 143-pound (65 kg) person with 12 percent body fat.

Reprinted, by permission, from J.H. Wilmore, D.L. Costill, and W.L. Kenney, 2008, *Physiology of sport and exercise*, 4th ed. (Champaign, IL: Human Kinetics), 49.

Because they provide energy in the form of calories, carbohydrate, protein, and fat are known as the energy-yielding nutrients. Vitamins, minerals, and water provide no calories whatsoever, but they are essential to bone and muscle health and overall body system integrity. Even more relevant is their role in enabling the body to access (i.e., use) carbohydrate, protein, and fat when needed, such as during exercise and recovery. Because of their critical role in energy production, vitamins, minerals, and water are often referred to as catalysts. They improve the efficiency of the chemical reactions that take place when the body needs to use the energy-yielding nutrients to perform a given activity. The fancy word for converting carbohydrate, protein, and fat to usable energy is *bioenergetics*, although most swimmers and coaches know it as burning calories.

Burning calories is a literal description of accessing and using stored and circulating nutrients for fuel, because all stored energy eventually degrades to heat energy. The conversion of each of the energy-yielding nutrients produces performance and heat. For reference, 1 kilocalorie is the amount of heat energy needed to raise 1 kilogram of water by 1 degree Celsius. When accessed for fuel, fat produces over twice as much energy as either carbohydrate or protein; 1 gram of fat provides 9 kilocalories, more than either carbohydrate or protein (both provide about 4 kcal per g).

The ability to access the energy-yielding nutrients is based on a number of factors: their availability in stored and circulating forms, the availability of catalysts, the intensity and duration of the work being performed, and, subsequently, the availability of oxygen. Oxygen availability is well established as a primary limiting factor when it comes to exercise performance, which really means that an energy cost is associated with exercise. This cost is directly related to intensity; to the number of kilocalories per gram for carbohydrate, fat, and protein; and to the way in which the body breaks down these nutrients to produce energy. Figure 14.1 illustrates several key points related to how a healthy, well-nourished swimmer needs and accesses fuel during exercise.

Let's draw a couple of important observations from figure 14.1:

- The total number of calories (carbohydrate plus protein plus fat) required to perform work (i.e., burned) increases with work intensity.

- Three sources of fuel are always contributing to the total caloric requirements of any workout. The relative contributions of these sources vary with work intensity (Coyle et al. 1997).

- Fat contributes the most to total caloric requirements during exercise at low intensity (Turcotte 1999). Fat is therefore the primary fuel source during easy and moderate workouts.

- Carbohydrate contributes the most to total caloric requirements during exercise of moderate to high intensity. Carbohydrate is thus the primary fuel source during moderate to hard workouts (Coyle et al. 1997).

- The contribution of protein to total caloric requirements during exercise is relatively small and unaffected by work intensity, provided that carbohydrate and fat are available in sufficient quantities to support the work.

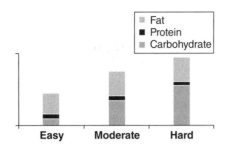

▶ **Figure 14.1** The amount of energy derived from the energy-yielding nutrients during easy, moderate, and high-intensity exercises. Note that a larger percentage of the energy to fuel performance at low intensity comes from fat, whereas the largest contributor to fueling performance at high intensity is carbohydrate.

Making the Connection

As mentioned previously, a swimmer's desired training outcome can be achieved through thoughtfully prescribed work that promotes a training response and adaptation. Training programs that address the development of the aerobic and anaerobic energy systems, fueling efficiency, muscle development, and neural processes related to swimming performance include pool and dryland workouts that are prescribed in quantities, intensities, and frequencies designed to

- enhance the ATP–CP renewal process (one component of anaerobic conditioning),
- enhance the body's ability to tolerate or delay the accumulation of lactic acid (another component of anaerobic conditioning),
- enhance the oxygen-carrying capacity of the blood (a component of aerobic conditioning),
- enhance the size and number of mitochondria in working muscles (another component of aerobic conditioning),
- improve the transmission of neural impulses that initiate movement (a component of power), and optimize the size and effects of muscle fibers (another component of power).

Conditioning all the energy systems and muscles to perform at their maximal capacity enables swimmers to perform at their best. But one of the most understated aspects of training is the fact that much of the adaptation that occurs in response to training occurs during and in combination with rest and recovery. Therefore, besides providing energy support, food provides the nutrients necessary to repair, rebuild, and maintain muscle tissue, blood, bone, and immune and nervous system elements that are taxed, stimulated, or jeopardized during training. Inadequate nutrient availability during exercise and rest can compromise the integrity of the immune, endocrine, and musculoskeletal systems in general (Burke, Louks, and Broad 2006).

Fueling Is a Skill

Strong fundamental skills are essential in any sport, and fueling for performance is no exception. Ensuring that the body has the nutrients it needs when it needs them is definitely a skill, one that moves athletes and their support teams beyond the concept of just counting calories. Fueling for performance is a matter of significantly affecting the quality of the work performed, the quality of the rest period, and ultimately the magnitude and direction of the adaptation and training response. A swimmer's nutritional needs and bioenergetics will be affected by that person's training status, training phase, dietary status, and overall health and state of mind (i.e., stress). Fueling for performance, therefore, is a matter of maintaining a daily food and fluid routine that is sufficient and appropriate in calories and nutrients taken at the appropriate times to support high-quality training, promote optimal adaptations, and sustain overall health.

How Much of What Should I Eat and Drink and When?

To maintain quality within the training program, a swimmer must learn to balance training-based fueling requirements with dietary intake. A healthy understanding and acknowledgment of how many calories are required to maintain a healthy and efficient body weight and composition is an important first step in ensuring this energy balance. The energy balance is the relationship between calories consumed through diet and those expended through training and the activities of daily living. Athletes can find themselves in one of three scenarios:

1. Positive energy balance: Energy intake is greater than energy expenditure.
2. Neutral energy balance: Energy intake equals energy expenditure.
3. Negative energy balance: Energy intake is less than energy expenditure.

Ignoring the role of energy balance can jeopardize a swimmer's adaptation to training and performance. For example, negative energy balance (i.e., when energy intake is less than and therefore does not support energy output or energy expended), forces the body to use an above-normal proportion of stored protein for fuel during exercise. This use of protein can lead to a loss of lean tissue, including muscle and its associated strength and endurance qualities (Burke, Louks, and Broad 2006). Chronic negative energy balance can lead to nutrient deficiencies and subsequent metabolic dysfunctions. Ultimately, these conditions become a primary limiting factor on exercise quality and therefore training adaptation.

The 2009 joint position statement on nutrition and athletic performance, published by the American Dietetic Association, Dietitians of Canada, and American College of Sports Medicine (Rodriguez, DiMarco, and Langley 2009) emphasizes the need for athletes to consume an amount of calories during periods of high-intensity or long-duration training that maintains body weight and health and maximizes training effects (neutral or slightly positive energy balance). Calculating these caloric requirements can be difficult, and without the guidance of a qualified professional, such as a board-certified specialist in sports dietetics, it can become a source of frustration and stress. The most commonly used tool for determining the necessary caloric intake for an athlete is the Harris-Benedict equation (Harris and Benedict 1919). Although the Harris-Benedict equation dates back to the early 1900s, it is still reliable and practical, and therefore it is widely used by sports dietitians to estimate basal metabolic rate (BMR, the energy needed to sustain base bodily functions) and subsequently determine an athlete's total caloric expenditure.

Harris-Benedict equation for BMR, men

$$BMR = 66.5 + (13.75 \times \text{weight in kg}) + (5.003 \times \text{height in cm}) - (6.775 \times \text{age in years})$$

or

$$BMR = 66 + (6.23 \times \text{weight in lb}) + (12.7 \times \text{height in in.}) - (6.76 \times \text{age in years})$$

Harris-Benedict equation for BMR, women

$$BMR = 655.1 + (9.563 \times \text{weight in kg}) + (1.850 \times \text{height in cm}) - (4.676 \times \text{age in years})$$

or

$$BMR = 655 + (4.35 \times \text{weight in lb}) + (4.7 \times \text{height in in.}) - (4.7 \times \text{age in years})$$

Harris-Benedict equation for total energy expenditure, men and women

$$\text{Daily energy expenditure} = BMR \times \text{activity factor}$$

where

Activity factor = 1.2 for little or no exercise

Activity factor = 1.375 for light exercise (one to three days per week)

Activity factor = 1.55 for moderate exercise (three to five days per week)

Activity factor = 1.725 for heavy exercise (six or seven days per week)

Activity factor = 1.9 for very heavy exercise (twice per day, extra heavy workouts)

Within-Day Energy Balance

So far, energy balance has been described in the context of a day. But equally important is an athlete's within-day energy balance (Duetz et al. 2000). Succumbing to the pressures of time and weight management, many athletes, including swimmers, suffer from an eating pattern characterized by oversized or infrequent morning and afternoon meals and snacks, followed by a large meal at the end of a long day. Through the physiology of food digestion, this pattern of eating promotes dramatic fluctuations in blood sugar, which inevitably leads to difficulty with body weight and composition management. The ideal scenario for an athlete is one in which calories are consumed throughout the day in amounts and with proper timing to offset the energy expended during training. Ironically, an athlete's desire to exert some control over body weight or composition is often the trigger to seek negative energy balance. Like many other athletes, swimmers naturally and deliberately pursue negative energy balance when put under pressure to lose weight or body fat. Without proper guidance and instruction, swimmers who pursue performance improvements through body weight and fat reduction can (and quite often do) easily and inadvertently compromise training quality and improvement altogether (Maughan 2010).

An additional element, and often a more productive approach, to promoting healthy and efficient body weight and composition involves discussions about the foundations of good nutrition specific to consumption of performance-related nutrients and its timing.

Energy-Yielding Nutrient Requirements

The roles and value of carbohydrate, protein, and fat in training and adaptation are well established and accepted. Current research and practice still support the use of the following daily intake recommendations for these macronutrients. Break out your calculator, because the requirements tend to be based on an athlete's body weight, but take comfort in the fact that after you go through this exercise several times, you will get a feel for how much food and what types of food will get to the recommended amounts:

Carbohydrate: 6 to 10 grams per kilogram of body weight per day

Protein: 1.2 to 1.4 grams per kilogram of body weight per day, up to 1.7 grams per kilogram of body weight per day

Fat: 20 to 35 percent of total energy intake per day

The ranges provided in these daily intake recommendations reinforce the notion that all food and fluid routines for serious athletes must be based on individual needs. Besides current training status, training phase, dietary status, and overall health and state of mind, a swimmer's individual needs can vary with current biological age, gender, and training volume and intensity. Because training volume and intensity are easily interpreted and tend to change more readily and frequently than any of the other factors, it is practical to use them to anchor the daily macronutrient requirements (see table 14.2).

Carbohydrate Intake

Most pool and dryland workouts tend to be in the moderate- to high-intensity range, so carbohydrate serves as the swimmer's primary training fuel source

Table 14.2 Sample Daily Macronutrient Requirements

Swimmer's body weight, lb (kg)	Current training volume and intensity	Carbohydrate (g/day)	Protein (g/day)	Fat (g/day)
100 (45.5)	Low to moderate	273	55	Varies with total caloric expenditures calculated by Harris-Benedict equation.
	Moderate to high	450	77	
150 (68.2)	Low to moderate	409	82	
	Moderate to high	682	116	
200 (90.9)	Low to moderate	545	109	
	Moderate to high	909	155	

(Stellingwerff and Boit 2007). The representation of carbohydrate in the media and fad diet promotions, however, has undermined its importance in the athlete's diet. Consequently, these reports and this misinformation have led many athletes and coaches to question its reputation. This circumstance is unfortunate because besides its role as an energy-yielding nutrient, carbohydrate plays a number of key roles in exercise physiology.

Adequate carbohydrate intake maintains glycogen stores and therefore maintains plasma and muscle glutamine levels. Glutamine is a fuel source for immune system cells. Adequate carbohydrate intake keeps glutamine levels higher during intense training and helps return levels to normal after exercise.

Adequate carbohydrate intake reduces the effects of the cortisol response to exercise (Gleeson 2006). Cortisol is a stress hormone released in response to physical and emotional pressure. Long term, cortisol can interfere with immune system function and proper storage of the energy-yielding nutrients.

Ideally, carbohydrate during exercise is used to maintain blood sugar levels, not to synthesize glutamine. Maintaining blood sugar levels during exercise spares protein, allowing protein to be used for building rather than for fuel.

A diet low in carbohydrate and high in protein may create a condition of acidosis, which requires buffering with glutamine, reducing glutamine's availability and increasing long-term susceptibility to illness.

When carbohydrate reserves are low, the body turns to fat, increasing fat oxidation and lipolysis. This process is facilitated by decreased levels of insulin and increased levels of epinephrine, norepinephrine, cortisol, and growth hormone.

Note that although bread, cereal, rice, pasta, and potatoes are excellent sources of carbohydrate, they should be balanced with other sources of carbohydrate, such as colorful fruits and 100 percent juices, corn, sweet potato, yogurt, and milk. Only then will the body also receive the appropriate mixture of vitamins and minerals required to store and access carbohydrate efficiently.

Fat Intake

Besides reacting to rumors about carbohydrate, many athletes have a fear of dietary fat and a corresponding tendency to place strict limits on dietary fat intake. Some try to avoid dietary fat altogether. But fat is an essential part of the athlete's diet. The key is to understand the role of fat in the body and the way to make healthy choices about its intake.

Fat provides the body with the fat-soluble vitamins A, D, E, and K. Some fat is required in processes associated with growth, reproduction, and cell membrane structuring. Some fat can offer protection against excessive loss of water and damage from the sun's radiation. Some fat must be supplied in fat-containing foods because the human body cannot make it.

Fat gives food its taste. If all the fat were removed from beef, chicken, lamb, and goat meat, it would be impossible to taste the differences between them. Fat causes food to stay in the stomach longer, creating feelings of fullness. Some fat in the diet can actually be a helpful element of a weight-loss strategy.

Fat is a concentrated source of energy. For athletes who have high daily caloric requirements, fat can provide some of those calories in smaller amounts of food. Without fat, some athletes would not be able to eat all the food needed to take in the calories required.

All types of fat (saturated, monounsaturated, polyunsaturated) provide nine kilocalories per gram, but these different types of fat function differently after they are inside the body. Saturated fat and cholesterol (a fatlike substance found predominantly in animal products) tend to be associated with health problems, whereas unsaturated fat, especially polyunsaturated fat, is generally recommended in balanced quantities. Swimmers should feel comfortable and confident eating healthy fat-containing foods such as olive oil, peanut butter, fish, and avocados. Coaches and parents should not advocate a fat-free diet for any athlete.

Protein Intake

Because protein does not typically contribute as a fuel source during exercise, its requirement in an athlete's diet is based largely on the effects of the exercise on the stored protein elements themselves. Therefore, when developing a workout, the coach must consider the anchoring elements of training—training volume and intensity—and assess how they will affect the body's protein environment. For example, a period of intense pool training accompanied by intense strength training is typically associated with periods of muscle tissue breakdown, known as catabolism. To optimize the desired training adaptations (gains in muscle mass or function that translate to strength, power, and so on), the protein environment must limit the amount of time that the swimmer spends in the catabolic state and promote a state of tissue repair and growth (anabolism).

The amount of dietary protein required to keep up with this magnitude of protein turnover will usually be close to the upper limit of the daily requirement, possibly near two grams per kilogram of body weight per day (Campbell et al. 2007).

Vitamin and Mineral Requirements

The most recent set of dietary recommendations established by the Food and Nutrition Board of the U.S. Department of Agriculture's Institute of Medicine and Health Canada are the dietary reference intakes (DRIs). Recent studies suggest that athletes from a variety of sports continue to consume less than the recommended daily intake for folate, vitamin D, calcium, iron, potassium, and magnesium (Knez and Peake 2010; Heaney et al. 2010) or practice "just in case" vitamin supplementation for those nutrients, as well as the antioxidants vitamin C and vitamin E (Knez and Peake 2010). Table 14.3 summarizes the daily intake recommendations for various vitamins and minerals necessary for health and swimming performance.

Table 14.3   Dietary Reference Intakes for Performance-Related Vitamins and Minerals

Nutrient	Role and function	DRI for females 19- to 50-years old	DRI for males 19- to 50-years old	Common food sources
Folate	Production of red blood cells, protein synthesis, central nervous system tissue repair	400 µ g/day	400 µ g/day	Black-eyed peas, lentils, okra, kidney beans, great northern beans, broccoli, iceberg lettuce, beets, lima beans, sunflower seeds, spinach, brussels sprouts, corn, asparagus, baked beans, green peas, baked potato, cabbage, avocados, peanuts, romaine lettuce, tomato juice, orange juice, strawberries, oranges, eggs, bananas, fortified cereal and milk, enriched bread, enriched rice, and enriched pasta
Vitamin C	Protection of cell membranes from oxidative damage	75 mg/day	90 mg/day	Red berries, kiwi, red and green bell peppers, tomatoes, broccoli, spinach, all citrus fruits and juices
Vitamin E		15 mg/day	15 mg/day	Wheat germ oil, almonds, safflower oil, corn oil, soybean oil, turnip greens, mango, broccoli
Vitamin D	Calcium absorption, bone health	15 µ g/day	15 µ g/day	Cod liver oil, salmon, mackerel, tuna, sardines, fortified milk, fortified cereal
Calcium	Maintenance and repair of bone, blood calcium levels, muscle contraction, nerve conduction, blood clotting	1,000 mg/day	1,000 mg/day	Yogurt, milk, cheese, salmon, tofu, rhubarb, sardines, collard greens, spinach, turnip greens, okra, white beans, baked beans, broccoli, peas, brussels sprouts, sesame seeds, bok choy, almonds
Iron	Formation of oxygen-carrying proteins, hemoglobin, myoglobin, energy production catalyst	18 mg/day	8 mg/day	Liver, beef, pork, lamb, oysters, clams, tuna, salmon, kidney beans, lima beans, black beans, collard greens, kale, spinach, tofu, swiss chard, fortified cereal
Potassium	Fluid balance, nerve transmission	4.7 g/day	4.7 g/day	Meat, poultry, fish, apricots, avocado, banana, kiwi, lima beans, vegetable juice, potatoes, tomatoes, carbohydrate-electrolyte drinks
Magnesium	Macronutrient metabolism, membrane stability, immune system function	310–320 mg/day	400–420 mg/ day	Nuts, barley, oat bran, wheat flour, cornmeal, avocado, soy beans, spinach, swiss chard, quinoa, oatmeal

Data from Food and Nutrition Information Center, USDA National Agriculture Laboratory (http://fnic.nal.usda.gov/dietary-guidance/dietary-reference-intakes). Dietary Reference Intakes are developed and published by the Institute of Medicine of the National Academies.

Although the vitamin and mineral needs of athletes may be slightly higher than the DRI in some cases or at certain times of the year, research continues to support the notion that the proportions of those needs are easily accounted for within the higher energy intakes of athletes. Therefore, for athletes who consume a calorically adequate and nutrient-rich diet and do not demonstrate signs of nutritional deficiency, the practices of supplementation to improve performance and "just in case" vitamin and mineral supplementation remain unwarranted (Woolf and Manore 2006). But for a couple of vitamins and minerals, evidence indicates that the risk of deficiency in certain swimmers remains high.

Special Considerations for Iron

Iron deficiency continues to be one of the most commonly detected and addressed nutritional deficiencies in athletes (Haymes 2006). Characterized by low available iron, low iron stores (low ferritin), poor iron use, low red blood cell count, and low hemoglobin concentration, most cases of anemia are preceded by a period of iron deficiency. Although iron deficiency itself does not affect performance to a large degree, the low availability of iron and related markers in the blood that accompanies anemia can have a significant detrimental effect on performance. The physiology to exercise becomes unavailable, recovery suffers, and training does not result in adaptation or improvement.

In swimmers, reports of iron stores well below the acceptable range (ferritin, 30 ng/ml for females, 35 ng/ml for males) are not uncommon. Ferritin, the storage form of iron in the body, is a solid indicator of internal iron activity. Although ferritin levels lower than 30 nanograms per milliliter are acceptable in recreational athletes, competitive swimmers rely on adequate ferritin levels to support regular extended endurance workouts, support double- and triple-session training days, manage lactate accumulations, and experience the physiological benefits of altitude training. A common symptom of anemia is fatigue. Female swimmers may be at greater risk because of significant body iron loss during menstruation and the consumption of smaller portions of iron-rich foods, such as red meat, in an effort to maintain energy balance or manage body weight. But male and female swimmers are equally susceptible to iron loss in sweat and rapid growth, poor iron absorption, and low intake of iron-rich foods in the diet.

Most athletes who suffer chronic iron deficiency or anemia require iron supplementation, but only after confirmatory diagnosis by a physician. Although maintaining adequate iron intake and ensuring adequate ferritin levels promotes health, long-term elevations in body iron can be detrimental. Iron supplements themselves can be toxic and ultimately deadly if a deficiency and a need for high doses are not confirmed. Naturally elevated and prolonged high ferritin levels can indicate a serious medical condition, such as hemochromatosis.

Anemia takes various forms, but most are related to poor dietary habits or excessive blood loss through menstruation. The key to maintaining healthy iron intake and stores is monitoring. Any athlete with inadequate iron in the diet or females who have heavy menstrual periods should have routine blood tests to screen for iron deficiency anemia. Protein-rich foods such as red meat, fish, poultry, legumes, and fortified cereals are excellent dietary sources of iron that do not generally have the potential for toxicity that iron supplements can present when taken without the guidance and instruction of a qualified sport dietitian or physician. Children should never have access to iron supplements.

Special Considerations for Vitamin D

Unlike iron deficiency, vitamin D deficiency does not receive the attention it probably deserves in the minds of athletes (Holick 2007; Vieth et al. 2007; Willis, Peterson, and Larson-Myer 2008). Although the risk of vitamin D deficiency is likely higher only for swimmers who train in indoor pools rather than outdoor pools, vitamin D is a dietary requirement for all athletes. The complication is that the variety of foods that supply it is limited.

Most people meet at least some of their vitamin D requirement through exposure to sunlight. Although vitamin D deficiency is rare in the general population, swimmers whose sun exposure is limited should consider making an extra effort to ensure a regular intake of foods that contain this nutrient, which is vital to supporting calcium and bone health. Some have suggested that this recommendation is especially important in a sport in which a large portion of the exercise is non-weight-bearing. Because of the integration of turns and dryland workouts into the sport, evidence to support this point is not conclusive.

Water and Hydration

Exercise raises body temperature, even in the pool. Fortunately, sweating offers an efficient way to remove excess heat from the body. Swimmers have been reported to sweat at a rate of 0.37 liters per hour (Cox et al. 2002). Although swimmers may sweat at a rate much lower than athletes in other sports do (Sawka et al. 2007), the effects of hydration and dehydration are no less important. Because the body produces heat and sweat in response to work, the blood must respond by delivering nutrients to exercising muscles, transporting metabolic by-products for removal, and delivering sweat to the skin. Over time, if sweating continues over the course of a two-hour workout, for example, total body fluid decreases, leading to a condition of dehydration. Any sweat loss from the body also removes electrolytes such as sodium, potassium, and chloride from the body.

Research suggests that dehydration from body fluid loss that results in a loss of body weight of more than 2 percent impairs aerobic exercise performance and mental agility, especially in a warm environment (Casa, Clarkson, and Roberts 2005; Cheuvront, Carter, and Sawka 2003).

To limit dehydration, swimmers are encouraged to incorporate hydration practices into the daily dietary routine. They should hydrate before, during, and after workouts according to the guidelines presented in table 14.4.

Table 14.4 Fluid and Electrolyte Recommendations

	How much?	What?	Examples
Before workout	5 to 7 ml/kg body weight	Water or 6 to 8% carbohydrate-electrolyte drink	2 cups at 2 to 3 hours before, then 1 cup at 1 hour before, then 1/2 cup at 15 minutes before
During workout	370 ml/hr, assuming a sweat rate of 0.37 L/hr	If more than 60 minutes, 6 to 8% carbohydrate-electrolyte drink. If less than 60 minutes, water may be sufficient	1 or 2 mouthfuls every 10 to 20 minutes
After workout	450 to 675 ml × 2% body weight within first 2 hours	Water, juice, or 6 to 8% carbohydrate-electrolyte drink	For a 160 lb (73 kg) swimmer, 2 1/2 cups taken evenly over the first 2 hours after a moderate workout, up to 4 cups taken over the first 2 hours after a very hard workout

Data from M.N. Sawka, L.M. Burke, E.R. Eichner, R.J. Maughan, S.J. Montain, and N.S. Stachenfeld, 2007, "American College of Sports Medicine position stand: Exercise and fluid replacement," *Medicine & Science in Sports & Exercise* 39(2): 377–390.

The purpose of drinking fluids during exercise is twofold:

1. To maintain adequate body fluid to help blood disperse heat and transport nutrients

2. To provide a source of fuel that will help maintain mental agility (because the brain relies heavily on blood sugar for fuel) and spare protein

Although water alone may accomplish the first objective, it cannot provide additional fuel. Carbohydrate-electrolyte drinks with carbohydrate content between 6 and 8 percent (by weight) are ideal. This concentration is low enough to promote fluid absorption in the gastrointestinal tract yet strong enough to deliver sugar to the bloodstream in a quantity that is effective in supporting the working body's use of carbohydrate as a fuel source, thereby sparing protein.

Timing Is Everything, and Recovery is Critical

Fueling for performance is a skill that athletes must practice. For swimmers, maintaining energy balance during a typical training day means keeping up with multiple fluctuations in energy demand and energy expenditure that accompany training. Eating in response to hunger (not a skill) is not enough to ensure adequate fuel sources and energy balance within each training day and throughout entire training cycles. Competitive swimmers must take eating to a more sophisticated level and become proactive with their eating plans and patterns. Eating must become a practiced skill. Similar to hydrating, fueling requires eating before, during, and after workouts.

Before a workout, ordinary meals and snacks should prepare a swimmer for the pending activity. More specifically, food and fluid taken during the four-hour period before exercise should combine carbohydrate and protein in such a way that the swimmer feels satisfied at the onset of the workout (i.e., no hunger, no undigested food in the stomach, no gastrointestinal distress). During a workout, the purpose of fueling is to provide a source of fuel that will help maintain mental agility, maintain blood sugar levels, improve performance quality, and spare protein. Despite perfect fueling during workouts, some accumulation of tissue damage is inevitable with high-level training. Therefore, replenishing fuel stores after every workout is critical to maintaining energy reserves from one workout to the next and limiting the amount of tissue damage over time (Rowlands et al. 2008; Koopman et al. 2007). A quality workout relies on the replenishment of fuel stores and hydration levels reduced during previous sessions. This replenishment is most critical during the first 20 to 120 minutes after the workout. Table 14.5 provides an overview of fueling schedule recommendations and guidelines for swimmers.

Table 14.5 Fueling Schedule Recommendations and Intake Guidelines

	Goal	Considerations	What?	Notes
Before workout	Prepare for fueling requirements of upcoming activity; stave off hunger during performance	Size of meal, time until performance, performance duration, performance intensity	High carbohydrate, moderate protein, low fat, low fiber Mixed meal with 200 to 300 g of carbohydrate and protein if 3 to 4 hours before performance	Stick with familiar food the swimmer has practiced with. Decrease meal size and protein content as workout approaches.
During workout	Maintain blood sugar levels, improve performance quality	Time of day, nutritional status before workout, dieting	If workout longer than 60 minutes, 0.7 g/kg body weight of glucose in liquid, gel, or solid form or 30 to 60 g/hr	Distribute equally at 15- to 20-minute feeding intervals.
After workout	Replace muscle glycogen, ensure rapid recovery	Extent of glycogen depletion or tissue damage (both related to duration and intensity), time until next workout	First priority: ensure carbohydrate intake of 1.0 to 1.5 g/kg body weight (0.5 to 0.7 g/lb) Second priority: add protein of 25 to 45% of mix with carbohydrate	Eat within first 30 minutes after workout. Repeat every 2 hours for 4 to 6 hours.

Data from Rodriguez, DiMarco, and Langley 2009; Jeukendrup 2007; Currell and Jeukendrup 2008; Jentjens and Jeukendrup 2003; Beelen et al. 2010; Cox et al. 2010; Rowlands et al. 2008.

Starting Recovery

The magnitude and direction of any training adaptation is influenced heavily by the environment resulting from the integration of available protein, carbohydrate, fat, vitamins, minerals, and water during rest and recovery (Burke 2010; Maughan 2010). The 2009 joint position statement on nutrition and athletic performance states,

> *After exercise, dietary goals are to provide adequate fluids, electrolytes, energy and carbohydrates to replace muscle glycogen and to ensure rapid*

recovery. A carbohydrate intake of 1.0–1.5 g/kg body weight (0.5–0.7 g/lb) during the first 30 min and again every 2 h for 4 to 6 h will be adequate to replace glycogen stores. Protein consumed after exercise will provide amino acids for the building and repair of muscle tissue. (Rodriguez, DiMarco, and Langley 2009, p. 710)

Table 14.6 provides a collection of recovery food ideas, most of which match the recommendations established by ACSM, ADA, and Dietitians of Canada.

Special Considerations for Competition and Travel

A swimmer's individual fueling routine should include fueling on the road. Even swimmers who follow excellent performance-based nutrition programs at home face certain fueling challenges on the road. The most practical recommendation for getting the right foods while on the road involves being prepared with back-up snacks and drinks from home, as well as being proactive in learning what type of food arrangements will be available at the destination (dining halls, restaurants, grocers, delis, convenience marts). Swimmers are advised to check with competition hosts or their event team managers for information about food arrangements. Lots of nutrition information for restaurants is available online.

Table 14.6 Summary of Recovery Food Ideas

Take one within the first 20 minutes postworkout.

	Food	Amount	Carbohy-drate (g)	Protein (g)	Ratio (carbohydrate: protein)	Fat (g)	Sodium (mg)	Potassium (mg)
Solids	Bagel with peanut butter	1 with 2 tsp	49	16	3.1	17	558	345
	Yogurt with Grape Nuts	8 oz with 1/2 cup	58	13	4.5	4	242	596
	PBJ (white bread)	1 sandwich	44	12	3.7	18	415	287
	PBJ (wheat bread)	1 sandwich	46	13	3.5	18	481	370
	PowerBar	1 bar (65 g)	45	10	4.5	2	90	190
	ClifBar	1 bar (68 g)	48	8	6.0	3.5	110	210
Liquids	Milk 2%	8 oz	12	8	1.5	5	122	375
	Milk with chocolate syrup	8 oz with 2 tsp	24	9	2.7	5	170	407
	Carnation Instant Breakfast	1 can (10 oz)	37	12	3.1	2.5	230	610
	Boost	1 can (8 oz)	41	10	4.1	4	130	400
	Ensure	1 can (8 oz)	40	9	4.4	6	200	370
	Slimfast	1 can (11 oz)	40	10	4.0	3	220	600

A little research will help identify opportunities for individualized meals, special food substitutes, and special food preparations. Competition fueling should be part of the routine, not a new experiment!

Traveling to Altitude

Training and competing high above sea level present a unique set of nutrition-related challenges. Altitude decreases the partial pressure of inhaled oxygen (P_iO_2) in the lungs. When this pressure forcing air from the lungs into the bloodstream decreases, so too does the amount of oxygen reaching (saturating) the blood. Within 24 hours of altitude exposure, the body recognizes this change in oxygen availability and begins forming new red blood cells to compensate for the decline in the oxygen-carrying capacity of the blood. One of the ingredients in forming new red blood cells is ferritin, which again ties into the importance of maintaining adequate iron stores in the body.

Besides the physiological changes, travel to altitude is often associated with training camps and competitions involving higher-than-usual activity levels, harder workouts or more intense performances, and meals offered at restaurants or large dining halls. Swimmers can prepare for the potential effects of altitude during training camps and competitions by following several simple guidelines both before and during the training or event:

Before traveling to altitude

- Make healthy eating and drinking strategies at home routine. Adequate and stable hydration and nutrition status allows the body to deal with initial altitude exposure and to adjust during the visit.

- Get any asthma-related or other breathing restrictions or tendencies addressed and under control.

- Include iron-rich foods in daily food choices at home to help stabilize iron stores. Examples of iron-rich foods are red meat, shrimp, fish, beans, peas, whole grains, tofu, dark leafy greens, and fortified cereals.

- Prepare mentally and physically for the common initial symptoms of exposure and plan the first few days of the visit accordingly. Anticipating the side effects makes them seem less dramatic when they are actually experienced.

During the altitude visit

- Stay hydrated. Drink fluids intermittently before, during, and after workouts. Avoid alcohol and limit caffeine.

- Eat plenty of carbohydrate, protein, and iron by including bread, pasta, fruit or fruit juice, meat, fish, milk, yogurt, beans, and dark salads in daily food choices.

- Be smart about fat by choosing healthy fat sources such as olive oil, nuts, avocados, and peanut butter and avoid wasteful fat sources such as french fries, pie, ice cream, and alfredo sauce.

- Get enough rest. Adequate sleep during the night and short naps during the day can decrease stress hormones and promote recovery and tissue regeneration.

Swimmers staying at altitude more than five days who seek to experience the physiological benefits of altitude training should consider an iron status screening by a physician or health care center before the start of the training camp. An iron status check typically includes a profile of a complete blood count (CBC), serum iron, total iron binding capacity (TIBC), and ferritin. Ferritin levels greater than or equal to 30 nanograms per milliliter for females or greater than or equal to 35 nanograms per milliliter for males are considered adequate. Note: This testing will be useful only if it is done at least six weeks before the altitude visit because even a mild deficiency can take at least six weeks to correct.

Performance-Centered Nutrition and Disordered Eating

Despite the tremendous amount of educational material available and the many avenues through which this information is disseminated, disordered eating continues to challenge many athletes whose sports carry a strong aesthetic element (Beals and Hill 2006). Swimmers are not alone in battling unhealthy eating behaviors as well as the internal and external pressures they experience in trying to mold themselves to the expectations and perceptions of what it means to be an athlete today. Although clinicians agree that disordered eating is psychologically based, the fact remains that restricting foods, binging, purging, using laxatives and diet pills, and engaging in compulsive or excessive exercise are nutrition related. Unfortunately, these issues often stem from an athlete's desire to lose weight in the name of appearance, and the behaviors may have little to do with performance in the pool.

The challenges for athletes who, unguided and unsupervised, attempt to lose weight or change body composition for the sake of appearance include such things as

- inadequate caloric intake (negative energy balance),
- overreliance on protein and fat and underreliance on carbohydrate,
- too many dietary substitutes such as dietary supplements or ergogenic aids,
- poor recovery,
- failure to practice eating and drinking in a manner that supports health and performance, and
- failure to plan daily food intake.

Although the desired physical changes may be realized, the integrated collection of physiological consequences can be devastating to a swimmer's performance: loss of metabolic muscle mass, lower metabolic rate (i.e., lower ability to burn calories), lower endurance, poor recovery, and a higher risk of injury, illness, and complications associated with nutrient deficiencies.

Addressing these challenges requires solid acceptance of the facts: Appearance is important, nutrition affects performance, food is fuel and should not be feared, chronic undereating slows metabolism, and nutrition can and should be planned to support performance. After all, everything that swimmers do in training is focused on performance, so nutrition should be too. Performance-centered nutrition incorporates the foundations of sport nutrition with the elements of sport performance:

- Eat a variety of foods from all the food groups. There are no magic foods or food groups for enhancing performance or losing or gaining weight.

- Eat colorful foods, especially during recovery. Vitamins give fruits and vegetables their bright colors. Always have at least two brightly colored fruits or vegetables on the dinner plate. Take advantage of the postexercise insulin response to replenish glycogen, attenuate tissue breakdown, and promote tissue accretion.

- Eat enough, frequently, and don't get hungry. Eat foods that support daily training requirements in terms of total energy, fuel sources, and metabolic catalysts. Obtain calories from sources that enhance metabolism and minimize waste and unnecessary hormonal responses. Avoid restricting calories by more than 10 to 20 percent of normal intake. Avoid dropping fat intake to less than 15 percent of total daily caloric intake. Time calorie intake to maximize use and storage. Hunger is a sign of an energy deficit and possible hormonal fluctuation. A healthy approach is to eat smaller meals and several snacks throughout the day, feeding the body every three to four hours, even on competition days.

- Drink enough, often enough, and don't get thirsty. Thirst is a sign of existing dehydration, which can impair mental and physical performance.

Summary

The best nutrition plan is the one most tailored to the unique needs of the individual swimmer. These needs are a function of age, gender, body size, training, and food preferences and tolerances. Performance-centered nutrition reflects a flexible, achievable, and sustainable approach to eating that allows athletes to overcome nutrition- and food-related challenges that can increase mental stress. Adopting a healthy and practical approach to weight management can help swimmers achieve the healthiest balance among body weight, body composition, food, and athletic performance.

CHAPTER 15

Performance Enhancers and Doping Control

—Jennifer L. Reed, PhD, MEd CS, and Andrew L. Pipe, CM, MD

No presentation of factors affecting elite swimming performance would be complete without a discussion of approaches to performance enhancement. All competitors have the laudable goal of enhancing their abilities, skills, and performance. In the pages that follow, we identify and review a series of methods that have been reputed to enhance performance, and we identify those that have been proved effective. We cannot stress enough that optimal approaches to training involve careful attention to the fundamental principles of nutrition—not exotic, unproven dietary practices—in association with the recognition that rest and recovery are essential elements of any training program. Success most often occurs by paying careful, methodical attention to the seemingly mundane, not by seeking the miraculous!

Performance enhancers, in our discussion, involve the use of substances, methods, or other phenomena. They have included warm-up exercises, hypnosis, stress management techniques, music, motivational strategies, nutritional practices, oxygen inhalation, application of extrinsic biomechanical aids, and other approaches thought likely to improve training or competitive performance. In this chapter we critically examine a number of commonly employed nutritional supplements. We emphasize that a remarkably low level of evidence supports the use of many of these highly advertised, often costly products whose use may also pose significant risk to competitive swimmers.

At the same time we realize that some people seek to enhance performance using illicit techniques. We recognize that an examination of issues surrounding doping and doping control is also of interest to those in the swimming community.

We thank Joshua Stern and Shain Thakrar, medical students at the University of Ottawa, for their assistance in preparing this chapter.

Unfortunately, prohibited approaches have compromised fair competition in swimming and have included the use of drugs, hematological manipulations, and other illicit methodologies. The use of foreign substances to enhance performance is an age-old practice that dates back to ancient Greece, to a time when athletes used special diets and stimulating potions in attempts to enhance athletic performance. In this chapter we discuss antidoping rule violations in elite swimming, comment on doping behaviors among athletes and coaches, and discuss new advances in doping education and control. We discuss aids related to aerobic performance (e.g., blood doping) and anaerobic performance (e.g., blood buffering) and prohibited drugs (e.g., anabolic steroids, B_2-agonists).

Nutritional Supplements

Nutritional supplementation is a common practice among elite athletes (Juhn 2003; Maughan, King, and Lea 2004). It has been noted that 65 percent of Canadian Olympic athletes at the Atlanta and Sydney Olympic Games and 89 percent of American collegiate-level athletes reported using nutritional supplements as part of their training regimens (Froiland et al. 2004; Huang, Johnson, and Pipe 2006). Supplement use reflects popular trends. New supplements, often highly publicized and luridly advertised, emerge in the marketplace and become popular, while others lose their luster and disappear altogether. From the outset, it is important to note that the scientific evidence supporting the use of most supplement products is limited or nonexistent. Nevertheless, supplements are heavily advertised, frequently employing scientific-sounding and highly exaggerated claims!

Nutritional supplements may be consumed in an attempt to manage large training volumes, maximize recovery, increase energy levels, reduce fatigue, increase strength, overcome muscle cramps, avoid illness, boost immune function, maintain good health, and improve performance (Juhn 2003; Maughan, King, and Lea 2004; Dascombe et al. 2010). Supplements may also be consumed because of sponsorship agreements and endorsement obligations, travel requirements, recommendations of peers or influential figures, or as part of a self-established routine (Dascombe et al. 2010).

Numerous supplementation practices have been reported among elite swimmers including the consumption of caffeine, sports drinks, isotonic drinks, vitamins, minerals, multivitamins, antioxidants, herbal preparations, glucosamine, iron, creatine, protein-carbohydrate mixes, amino acids (protein), garlic, horse radish, fish oil, carnitine, conjugated linoleic acid, cytochrome, inosine, ginseng, bee pollen, oxygenated water, vanadium, coenzyme Q10, pyruvate, dimethylglycine, and bicarbonate (Dascombe et al. 2010; Baylis, Cameron-Smith, and Burke 2001; Zenic et al. 2010; Rodriguez, DiMarco, and Langley 2009; Momaya, Fawal, and Estes 2015). Sports drinks provide an appropriate source of energy and nutrients to meet the nutritional needs of training and competition. The principal reason for the consumption of sports drinks is to increase energy intake (Lun et al. 2012; Slater, Tan, and Teh 2003). Although appropriate energy intake is important because inadequate energy levels can impair swimming performance (Vanheest et al. 2014), for most swimmers competing in short events the ongoing administration of calories (the most common ingredient of sport drinks) is largely unnecessary. Multivitamins and vitamin C are reported as the most popular vitamin supplements used by elite swimmers (Baylis, Cameron-Smith, and Burke 2001); echinacea has been reported as the most common herbal product consumed by swimmers (Baylis, Cameron-Smith, and Burke 2001). Antioxidant supplementation may have a role (vitamin C and E) during periods of adaptation to increased training stress (Baylis, Cameron-Smith, and Burke 2001). But no conclusive proof of health benefits or enhanced performance is available, and any improvement in performance is likely to be small and mediated by the placebo effect (Baylis, Cameron-Smith, and Burke 2001). The body maintains exquisite control over the level of many vitamins, so an increased intake of water-soluble vitamins is immediately met with an increase in the excretion of that same vitamin, leading to the sarcastic observation that many athletes produce the most nutritious urine in the world!

Despite the number of readily available supplements and the number of elite swimmers who consume these products, there is limited data to suggest that nutritional supplements (e.g., vitamins and minerals) enhance performance (Rodriguez, DiMarco, and Langley 2009; Volpe 2007). Moreover, the production and marketing of the vast majority of nutritional supplements is unregulated. Athletes risk the inadvertent ingestion of prohibited substances which may be often added to these products without any identification of their presence on the label. Such incidents occur with increasing frequency on a worldwide basis. Supplement use comes with little evidence of benefit—there are some exceptions—and considerable risk (Outram and Stewart 2015; Maughan 2013; Judkins and Prock 2012; King et al. 2012).

Elite swimmers typically seek information from a variety of sources when deciding whether to take a supplement. The role of self-styled nutritional gurus, strength and conditioning coaches, and others with little formal training in nutritional science can be problematic. For many, nutrition is more a religion than a science, and, tragically, each year a significant number of competitors in a variety of sports are found to have ingested prohibited substances because of the ill-advised use of nutritional supplements. Although dietitians, doctors, pharmacists, nutritionists, sport scientists, coaches, and naturopaths are often thought to be the principal sources of information for athletes when they consider whether to take a supplement (Dascombe et al. 2010; Baylis, Cameron-Smith, and Burke 2001; Zenic et al. 2010; Sajber et al. 2013), it is frequently noted that athletes are more likely to discuss supplement use with the staff of health food shops, herbalists, supplement salespersons, peers, family, and friends (Huang, Johnson, and Pipe 2006; Dascombe et al. 2010; Zenic et al. 2010). This circumstance is a concern because many such individuals lack in-depth knowledge regarding nutritional supplements. Sadly, nutritional scientists and dietitians are less frequently consulted or heeded! Misinformation regarding nutritional supplementation places athletes at a higher risk of positive doping violations. The billion-dollar nutritional supplement industry is almost completely unregulated in the United States, the source of a substantial proportion of the world's nutritional supplement products. The nature of the ingredients, labeling practices, quality controls, and manufacturing and marketing processes surrounding these products is generally open to suspicion. Inadvertent doping occurs when an athlete records a positive drug test after ingesting a banned substance as an unrecognized ingredient of such products. Many cases occur because of the consumption of products by unsuspecting athletes who have followed the advice of perhaps well-intentioned, but frequently ill-informed, advisors or coaches.

Most countries have national antidoping organizations (NADOs) that provide education and guidance to athletes regarding the use of medications and supplements. But in most instances there is no way to guarantee the safety or contents of nutritional products from countries (most commonly the United States) where the supplement industry is unregulated. Athletes assume absolute liability for anything they place in their bodies, and antidoping sanctions are typically applied in cases in which a prohibited substance is detected even though it was consumed, in error, in a supplement. Sadly, competitors can be disqualified from sport and face public humiliation as a doping athlete following the consumption of a contaminated nutritional supplement (Baylis, Cameron-Smith, and Burke 2001). All athletes must be aware of the risks of using nutritional supplements.

Unfortunately, some researchers have noted that few elite swimmers (less than 4 percent) believe that their sport is doping free (Sajber e al. 2013). A recent report suggested that one in five swimmers would use doping products if they would ensure sport success without negative health consequences (Zenic et al. 2010). Swimmers who believe that doping practices are commonplace in their sport are more likely to have a tendency toward doping usage (Zenic et al. 2010). Approaches that would create a competitive environment in which doping behavior is seen by athletes as being socially unacceptable are important in the fight against doping.

Caffeine

Caffeine is a substance, not prohibited, that most adults consume daily. The widely available foods, drinks, and nonprescription medications that contain caffeine have increased the opportunities for athletes to consume caffeine as an ergogenic (performance-enhancing) aid. Table 15.1 shows the caffeine content of common foods, drinks, and nonprescription preparations (Burke 2008; caffeineinformer 2014).

The effects of caffeine in reducing fatigue and increasing wakefulness are well documented (Burke 2008). In healthy adults, moderate caffeine intake of up to 400 milligrams per day (6 mg per kg of body weight) is not associated with adverse effects (Burke 2008).

Table 15.1 Caffeine Amounts in Food, Drinks, and Nonprescription Preparations

	Serving	Caffeine (mg)
FOODS		
PowerBar Acticaf performance bar	65 g	50
PowerBar caffeinated sports gel	40 g sachet	25
PowerBar double caffeinated sports gel	40 g sachet	50
GU caffeinated sports gel	32 g sachet	20
SumSeeds energized sunflower seeds	3.5 oz (1 bag)	120
Morning Spark energy instant oatmeal	1 packet	60
Chocolate milk	60 g	5 to 15
Dark chocolate	60 g	10 to 50
Perky jerky	1 oz	150
Penguin caffeinated mints	1 mint	7
Jolt gum	1 piece	45
DRINKS		
Instant coffee	250 ml (8 fl. oz) cup	60 (12 to 169)
Brewed coffee	250 ml (8 fl. oz) cup	80 (40 to 110)
Short black coffee or espresso	1 standard serving	107 (25 to 214)
Iced coffee	500 ml bottle (16 fl. oz)	30 to 200
Tea	250 ml (8 fl. oz) cup	27 (9 to 51)
Hot chocolate	250 ml (8 fl. oz) cup	5 to 10
Coca-cola	355 ml (12 fl. oz) can	34
Pepsi cola	355 ml (12 fl. oz) can	38
Sunkist orange soda	8 fl. oz	28
A&W cream soda	12 fl. oz	29
Red Bull energy drink	250 ml (8 fl. oz) can	80
V Energy drink	250 ml (8 fl. oz) can	50
Vitamin Water (energy citrus flavor)	20 fl. oz	42
NONPRESCRIPTION PREPARATIONS		
Excedrin	1 tablet	65
One-a-Day Energy	1 tablet	120
Midol Menstrual Complete	1 tablet	60

Caffeine was removed from the World Anti-Doping Agency's (WADA's) list of prohibited substances and methods in part because of its widespread, global presence in a variety of commonly consumed foodstuffs and beverages. Athletes are therefore able to consume caffeine either in their diets or for specific performance-enhancing purposes. Caffeine levels in the urine samples collected in the course of doping controls are monitored carefully by the WADA to detect patterns of misuse in sport. Caffeine is on the list of restricted substances (urine samples exceeding 15 micrograms per ml of caffeine) for the National Collegiate Athletic Association (NCAA).

The habitual social intake of caffeine and its specific use in relation to a training session may benefit elite swimming by prolonging an athlete's capacity to undertake the physical and mental components of a workout (Burke 2008). Several researchers have examined the effect of caffeine on swimming (Burke 2008;

MacIntosh and Wright 1995). Caffeine has been shown to enhance performance in sustained high-intensity swimming events lasting from 1 to 20 minutes (Burke 2008). In controlled research trials involving 1,500-meter freestyle swimming, caffeine ingestion (6 mg per kg of body weight) resulted in faster performance times (23-second improvement) in an event that is completed in less than 25 minutes (MacIntosh and Wright 1995). Further, caffeine ingestion (205 mg; 4 mg per kg of body weight) 60 minutes before 100-meter swim races leads to enhanced swim velocity (meters per second) in trained swimmers (Collomp et al. 1992). Caffeine appears to mediate improvements in performance through increased lipolysis (lipid breakdown) and fat oxidation, decreased muscle glycogen breakdown (Kovacs, Stegen, and Brouns 1998; Cole et al. 1996; Costill, Dalsky, and Fink 1978; Ivy et al. 1979), and lessening of the subjective perception of effort (Ivey et al. 1979). Not generally appreciated is that individual sensitivity to and metabolism of caffeine can vary widely. Beyond a certain intake, symptoms of caffeinism such as irritability, restlessness, and agitation may develop, possibly reducing performance capacity.

Blood Buffers

Bicarbonate is generally thought to provide a definite benefit to sport performance when used in a specific protocol for a specific event (Baylis, Cameron-Smith, and Burke 2001). In short-term, all-out performance in which nonoxidative energy sources provide most of the energy for muscle contraction, the focus of attention shifts to the buffering of hydrogen ions (H^+) released from the muscle. Elevations in H^+ in muscle can decrease the activity of phosphofructokinase (PFK), which may slow the breakdown of glucose, a muscle fuel; interfere with excitation-contraction coupling events by reducing Ca^{++} efflux from the sarcoplasmic reticulum, impairing muscle function (Fuchs, Reddy, and Briggs 1970); and reduce binding of Ca^{++} to troponin, further impairing muscle function (Nakamaru and Schwartz 1972). Not surprisingly, therefore, decreases in muscle force development have been linked to increases in muscle H^+ (Tesch et al. 1978).

The primary means by which H^+ is buffered during exercise is through its reaction with the plasma bicarbonate reserves to form carbonic acid, which subsequently yields carbon dioxide (CO_2) that is exhaled during normal respiration. As bicarbonate stores decrease, the ability to buffer H^+ is reduced and the plasma H^+ increases, producing a state of acidosis (Powers and Howley 2012). Systemic alkalosis (decreased H^+ concentration) induced through the ingestion of bicarbonate has been shown to improve exercise performance and delay the onset of fatigue (Lindh et al. 2008; Mero et al. 2004). The findings of Lindh et al. (2008) revealed that 200-meter swim performance time was faster after consuming sodium bicarbonate (300 mg per kg of body mass) than in control or placebo conditions (1:52.2 ± 4.7 sodium bicarbonate; 1:53.7 ± 3.8 control; 1:54.0 ± 3.6 placebo; min:ss; $p < 0.05$). Mero et al. (2004) demonstrated that combining sodium bicarbonate and creatine supplementation (0.3 grams per kg of body weight) enhances interval swimming performance in elite swimmers (100-meter freestyle swims) by 0.9 seconds when compared with the administration of a placebo.

The use of blood buffers to induce alkalosis is not without risk. Large doses of sodium bicarbonate can cause diarrhea and vomiting, which can obviously have an adverse effect on performance.

Creatine

Creatine (methyl guanidine acetic acid) supplementation is a common practice among elite swimmers (de Silva et al. 2010). Creatine supplements were first brought to broad public attention following the 1992 Olympics in Barcelona. Annual worldwide consumption of creatine is estimated at more than 2.7 million kilograms (Baylis, Cameron-Smith, and Burke 2001). Creatine is synthesized by the body, and it plays an important role in energy metabolism. Inside the muscle cell, creatine is phosphorylated to generate phosphocreatine (PCr), an energy substrate that undergoes dephosphorylation to resynthesize adenosine triphosphate (ATP) from adenosine diphosphate (ADP) in the following reaction:

$$PCr + ADP + H^+ \leftrightarrow Cr + ATP$$

The degree to which skeletal muscles use PCr in the regeneration of ATP (a principal source of muscle energy in short-duration activity) depends on exercise intensity and duration. The breakdown of ATP in muscle cells releases energy for muscular contraction. The supply of PCr is limited; total combined ATP and PCr stores are capable of sustaining all-out maximal effort for 5 to 10 seconds. Fatigue may be attributed to the rapid decrease in PCr and a diminished rate of ATP regeneration (Silva et al. 2007).

Creatine supplementation has been shown to increase resting concentrations of creatine in skeletal muscle, which consequently increases PCr concentrations by 12 to 18 percent (Juhn 2003; Branch 2003), thus facilitating regeneration of ATP during intense exercise. Typical creatine supplementation practices involve oral creatine intakes of 20 grams per day for five days as a loading dose, followed by 5 grams per day as a maintenance dose. But athletes often take more than needed. Two grams per day is enough to maintain optimally elevated creatine concentration in skeletal muscle (Juhn 2003). Many athletes are nonresponders, and the administration of creatine produces no discernible benefit. Creatine is typically found in certain animal proteins, so those with an inadequate intake of dietary creatine are more likely to derive additional benefit from its ingestion.

The generation of peak nonoxidative power and nonoxidative capacity during short-term, high-intensity exercise may depend on endogenous levels of ATP and PCr. An increase in total muscle PCr through exogenous creatine supplementation may provide an ergogenic effect by enhancing the rate of ATP synthesis during this type of exercise.

Performance enhancements observed in laboratory experiments may not be present during actual swimming activities. The literature is conflicting regarding the effect of creatine supplementation on swimming performance. The inconsistencies in the literature about the effects of oral creatine supplementation on either performance or body composition may result from the variety of protocols (number of grams, number of days, time between dosing and event) used or groups of participants (trained, untrained, males, or females) used to investigate the effects (Silva et al. 2007). Some studies have reported improved swimming performance (Peyrebrune et al. 2005), but others have reported no influence of creatine supplementation in either a single swim situation or repeated interval swimming bouts (Silva et al. 2007). For example, creatine supplementation when compared with placebo supplementation has not been shown to improve swimming performance in events less than 150 seconds in duration (Branch 2003).

Creatine is osmotically active—it draws water into the tissues in which it is found in excess—leading to slightly swollen muscles, weight gain, heavier limbs, changed hydrodynamics, and increased drag. These latter features may explain why in sports in which it is necessary to propel oneself through or over the water (swimming and rowing), creatine use has frequently failed to show any performance-enhancing benefits (Juhn 2003). This increased quantity of water in the muscle of creatine users also explains why creatine supplementation has been found to cause a significant increase in total and lean body mass; average increases were $1.2 \pm 0.3\%$ and $2.2 \pm 0.7\%$, respectively (Branch 2003). Creatine supplementation has been found to improve the performance of specific isolated tasks such as isotonic lifting (rapid repetitions), isometric exercise, leg ergometer power, and other forms of work that primarily use nonoxidative glycolysis as a principal energy source (Branch 2003). The ergogenic potential of creatine supplementation diminishes with increasing duration of activity (Branch 2003).

Other documented adverse effects of creatine supplementation include increased muscle compartment pressure, which has the potential to impair blood flow in certain muscle groups. Because skeletal muscle has a threshold beyond which no more creatine can be stored, athletes should be informed that more is not better. In fact, increasing levels of creatine ingestion are associated with an increased incidence of adverse effects (Juhn 2003). Gastrointestinal disturbances and muscle cramps are frequent and common side effects of creatine intake.

Dietary Nitrate

In recent years, considerable interest has been directed to the use of nitrate and its role in enhancing the efficiency of muscle contraction. Evidence is accumulating that the ingestion of nitrates or beetroot juice (which is nitrate rich) rapidly increases the levels of nitrite and enhances the production of nitric oxide, a potent regulator of muscle blood flow (Vanhatalo et al. 2010; Larsen et al. 2007, 2010). The result appears to be an increase in muscle efficiency and a reduction in muscular oxygen consumption during a maintained level of power output (Larsen et al. 2010). Investigators have demonstrated that beetroot juice ingestion increases endurance exercise capacity (Bailey et al. 2009, 2010). Consequently, the consumption of this product has soared in many athletic circles. An increase in the level of nitric oxide can also be induced by the consumption of l-arginine, and its use has been associated with improved muscular efficiency (Bailey et al. 2010). The evidence of the health benefits of nitrate ingestion continues to grow, but at the same time it is acknowledged that overdosing with these agents may have health consequences (Archer 2002; Derave and Taes 2009).

Amino Acids and Beta-Alanine

Protein and amino acids, the building blocks of protein, play an important role in the development of strength. Elite swimmers commonly use these sport supplements (Paschoal and Amancio 2004). Athletes have a greater daily protein requirement than sedentary individuals do. The recommended dietary allowance of protein is 0.8 gram per kilogram of body weight per day for adults, but for athletes it ranges from 1.2 to 1.7 grams per kilogram of body weight per day; the higher values are reserved for strength athletes (American College of Sports Medicine 2013). Despite recognition of the additional protein needs of athletes, most athletes eat well enough to achieve an appropriate dietary intake; there is little convincing evidence to support additional consumption of protein or amino acids as performance enhancers (Juhn 2003). Excess protein or amino acid intake may lead to adverse health outcomes such as increased urinary calcium excretion, which may compromise bone mineralization, especially in elite swimmers who typically present with bone mineral densities lower than those of endurance or strength athletes (Paschoal and Amancio 2004).

Interest continues to grow about the effectiveness of beta-alanine, an amino acid that appears to increase muscle levels of carnosine, an intracellular buffer, thereby enhancing performance in situations in which muscle acidity increases because of exercise. Much of the research surrounding the effectiveness of many nutritional supplements has involved an examination of the effects of these substances in improving performance in nonelite participants. Beta-alanine is no different in this respect, and many of the studies evaluating its effectiveness have no clear relevance to high-performance sport. A carefully constructed examination of the effect of beta-alanine supplementation on swimming performance involving elite competitors failed to identify any performance benefits following 10 weeks of beta-alanine supplementation (4.8 grams per day over a four-week loading phase, 3.2 grams per day during a six-week maintenance phase) (Chung et al. 2012). Similar results have been reported in an investigation involving elite 400-meter runners (Derave et al. 2007). The initial evidence of the ergogenic potential of this agent in the laboratory setting has not been replicated in the swimming pool or on the track.

Remember the Basics

Although numerous supplements are aggressively marketed, the majority making astounding claims, most have little or no effect on performance. Elite swimmers need to remember the basics: optimal energy, iron, and folate levels.

Energy Levels

The goal of training is to produce physical adaptations to achieve a higher level of athletic performance. High training loads (exercise energy expenditure) demand greater energy intake to maintain energy balance. The maintenance of energy balance has long been theorized as an essential component of maximal performance. In a recent report, Vanheest and colleagues (2014) demonstrated that significant decrements in performance in elite junior national-caliber female swimmers during a 12-week competitive season were associated with chronic ovarian suppression because of inadequate energy intake. Rigorous approaches to caloric restriction to limit weight gain frequently produce distinct changes in normal hormonal fluxes (Reed et al. 2011; Reed, De Souza, and Williams 2013) and decrements in performance (Vanheest et al. 2014; Gibbs et al. 2013; Gibbs et al. 2011). Women with subtle ovarian suppression and long menstrual cycles (oligomenorrhea) experienced reductions in sport performance as measured by a 400-meter swim time trial. In fact, sport performance declined by 9.8 percent in females with ovarian suppression, whereas performance improved by 8.2 percent in females with normal menstrual cycles. Communication of this message to coaches and athletes is essential because many people promote energy-restricting practices with the goal of improving performance (Vanheest et al. 2014). Adequate energy intake is also needed to reduce the risk for nutritional repartition that can lead to impaired menstrual, bone, and cardiovascular health (Reed et al. 2011; Nattiv et al. 2007; O'Donnell, Goodman, and Harvey 2011; De Souza et al. 2007, 2008; Hoch et al. 2011; Reed et al. 2015).

Iron and Folate

Iron is required for the formation of oxygen-carrying protein, hemoglobin, and myoglobin, and for enzymes involved in energy production (Rodriguez, Di Marco, and Langley 2009). Iron depletion (low iron stores) has been observed among elite swimmers, especially females (Brigham et al. 1993; Gropper et al. 2006). Iron deficiency, with or without anemia, can impair muscle function and limit exercise performance. In general, a diet that provides adequate iron intake can be said to be providing adequate intake of all essential nutrients. Paying careful attention to dietary iron intake is therefore almost a guarantee against the development of nutritional deficiencies.

The recommended dietary allowance for iron for men aged 19 years and older is 8 milligrams per day; the recommended dietary allowance for iron for women aged 19 to 50 years is 18 milligrams per day (Thompson, Manore, and Sheeshka 2005). Elite swimmers and those who are vegetarian or regular blood donors should aim for an iron intake greater than the recommended dietary allowance (Rodriguez, Di Marco, and Langley 2009). The high incidence of iron depletion among athletes is usually attributed to inadequate energy intake (Rodriguez, Di Marco, and Langley). Other factors that can affect iron status include vegetarian diets that reduce iron availability; periods of rapid growth; training at high altitudes; increased iron losses in sweat, feces, urine, and menstrual blood; intravascular hemolysis; regular blood donation; and injury.

Consistently poor iron intake can negatively affect health and physical and mental performance. Prompt medical intervention and ongoing monitoring is warranted. Some athletes may experience a transient decrease in serum ferritin and hemoglobin at the initiation of training because of hemodilution in response to a normal training-induced increase in plasma volume, a common phenomenon known as sports anemia. Such a state may not respond to nutritional intervention. These changes seem to be a beneficial adaptation to aerobic training and do not negatively affect performance (Powers and Howley 2012).

In athletes who are iron deficient, iron supplementation not only improves blood measures and iron status but also increases exercise performance as evidenced by increased oxygen uptake and endurance, reduced heart rate, decreased lactate concentrations during exercise, and reduced muscle fatigue. Ironically, many athletes, consumed by an appetite for esoteric nutritional supplements, ignore fundamental nutritional determinants of health and performance like iron. Success in the area of sport nutrition often consists of doing ordinary things extraordinarily well!

Folate is required for the production of red blood cells. The recommended dietary allowance for folate for men and women aged 19 years and older is 400 micrograms per day (Thompson, Manore, and Sheeshka 2005). Folate is frequently low in the diets of female athletes, especially those who are vegetarian or have disordered eating patterns (Rodriguez, Di Marco, and Langley 2009). Severe deficiency of folate may result in anemia and reduced exercise performance (Rodriguez, Di Marco, and Langley 2009). Folate supplementation is recommended for females of reproductive age; its use is associated with a significant reduction in the risk of certain birth defects in children born to those with appropriate levels of this nutrient.

Antidoping Activities in Swimming

Regulations against drug use in sport began in the 1920s and gained urgency after the amphetamine-related deaths of the Danish cyclist Knut Jensen during the 1960 Rome Olympics and the UK competitor Tommy Simpson in the 1967 Tour de France. Doping controls in Olympic competitions were introduced at the 1968 Mexico games. In the years that have followed, doping control activities have evolved considerably and are now the fundamental responsibility of the WADA, created in 1999 under the auspices of governments and the international sport community as an independent international organization to promote, coordinate, and monitor the fight against doping in sport. The WADA Code is the basis of antidoping policies and rules among sports organizations; the most recent version was adopted in South Africa in 2013, and it became active in January 2015. The WADA Code defines doping as the occurrence of one or more of the rule violations identified in the sidebar "Doping as Defined by the World Anti-Doping Agency Code" (World Anti-Doping Agency 2009).

Doping as Defined by the World Anti-Doping Agency Code

1. Presence of a prohibited substance or its metabolites or markers in an athlete's sample.

2. Use or attempted use by an athlete of a prohibited substance or a prohibited method.

3. Refusing or failing, without compelling justification, to submit a sample collection after notification as authorized in applicable anti-doping rules, or otherwise evading sample collection.

4. Violation of applicable requirements regarding athlete availability for out-of-competition testing, including failure to file required whereabouts information and missed tests that are declared based on rules that comply with the International Standard for Testing. Any combination of three missed tests or filing failures within an 18-month period as determined by the anti-doping organization with jurisdiction over the athlete shall constitute an anti-doping rule violation.

5. Tampering or attempted tampering with any part of doping control.

6. Possession of prohibited substances and prohibited methods.

7. Trafficking or attempted trafficking in any prohibited substance or prohibited method.

8. Possession by an athlete in-competition of any prohibited method or prohibited substance, or administration or attempted administration to any athlete out-of-competition of any prohibited method or any prohibited substance that is prohibited out-of-competition, or assisting, encouraging, aiding, abetting, covering up, or any other type of complicity involving an anti-doping rule violation or any attempted anti-doping rule violation.

Each year WADA publishes a list of substances and methods prohibited in sport called the Prohibited List. A list of these substance and methods can be found on the WADA website at www.wada-ama.org.

Athletes, coaches, and trainers at every level of competition need to be aware of the prohibited substances and methods. Equally important, all competitive swimmers need to understand their responsibility to ensure that training and competition take place in a manner consistent with the spirit of sport and ensure that nothing they ingest or are administered is considered a doping agent as defined by the Prohibited List. This point is of particular significance, as previously noted, when considering the use of nutritional supplements, which may contain prohibited substances and represent a veritable minefield for the competitor.

In cases when injury, illness, or established medical condition requires the use of otherwise prohibited medications, athletes and their doctors can apply for a

Therapeutic Use Exemption (TUE). A panel of medical experts with particular experience in the care and treatment of high-performance athletes carefully reviews the medical circumstances of the competitor and the necessity for the use of specific medication. With their approval, permission is granted for the use of the specific medication; the detection of that substance in the process of doping control will not be adjudged an antidoping violation when a TUE has been previously granted.

History of Doping in Elite Swimming

Competitors from the DDR (the former East Germany) dominated women's swimming in the 1970s and 1980s. At the 1976 Olympics in Montreal, East German athletes won 40 gold medals, including 11 of the 13 gold medals available in women's swimming events. For two decades, these women were nearly unbeatable in the pool. Following the fall of the Berlin Wall and the collapse of the East German regime in 1989, the truth of the East German state's systematic steroid program (State Plan 14.25), which involved administering performance-enhancing drugs to their athletes, became clear (Durham 2013). The drug program, administered with or without the knowledge of the athletes, resulted in numerous victories in national and international competition, and unfortunate consequences for many of these swimmers years later. Swimmers as young as 13 years of age were administered oral and injectable anabolic steroids. Coaches and trainers often represented the pills and injections as vitamin preparations (Durham 2013). In 1998 Carola Nitschke, who broke the world breaststroke record at age 14, became the first doped athlete to return her medals and ask that her name be stricken from the record books; Nitschke reported being given as many as 30 pills a day.

The current German government now estimates that 10 percent of the 10,000 doped athletes face serious health issues. The reported problems have included an array of hormonal side effects: excessive hair growth, deepening of the voice, and masculinization of the genitalia as well as gynecologic issues including infertility and breast cancer. Many of these unfortunate competitors have reported mental health issues or delivered children with birth defects, consequences, it is assumed, of the doping program that operated many years earlier. More than 20 years after their Olympic success in Montreal, former East German coaches, trainers, and officials faced criminal charges. In 2000 a Berlin court found the former East German sports chief, Manfred Ewald, and medical director, Manfred Hoppner, guilty of "systematic and overall doping" in East German competitive sports.

Antidoping Rule Violations in Swimming

The antidoping rule violations per year, country of origin of competitors, and the prohibited substances detected are shown in figures 15.1 to 15.3. These data were retrieved from Fédération Internationale de Natation's (FINA's) 2003 to 2013 antidoping reports, which can be found on the FINA website.

Anabolic Steroids

Anabolic steroids appear on the WADA's list of prohibited substances and methods, and they have been among the most commonly abused prohibited substances by elite swimmers (figure 15.3). It is well known that anabolic steroid use, while increasing lean muscle mass and improving sports performance, can lead to deleterious health outcomes. Possible adverse effects include, but are not limited to, increased levels of aggression, liver damage, premature long-bone growth plate closure in adolescents, menstrual irregularities, deepening of

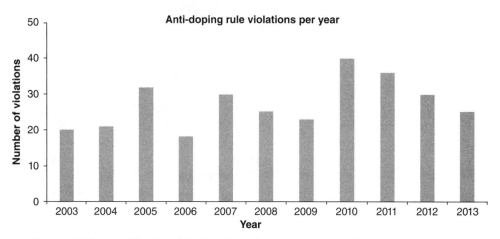

▶ **Figure 15.1** Antidoping violations in swimming, 2003 to 2013.

Data from Fédération Internationale de Natation (FINA). Available: www.fina.org.

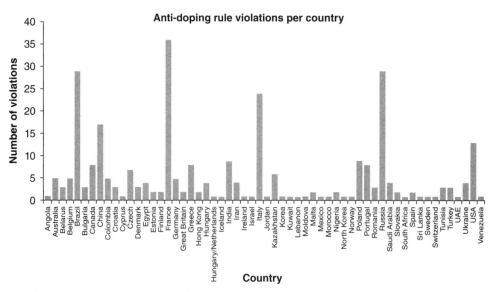

▶ **Figure 15.2** Antidoping violations by country of offender, 2003 to 2013.

Data from Fédération Internationale de Natation (FINA). Available: www.fina.org.

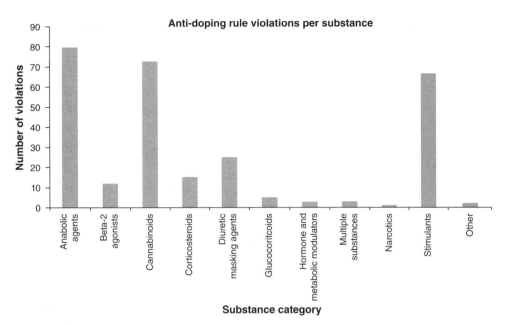

▶ **Figure 15.3** Prohibited substances detected in swimming doping controls, 2003 to 2013.

Data from Fédération Internationale de Natation (FINA). Available: www.fina.org.

the voice, cessation of breast development in women, increased rate of muscle strains and ruptures, high blood pressure, high cholesterol, decreased glucose tolerance, acne, male pattern baldness, depression, and thrombosis (Maravelias et al. 2005; Momaya, Fawal, and Estes 2015).

Blood Doping

Blood doping—the manipulation of certain blood elements, the red blood cells, by blood transfusion or hormonal stimulation of red blood cell production—enhances oxygen-carrying capacity and is clearly identified as a prohibited method. Although several well-controlled research trials have demonstrated that blood doping can improve exercise performance and maximal aerobic capacity ($\dot{V}O_2$max), there is general agreement that such practices have no place in modern sport. Competition should occur between swimmers, not hematologists!

Erythropoietin (EPO), a peptide hormone now available in recombinant forms, is naturally produced by the human body and is released from the kidneys. It stimulates red blood cell production by the bone marrow, thereby increasing their number and enhancing oxygen transport. The administration of this synthetic hormone produces the effects of blood doping—an increase in red cell numbers—without actual blood transfusion (Sawka et al. 1996). Its use provides a new challenge to antidoping authorities, who have responded by developing unique, sequential profiles of a competitor's blood values, which permit the identification of artificial manipulation. Athletes who train at altitude experience a natural increase in red blood cell production to compensate for the low oxygen levels (hypoxia). Training at altitude, however, usually results in a reduction in training intensity; the advantages of training in such locales have been greatly exaggerated.

Blood doping can have several adverse effects, including enhancing the likelihood of clot formation because of the increased viscosity of the blood (Momaya, Fawal, Estes 2015). The development of blood clots can obstruct blood flow to the heart and brain, resulting in a heart attack or stroke. The misuse of recombinant human EPO may also lead to autoimmune diseases and serious health consequences. Many deaths have been documented among athletes following the administration of EPO (Montagnana et al. 2008; Dhar et al. 2005; Momaya, Fawal, Estes 2015).

β_2-Agonists

More than 10 percent of elite athletes suffer from exercise-induced bronchospasm, a constriction of the airways that limits oxygen flow and athletic capacity (Wolfarth, Wuestenfeld, and Kindermann 2010). The risk of asthma is known to be higher in athletes training more than 20 hours per week (Nystad, Harris, and Borgen 2000). Repeated in-pool exposure to chlorine and related products irritates the airways and may itself promote the development of asthma (Wolfarth, Wuestenfeld, and Kindermann 2010). (Modern water treatment systems in swimming pools no longer employ chlorine or related chemicals.) Exercise-induced bronchoconstriction describes the acute transient airway narrowing that occurs during or after exercise. It is defined as a greater than 10 percent decrease in the ability to force air from the lungs in one second (the forced expiratory volume, or FEV_1) after an exercise challenge (Billen and Dupont 2008). The drying of the airways caused by increased rates of breathing during exercise is also a trigger for exercise-induced bronchoconstriction (Billen and Dupont 2008). Swimmers are at risk of exercise-induced bronchoconstriction because of the high volume of air managed by the lungs (described as a high respiratory minute volume) in association with swimming (Billen and Dupont 2008). The modern pharmacological management of asthma fundamentally involves the use of inhaled glucocorticosteroids to maintain optimal airway function and the use of bronchodilator therapy (e.g. β_2-agonists) to address or prevent any further increase of asthma symptoms. For those in whom exercise has been demonstrated to stimulate bronchospasm, the use of short acting β_2-agonists before exercise will substantially prevent exercise-induced asthma attacks (Wolfarth, Wuestenfeld, and Kindermann 2010; Billen and Dupont 2008).

The prevalence of exercise-induced asthma and bronchoconstriction is greater in elite athletes than it is in the general population (Rundell and Jenkinson 2002). Since 1984 the number of athletes using β_2-agonists to manage these conditions has increased (Wolfarth, Wuestenfeld, and Kindermann 2010). The use of β_2-agonists both in and out of competition is permitted when a clear diagnosis of asthma can be established. Use of the most common antiasthmatic medications (salbutamol, formoterol, and salmeterol) is allowed without obtaining a Therapeutic Use Exemption (TUE) if the levels of the medications do not exceed specified thresholds when identified in urine tests. The use of other antiasthmatic agents including terbutaline is permitted following the receipt of a TUE. When applying for a TUE for the use of certain antiasthmatic medications, evidence of the diagnosis of asthma in the form of the results of specific lung-function tests, a clear clinical history, and the documentation of the diagnosis by a physician must be submitted to a national antidoping organization or, in the case of an elite competitor, to FINA. There has been concern that inhaled β_2-agonists might have a performance-enhancing effect, but the evidence to support this concept is limited. A review of the literature performed in 2010 revealed that most randomized placebo-controlled trials in nonasthmatic elite athletes demonstrated no performance-enhancing effects of inhaled β_2-agonists (formoterol, salbutamol, salmeterol, and terbutaline), but lung function (FEV_1) was improved after inhalation of β_2-agonists in most of these studies (Wolfarth, Wuestenfeld, and Kindermann 2010; Kindermann 2007). The use of inhaled glucocorticosteroids is permitted; no ergogenic effect of these steroid preparations administered in this manner has been demonstrated to date (Billen and Dupont 2008). Note that one β_2-agonist, clenbuterol, is used in certain regions (e.g., South and Central America and China) to enhance muscle growth in farm animals. The ingestion of meat products by athletes in these countries has frequently resulted in the identification of clenbuterol in subsequent urine samples. This situation is of obvious concern to competitors and antidoping officials. Clenbuterol is not seen as a highly effective antiasthmatic agent, and it is used as such in only a few countries.

Remote Ischemic Preconditioning

Remote ischemic preconditioning (RIPC) is a method in which brief episodes of alternating ischemia (restriction of blood flow) and reperfusion (restoration of blood flow) induced in distant tissues or organs produces chemicals that protect muscles from the effects of ischemia (restriction of blood flow leading to reduced oxygen levels needed for cellular metabolism) that may occur in subsequent exercise (Przyklenk and Whittaker 2011). RIPC can be induced by cycles of inflation and deflation of a standard blood pressure cuff on a limb. Some literature suggests that RIPC may be used to enhance swimming performance through improvements in muscle tolerance to tissue hypoxia (Jean-St-Michel et al. 2011). In support, several investigators reported that RIPC of the legs has been shown to improve maximal performance by 1.6 percent and maximal oxygen consumption by 3 percent in healthy participants performing bicycle testing (de Groot et al. 2010). In highly trained swimmers, a recent report revealed that RIPC was associated with improved maximal performance (100-meter swims) (Jean-St-Michel et al. 2011). Although RIPC is possibly a promising method to enhance performance, the studies to date that have examined its effect on swimming performance have been limited to a small number of trained athletes in a few events. Future studies with athletes of varying performance levels from a range of sports are needed to gain a full evaluation of the effect of RIPC on performance.

Coaching Education

Coaches are critical to the creation of an environment in which scientific approaches to training and nutrition are the norm. Their attitudes toward doping practices are central to ensuring the development of appropriate sporting values among swimmers. Many coaches declare that self-education is their main source of information regarding nutritional supplementation and antidoping matters. None seem to be of the opinion that doping does not exist in elite swimming. Coaches also seem to know more about sport nutrition and doping than athletes do, and coaches express more support for stronger penalties following the detection of doping behavior than athletes do (Sajber et al. 2013).

In response to coaches' learning needs and demanding schedules, the WADA has taken a lead in launching CoachTrue, a computer-based, self-teaching antidoping tool, that can be found at www.wada-ama.org.

CoachTrue's elite-level module includes the following:

1. Pretest, an evaluation of a coach's current knowledge

2. Tutorials, a series of presentations that provide essential information on the health consequences of doping, the coach's accountability, results management, Therapeutic Use Exemptions, whereabouts, and decision making

3. Scenario-based activities, a practical application of acquired knowledge to likely real-life scenarios

4. Who wants to play true?, a fun way for coaches to test their knowledge on antidoping issues

5. Posttest and certification, a final assessment after coaches have completed all required learning steps, and a certificate of participation

This important resource is recommended for all coaches who want to enhance their understanding of how they can provide powerful leadership to their swimmers while creating a training environment in which doping practices are clearly and explicitly condemned.

New Strategic Approaches

Two new approaches to assist in the fight against doping that have emerged in the past few years are the athlete biological passport (ABP) and gene doping.

Biological Passport

The athlete biological passport (ABP) is an electronic record of test results based on the monitoring of selected parameters over time that indirectly reveals the effects of doping, as opposed to the traditional direct detection of doping by analytical means (Gilbert 2010; Sottas et al. 2011). The WADA executive committee first approved the WADA Athlete Biological Passport Operating Guidelines on December 1, 2009. A note from the WADA provides background on the biological passport:

> *The fight against doping relies on several strategies, including the direct testing of athletes as well as evidence gathered in the context of non-analytical doping violations. By combining these strategies, and seeking new ones to address emerging threats, the global fight against doping is more effective. The typical doping control approach based on the detection of prohibited substance or their metabolites in an athlete's sample remains an effective approach; however it has limitations when an athlete may be using substances on an intermittent and/or low-dose basis. Furthermore, new substances or modifications of prohibited substances (e.g., designer drugs) may be difficult to detect by conventional analytical means. In recent years, doping regimes have become much more scientifically planned and have taken advantage of the weaknesses in traditional protocols. This underscores the need for a more sophisticated and complementary strategy to effectively fight doping, namely, the Athlete Biological Passport. (World Anti-Doping Agency 2013)*

In 2012 FINA introduced a pilot ABP now involving 32 of the world's top-ranked swimmers, in several events, drawn from around the globe. Frequent blood testing of such competitors is ongoing, and hematological profiles have been developed. Additional blood tests involving these and other swimmers were performed immediately before the 2012 London Olympic Games; hundreds more blood samples were obtained at the time of the 2013 Barcelona FINA World Championships. The development of ABP profiles of FINA swimmers has begun. Sequential monitoring of the results of these samples permits the construction of an individual athlete's blood profile (figure 15.4). Careful examination of the profile permits the identification of any anomalous results and triggers additional reviews by hematological experts. The use of such approaches allows experts to conclude that manipulation of blood products has occurred. This technique permits the prosecution of cases without actual evidence of the presence of a prohibited substance in the blood or urine. Expansion of the FINA ABP program is expected to continue.

Gene Doping

Gene doping is defined by the WADA as the nontherapeutic use of cells, genes, genetic elements, or the modulation of gene expression, having the capacity to improve athletic performance (World Anti-Doping Agency 2014). Genes are composed of segments of DNA that provide a code for the production of various proteins. These proteins build our cells and instruct them how to function.

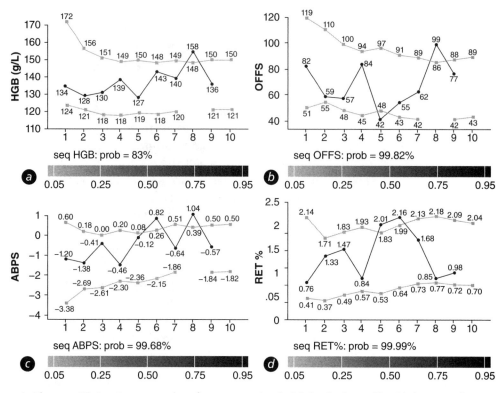

▶ **Figure 15.4** An example of a competitor's biological profile. Light gray lines represent the personally derived normal values for various blood elements or scores. Dark gray lines reflect changing levels of blood elements or calculated scores as revealed by ongoing blood testing.

The most common way to insert a gene into the body is to use a disabled virus that has been altered so that it is not itself harmful but can act as a vehicle for the delivery of DNA to a cell. An example of gene doping might include the use of gene therapies to increase muscle growth or blood-cell production, enhance oxygen-carrying capacity, or augment pain resistance. Notwithstanding the considerable expansion of our knowledge of genetics, it is doubtful that gene doping is currently a reality, although the WADA and its partners have already made it a research priority. In 2003 the prohibited list of substances and methods was amended to include gene doping, which has remained on the Prohibited List ever since. The WADA has collaborated with genetic scientists worldwide to initiate discussions and research projects that examine approaches to the detection of gene doping. Further, the WADA has undertaken education efforts to inform athletes that gene doping will be an imperfect science and dangerous (World Anti-Doping Agency 2014). The WADA's views on gene doping have been succinctly stated:

Gene doping represents a threat to the integrity of sport and the health of athletes, and as the international organization responsible for promoting, coordinating and monitoring the global fight against doping in sport in all its forms, WADA is devoting significant resources and attention to ways that will enable the detection of gene doping. (World Anti-Doping Agency 2014)

Summary

The continually growing popularity of swimming around the world is a testament to the appeal of this sport, its ability to ensure fitness, and the excitement that surrounds aquatic competition. The desire to enhance swimming performance and achieve competitive success is natural and commendable. All those involved in the care and coaching of swimmers must ensure that their preparation and training reflect sound scientific principles and take place in accordance with evidence-based best practice in an atmosphere that reflects an unwavering commitment to fair competition and doping-free sport.

CHAPTER 16

Swimming Psychology: Merging Mind and Body

—James Bauman, PhD

The subtitle of this chapter, "Merging Mind and Body," is meant to challenge the reader to adopt new ways of thinking about the mental side of swimming. The title seems to imply that the mind and body are disconnected or experience a changing degree of connectedness. It also implies that to swim faster, a swimmer's body and mind must be synchronized in the pool and must be able to disregard the disconnecting distracters associated with competing and performing on demand. Both statements are true. For swimmers to achieve their potential in the pool, the mind and body must work as one. Clearly, anatomical and physiological elements link the body to the mind or brain; we see these in the form of skeletal, muscular, organ, circulatory, neurological, and chemical connections. Although these physical connections exist, anyone who has competed knows that on some training and competitive days, there seems to be a complete disconnect—an absence of a connection between what the mind wants the body to do and how the body actually performs.

The matrix of connections linking the mind to the body continues to be unraveled and understood. Only recently have neuroscientists and practitioners discovered some ways in which these complex connections work, and they freely admit that there is much they do not yet understand. Ongoing research provides some answers into how the mind and body work together, but even those answers seem to create more questions. The space required to address the current body of knowledge on this topic would fill a textbook, and many questions would still be left unanswered. But we cannot wait for all the answers to be discovered. We need to convey to young athletes what the applied research and experience is currently telling us. That is the purpose of this chapter.

We have all listened to an athlete or coach being interviewed after a less-than-successful athletic performance. Athletes, in these instances, frequently say something like, "I wasn't mentally tough" or "I lost my focus," whereas coaches may say, "We made too many mental mistakes" or "We didn't come mentally prepared to compete." These kinds of responses lead us to believe that the mental part of competing is an important aspect of performance. On returning to training, however, little if anything is typically done to address the mental side of sport for either training or competition. Instead, the swimmers are usually back to the pool for more laps, more conditioning, more technical instruction, and other fixes that may or may not have anything to do with a poor performance. Merging the body and mind seems to get a lot of lip service in sport, but when push comes to shove, the idea does not typically find its way into the regular training regimen.

This chapter on sport psychology will be somewhat different from chapters in other books or the information on the growing number of websites selling repackaged concepts or never-before-disclosed magic steps to success. What follows is based on more than 24 years of practical experience and full-time applied work with developmental, collegiate, professional, and Olympic athletes across more than 60 sports, including swimming. The mental strategies described in this chapter are based on science, research, and applied practice. The emphasis is on the practical application of these strategies with athletes and teams. Coaches, athletes, and parents are provided user-friendly descriptions of the benefits of the body and mind connection, descriptions of the kinds of circumstances that contribute to the unraveling of those connections, and some proven strategies that can be taken to the pool to enhance performance. These understandable and easy-to-use strategies will help swimmers maintain and improve the connections between mind and body, which will ultimately result in consistently faster swimming in competition. The tone of this chapter is conversational. Interestingly, the concepts and constructs described in this chapter have been documented in the works of ancient philosophers, modern-day theorists, and other smart people long before they were published in today's performance books or the electronic media. As such, like much of what seems to be published, the information contained herein is probably not original; rather, it is a consolidation of the work of those great thinkers. The new ideas that many authors claim to offer may simply be restatements of what was said long ago, but in a new context—sport. The content of this chapter is primarily based on those old concepts and years of experience in applying practical approaches to sport in real situations.

Swimming faster can look different depending on the age group of swimmers being discussed. For example, we typically see large performance improvements in the beginning of an athlete's career. These advances gradually become smaller as the athletes approach their ultimate performance potential (talent). Although these later improvements are incrementally smaller, they are proportionately as significant as what occurred in the earlier stages. With only a slight variation in the language and attention given to age, developmental, and experience differences, the strategies to swim faster found in this chapter can be applied to swimmers of all ages.

Analogies are used throughout this chapter to illustrate points and concepts. An analogy shows similarities between concepts that might ordinarily seem unrelated. Analogies help provide insight into what could be a confusing or ill-defined subject or situation by using a subject or object that is more familiar or more easily understood. Analogies are an effective way to teach lessons about a variety of challenging subjects. Analogous tools will assist in describing the strategies to help swimmers stay on track and progressively swim faster. The tools and strategies to be discussed in this chapter include the following:

- Developing mental pliability (or plyability; see sidebar)
- Establishing a competition plan that has a high probability of success (beat personal average)
- Competing in the present (gravity)
- Paying attention to self-talk
- Identifying and managing pressure or distraction (hot water tanks)
- Managing physiological and psychological energy (tachometers)
- Going through yellow lights (fuel warning lights and traffic lights)
- Using the pit crew

The chapter is broken into sections to address each of these facets of mental preparation and performance.

Finally, although this chapter is about swimming fast, all of what is written can pertain to life in and out of the pool, as well as other sports. Sport psychology is about improving all facets of human performance, not only sport.

Mental Toughness or Mental Pliability?

To begin this section, let's first challenge some of the terminology that has been used in the field of sport psychology and offer a different perspective on the much-overused concept of mental toughness. Setting the stage for that challenge and using our first analogy, we can use basic computer terminology to describe the body (below the chin) as hardware and the mind (above the chin) as software. Although other chapters in this book look at the hardware involved in swimming in detail, this chapter focuses on the software.

Nearly every sport psychology book either addresses or refers to the concept of mental toughness and explains its necessity to elite sport performance. But is it mental toughness or some other attribute that is truly important for a swimmer? Being tough has long been a mainstay in the good-old-boy way of thinking about the mental side of sport performance. But mental toughness does not clearly describe that evasive characteristic commonly associated with elite athletes who consistently perform at higher levels. Vince Lombardi, the legendary coach of the Green Bay Packers, once said, "The difference between a successful person and others is not a lack of strength or lack of knowledge, but rather a lack of will." The "will" that Coach Lombardi was referring to may have been what others over the years have called mental toughness. Unfortunately, we will never know exactly what Lombardi was thinking when he fashioned that famous quotation. But I believe that within the field of sport psychology and possibly in the spirit of Coach Lombardi, we are overdue in developing more descriptive terms that clearly articulate the characteristics we see in athletes who just don't quit. We need a clearer mental picture of "will." Instead of mental toughness, I propose the term *mental pliability* to describe that special, necessary, and core ingredient seen in most elite performers—those who can perform on demand, under all circumstances, and with consistent high-end results. I see a difference between mental toughness and mental pliability. It's more than just semantics; the difference between the two concepts is the flexibility, adaptability, and "stick-to-it-ness" that mental pliability suggests.

Imagine a solid piece of wood with the same dimensions as a thick telephone book. Let's equate those objects to the concepts of mental toughness (wood) and mental pliability (telephone book). Being mentally tough generates images of someone who is thick-skinned, solid, hard, unshakeable, and seemingly unbreakable, like that solid piece of wood. Yet if one were to take that piece of wood and throw it against something harder, hit it on a sharp edge, or hit it with a hammer, the wood likely would crack, splinter, or break apart. Although, on the outside, the piece of wood appears rigid, solid, and strong, under the right conditions it is not so tough and not so unbreakable.

Mental Plyability

Another way to describe the psychological flexibility required to succeed in swimming is as mental *plyability*, bringing to mind the flexible strength of plywood as opposed to the rigid but breakable structure of a hardwood.

Now consider a phone book and envision how it would perform if thrown against something hard, hit against a sharp edge, or struck with a hammer. It wouldn't crack, splinter, or break apart like the wood. Instead, it would bend and temporarily change shape to absorb the shock and then return to its original shape. The phone book is malleable; it can change its shape, absorb or deflect force, handle repeated physical contact, and retain its original shape. In short, it demonstrates adaptability and resilience. The only way to break a phone book would be to methodically tear it apart a few pages at a time. Great athletes, like a phone book, can bend or adapt to many situations; they are resilient and do not break under pressure or contact. The ability to adapt to the situation and environment results in the development of resilient durability over time. More than mental toughness, this ingredient is necessary in competitive athletes. This is what I think Coach Lombardi was describing.

So should a swimmer be mentally tough or mentally pliable? Athletes who choose to be pliable will find strategies in this chapter to equip them to move in that direction. Athletes who want to be tough must be prepared to face the consequences of potentially breaking into pieces under those special circumstances that will challenge toughness and try to break them apart—competition! Mental pliability (or *plyability*), not mental toughness, will connect swimmers' software with their hardware in ways that get them to the wall faster than ever before.

Competing in the Present: Gravity and Autopilot

As previously mentioned, precisely defining the mind and body connection is difficult because science has not yet completed the entire puzzle. We still don't know exactly how all the pieces fit together. But the observable effects of the mind and body being connected or disconnected are easier to quantify or at least describe. Similarly, the next analogy used to illustrate the importance of that connection is gravity, which, by the way, is another difficult-to-define phenomenon. Gravity! How can the power of connecting the mind with the body have anything to do with gravity? Well, that is the spirit of the analogy. Although the similarity may not be apparent, that connection will soon become clear.

What is gravity? Newton (1729) said, "Every point mass attracts every single other point mass by a force pointing along the line intersecting both points." He described that effect as gravity. Newton's law of universal gravitation further stated, "Every massive particle in the universe attracts every other massive particle with a force, which is directly proportional to the product of their masses and is inversely proportional to the square of the distance between them." Now, doesn't that clear up the importance and power of connecting the mind and body in sport?

Actually, what Newton was describing is the incredible power of attraction between two objects in space, an attraction that exists even when those objects are in constant motion. To expand on this analogy, let's look at the power of gravity between the sun and the known planets in the solar system. Without the gravitational pull between the sun and the planets, all the planets would simply fly off into the universe. The powerful gravitational attraction between these massive objects keeps the planets invisibly connected to the sun, even as they orbit around it.

If we move to a smaller gravitational relationship and look at the forces that exist between the earth and the moon, we see similar effects. Just as we saw with the sun and the planets, the gravitational pull between the earth and moon prevents the moon from flying out into the universe. As a result, the moon remains in continuous orbit around the earth. What is also interesting is that the relationship between the earth and the moon affects not only what happens to the moon but also what occurs here on earth. For example, the gravitational pull of the moon on the earth creates ocean tides. We also know that the sun has an effect on the tides, but not nearly to the extent that the moon does. Research has found that the strongest gravitational pull occurs along an imaginary line drawn from the center of the moon to the center of the earth. Water is pulled toward this line, causing the tides. This line where the strongest gravitational pull occurs is continuously moving, following the moon throughout its entire orbit. Consequently, the tides ebb and flow, following the moon as it orbits the earth. Gravity is an amazingly powerful phenomenon!

Now let's consider an even smaller planetary relationship and look at the metaphorical and potential gravitational pull or attraction between the mind and the body. What if there were a similar and equally powerful connection between mind and body? What if there is a possibility that when we line them up, like the earth and moon, there is also an incredible gravitational effect? When the mind and the body are synchronized, athletes describe the strength and ease of performance that occurs. Just maybe, they are experiencing the metaphorical force of gravity.

Athletes frequently describe the experience of being in the zone, another commonly used description, when they perform amazingly well. At times, the mind and the body are in the same place, the same time zone, if you will. It is almost as if the athlete experiences, from a human perspective, the same invisible gravitational power that the earth and moon experience in every moment of every day. Elite athletes who understand that connection and that experience also understand how to increase the likelihood of experiencing it with increasing frequency. So, how do they do that?

Sport psychologists have consistently encouraged athletes to be in the moment. That encouragement is meant to persuade athletes to maintain a conscious, but subtle, mental focus and involvement in the experience of what is happening *right now*. Although the suggestion to focus on the present is easy to articulate, in practice, athletes often find it difficult to understand conceptually what being in the moment actually means, why it is important, and how to achieve it in competition on a consistent basis.

In working to help athletes understand how to get in the zone, let's first consider the three most generic time zones in life, as well as in and out of sport: the past, present, and future (figure 16.1).

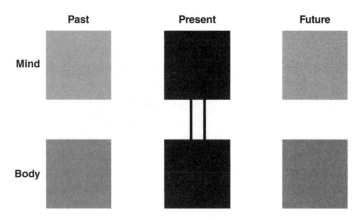

▶ **Figure 16.1** Three time zones in relation to mind and body connections.

Figure 16.1 illustrates that the body can be only in the present (lower dark square). I can think of only two situations in which the physical body can be in any time zone but the present: when in a time machine (we're still working on this apparatus) or while flying on a jet across time zones or datelines. Therefore, we can safely say that the body is always in the present. But the mind (thoughts and emotions) is free to wander and dwell on the past (upper-left light gray square), the present (upper-middle dark gray square), and the future (upper-right light gray square). Because the body can be only in the present time zone, for a swimmer to perform in the zone and achieve the necessary body–mind alignment, the mind must also be in the present. The two dark gray squares connected by the dark lines represent this body and mind connection, in the present moment. Right here, right now, and in this moment is where a swimmer wants to be when competing. When this happens, the swimmer is good to go and good to go fast! Maybe that is the gravitational connection experienced when a swimmer swims well and swims fast. Thinking about the past or the future takes the mind out of alignment with the body, so performance decreases. In these cases, the swimmer is not good to go, or at least not to go fast! We seem to be fighting thinking and emotional gravity in that case.

Unlike the body, the mind can easily move across all the time zones. In fact, that movement of thought and emotions can travel across those time zones regularly leading up to, during, and even after a competition. For example, it is not unusual for athletes to begin to question whether they prepared well enough or long enough (past); to ask themselves what they will do if they have a bad start, a bad turn, or run out of energy (future); to think that other swimmers look more fit and therefore will swim faster (future); to think that other swimmers have better times and therefore will swim faster (future); or to think they don't belong here (present). All these thoughts, including the one specific negative example in the present, are chances for an athlete's mind and body to disconnect. Any thoughts about what should or could have been (past) or concern about what should or could happen (future) will result in a temporal misalignment of body and mind and a decrease in the synergistic power (gravity) that occurs when the body and the mind are in the present. But when thoughts are focused on the job in this moment (present), the likelihood that the swimmer will encounter an in-the-moment experience increases. All that distracting thinking begins to fade away, and all thoughts turn inward and toward the task at hand—technique, tactics, it's time to go, and it's time to swim fast!

Outstanding swimmers regularly report that swimming in the present is a powerful experience that feels effortless, quiet, fluid, and rhythmic. We associate these descriptions with swimming in the zone. If, while preparing for or swimming an event, an athlete focuses on a mistake made in a past race or dwells on the expectations of needing to swim a personal best to make a team (future), performance will likely not be its best. But a swimmer who is able to prepare and swim moment by moment, stroke by stroke according to an established race plan will likely have better swims. An athlete who swims in the moment will progressively focus on getting an explosive start while on the blocks, then generating powerful and efficient underwater kicks, then settling in to establish a rhythmic breathing pattern and powerful stroke rate, then preparing for and completing a quick and powerful turn off the wall, performing the underwater kick again, recapturing the rhythm of breathing and stroke rate, and finally taking a last breath with a long and powerful reach and touch to the finish. When a race is swum progressively (biomechanically and mentally), the swimmer will have stayed in the moment while progressing through the event. Being mindful of the present allows athletes to take advantage of synchronizing their thoughts with their motor movements in the pool. Remember how the gravitational relationship between the moon and the earth is constantly changing as the moon slowly orbits the earth? Similarly, a swimmer's mental focus must also change throughout a swim to draw on the power that comes from having the body and mind perfectly aligned in the present as the swimmer moves through the race. The moon can't look back to where it was or could have been, or forward to where it is going or where it might go; neither should the swimmer.

Let's consider another analogy and think about how jumbo jets fly and transport people all over the world, moving us through time. Although air travel may seem like a complicated task, much of what goes on in the air happens under the guidance of the plane's autopilot. The onboard computer (autopilot) has been programmed to increase the speed so that the plane takes off, climbs to the right altitude, maintains the correct altitude, goes in the right direction, decreases the altitude for landing, and then slows down for landing. Although highly qualified pilots are necessary to manage the takeoff, monitor the flight, and manage the landing, the onboard computer essentially flies the plane. The same applies in the pool. Every swimmer has an on-board computer (the brain) that is programmed through hours and hours of training. When it comes time to race, the best swimmers have an already-developed race plan that has been programmed into their brains. As they approach the start and step on the blocks, they activate their autopilot and then just go. Like airline pilots, they are the onboard pool pilots who monitor the autopilot (their competitive routine) and sometimes make fine adjustments to the race plan (flight plan) to stay on course and finish the race (flight). Swimmers and pilots alike get into trouble when they start to question their flight instruments and then interfere with the onboard computer. By progressively staying in the moment as a race unfolds, swimmers become like airline pilots. They trust their training, their preparation, and their machine; what is left is only monitoring and making adjustments, but the computer (the brain) is really flying the body.

The ease at which a swimmer can swim depends on the swimmer's ability to trust the computer to carry out the flight plan. A swimmer who starts messing with the controls (thinking out of the moment and into the past or future) will likely experience a loss of power. When the mind slips to the past or future, even for just a few seconds, technical proficiency can deteriorate. A cascading effect then occurs; the swimmer begins to lose technical proficiency in the water, becomes less streamlined, creates more drag, and has to work harder to maintain a given speed.

Coaches can introduce the idea of gravity and autopilot as a way of describing the potential power of staying in the moment. Using a concept from physical science (gravity) can help swimmers understand the importance of focusing on the present when competing. Going on autopilot for competition will free up an athlete to focus on technique and race tactics rather than the distracting past and future thoughts (self-talk) that routinely contribute to less-successful swims. There will be more on self-talk later in the chapter. For now, the goal should be to help swimmers focus on here and now. Talking to athletes about this concept should be easy, but many will forget the teachings when it comes time to compete. The use of cues or visual reminders can help remind swimmers to stay in the present. Cue words can be written on note cards, wristbands, or the backs of the hands or tops of the feet. For cues to be useful, they must be in the swimmer's visual field when the swimmer needs to remember and implement the time zone (gravity) and autopilot strategies. Here is a list of cue words:

Cue Words

F: fun (early on), fluid, free, fast, flow, fuel (use pressure to fuel you), finish

A: average (beat it!), aspirations, always pliable, autopilot, adaptable

S: self-talk (constructive), simple, solution-oriented, speed, sleek

T: time zones (be in the present), technique, tactics, tachometer

E: effortless, efficient, enjoyable, easy

R: resilient, run the yellow lights

Goals: Beat Your Average (>$\bar{X}$)

Now that three basic premises have been established about the importance of merging the mind and body (pliability, gravity, and autopilot), we are ready to establish some direction or a plan for the competitive season. Scientists and psychologists began studying goals and aspirations in the United States in the 1940s (Lewin, et al. 1944). Atkinson (1958) began to associate the difficulty of a goal with the probability of achieving that goal. His studies concluded that, within limits, the more difficult the goal is, the higher the probability is of achieving that goal. Later, Edwin Locke (1967) began more than 40 years of research in developing his theory of goal setting and task motivation (Locke and Latham 2002). T.A. Ryan (1970) explored the notion that motivation was the cause of human action. If a person was motivated, things got done. If motivation was lacking, things didn't get done. Still later, George Duran (1981) seems to have been the first to document the popular mnemonic SMART (specific, measureable, attainable, relevant, and time bound), which described what he considered the key components to establishing and achieving goals. Since that time, many people have researched, written, and talked about their versions of the pioneering work in goal setting.

Goals seem to affect performance through at least four processes:

1. Goals provide a direction for attention, effort, and activities that are relevant to achieving the goal.

2. Goals provide an incentive or inspirational force that moves us to action. The higher the goal is, the greater the effort required is to accomplish the goal. Lower goals will see less effort associated with pursuit of those goals.

3. Having goals affects persistence, particularly when people encounter the obstacles that typically block their way in the pursuit of goals.

4. Goals directly and indirectly affect arousal levels, personal discovery, and using task-relevant knowledge and strategies in efforts to achieve (Locke and Latham 2002).

Earlier in the chapter, the term *mental pliability* was used to replace mental toughness. Similarly, we can use the term *developing a game plan* as a more effective description of what most have come to understand as goal setting. Just as a company develops a business plan to guide its efforts to become successful and profitable, the athlete needs to have a game plan for the competitive year and know how to execute it to be successful and profitable in the pool. Profitability for a swimmer is constant progress. If progress is maintained over time, the more regularly the socially defined metric of success (winning) will begin to happen. But if the goal or focus is only on winning, swimming faster will likely occur only occasionally. Game plans can include athletic, academic, career, interpersonal, social, and personal aspirations. Often, game plans include times for each event that an athlete plans to achieve each year. Other parts of the game plan could be qualitative in nature, and improvement might be based on feel rather than numbers.

In working with athletes, including swimmers, for more than 24 years, I have heard many interesting perspectives concerning game plans. With only a few exceptions, swimmers have been indoctrinated, beginning at an early age, with the idea that goals are important to provide some sense of forward progress and are necessary to achieve success as a swimmer. But the practices that many athletes put in place to establish and pursue goals are less than optimal. Seasonal goal-planning sessions between coaches and athletes are often inconsistent and sometimes unrealistic. Goals are often reviewed by athletes and coaches only at the start and end of the competitive season. Athletes typically set yearly goals that read something like "Set a new personal best for each event." No real dialogue or specific planning occurs about how they will achieve those goals. If a personal best is achieved during the season, the trend is usually just to change the goal to reflect a new best time.

Experience and research have shown us that goals are probably necessary in sport, but how they are woven into the training and competitive season is often fragmented and inconsistent. As long as athletes chant the mantra, "My goal is to set a personal best," most seem to be content with that level of perceived motivation. Practical experience and probability, however, do not favor that approach toward developing a swimming game plan. Although swim times are important and are an objective measure of overall progress, they can also become a source of anxiety and create unnecessary pressure to perform. So, instead of swimming faster, many athletes end up swimming slower because of the added pressure of the expectations built up around the goal of beating a personal best.

In major competitions, athletes have consistently expressed that they believe they must have an exceptional performance that day or do something special to be successful. In their words, success is synonymous with winning. As soon as athletes begin to focus on the results—winning—they take themselves out of the game. By focusing on the outcome, not the process of getting there, swimmers may lose the ability to swim in the moment. They sabotage the autopilot plan that they put in place.

Encourage swimmers to have a game plan that allows the objective measurement of progress, includes aspects that have a high probability of being successfully completed, and can be implemented without adding the psychological pressure that often accompanies beating a personal best. With all these things in place, athletes will progressively swim faster. An approach to accomplishing this came out of a set of disappointing performances for some USA athletes in the 2000 Sydney Games.

Following those Olympic Games, interviews were conducted with several athletes from a variety of sports whose performance could be objectively measured (stopwatch, horizontal or vertical distance) and who were supposed to do well at the Games but didn't. The questions asked were formulated to gain a better understanding of why they had performed at a level lower than what they knew they could do and had previously proved they could do. We wanted to know what had happened and why. Almost without exception, the major reason the athletes gave for performing at a level below their realistically expected performance was pressure. Pressure came in many forms, but it seemed to cluster around real and perceived expectations of family or friends, sport organizations, sponsors, coaches, teammates, the media, and themselves, and an overwhelming belief that they would need to have the best performance of their lives. Here they were at the biggest sporting event, and the athletes described a nearly complete abandonment of everything they had done to get themselves to this place. Suddenly, the Games had changed their game plan and wrapped it in a shroud of anxiousness that took them out of their usual performance preparation and routine. What was also interesting was that every athlete interviewed was clearly concerned about the time, height, or distance they believed they needed to achieve to be successful, to win a medal. Among those disappointed by their performance as measured with a stopwatch or measuring stick were athletes who became too focused on those results, athletes who forgot the game plan, athletes who unconsciously abandoned the game plan, and athletes who couldn't execute the game plan. These athletes all said that if they had been able to reduce the anxiety that they experienced in the hours, minutes, and seconds right before the event, they would have and could have performed differently.

Anxiety is really a symptom of a wide range of other issues. To decrease anxiety, we first have to identify the source of that anxiety. If we attempt to decrease the symptoms of anxiety without addressing the reasons for that experience, we will not be successful. Simply put, as in the field of medicine, if we treat only the symptoms of a problem rather than the problem itself, the symptoms will continue to be present.

Athletes experience anxiety for many reasons, but one in particular seemed to be common among all athletes who saw anxiety adversely affect their performances. What came from the interviews with the Olympic athletes was some compelling information regarding their beliefs about themselves when they competed. They believed that they had to do something special. For them, that meant performing at a level that would result in a personal best or beyond.

When attempting to understand more about what these athletes were saying, we learned that there was a real sense of doubt that they could achieve the expectations, or goals, that they had placed on themselves. The chances of setting a personal best in the company of other great athletes seemed suddenly small to them. Clearly, these athletes were focusing on a goal with a low probability of success, and they knew it! In fact, many of these athletes indicated that for them to be successful in a field of other extremely talented athletes, they would need to surpass their previous personal best by far. At that point, they entered a zone, but it was more like a twilight zone, not a performance zone.

Part of changing an athlete's perspective about performance is to look at statistics and performance trends. One strategy to reduce anxiety is to teach athletes about performance probability and incorporate that concept into their game plans (goals), their training, and competition. Let's talk briefly about probability. One of the more common ways to illustrate the chances that something will occur (probability) is by using a frequency distribution. A frequency distribution illustrates the frequency at which various scores occur over time. A normal distribution, or the bell-shaped curve (figure 16.2), named after its relative bell-shaped appearance, is used to illustrate any variable (e.g., an athlete's swim times for a given event) with how many times each race time has occurred (frequency) over a particular period.

As we look at frequency distributions, probability tables, and statistical formulas to calculate the chances that particular scores (swim times) will occur (standard deviations), we find that performance scores tend to cluster around the average time for any particular event. That statement simply means that it is easy to calculate the probability of what an athlete might swim on any given day. Just know the swimmer's average time for that event. The average of a swimmer's times in an event is calculated just like a scholastic grade point average. Simply add up all of a swimmer's times in an event and then divide by the number of times that event was swum. That result is an average time for the event. The symbol $\bar{X}$ (X-bar) is used to represent the average swim time.

To understand swim time probabilities as percentages shown in figure 16.2, we can break swims down into five categories:

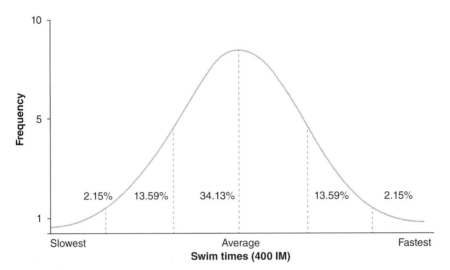

▶ **Figure 16.2**   Frequency distribution illustrating sample format for swim times with frequency of times and probability of occurrence of those times, as measured by percentages.

1. Good swims, those times clustered around and on either side of the average time, occur about 68 percent of the time.

2. On the slower side of the swim average, mediocre swim times (well below the average time, but not the worst) occur about 14 percent of the time.

3. Suck swims, to use a swimmer's vernacular (the slowest ever times), occur about 2 percent of the time.

4. On the faster side of the swim average, really good swims (faster than the average swim time for an event but still short of a personal best) occur approximately 14 percent of the time. Note that these swims occur about as often as the mediocre swims on the slower side of the curve.

5. Finally, the category of great swims (equal to or greater than a personal best) occurs about 2 percent of the time. These swims occur with about the same probability as the worst swims.

All this is meant to illustrate that if swimmers have the goal of setting a personal best each time they swim, they have only about a 2 percent chance of doing that! No wonder athletes go to the start with doubt, anxiety, pressure, and fear of what is likely to happen. You aren't doing the statistical analysis, but you have a feel for your chances of having a spectacular swim. That is what can get into your head!

What statistics do not take into account are other potential negative human factors (e.g., what the swimmer is thinking and feeling, illness, injury, what's at stake, and so on) or potential positive human factors (e.g., having and following a game plan, pliability, swimming in the moment, having successfully done this before, having a genuine feeling of being ready, and so on). These factors are left out of probability tables, but they clearly affect times and performances. Instead, probabilities are based on the cold hard facts of scores (swim times). But think about it. If a swimmer could reduce any sense of anxiety that is experienced before a swimming event, doesn't it make sense to generate a completely different set of scores? That's exactly what the 2000 Sydney athletes were looking for in those Games, but unfortunately they didn't find it when they needed it.

Again, by reflecting on the average swim rather than a personal best swim, the probability of beating the average time is nearly 70 percent. Swimmers can go into a swimming event knowing that the game plan of beating their average has more than a 70 percent chance of being successful. That probability of success is certainly much higher than the 2 percent probability of setting a personal best! Experiencing consistent success is important, and this strategy of beating the average sets the stage for that to happen on a regular basis.

When the concept of beating their average (greater than $\bar{X}$) is first introduced to athletes, they are often skeptical and think that the approach is too easy. They become skeptical because they have not been conditioned to think that way and they have not approached developing a game plan that way. After all, beating their own average is no big deal, or so they thought. But consider this. As with an academic grade point average, the higher the average is raised, the more challenging it becomes trying to beat it. In the case of a swimmer, the average time is getting faster, or lower. Imagine training and competing all year with the plan of beating your average time each time you swim. By the end of the year, you will have decreased your times and established a new performance mantra—beat my average. Instead of an anxiety-filled statement such as "I need to do something special and set a personal record," the swimmer becomes conditioned to put less emphasis on the outcome by having the same game plan each week. Athletes who are able to do that can calm down and focus on what really makes them swim faster (technique, biomechanics, tactics, and the game plan in the pool). Even more exciting is that, almost without exception, those athletes who put less emphasis on setting personal bests actually begin to set personal bests more frequently. When that begins to happen, we change the game plan by averaging the swimmers' personal bests, and that is what they beat! It's like a student going to graduate school and leaving behind his undergraduate scores and grade point average. Those undergraduate numbers just aren't relevant in graduate school. The same applies to leaving behind the old swim times.

Some U.S. athletes implemented and used this strategy of beating the average in preparing for and competing in the 2004 Athens, 2008 Beijing, and 2012 London Olympic Games. The plan must be used day in and day out in both training and competition. Attempts to use this way of thinking only in competition without practicing it throughout the year in training have less probability of working. A consistent finding in Athens, Beijing, and London was that athletes approached the Games with a calmer and more focused belief system that was based on a high probability for success ("All I have to do today is beat my average, focus on my game plan, and maintain great biomechanics"). That approach led to more medals and personal bests, simply because these athletes had learned about probability and pursuing self-talk and belief systems that gave them the best chance to be successful. They also reported that they were keenly aware that many of their competitors were struggling with the issues they had finally been able to let go. Many of our athletes became creative in wearing the visual cue (> $\bar{X}$) on a hand or foot as a regular reminder to keep them on track when they competed.

Self-Talk

Most of our waking moments are consumed with what we call self-talk. Self-talk is the internal monologue we carry on with ourselves, whenever we are not actually talking aloud with others. The body of knowledge associating self-talk with performance outcomes in athletics and achievement is growing (Weinberg et al. 1984; Goodhart 1986; Gould, Eklund, and Jackson 1992; Van Raalte et al. 1994; Hardy, Gammage, and Hall 2001). In the cited research, self-talk generally has been used to self-calm or relax, self-educate, self-motivate, focus, self-reward, self-criticize, and pass time. Self-talk can be directed inward or at others. It can be constructive, destructive, positive, negative, and move us to or away from action. Self-talk can be neutral or, in some cases, so quiet that we are not consciously aware of the conversation being held. Lastly, self-talk can be believable or not to the person carrying on the internal dialogue.

We often hear coaches or teammates encourage athletes to think positive, focus, see themselves being champions, and more. But the extent to which athletes truly believe what they are being encouraged to say to themselves has a direct effect on whether the self-talk will have any bearing on their performances. Self-talk that is positive and constructive in nature, when channeled in the right direction, can result in improved performance. Unfortunately, self-talk that is negative and destructive in nature will have a detrimental effect on performance. As illustrated earlier in the gravity discussion, nonproductive self-talk tends to be about the past or future, whereas constructive self-talk is aligned with the present ("My job is to swim fast"). The objective of most sports is really pretty simple; in the case of swimming, it's to swim fast.

Most swimmers, thinking back to when they were younger, remember that swimming fast was fun, even though they may not have recognized that they were swimming in the moment or not really caring about the past or what might lie ahead. Swimming for fun was as important as swimming fast. In fact, fun and fast were often synonymous in the minds of great athletes. Unfortunately, the business of sport has a way of systematically driving the fun out of sport and replacing it with a prime focus of swimming fast, swimming faster, working hard, making money, and always setting personal bests. These seeds have been planted, and they often grow into a full crop of negative self-talk that we deal with in sport and in life. It is as if fun, hard work, and progressive improvement cannot occur at the same time as swimmers become more seasoned and move toward higher levels of competition. I wholeheartedly disagree with that assumption. If fun is left out of the equation to swim fast, attempts to swim fast will feel gravitational resistance. It's like swimming against a current rather than swimming with the current or being pulled through the water. The fast suits have been taken out of the pool. If you want swimmers to swim fast, help them put on fun suits. You will be amazed at the progress they make! Swimming fast means teaching and learning the fundamentals of swimming. Sometimes the key ingredients are obvious, but we forget to include them. Fun and the mental part of swimming need to be included.

Swimming fast means reverting to the way of thinking we had when we were younger, when we focused on the feeling of swimming fast rather than the absolute and driven objective of swimming faster than everyone else in the pool. The key is to swim faster than you did before. Own your lane! When a swimmer can begin to do that, swimming faster will begin to take on an impressive life of its own.

In the meantime, we have to contend with and remedy the culture associated with competitive sport that has evolved over the years. Unfortunately, a less-than-positive atmosphere that often encourages the development and use of negative self-dialogue has been unintentionally created for swimmers. The following are some of the more common self-talk errors, as well as suggestions to help swimmers convert negative self-talk statements to positive, constructive, and productive self-talk statements.

Focusing on the Past or the Future

"I can't believe I swam so terribly in my first event" (past) or "Now, every stroke and turn of this next event has to be perfect to make up for my earlier bad swim" (future). Not letting go of a mistake or poor performance takes the thoughts and focus away from where they need to be—on the present moment and in the present event! Continuing to carry on these past and future self-conversations clutters up the connection between the body and the mind—physiologically, biomechanically, and psychologically. This kind of self-talk often evolves into a series of errors that contribute to unsuccessful performances. Instead, swimmers should strive to let the past performance go before even heading to the pool for the next event. They need to focus on competing right here, right now, and in this event.

Focusing on Real or Perceived Weaknesses During the Competition

"I am the most inexperienced athlete here," "I've never beaten her before," or "I should have trained harder." Any of these statements might be true, but all are irrelevant at the time of competition. During competition, swimmers who dwell on what they don't have may as well be tying weights to their ankles. Competition is a time when self-talk and mental focus should be fully directed to areas such as being technically and tactically proficient and sticking to the race plan. Swimmers who think that they are at 80 percent of where they should be as swimmers need to give the full 100 percent of that 80 percent (John Wooden and Paul "Bear" Bryant). Thinking about or focusing on what they don't have (skills, absolute feel for the water, and so on) will simply take their swim times to the slow side of the curve. The most logical way to increase performance percentage is through additional deliberate training. Swimmers will not magically create more without investing the time required to improve the requisite skills or fitness level. Simply trying harder is not the answer. The key to swimming faster is to work harder and smarter in training and then replicate that in competition. Self-talk is most productive if swimmers think more about what they are bringing to the pool rather than what they aren't, or think they aren't, bringing to the pool. They will reach a point in their swimming careers where what they have is enough to be successful. The trick is for them to focus on what they have and then give that in the pool with an unwavering commitment.

Focusing on Ultimatum Outcome or Profit Only

"I must win," "I have to finish in the top two," or "I have to beat him." Make no mistake, in sport, as in any business, something is at stake! But the relationship between what is at stake and how important that really is to a swimmer is most clearly found in how healthy the swimmer's perspective is about why she competes. No doubt, every business must be profitable to stay afloat. But if profit (winning) is the bottom-line reason that an athlete competes in sport, profits will be lean and hard to come by many of the years of competition. Swimmers need to understand, know, and revisit the real reasons that they compete. If it is only about winning, they will regularly be one stroke, one turn, or one hand short of touching the wall behind those who understand the deeper levels of this relationship. Focusing on the result (future) will take them out of the moment and negatively affect their performance. When swimmers stay in the moment and the process (swimming right now), then the probability of an outcome (profit or success) will occur more frequently. If the focus is on the outcome (future), the water just seems to get more difficult to move through as the event unfolds. In the end, swimmers need to create a clear definition of how they define success, in and out of the pool. Success isn't always defined as winning. Swimmers have all won races with a performance that they weren't satisfied with. They have all had races that they didn't win but that felt great. And they might have had a great time as well. The best race occurs when the swimmer has a great swim, feels great, and wins! Success comes in a variety of forms. To stay in the game and be profitable, swimmers need to focus on the process and in that moment.

Focusing on Uncontrollable Factors

"I don't like this pool," or "I don't like this lane," or "I don't like this suit." Thoughts such as these are a waste of precious emotional energy because they focus on elements that are sometimes just out of the swimmer's control. Uncontrollable factors are just that—out of the swimmer's control. No matter how much a swimmer complains about the pool, lane, water temperature, equipment, and so on, it doesn't change anything except that person's attitude and energy level. A good rule when planning is to expect things not to be perfect. That is the business of performance and life. If something is not quite right, the message should be "It is what it is" (Navy SEAL mantra). Get over it and get back in the moment. Be solution oriented in responding to adversity. When encountering an obstacle or challenge, a true competitor sees only two choices—ignore it or fix it, but always move on!

Demanding Perfection

"I have to have a perfect race," "I have to hit exactly the right splits," or "I have to look perfect." Sport is about pursuing perfection, and that is all we really do—pursue it. We can only approximate perfection. That is why every sport has the built-in flexibility of not requiring participants to be perfect. The size of a basketball hoop is larger than the basketball; a golf cup is bigger than the golf ball. Except for the 25- and 50-meter events, swimmers have multiple pool lengths to make up for a slightly missed turn or stroke. Striving for perfection is a great attitude; demanding it is not. We just need to make a personal demand to strive for it!

Identifying and Managing Pressure (Hot Water Tanks)

Pressure to perform at higher levels throughout the year seems to be a common characteristic of sport. Pressure is often considered the cause of failing to perform on demand. As baseball manager Tommy Lasorda once said, "Pressure is a word that is misused in our vocabulary. When you start thinking of pressure, it's because you've started to think about failure." Because this topic is a popular point of discussion, I want to introduce another analogy to explain where pressure comes from, how that pressure is regulated, and what happens if we don't manage and rechannel the pressure in a constructive way leading up to and during an athletic event.

All of us experience and appreciate the convenience and comfort of hot water for baths, showers, and sinks. We can thank Benjamin Maughan, an English engineer, who developed the modern version of the hot water heater in about 1868. In about 1889 Edwin Rudd, a Norwegian mechanical engineer, used Maughan's designs to develop a container-based apparatus similar to what we use today.

Most hot-water tanks are closed containers made of a fiberglass material. Residential hot water tanks are typically large enough to hold 50 to 60 gallons (190 to 230 L) of cold water that is heated by a heat source (gas or electricity). A thermostat on the hot-water tank senses the temperature of the water in the tank. As hot water is used, more cold water enters the tank to keep the tank full. As the cold water is added to the tank, the water temperature falls below a certain level, the thermostat senses the drop in temperature, and it restarts the heat source so that hot water will be available the next time it's needed. As the water temperature increases and reaches the temperature set on the thermostat, usually about 125 degrees Fahrenheit (52 degrees Celsius), the thermostat senses that change and turns off the heat source. But what happens if the thermostat malfunctions or is set too high? Physics tells us that if we continue to heat a liquid in a closed container, the pressure in the container continues to rise. In the hot-water heater, the pressure could rise to a level that exceeds the structural ability of the water tank to handle the increasing inside pressure. In that case, the tank would split or crack, and about 50 gallons of hot water would spill all over the floor.

Recognizing this problem, today's hot-water tanks include a safety device called a pressure relief valve that is attached to the tank. When excess pressure develops, the pressure relief valve automatically senses the problem. The valve opens and allows the excess pressure (steam) to be released from the tank. This system prevents the tank from breaking and spilling water all over the floor. The problem will continue to present itself, however, if the temperature setting on the thermostat is not corrected or the faulty thermostat is not replaced.

What does this have to do with athletes or swimming? Imagine that athletes, like hot-water tanks, are closed containers filled with a liquid that can build up pressure. Swimmers also have various sources of heat—coaches, parents, media, sponsors, injuries, illness, life circumstances, travel, teammates, organizations, possible financial gain or loss, the possibility of making a team—that can cause pressure to build. The swimmer's thermostat refers to the swimmer's ability to sense pressure when it is building and manage it in a way that does not interfere with performance. An additional function of the performance thermostat is to develop a set of strategies that can be used to develop and maintain a healthy perspective on performance.

Also, like the hot-water tank, swimmers may have a pressure relief valve that serves as a backup for the thermostat. Pressure relief valves can be coaches and support staff that can assist when an athlete's personal strategies don't seem to be working. When swimmers heat up from pressure, they expect the thermostat (mental coping strategies) to kick in and take care of the increasing heat. These strategies are addressed in this chapter. For those with an ongoing awareness about healthy perspectives and regular applications of effective strategies, the pressure is naturally monitored, managed, and channeled into constructive behavior. For those who do not use these strategies, pressure can continue to increase and have dramatic negative effects on performance as the athlete nears the point of coming apart. Unfortunately, when the thermostat (strategies) isn't used and swimmers don't check in with the pressure relief valve (coaches and other support resources), the results can include panic, choking, anxiety, fear response, increased vulnerability to illness or injury, slow recovery from injury, decreased swimming technique, changes in mood, substance use or abuse, quitting sport, and more.

Pressure itself is not entirely a negative element. Some athletes are able to reframe, relabel, and use pressure to create more fuel for higher performances. Some swimmers actually need more heat (pressure) to access performance levels that they cannot tap into any other way. They don't need a pressure relief valve. They need more heat for higher performance.

All athletes need to identify and understand the sources of heat and pressure, as well as the extent to which they affect mind-set and performance in either productive or counterproductive ways. Athletes need to create a working set of strategies (thermostat) to regulate their internal response to pressure. Finally, they need to identify people who can serve as the pressure relief valve and assist them in adjusting or reapplying performance strategies to get back on track. It then becomes possible to either decrease the intensity and its negative effect on performance or convert it into performance fuel.

Great athletes who consistently perform well understand that the real drug of sport is that amazingly unique and energizing anticipatory excitement they experience leading up to and right before the start. They know it is coming, and they expect it to be there. They need it for that extra gear that training cannot give them. It is the fuel of champions, and they have learned to embrace and use it.

All swimmers can choose to use that special fuel to push or pull them through the water (positive), or they can choose to use it to make them feel as if they are pulling weights and swimming upstream! What's more amazing is that athletes can learn how to make the right choice. Having great technique and great endurance takes time, smart work, hard work, and practice. Seeing and using the pressure of competition as fuel takes practice, too.

Energy Management (Tachometers)

A tachometer is a gauge typically found on the instrument panel of a car. It tells how many revolutions per minute (RPMs) the engine is turning at any giving point. The higher the RPMs are, the harder the engine is working. The tachometer reads 0 RPMs when the car is off, but when the car is started, the tachometer needle jumps right up to around 1,500 to 2,000 RPMs before settling back down to a quiet idling rate of about 900 RPMs. This idle speed simply keeps the engine on, warm, ready, and using only enough fuel to stay running.

When the driver pushes down on the gas pedal, the tachometer needle immediately jumps to a higher number on the gauge, indicating that the engine is increasing its RPMs. Typically, the speed of the car is increasing as well. When a car is in its top gear and just cruising along, most tachometers will read somewhere around 3,000 RPMs. If the engine is pushed too hard, the tachometer will begin to register in the higher numbers on the gauge, which typically are in bright orange or red, colors widely recognized for warning! In this case, the tachometer is warning the driver that the engine RPMs are dangerously high. Malfunctions, poor performance, and even damage to the engine are likely. Hitting that orange or red area on the gauge is a warning to shift gears so that the RPMs get back down to a cruising range for the engine.

What does this have to do with swimming faster? In 1908 Yerkes and Dodson developed the inverted U hypothesis, which offered a description of their research describing the relationship between anxiety and performance (figure 16.3). Briefly, they hypothesized that increasing anxiety (excitement or energy) was positively and directly related to increasing performance to a particular point. When the anxiety (excitement or energy) passed a certain threshold, performance began to decline, proportionate to the increasing anxiety.

Later, Hardy and Fazey (1987) and Hardy and Parfitt (1991) expanded on the earlier work and developed the catastrophe model, which considered both physiological and psychological energy, rather than anxiety. By combining two variables with performance, the catastrophe model alters the inverted U diagram somewhat, but both hypotheses clearly propose an important relationship between energy level (physiological and psychological) and performance. Athletes need to identify their optimal energy level. Too little energy will result in a flat performance, and too much energy will result in decreased performance because of high anxiety (energy). Each sport and each athlete has a different level of energy associated with performance needs. Distance swimmers have their best energy levels to the left of midline on the inverted U, sprinters more to the right, and middle-distance swimmers probably more toward the center of the curve. Energy levels will need to be practiced through trial and error. Just as car engines have a variety of RPM levels for peak performance, so do swimmers.

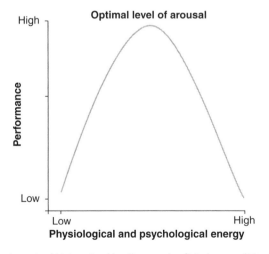

▶ **Figure 16.3** An inverted U, inspired by the work of Yerkes and Dodson, that illustrates the relationship between physiological and psychological energy and performance.

As with most research and hypotheses, subsequent research often challenges earlier findings. The work done by Yerkes and Dodson and Hardy is no exception. From an applied perspective, however, the relationship between levels of physiological energy, psychological energy, and performance plays out every day. Therefore, in my work, these models are valuable, and they make sense to practitioners, coaches, and athletes.

Imagine superimposing the inverted U on a tachometer. You will quickly see the relationship. Lower numbers on the tachometer correspond to lower levels of energy on the inverted U. Redlining the tachometer corresponds to higher energy and decreasing performance on the inverted U. The analogy of a tachometer to represent things such as heart rate or physiological and psychological energy is a good metric for engine performance, in cars and in swimmers.

As swimmers train and compete, they should begin to use an energy scale similar to a tachometer to evaluate their performance. Imagine an internal tachometer numbered from 1 to 8. The lower numbers are energy levels associated with being on idle, and the higher numbers are redlining, or being way too energized. Each swimmer should find a number on the tachometer that represents the cruising setting. Athletes need to think about really good performances and associate them with a number on their tachometers. Before swimmers compete, they can check their emotional energy by maintaining awareness of their internal tachometers. As swimmers prepare to perform, their energy levels should begin to rise to the cruising numbers, but not as far as the higher numbers (redline.) Some well-known mechanisms to regulate energy include listening to music and performing breathing exercises. Swimmers should use this tachometer strategy before races and even during the races themselves. They can also regularly monitor their anxiety levels using this strategy. The more practice athletes get using this approach, the more likely they will be to monitor and raise or lower their energy level to achieve the necessary arousal level when they step on the blocks.

Yellow Lights

Early in my driving career, I was taught that when approaching an intersection, if the traffic light turned yellow, I was supposed to slow down and stop. Obviously, traffic intersections would be a bigger mess than they are now if we didn't have traffic lights to clear intersections. So, for years I believed that yellow lights meant to slow down and stop. Later, I moved from rural America to southern California and took my driving skills and beliefs about the rules of the road with me. I soon realized, however, that the beliefs about driving in California were much different from those in rural America. Yellow lights did not mean slow down. They seemed to convey the message to speed up and get through the intersection! In one of my first intersection experiences in California, I slowed down for the yellow light and all the cars in the surrounding lanes flew through the intersection. Simultaneously, I looked in my rearview mirror. Directly behind me was a car fishtailing and braking hard to avoid rear-ending me. I could clearly make out the obscenities that driver was yelling at me through his windshield. The lesson I learned in California was that yellow has a much different meaning attached to it than what I had learned back home. Yellow means "go," and anyone who doesn't go will be left at the light while everyone else moves on.

What does this have to do with sport? The same beliefs about yellow lights and slowing down hold true when thinking about performance. As athletes get tired from physical exertion, they begin to receive warnings (yellow lights) from their bodies and they naturally begin to think about slowing down to relieve that discomfort.

These uncomfortable intersections, which can occur at various points in different events, represent times when athletes have an opportunity to decide what their bodies are really telling them. "Should I slow down or swim through the yellow lights that my body is giving me?" What the body is really saying is that here is an opportunity to go! Just like the yellow traffic lights in California, if a swimmer slows down for the yellow, other swimmers (who likely are experiencing the same yellow warning lights) will likely continue and may even speed up to make it through the intersection.

Each time swimmers choose to run the yellow light in the pool, they move closer to becoming a different athlete. Each time they give in and decide to slow down for the yellow light, they will likely end up touching the wall behind the other competitors, knowing all the while that they really could have pushed through the yellow. Unfortunately, in the latter case, the swimmer will climb out of the pool unchanged, the same athlete who dove in at the start. For swimmers to be different every time they swim, they need to run the yellow lights in the pool. A necessary ingredient to move from the current level to a higher level of performance is to push regularly to an uncomfortable level (run the yellow light). There will be some resistance to being uncomfortable, but athletes really have two clear choices. The first, as a swimmer, is to continue to push through times of being physically and psychologically uncomfortable and get better. The second, as a swimmer, is to remain at the current level of comfort and simultaneously remain at the current performance level. The swimmer makes the choice!

Fuel Gauges

We've already discussed one gauge in the performance dashboard of a car (tachometer); another important indicator of a car's performance and status is the gas, or fuel, gauge. The fuel gauge provides a rough idea about how much fuel is left in the tank. Most fuel systems in today's cars also have an indicator that illuminates when the car is low on fuel. When that light comes on, we usually think we are nearly out of fuel and had better head to the gas station to fill up. When the light comes on, we may frantically change our driving plans and start looking for a gas station so that we don't run out of gas. But that light is just another yellow orange warning light, one to be considered, but not necessarily one that requires us to change our plans. Specifically, it tells us that we are low on fuel and that we are now using reserve fuel to keep the car moving.

Nearly every athlete has experienced those sinking thoughts and self-talk about being nearly out of fuel, during either a difficult training session or an all-out competition. "Do I have enough fuel left to finish this set or race?" "What if I don't have enough fuel to finish and I don't?" "How embarrassing is this going to be if I just get smoked in this race?" "I'd better slow down so that I can at least finish strong." But if swimmers knew how far they could go after the low-fuel light comes on, they would be able to push through that light to use every last drop of gas without fear that they would run out before the race was over. This information—how far we can go after the fuel light comes on—comes from careful monitoring and self-testing during training.

For example, when I buy a vehicle, I fill up my 1-gallon (3.8 L) lawn mower gas container, put it in the trunk of the car, and start driving. When the low-fuel light illuminates, I push in the odometer button and reset the trip mileage to zero. Then I drive until my car runs completely out of gas, the engine stops, and I coast to a stop. A quick glance at the odometer tells me how many miles I have driven since the fuel light came on. I now know exactly how far I can drive on my reserve fuel. This piece of information is important to have for any machine, including the body. When swimmers know how far they can go before the tank runs out of gas and how fast they can swim to get there, a whole new realm of racing options presents itself. Knowing this generates a new kind of self-talk: "I have plenty in reserve, so let's just kick it up a gear!"

Remember that yellow lights and low-fuel gauges are signals to keep going, not to slow down or start worrying. Swimmers should challenge those old beliefs by challenging the lights. Each time they make that decision, they will be on their way to becoming a different and faster swimmer.

Pit Crews

Imagine what it would be like for a NASCAR or Indy race car driver to run a race without a pit crew. That's the way it was in the early days of racing (pre-1950s). During the 1950s, the Wood Brothers were the first to choreograph pit stops for their drivers. Before then, drivers raced the race and serviced their own cars. As race distances increased, tracks got faster (dirt to asphalt and flat tracks to banked curves), engines got bigger, speeds increased, and money for the winner grew, just as it did for swimmers. A support crew became a necessity for any driver who wanted to be successful. From that point on, the best crews became a significant part of a racer's success.

Efficiency and safety for the crewmembers soon became paramount. Regulations began to limit the number of people allowed on the track to service the driver and the car. In other sports, rules or available credentials restrict the number of people in the competition area. The main ingredients to keeping the car on the road seemed to be tires and fuel. So the pit crew became the jack man, front-tire changer, front-tire carrier, back-tire changer, back-tire carrier, gasman, and gas catcher. Every crew has a crew chief to coordinate the work of the crew, but the chief is overseeing all that work from behind the wall.

The on-track crews are critical to the driver and the car for the preparation leading up to the race, during the race, and after the race. But the driver and the race team rely on the support of many essential off-track people, sponsors, and organizations. In all sports, the evolution of athletes (bigger, stronger, faster, and competing over longer durations and distances) and athletic competition (more risky) has required increasing levels of efficiency in athletes, their equipment, and the support crews.

In athletics, the pit crew concept is alive and well, but until now the similarities between car racing and other sports have not been highlighted. Years ago, swimmers typically had their lone pit crewmember, the coach. The coach provided everything the athlete might need to compete. But like NASCAR, competitive swimming has changed; a crew of people is needed to support an athlete in today's competitive environment. A swimmer's crew consists of coach, assistant coaches, strength and conditioning coach, physiologist, biomechanist, high-speed video technologist, medical staff, sport psychologist, sport nutritionist, chiropractor, and massage therapist.

Like the NASCAR pit crew, these key players for a swimmer must also be choreographed to provide the swimmer with the highest level of science and collaborative effort to keep the swimmer in the race. Just as in NASCAR, a host of others never seen by the casual observer are behind the wall, people just as necessary to the swimmer's success—family, friends, relationship partners, teammates, clubs, organizations, other coaches, financial supporters, agents, and more. Just like the pit crew, these supplemental support systems are important to the overall effort to assist the athlete. Earlier in the discussion about hot-water tanks, I mentioned the pressure relief valve as a backup to the thermostat (personal strategies). All the pit crewmembers are the swimmer's relief valves. Swimmers should use them!

Summary

A swimming career is long and arduous. Being successful takes a lot of blood, sweat, and tears. In the end, however, a swimming career can be one of the most rewarding and fun-filled careers that any athlete can experience. Swimmers learn lessons about themselves, life, where they have been, where they are going, and how they will get there. To synchronize their minds with their bodies and swim faster, swimmers need to practice and use the strategies outlined in this chapter. They can maintain an effective mind and body connection by

- adopting a new perspective of mental pliability,
- consistently recalculating and beating their average times in events in which they compete ($\bar{X}$),

- keeping their thoughts in the present time zone (using the force of gravity),
- moving toward and maintaining constructive thoughts (self-talk),
- identifying and managing sources and intensities of pressure (hot-water tank),
- understanding and managing physiological and psychological energy levels (tachometer),
- challenging the yellow lights that occur during competitions (running the yellow lights),
- knowing what's in their reserve fuel tank (low fuel light), and
- using their pit crew!

CHAPTER 17

Growth and Development

—Anne Pankhurst, PhD

This chapter is concerned with the growth, maturation, and development of every child and young person on the path to becoming an adult. Therefore, the information is not only about swimmers or even young athletes but also about the growth and development process that every young person goes through. Certainly, for swimming coaches to work appropriately and effectively with young people, they must be knowledgeable about growth and development and, more important, be able to apply those concepts in their daily activities and behaviors. Parents and sport or club officials are also stakeholders in the process of developing young people in sport; they, too, should be aware of the information and understand its implications for every young athlete in a coaching program.

This chapter first discusses growth, maturation, and development as it relates to young athletes, and it then outlines the implications of each for coaches. The final section of the chapter discusses how practice should be structured at different stages of athlete development to provide a developmentally appropriate swimming experience.

Defining Growth, Maturation, and Development

Two important issues deserve some discussion and clarification before we move forward. First, the terms *growth*, *maturation*, and *development*, although linked, are distinct entities. Therefore, they will be defined and discussed individually. In terms of coaching young athletes, however, the close links they have to each other and the manner in which they affect each other are important for any coach who works with developing swimmers to know and understand.

Additionally, although every child follows the same general pattern of growth and maturation, each child is an individual in the sense that the timing and tempo of her progress through the stages of growth and maturation will be unique. The fact that the timing of progress toward adulthood takes place individually is a central tenet to this chapter. Because of the nonuniformity of individual athlete development, coaches, parents, and systems find it extremely difficult to compare one child with another, especially during periods of rapid growth such as puberty. As athletes grow and mature, each child likely will be at a different stage of development than others within his peer group (Baxter-Jones and Sherar 2007; Buenen and Malina 2008). These differences can be especially marked during puberty and can persist until the growth and development process has concluded (i.e., adulthood).

A key item for coaches to realize is that because each child has the potential to progress at a different tempo than other swimmers in the same training group, they may need to adjust their coaching styles, techniques, and areas of focus to provide a developmentally appropriate training and competitive experience. Realistically, only as adults can people be accurately compared in terms of athletic performance. But that does not seem to prevent people from making comparisons and making decisions about talent when athletes are very young! To give a practical example, two 12-year-olds competing at a swim meet could appear to have the same technical abilities and skills. But because they are in different stages of growth and maturation (perhaps one is small and immature and the other is tall and nearing adulthood), their ability to perform will be influenced simply by their physical size and abilities, their different levels of strength and speed. To compare them in terms of the outcome of the race, or worse, to state that one is more talented than the other based on physical ability is inappropriate. Because of the training and competitive requirements of sport, the individual's rate of growth and maturation has a tremendous effect on performance.

Consequently, anyone involved in youth or junior sport should understand the processes of growth, maturation, and development because those elements will affect every young person. Coaches and parents are the stakeholders most closely associated with young athletes. For them, this knowledge and understanding is crucial if young people are to develop their potential, whether as Olympic champions or as recreational swimmers. Both parents and coaches influence athlete development all along the developmental pathway. How then are the terms *growth, maturation,* and *development* defined, how are they manifested, and what are their implications for coaching practice?

Growth

Growth refers to increases in the size of a person, in terms of either the body as a whole or the individual limb segments (arms, legs, and trunk). Typically, growth results in an increase in height (stature), weight (body mass), organ size (e.g., heart and lungs), and the size of the skeletal system (Malina, Bouchard, and Bar-Or 2004). Therefore, growth is a dynamic and actual change in the size, shape, and structure of the body itself or its parts. Some elements of growth such as height (stature), size of segments, and weight (body mass) are observable and measurable. These variables normally are tracked for young people regularly by medical practitioners. But growth in young athletes can (and should) be measured regularly by coaches as well to determine the approximate stage of development of each swimmer. Some previous knowledge of normal growth and development is useful for a coach and can provide some insight as to what each athlete will look like in the future. For example, on average girls reach 75 percent of their adult height by 7.5 years of age and boys by 9 years of age. Typically, girls have attained 90 percent of their adult height at 11.5 years and boys at 13.5 years. In the case of stature or height, predicting full adult height is relatively easy (Beunen 2001) using straightforward testing or medical records.

One of the keys for coaches to understand and take into account is that growth is not steady throughout childhood or adolescence; the velocity of growth (rate of increase) is different at different stages. Whether a swimmer is experiencing a period of rapid or slow growth can affect training and competitive success.

Five stages of growth before adulthood are recognized, and each has a different rate-of-growth pattern. Note that all age ranges given here are averages, so take care in deciding how individual children fit into the stages.

1. From birth until 2 or 3 years of age, the child grows rapidly and increases in stature, up to 12 inches (30 cm) in the first year. By the age of 2, the average child has attained 50 percent of her adult stature.

2. During childhood (defined as 4 to 10 years of age), the growth rate decelerates considerably and settles in to a steady rate of around 2 to 3 inches (5 to 7.5 cm) per year, although many 6- to 8-year-olds experience a midgrowth spurt during which the rate of growth increases slightly.

3. During the prepubertal stage (between the ages of 8 or 9 and 12, although it may occur earlier or later depending on gender), the young person begins the growth spurt. This is called the onset of peak height velocity (PHV).

4. During puberty, the growth spurt is characterized by another rapid increase in height until the person achieves PHV, the period of most rapid growth.

5. The postpuberty period follows the growth spurt and PHV. This period of slower growth continues until adulthood.

Increases in body mass (weight) follow the same general pattern described for increases in stature, but they come later and are delayed relative to the increases in height (height gains precede weight gains). The term peak weight velocity (PWV) is given to the peak rate of increase in body mass (Baxter-Jones and Sherar 2007). On average, boys ultimately end up being both taller and heavier than girls.

Coaches and parents need to understand that although these stages are often linked to chronological age, the data indicate only the average age when these growth phases occur. The fact that most children and young people are not average means that many will be either ahead or behind the average age.

For example, a swimmer who is experiencing normal growth can be shorter or taller than another child at the same chronological age and can weigh less or more. These growth factors have implications for swimmers and their ability to perform specific skills because both PHV and PWV affect physical development.

The velocity of the increase in stature is a more important measure than the actual increase in height because it gives a real indication of the onset of puberty. Puberty is marked by a rapid increase in height, but the rate of this increase is what matters most in terms of coaching. We have already seen that children under 8 or 10 years of age (remember, this is the average age) are growing steadily and slowly. As the rate of growth increases, the difference between one height measurement and the next can be measured and recorded. The point at which the rapid increase in velocity begins is known as the onset of PHV, and it signals the start of the growth spurt. For a varying period of months, every young person will grow rapidly until he reaches peak height velocity (PHV), the point at which growth rate is maximal and then starts to slow down.

During growth, maturation is also taking place. The period of much slower steady growth that follows the growth spurt can continue until 16, 18, or even 20 years of age, depending on gender. This stage is known as postpuberty. Adulthood is indicated when growth (and maturation) is finally complete.

Maturation

Maturation is the term used to define the coming of age processes experienced by the biological systems of the body—the skeletal, sexual, hormonal, and neural systems—as they develop. Maturation is a dynamic process of change because the various systems progress toward the adult biological state at different rates and tempos, both within the same person (i.e., not all systems may develop at the same rate) as well as between people (i.e., individuals may mature at different rates).

The stages of maturation are similar to and parallel to those listed for growth. As examples of this, childhood (ages 4 to 10) is the stage at which maturation of the skeletal and neural systems primarily occurs. Additionally, maturational changes to the sexual and hormonal systems are known to begin in prepuberty and are particularly evident during puberty. These maturational processes affect every young person, but the timing and tempo take place on an individual timetable and therefore will be different for each person in a manner similar to growth.

The indicators of maturation are clearly different for boys and girls (see the section on gender for more information). For example, girls have a biological marker similar to that of PHV that will signal the maturation of the sexual system: the onset of the menstrual cycle (menarche), which, for the vast majority of girls, takes place within a few months of PHV. The sexual characteristics of boys (e.g., genital changes, body hair, and voice changes) all mature at different stages and not necessarily in the same order for each male, making it difficult for all but qualified medical practitioners to judge a boy's stage of maturation.

Coaches should keep a watchful eye for elements of growth and maturation that can be observed even if they cannot be measured. Observation assumes that coaches know what to look for and can understand the implications for coaching practice in what they observe. In addition, in exactly the same way that growth occurs, maturation takes place at different times for young people of the same age. Young athletes can be either early, average, or late maturers in relation to their peers of the same age. Parents are a useful resource for coaches; parents naturally will be more aware of maturational changes than coaches, and they can help coaches understand where a swimmer stands in the maturational process (another reason for maintaining good relationships with parents).

Clearly, the two processes of growth and maturation are biological in nature and unavoidable in practice; they take place at some stage in every young person. Maturation has implications for a young athlete's ability to perform specific skills in sport, especially when athletes are grouped with others of the same age. Young people may also temporarily lose skills as they mature and move through puberty because of, for example, increases in limb lengths and changing body proportions that affect coordination.

Development

Development is a different concept from either growth or maturity. It refers to two distinct factors in the progress of young people toward adulthood. First, the term signifies the status of the various biological systems of the body as the young person gets older. Second, it relates to athlete behavior and skill development, elements that can be observed and assessed in terms of the acquisition and increasing competence in various skills over time. In particular, coaches can witness this as young athletes develop and expand their repertoire of physical, physiological, emotional, intellectual, and social skills. Two issues are important for coaches:

1. The rate of development in the various factors is nonlinear. A swimmer's ability in one factor is unrelated and inconsequential to his ability in another. For example, just because a young athlete has advanced physical skills, there is no reason to assume that he will have advanced or even normal social skills or emotional control. In reality, although this young person may be growing and maturing physically ahead of his peer group, his mental or emotional skills may lag behind or be more developed than his physical abilities.

2. Every child or young person acquires skills and abilities at a different age and stage, often depending on her environment. Each athlete is unique in terms of how she will progress through growth, maturation, and development.

Implications for Coaches

The processes of growth, maturation, and development are at work in all young children and adolescents. Certainly, these processes should affect coaching practice and behavior. Those implications are discussed in detail throughout this section.

The fact that young athletes grow and mature at different rates and chronological ages is theoretically and practically important for coaches. The implication for the young athlete is that the playing field will always be uneven until everyone has reached adulthood. Only then can an apples-to-apples comparison truly be made.

Furthermore, at least initially, that unevenness will largely be tipped in favor of children who grow and mature earlier than others do. In some aspects, the early maturers keep their perceived advantage into adulthood, but coaches need to work out where each young athlete is on the developmental pathway and take that into account when designing training plans, scheduling competition, and building relationships. For example, the coach must consider whether coaching adolescent athletes in chronological age groups constitutes best practice. The more beneficial approach may be to give athletes an opportunity to train with a group of developmentally comparable swimmers. To confuse the situation further, physical and physiological development do not necessarily match the rate of a young swimmer's psychological development, so being placed in a different chronological age group may not be the right solution for a young person. Often, the advantages of height and maturity mean that these youngsters are likely to be more successful and so could or should be in a different (higher-level) training group. Coaches also may believe they should select the more successful young athletes for *more* training and competition without considering that they are still immature in other respects. The athlete's level of mental, emotional, or social maturity may mean that training with his peer group is more enjoyable, despite the differences in physical ability.

To compound the issue even further, because young people gain confidence from success and success is perceived to be indicator of competence, late maturers who are not successful can lose confidence when their more successful peers are in the same training or competition group. Such actions can be discouraging for the late developers who are not selected for the all-star team or the elite group. Consequently, many leave a sport in which they perceive themselves to be inferior to their peers. If these same late maturers are looked after, however, they often catch up and become more successful than the early maturers, if they are still in the sport. So placing young athletes in groups can make for tough coaching decisions. Clearly, coaches face a formidable challenge in providing all developing swimmers with an environment that will foster long-term enjoyment and success.

Monitoring Young Athletes' Performance

The implications of growth and maturation are that coaches need methods for monitoring the stage of development of each young person to know where he is in the development curve (Malina and Beunen 2008). If involvement in the sport is increasing and moving from recreational to competitive participation, the frequency of this monitoring should increase and go deeper than mere observation. Regular height and weight measurements that are recorded and monitored can be important and useful. As previously mentioned, measuring the rate of height increase can be a valuable tool for identifying where the youngster is in the growth and maturation process as a whole or in the growth spurt in particular. A steady increase in weight should be expected and recorded, especially for young athletes who have a high training load. A loss of weight in any young athlete should raise a red flag and be investigated. Recording the rate of growth (i.e., the change in height or weight over a consistent and regular time interval), performing and recording regular skill testing, maintaining injury records, and keeping regular contact with parents will help coaches determine where a young athlete is on the developmental pathway (Beunen 2001). Good practice in coaching young people means that coaches should have sound evidence of where each athlete is in terms of development and not rely on chronological age as the sole indicator.

The biological outcomes of growth and maturation also affect what can, and should, be trained and when. The athlete development research indicates that biological age—where the athlete is developmentally—is much more important than the chronological age of a young athlete (Bloom 1985; Bompa 2000). Physical skills and capacities, for example, are affected by growth and maturation, and therefore any training of them should be linked to the growth spurt and biological age, not the swimmer's chronological age. Differences will also be found between genders, but less research has been done on the development of physical capacities in girls than in boys. Take into account the following:

- A young person who is growing rapidly may be taller but not necessarily stronger or faster and will almost certainly lose some coordination temporarily as limb lengths increase and are out of proportion to the trunk.

- Different types of strength, or strength attributes, develop at different rates and times, and coaches need to understand all of them to train them effectively. Muscular, static, and explosive strength development in boys begins during the growth spurt and reaches a peak up to a year after PHV.

- Muscle growth takes time to catch up with skeletal growth (skeletal growth precedes muscle growth), and care should be taken with any strength training of young athletes during puberty.

- The increase in weight (PWV) comes after PHV. Coaches need to remember that the body first increases rapidly in stature (PHV) and then increases in overall size—muscle mass, weight (PWV), and strength (PSV).

- The best opportunities to improve and increase flexibility and speed of the limbs and the body as a whole precede PHV. Therefore, flexibility and speed should be developed before strength (Beunen and Malina 2008).

- The propensity for injury increases, especially during puberty, if training type and volume is too high or is too repetitive of the same skills.

- Young people tire more quickly and easily, so rest and recovery are even more important (see section later in this chapter).

- Consequently, the development of strength, speed, flexibility, and other physical capacities must be carefully monitored by coaches during puberty and postpuberty. Specific physical tests can be used to monitor the development of all physical capacities.

Clearly, when working with groups of young athletes on physical development, variations will occur in who can do what and when. One method of overcoming this issue is to have swimmers train physical skills in specific groups—prepuberty, puberty, and postpuberty—to ensure that the training methodology, volume, and intensity of work are appropriate. All these factors can be incorporated under the banner of providing developmentally appropriate training.

Physiological Factors That Affect Training

Besides physical factors, a number of physiological parameters affect the ability of a young maturing athlete to train and compete. The processes of growth, maturation, and development have a major effect on the ability of young athletes to leverage the physiological attributes that are commonly seen as a normal part of adult performance. An important mantra to follow is that young athletes are not simply miniature adults and should not be expected to behave in the same way. Junior athletes develop physiological attributes and capacities as they grow and mature. As an example, although aerobic function is a key contributor to performance in all athletes, aerobic capacity is not fully developed in young athletes and therefore it should not be trained in the same way that it is in adults. Consider the following:

- Younger athletes have smaller hearts and lower blood volume.
- Developing athletes have a higher heart rate and a lower stroke volume (the amount of blood ejected from the left ventricle per cardiac contraction) compared with adults.
- Children and adolescents have less ability to extract oxygen from the air as they work. The result is that they have to take faster breaths to deliver the same amount of oxygen to working muscles as adults do.
- Prepubescent athletes have a less efficient energy system in terms of producing lactate because they use more fat than glycogen or glucose to fuel performance compared with adults.
- Younger athletes are often less aware of the effect of a training load and the need for rest.
- Children have a lower proportion of muscle in relation to body mass, so they have to work harder to achieve the same or lower outcome of work as an adult at the same task.

Taken as a whole, these factors affect how a coach trains a young swimmer compared with athletes who have gone through puberty.

Fluid Balance and Temperature Regulation

Even when taking their smaller size into account, children and prepubertal athletes have greater skin surface area, relative to adults, and experience higher blood flow to the skin than pubertal athletes or adults do. Because the skin is exposed to the environment, young athletes consequently have greater difficulty with thermoregulation, or the ability to regulate their temperature, than older athletes do. In addition, young athletes take longer to acclimate to changes in ambient temperature than adults do (Williams 2007). Although children can typically tolerate exercise in normal temperatures, in hot or cold temperatures their thermoregulation is limited and more difficult; consequently, they are less able to tolerate exercise in hot or cold conditions.

Finally, children and young athletes are poor at recognizing thirst and thus fluid deficiency. They become dehydrated more easily and more frequently than adults do. Coaches need to build rest and fluid breaks into the training schedule and sessions and then monitor the amount of fluid that they consume.

Psychological Development

Growth and maturation also affect the development of mental, emotional, and social skills, which follow a pattern similar to that of physical development. With that said, a number of psychological skills can be developed at various ages in immature and developing young people (MacNamara, Button, and Collins 2010). For example, perceived competence, commitment, self-confidence, self-reliance, and coping under pressure can begin to be developed during puberty (Eklund and Gould 2008; MacNamara, Button, and Collins 2010; Weiss, Bhalla, and Price 2008). Coaches should know how to develop those skills by using appropriate coaching practices and coaching environments at different stages of the developmental pathway.

Training and Competition

The processes of growth and maturation obviously affect both training and competition. Bloom (1985) and Bompa (2000) suggested that coaches should always take into account an athlete's biological age in designing a plan to develop her physical and technical skill base appropriately and successfully. Balyi and Williams (2010) also suggested that knowing the athlete's biological age would help coaches deliver developmentally appropriate training and competition. The evidence given thus far in this chapter is that technical development will be either limited or enhanced by the level of physical development. Young people moving through puberty will not have the same range of physical skills that fully mature athletes do, and they will also find that their skills and abilities will ebb and flow during periods of rapid growth. Even young children can experience balance problems because of the relative size and weight of their heads during childhood.

Organizing and conducting training and practice is obviously part of the coach's role. The research in the area of practice and training design is clear: The age and stage of athlete development is an important consideration in determining practice and training programs for young athletes. Again, but in a different context, growth, maturation, and development affect the type, volume, and purpose of training. Consider the following coaching points that can be integrated into a swimming training and competitive framework:

- Developmentally, prepubescent children need a more fun and playful environment. Short periods of varied activities will fit their psychosocial needs (Baker and Côté 2006; Côté and Lidor 2013).

- Learning basic skills is easier and more productive during the steady growth of either childhood or postpuberty than it is when the athlete is growing and maturing rapidly (e.g., puberty).

- During childhood, children need to experience a wide variety of sports at a low overall volume.

- As young athletes increase in maturity and develop a higher-quality skill base, deliberate practice among developing swimmers can be effective. Deliberate practice (characterized by increased training volume, intensity, and lack of immediate reward) is certainly a more appropriate form of practice for young people in puberty and postpuberty than it is for children and prepuberty young people. Before volume is added (deliberate practice involves repetition and long periods of the same practice; Hambrick et al. 2013), coaches should devise different types of practice methods that specifically improve performance and skills for young athletes.

- The ratio of practice to competition should be an important consideration for coaches. Practice volume, and especially competition volume, should be lower in childhood and prepuberty compared with later stages of development.

Finally, within this context are the concepts of trainability and readiness. Trainability refers to the actual ability of the athlete to respond to training of a specific skill, meaning that the athlete has the physical and physiological capability to learn that skill at that time. Clearly, trainability links to the stage of growth, maturation, and development of the individual athlete. Readiness, however, also links to the psychosocial development of the athlete, which, as discussed earlier, may or may not be in line with biological growth and maturation. Readiness is linked to trainability, but both concepts affect the training of young people.

Proper Training

Proper training techniques for the young athlete are imperative. To become well-rounded athletes and people, children need to be taught the skills of various sports. As a foundation, before young athletes can excel in any sport they first need to learn the basics of movement and have opportunities to develop a variety of skills. The outcome is that they acquire coordination (the organization of motor firing patterns that lead to efficiency of muscle activation), body control when moving and changing direction (agility), and static and dynamic balance in a variety of ways. Evidence indicates that concentrating on one sport too early in life can be detrimental to the development of athletic skills. Coordination, agility, and balance underpin the biomechanics of swimming technique, and the mastery of these skills can enhance performance in adolescence and over a lifetime. Besides providing a greater skill base, multisport involvement early in life can help to decrease the risk of injury in young athletes. In contrast, improper learning and concentration on one sport in childhood can lead to injury.

Young Athletes and Competition

Competitive success or failure in young athletes is significantly influenced by their level of maturation and development. Coaches need to appreciate that fact, because although success is important, *why* a particular young person is successful is potentially a more important piece of information. Is it because the athlete was simply bigger and stronger? In that case, success could be temporary until the late maturers catch up. Is it because that athlete had more coaching? In that case, the skill level *should* be higher. Or is it because the athlete has real potential? To answer this question, the coach must understand what potential and talent are and how they are manifested in young athletes.

Baxter-Jones (1995) determined that junior competitive success cannot be used as an indicator of talent or future successful performance. The reality of junior competition is that young athletes perform inconsistently as they progress through puberty. Early maturers have such physical advantages over their peers that they succeed initially but only temporarily. The existing junior competitive framework, except in rare instances, does not takes into account the skeletal or biological age of young athletes (Bompa 2000). These ages and their influence on performance and training design are discussed in the next section.

In addition, coaches need to be sure of the purpose of competition for junior athletes and make sure that the reasons driving competition are developmentally appropriate. Adult and junior competitive systems have different characteristics. Junior athletes normally compete in competitive systems that are chronologically age based, usually with two-year age banding, a feature that is absent in adult competition. Further, the relative age effect (RAE), discussed in the next section, highlights the fact that differences in success can be attributed, in some cases, simply to the month in which a child was born. Often, competitive outcomes are taken as an indication of talent in a young athlete, although the evidence indicates little connection between junior success and adult success (Pankhurst and Collins 2013). Thus, coaches need to be sure that they relate competitive success to each young athlete's status in terms of growth, maturation, and development.

Different Ages in Athlete Development

The processes of growth, maturation, and development have further ramifications in creating a number of age classifications for young people. We have already referred to the fact that junior competition tends to takes place in chronological age groups. But the previous discussion of the various aspects of growth and maturation has already indicated that chronological age can be a poor determinant of the real age of a young person. Bompa (2000), for example, discusses anatomical (skeletal) and biological age. The phenomenon of the relative age effect is well known in junior sport research and practice. Sport age should also be added to this list. Every coach who works with young people should understand the effect of each of these ages to the extent that it affects and guides coaching practice.

Chronological Age

Chronological age is the age on the birth certificate and the age used in competition in almost all junior sport. Therefore, competition will clearly favor the early maturer who will inevitably be bigger, stronger, and faster than the late maturer of the same chronological age. But growth and maturation are constantly changing. Malina, Bouchard, and Bar-Or (2004) pointed out that performance of prepubertal and puberty athletes of the same chronological age varies over even short periods. Thus, competitive results during these two developmental stages are almost random in nature. Coincidentally, these factors highlight major flaws in any selection process that ostensibly tests for talent in young, immature athletes.

Skeletal Age

Skeletal age provides an estimate of maturation of the skeletal system by measuring aspects of bone length and structure. Skeletal maturation is indicated by increased bone development and a decrease in cartilage. Skeletal age can be assessed by experts using various measurement methods. The most common is to use a plain radiograph of the left hand and wrist to evaluate bone age and examine the growth plates. (When growth has ceased, the growth plates between the long bones and the ends of the bones will fuse.) Skeletal age is important in sport because it affects the ability of young athletes to train for, develop, and perform specific athletic skills.

Biological Age

In a similar manner to skeletal age, the biological age of a young person does not necessarily follow birthdays (chronological age) or the calendar. Biological age indicates the level of maturation of the various biological systems. It can be determined only by a thorough understanding of the processes of maturation and development of those systems. Again, in terms of athlete development, biological age is more important than chronological age. Much athlete development research (Bloom 1985; Bompa 2000) suggests that coaches should always take account of biological age to develop an athlete's physical and technical skill base appropriately and successfully. Balyi and Williams (2010) took this further in indicating that coaches should know how to deliver developmentally appropriate training and how to set up a competitive schedule appropriate to the athlete's biological age.

Relative Age

Research and experience both indicate that children born at the beginning of a year are inevitably more mature than those born at the end. This phenomenon is known as the relative age effect (RAE). It follows that the younger the child is in the same chronological year, the greater the propensity will be for differences to be seen in the levels of maturity between him and children born earlier in that year. Note that the year does not necessarily run from January to December; it may be the school year from August to July or a sport year from September to August. Education systems have understood the outcomes of RAE for many years. Children who are born later in the year are inevitably younger and often understandably less able than their peers are. Research (Edgar and O'Donoghue 2005; Morris and Nevill 2006; Musch and Grondin 2001) on the effect of relative age in the junior competitive context is both extensive and important for coaches and parents. Actual results are clear—children born in the first half of the sport year are far more likely to achieve competitive success than those born later, and this advantage often carries on beyond puberty. The age-group competitions typical of junior sport are often in two-year age bands, further compounding the issue. A child born at the end of the two-year cycle can be nearly two years younger than a child born at the beginning of the cycle. Coaches need to understand that RAE is a factor that can be compounded even more by early and late maturation.

Sport Age

Inevitably, young people take up a sport at different (chronological) ages and times. Therefore, in a given period, they will have had more or fewer opportunities to learn the necessary skills. Some will have had more coaching and more access to facilities than others, so their experience or abilities should be greater. When making value judgments about young people's abilities in a sport, coaches need to take into account the sport age of each individual and link that to biological age.

Implications of Different Ages in Athlete Development

It would seem obvious that coaches should understand and take into account different ages when designing training and competition environments because they will affect a young athlete's ability and enjoyment in a sport at a given time.

But it is often the case that the implications of skeletal age, RAE, and sport age are either unknown or misunderstood by coaches and therefore are not taken into account in coaching practice. This issue is especially important when coaching a group of young people of chronological ages 9 to 11. Within that group could be young athletes with biological ages ranging from 8 (late maturers) to 14 (early maturers). Some could be born in January of one year, and others could be born in December of the following year; some could have been taking part in the sport for four years, and others just one. In terms of mental and emotional development, some in the group will be children and others will be in the middle of puberty. Coaches who are trying to conduct quality coaching in such circumstances can and must treat every person as an individual, but they also need to be aware of making judgments about standards of performance and contrasting one person's abilities with another's.

Notes on Gender

The effects of the obvious gender differences become more apparent and important in the coaching context as young male and female athletes grow and mature. Consider the following examples and differences between boys and girls and the way in which they develop:

- In terms of growth (Baxter-Jones and Sherar 2007), girls reach PHV up to two years ahead of boys.

- In terms of final stature, however, boys usually end up being between 5 and 6 inches (between 12.5 and 15 cm) taller than girls. The principal reason for this is that boys have a longer growth window compared with girls; they experience continued, steady growth while girls are in their growth spurt. The result is that after boys have completed their own growth spurt (two years later), they have had a longer opportunity to experience growth.

- Children of both genders typically have a body-fat level of 16 to 18 percent. But when discussed in terms of developmental increases and distribution of weight, although young people of both genders become heavier during periods of growth, for boys the increase in weight comes primarily from increases in muscle mass and skeletal tissue. For girls, the increase in muscle mass is less compared with boys, and a much greater increase occurs in fat mass. Boys may even decrease their body-fat percentage with growth and maturation. The percentage of fat mass is an indicator of gender; females have a higher percentage (24 to 28 percent) than males (16 to 18 percent) do postpuberty.

- Partly because of the distribution of fat mass, girls tend to have both a lower center of gravity and a different body shape than boys. This body shape is evidenced by wider shoulders (an increase in the biacromial diameter) and more muscle for boys and wider hips (an increase in the biiliac diameter) for girls. The differences in muscle mass in the shoulder girdle between the genders accounts for strength differences after puberty, and the lower center of gravity for girls gives them better balance.

- The increased width of the hips in females does increase the Q angle (the angle of the knees in relation to the hips) and can affect quadriceps muscle development. Differences are also seen in trunk length (boys have longer trunks than girls) and in arm length (again longer in boys).

- Postpuberty, physiological differences also become apparent between males and females. Males have larger hearts and lungs. Testosterone increases the blood hemoglobin and the number of red blood cells, so males can carry 11 percent more oxygen per liter of blood on average compared with females.

- The onset of the menstrual cycle for girls occurs at PHV (Rogol 2008). Often the menstrual cycle means that girls need more iron (because they lose iron during menstruation) and calcium, so diet becomes very important for female athletes.

Coaches need to be aware of the information relating to gender differences. Although these differences are almost nonexistent in children, they are very apparent postpuberty. These differences affect physical and physiological performance. The items described here relate principally to issues of growth and maturation, but psychological, mental, and emotional differences between the genders are known to exist and will also affect performance and thus coaching practice. Although coaching practice for girls and boys prepuberty can be similar, during and after maturation coaching practice should recognize the differences between the genders.

Ethnicity

Recent research on the age of sexual maturation indicates a lowering of the age at which boys mature in different ethnic groups, adding to previous and similar research on girls (Herman-Giddens et al. 2012). For girls the average age for the onset of puberty, which was 12.5 years in 1980, shifted to 10.5 years in 2010. The figures for boys are similar, but on average lag a year behind the girls. This research also indicates that the average age of maturity varies for different ethnic groups; the maturation of African American girls can now begin at 8.8 years of age, earlier than it is for white Caucasian girls (9.9 years). For boys the trend is similar in the United States. African American boys mature first, and Hispanic boys mature a little earlier than white Caucasian boys do. Current practice indicates that such research is unknown to coaches and that the implications are misunderstood by sport organizations, coaches, and parents alike.

Differences in ethnicity have been shown to affect growth, maturation, and development. The consequence is that coaches need to take account of ethnic background and reconsider their thinking on age and stage of development in relation to physical and physiological training and what is possible and when for different athletes.

Coaching Practices at Different Ages

The knowledge, techniques, and behaviors that coaches use at different stages and ages of athlete development can affect the enjoyment and performance of the swimmers they teach. High-quality coaching based on an understanding of growth and development and infused with developmentally appropriate teaching is especially important to the process of shaping young people as well as athletes. Côté et al. (2010) noted that coaches need different skills to meet the needs of young athletes at different stages of the performance pathway. This chapter has given information on the importance of coach knowledge about the processes of growth, maturation, and development and has provided some examples of how growth and development principles can be integrated into a training and competition plan. But all the knowledge available will not compensate for an absence of other critical coaching behaviors. The overall environment created by coaches is vitally important:

- Weiss, Bhalla, and Price (2008) suggested that the environment must focus on giving optimal, attainable challenges for self-improvement if young athletes are to develop the perceived competence and motivation associated with success. As stated throughout the chapter, coaches need to understand the relationship of growth, maturation, and development and the ways that they contribute to success.

- Weiss, Bhalla, and Price (2008) also highlighted the importance of appropriate goal setting (defined as the age-appropriate number and type of goals and periods) that meets the developmental needs of each athlete.

- Research by Martindale and Mortimer (2011) noted that the coaching environment for young athletes is key to their retention, enjoyment, and success in any sport. That environment requires coach behavior based on mastery-oriented coaching in which the young athlete is working to achieve quality performance and is not unduly concerned with success.

- Coaching practice must also be supportive and positive. Coach reactions to mistakes should take a positive turn by noting what the young athlete did well and encouraging a repeat of that behavior. In this context, Weiss, Bhalla, and Price (2008) showed that coaches need to support young athletes in developing their self-esteem and self-efficacy, in particular, by giving positive and specific feedback that does not focus solely on correcting errors.

Unsurprisingly, factors similar to those considered when creating a good environment for athletes should also be taken into account when thinking about the coach. Cassidy, Jones, and Potrac (2004) suggest that coaches who continually question their own knowledge and competence are more likely to deliver positive messages to young athletes and to create the positive environment that contributes to success. Research also indicates that the role and influence of the peer group on young athletes is more or less important at different stages of development (Bruner, Eys, and Turnnidge 2013).

As a final note, coaches also need to be aware that the sources of competence change with, and are related to, age changes in terms of the relative importance of parents and peer groups and levels of success. Coaches who work with competitive swimmers who are growing and developing through childhood and puberty need to find ways to develop the swimmers' confidence and ability to handle training and competition in line with their maturational age. Understanding the implications of growth, maturation, and development will set that process in motion.

Summary

The topic of growth and development underlies all aspects of sport performance. Understanding how a young athlete grows and matures is critically important for coaches as they develop training programs and establish environments that meet the athletes where they are. Young athletes are not simply miniature adults; they have different physical and physiological capacities, their mental and emotional capabilities are not developed to adult levels, and they experience growth spurts that can completely throw off coordination and motor skills. Yet coaches often attempt to fit young athletes into an adultlike competition and training model, potentially compromising performance while providing a less-than-enjoyable experience for the athletes.

On paper, it is easy to understand that athletes of dissimilar ages are in fact different from one another and that it makes sense to provide different training stimuli that match their abilities and skill sets. But when it comes to putting growth and development principles into practice on the pool deck, things quickly become more complicated. How do you break athletes into groups to provide the proper training or social experience? What happens when you do not have enough lanes to do things exactly right for everyone? How do you handle it when every athlete in the pool is in need of something slightly different to optimize his experience in the pool? These issues are a lot to handle and digest, but one of the most important things that a coach can realize is that differences do exist and that athlete behaviors and activities might need to be viewed more often through a growth and development lens. Simply understanding how athletes grow and develop will help coaches create a developmentally appropriate training environment and interpret what they see in athletes in and out of the pool.

This chapter has presented a great deal of information on the topics of athlete growth and development that can improve your coaching. Use it in your program to provide swimmers a developmentally appropriate athletic experience that focuses on the athlete's long-term development.

CHAPTER 18

Sports Medicine: Swimming Injuries and Prevention

—Courtney Dawson, MD, and Scott A. Rodeo, MD

Musculoskeletal injuries encountered among competitive swimmers tend to arise from repetitive overuse and improper stroke mechanics. The shoulder is the area of the body most commonly affected by injury because greater than 90 percent of the propulsive power in swimming comes from the upper extremity. But the spine, knee, and core (abdominal, trunk, and back) are also frequently injured in swimmers (Pink and Tibone 2000). Awareness of potential injury patterns and prevention strategies can help keep swimmers active and in the water. This chapter provides an overview of common as well as relatively uncommon injuries in swimmers and aims to provide the treating physician or other medical practitioner with the tools necessary to care for the swimming athlete.

Initial Evaluation

Whether a physician has been working with a swimmer for years or has just met the athlete, the first step for understanding the nature and extent of the injury involves an initial evaluation. The approach to the initial evaluation of the swimming athlete who presents with pain should follow several standard principles:

• **Take an athlete history.** All patients require a careful history to elicit an understanding of the demands of the sport-specific training regimen. The athlete history should help the physician gain an understanding of training load because many of the injuries sustained within this population will be because of repetitive overuse. They may present as a picture of tendonitis, bursitis, impingement, or muscle imbalance because of fatigue from overtraining.

• **Perform a shoulder-specific exam.** The shoulder-specific exam should focus on range of motion, muscle balance and imbalance, scapulothoracic motion, and laxity. Throughout the course of a season, the competitive swimmer performs nearly 500,000 strokes with each arm (Richardson, Jobe, and Collins 1980). This workload predisposes the athlete to repetitive overuse injuries of the upper extremity.

- **Evaluate the core of the body.** Comprehensive evaluation should always include trunk strength, core stability, and flexibility (Heinlein and Cosgarea 2010) because deficits in core strength and stability are known to contribute to injuries further along the kinetic chain (e.g., shoulder).

- **Understand and evaluate the stroke mechanics.** Although not every physician will have in-depth knowledge of swimming technique, watching video of the swimmer with the athlete and coach will help give an understanding of the underlying injury mechanisms.

Shoulder Injuries

The most common musculoskeletal complaint in swimmers is shoulder pain. The repetitive overhead motion of the swimming stroke predisposes the shoulder to overuse injury and pain. Several underlying anatomic factors can increase the risk of the development of shoulder pain. Shoulder motion, strength, and stability all depend on the function of numerous muscles around the shoulder girdle, including the rotator cuff and muscles around the upper back and scapula (shoulder blade). Several factors should be considered in the evaluation of shoulder pain in the swimmer.

Overuse Injuries of the Shoulder

Muscle fatigue and dysfunction that arise because of the demands of swimming stroke mechanics can lead to overuse injuries, specifically of the shoulder girdle. Among elite-level athletes, the literature reports the prevalence of shoulder pain to be as high as 80 percent (Brushoj et al. 2007). During both freestyle and butterfly stokes, the pectoralis major, latissimus dorsi, and serratus anterior muscles are responsible for the pull-through, or propulsive phase of the stroke (Heinlein and Cosgarea 2010). The subscapularis and teres minor muscles are also active throughout most of the pull-through phase and thus are prone to fatigue (Pink and Tibone 2000; Heinlein and Cosgarea 2010). As these muscle units fatigue, they become more susceptible to injury and shoulder kinematics can be adversely affected. The rotator cuff consists of four muscles (supraspinatus, infraspinatus, subscapularis, and teres minor) and provides stability to the shoulder girdle. Because of the demands placed on the glenohumeral joint during the swimming stroke, the rotator cuff plays a major role in stabilizing the humeral head in the glenoid (shoulder socket) and avoiding impingement of the rotator cuff tendons. When fatigued, the rotator cuff complex is unable to function normally and the athlete may alter stroke mechanics because of pain.

The condition known as swimmer's shoulder was first described by Kennedy and Hawkins as a "common painful syndrome of repeated shoulder impingement in swimmers" (Kennedy and Hawkins 1974; Sein et al. 2010). The complaint expressed by swimmers is often one of vague pain around the front of the shoulder that may be difficult to define specifically, making diagnosis challenging. But the treatment algorithm remains the same, centered on an extensive course of conservative therapy that focuses on strengthening the rotator cuff and periscapular muscles in addition to addressing improper stroke mechanics.

Shoulder Laxity

Shoulder function depends on a delicate balance of mobility and stability. Stability of the shoulder joint should provide a balance for proper joint mechanics, but in the case of competitive swimmers, an element of laxity may prove beneficial for improved stroke mechanics. Shoulder stability is provided by the capsule (static stabilizers) and rotator cuff musculature (dynamic stabilizers), which act in combination to provide shoulder stability during overhead activity. An imbalance because of excessive shoulder joint laxity can lead to rotator cuff overload, fatigue, and subsequent injury. Many studies have documented the presence of underlying shoulder laxity among both competitive and recreational swimmers (Brushoj et al. 2007; McMaster, Roberts, and Stoddard 1998; Zemek and Magee 1996; Bak and Fauno 1997).

There is a fine line between normal shoulder laxity and abnormal or pathologic shoulder instability. Many swimmers and other overhead athletes may have elements of both inherent and acquired laxity because of the demands of training, and after a threshold is reached, instability may prevail, predisposing the athlete to injury (McMaster, Roberts, and Stoddard 1998; Zemek and Magee 1996; Bak and Fauno 1997). The pattern of instability might be either anteroinferior (in which the humeral head moves excessively forward) or multidirectional. The condition must be assessed on an individual basis. The most challenging aspect for the treating physician is differentiating between normal laxity and abnormal instability in this population.

Impingement

Swimmers, like other overhead athletes, can present with typical symptoms of impingement of the rotator cuff tendons because of altered stroke mechanics (Rodeo 2004). Impingement on the top surface of the rotator cuff tendons by the overlying acromial bone can occur with forward flexion and internal rotation in the recovery phase of the stroke. Impingement can also occur between the biceps tendon or deep surface of the rotator cuff and the glenoid and labrum with the arm in forward flexion, adduction, and internal rotation during hand entry in freestyle and butterfly.

Less commonly, impingement can occur in swimmers between the coracoid bone in the front of the shoulder and the subscapularis tendon. The provocative position is usually forward flexion, adduction, and internal rotation where the coracoid process may impinge on the underlying subscapularis tendon and lesser tuberosity of the humerus. Each of these specific types of impingement can be exacerbated by excessive joint laxity and altered stroke mechanics because of overload and muscle fatigue.

Jobe, Kvitne, and Giangarra (1989) hypothesized that repetitive overhead activity can lead to chronic microtraumatic injury to the shoulder capsule and subsequent laxity. This condition may cause stretching of the capsular structures and subsequent mechanical impingement (Sein et al. 2010). Although the evidence in the literature to support this hypothesis is incomplete, the possibility brings to light the integral relationship between repetitive activity and subsequent injury.

Os Acromiale Stress Reaction

A much less commonly reported cause of shoulder pain in the competitive swimmer is a stress fracture in the acromion ("os acromiale"). Bedi and Rodeo (2009) reported on a case of a collegiate swimmer who presented with insidious onset of shoulder pain in the nondominant arm without a history of instability or trauma. Her initial diagnosis was "swimmer's shoulder," and symptoms recurred immediately after she returned to competitive swimming after a course of physical therapy and rest. Her exam was consistent with impingement and showed no evidence of instability. Further workup including cross-sectional MRI imaging revealed an os acromiale with inflammation at the site of the stress fracture. Given the failure of conservative treatment and her desire to return to competitive swimming, the swimmer elected to undergo surgical stabilization. She was able to return to competition five months after surgery with complete resolution of her symptoms. Despite this relatively rare case of shoulder pain, it must be considered in the workup and diagnosis of a swimmer who presents with shoulder pain.

Spine Injuries

Low-back pain is another common complaint among swimmers. The muscles of the trunk and lower back are continuously active to maintain posture in the water during swimming. Similar to the muscles of the shoulder, the major muscles around the back and spine play a critical role in providing spinal stability. Overuse and fatigue of these muscles can lead to back pain. Back pain can arise from several sources.

Spondylolysis

Hyperextension forces in strokes such as butterfly and breaststroke can lead to overuse injuries and pain. Despite the fact that swimming is often a recommended form of exercise for patients with low-back pain, competitive swimmers may present with complaints of pain because of their level of training intensity and repetition. Often, the specific cause of the low-back pain may not be elucidated. Nyska et al. (2000) reported on four elite adolescent swimmers with low-back pain who were diagnosed with a stress reaction of the spinal vertebra (spondylolysis). Three of the patients were butterfly or breaststroke swimmers. Treatment consisted of activity modification and bracing with complete resolution of symptoms and return to swimming.

Lumbar Disk Disease

Lumbar intervertebral disk degeneration is another potential cause of low-back pain in elite swimmers. In a study of the Japanese national swimming team, 25 percent of the elite swimmers had symptoms associated with low-back pain (Katayama et al. 2000). Kaneoka et al. (2007) conducted a case control study that examined the prevalence of lumbar disk degeneration among elite swimmers. They found that 68 percent of the elite swimmers had degenerative disks at various levels compared with 29 percent of recreational swimming controls. The prevalence was highest in the lower lumbar spine at the L5–S1 level (Kaneoka et al. 2007). Risk factors that may predispose to low-back pain in swimmers include an increase in swimming volume, weight training, stroke mechanics, and swimming training devices such as fins, kickboards, and pull-buoys that may lead to excessive hyperextension of the lumbar spine (Nyska et al. 2000).

Knee Injuries

Knee problems are less commonly caused by swimming. Knee pain by itself, however, is rather common in athletic people, especially young females. Thus, although the pain may not be caused by swimming per se, knee pain may be reported by the swimmer.

Pain on the inner (medial) side of the knee can be a common complaint among competitive swimmers, usually breaststrokers. Kennedy, Hawkins, and Krissof (1978) reported on a cohort of Canadian swimmers in 1978 and found that knee pain occurred in 27 percent and that over 70 percent of that subgroup consisted of breaststroke swimmers (Rodeo 1999). Knee pain, like other injuries in this population, is most often associated with repetitive overuse. The mechanics of the breaststroke kick place tremendous loads on the knee. Hydrodynamic forces can add to the cumulative stress and lead to injury. Rovere and Nichols (1985) reported that knee pain in breaststrokers was related to the number of years of training and training volume in addition to increasing age and caliber of swimmers (Rodeo 1999).

The patellofemoral joint (kneecap) is also exposed to abnormal repetitive loads during swimming training. Pain arising from the patellar area can be due to an imbalance in muscle strength about the knee or poor stroke and kick mechanics. Increased patellofemoral contact stresses are generated during wall push-off and repetitive quadriceps muscle contraction with the flutter kick (Rodeo 1999).

Several intrinsic factors must also be considered in the evaluation of a swimmer with anterior knee pain such as generalized ligamentous laxity and knee hyperextension ("genu recurvatum") (Rodeo 1999).

Less Common Injuries in Swimmers

As discussed earlier, shoulder pain is common in swimmers. Although the most common cause appears to be rotator cuff muscle fatigue and overload with resultant secondary impingement, other causes should be considered. Sometimes shoulder pain in swimmers is accompanied by paresthesias (numbness and tingling) in the hand and fingers. Although shoulder instability can sometimes be associated with such symptoms, other diagnoses should be considered.

Upper-Extremity Venous Obstruction

Vogel and Jensen (1985) have described a case report of "effort" thrombosis (blood clot) of the subclavian vein in a competitive butterfly swimmer. This presentation of shoulder and arm pain in a swimmer is extremely unusual. The typical incidence seems to be young, physically active male patients. Symptoms may be subtle at presentation. They are exacerbated by activity and are generally resolved after a period of rest. Venography is required for confirmatory diagnosis.

Sanders and Rao (2007) presented a case series of six patients with obstruction of the axillary vein by the pectoralis minor muscle in the front of the shoulder. All patients presented with symptoms of arm swelling and pain, as well as weakness, numbness, and tingling in the arm and hand because of decreased blood flow to the arm. Symptoms resolved after surgical release of the pectoralis minor muscle. Despite the fact that none of the patients in this case series were swimmers, the senior author has seen this in a swimmer. The diagnosis of either axillary or subclavian vein obstruction must be considered in patients presenting with neurovascular symptoms, possibly because of repetitive overhead use of the arms or overuse syndromes.

Rib Stress Fractures/Slipping Rib Syndrome

Rib stress fractures have been described in elite rowers, but Taimela, Kujala, and Orava (1995) have also presented a case of two consecutive rib stress fractures in a female competitive swimmer. No trauma preceded either of the fractures, 15 months apart, so stroke biomechanics and her training regimen were believed to be responsible for the injury. With accurate diagnosis, the rest period for healing and recovery can be short and the athlete can return to competition in a timely fashion.

Another uncommon but reported injury pattern in competitive swimming is the slipping rib syndrome described by Udermann et al. (2005). Slipping rib syndrome has been described as hypermobility of the anterior ends of the false rib costal cartilages, which may lead to slipping of the affected rib under the adjacent superior rib (Gregory, Biswas, and Batt 2002). A case report describes a 20-year-old competitive female swimmer who presented with anterior rib cage pain during a warm-up. There was no history of trauma. After nine months of failed conservative treatment, multiple imaging studies and specific physical exam findings verified the diagnosis. The swimmer successfully returned to competition after surgical intervention.

Thoracic Outlet Syndrome

Although less common, thoracic outlet syndrome should be considered in the evaluation and diagnosis of shoulder pain among competitive swimmers. Thoracic outlet syndrome refers to compression of the nerves and blood vessels in the region between the neck and arm. This condition can occur because of a combination of shoulder laxity and changes in shoulder girdle mechanics and posture. It presents as pain, numbness, and tingling in the shoulder and arm. Several studies have described cases of neurogenic thoracic outlet syndrome in this population (Richardson 1999; Katirji and Hardy 1995; Fraxino de Almeida and Meyer 2007). Freestyle, butterfly, and backstroke all involve significant force for pull-through at the extremes of arm abduction, placing the arm in a precarious overhead position (Richardson 1999). The result may be compression of the neurovascular structures in the neck and near the first rib. Neurogenic thoracic outlet syndrome typically affects the nerve roots of the lower cervical spine, most commonly C8 and T1, because of anatomic positioning. Symptoms of thoracic outlet syndrome can be either neurogenic, vascular, or less commonly, both. They may consist of the inability to keep the fingers together during the pull-through phase of the stroke because of weakness of the intrinsic muscles in the hand or coolness and pain in the upper extremity.

An association between multidirectional instability of the shoulder and the development of thoracic outlet syndrome has recently been recognized. Competitive swimmers often possess some degree of shoulder laxity, which may alter the anatomical relationship between the joint and neurovascular structures of the neck and arm during the extremes of shoulder motion. The presence of thoracic outlet syndrome may be missed in patients with multidirectional instability, so accurate evaluation and diagnosis is crucial when treating this population (Schenk and Brems 1998).

Sternoclavicular Joint Subluxation

The sternoclavicular joint, where the inner end of the clavicle connects to the sternum (breastbone), is the primary connection between the shoulder girdle and the axial skeleton. With the involvement of the shoulder in the biomechanics of the swimming stroke, the sternoclavicular joint may be susceptible to the same overuse and repetitive use injuries that the glenohumeral joint is prone to with swimming training. Sternoclavicular joint subluxation (partial dislocation) is uncommon, but it has been described in the literature among competitive swimmers. Echlin and Michaelson (2006) present a case report of a 14-year-old competitive butterfly swimmer with bilateral subluxing sternoclavicular joints without a history of antecedent trauma. In this case, as in most others presenting with atraumatic subluxation, the patient's exam also revealed generalized joint hypermobility and laxity.

Exertional Compartment Syndrome of the Forearm

A rare cause of pain and numbness in the hand and arm that has recently been reported in a swimmer is exertional compartment syndrome of the forearm that required surgical release (Seiler et al. 2011). Compartment syndrome results from increased pressure in a muscle group because of incomplete venous outflow from the muscle during exercise, leading to pain. The patient was a 19-year-old collegiate swimmer with forearm pain, tightness, and hand numbness that occurred during swimming. The diagnosis was verified by elevated muscle compartment pressures, and the patient returned to competitive swimming after surgical release of the fascia around the muscle compartment.

Injury Prevention in Swimming

The most important factor in the management of musculoskeletal injuries in swimming is prevention. A comprehensive program of appropriate stretching, strengthening, endurance training, development of muscle balance and proprioception, and instruction on stroke-specific mechanics should form the foundation of the training regimen for competitive swimmers. Because overuse injury is the most prevalent etiology of musculoskeletal pain among this population, careful monitoring of training volume and duration by coaches and physicians will help minimize repetitive use injuries and identify athletes at risk. Specific training regimens should focus on rotator cuff strengthening and scapular stabilization exercises in addition to a core stabilization program to address deficiencies in low-back, abdominal, and pelvic muscle strength. Evaluation of stroke mechanics allows the identification of imbalances and weaknesses that may predispose a swimmer to overuse injury. Instruction on proper mechanics will improve performance and help prevent injury.

Summary

Because of the high demands of training, swimmers are prone to repetitive use injuries. Shoulder pain, an almost universal complaint in this population, is related to overuse and subsequent fatigue, glenohumeral laxity, and the mechanics of the swimming stroke. Swimmers can also present with complaints of low-back pain or knee pain because of the repetitive stress of stroke-specific mechanics. Proper evaluation will help identify the at-risk athlete and is essential in accurate diagnosis and management of musculoskeletal injury in the swimmer.

Physicians should also be aware of several less common injuries that have been reported in competitive swimmers, such as thoracic outlet syndrome, sternoclavicular joint subluxation, proximal vascular obstruction due to muscle hypertrophy or cervical ribs, and stress reactions of the acromion and ribs. Knowledge of these conditions will assist in comprehensive evaluation, work-up, and management of swimming athletes. Prevention of such injuries is critical in keeping these athletes in the water and avoiding lost time in training and competition.

CHAPTER 19

Sports Medicine: Illnesses and General Health

—Margo Mountjoy, MD, CCFP, FCFP, Dip Sport Med

Much attention is given in aquatic sports medicine to the prevention and treatment of injuries. As any aquatic team physician knows, illness can also have a negative effect on performance as well as the overall health of the athlete. Evidence from a surveillance study on injury and illness prevalence in elite swimmers during a FINA World Championships (2009) supports this premise (Mountjoy et al. 2010b). Protection and promotion of the health of the swimmer is an important consideration for maximizing performance in the pool. Early identification of and effective intervention for medical issues is essential for the preservation of the well-being of the athlete (Mountjoy et al. 2010a).

Common health issues facing the swimmer include asthma, overtraining syndrome, iron deficiency, the female athlete triad, eating disorders, travel-related health issues, and consequences of pool chemical exposure. The aquatic team physician needs to be familiar with these conditions, proficient at implementing prevention policies, and adept at applying effective treatment regimens. Optimizing a swimmer's overall health and well-being as the swimmer attempts to achieve fast performances in the pool also requires attention to the proper nutrition and psychological training of the athlete. An effective high-performance training program must consider all these factors to optimize performance.

Role of the Aquatic Team Physician

The effective aquatic team physician has a multifaceted role in the management of illness and the promotion of general health of the athlete. This role can be broken down into three components, as highlighted in figure 19.1: performance enhancement, prevention of illnesses and injuries, and protection of the athlete.

Performance	• Illness intervention • Return-to-play guidelines • Long-term athlete development • Translation of sport science
Prevention	• Preparticipation examination • Prevention programs • Prevention research
Protection	• Antidoping • Sexual harassment and abuse • Fundamental principles of medical care

▶ **Figure 19.1** The role of the aquatic team physician in promoting performance and athlete health.

Performance

The swimmer's performance in the pool can be enhanced by many factors including specialized training, expert coaching, and a sophisticated nutritional program. The swimmer's performance also will be enhanced by a team physician who responds efficiently and effectively to health issues, employs evidence-based return-to-play guidelines, and takes a long-term athlete development perspective when developing an appropriate performance and illness and injury prevention program. A team physician can assist by translating the latest sport science and sports medicine into practical advice for the coach and swimmer. Let's look at each of these in more detail.

Effective Illness Intervention

A swimmer with an acute illness can benefit from proficient intervention by a team physician. The team physician should be readily accessible so that the swimmer can access medical care expediently. Medical intervention with appropriate investigations and effective treatments derived from evidence-based guidelines will expedite recovery, minimize time lost from the pool, and maximize the health of the athlete.

Return-to-Play Guidelines

The swimmer who returns to training before recovering fully from an illness or injury is vulnerable to relapse and recurrence of the original illness. This typically results in longer absences from training, frustration for the athlete and coach, interference with performance, and potentially even further health compromise. The aquatic team physician can minimize this risk to the athlete by ensuring that evidence-based return-to-play guidelines are followed. A graduated return-to-swimming program with a stepwise progression of both endurance and intensity will help prevent relapse. During this time of recovery and reintegration to full training, regular medical reviews to evaluate progress facilitates the successful return to sport. Involving the coach and trainer in the return-to-swimming planning following illness will help to ensure compliance and increase the understanding of all the members of the athlete's high-performance team. Keep in mind that the specific return-to-swimming guidelines depend on the illness or injury encountered by the athlete. The best course of action is to consult with the team physician so that all parties (coaches, parents, athletes, agents, and so on) are aware of the appropriate course of action.

Long-Term Athlete Development Program

All successful swimmers were once developing child athletes. An aquatic champion is one who underwent a carefully planned, safe, age-appropriate sport development program. The child athlete has unique physical, psychological, and social needs depending on the stage of maturation and development. Training programs should take into account the structures in the body that are vulnerable to injury in a developing athlete: articular cartilages, bone structures, growth plates, and other areas where a disparity is present in the rate of growth between bone and soft tissues. Scientific guidelines for aerobic, anaerobic, and strength training of the child athlete should be followed when developing the training program for the youth swimmer.

The psychological training of the youth swimmer is also an integral component of the long-term athlete development model. Similar to the physical training requirements, the psychological training program varies depending on the stage of maturity. This training is different from the psychological training of the mature athlete. In addition, the youth athlete has distinctive hydration requirements that differ from those of the mature swimmer. Attention must be directed to those needs to avoid medical issues related to dehydration. In addition, provisions in the nutritional program of the youth athlete must ensure adequate intake of energy and the micro- and macronutrients required to meet the demands of growth, health maintenance, and exercise. Read more about age-appropriate physical, physiological, and psychological training in chapter 17. The aquatic team physician can play an integral role in helping the coaching staff design appropriate training programs for the developing child swimmer (Mountjoy et al. 2008).

Translation of Sport Science Knowledge

Considerable advances continue to be made in aquatic sport science and medicine, advances that have the potential to aid in swimming performance. The team physician can assist the coach by translating this science into practical advice to guide the training programs for the elite aquatic athlete both in and out of the water.

Sports Medicine Team

Take the time to identify a sports medicine team in your area, which can include a general practitioner, physical therapist, and orthopedist. Identify professionals before you need them so that when a need arises you can quickly connect them to the athlete. When searching for the right team physician, consider the following:

- Ask around and find someone who has delivered quality care to swimmers in the past.

- Find someone who is familiar with the demands of elite sport, preferably someone who has experience with swimming. This person will be better able to optimize the goals of the athlete, taking into consideration your goals as a coach and the medical provider's goals of restoring the athlete to health.

- Encourage this person to get involved with the team, perhaps by attending workouts; giving presentations to coaches, athletes, and their parents; or even traveling with the team to selected events.

Prevention

Besides enhancing performance through the early and effective management of health issues in the swimmer, the team doctor also has a role in the care of the elite swimmer to prevent the occurrence of those issues. Prevention principles implemented by the aquatic team physician will lead to better overall athlete health, a decrease in illness rate, a decrease in loss of time from training, and ultimately faster swimming.

Preparticipation Examination

One of the most important opportunities for the sports physician to prevent illness in athletes is the preparticipation examination (PPE). The PPE should be mandatory for all elite swimmers. The purpose of the PPE is to identify athletes whose health may be at risk from sport participation. An example would be the identification of risk conditions for sudden cardiac death such as arrythmogenic right ventricular cardiomyopathy, coronary artery abnormalities, or hypertrophic cardiomyopathy (Corrado et al. 2006). The PPE also identifies athletes who may have health conditions that affect performance, such as early iron deficiency anemia, but have not yet shown overt clinical signs. The PPE provides the team physician the opportunity to ensure that the athlete is receiving appropriate care for ongoing current medical illness such as asthma. The PPE also helps develop the athlete–physician relationship. Finally, the PPE enables the physician to reinforce the antidoping culture of the team.

The PPE should be performed on an individual basis during the off-season so that appropriate interventions can occur in sufficient time before the competitive season. In addition to screening for common injuries seen in swimmers, the aquatic-specific PPE should assess for the presence of asthma, complications from prolonged water or chlorine exposure (irritation of the eye such as conjunctivitis or ear infection), iron deficiency anemia, the female athlete triad (defined later in the chapter), and eating disorders.

To complement the medical component of the PPE, the examination should include an assessment of the athlete's strength, flexibility, body composition, nutritional status, and psychological health. These assessments will help identify any current or potential health issues that could affect training and performance. Periodic examinations throughout the training season offer the opportunity for monitoring and the early identification of health issues (Ljungqvist et al. 2009).

The PPE should serve to determine whether any risks or underlying health issues need to be addressed or otherwise known when determining whether an athlete is healthy enough to engage in a rigorous training program. A PPE should include information from the following areas:

- Medical history documenting past illnesses, allergies, and injuries
- Family history of illnesses and injuries that could provide evidence of increased risk in certain areas
- Comprehensive physical exam
- Sign-off from the physician indicating that the athlete is cleared to participate in sport

Most physicians have their own PPE forms, but a sample form can be found at www.olympic.org/Documents/Commissions_PDFfiles/Medical_commission/Athlete_PHE_form.pdf.

Prevention Programs

An effective aquatic team physician not only reacts to health issues as they arise but also implements prevention programs to prevent health issues before they occur. To complement the prevention programs for injuries discussed elsewhere in this book, the team physician should implement prevention programs for illnesses specific to athletes' ages, athletic level, and gender. In particular, the team doctor, working in conjunction with other sport science professionals such as a sport nutritionist and sport psychologist can implement appropriate nutritional and body image programs for adolescent female athletes to help prevent the development of the female athlete triad or eating disorders (International Olympic Committee 2005; Mountjoy 2008; Nattiv et al. 2007). A balanced nutritional program also helps prevent the development of iron deficiency anemia and deficiencies in other micronutrients such as calcium and vitamin D (Peeling et al. 2008).

During the influenza season and when the team is traveling, the team physician should implement a preventative hygiene educational program for swimmers to decrease the transmission of influenzas or gastroenteritis on the team (Spence et al. 2007). Finally, some athletes on the team may benefit from the implementation of a stress-management program in cooperation with the team sport psychologist to help them cope with the pressures of high-level training and competition.

Prevention Research

An important aspect of improving the performance of aquatic athletes is the application of scientifically valid prevention intervention programs. To determine effective prevention interventions, first ascertain the prevalence of the health issue and the causative factors (van Mechelen, Hlobil, and Kemper 1992). Although little illness surveillance data has been published about aquatic athletes, one study completed at the 2009 FINA World Championships (Aquatics) showed that more illnesses than injuries occurred in elite swimmers during the course of the championships (Mountjoy et al. 2010b). Swimmers suffered more illnesses in comparison with the other aquatic disciplines of diving, water polo, synchronized swimming, and open-water swimming. Analysis of the injury surveillance data guides the development of prevention programs that can potentially decrease illness in the future. The aquatic team physician can become involved by participating in or conducting prevention research projects and by applying the results of published scientific data on illness prevention in his aquatic sports medicine practice. According to van Mechelen et al. (1992), the first step to preventing injuries is to conduct surveillance studies to determine the prevalence and cause of the injury (figure 19.2).

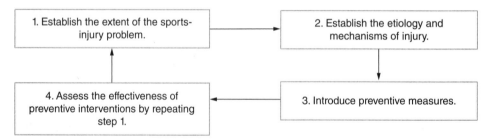

▶ **Figure 19.2** Injury prevention model.

Protection

The third component of the role of the aquatic sports physician is one of protection. An important but less commonly recognized role for the team physician is to educate and protect athletes from other threats to their health. This includes educating athletes about the risks of performance-enhancing substances and about recognizing and avoiding sexual abuse.

Antidoping

The team physician is responsible for protecting not only the health of the athlete but also the integrity of the sport. These goals can be accomplished by observing and promoting the principles of antidoping in sport as outlined in the World

Anti-Doping Agency (WADA) Code (World Anti-Doping Agency 2015). Using prohibited substances and methods is harmful not only to the health of the athlete but also to the integrity of sport. The team physician plays an integral role in protecting the athlete from doping by creating a culture of fair play in which the practice of doping is unacceptable. As part of this, the team physician must be intimately aware of the rules and regulations regarding illegal and performance-enhancing medications as well as the appropriate documentation and reporting of the use of performance-enhancing medication deemed medically necessary. Evidence from public health antismoking campaigns teaches us that a cultural attitude shift to one of nonacceptance of unhealthy or unacceptable behaviors is an effective deterrent against the unhealthy behavior.

The World Anti-Doping Agency (WADA) changes the Prohibited List of Substances and Methods yearly. In addition, the testing protocols and the rules and regulations for granting permission to use prohibited substances and methods, known as Therapeutic Use Exemptions, also change regularly. The team physician should be aware of these changes and should educate swimmers as new modifications are published to encourage deterrence and to protect the athlete from inadvertent doping.

Sexual Harassment and Abuse

The aquatic team physician also can help protect swimmers from sexual harassment and abuse. Besides being aware of the signs and symptoms of sexual abuse, the team physician should have an appropriate intervention strategy should an incident arise and ensure that the team has preventative policies and codes of conduct in place, including standards of behavior for members of the athlete's entourage and support team.

Sexual harassment and abuse in sport occur in all sports and at all levels, although prevalence studies show that they occur more frequently in elite sport (International Olympic Committee 2008). Aquatic sports are not immune to this issue (Brackenridge 2008). Perpetrators more often are male than female and are always in a position of power and authority, usually as a member of the athlete's entourage or as a senior teammate. Sexual abuse in sport occurs when athlete protection is absent, perpetrator motivation is high, and athletes are highly vulnerable. Sexual abuse not only negatively affects the physical and psychological health of the athlete but also leads to impaired performance, athlete dropout, and an unhealthy sporting environment for other athletes (International Olympic Committee 2008).

Fundamental Ethical Principles of Medical Care

The final component of the aquatic team physician's role in protecting the general health of the athlete relates to the actual level of the physician's ethical standard of medical care. All actions of the aquatic team physician should be guided by the fundamental principles outlined in the FINA Sports Medicine Rules, which can be found at www.fina.org/H2O/docs/rules/FINAmedicalrules_20132017.

pdf. These rules are based on the Olympic Movement Medical Code (OMMC), which can be found at www.olympic.org/PageFiles/61597/Olympic_Movement_Medical_Code_eng.pdf. The OMMC serves as an ethical guideline for the protection of the health of the elite athlete. The OMMC reviews the intricacies of the unique relationship between athletes and their health care providers. The athlete's rights to informed consent, confidentiality, and freedom of choice in medical care are emphasized. The team physician's obligation to practice evidence-based ethical medicine, treat athletes with dignity, and alleviate unnecessary suffering is highlighted. The OMMC reviews the unique principles for the protection and promotion of the athlete's health during training and competition. Adhering to these ethical guidelines serves to ensure that the athlete receives appropriate and effective care, which will result in protecting the health of the athlete and subsequently in promoting better performance in the pool.

Swimming-Specific Health Issues

The illnesses and injuries common to swimmers are considered in detail in this section. Specific interventions or prevention strategies can be employed to promote health and enhance performance.

Asthma

During the 2008 Beijing Olympic Games, swimming had the third highest incidence of asthma in comparison with all summer sports. The incidence of asthma was 19.1 percent in swimming, coming in behind triathlon at 25.7 percent and synchronized swimming at 21.2 percent. In contrast, the overall incidence of asthma at the Olympic Games was 7.2 percent. The high incidence of asthma in swimming can be attributed to the chronic exposure of the lungs to environmental irritants while breathing deeply and rapidly during endurance training. In addition, the exposure of the lungs to chloramines, a by-product of the chemicals used in pool water, has been implicated as a causative factor for the development of asthma in swimming (Fitch et al. 2008). Evidence shows that on retirement from competitive swimming, the asthmatic swimmer can achieve partial reversibility of the airway obstruction (Helenius et al. 2002).

The swimmer with asthma may present with bronchospasm, chronic cough, or chest tightness with performance. The athlete may reveal a history of childhood atopy or allergy. Although the physical examination is often normal, there may be evidence of bronchospasm. Radiographic evaluation is often normal. Spirometry (FEV1) measured both before and after bronchodilator challenge may show reversibility of airway obstruction. In the absence of airway obstruction, bronchial provocation tests may be conducted to identify airway hyperresponsiveness. Substances used in the bronchial provocation tests may include methacholine, mannitol, hyperosmolar saline, and histamine. Eucapnic voluntary hyperpnea and a controlled exercise challenge may also be used to induce bronchospasm to facilitate the diagnosis of asthma (Helenius et al. 2002).

Pulmonary Function Testing (PFT)

A large percentage of swimmers experience exercise-induced asthma or bronchospasm because of the harsh effects of swimming in a chlorine-rich environment. As such, these athletes could likely benefit from using asthma medications. Many of these medications, however, are banned by U.S. and international antidoping agencies as performance-enhancing drugs. Even so, athletes can take these medications if they truly have asthma. To document this, an athlete can undergo a pulmonary function test (PFT) that measures lung volume before and after exercise and documents any arising airway restrictions. The athlete must then file a Therapeutic Use Exemption (TUE) form, signed by the testing physician, with the U.S. Anti-Doping Agency (USADA) to request use of these medications. Information on TUEs can be found on the USADA website at www.usada.org/substances/tue/.

The treatment of asthma in the swimmer is based on the same treatment principles used for the nonathlete. Attention should be given to decreasing environmental allergens, improving education, and treating comorbidities such as gastroesophageal reflux disorder. Exercise in environments with poor air quality or extreme heat or cold should be avoided. Because of the chronicity of asthma and its varying course over time, pharmacotherapy should be individualized for each athlete. Reassessment at regular intervals is recommended. The cornerstone of pharmacotherapy is the regular use of inhaled glucocorticosteroids and the use of fast-acting beta-2 agonists for treatment of breakthrough symptoms. Fast-acting beta-2 agonists are also indicated for pretreatment for the prevention of exercise-induced bronchospasm. Leukotriene antagonists and long-acting beta-2 agonists may be useful adjuncts in more severe cases. The swimmer who is well controlled should have an absence or minimum of day and night symptoms and no limitation on exercise. Athletes who are not well controlled may have been misdiagnosed, may be receiving incorrect treatment, may not be complying with the treatment plan, or may have uncontrolled exposure to exacerbating factors (Fitch et al. 2008).

The aquatic team physician should be aware of the latest WADA requirements for Therapeutic Use Exemptions for asthma medications because both beta-2 agonists and glucocorticosteroids are on the WADA Prohibited List (World Anti-Doping Agency 2013). These requirements change regularly, so the health care provider needs to stay abreast of these changes by regularly accessing the USADA and WADA websites. Large-scale changes to the antidoping code typically are voted on late in the calendar year and then take effect on January 1 of the following year.

Female Athlete Triad

The female athlete triad refers to "the interrelationships among energy availability, menstrual function, and bone mineral density, which may have clinical manifestations including eating disorders, functional hypothalamic amenorrhea, and osteoporosis" (Nattiv et al. 2007). Energy availability is defined as the dietary energy intake minus exercise energy expenditure. The female swimmer runs into difficulty when the energy expenditure exceeds the energy intake through a clinical eating disorder, disordered eating, or excessive exercise. In response to the energy deficit, the hypothalamus suppresses hormonal function, which results in a variety of menstrual disturbances ranging on a continuum from eumenorrhea to amenorrhea. Subsequently, bone health is affected, ranging from suboptimal bone density to osteoporosis (figure 19.3). Stress fractures are more likely to occur in the athlete with a menstrual disturbance or with low bone mineral density (Bennell et al. 1999; Torstveit and Sundgot-Borgen 2005).

Because swimming is an endurance sport and a sport in which the athletes' bodies are on display, body image issues may make female swimmers vulnerable to the development of the female athlete triad (Sundgot-Borgen and Torstveit 2004).

The treatment of the female athlete triad requires a team approach that includes the team physician, a sport nutritionist, and a sport psychologist. Restoration of menstrual function through the correction of energy balance is essential in the treatment of menstrual disturbances and decreased bone density.

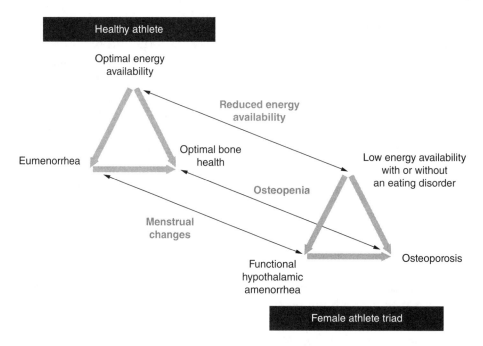

▶ **Figure 19.3** The female athlete triad model. Narrow arrows indicate energy availability, menstrual function, and bone mineral density along a continuum. The athlete travels along each continuum depending on diet and exercise habits. Thick arrows indicate the effects on bone mineral density by energy availability and menstrual function.

Reprinted, by permission, from M. Mountjoy, 2009, "Injuries and medical issues in synchronized Olympic sports," *Current Sports Medicine Reports* 8(5): 255–261. Adapted, by permission, from A. Nattiv, A.B. Loucks, M.M. Manore, et al., 2007, "American College of Sports Medicine position stand: The female athlete triad," *Medicine & Science in Sports & Exercise* 39(10): 1867–1882.

This goal is accomplished by increasing nutritional intake or decreasing energy expenditures (Drinkwater et al. 1986). Athletes with disordered eating or clinical eating disorders require more specific treatment interventions. Nutritional counseling should ensure the availability of macro- and micronutrients (calcium, vitamin D, and vitamin K) required for the restoration of bone health. Athletes have higher protein needs than nonathletes (Nattiv et al. 2007). Early intervention has been shown to be effective in preventing the development of more serious symptoms (Kohrt et al. 2004).

Eating Disorders and Disordered Eating

Disordered eating is defined as various abnormal eating behaviors, including restrictive eating, fasting, frequent skipping of meals, overeating, binge eating followed by purging (vomiting), and using diet pills, laxatives, diuretics, or enemas (Nattiv et al. 2007). An eating disorder is a clinical mental disorder defined by criteria outlined in *Diagnostic and Statistical Manual-V* (*DSM-V TR*) and needs to be addressed by a team of qualified and experienced professionals including the team physician, a sports nutritionist, a sport psychologist or psychiatrist, and the coach (Sanborn et al. 2000). Eating disorders are characterized by abnormal eating patterns that often are focused on altered body image, irrational fear of weight gain, and attempts at weight loss (Nattiv et al. 2007). There are three classifications of eating disorders (American Psychiatric Association 2000):

1. Anorexia nervosa (AN) is characterized by restrictive eating behaviors and low body weight.
2. Bulimia nervosa (BN) is characterized by overeating followed by purging.
3. Eating disorders not otherwise specified is used for athletes who do not fully meet the criteria for AN or BN.

The prevalence of eating disorders in sport is greater in female athletes than in male athletes, and it is higher in sport (15 to 31 percent) than in the general population (5 to 13 percent). Again, because swimming is an endurance sport in which body image is important, swimmers are at particular risk for the development of eating disorders (Sundgot-Borgen and Torstveit 2004). Abnormal eating behaviors can potentially be identified in the swimmer by a trained professional during the PPE (Ljungqvist et al. 2009). The physical examination of the swimmer identified by history as being at risk for an eating disorder should be focused on looking for secondary signs of eating disorders, which often are absent in the early stages of the illness (Rumall and Lebrun 2004). Laboratory evaluation should include a complete blood count (CBC), a chemistry profile, and a hormone profile. A 12-lead ECG will help identify athletes at risk for a potential lethal cardiac arrhythmia such as bradycardia or ECG changes induced by electrolyte disturbance. Bone mineral density should be considered for the amenorrheic athlete to assess bone health, and a nutritional analysis is helpful to ascertain the status of macro- and micronutrients (Ljungqvist et al. 2009).

A number of self-reporting tools can be used to identify eating disorders in athletes, including the Eating Disorder Inventory (EDI) (Garner 2004), Eating Disorder Examination-Questionnaire (EDE-Q) (Carter, Steward, and Fairburn 2001), Eating Disorder Screen for Primary Care (ESP) (Cotton, Ball, and Robinson 2003), and the SCOFF Questionnaire (Luck et al. 2002). The accuracy of any screening can be further enhanced by including a clinical interview session following the self-reporting questionnaire (Beals 2003). Swimming coaches should not administer these tools as part of their coaching. But coaches should be aware of the warning signs accompanying eating disorders and disordered eating (figure 19.4) so that they can involve a professional should a need arise in this area.

The first clinical decision should be to ascertain the risk of life-threatening conditions associated with eating disorders, conditions that may require emergency hospitalization and would preclude a return to swimming, such as cardiac arrhythmias, electrolyte disturbances, suicide risk, hypotension, or significant weight loss (Yager 2007). The treatment plan for the swimmer with an eating disorder should include psychotherapy and nutritional counselling. Pharmacotherapy may be used as an adjunct to psychotherapy for the treatment of eating disorders and should be used to treat an athlete with any comorbid psychiatric illness such as depression, anxiety, obsessive-compulsive disorder, or suicidal ideation (Yager 2007). Including the swimmer who is unable to train in team functions and meetings is beneficial in facilitating the integration of the swimmer back to sport (Thompson and Sherman 2010). Recognize that although most people think of females as the only athletes who suffer from eating disorders and body image issues, male athletes encounter these challenges as well.

Low body weight

Lanugo

Petechiae

Sub-conjunctival hemorrhages

Erosion of tooth enamel

Peripheral edema

Parotid gland swelling

Bradycardia

▶ **Figure 19.4** Physical signs of eating disorders.

Overtraining

Improvements in swimming speed result from the body's adaptation to training and competition stress. Not allowing adequate time for the body to recover from these stressors results in overtraining. In addition to these physical stresses, psychological factors play a role in the development of overtraining. Although a full discussion of overtraining and the symptoms associated with it is presented in chapter 13, some of the key points are restated here:

- The swimmer may complain of excessive fatigue, insomnia, anorexia, myalgias, mood changes, and persistent or recurrent minor illnesses.

- A thorough history and physical examination is required to rule out other causes for the symptoms.

- A comprehensive psychological screening will help identify psychological stressors both inside and outside sport that may be contributing to the athlete's stress. Although there is no specific or sensitive laboratory test to identify the presence of or predict recovery from overtraining, minor elevation of muscle enzymes and ECG changes may be evident on initial screening.

- The basis of therapy (and prevention of overtraining in the first place) should be ensuring that the athlete gets adequate rest and recovery from training.

- Regular assessments to monitor recovery and to support the athlete are recommended. Counseling to assist with extraneous psychological stressors may be indicated. The period of rest required for full recovery is often prolonged.

- The team physician needs to educate the athlete and the coach about the warning signs and provide support (Meeusen et al. 2013).

Iron Deficiency Anemia

Iron deficiency anemia is a common illness in female athletes. The cause of iron deficiency in female athletes is thought to be multifactorial including insufficient dietary intake, menstrual losses, hemolysis, gastrointestinal losses, sweating, and hematuria (Fallon 2004). Research by Peeling et al. (2008) suggests that the acute phase response to exercise results in a release of cytokines that stimulate the production of hepcidin, a peptide produced in the liver that is a key regulator of iron metabolism. Hepcidin has a negative effect on erythopoesis in the liver. More research is needed to define this physiological response to exercise.

Regular screening of the female athlete to track the parameters of hemoglobin, hematocrit, and serum iron and ferritin will help identify the athlete at risk for iron deficiency early, thus preventing significant morbidity and performance deficits. Nutritional counseling for female athletes should emphasize the importance of adequate iron intake to prevent iron deficiency.

Treatment of iron deficiency anemia includes the restoration of iron deficits and interventions to correct the causative factor to prevent a recurrence. These actions should be instituted under the direction of a physician. If rapid restoration of iron deficits is required because of the severity of the iron deficits or the timing of critical competitive events, consideration should be given to parenteral forms of iron replacement such as intravenous iron infusions or intramuscular injections. These routes may also be used if the athlete is intolerant of oral iron. If excessive, menstrual losses should be treated by a gynecologist to minimize the iron deficit. Close monitoring of blood parameters in the female athlete at risk is recommended.

Eye, Ear, Nose, and Throat (EENT)

The main cause of illness of the eye, ear, nose, and throat (EENT) system is chronic exposure to water during training. Otitis externa ("swimmer's ear") is caused by the overgrowth of bacteria in the ear canal from the trapping of water. The swimmer with otitis externa often complains of pain and itching in the ear canals, which can be quite severe. Using earplugs during training and instilling acetic acid drops after training are helpful in preventing this condition.

Chlorine-induced conjunctivitis is now rare because of the widespread use of goggles. Athletes who train in outdoor pools are at risk for the development of pterygium in the eye from exposure to ultraviolet light, wind, and sand. A pterygium is a benign growth of tissue that extends from the corner of the eye to the pupil. Because vision may be affected, surgical removal may be necessary (Meeusen et al. 2013).

Aquatic Dermatological Complications

Prolonged exposure of the skin to water can leave the skin prone to various infections. Tinea pedis (athlete's foot) and tinea cruris (jock itch) are caused by a fungal skin infection. Infections can be prevented by the practice of judicious drying after training and applying antifungal powders. Prerace shaving of the skin to improve speed by reducing drag can cause a bacterial folliculitis. Viral plantar verrucae are common in swimmers from exposure of the feet to the virus on the pool deck. This can be prevented by the use of deck shoes in the changing rooms, showers, and pool deck. Some athletes develop an itchy allergic urticarial rash caused by exposure to pool chemicals or cold water. This rash can be treated with oral antihistamines (Meeusen et al. 2013).

Travel Health

Besides the medical issues that can occur during training, the swimmer is vulnerable to medical issues resulting from traveling to competitive events. To minimize the risk of developing these medical issues, the aquatic team physician should be proactive in developing preventative initiatives relevant to the particular health risks of the country or countries of destination. Immunization requirements vary around the world and may include tetanus, diphtheria, polio, hepatitis B and C, yellow fever, typhoid fever, and malaria prophylaxis.

Prophylactic immunization protocols for the swimmer should occur in sufficient time to ensure adequate immunity at the time of exposure at the competition or training destination. The information on the immunizations to receive is too lengthy to list here, but a team physician should be able to provide a swimmer and coach with appropriate guidelines for international travel. The coach should be sure to notify the team physician of any international travel plans well in advance in case any timing-dependent medications or immunizations must be administered. The Centers for Disease Control (CDC) maintains information on the immunizations recommended for international travel at www.cdc.gov/travel/.

The aquatic team physician also can be instrumental in educating swimmers on preventative measures in response to the environmental risks unique to the country of the event or training camp such as pollution, extremes of temperature, sun exposure, and altitude variations. Medical advice to minimize jet lag and facilitate acclimatization also can be provided by the team physician. The team physician should be proactive in arranging clean drinking water and ensuring an appropriate, familiar, and safe food supply for the team in the hotel in the country of destination. Street safety is another travel issue that should be considered in the preventative health program for the traveling swim team.

Competition Health and Infectious Disease

Swimming faster at the time of competition is what counts! Maximizing swimming performance during competition is an important component of the aquatic team physician's role. Studies have been published on the injury risks in swimming during competition from the 2008 Beijing Olympic Games (Junge et al. 2008) and during the 2009 FINA World Championships (Aquatics) (Mountjoy et al. 2010b). To date, only one study outlines the medical illnesses that occur during a competition (Mountjoy et al. 2010b). During the 2009 FINA World Championships (Aquatics), 184 acute illnesses were reported, making up 7.1 percent of all registered athletes during the championships. Thirty (16.3 percent) of these illnesses were expected to result in a time loss from sport, although no illness was expected to require more than one week's absence from sport. Although an absence of less than a week may seem like a minor illness, it would be disheartening if this period included the athlete's major competitive events.

The respiratory system accounted for approximately half of the illnesses ($n = 91$; 50.3 percent) and the gastrointestinal system accounted for a fifth ($n = 36$; 19.9 percent). The most frequent diagnoses affected the upper respiratory tract including otitis or middle ear inflammation (16.8 percent) and tonsillitis (9.8 percent). The most commonly reported symptom was pain, and the cause was classed as infection (49.2 percent) or environmental (27.6 percent) (Mountjoy et al. 2010b). A prospective study on upper respiratory tract infections (URIs) in athletes during training and competition shows that URIs are more common in elite athletes than in noncompetitive athletes. This higher rate of infection is thought to be due to the increased susceptibility to infection resulting from overtraining-induced immunosuppression and from crowding at competition venues. The data from the 2009 FINA World Championships support this latter premise because it was found that swimming had the highest illness rates in comparison with the other aquatic disciplines of diving, synchronized swimming, water polo, and open-water swimming. The higher rates were postulated to be due to the relative larger numbers of swimmers, leading to significant crowding in the warm-up and rest areas around the swimming competition venue. Ear infections are thought to be common in swimmers because of exposure of the ears to water-borne pathogens (Beck 2000). These data illustrate the importance of application of infection control principles to prevent illness in competing athletes. The aquatic team physician should instruct the athletes and support members of the athlete's entourage on infectious disease prevention practices (figure 19.5) while traveling.

Nutritional Supplements in Aquatics

The sport nutritional supplement industry is a multimillion dollar business in Western countries. Sports medicine professionals have focused increasing attention on the use of nutritional supplements. Athletes take nutritional supplements for various reasons including the promotion of adaptation to training, the promotion of recovery, the maintenance of health to reduce training interruptions because of illness or injury, and the enhancement of competitive performance.

Although the promotional materials for these products claim performance and health benefits, the sport science fraternity recognizes that ingestion of these products can result in harm to health and may trigger a positive doping control result. Because of the nonregulation of the nutritional supplement industry, the manufacturer has no legal responsibility to ensure the quality and purity of the supplement. In several documented cases, elite swimmers who tested positive for anabolic steroids attributed the presence of the substance in their urine to their use of nutritional supplements. These cases clearly illus-

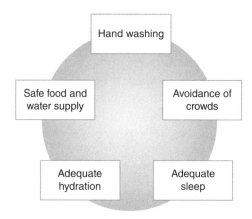

▶ **Figure 19.5** Strategies to prevent infectious disease.

trate the risk that athletes take when they consume nutritional supplements. Swimmers need to be reminded of the strict liability premise established in the World Anti-Doping Code whereby the athlete is responsible for any substance found in her biological sample. Ignorance is not an accepted excuse (World Anti-Doping Agency 2009).

Swimmers are large consumers of nutraceuticals (a food or beverage that provides health or medical benefits) as evidenced by a study of medication and nutritional supplement use during the 2003 FINA World Championships (Aquatics) in Barcelona, Spain. A retrospective analysis of 308 doping control forms was completed to identify and classify the use of declared medications and supplements during the three days before the doping control test completed at the time of competition. The results show that 176 athletes (57 percent) declared the use of a vitamin preparation, 51 athletes (17 percent) declared the use of a mineral, 80 athletes (26 percent) declared the use of a supplement, and 34 athletes (11 percent) reported the use of an herbal preparation (Pipe, Corrigan, and Mountjoy 2005).

Nutritional supplements that may have a performance effect include creatine, caffeine, bicarbonate, and beta-alanine. Creatine can increase the high-energy creatine phosphate found in muscles, leading to improvement in single or multiple sprints. Creatine may also produce gains in muscle strength or mass. No health risks have been identified with its use other than the potential increased risk for cramping and dehydration.

In small amounts (about the amount found in one cup of coffee), caffeine may improve performance in prolonged exercise and may be helpful in events of shorter duration. Larger amounts of caffeine have not been shown to be more effective and may result in unwanted side effects.

Bicarbonate is an effective buffering agent against the buildup of lactic acid in events lasting from 30 seconds to 8 minutes. Gastrointestinal discomfort is a common side effect from the use of bicarbonate. Likewise, beta-alanine has been shown to be an effective buffer for use in high-intensity events through the enhancement of muscle levels of carnosine (International Olympic Committee 2010).

Swimmers who consume a well-balanced, nutrient-rich diet should not need to use nutritional supplements. The aquatic team physician has a responsibility to educate swimmers about the risks of consuming nutritional supplements. In fact, coaches, athletes, and any health care professionals who work with athletes need to be aware of the rules and regulations about nutritional supplementation as well as the risks involved in using these substances, even those that on the surface are identified as legal.

Proper Nutrition

The swimmer's diet has a large influence on training and can affect performance. A discussion of illness and general health in the promotion of swimming faster would not be complete without attention to nutrition. Although more detailed nutritional information can be found chapter 14, several important highlights related to the health of the athlete are reviewed here:

- A swimmer's nutritional prescription should be individualized with respect to age, maturation, size, energy output, time of competitive season, and gender.
- Attention should be given to ensuring adequate energy intake to balance energy output.
- Adequate provision of carbohydrate as a fuel source and for optimizing glycogen recovery after exercise is essential in the aquatic athlete.
- Sufficient protein intake provides the necessary building blocks for muscle development and hormone and enzyme production. Protein is also essential for the repair of damaged tissues.
- Vitamins and minerals including iron, calcium, copper, manganese, magnesium, selenium, sodium, zinc, and vitamins A, C, E, B_6 and B_{12} are particularly important for athlete health.
- Appropriate hydration preexercise, during exercise, and postexercise for recovery can positively affect performance.
- For endurance swimming events or practices longer than one hour, hydration should include carbohydrate as an energy source and electrolytes to replace salt losses from sweating in addition to the replacement of fluid losses. Hydration status can be monitored by evaluating body weight pre- and postexercise. The color of the urine is another indicator of hydration status; concentrated or dark urine indicates dehydration. Urine color charts are available online. Keep in mind that these charts are helpful tools but are not foolproof. Some nutritional supplements will cause a change in urine color regardless of hydration status; any interpretations made about hydration should consider this point.

Special nutritional modifications for swimmers training or competing while fasting during the month of Ramadan should be addressed.

The youth swimmer has unique nutritional demands regarding altered thermoregulation and hydration homeostasis relative to the adult athlete. The youth swimmer must also ingest sufficient energy and nutrients to sustain growth in addition to meeting exercise demands. The young swimmer is at an impressionable stage when lifelong healthy nutritional habits and a healthy body image can be encouraged.

The female swimmer's nutritional prescription should include balanced energy intake in addition to adequate iron to replace menstrual losses and calcium to maximize bone health. Attention to healthy strategies for reducing body fat may be necessary in some female athletes. Endurance female swimmers should have a balanced energy intake to reduce the risk of developing the female athlete triad.

An important component of enhancing swimming performance during competition is careful attention to nutrition. During travel, the swimmer should maintain good hydration status. Arrangements should be made with the accommodating hotel to provide safe and high-quality food and water for the team. Swimmers can be encouraged to bring familiar snacks from home such as cereal, breakfast bars, rice cakes, crackers, pretzels, spreads, and nuts and dried fruit.

Swimmers who compete in endurance events (800 meters and longer) should pay special attention to the nutritional demands of the prolonged duration of these events. Because carbohydrate is a key source of energy, adequate intake during the six hours before the swim is advantageous. The swimmer should ensure adequate water and salt intake preevent, often finishing the last drink 60 to 90 minutes before competing. During long swims, fluid, carbohydrate, vitamin, mineral, and electrolyte replacement should occur throughout the event to ensure energy balance and replace losses through excessive sweating.

Because of the short duration of sprint events, fluid and carbohydrate levels have less influence on performance. But because of the competition structure that includes heats, semifinals, and finals and long periods between events, attention should focus on maintaining fluid and energy levels.

Psychological Health

The margin that separates athletes today is so small that a swimmer truly needs to develop a psychological edge as well as a physical edge over his competitors. A huge percentage of success can be attributed to psychological skills, because in the end, the way in which an athlete prepares mentally goes a long way to determining performance, especially at the elite level in which many athletes are working with similar levels of physical skill. The elite swimmer has to be committed and devoted to developing a psychological strategy to achieve the ultimate goal of success.

Chapter 16 focuses specifically on the development of mental skills to enhance swimming performance. Attention to the swimmer's psychological health is not only a key to physical performance but also a critical component to maintaining health. As with all people in society, the swimmer may suffer from psychological illnesses or challenges that require special attention in the team and competitive venues.

Summary

A successful elite aquatic athlete requires a complex integrated training program of sport science, psychology, and sports medicine. The aquatic team physician plays an integral role in enhancing performance, preventing illness, and protecting the athlete. Swimming faster requires attention to medical issues in the aquatic athlete. Early diagnosis and institution of effective treatments for commonly occurring medical illnesses in swimmers will help decrease time lost from training and competition. Instituting surveillance and prevention programs will help prevent many of the medical issues that face elite swimmers. The team doctor plays an integral role in collaborating with and coordinating the interventions of other members of the high-performance team, including the sport nutritionist and the sport psychologist. Promoting and protecting the health of the elite swimmer will ultimately result in faster swimming.

CHAPTER 20

Strength and Conditioning for Performance Enhancement

—Scott Riewald, PhD, CSCS

Most, if not all, of the top swimmers today engage in some sort of strength training. Not long ago swimmers and coaches debated whether strength training was beneficial or harmful to swimmers, yet today many would argue that it is an integral part of a swimmer's overall preparation strategy.

The term *strength training* is a somewhat ambiguous term in the world of swimming, and it is not necessarily synonymous with the term *dryland training*. Strength refers to a person's ability to generate or resist force. At its core, strength training centers on training against resistance, whether that resistance is found in the pool or in a weight room. The resistance underlying strength training can take various forms. One swimmer might use body weight or elastic tubing to provide the resistance, whereas another might use weight machines or devices in the pool to increase drag and apply the necessary resistance to promote strength development. All of these strength-training modalities have a place in swimming. In fact, most swimming strength-training programs provide a combination of dryland training (exercises performed out of the water) and in-water training, and each element is designed to develop a specific aspect of strength.

Besides building strength, swimmers need to develop power, or the ability to produce large forces quickly. In every race or competition, the ability to generate power comes into play. Even distance swimmers, long thought to need only muscular endurance, can benefit by adding exercises designed to improve power to their training plans.

In theory, increased strength should lead to increased ability to generate propulsive forces in the water. Although this statement makes logical sense, we need to recognize that increased dryland strength does not always lead to increased propulsive force in the water, nor does it necessarily translate to improved swimming performance. The ability to produce propulsive force in the water is a multifaceted, complex task that incorporates proper timing, technique, body position, and subtleties of hand and arm position, in addition to strength. Strength is just one of the myriad variables that contribute to performance in the pool, yet it is an important variable.

Although research has shown that it is difficult to establish strong correlations between an athlete's maximal strength and swimming performance, whether a swimmer is able to tap into her maximal strength is in many ways irrelevant. Swimmers can still benefit and improve in-water performance by participating in a well-structured strength and conditioning program, regardless of whether they are able to pull or kick harder. Although on the surface this statement may appear to be confusing or contradictory, consider the following:

- Swimmers can experience strength and flexibility imbalances, but engaging in a strength and conditioning program can restore that balance, which can help prevent injuries and reduce the number of lost or poor-quality training days. Through this mechanism alone, strength training can enhance training and performance. If nothing else, swimmers should perform foundation-focused strength training exercises to maintain proper balance throughout the body and assist in the prevention of common swimming injuries, including swimmer's shoulder.

- Even without increasing propulsive force, better muscle strength and control can help swimmers maintain better body position in the water, thus reducing drag and thereby improving performance. Maintaining better control of the body in the water can have a profound effect on performance. In chapter 1 it was shown that swimming speed can be increased by reducing resistance, so any improvement in body position should result in increased swimming velocity.

Maximal strength may not be important in swimming. Instead, swimmers may need only a necessary level of strength to succeed at the elite level. Among the myriad factors that affect performance are what could be called correlational factors, meaning that a strong correlation is present between the variable and a given performance outcome, such as swimming velocity. The assumption in this type of a relationship is that more of something is better. Alternatively, there can be what are best called threshold variables, in which a certain level is needed to achieve high-level performance. Above that threshold a poor correlation is found between increased gains in that area and performance. Kondraske (2008) has proposed the idea that a threshold relationship exists between some basic performance variables and real-world performance outcomes. He has advocated that attempts to draw strong correlation relationships may not make sense for every factor that contributes to performance. Instead, he puts forward the notion that commonalities will appear among all top performers in that they all achieve at least a baseline level of aptitude in certain critical areas. As part of the discussion on swimming performance, it is worth considering that strength may be one of those threshold variables. Although more strength is not necessarily better, swimmers may need to achieve at least a baseline level of strength to achieve peak performances at any level.

This chapter shares what the research says about strength in swimming and how it contributes to swimming performance. In addition, it looks at how the knowledge about strength training can be put to use in the development of programs to improve swimming performance and minimize the risk for injury.

Understanding the Demands of Swimming and the Potential Role of Strength and Conditioning

Training for swimmers, both in and out of the water, needs to reflect the demands of the sport and prepare the body appropriately for competition. The importance of a well-designed strength-training program comes into focus when we reflect on the physical demands of swimming. Consider the following factors that affect swim performance:

- **Demands of the stroke.** Swimming encompasses four different strokes that use, in some instances, markedly different muscle groups. Stroke-specific exercises will help build the strength, power, and flexibility needed to excel in particular events.

- **Demands of the race.** Within a given stroke, the competitive swimming events range dramatically in distance, from 50 to 1,500 meters in the pool and as far as 25 kilometers in open water events. An athlete's strength-training program needs to be adapted to the demands of the race.

- **Individuality of the athlete.** Every athlete is different in body size, shape, and physiology. Therefore, what works well as a strength program for one athlete may not be optimal for another. Strength training needs to be adapted to the individual needs and unique aspects of each swimmer to maximize performance in the pool.

- **Uniqueness of performing in water.** Swimming places demands on the core of the body that are unlike those seen in any land-based sport. Because swimmers need to generate force and propulsion by pressing against a fluid surface, they need to be even stronger and more stable through the core than athletes who compete in land-based sports. Strength training, particularly exercises done in the water, can help improve an athlete's feel for the water and improve the ability to produce propulsive force with the upper and lower body.

- **Repetitive nature of the strokes.** An elite freestyler may take between 20 and 25 stroke cycles every 50 meters. A swimmer who trains 8,000 meters per day will take between 3,200 and 4,000 stroke cycles every day. If this same swimmer trains six days a week, each arm will pull as many as 1,000,000 times over the course of a year. Although any one stroke does not cause an injury, the repetitive damage that builds up over time with each incorrect stroke can easily sideline a swimmer. Strength training can help prevent these overuse injuries from occurring.

- **Tendency for imbalances to be formed.** The repetitive nature of swimming predisposes athletes to developing strength and flexibility imbalances (McMaster 1999; Bak 2010; USA Swimming Task Force on Injury Prevention 2002; Rodeo 2004; Spiegelman 2006; Torres and Gomes 2009). Common imbalances seen in swimmers include but are not limited to the following: shoulder internal rotator strength greater than shoulder external rotator strength, trunk flexor strength greater than trunk extensor strength, glenohumeral internal rotation deficiency (GIRD) that limits the internal rotation that can be achieved in the shoulder, and hip flexor tightness that induces anterior pelvic tilt and alters body position and kicking efficiency in the water.

The preceding factors, among others, make swimming unique in the world of sport. For all those reasons, it becomes apparent that strength training is needed to prepare the body for training and competition. Note that swimming in and of itself will build strength, but only to a point. The argument can be made that the swimmer will never fully develop the strength necessary to achieve maximal performances simply by participating in the sport. In fact, not engaging in strength training to complement swimming can be detrimental to health and performance. The repetitive and unbalanced nature of swimming often causes the muscles and structures on the anterior side of the body to become disproportionately stronger than those on the posterior side of the body. These imbalances contribute to a number of the injuries seen in swimmers (McMaster 1999; Bak 2010; USA Swimming Task Force on Injury Prevention 2002; Rodeo 2004).

Goals of a Strength-Training Program and the Factors Contributing to Strength Development

A strength program can be designed to target the development of specific strength attributes, some of which are better suited to swimming performance than others (Baechle and Earle 2008). Research and practical experience have identified various strategies that should be used based on the physical attribute being targeted. The strength attributes that could be targeted are identified here.

- **Maximal strength.** Maximal strength refers to the greatest amount of force that a swimmer could generate in one all-out effort. Maximal strength is commonly measured as the amount of weight a person could lift (or force that can be generated) in a one-repetition max test (1RM). Swimmers typically are not focused on developing maximal strength in any muscles or muscle groups in the body.

- **Strength endurance.** Strength endurance is the ability to produce a specified level of force repeatedly without fatigue. Typically, the level of force generated in any one contraction is not maximal, but it may represent a high percentage of a swimmer's maximum force-generating capacity in specific muscles or muscle groups. Strength endurance is critically important for swimmers because of the repetitive nature of the sport; for a swimmer to perform well and remain free from injury, many muscles need to have strength endurance. Some specific muscles or muscle groups that come to mind are the scapular stabilizers (which control the shoulder blades and maintain proper positioning of the shoulder joints), the core muscles (which control body posture in the water), the muscles of the rotator cuff and upper back (which are responsible for generating upper-body propulsion), and the muscles of the hip (which drive the propulsive kick). Strategies to develop strength endurance should be incorporated into strength-training plans for these muscle groups.

• **Power.** As discussed earlier, power is the ability of the neuromuscular system to produce large forces in a short time. Mathematically, muscle power equals muscle force multiplied by contraction velocity. Power is an important aspect of performance in swimming, especially in certain muscle groups where explosiveness is required to achieve optimal performance. For example, powerful lower-limb extensor muscles are needed to drive the start or push-off from the wall following a turn. Power in the upper-body musculature is beneficial to sprint performance and to the ability to shift into another gear at the end of a long race.

• **Muscle hypertrophy.** Hypertrophy training is designed to maximize muscle size, not necessarily strength. In general, strength training designed for swimmers should not be focused on gaining muscle size.

Strength can also be categorized based on the role that it plays in the execution of a sport. Strength can be thought of in two common ways as it relates to swimming performance—foundational strength and swimming-specific strength.

Foundational strength may also be thought of as general strength, or the strength base needed simply to play the sport. The goal of building foundational strength should not be to develop maximal strength, but instead to build a strength base on which the swimmer can build power and swimming-specific strength.

Swimming-specific strength describes the strength needed to execute the four strokes and excel while doing it. Each of the four strokes has specific demands that require different muscles to be used in different ways. Some coaches refer to swimming-specific strength as functional strength, but the terms are essentially synonymous and refer to developing in-water strength specific to maximizing performance.

Table 20.1 identifies general strategies for developing muscular strength, maximizing power, increasing muscle size and growth (hypertrophy), and building strength endurance. These strategies hinge on delivering the right stimuli to the muscles—the best combination of load (represented as the percentage of an athlete's 1RM load), repetitions, sets, rest and recovery between sets, exercise speed, and the number of training sessions per week to maximize the gains seen by the athlete.

Table 20.1 Means for Developing Various Strength Attributes in Swimming

Training variable	STRENGTH ATTRIBUTE			
	Strength	Power	Hypertrophy	Endurance
Load (% of 1RM)	>85	45–60	65–85	40–65
Repetitions per set	1–5	1–5	6–12	>12
Sets per exercise	2–6	3–5	3–6	2–3
Rest between sets	2–5 min	2–5 min	30–90 sec	<30 sec
Speed per repetition (% of max)	60–100	90–100	60–90	60–80

Data from T.R. Baechle, R.W. Earle, and D. Wathen, 2008. Resistance training. In *Essentials of strength training and conditioning*, 3rd ed., edited for the National Strength and Conditioning Association by T.R. Baechle and R.W. Earle (Champaign, IL: Human Kinetics), 381–412; M.C. Siff and Y.V. Verkhoshansky, 1999, *Supertraining*, 4th ed. (Denver: Supertraining International); and V.M. Zatsiorsky and W.J. Kraemer, 2006, *The science and practice of strength training*, 2nd ed. (Champaign, IL: Human Kinetics).

Depending on the muscle group being strengthened or the event that the swimmer is training for, a swimmer may adopt a training plan that emphasizes endurance or speed and power. To develop strength endurance, the swimmer performs fewer sets but executes more repetitions than the swimmer who is training to develop power or speed. To develop power and speed, athletes typically perform more sets using relatively low loads, which promotes production of higher speeds. Although swimmers may focus on developing strength endurance at times, they will still integrate workouts that emphasize strength and power development. The process of structuring training across a season to include these various elements is called periodization. This topic is the focus of chapter 9. As a rule, swimmers should not have muscle hypertrophy as a strength goal. These principles should drive how coaches develop strength-training regimens for the swimmers they work with.

Developing Power in Swimming

The focus of power training should be to find the optimal balance between strength and speed and then carry that power over to athletic performance. Sport-specific power development is difficult in any sport, but because swimmers need to be able to generate this power against water, an unstable surface, as opposed to the ground, power training can become even more complicated. The force that a runner applies to the ground translates into nearly 100 percent propulsive force, but in swimming some of the force applied to the water puts the water in motion, resulting in a lower percentage of the force going toward propulsion. One of the most difficult tasks for a swimmer is learning to apply force in a manner that maximizes the resultant propulsive action.

The thinking in the past was that power was best developed by lifting heavy loads for a small number of repetitions. But this way of training does not address the speed component of the power equation, just the force component. Consequently, recent thinking about building power in athletes has changed somewhat to incorporate several new paradigms. Now, strength and conditioning programs designed to maximize a swimmer's power should contain three components:

1. Some strength training using heavy resistance
2. Plyometric exercises that work on developing the rate of force development, or the speed at which the muscles can contract and produce force
3. Speed-based strengthening that uses lower resistance but emphasizes performing the exercises as quickly as possible and through the greatest range of motion possible

Swimmers often need to develop endurance and power simultaneously to maximize performance. This effort creates a problem, because large amounts of endurance training can inhibit muscle strength and power (Sharp, Troup, and Costill 1982; Costill 1999; Sharp 1986) and vice versa. Training must be periodized so that speed and power training is integrated appropriately with endurance training to optimize muscle function for swimming.

Relationship Between Strength and Swimming Performance

Before going much further into a discussion of how to design a swimming-specific strength-training program, let's look at what the research has to say about the effect that improvements in swimming strength have on performance. To ground this discussion, we can restate the goals of a strength-training program in swimming: to enhance performance and reduce the risk of injury. Note the following points about the nature of the existing research and the way in which it should be interpreted:

- Compared with the other areas of sport science and sports medicine that have been studied in relation to swimming, the body of research about strength and swimming performance is limited. A body of work from the 1980s exists, but little systematic research has been conducted since.

- The proficiency of the swimmers studied in the existing literature encompasses the full spectrum of ability, from developmental to elite athlete, making comparisons and the ability to draw definitive conclusions difficult. As might be expected, the research shows the greatest correlation between strength and performance when looking at groups of athletes that include a wide range of proficiency in the water. As the groups become more homogenized with respect to swimming proficiency, the correlations between strength and swimming performance decrease (Sharp, Troup, and Costill 1982).

- Given the complexities of the swimming stroke and the way that propulsion is generated, teasing out the exact contribution that strength gains make to performance is difficult. This issue pertains as well to the analysis of other performance factors, but note that in addition to strength gains that may occur from training, other factors are changing that can affect the observed results.

As a result of these factors, the results coming from the literature are that no definitive statement can be made that strength training definitely has "this effect" or "that effect" on performance (Tanaka and Swensen 1998). But the evidence is sufficient to suggest that improved strength and power can affect performance in the pool. This idea is especially true if we consider the point made in the introduction to this chapter that strength may be a threshold variable; in this light, strength training is not about making swimmers as strong as they can be; rather, it is about getting them to a threshold level of strength that any swimmer needs to succeed (Kondraske 2008).

With that stated, let's look at the research to understand whether strength training contributes to these areas. Rather than run through pages of text, the approach taken here is to summarize key findings from research and identify the take-home message for coaches.

When looking at the correlation between dryland (out-of-water) strength tests and in-water performance, studies have not shown many conclusive results. But the research has shown a relationship between peak isokinetic shoulder torque (Miyashita and Kanehisa 1983) and swimming time in the 100 meter FR as well as between arm power measured on a swim bench and performance in a 25-meter sprint (Sharp, Troup, and Costill 1982). Vorontsov (2011) found that dryland strength measures of maximum pulling force and power, as measured on a swim bench, were the only variables to correlate with in-water performance in a selected group of female swimmers, and even then, these variables correlated only to performance in sprints (50-meter and 100-meter swims), not in longer distance performances. In more recent studies, Girold and colleagues (2007) have found that swimmers experience significant increases in strength as well as swimming velocity following a 12-week dryland strengthening program focused on developing strength in the upper body, primarily, as well as the core and legs. Garrido et al. (2010) have also shown correlations between various dryland strength and power measures and sprint performance.

Although the correlations between strength and power and performance may not show a statistically significantly relationship, studies conducted in the early 1980s on national-caliber swimmers found that sprinters generated the highest levels of upper-body power, as measured on a swim bench, compared with middle-distance swimmers (next highest group) and endurance swimmers (Sharp, Costill, and King 1983). Additionally, the male swimmers produced more power than the females did in the study. Within these groups, however, power did not correlate with performance (meaning that the strongest sprinter did not necessarily swim the fastest times in the pool), lending credence to the idea that strength and power may be a threshold variable, as suggested earlier when discussing the research of Kondraske (2008).

The research focused on lower-body strength and the relation to performance is even more limited. One study showed a correlation between knee extension leg power and swimming velocity in a 200-meter FR (Bardzukas et al. 1992). Given the broad age range of the swimmers involved, the results likely reflect differences in age and swimming proficiency rather than differences in leg strength.

Investigations that centered on comparing in-water strength measures with performance show more-promising results. Several studies have shown that the peak pulling force, as measured in tethered swimming, correlates with performance across a range of swimming distances (Sharp 1986; Vorontsov 2011; Sharp, Costill, and King 1983; Girold et al. 2006; Toussaint and Vervoorn 1990). Girold and colleagues (2006) showed that swimmers achieved faster swimming velocities following three weeks of either in-water resisted-swimming training (swimming *against* elastic resistance) or swimming-assisted training (swimming *with* the assistance of elastic tubing). But the greater performance gains, as assessed by a 100-meter FR time trial, were seen in the athletes who participated in the resisted-swimming group. Toussaint and Vervoorn (1990) also showed that resisted sprint training for 10 weeks contributed to improved performances in race distances ranging from 50 to 200 meters.

Considering all this, a strong argument can be made that strength training, and developing strength on dryland or in the water, can have a positive effect on swimmers, even when looking only at performance. When considering injury prevention, the case to be made for integrating strength training with in-water swimming becomes even stronger, as will be seen later in this chapter.

Dryland Strength-Training Modalities for Swimmers

Coaches and swimmers have many options when it comes to designing and implementing a strength-training program that will maximize performance in the pool while also minimizing the risk of injury. Each strength-training modality has pros and cons, such as cost, ability to travel with the equipment, swimming specificity, and so on, and coaches and athletes likely will favor certain approaches over others. This section presents some of the more common modalities that can be used as part of a comprehensive strength-training program along with the pros and cons of each. Note that there not a gold standard when it comes to strength training. The most successful strength-training programs integrate aspects from various modalities to provide the best environment for developing swimming-specific strength.

Elastic Resistance

Strength training against the resistance of elastic tubing has been part of swimming for decades. Elastic tubing is easy to use and portable, and it allows swimmers to mimic swimming-like motions as a dryland exercise.

One downside of using elastic tubing, or bands, for strength training is that the resistance it provides is not constant; the more the tubing is stretched, the greater the resistance it provides. Typically, the resistance increases as a swimmer progresses through the full range of motion of an exercise. In some instances this may be appropriate for developing swimming-specific strength (e.g., force builds through the execution of a swimming pull), but in others it may not be (e.g., in many exercises designed for injury prevention).

Elastic resistance also can be used in the pool in tethered swimming, in which the swimmer must swim against added resistance (Vorontsov 2011; Sharp, Costill, and King 1983). More information on in-water resistance training is provided later in this chapter.

Swim Bench Training

Swim benches provide isokinetic or isotonic resistance while allowing swimmers to model the in-water stroke. Some swim benches require the athlete to use body weight as the resistance, whereas others force the swimmer to pull against an extra load. When doing any of these exercises, swimmers must try to mimic the stroke that they race with. They should maintain the appropriate stroke rate and mechanics to engrain the proper neuromuscular patterns.

Suspension System Training

In recent years a number of suspension training systems have come on the scene. Both recreational and professional athletes use these systems. The basic premise behind suspension systems is that the athlete is required to control body position by engaging the core and other stabilizing muscles to perform an exercise. In short, these strength-training systems provide an additional balance challenge to athletes as they are performing otherwise traditional exercises. This type of training stimuli is particularly appropriate for swimmers because of the need for core and scapular stability to perform optimally in the pool. Given the relative newness of suspension systems and their integration into mainstream strength training, few resources are available that specifically target swimmers, although more education and information targeting swimmers is now becoming available.

Free Weights and Strength-Training Machines

Almost every weight room provides both free weights and machines as training options. As with other training modalities, these tools have advantages and disadvantages. Both are designed to help athletes improve strength, but free-weight exercises place added premium on stability and control in the joints involved in the movement because the movement path is not constrained as it is in many weight machines. But machines are relatively easy to use, are thought to be a safer alternative to free weights, and allow the user to perform some exercises that are difficult or impossible to execute using free weights (Baechle and Earle 2008).

Olympic Lifts

Olympic lifts such as the snatch and the clean and jerk are a class of exercises used in Olympic weightlifting competitions. These multijoint exercises build full-body strength and explosive power, but they require a high level of technical expertise to perform correctly. Several simple modifications (e.g., the hang clean and high pull) can be made to the Olympic lifts to give swimmers a series of exercises that they can use to develop further power and explosiveness. These advanced exercises should be performed in a weight room, not necessarily on the pool deck. In addition, a certified strength and conditioning specialist should be enlisted to provide instruction on proper lifting technique.

Stability Training

Stability training involves performing exercises that contain an element of balance. Such exercises range from those performed while standing or sitting on an unstable surface (e.g., rowing while seated on an exercise ball or performing a shoulder external rotation exercise while standing on a balance pad) to distal movements executed with the arms and legs while maintaining a stable body position (e.g., side plank with a single-arm row). Because they provide an added challenge to the body, stability exercises are an advanced form of exercise. For example, a standing external rotation exercise using elastic tubing with the elbow at the side becomes increasingly challenging when the shoulder is abducted 90 degrees so that the scapular stabilizers need to become engaged at a higher level. (See the standing external rotation and catch position external rotation exercises later in the chapter for comparison between the two techniques.)

In-Water Strength-Training Modalities for Swimmers

In-water strength training provides swimmers the benefit of developing sport-specific strength while training actual swimming movements. Arguably, these types of in-water exercise are most beneficial for improving swimming performance because they provide a progressive overload and a high degree of transferability between the exercise and the swimming strokes (Tanaka and Swensen 1998; Girold et al. 2007; Sharp, Costill, and King 1983; Girold et al. 2006; Toussaint and Vervoorn 1990).

Coaches can add resistance in any number of ways to create in-water resistance sets, yet swimming against resistance should be treated as any other training exercise (e.g., considering volume, intensity, rest, frequency). Whatever training method is used, care should be taken to ensure that the exercise does not negatively affect the swimmer's stroke technique. Nevertheless, swimming against added resistance will likely change stroke mechanics. Maglischo et al. (1995) found that swimming against resistance typically causes the swimmer to swim with decreased stroke rate and decreased stroke length. Treating these exercises as strength-training exercises and structuring sets in the manner of a free-weight exercise will produce a strengthening effect. Doing these exercises in large doses, however, can lead to stroke alterations and bad technique habits.

Swimming Against Added External Resistance

Swimming against extra resistance (e.g., tethered swimming or swimming with parachutes) allows a swimmer to use proper stroking mechanics while building strength. The swimmer maintains a feel for the water, and loads can be increased incrementally to provide progressive overload. Swimmers also may have access to a power rack, a weight stack that can be tethered to a belt placed around a swimmer's waist. As the swimmer swims down the pool, he lifts the weight stack and swims against a defined level of added resistance.

Vertical Kicking and Using Fins or Paddles

Vertical kicking sets can be used to develop lower-body power by having swimmers hold their hands or a small medicine ball above the head. Additionally, fins can provide additional resistance and progressive overload when kicking. The key with using fins, or paddles for that matter, is to treat them as strength-training exercises. Sets can be designed to target specific aspects of strength development (e.g., power). Athletes should work at the required intensity to reap the benefits of this type of training.

Assisted Swimming

Swimming with assistance can provide another means for developing swimming speed and sport-specific strength. In short, assisted swimming works on developing speed and getting the body accustomed to the feel of swimming fast. Swimming with assistance trains the neuromuscular system for race-paced performances.

The easiest way to perform assisted swimming is to attach a long piece of elastic tubing to one end of the pool and the other to the swimmer's waist. The swimmer should pull or swim to the other end of the pool, let go, and allow the band to pull her along as she swims. A partner can assist by pulling in the slack tubing as the swimmer swims. This overspeed training allows swimmers to train with a desired race stroke rate and get a feel for what it is like to swim faster than they can on their own (Girold et al. 2006; Maglischo et al. 1995).

In-Water Stability Training

Just as stability training can be done on dry land, it can be done in the water. Stability training in the water is often more effective because water is an extremely unstable surface. Swimmers can be challenged to balance on kickboards or find creative ways to balance on stability balls in the pool. Ultimately, these types of exercises provide swimmers with additional body control that will help minimize drag and allow the transference of power from one part of the body to another, thereby assisting with propulsion.

Creating a Strength-Training Plan for Swimming

When creating a strength plan for swimmers, coaches need to consider some foundational principles of program design. These principles have been modified to reflect the specific demands and challenges of swimming, and the points made here should be considered when designing a training plan to optimize performance and reduce the risk of injury.

Using these principles as a guide, coaches should be able to put together a strength-training program that will enhance swimming performance. Refer to table 20.2 and the resources referenced in the table to understand the types of exercises that can be included in a strength and conditioning program that will develop foundational strength and then progress to building swimming- or stroke-specific strength and power. Additionally, refer to chapter 9 on periodization to understand how training sessions can be structured and organized to achieve specific strength gains and performance outcomes.

Progressive Overload Principle

The body is remarkable in that it will respond and adapt to the physical and physiological demands imposed on it, at least to a point (Baechle and Earle 2008). Exercising against resistance stimulates muscles to grow so that they can produce more strength. But any new physical stimuli should be imposed progressively, providing small increases in training to avoid overwhelming the body. Additionally, subsequent challenges must be applied only after the body has had time to adapt to the initial overload. Increasing training load too much or too quickly can lead to fatigue and increase an athlete's risk of injury.

General Adaptation and Recovery

Tied to the concept of progressive overload is the general adaptation syndrome, which describes how the body responds to stress (Baechle and Earle 2008). In general, the body responds physically and physiologically to stress with a period of alarm. When considering strength training and swimming, this alarm response includes slight muscle breakdown, mild inflammation, bone remodeling, and so on. But when the stress is removed and the body has an opportunity to recover, it will become stronger and better able to withstand subsequent stressors. Repeated stress without time for recovery will continue to break down the body, potentially putting an athlete in an overtrained state. The need for recovery is discussed in chapter 13. All coaches and athletes need to understand how to walk the fine line between providing an appropriate training stimulus and overtraining.

Exercise Specificity

A certain level of sport specificity should accompany strength training; the strength training for a given sport must complement the actual sport training and match the demands of the sport. This point is thought to be especially pertinent to swimming, which includes the challenge of transferring strength created on dry land to augment performance in the water. Although some strength can be transferred from one activity to another, swimmers generally want to engage in activities that simulate swimming (e.g., swimming against parachutes or a power rack) in addition to any dryland work. This approach will help to consolidate dryland strength gains while also building swimming-specific strength.

Exercise Selection and Appropriate Progressions

The goals in strength training for swimming are twofold: to enhance performance and to prevent injury. Typically, the injury prevention component should be addressed first to eliminate strength and flexibility imbalances at key locations throughout the body. After this foundational strength is established, the focus can be directed to improving swimming-specific strength for performance. Many exercises build on each another, so without a proper foundation of strength and control, a swimmer will be unable to realize the gains that could come from more advanced exercises and may be at a greater risk for injury when performing them. Take, for example, the muscles that control the shoulder blade kinematics. Adequate strength is needed in these muscles to ensure that correct shoulder kinematics is in place before attempting to develop strength that would contribute more directly to propulsion.

Table 20.2 highlights a variety of strength-training exercises, categorizing them as either foundational, stroke specific, core, or focused on injury prevention. The table also identifies the body parts and muscle groups affected by the exercises. This chapter cannot provide step-by-step descriptions for all these exercises, but selected core training and injury prevention exercises are described later in the chapter. Refer to these additional resources to obtain detailed descriptions of how these exercises should be performed: USA Swimming Task Force on Injury Prevention 2002; Baechle and Earle 2008; Salo and Riewald 2008; McLeod 2010.

Demand Proper Technique

Swimmers need to perform proper technique on every repetition of every strength set. Not doing so can subject them to unnecessary injury risks. Consider a relatively basic rowing exercise. To ensure the health of the shoulder and maximize performance gains, the shoulder blades need to be set and retracted for each rowing repetition. Failure to do this does not train the muscles to stabilize the shoulder girdle appropriately. Similarly, to build power through higher-intensity exercises such as Olympic lifts or plyometrics, technique is critically important to avoid inappropriate overloading of the structures of the body.

Table 20.2 Strength-Training Exercises for Swimming

Exercise name	PRIMARY STRENGTH EMPHASIS				FOCUS			Muscle groups affected	References for instruction
	Foundation	Stroke specific	Core training	Injury prevention	Endurance	Power	Flexibility		
Scapular retraction	✔			✔	✔			Scapular retractors	Salo and Riewald 2008
Scapular retraction with external rotation	✔			✔	✔			Scapular retractors, shoulder external rotators	USA Swimming Task Force on Injury Prevention 2002; Salo and Riewald 2008
Full can exercise	✔			✔	✔			Deltoid, general rotator cuff	USA Swimming Task Force on Injury Prevention 2002
Ball on the wall				✔	✔			Scapular stabilizers, general rotator cuff	USA Swimming Task Force on Injury Prevention 2002
Seated rowing	✔			✔	✔			Upper back, scapular stabilizers	USA Swimming Task Force on Injury Prevention 2002; Salo and Riewald 2008
Hitchhiker				✔	✔			Upper back, scapular stabilizers	USA Swimming Task Force on Injury Prevention 2002
Push-up with a plus	✔			✔	✔			Serratus anterior, scapular stabilizers	USA Swimming Task Force on Injury Prevention 2002
Chest punch	✔			✔	✔			Serratus anterior, scapular stabilizers	Salo and Riewald 2008
Upper-body press-up	✔			✔	✔			Serratus anterior, scapular stabilizers	Salo and Riewald 2008
Scapular push-up				✔	✔			Serratus anterior, scapular stabilizers	McLeod 2010
Scapular dip				✔	✔			Scapular stabilizers	McLeod 2010

(continued)

	PRIMARY STRENGTH EMPHASIS				FOCUS				
Exercise name	Foundation	Stroke specific	Core training	Injury prevention	Endurance	Power	Flexibility	Muscle groups affected	References for instruction
Standing external shoulder rotation	✔			✔	✔			Shoulder external rotators	Salo and Riewald 2008
Catch position external rotation	✔			✔	✔			Shoulder external rotators	Salo and Riewald 2008
Hollow hold			✔	✔	✔			Abdominals, general core	McLeod 2010
Prone bridge (variations)			✔	✔	✔			Back extensors, general core	Salo and Riewald 2008; McLeod 2010
Back bridge (variations)			✔	✔	✔			Abdominals, general core	Salo and Riewald 2008
Leg drop (variations)			✔	✔	✔			Obliques, general core	Salo and Riewald 2008
Knee to chest (variations)			✔	✔	✔			Abdominals, obliques, general core	Salo and Riewald 2008
Dead bug exercise	✔		✔	✔	✔			Abdominals, general core	USA Swimming Task Force on Injury Prevention 2002; Salo and Riewald 2008
Bird dog or quadruped	✔		✔	✔	✔			Back extensors, general core	USA Swimming Task Force on Injury Prevention 2002; Salo and Riewald 2008
Y exercise	✔		✔	✔	✔			Back extensors, scapular stabilizers	McLeod 2010
Front balance drill			✔	✔	✔			Back extensors, general core	Salo and Riewald 2008
Back balance drill			✔	✔	✔			Abdominals, general core	Salo and Riewald 2008
Back extension (variations)		✔	✔	✔	✔			Back extensors	Salo and Riewald 2008; McLeod 2010

Exercise name	PRIMARY STRENGTH EMPHASIS				FOCUS			Muscle groups affected	References for instruction
	Foundation	Stroke specific	Core training	Injury prevention	Endurance	Power	Flexibility		
T exercise			✔	✔	✔			General core	Salo and Riewald 2008
Abdominal crunch with rotation			✔	✔	✔			Abdominals, obliques	Salo and Riewald 2008
Stability ball prone super-man			✔	✔	✔			Back extensors, general core	McLeod 2010
Seated medicine ball chest pass			✔			✔		General core	Salo and Riewald 2008
Seated medi-cine ball toss (variations)			✔			✔		Obliques, general core	Salo and Riewald 2008
Squat (variations)	✔				✔			General lower-body strength	Salo and Riewald 2008; McLeod 2010; Baechle and Earle 2008
Lunge (variations)	✔				✔			General lower-body strength	Salo and Riewald 2008; McLeod 2010; Baechle and Earle 2008
Monster walk	✔				✔			Hip abduc-tors	Salo and Riewald 2008
Ankle dorsi-flexion	✔				✔			Ankle dor-siflexors	Salo and Riewald 2008
Calf raise	✔				✔			Ankle plantar flexors	Salo and Riewald 2008
Seated ham-string curl with elastic resistance	x				✔			Knee flexors, hip extensors	Salo and Riewald 2008
Step-up	✔				✔			General lower-body strength	Salo and Riewald 2008; McLeod 2010
Single-leg deadlift or Romanian deadlift	✔				✔			Hip exten-sors, back extensors	Salo and Riewald 2008; McLeod 2010; Baechle and Earle 2008

(continued)

Table 20.2, *continued*

Exercise name	PRIMARY STRENGTH EMPHASIS				FOCUS			Muscle groups affected	References for instruction
	Foundation	Stroke specific	Core training	Injury prevention	Endurance	Power	Flexibility		
Single-leg squat	✔			✔	✔			General lower-body strength	Salo and Riewald 2008; McLeod 2010
Star drill	✔			✔	✔			General lower-body strength	Salo and Riewald 2008
Elastic band kick	✔				✔			General hip strength	Salo and Riewald 2008
Pull-up	✔				✔			Shoulder adductors, upper back	Salo and Riewald 2008; McLeod 2010
Lat pull-down	✔				✔			Shoulder adductors, upper back	Salo and Riewald 2008; McLeod 2010; Baechle and Earle 2008
Core chest press	✔		✔		✔			General upper-body strength	Salo and Riewald 2008
Posterior chain exercise (variations)	✔		✔	✔	✔			Back extensors, scapular stabilizers	Salo and Riewald 2008; McLeod 2010
Upright row	✔				✔			Shoulder abductors	Salo and Riewald 2008
Triceps extension	✔				✔			Elbow extensors	Salo and Riewald 2008; McLeod 2010; Baechle and Earle 2008
Wrist flexion	✔				✔			Wrist flexors	Salo and Riewald 2008; Baechle and Earle 2008
Wrist extension	✔				✔			Wrist extensors	Salo and Riewald 2008; Baechle and Earle 2008
Dumbbell kickback	✔							Elbow extensors	Salo and Riewald 2008; McLeod 2010

	PRIMARY STRENGTH EMPHASIS				FOCUS				
Exercise name	Foundation	Stroke specific	Core training	Injury prevention	Endurance	Power	Flexibility	Muscle groups affected	References for instruction
Biceps curl	✔							Elbow flexors	Salo and Riewald 2008; McLeod 2010; Baechle and Earle 2008
Chest press or bench press	✔				✔			Pectoral muscles	Salo and Riewald 2008; McLeod 2010; Baechle and Earle 2008
Standing Zeus	✔		✔		✔			Obliques, upper back	McLeod 2010
Hamstring curl	✔				✔			Knee flexors, hip extensors	McLeod 2010; Baechle and Earle 2008
Ankle inversion or eversion	✔				✔			General ankle strength	McLeod 2010
Standing hip internal rotation	✔				✔			Hip internal rotators	McLeod 2010
Standing hip external rotation	✔				✔			Hip external rotators	McLeod 2010
Reverse fly (variations)		FL			✔			Posterior deltoid, upper back	Salo and Riewald 2008; McLeod 2010
Kicking with fins		BA, FL, FR			✔			General lower-body strength	Salo and Riewald 2008
Swimming with parachute		BA, BR, FL, FR			✔			Swimming-specific strength	Salo and Riewald 2008
Swimming against resistance		BA, BR, FL, FR			✔			Swimming-specific strength	Salo and Riewald 2008
Walking lunge with rotation		BA, FR	✔		✔			General lower-body strength, obliques	Salo and Riewald 2008
Kicking with ankle weights (variations)		BA, FR			✔			General hip strength	Salo and Riewald 2008; McLeod 2010

(continued)

Table 20.2, *continued*

Exercise name	Foundation	Stroke specific	Core training	Injury prevention	Endurance	Power	Flexibility	Muscle groups affected	References for instruction
		PRIMARY STRENGTH EMPHASIS			FOCUS				
Back extension with rotation		BA, FR	✔		✔			Back extensors, obliques	Salo and Riewald 2008
Medicine ball handoff		BA, FR	✔					Obliques	Salo and Riewald 2008
High to low chop		BA, FR	✔			✔		Obliques, abdominals	Salo and Riewald 2008; McLeod 2010
Low to high chop		BA, FR	✔			✔		Obliques, abdominals	Salo and Riewald 2008
Alternate-arm superman		BA, FR	✔		✔			Back extensors, upper back	Salo and Riewald 2008
Russian twist		BA, FR	✔		✔			Obliques, general core	Salo and Riewald 2008; McLeod 2010
Straight arm row		FL, FR		✔	✔			Shoulder extensors	Salo and Riewald 2008; McLeod 2010
One-arm medicine ball throw-down		BA, FR	✔			✔		Shoulder adductors, arm extensors	Salo and Riewald 2008
Medicine ball throw-down		FL, FR	✔			✔		Shoulder adductors, arm extensors	Salo and Riewald 2008
Medicine ball leg lift		BR, FL			✔			Abdominals, general core	Salo and Riewald 2008
Good morning		BA, BR, FL, FR			✔			Back extensors, hip extensors	Salo and Riewald 2008; Baechle and Earle 2008
Hip extension		FL, FR			✔			Hip extensors	Salo and Riewald 2008
Hip flexion		FL, FR						Hip flexors	Salo and Riewald 2008
Medicine ball V crunch		BR, FL	✔		✔			Abdominals, general core	Salo and Riewald 2008
Bent-over row		FL, FR			✔			Upper back	Salo and Riewald 2008; Baechle and Earle 2008

Exercise name	PRIMARY STRENGTH EMPHASIS				FOCUS			Muscle groups affected	References for instruction
	Foundation	Stroke specific	Core training	Injury prevention	Endurance	Power	Flexibility		
Bent-over lateral raise		FL, FR			✔			Posterior deltoid	Salo and Riewald 2008; Baechle and Earle 2008
Sumo squat		BR, FL			✔			General lower body strength	Salo and Riewald 2008
Chest fly		FL, FR			✔			General upper-body strength	Salo and Riewald 2008; Baechle and Earle 2008
Catch position sculling		BR, FL, FR			✔			General forearm and shoulder	Salo and Riewald 2008
Sculling: midpull		FR, FL			✔			General forearm and shoulder	Salo and Riewald 2008
Forward deltoid raise		BA			✔			Anterior deltoid, shoulder flexors	Salo and Riewald 2008; McLeod 2010
Lateral dumbbell raise		FL, FR			✔			Middle deltoid, shoulder adductors	Salo and Riewald 2008; McLeod 2010
Skipping						✔		General lower-body power	Salo and Riewald 2008; Baechle and Earle 2008
Bounding						✔		General lower-body power	Salo and Riewald 2008; Baechle and Earle 2008
Lateral line hop						✔		General lower-body power	Salo and Riewald 2008; Baechle and Earle 2008
Jump turn						✔		General lower-body power	Salo and Riewald 2008
Box jump						✔		Hip, knee, and ankle extensors	McLeod 2010; Baechle and Earle 2008
Shoulder pullover						✔		General upper-body power	Salo and Riewald 2008

(continued)

Exercise name	PRIMARY STRENGTH EMPHASIS				FOCUS			Muscle groups affected	References for instruction
	Foundation	Stroke specific	Core training	Injury prevention	Endurance	Power	Flexibility		
Streamlined jumping						✔		General lower-body power	Salo and Riewald 2008
Seated medicine ball twist			✔			✔		Obliques	Salo and Riewald 2008; McLeod 2010
Figure-eight medicine ball throw			✔			✔		Obliques	Salo and Riewald 2008
Plyometric sit-up			✔			✔		Abdominals, general core	Salo and Riewald 2008; McLeod 2010
Plyometric leg lift			✔			✔		Abdominals, general core	Salo and Riewald 2008
Explosive wall chest pass			✔			✔		General upper-body power	Salo and Riewald 2008; Baechle and Earle 2008
Explosive rotational medicine ball throw			✔			✔		Obliques	Salo and Riewald 2008
Medicine ball squat with chest throw						✔		General lower-body power, general upper-body power	Salo and Riewald 2008
Medicine ball squat jump						✔		General lower-body power	Salo and Riewald 2008
Power drop						✔		General upper-body power	Salo and Riewald 2008; Baechle and Earle 2008
Overhead medicine ball throw						✔		General upper-body power	Salo and Riewald 2008; Baechle and Earle 2008
Hang clean						✔		Full-body power	Salo and Riewald 2008
High pull						✔		Full-body power	Salo and Riewald 2008
Overhead single-arm bounce with medicine ball						✔		Scapular stabilizers, rotator cuff	McLeod 2010

Exercise name	Foundation	Stroke specific	Core training	Injury prevention	Endurance	Power	Flexibility	Muscle groups affected	References for instruction
		PRIMARY STRENGTH EMPHASIS			FOCUS				
External rotator catch and toss		BA, FL, FR		✔		✔		Shoulder external rotators	Salo and Riewald 2008
90/90 plyometric ball drop		BA, FL, FR		✔		✔		Shoulder external rotators	Salo and Riewald 2008
Hamstring stretch				✔			✔	Knee flexors, hip extensors	USA Swimming Task Force on Injury Prevention 2002; Salo and Riewald 2008; Baechle and Earle 2008
Neck stretch							✔	Lateral flexors of the neck	USA Swimming Task Force on Injury Prevention 2002; Salo and Riewald 2008; Baechle and Earle 2008
Hip flexor stretch				✔			✔	Hip flexors	Salo and Riewald 2008; Baechle and Earle 2008
Calf stretch (variations)							✔	Ankle plantar flexors, knee flexor	Salo and Riewald 2008; Baechle and Earle 2008
Ankle dorsi-flexor stretch							✔	Ankle dorsiflexors	Salo and Riewald 2008
Figure-four stretch							✔	Hip internal rotators	Salo and Riewald 2008
Hip adductor stretch							✔	Hip adductors	Salo and Riewald 2008
Quadriceps stretch (variations)							✔	Knee extensors	Salo and Riewald 2008; Baechle and Earle 2008
Knee to chest stretch							✔	Low back extensors	Salo and Riewald 2008; Baechle and Earle 2008

(continued)

423

Table 20.2, *continued*

Exercise name	PRIMARY STRENGTH EMPHASIS				FOCUS			Muscle groups affected	References for instruction
	Foundation	Stroke specific	Core training	Injury prevention	Endurance	Power	Flexibility		
Seated groin stretch							✔	Hip adductors, hip internal rotators	Salo and Riewald 2008
Spinal twist							✔	Lateral rotators of the spine	Salo and Riewald 2008; Baechle and Earle 2008
Hip twist							✔	Lateral rotators of the spine, hip external rotators	Salo and Riewald 2008
Upper-back stretch							✔	Shoulder extensors, shoulder adductors	Salo and Riewald 2008
Streamline stretch							✔	Lateral flexors of the trunk	Salo and Riewald 2008
Triceps stretch							✔	Elbow extensors	Salo and Riewald 2008; Baechle and Earle 2008
Chest stretch				✔			✔	Pectoralis muscles	Salo and Riewald 2008
Cross-arm stretch				✔			✔	Posterior shoulder	Salo and Riewald 2008; Baechle and Earle 2008
Sleeper stretch				✔			✔	Shoulder external rotators	Salo and Riewald 2008
Towel stretch				✔			✔	Shoulder external rotators	Salo and Riewald 2008

Train Movements, Not Just Muscles

Muscles and muscle groups work together to produce movements; few (if any) muscles work in isolation during the execution of a swimming stroke. A swimmer will have muscles of the arms, upper back, core, and legs all working together. Although the complete demands of a swimming stroke cannot be mimicked entirely in one exercise, the muscles should be trained to work together in patterns of movement. For that reason, full-body exercises and exercises that require core stability when executing a distal movement can be extremely powerful in training swimmers. These types of exercises train muscles to act synergistically, not in isolation.

Train the Correct Energy Systems

Although energy systems are closely associated with in-water training, they also need to considered when developing strength-training programs. Should certain muscle groups be trained for muscular endurance? Absolutely. Take, for example, the muscles of the rotator cuff and the scapular stabilizers; these muscles should be trained so that they can generate the necessary force repeatedly with limited fatigue. Should other muscle groups be trained for explosive power? Unquestionably. The leg extensors that propel the start and wall push-offs, for example, need to be trained in a different manner to promote optimal performance in the pool.

Exercise Intensity and Volume

Tied to the idea presented in the previous section, to develop muscular endurance, muscles should be trained using a lighter weight but for a higher number of repetitions. When training for power, besides reducing the number of repetitions and increasing the rest interval between sets, the exercises should be performed when the swimmer is completely fresh to maximize the benefits. This requirement may mean restructuring some aspects of training sessions to keep from putting power training at the end of the workout.

Periodization and Complementing In-Water Training

Training should be planned and periodized to apply appropriate stimuli while also allowing for recovery. This approach will facilitate long-term athlete development and at the same time maximize performance at key competitions. With that said, any strength training should complement the work being done in the pool. In-water training and strength training are too often seen as independent activities, so little consideration is given to how a heavy strength-training session might affect the in-water work and vice versa. Coaches must consider how all aspects of a training plan interweave to maximize the performance and health of the swimmer.

Understanding the Kinetic Chain and Swimming

When planning a strength and conditioning program, coaches need to consider how the body works and how strength and conditioning can help it work more effectively. The body is made up of a series of segments that are linked together to function so that what happens (or does not happen) in one part of the body affects what occurs elsewhere (Kibler, Press, and Sciascia 2006; Kibler 1998). This concept, that the body is liked together functionally, has been termed the *kinetic chain*. Swimmers who have a strong kinetic chain gain a tremendous benefit because they can tap into strength throughout the body to generate propulsive force. For example, power can flow from the legs to the upper body or from the right side to the left to assist in generating propulsion. But a broken link in the chain, whether it results from lack of strength, poor muscular control, or fatigue, compromises the integrity of the entire chain and results in added physical demands being placed on muscles or structures elsewhere in the body. For swimmers, in many instances, greater demands are placed on the structures of the shoulders, increasing the risk of injury. The muscles of the torso, those that control the motion of the pelvis and link the upper and lower halves of the body, make up one critically important link in the kinetic chain.

The Core in Swimming

Strength and stability in the muscles surrounding the core of the body are key to maintaining the integrity of the kinetic chain. The ability to engage the core musculature in the body can have an effect on performance and injury prevention. We can think of the core as a muscular cylinder surrounding the middle third of the body made up of all the muscles that surround the body's center of mass:

- The erector spinae muscles in the lower back contract to extend the lower back and provide stability to the pelvis.
- The internal and external oblique muscles in the abdomen work together to rotate the torso, assist in side bending, and provide stability to the pelvis. The right internal oblique and the left external oblique contract simultaneously to produce rotation to the right, and vice versa.
- The transverse abdominis in the lower abdominal region runs laterally across the abdomen and acts as a corset to provide stability to the pelvis.
- The rectus abdominis muscle forms the six-pack and functions to flex the trunk and produce forward bending.

In addition, the other muscles that attach to and control the pelvis, spine, and shoulder girdle can be considered part of the core. Taken together, these muscles facilitate a wide range of movements throughout the middle third of the body and provide stability to the pelvis, spine, and shoulder girdle.

A strong and stable core can enhance in-water performance in several ways (Vorontsov 2011; Salo and Riewald 2008):

 • **Maintaining a streamlined body position in the water.** A strong and stable core helps swimmers maintain a consistent and efficient body posture in the water, minimizing unwanted movements and resistance.

 • **Establishing a stable base of support.** A strong core helps swimmers develop a stronger pull and kick. It's been said that core stability allows limb mobility (Kibler, Press, and Sciascia 2006). In other words, having core stability allows swimmers to use their arms and legs for what they're meant to do—to generate propulsion. Core stability is more important in swimming than it is in land-based sports in which an athlete interacts with the ground. The grounding effect seen in land-based sports allows large forces to be generated between the feet and the ground that can then be transferred through the body. This energy can power a forehand in tennis or help an offensive lineman drive into his block. In the water, swimmers have no rigid surface to push against; they are essentially trying to pull or kick against a surface that is always trying to move out of the way. Core stability provides the base of support needed to generate efficient movement and propulsion from the arms and legs.

• **Linking the lower body to the upper body.** Consider the difficult task of pushing a string across a desktop. In many ways, this feat is analogous to trying to generate propulsion from a kick when core stability is poor. A weak core makes the body function like the floppy string. Creating a rigid link between the upper body and the lower body allows the swimmer to use the legs to push through the water rather than rely entirely on the arms to pull the body through the water.

• **Contributing to body roll in freestyle and backstroke.** Although a number of factors contribute to body roll, including the kick and a drive from the hips, the muscles of the body's core also play a role. This body rotation is necessary for efficient pulling (and kicking) in freestyle and backstroke.

• **Driving the undulation in butterfly and breaststroke.** Core stability is important not only for freestyle and backstroke but also for butterfly and breaststroke. A strong core allows the propulsion of the kick to drive the body forward and adds to the power from the upper body.

Overall, having a stable core will help an athlete swim faster by promoting more effective and efficient propulsion while also reducing the amount of drag experienced in the water.

Dryland Training for the Core

Swimming places extra demands on the core and increases the need for dynamic stability. The focus of core training should be on developing stability, which incorporates elements of both strength development and control, not just strength. Strong core muscles are important, but even the strongest muscles are useless if they are activated at the wrong time or in the wrong order. Swimming-specific core exercises should challenge the swimmer to maintain balance and control of the muscles while also developing strength. This kind of core training work should translate more readily to performance in the pool. Many athletes have experienced success engaging in unbalanced training both in and out of the water.

Several examples of exercise progressions that challenge the core and build stability are presented in the following section (USA Swimming Task Force on Injury Prevention 2002; Salo and Riewald 2008). The exercises presented here are general in nature. They establish a foundation of core strength and stability and progress to increased strength and power development. In addition, specific strength programs and exercises can be used to develop specific attributes of core stability that relate to a specific stroke or athlete. Additional resources are available that provide more detail and a greater diversity of exercises that can be used to develop core stability.

Prone Bridge Progression   Prone bridging (figure 20.1) involves controlling the core to maintain a consistent body line, much like swimmers need in the water. The focus of these exercises is to maintain a straight line from the ankles through the hips to the shoulders while balancing on the forearms and toes. Athletes should work to maintain this form even as balance becomes challenged and the stabilizing muscles become fatigued.

▶ **Figure 20.1**   Prone bridge progression. The prone bridge challenges the core musculature increasingly as the athlete reduces the points of contact with the ground. In this case, the athlete progresses from (a) having the toes and forearms in contact with the ground to (b) having the toes or elbows in contact with an unstable surface such as a stability ball.

Back Bridge Progression Back-bridging exercises (figure 20.2) target the entire core, requiring those muscles to help maintain a consistent body line from the shoulders through the hips to the knees and ankles. Again, as the exercise increases in difficulty, the core will be required to stabilize the body in increasingly demanding, dynamic situations.

▶ **Figure 20.2** Back bridge progression. The back bridge challenges the core musculature increasingly as the athlete adds limb movements to the exercise. The athlete progresses from (a) performing a basic back bridge to (b) executing alternate knee extensions while maintaining a consistent body position through the core.

Side Bridge Side bridging (figure 20.3) develops strength in the muscles that make up the sides of the core. Because these muscles also help a great deal with initiating and controlling body rotation, developing strength and stability in this area is critical. To increase difficulty and challenge stability, athletes can perform single-arm rows using elastic tubing while maintaining the side bridge position.

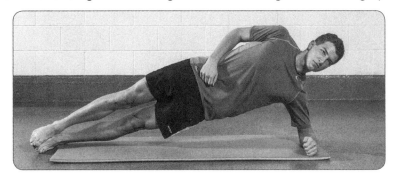

▶ **Figure 20.3** Side bridge. The side bridge challenges the oblique muscles while the athlete tries to maintain a constant body line.

Bird Dog Progression   The bird dog exercise is designed to improve strength and control of the core muscles, particularly the muscles of lower back, while requiring the swimmer to produce movement of the arms and legs (figure 20.4). Additional challenges can be added by forcing the swimmer to perform the exercise while balanced on an unstable surface.

▶ **Figure 20.4**   Bird dog progression. The bird dog exercise challenges the extensor muscles in the lower back and becomes increasingly difficult as the stability of the surface that the athlete interacts with changes. In this case, the athlete progresses from (*a*) having one hand and knee in contact with the ground to (*b*) having only the toes and hand in contact with the ground while balancing the torso on a stability ball.

Leg Drop Progression   The leg drop (figure 20.5) requires core stability with rotation and carries over well to performance in the pool. The basic premise of the exercise is that the swimmer allows the knees to drop to the side of the body in a controlled manned, requiring activation of the obliques and other core muscles. Additional challenges are provided by lifting the feet off the floor.

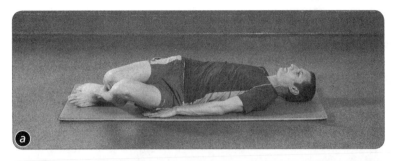

▶ **Figure 20.5**   Leg drop progression. The leg drop progression requires the swimmer to maintain stability with torso rotation. (a) The basic form of the exercise is to control rotation as the knees drop to the floor while both feet are in contact with the ground. (b) Difficulty is added by controlling the knee drop after lifting the feet off the floor.

After a base level of strength is developed in the core, additional challenges can be provided by performing more advanced, dynamic exercises that require higher forces, high movement velocity, or an increased need for stability. The following are some examples of more advanced exercises:

Partner-assisted medicine ball toss

High to low chop

Low to high chop

Plyometric sit-up

Plyometric leg lift

Russian twist

Overhead medicine ball throw

Figure-eight medicine ball throw

In-Water Core Training Exercises

Because swimmers train and compete in the water, they often benefit by engaging in some strengthening exercises that take place in the water. Placing swimmers in an unbalanced situation in the water will help facilitate the development of swimming-specific core stability.

Front-Side and Back-Side Balance Drill   The front-side balance drill (figure 20.6a) requires the swimmer to maintain a streamlined position on the belly while balancing on a floatation device designed to introduce greater instability than what the water provides on its own. The back-side balance drill (figure 20.6b) is performed much like the front-side exercise except that it requires the swimmer to maintain a streamlined position on the back while balancing on a floatation device. As swimmers become more proficient at these exercises, they can add more kickboards to the stack that they are balancing on. The increased buoyancy provides more instability while continually challenging the core. An even greater challenge can be achieved by having the swimmers balance on a stability ball in the water.

▶ **Figure 20.6**   Front-side and back-side balance drill. Swimmers should be encouraged to work on their balance in the water. A way to do this is to ask the swimmer to balance on a kickboard or stack of kickboards floating (a) on her front or (b) on her back. Difficulty can be increased by adding more kickboards to the stack.

Strength and Conditioning for Injury Prevention

Chapter 18 deals specifically with injuries in swimming. Strength training can help prevent these injuries, particularly injuries to the shoulder. Although improper technique definitely contributes to shoulder injuries, so do strength and flexibility imbalances in the shoulder, upper back, and core. In swimmers, the shoulder internal rotators are often stronger than the external rotators, creating a strength imbalance within the rotator cuff. Additionally, the external rotators tend to fatigue more quickly when this strength imbalance exists. The fact that the internal rotators are preferentially stronger makes sense given the degree to which they are used in the competitive swimming strokes; the external rotators are hardly activated. Maintaining a strength balance in the shoulder is important because both muscle groups work together to keep the ball-and-socket joint properly aligned. When the normal force balance is upset in the shoulder, the risk of impingement increases. Swimmers need to take deliberate steps to strengthen the external rotators to restore normal strength balance in the shoulder while also building endurance to allow the shoulder to function properly.

When shoulder pain does occur, the assumption naturally made is that the root cause of the pain lies in the ball-and-socket joint itself. Recall, however, that a weak link or break anywhere in the kinetic chain can place undue stress on the shoulder. Fatigue or weakness in the scapular stabilizers, which causes a breakdown in scapular kinematics, often contributes to shoulder pain (McMaster 1999; Bak 2010; USA Swimming Task Force on Injury Prevention 2002; Rodeo 2004; Scovazzo et al. 1991). For the ball-and-socket joint to function properly, a swimmer needs to have excellent strength and control of the muscles that control the shoulder blades. In a healthy shoulder in which the scapular stabilizers are strong, the shoulder blades stay flush against the torso throughout the movement, thus maintaining proper alignment of the glenohumeral joint.

The serratus anterior is one scapular stabilizer that deserves special attention. This muscle wraps around the rib cage and is active throughout much of the freestyle stroke cycle. The serratus anterior has been found to fatigue quickly in swimmers with shoulder pain (Scovazzo et al. 1991). Most traditional strengthening exercises do not target this muscle, so exercises for this muscle need to be specifically included in a swimmer's strength-training plan.

Strength Training to Prevent Shoulder Injury

A swimmer can do a number of strengthening exercises to protect the health of the shoulder (USA Swimming Task Force on Injury Prevention 2002; Salo and Riewald 2008). The ones presented here have been selected because they target the strength imbalances and areas of weakness most often seen in swimmers and they promote healthy joint function while also strengthening the kinetic chain.

Swimmers should follow some general guidelines when performing these exercises:

- Use very light weights. The muscles being trained are small. Using weights that are too heavy will engage other muscles.

- Focus on endurance. Swimmers should perform two or three sets of 15 to 25 repetitions of each exercise.

- Control the movements. Swimmers should not race to see who can perform these the fastest. They should use slow, deliberate movements and focus on retracting and setting the shoulder blades at the start of each repetition.

- Develop consistency. These exercises should be performed at least two or three times per week. Doing these exercises is important even if a swimmer is not injured. Injury prevention should be a priority at all times of the year.

- Maintain proper form. If a swimmer cannot maintain the correct technique, the exercise should be stopped.

- Avoid pain. If a swimmer has a preexisting injury or if any of these exercises cause pain, the activity should be stopped. Although these exercises should produce a muscle burn, they should never cause pain.

Scapular Retraction: Setting the Shoulder Blades This exercise (figure 20.7) strengthens the scapular stabilizers in the upper back. It is the most basic of the upper-back exercises and serves as the starting point for many of the rotator cuff and upper-back exercises that follow. The instructions to the athlete should be to pinch the shoulder blades together in the middle of the back.

▶ **Figure 20.7** Scapular retraction. Setting the shoulder blades through scapular retraction should be the first step of any upper-back or rotator cuff exercise. These images show (a) the starting position and (b) the ending position of the exercise. This exercise can be easily performed using elastic bands or tubing.

Shoulder Retraction With External Rotation   This exercise (figure 20.8) takes scapular retraction to a new level and strengthens the shoulder external rotators in the rotator cuff and the muscles in the upper back that control the shoulder blades.

▶ **Figure 20.8**   Scapular retraction with external rotation. In this exercise the swimmer sets the shoulder blades while also producing shoulder external rotation. These images show (a) the starting position and (b) the ending position of the exercise. This exercise can be performed using elastic bands or tubing.

Standing External Rotation   This exercise (figure 20.9) builds strength in the external rotators of the rotator cuff. As with all rotator cuff exercises, the athlete should retract the scapulae before each repetition.

▶ **Figure 20.9**
Standing external rotation. In this exercise, the swimmer keeps the elbow at the side while externally rotating the shoulder against resistance. These images show (a) the starting position and (b) the ending position of the exercise. This exercise can be performed using elastic bands or tubing.

Catch Position External Rotation   This exercise (figure 20.10) strengthens the external rotators of the rotator cuff. It is more complicated than the standing external rotation exercise because the swimmer is required to stabilize the shoulder and shoulder blades to a greater degree. But this exercise is more swimming specific because the movement mimics the shoulder action during the catch in freestyle and butterfly. If the exercise is done correctly, the upper arm should not move during the execution of the exercise.

▶ **Figure 20.10**
Catch position external rotation. In this exercise, the swimmer abducts the shoulder 90 degrees before externally rotating the shoulder against resistance. These images show (a) the starting position and (b) the ending position of the exercise. This exercise can be performed using elastic bands or tubing.

Full-Can Exercise

This exercise (figure 20.11) strengthens the muscles of the rotator cuff and improves overall shoulder stability. Swimmers should stay away from the empty-can exercise, in which the thumbs are pointed downward (shoulders internally rotated) through the movement because this action can create additional irritation for the tendons in the shoulder.

▶ **Figure 20.11** Full-can exercise. In this exercise, the swimmer abducts or flexes the shoulders against resistance until the hands reach shoulder height. The shoulders should be externally rotated during this exercise so that the hands are positioned in such a way that it looks as if they are holding cans. These images show (a) the starting position and (b) the ending position of the exercise. This exercise can be performed using elastic bands or tubing.

Chest Punch This exercise (figure 20.12) preferentially targets and builds strength in the serratus anterior muscle that runs around the rib cage and controls the shoulder blades. The exercise can be performed with both arms at the same time (figure 20.12a and b) or with each arm independently (figure 20.12c and d). All of the motion in this exercise comes from pressing the arms upward and protracting the shoulder blades.

▶ **Figure 20.12** Chest punch. This exercise targets the serratus anterior muscle and is important for maintaining shoulder stability. These images show the starting and ending positions of the exercise when (a and b) both sides of the body are worked simultaneously and when (c and d) just one arm is used.

Upper Body Press-Up With a Plus

This exercise (figure 20.13) also targets the serratus anterior muscle and serves to build dynamic stability in this muscle, which controls the shoulder blades and the orientation of the glenohumeral joint when swimming.

▶ **Figure 20.13** Upper-body press-up with a plus. From a push-up position and while maintaining a constant body position, the swimmer puts one hand on a raised surface. She then follows by bringing the second hand on to the raised surface and pushes the upper body away, rounding the upper back across the shoulders. These images show (a) the starting position, (b) the midpoint position, and (c) the finish position of the exercise.

Rowing Rowing exercises (figure 20.14) are extremely beneficial for strengthening the upper back and protecting the health of the shoulders. A swimmer could perform many variations of rowing exercises, but the one constant is that the athlete needs to set the shoulder blades before each repetition.

▶ **Figure 20.14** Rowing variations. These images show the starting and ending positions of (*a* and *b*) a seated row performed on a stability ball and (*c* and *d*) a straight arm rowing exercise. These exercises can often be performed using elastic bands or tubing.

Strength Training for Prevention of Other Injuries

Besides the shoulder, the next most common injury sites are the knee (patellofemoral pain and medial collateral ligament sprains) and the back. The most common injuries in these areas seem to result from a combination of overuse, muscle weakness, and poor flexibility, all of which can be addressed through a strength and conditioning program that targets strength development, the appropriate balance between muscular endurance and power, and flexibility.

For the knee, balanced strength needs to be developed through the legs. In many instances, the swimmer needs to build overall leg strength and strength in the hamstrings in particular to maintain a normal flexor-to-extensor strength ratio around the knee. Table 20.2 provides additional exercises that can be used to develop foundational strength in the lower body and help prevent injury.

For back health, the muscles of the core need to be strengthened to provide stability to the pelvis and maintain an appropriate posture in the water. In many instances, swimmers demonstrate tight hip flexors, resulting in an anterior pelvic tilt and the adoption of a kyphotic posture in the lower back (excessive curvature). This position not only compromises body position and the ability to generate an effective kick but also contributes to lower-back pain. Static stretching of the hip flexors (figure 20.15) can help restore normal hip posture, positively affecting both health and performance.

▶ **Figure 20.15** Hip flexor stretch. Developing adequate flexibility through the hip flexors will help the swimmer maintain proper body position in the water as well as improve the efficiency of the flutter or butterfly kick.

Flexibility Training for Swimming

Stretching often goes hand in hand with discussions on strength training. Optimal muscle function is based on establishing a balance between strength and flexibility. Having muscular strength is important, but being able to produce force through a full range of motion is what allows swimmers to become truly proficient in the water. As such, flexibility training is just as important to a swimmer's performance as strength training.

Just as swimmers develop strength imbalances throughout the body, many also develop flexibility imbalances. Flexibility imbalances can be seen in the shoulders of many swimmers, particularly in the direction of internal rotation (Spiegelman 2006; Torres and Gomes 2009). Nonathletes commonly have 70 degrees of internal rotation at the shoulder, but research conducted on a group of collegiate swimmers showed that they had only 49 degrees of internal rotation, a deficit of more than 20 degrees (Spiegelman 2006). This deficit is even greater than what has been found for athletes who participate in sports such as baseball and tennis that are thought to place more stress on the shoulder. Although these swimmers exhibited slightly greater external rotation than nonathletes did, they still showed an overall range-of-motion deficit of 10 degrees at the shoulder. In sports such as tennis, similar internal rotation deficits develop over time and are linked to increased risk of injury. Internal rotation flexibility deficits will likely continue to worsen in swimmers unless flexibility training is used to improve range of motion.

Swimmers often experience tightness of muscles on the anterior (front) side of the body, including the hip flexors. When these muscles are tight, they pull the pelvis into a position of anterior pelvic tilt, which affects performance both by inhibiting an athlete's ability to maintain a streamlined position (increased drag) and by reducing the ability to produce an effective and propulsive kick (reduced propulsion).

With that said, in all instances swimmers should strive to achieve a normal range of motion about the joints. Swimmers have an optimal range of flexibility that places them at the lowest risk of injury. If a swimmer falls outside this normal range, either because muscles are extremely tight or because joints are hyperflexible, the risk of injury increases. Regular stretching should be a regular part of a swimmer's training to maximize performance and reduce injury risk.

Flexibility is a term used to describe the elasticity of muscles and other structures that surround a joint. Static flexibility is the range of motion measured at a joint while maintaining a stationary position. In other words, no movement occurs. Most athletes are familiar with static stretching, which typically involves stretching a muscle or muscle group and holding that position for 20 to 30 seconds. Dynamic flexibility is flexibility with movement. It can be thought of as the range of motion available to swimmers while they are actually swimming. Although dynamic flexibility may seem to be the more important component for swimmers, both types of flexibility are important to swimmers. Regular static stretching is an important and necessary first step toward developing greater dynamic flexibility and improving in-pool performance.

Static stretching should be performed at the end of a practice, not before. Muscles are most pliable when they are warm, so the end of practice is an ideal time to work on flexibility training. In addition, static stretching before a practice or event may actually impair performance. Recent research has shown that static stretching can impair the ability of a muscle to generate peak forces and power for as long as an hour after the stretch is performed. In a sport such as swimming, which requires virtually all the muscles in the body to produce force and power, static stretching before a workout has the potential to limit performance. Although this phenomenon has not been studied specifically in swimming, the results of swimming-specific research would be unlikely to produce results that are different from what has been seen in other sports.

If swimmers need to stretch before a training session or competition, they should try to stretch at least one hour beforehand to allow the muscle contractile properties that contribute to optimal performance to be restored.

The following are some additional guidelines for static stretching:

- Stretches should be performed two or three times and held for 20 to 30 seconds. This approach will produce the greatest gains in flexibility. Holding the stretch longer does not seem to produce any additional benefits.

- Flexibility training should be treated as a part of a swimmer's overall training program. Flexibility does not improve overnight. Making a change requires including flexibility training in the daily routine. Try to devote 10 to 15 minutes every day to stretching. Although a single stretching session can improve flexibility for up to 90 minutes, we are looking for long-term flexibility gains that come only with time.

- Stretch both sides of the body. Swimming is a bilateral activity, so the muscles on both sides of the body need to be stretched.

- Stretch progressively and within limits. Athletes should not try to do too much or stretch a muscle group too vigorously. Additionally, they should avoid bouncing to try to get a deeper stretch in a muscle.

- Stretching should never be painful. Swimmers should feel tension in the stretched muscle, but stretching should never hurt. If athletes do feel pain, they should stop the stretch.

One of the most beneficial stretches for improving or maintaining range of motion at the shoulder is the sleeper stretch (figure 20.16). This stretch targets the external rotators and posterior shoulder capsule, thus improving the range of motion into internal rotation.

Note that in some people, being too loose in the shoulder (a condition called hyperlaxity), not being too tight, is what contributes to injury. The shoulder joint is surrounded by a joint capsule. This structure provides some stability to the joint and keeps the ball-and-socket positioned correctly. When the front

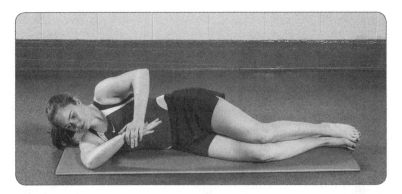

▶ **Figure 20.16** Sleeper stretch. The sleeper stretch helps improve the degree of internal rotation range of motion in the shoulder.

part of the shoulder joint capsule becomes overstretched, the shoulder does not move properly and impingement is more likely to occur. Many swimmers unknowingly contribute to this condition by performing the arms behind the back shoulder stretch (figure 20.17). This stretch can be detrimental to the health of the shoulder because it primarily stretches the joint capsule and not the chest or shoulder muscles.

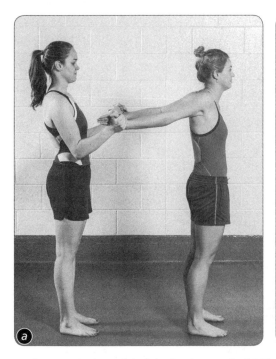

▶ **Figure 20.17** Behind the back stretch. (a) The behind the back stretch shown here is contraindicated for swimmers because it tends to stretch the anterior joint capsule of the shoulder. (b) An alternative stretch, which appropriately targets the pectoralis muscles, is the chest stretch.

The Warm-Up and Swimming

The warm-up is often thought of as a part of a strength and conditioning program. It can provide many benefits in swimming. The basic purpose of the warm-up is literally to warm the body by increasing muscle and core body temperature. When the body is warm, the muscles are able to function more efficiently because they contract with greater force through a greater range of motion. A good warm-up also does a number of other things to get the body physically ready for high-intensity swimming:

- The warm-up primes the cardiovascular and respiratory systems, enhancing the body's ability to pump blood and deliver oxygen to the working muscles.
- The warm-up develops dynamic flexibility or flexibility with motion. It puts muscles and joints through their range of motion, actively enhancing flexibility and improving stroke efficiency.
- It gets the body's biochemistry working optimally. All of the body's physiological systems need to be warmed up to optimal levels to support high-intensity swimming.
- It gets the mind talking with the muscles, improving coordination and the efficiency of movement.
- It helps reduce the risk of injury. Jumping right into high-intensity swimming without warming up puts the body at increased risk of injury ranging from muscle pulls to heart complications. Easing into a practice by using a warm-up can help reduce those risks.

Conducting an in-water warm-up immediately before a competition event is often not possible. Although swimmers typically are able to warm up before the start of competition, not every event provides a warm-up pool where athletes can warm up between races. In these cases, performing a dryland dynamic warm-up is beneficial. Dynamic warm-up exercises involve movement and are designed to improve dynamic flexibility while also elevating body temperature (Salo and Riewald 2008). The exercises selected should target the specific muscle groups used in swimming, and each exercise should be performed for 15 to 30 seconds. The total dynamic warm-up should take 5 to 10 minutes to complete. Rubber tubing can be used to facilitate dynamic exercises, which can be swimming specific and therefore enhance the dryland warm-up procedure.

Special Considerations for the Young Swimmer

Many questions have been asked about the appropriateness of having young, prepubescent athletes engage in strength training. Concerns exist about increasing the risk of injury, stunting growth, and negatively affecting normal growth and development. But the American College of Sports Medicine (Faigenbaum and Micheli 2013), the American Academy of Pediatrics (Council on Sports Medicine and Fitness 2008), and the National Strength and Conditioning Association (Faigenbaum et al. 2009) have all issued position papers or public comments stating that strength training is appropriate and safe for children if proper supervision and technique instruction are provided. The American College of Sports Medicine in *Current Comment on Youth Strength Training* states,

> *Contrary to the traditional belief that strength training is dangerous for children or that it could lead to bone plate disturbances, the American College of Sports Medicine (ACSM) contends that strength training can be a safe and effective activity for this age group, provided that the programs are properly designed and competently supervised. (Faigenbaum and Micheli 2013)*

This sentiment has been echoed by all other organizations and professionals in the strength-training community (Faigenbaum 2012). The National Strength and Conditioning Association, in their position statement on youth resistance training, put forward seven key statements to describe a properly designed and supervised resistance-training program:

1. It is relatively safe for youth.
2. It enhances the muscular strength and power of youth.
3. It improves the cardiovascular risk profile of youth.
4. It improves motor skill performance and may contribute to enhanced sports performance of youth.
5. It increases a young athlete's resistance to sports-related injuries.
6. It helps improve the psychosocial well-being of youth.
7. It helps promote and develop exercise habits during childhood and adolescence.

Another question that often comes up with younger swimmers is, "Does strength training actually help a young swimmer?" The short answer is, "Yes, it does." Although testosterone, a steroid produced naturally in the body predominantly after puberty, is necessary to build muscle mass and strength, young athletes can see improvements in motor control and strength after being engaged in a strength and conditioning program. Several benefits to young athletes have been documented:

- Increased strength and coordination through improved neuromuscular function
- Increased bone density
- Improved self-image and self-confidence
- Potential to prevent injuries

All these attributes should be appealing to young swimmers.

Kraemer and Fleck (2005) capture all these ideas in their youth strength-training progression model in which they lay out appropriate exercises and training techniques for athletes of various ages. Their model offers the following key take-home messages:

- Athletes 7 years old and under should perform exercises with little or no weight and focus on learning proper technique. As they develop physically and emotionally, the complexity of the exercises and the volume and intensity of the training should increase.

- From 8 to 10 years of age, athletes should gradually increase the number of exercises, the number of repetitions, and training volume while still performing relatively simple exercises.

- From 11 to 13 years old, athletes can do more advanced exercises, but they should be done with no weight while technique is emphasized.

- From 14 to 16 years old, athletes should continue to increase training volume while adding sport-specific exercises to the training plan.

- Above 16 years of age, athletes should progress into an adult-style program but only after they have mastered all techniques and have adequate training experience.

Coaches need to set appropriate strength and conditioning goals when working with young swimmers. The general themes surrounding strength training for the young athlete should be preventing injury, building athleticism, engraining proper exercise technique, and developing endurance. The technique work put in during this developmental phase lays the foundation for more advanced training down the road as the swimmer gets older. Although power development may be an appropriate goal for an older athlete, it should not be the focus of the training plan for a young swimmer because of the loads that this type of training can place on the body. When proper technique is emphasized and every strength-training session is conducting by a qualified and certified strength coach, young swimmers who are engaged in a strength-training program have a very low risk of injury.

When looking specifically at the research on strength training for the young swimmer and its effect on swimming performance, limited data are available to draw from. Several studies, however, show favorable improvements in performance following strength training (Bulgakova, Vorontsov, and Fomichenko 1990; Blanksby and Gregor 1981), although results from at least one other study have shown no positive relationship between development of power and flip turn performance (Cossor, Blanksby, and Elliot 1999).

Summary

This chapter provides a number of take-home messages that can help coaches develop and modify a strength and conditioning program for swimmers.

Strength gains made on dry land or in the water can positively affect swimming performance. The relationship between strength and propulsion should not be the sole focus, because performance gains can also be realized when a swimmer maintains a good, consistent body line in the water, thereby reducing drag.

Strength training for injury prevention should be targeted to areas of the body where strength imbalances frequently exist (e.g., shoulders and scapular stabilizers) or where the links in the kinetic chain are weak (e.g., core).

An appropriate strength-training program for swimmers should integrate multiple training modalities that include dryland and in-pool training. Resisted swimming exercises are a sport-specific training modality that positively correlates with swimming performance. Coaches should build foundational strength in swimmers before working on swimming-specific strength exercises or power exercises.

Don't be afraid to engage even the youngest swimmer in a strength-training program. Focus on teaching technique and building foundational strength, using exercises that require little or no weight. Engrain the concepts behind strengthening for injury prevention and lay a foundation that will be useful to the athletes as they develop.

Do not forget about flexibility training but be sure to conduct static stretching at the end of training, not before. Full-body flexibility is important, but the focus should be on areas where flexibility imbalances are known to develop in swimmers (shoulder internal rotation, hip flexor tightness). Also, strive to achieve normal ranges of motion about joints; excessive flexibility can be just as damaging to performance and joint health as too little flexibility.

Finally, be creative and have fun. You can train strength in swimmers in many ways. Strength training should be an enjoyable experience that never gets old. Enjoy applying this information with your swimmers.

Considerations for Special Groups

CHAPTER 21

Adolescent Swimmers

—Jordan D. Metzl, MD, and Morgan A. Busko, MD

Adolescent swimmers face a variety of unique issues because of the demanding nature of the sport and the uniqueness of the developing adolescent body. Parents, coaches, and athletes should be aware of the physical, psychological, and physiological changes that young swimmers undergo and the way in which these changes affect their athletic performance. This chapter discusses the demands of swimming on the developing body, health concerns specific to the adolescent swimmer, and the most common injury patterns and medical concerns seen in these athletes. It provides the latest research on the recommended training volume as well as various types of preventive strength training for adolescent swimmers. The goal of this chapter is to discuss methods of ensuring health and safety for adolescent swimmers.

Sport Specialization

Should adolescent swimmers be committed to swimming year round at the expense of engaging in other sports? Year-round training in a single sport during the adolescent years is becoming increasingly common, particularly among youth swimmers. In a study of university-aged female athletes, swimmers stood out among the diving, tennis, golf, track and field, basketball, and volleyball athletes as being the only athletes who had their first organized sport experience in their current sport (Malina 2010). In short, swimmers enter the sport early and stay with it. Additionally, the general perception is that to succeed at swimming, early sport specialization is beneficial for most swimmers.

Too much of a good thing, however, can cause problems. Year-round swimming without involvement in other sports is one of the leading causes for adolescent swim injuries. New evidence has shown that the sheer quantity of strokes and the length of time involved in the sport, two measures of training volume, are the two best predictors of overuse injury in swimming (Bak 2010). Choosing to specialize in swimming at an early age often results in repeated microtrauma and persistent loading of tissues that are not yet at full strength or development.

To prevent pediatric overuse injuries, the American Academy of Pediatrics and the National Athletic Trainer Association both recommend that adolescent athletes not be committed to one sport year round until midadolescence (American Academy of Pediatrics 2000). Coaches and parents should encourage adolescent swimmers to join other sport teams or engage in other activities that enhance their motor development and allow their swimming-specific muscles to rest.

United States Swimming has recommendations for the maximum training volume for adolescent swimmers, which directly address the issues of swim volume in growing teens. For 11- to 14-year-old swimmers who are developing basic skills, no more than 4 to 6 sessions per week (60 to 90 minutes per session) are recommended. If athletes are participating year round, simultaneous activities should be encouraged to decrease the time in the water and increase weight-bearing exercise. Adolescents who are participating only in swimming should take two to three months, preferably nonconsecutive, off from competitive swimming. For 13- to 18-year-olds, the maximum training load is 6 to 10 sessions per week (90 to 120 minutes per session). This age is the time of youth when many swimmers commit to year-round competition, but sport specialization is encouraged only for advanced swimmers 14 years or older who demonstrate the potential to reach an elite level. For this small group of elite adolescents, the USA Swimming organization recommends a maximum of 8 to 10 sessions per week (90 to 120 minutes per session) and recognizes that year-round competition with short periods of rest is essential to avoiding loss of aerobic fitness (USA Swimming 2010).

Parents and coaches often question whether their children or athletes can compete at an elite level if they are not swimming at a high training volume year round, but the reality is that few adolescent swimmers have the potential to reach that elite level. Because of the fragile nature of the human body during development, adolescents who choose to specialize in swimming at an early age may be more prone to injury, burnout, and long-term health issues, as discussed later in the chapter.

The Developing Adolescent Athlete

The adolescent years are a period of great importance in the development of the adult skeleton and the mature athlete. Adolescent development is a combination of physical, physiological, and psychological changes during the teenage years that have a large effect on athletic performance. The physical changes of the body are most significant during puberty, a time marked by sexual development, an increase in gender-specific hormones, and rapid growth. Surging levels of the steroid hormone estrogen in females and rising levels of testosterone in males are responsible for the constant state of evolution during this time, which is easily seen in rapid changes in height, weight, and physique (Metzl and Shookhoff 2002).

The changes in height, weight, and body contour are the result of rapid growth of the bones and muscles. The long bones in the body have epiphyseal plates, known as growth plates, which are regions of cartilage present only until the body stops growing. Around the end of puberty, the cartilage cells in the growth plate stop replicating, and the plate is slowly replaced by bone until it becomes the epiphyseal line, which no longer has growth potential. These growth plates are the weakest part of the skeleton, and their fragility makes them a common site of injury among young athletes. The plates are often weaker than the ligaments and tendons that surround them, so injuries that might result in a joint sprain for an adult can cause a growth plate fracture in an adolescent (Metzl and Shookhoff 2002).

During these periods of rapid skeletal growth, the muscles are also growing, but they may not grow at the same pace as the bones. The result can be a noticeable loss of flexibility. The slower muscular growth leads to increasing tension, tightness, and aches. Stretching is the most important remedy to prevent muscular injury as this natural phenomenon occurs. Because of the delicate nature of the developing body, adolescent athletes must take special precaution to protect their bones, muscles, and ligaments (Metzl and Shookhoof 2002).

Physiological changes related to growth and development accompany the more apparent pubertal changes. Adolescent athletes experience noticeable gains in their maximal oxygen uptake ($\dot{V}O_2$max), anaerobic capacity, and muscular strength (Geithner et al. 2004). $\dot{V}O_2$max is the maximum capacity of a person's body to transport and use oxygen during exercise of increasing intensity. Oxygen, which is carried in the blood, is the limiting factor in endurance exercise because it is required for the generation of adenosine triphosphate (ATP), which is the form of energy that muscles use. As the heart muscle gains strength during adolescent development, it is able to pump more oxygen through the blood to the rest of the muscles in the body. Therefore, $\dot{V}O_2$max is a strong reflection of a person's physiological fitness, and it is considered the single best indicator of cardiovascular fitness and maximal aerobic power in adolescents. An increase in $\dot{V}O_2$max as adolescents mature is one of the driving forces behind improved performance in endurance sports such as swimming, cycling, rowing, cross-country skiing, and running. As adolescents grow and mature, they are stronger and more physiologically able to tolerate longer periods of exercise and activity (Geithner et al. 2004).

Health Concerns Specific to the Adolescent Swimmer

Adolescent athletes in every sport take certain precautions to prevent injury and damage to the body during the growing years. A variety of health concerns are specific to the adolescent swimmer. Low bone mineral density, the female-athlete triad, and exercise-induced bronchospasm are three of these health concerns. In addition, specific musculoskeletal injuries are prevalent among adolescent swimmers because of the repetitive nature of the sport. Young athletes, parents, and coaches should be familiar with these health concerns so that athletes can participate in exercises and routines that will help to prevent them.

Bone Mineral Density

Why should adolescent swimmers be concerned about their bone mineral density (BMD)? Bone mineral density is the ratio of weight to the volume or area of the bones. Low BMD and osteoporosis (decreased bone density) have a positive association, so BMD is an indirect indicator of fracture risk. During adolescence, more bone is deposited than is withdrawn, so an increase in bone density parallels the growth in bone size. Peak bone mass is the greatest amount of bone mass that will be present throughout life at a specific site in the skeleton. Bone mass increases during childhood and puberty, reaches a peak around the age of 30, and then declines with age (Rizzoli et al. 2010). Therefore, the bone being formed during the adolescent years determines the athlete's eventual BMD, which is a key determinant of adult skeletal health (Rizzoli et al. 2010).

Adolescent swimmers are at particular risk for low BMD because the sport does not involve any weight-bearing activity. Weight-bearing exercise is any force-generating activity that creates a large compressive force on the bones, which has a positive effect on osteogenic (formation of new bone) activity (Whalen and Carter 1988). Evidence indicates that the effects of weight-bearing exercise on bone are more effective if the exercise occurs before or at the time of the adolescent growth spurt (Witzke and Snow 2000). Several studies have compared the total body BMD and regional BMD (lumbar spine, femoral neck, and leg) of adolescents who are participating in either weight-bearing or non-weight-bearing exercise. These studies demonstrate that runners and athletes who participate in weight-bearing sports have significantly higher total body BMD and regional BMD than swimmers (Silva et al. 2011; Pettersson et al. 2000).

Because of the non-weight-bearing nature of the sport, both male and female adolescent swimmers who are not participating in other weight-bearing forms of exercise are at a higher risk for osteoporosis and osteopenia (an early stage of osteoporosis) later in life. The American College of Sports Medicine recommends that adolescent swimmers incorporate into their weekly training plans at least three days of 10 to 20 minutes of impact activity (Kohrt et al. 2004). In addition, swimmers can promote bone growth by engaging in weight-bearing sports during swimming's off-season.

What else can adolescent swimmers do to maximize their BMD during this critical period of growth? Numerous studies have demonstrated that BMD increases with increasing muscle strength (Nichols, Sanborn, and Love 2001). Strength training stimulates an increase in BMD beyond what occurs naturally; these positive results have been seen with both resistance training and plyometric jump training (Blimkie et al. 1996; Witzke and Snow 2000). Strength-training exercises that are recommended specifically for adolescent swimmers are discussed later in this chapter.

Several cross-sectional studies show that weight-bearing exercise must be coupled with sufficient calcium intake to have a positive association with BMD (Kanders, Dempster, and Lindsay 1998; Chan 1991). When the body is not receiving adequate calcium, it takes calcium from the only source that it has—the bones. The U.S. national recommendations for calcium intake for 11- to 24-year-olds is 1,300 milligrams per day, which can be obtained through four servings of calcium-rich foods or drinks, such as milk, yogurt, and cheese (French, Fulkerson, and Story 2000). Nonfood calcium supplements containing between 300 and 1,000 milligrams have also demonstrated positive effects on BMD during the adolescent years (Lloyd et al. 1993; Nowson et al. 1997). Therefore, besides eating calcium-rich foods, young swimmers should take a calcium supplement with added vitamin D every day to protect their bones.

Female Athlete Triad

Adolescent female swimmers with low BMD are subject to the female athlete triad, which is a serious health concern that is being seen with increasing frequency (Golden 2002). This topic is discussed in detail in chapter 23, but to review here, the three components of the triad are anorexia (insufficient caloric intake), amenorrhea (absence of menstrual periods), and osteoporosis (decreased bone density). Sustained anorexia leads to a significant decline in available energy, which causes the amenorrhea and osteoporosis because of the body's physiological response to decreasing body fat percentages that result from energy deprivation. Energy availability is the energy consumed through the diet minus the energy expended through exercise. Figure 21.1 demonstrates the range of energy availability, which is the amount of energy available after exercise for the remainder of bodily functions such as cellular maintenance, thermoregulation, growth, and reproduction (Nattiv et al. 2007).

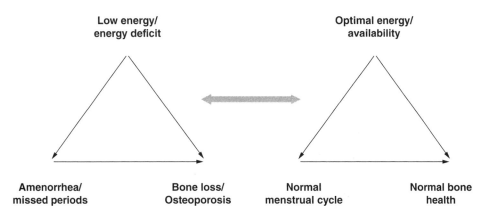

▶ **Figure 21.1** Energy availability spectrum. Energy availability is the energy consumed through the diet minus the energy expended through exercise.

Energy deficiency can be a result of the disease anorexia nervosa, an eating disorder depicted by conscious restrictive eating and distorted body image. Sustained low energy availability because of long-term anorexia nervosa can lead to complications involving the cardiovascular, endocrine, reproductive, skeletal, gastrointestinal, renal, and central nervous systems (Nattiv et al. 2007). This psychological issue needs to be addressed by a multidisciplinary team of health care professionals, a registered dietitian, the family and coach of the athlete, and a mental health practitioner.

Not all athletes with low body fat percentages have an eating disorder. Low energy availability may also be unintentional, which is common among rapidly growing, active females who perform high training volumes, such as adolescent swimmers during puberty. When young females remain in low energy states, depicted by the triangle on the left of figure 21.1, the hormones that stimulate bone formation are decreased and the estrogen no longer performs its normal role in preventing bone resorption. These hormonal alterations are responsible for the poor bone health characteristic of the female athlete triad. An athlete's BMD is a reflection of her menstrual history and her current and past energy availability (Nattiv et al. 2007).

Low energy availability before puberty has been shown to delay sexual development and suppress growth. Primary amenorrhea is the absence of menstruation after the age of 15 or after the athlete has gone through other pubertal changes, and it can be a red flag for the female athlete triad. Secondary amenorrhea is characterized by more than three months of no menstrual cycles after having normal menstrual cycles. Amenorrhea has many causes, but the absence of menses in the female athlete triad occurs because the pituitary gland is not secreting pulses of luteinizing hormone, which is normally secreted at specific intervals throughout the day. Young swimmers can experience amenorrhea even without dietary restriction if their volume of habitual, strenuous physical activity is too high.

Coaches, parents, and athletes should all be aware of the female athlete triad so that it can be addressed early to minimize the negative effects of the energy deficit on the body. Restoring regular menses will not return a young female to her best possible bone health, but her BMD will start to improve as the hormones return to normal function. Health care professionals stress prevention, early recognition, and treatment of the female athlete triad because the consequences of these conditions are potentially irreversible (Wade, Schneider, and Li 1996).

Exercise-Induced Bronchospasm

What is exercise-induced bronchospasm (EIB), and why is it so common among adolescent swimmers? EIB is a temporary condition of respiratory difficulty because of a sudden constriction of the muscles in the walls of the lung's bronchioles. Although 90 percent of asthmatics experience EIB, 10 percent of the nonasthmatic population is also subject to this condition. It can be caused by medical conditions, medications, and environmental factors, and it is triggered by aerobic exercise. The diagnosis of EIB is based on a demonstrated reduction in an athlete's forced expiratory volume in one second (FEV1), as well as a thorough history that indicates shortness of breath during exercise, tight chest, coughing, wheezing, and decreased exercise endurance. The physical exam of an athlete with EIB will usually present as normal.

Studies indicate an increased prevalence of EIB among swimmers, and adolescent swimmers are particularly prone to this condition for several reasons (Helenius et al. 1998). The first is the demanding nature of the sport on the lungs. During exercise, particularly endurance training, increasing ventilation leads to the loss of heat and water through respiration, which causes the bronchial constriction. After years of training, the respiratory mucosa becomes increasingly inflamed and the epithelium can be damaged, causing symptoms to worsen over time.

The training environment of adolescent swimmers is the second reason that they are at increased risk of EIB. Training in chlorinated pools, in which chloroform and other organic compounds are formed, is an environmental cause for EIB (Drobnic et al. 1996). Evidence for this is found in studies that demonstrate significantly higher onset of EIB among swimmers when compared with runners and cyclists (Williams, Schwellnus, and Noakes 2004). Despite the fact that chlorine concentrations in pool environments are kept at acceptable levels, extensive exercise in the presence of these "safe" chlorine levels produces abnormal levels of exposure to the toxin chloroform. A direct association is seen between the water chloroform level, the chloroform concentration in the environmental air, and the chloroform level in the blood plasma (Aiking et al. 1994). Swimming in a poorly ventilated indoor swimming pool increases the assimilation of these harmful toxins, which can trigger EIB. According to the U.S. National Institute for Occupational Safety and Health, chronic exposure to chloroform can also damage the liver and kidneys.

Although adolescent swimmers train in the same environment as their elders do, adolescents are at a greater risk for EIB because they inhale more air per unit of body weight and have less-developed immune systems. Therefore, they absorb a greater amount of toxins, primarily chloroform, during a training session. Multiple training sessions prevent the clearing of toxins because at least one night is needed for absorbed substances to be removed from the body (Cammann and Hubner 1995). For that reason, the onset of EIB in adolescent swimmers may follow sudden increases in training volume or a transition to two-a-day practices.

Adolescent swimmers with symptoms of EIB should be evaluated by a doctor to determine how serious their condition is and to initiate effective management of the condition (Sinha and David 2003). Swimmers should be aware of the nature of EIB, the triggers that are specific to their case, and the ways that they can avoid or control bronchospasm without medication. One way to prevent bronchial hyperresponsiveness during these acute attacks is to warm up properly before performing vigorous exercise (Reiff et al. 1989). In addition, adolescents should seek opportunities to train outdoors because the chloroform exposure of outdoor pools is much less than that of indoor pools (Aiking et al. 1994).

Musculoskeletal Injuries

The muscles and tendons of the developing body are particularly fragile during adolescence as they adapt to the maturing skeleton. Chapter 18 looks in depth at orthopedic injuries in swimming, but this section deals specifically with orthopedic issues in the developing athlete.

Shoulder pain is the most common musculoskeletal complaint among swimmers of all levels, so athletes, coaches, and parents need to understand how the shoulder works. The shoulder is a ball-and-socket joint that has 180 degrees of rotation. The humerus (the upper-arm bone) is the ball portion of the joint, and the scapula is the socket. These bones are held together by the glenohumeral capsular ligaments and the four rotator cuff muscles. Stability in this region is important for maintaining a healthy ball-and-socket. The glenohumeral ligaments in the shoulder provide static stability, which holds the bones together. The rotator cuff muscles (supraspinatus, infraspinatus, teres minor, and subscapularis) provide dynamic stability when the shoulder is in motion. Shoulder stability depends on a combination of both dynamic and static stabilizers. This stability can be compromised if muscle strength and endurance are inadequate during the period of rapid skeletal growth.

When 993 10- to 18-year-old swimmers were evaluated, 47 percent reported a history of pain in the shoulder, referred to as swimmer's shoulder (McMaster and Troup 1993). The term *swimmer's shoulder* was first used in 1974 to describe anterior shoulder pain felt by swimmers during and after training. It has since become a nonspecific term referring to a variety of injuries that occur in the shoulder region. Shoulder pain in swimmers is generally assumed to result from subacromial impingement, whereby the rotator cuff tendons impinge against the overlying acromion bone, which results in rotator cuff tendonitis. Tendonitis is the inflammation of a tendon because of irritation. The tendons of the rotator cuff muscles pass through a relatively narrow space between the acromion process of the scapula and the head of the humerus, which can apply pressure on these tendons if the space is constricted. In the case of swimmer's shoulder, the tendons of the rotator cuff and associated bursa often become inflamed because of impingement caused by the repetitive overhead arm motion of the freestyle stroke.

Impingement can occur during the pull-through phase or during the recovery phase of freestyle. If a swimmer's hand enters the water across the midline of the body at the beginning of the pull-through phase (known as hand entry), the shoulder is placed in a position of horizontal adduction, which results in a mechanical impingement. Impingement can also occur during the recovery phase of freestyle, which starts when the arm exits the water and ends with hand entry. During this phase, fatigue often becomes evident as swimmers find it more challenging to lift their arms out of the water with each stroke. Adolescent swimmers are more prone to fatigue during this phase when their muscles lack full strength during maturation. In addition, swimmers with shoulder impingement have been shown to minimize their follow-through, eliminating the extreme internal rotation by pulling their hands out of the water too early. This action may be contributing to the impingement, or it may be a result of their subconscious effort to minimize pain from the injury. All these stroke alterations result in decreased efficiency of the rotator cuff muscles and mechanical impingement of the supraspinatus tendon.

What predisposes adolescent swimmers to swimmer's shoulder? Lax ligaments, poor technique, and overtraining are the most common causes of swimmer's shoulder. Because of the nature of the sport, loose ligaments in the shoulder are common among swimmers. Young swimmers who have naturally lax ligaments, most commonly seen in those with underlying generalized ligamentous laxity, are subject to loose shoulders that may slip out of their sockets because of a lack of static stability. In this setting, the rotator cuff is overloaded because of reliance on the dynamic stabilizers. If these athletes identify this condition early, they can focus on strengthening the rotator cuff muscles, which will increase their dynamic stability to compensate for the lack of static stability.

Poor technique can also lead to impingement over a short period because of the repetitive nature of the sport and the increased likelihood of microtrauma during growth and development. Crossing the hand over the midline on hand entry, as discussed previously, and pointing the thumb down with the palm facing outward are two common mistakes made, particularly by young swimmers who have not yet had extensive years of technique training.

Overtraining or underrecovery is another leading cause of swimmer's shoulder. Swimmers in year-round youth swim programs average between 6,000 and 10,000 meters per day and practice five to seven days per week. Assuming that their average stroke count is between 8 and 10 strokes per 25 meters, swimmers are rotating each shoulder around 30,000 times per week. The muscles of a growing body are more prone to fatigue than those of fully developed athletes, which causes them to work less efficiently. The muscles are then forced to work harder with less strength, and athletes will increase their stroke frequency in an attempt to compensate. To minimize their chances of developing an overuse injury, adolescent swimmers should avoid swimming seven days per week, rapidly increasing their training volume, or specializing in a sport year round.

Studies have shown that strengthening the rotator cuff muscles, scapular muscles, lower trapezius, and core muscles will significantly decrease an athlete's risk for developing swimmer's shoulder (Faigenbaum et al. 2009).

Strength Training for Adolescent Swimmers

Despite the old misconception that youth strength training was unsafe and ineffective, major health organizations such as the American College of Sports Medicine (ACSM), the American Academy of Pediatrics (AAP), and the National Strength and Conditioning Association (NSCA) are now advocating appropriately designed and properly supervised strength-training programs for adolescents.

Strength training is now recognized as a vital component of youth athletic programs, injury prevention strategies, and long-term health promotion. As adolescents become more active in sport and conditioning, accountability for their cumulative workload is often lacking. Age-appropriate guidelines for strength training have been established to reduce the risk of sports injuries and improve athletic performance. Figure 21.2 presents guidelines for youth strength training; for additional information, see the NSCA position statement for youth resistance training as well as the NATA position statement on the prevention of pediatric overuse injuries (Faigenbaum et al. 2009; Valovich McLeod et al. 2011).

Strength training prevents poor conditioning and muscular imbalance, which are two major causes of acute and overuse injuries. Well-designed strength-training programs that include a combination of resistance training and plyometrics have been proved to reduce sports-related injuries in adolescent athletes (Valovich McLeod et al. 2011).

- ◆ All strength-training sessions should be supervised by a quality instructor.
- ◆ Each training session should begin with a 5- to 10-minute warm-up or dynamic warm-up and end with a cool-down session.
- ◆ Young athletes should use light loads or body weight as resistance. Loads should increase gradually as the athlete becomes more proficient and stronger.
- ◆ All exercises should be performed with an emphasis on using proper technique.
- ◆ Injury prevention is key. Swimmers should focus on building strength in the muscles of the shoulder and rotator cuff, upper back, and core.
- ◆ Muscle balance and full-body strengthening are also important, so athletes should incorporate a mix of upper-body and lower-body exercises.
- ◆ Young athletes should not attempt to perform maximum lifts in any exercise. Additionally, strength training is not a contest to see who can lift or do more.
- ◆ Proper recovery is key, so athletes should not strength-train the same muscle groups on consecutive days. Performing two or three strength-training sessions per week is appropriate.
- ◆ Low-level plyometric exercises (hopping, skipping, bounding) are appropriate for young athletes.
- ◆ Progress should be monitored and evaluated regularly.
- ◆ Athletes should be encouraged to let the coach know if anything hurts or does not feel right.
- ◆ Strength can be developed in the pool in various ways, such as fins, vertical kicking, pulling, and so on.
- ◆ Remember that resistance training places stress on the body, so it should be considered part of the athlete's overall training volume.
- ◆ The athletes should have fun but should also bring maturity to strength training for it to be safe and successful.

▶ **Figure 21.2** General guidelines for strength training in adolescents.

Strength training is the use of resistance to muscular contraction from light weights or body weight designed to build strength, anaerobic endurance, and the power of skeletal muscles. Strength training provides functional benefits for athletes of all ages, but it is particularly beneficial during adolescence because it improves bone density; increases the strength and resilience of muscles, tendons, and ligaments; improves joint function; raises the level of good cholesterol (HDL) in the body; improves cardiac function; triggers a temporary increase in metabolism; and reduces the potential for injury.

Among the different forms of strength training are weight training, resistance training, isometric training, and plyometrics. Weight training and resistance training are similar in that they use gravity or elastic resistance to oppose muscle contraction. Elastic resistance provides the opportunity to increase strength while also allowing athletes to expand their range of motion (Duchateau and Hainaut 1984). Isometric (or constant length) training differs in that the length of the muscle and the joint angle remain constant during a contraction. Isometric training increases strength at the specific joint angles where the exercise is carried out and, to a lesser extent, at additional joint angles, whereas dynamic training increases strength through the muscle's complete range of motion.

Note that strength training and power lifting are not the same. Strength training is repetitive lifting of light weights, designed to increase baseline strength by developing more muscle fibers, whereas power lifting is heavy lifting designed to maximize muscle mass. Power lifting, as well as heavy lifting of any kind, is potentially dangerous to the open growth plates in adolescents, so it is not recommended for young athletes.

Plyometric training is an alternative form of conditioning designed to improve neuromuscular nervous system for the purpose of improving athletic performance. Plyometrics generates fast, powerful movements through repeated loading and contracting of the muscle, which increases the speed or force of muscular contractions. Plyometric jump training creates ground reaction forces that are four to seven times body weight, which provides benefits to the growing skeleton during adolescence (Whalen and Carter 1988). This aspect is of particular importance for swimmers, who must seek opportunities outside their sport for weight-bearing activity.

Dryland training is the term that swimmers use to refer to strength-training exercises, which can include bodyweight exercises (calisthenics), stretch cords, medicine balls, and machines. Consistent dryland workouts are the foundation for success in the sport, particularly for adolescent swimmers. The muscles of the core, back, and shoulders are of particular importance and should be the focus of a strength-training program. Electromyographic stroke analysis has demonstrated that the scapular muscles (serratus anterior, subscapularis, and lower trapezius) are used continuously throughout the entire stroke. Therefore, they are most susceptible to fatigue if they are not properly strengthened. When fatigued, swimmers tend to compromise the upward rotation of the scapula, which is a leading cause of shoulder impingement.

The following are some recommended dryland exercises for adolescent swimmers, designed for both improving performance in the water and preventing injuries.

Plank The plank is an isometric exercise that builds endurance and strength in the abdomen, back, shoulder, and stabilizer muscles. Prepare for planks by lying face down and resting on the forearms. Push up off the floor, raising the body on to the toes and elbows (figure 21.3). Keep the back flat so that it remains in a straight line from head to heels. If the butt is sagging or sticking up in the air, contract the abdominal muscles to maintain proper form. Hold for 60 seconds, lower, and repeat.

▶ **Figure 21.3** Plank position.

Side Plank The side plank strengthens the shoulder girdle, wrist and elbow joints, abdomen, and back. Prepare for side plank by lying on your side. Lift your body off the ground and balance on one forearm and the side of one foot (figure 21.4). Raise the opposite arm in the air as if you are reaching for the ceiling. Hold for 60 seconds, switch sides, and repeat.

▶ **Figure 21.4** Side plank position.

Stability Ball Reverse Fly   Reverse flys work the muscles in the shoulders (rear deltoids) and the upper back (trapezius and rhomboids). Prepare by lying face down with the chest supported on a stability ball. Keep the feet wider than shoulder-width apart to maintain stability. Hold a dumbbell in each hand with palms facing each other. Start with dumbbells resting on the floor directly under the shoulders (figure 21.5a). Bend the elbows slightly while lifting the dumbbells to shoulder level and squeeze the shoulder blades together at the top of the movement (figure 21.5b). Slowly, with control, return to the starting position. Inhale on the way up and begin exhaling at the top of the movement.

▶ **Figure 21.5**   Stability ball reverse fly: (a) starting position; (b) peak position.

Goblet Squat This exercise improves hip mobility and ankle dorsiflexion while also building stability and overall strength. Prepare by standing up straight while holding a light medicine ball or weight close to the chest. Squat down as if sitting on a chair, without allowing the knees to bend beyond the feet at any time. At the bottom of the squat, pause and use the elbows to push out the knees (figure 21.6). Return to the starting position and repeat. Keep the back straight and the head up throughout the entire exercise.

▶ **Figure 21.6** Goblet squat.

Russian Twist With a Medicine Ball Russian twists work all the muscles in the abdomen. Prepare by sitting tall with the legs extended in front of the body and the knees bent. Hold a medicine ball in both hands. Rotate the torso to the left and bring the medicine ball to the ground near the left hip (figure 21.7). After lightly tapping the ball to the ground but without resting it there, rotate the torso to the right and tap the medicine ball to the ground near the right hip. Repeat this rotation without pausing in the middle.

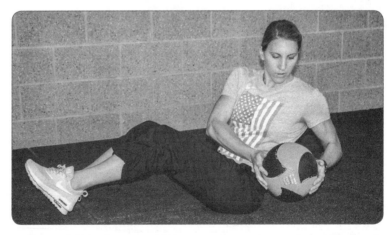

▶ **Figure 21.7** Russian twist.

Push-Up Plus   This exercise distinguishes itself from the standard push-up by placing extra emphasis on the serratus anterior muscle, which is of particular importance to swimmers. Strengthening the serratus anterior will reduce the risk of shoulder injuries and improve posture. Prepare by assuming a push-up position. Have the arms straight and place the hands slightly wider than shoulder-width apart. Keep the body in a straight line from the head to the ankles. Lower the body until the chest nearly touches the floor. Pause here for one second. Push back up (figure 21.8a), but as the arms straighten, push the upper back toward the ceiling (figure 21.8b) and pause for one or two seconds before lowering to starting position. Repeat.

▶ **Figure 21.8**   Push-up plus: (a) coming up from lower end of push-up; (b) pushing upper back toward the ceiling at top end of push-up.

Summary

This chapter provided a comprehensive view of the adolescent swimmer. Coaches, parents, and athletes who understand the health concerns specific to the adolescent swimmer can take proper precautions to prevent injury and promote safety in this population of athletes. Through a combination of adequate strength training and appropriate training volume, adolescent swimmers can improve year to year while remaining healthy and reducing the risk of injury.

CHAPTER 22

Masters Swimmers

—James W. Miller, MD

Swimming is an incredible sport that athletes of all ages can enjoy. The sport carries with it some tremendous health benefits because it provides a mix of aerobic and anaerobic conditioning that drives gains in fitness, motor control and technique, and power production. Additionally, a well-designed aquatic fitness program addresses a number of factors that are important to older athletes: the low-impact nature of swimming, the ability of water to support aging joints, the development of aerobic and anaerobic fitness, and a socially supportive environment that includes the opportunity for supervised, coached training sessions. In short, swimming offers a unique experience to adults of all ages and ability, whether a person wishes to engage in a fitness program or compete in organized swim meets. For those looking to race, competitions are available worldwide. These competitions may be conducted in a pool or open water, and they can serve as a stimulus to motivate training or as a measurement of a person's level of training or conditioning.

Masters swimming does not come without its challenges. The competitive nature of swimming requires a strong commitment from athletes at any level, but the masters swimmer faces the added challenges of work, family, and (unfortunately) aging. Despite these challenges, masters swimmers across the country and around the world continue to improve their performances and use swimming to fuel a healthy lifestyle. One thing that underlies any successful masters swimming endeavor is consistency—training with regularity and doing the things necessary to achieve health and performance goals.

Courtesy of U.S. Masters Swimming www.usms.org. Photographer: Allison Tolpa.

▶ **Masters swimmers celebrating their accomplishments.**

Overview of Masters Swimming

Before diving headlong into a discussion of masters swimming and ways to maximize performance, we need to define several terms commonly used in the sport.

Defining Masters Swimming

Masters swimming is an internationally organized sport for athletes who are 25 years of age and older. Note that in the United States, the beginning age is younger; athletes can start swimming in masters events at 18 years of age. The difference in the United States comes in part from the university system and the career paths available to swimmers. In the United States athletes typically enter a college or university setting at 18 years of age. The age for participation in masters was reduced to coincide with that age, allowing athletes to continue their involvement as they transition from a high school program to either higher education or work.

Masters swimming competitions are divided into 5-year increments. Competitive age groups are established for ages 25 to 29, 30 to 34, 35 to 39, and so on all the way up to 100 to 104 years of age. In the United States, an added age group captures the 18- to 24-year-old swimmers. The approaches described here underscore the main philosophy of masters swimming—the promotion of fitness for life. The mission statement of United States Masters Swimming says it best: "To promote health, wellness, fitness and competition for adults through swimming."

Defining the Competitive Athlete in Masters Swimming

The term *competitive athlete* applies to all masters swimmers who engage in pool-based competitions, open-water swims, or triathlons. The pool events available to masters swimmers in competition typically include all the traditional strokes and distances. Also available is a full array of open water distance events, which are swum in lakes, rivers, bays, and beach environments. Triathlon events include a range of distances, from sprint-distance triathlons all the way up to the Ironman and ultramarathon distance races.

Defining the Fitness Athlete in Masters Swimming

The term *fitness athlete* applies to anyone who swims and trains to maintain health and fitness but not necessarily to compete in organized competitions. When discussing the importance of swimming as a life habit, even the most accomplished Olympic athlete lists fitness as a top reason for swim training.

▶ **A winning mixed relay from the Tamalpais Aquatic Masters swim team.**

Superficially, the differences between the competitive and fitness sides of the masters swimming spectrum may seem significant, but the athletes themselves perceive those differences to be small. Masters swimming is really all about fitness for life. It is a culture that embraces the philosophy of fitness.

There is more to consider when exploring why adults train in swimming. Fitness and love of the water are the obvious reasons for many. Physicians recommend aquatic programs to address a wide range of medical problems, as discussed in detail later. In addition, the social side of masters training is a fundamental draw to many who participate in the sport. As in most sports, differences in social, ethnic, and religious backgrounds disappear, and all participants enjoy a common language and interest. Recent remarks at the US Masters Swimming National Championships frequently included the desire to catch up with old friends and meet new ones as a prime reason for attending the four-day competition.

Swimming Is Unique: The Healing Waters

Many aspects of swimming are unique among the types of exercise that adults can pursue throughout their lives. The aquatic medium offers features for both athletes and health care professionals who are attempting to motivate patients (athletes) to adopt a healthier lifestyle.

First, water supports the body in a suspended state, which minimizes the problems of balance and impact on the body. If a swimmer loses balance in the pool, the consequences are few, whereas an athlete who falls while exercising on land may face contusions, lacerations, or fractures that may result in considerable time lost from activity and even loss of independence. People who have arthritic joints may have difficulty on land, but they frequently enjoy much freer function when their joints do not have to bear body weight. Aquatic rehabilitation of musculoskeletal injuries or following joint replacement is common. Aquatic support decreases the impact of body weight on the joint, and the patient can slowly progress back to land-based activity.

Second, temperature regulation is unique to water. In a well-controlled aquatic environment, water temperature is tightly monitored to suit the needs of the athlete. Water temperatures of 81 degrees Fahrenheit (27.2 Celsius) or less are ideal for the heavy aerobic demands of competitive swimmers who are attempting to maximize their time in the pool with an aggressive program. This water temperature allows athletes to maintain high levels of training without having their core temperature rise. Consequently, they can more easily control their heart rate. This aspect is important to those who have underlying blood pressure and cardiac problems, as well as to pregnant athletes.

Differences in the size of the masters athlete also come into play when discussing temperature regulation. The greater an athlete's surface area is relative to weight, the easier it is for the athlete to dissipate heat. Following adolescence, the ratio of surface area to weight tends to decrease, making heat buildup a greater problem. Training at the correct water temperatures helps the masters athlete keep core temperature and heart rate in a safe range. Temperatures closer to 88 degrees Fahrenheit (31 degrees Celsius) provide a warm environment conducive to instruction and rehabilitation. Between these two temperature extremes is a range for other aquatic activities, but at 83 degrees Fahrenheit (28.3 degrees Celsius) and above, athletes who are steadily moving have increasing difficulty controlling heart rate as core body temperature rises.

Third, exercising in the horizontal position is another unique aspect of swimming. Being horizontal allows blood to be more equally distributed throughout the lungs and optimizes oxygen delivery to the blood because there is no oxygen blood inequity as exists in the upright position. To be clearer, when the body is upright, more blood is in the bases of the lung than at the top. This situation is equalized in the supine position. Skeletal stresses are more equally distributed in this plane as well, because gravity is not a factor.

Fourth, humidity has long been thought to be an advantage for athletes with asthma or other lung diseases. Humidity tends to improve the viscosity of mucous secretions, making them much easier to handle. The reverse environment, which is notorious for being the worst for the pulmonary system, is cold, dry air, which can induce an asthma attack in athletes who are prone to this risk. Altitude magnifies the problems with cold, dry air. Although warm humidity is advantageous for lungs, the by-products of chlorine, bromine, and other chemicals may offset some of this advantage. Thus, the entire aquatic environment has to be considered when assessing the benefits of humidity on the lungs. The air-handling system of an indoor or outdoor aquatic complex, water temperature, water chemical balance, and temperature differences between air and water all contribute to the aquatic environment.

The bottom line is that the aquatic environment is a unique place to exercise. The support for the body, humidity, and heat dissipation for training give advantages to athletes of all ages.

Offsetting the Effects of Aging

As much as people would like to think that they can steal from Father Time, evidence abounds to the contrary. The effect of aging is real, whether it is a decrease in muscular strength or an increase in arthritic joint pain. Can we alter the progression of aging through regular exercise such as swimming? In short, the answer is yes, but we should examine what the research says about aging and the effect of engaging regularly in swimming. In the process we will look at these specific questions:

- What are the physical, physiological, and other benefits that can come from being a part of a masters swimming program?
- How should an older athlete train to either maintain health or maximize performance? Do the methods of training need to change compared with what a younger athlete would do?
- Do masters athletes need to prepare differently or approach recovery from a different perspective? Are the guidelines different?

Courtesy of U.S. Masters Swimming www.usms.org. Photographer: Cokie Lepinski.

▶ **Masters swimming provides the opportunity for fitness to adults of all ages.**

The preceding questions are a lot to consider. Obviously, it is not as simple as saying to the enthusiastic new athlete, "Push off and let's see how it goes."

Aging people certainly deserve attention because they are the most rapidly growing sector of the population. In 1990 there were 33 million people over the age of 65. Those over the age of 85 were the most rapidly growing segment of the population. The U.S. population grew by 11 percent in the 1990s, but the number of people over 85 years old grew by 44 percent. If we fast-forward to the projections of the U.S. Census Bureau, between 2000 and 2030 the population of those 65 and over will grow by 204 percent in the United States. This growth will likely translate into many masters swimmers who want to remain independent and enjoy an active lifestyle. Coaches need to understand how to train this group of people. Additionally, facilities and coaches need to be prepared for the demands that will be placed on them in the coming years.

What Is Aging?

Researchers have various definitions of aging, from the cellular level to the organ system level. Microscopically, a loss of cell water accompanies a fundamental change to the cell's DNA. Simply stated, wrinkled cells come from wrinkled people. Whether from the loss of water or a change in the contents of the cells themselves, a decline in the elasticity of the cellular fibers occurs throughout the body with aging.

If we consider specific organ systems, which is a common way to look at the phenomenon of aging, it is often beneficial to consider each one separately to get the best picture of how the aging process affects the body. On average, we can expect to lose approximately 10 percent of function per decade during the normal aging process. Usually, this rate seems to accelerate at a certain age. The target age at which the aging process seems to accelerate is system dependent, not person dependent. Little research has been done about how aerobic or anaerobic training affects the target age, but it is known that regular exercise, and swimming in particular, can delay or considerably slow the aging process overall.

Organ Systems and the Benefits of Aquatic Fitness

We have seen masters swimmers stay actively engaged in the sport well into their 80s and 90s and even 100s. So, what occurs, system by system, when the human body ages (see table 22.1), and how can swimming affect this process? The overall effect of a vigorous exercise program on the body are far reaching indeed. In a study conducted by the Cooper Clinic, Steven Blare followed 40,547 adults between the ages of 20 and 70 over a 13-year period, looking at all causes of mortality. He broke the group into categories based on the activities (or lack thereof) in which the individuals participated. The study participants were classified as sedentary (15,883), runners (3,746), walkers (20,356), or swimmers (562). The observations and the subsequent conclusions that were drawn from this study were surprising, especially the finding that the mortality rates over those 13 years were 11 percent for the sedentary people, 7.8 percent for walkers, 6.6 percent for runners, and 1.9 percent for swimmers (Whitten 2010). Why is this the case?

Let's look at how masters swimmers train. Masters athletes typically exercise year round and engage in three or more pool or open water practices per week, all of which is considered vigorous exercise. This type of activity exceeds the recommendations put forward by the American College of Sports Medicine (ACSM) and U.S. government studies. Historically, the benefits derived from exercise were demonstrated in 1970 when evidence was found linking vigorous physical exercise to improvement in maximal aerobic power ($\dot{V}O_2$max). In 1978 ACSM defined vigorous exercise as 60 to 90 percent of maximum predicted heart rate (American College of Sports Medicine 1978). Data collected between 1985 and 2000 further substantiated the effect that moderate exercise has on cardiovascular disease risk factors and all causes of cardiac mortality. At that time, the recommendation that people engage in 30 minutes of moderate exercise was promoted (U.S. Department of Health and Human Services 1996). In 2002 the Food and Nutrition Board of the Institute of Medicine countered that advice by increasing the exercise recommendation to 60 minutes, though still

Table 22.1 Commonly Accepted Age-Related Organ System Changes

Organ system	Structural changes	Functional changes
Body composition	Decline in total body water Doubling of body fat between 25 and 75 years of age Decline in skeletal bone Decline in height (inevitable) and weight (ideally)	
Skin	Thinning of all three layers Diminished melanocytes Diminished sweat glands Decreased elasticity Decreased connective tissue support	Fragile skin Graying of hair and less tanning capacity Decreased heat tolerance Slower wound healing Easier bruising and fragile skin
Cardiovascular	Increased vessel stiffness Sclerosis of heart valves Decreased muscle contractility	Tendency for increased systolic blood pressures Decrease in maximum heart rate achievable
Pulmonary	Decreased elasticity Increased chest wall stiffness Thickened alveolar membranes Decreased ciliary function	No change in total lung capacity Decrease in forced vital capacity (25 ml/yr after age 20) Decreased maximal oxygen uptake (PaO2 at rest declines $100 - 0.33 \times$ age) Diminished cough reflex Impaired mucus clearance Increased risk of aspiration
Renal	Loss of glomeruli Decreased renal blood flow	Decreased creatinine clearance $140 -$ age (weight in kg) $/ 72 \times$ Scr Decrease in maximum urine osmolality
Gastrointestinal	Decrease in peristalsis throughout to varying degrees Decrease in gastric acid production Decrease in salivary production	Increase in constipation because of motility and immobility
Musculoskeletal	Bone loss (multifactorial) Diminished selective muscle mass Decrease in articular cartilage and elasticity	Osteoporosis and fractures of spine and hip Kyphosis
Vision	Decrease in pupil size Thickening of lens and loss of elasticity Loss of cones Diminished tearing	Decreased visual accommodation Hyperopia Decreased acuity Decreased color sensitivity Decreased night vision Dry eyes
Hearing	Degenerative changes of ossicles Atrophy of cochlear hair cells Loss of auditory neurons Decrease in cerumen and drying	High-frequency hearing loss Poor speech discrimination
Taste	Decline in number of taste buds	Increased intake of salt and sugar
Bone marrow	No absolute change in number of cells Decreased ability to respond to a stress such as overwhelming infection or a toxin	Increased risk of severe infections
Immune system	Decreased T-cell activity Impaired febrile response	Increased risk of infection and its consequences
Nervous system	Decrease in coronal neurons Decrease in neurotransmission time and central processing Decrease in natural melatonin levels	Increased motor and sensory processing time, resulting in instability and slowed reaction time Decrease in complex learning Decline in cognitive function Decline in REM sleep and restorative sleep
Endocrine system	Increased insulin resistance (multifactorial) Decline in sex hormones	Elevation of blood sugar Menopause and andropause

at a moderate level (Institute of Medicine of the National Academies of Science 2002). In 2008 the activity recommendation changed to an expectation of 150 minutes of moderate activity per week or 75 minutes of vigorous activity per week based on research of a scientific council (U.S. Department of Health and Human Services 2008). Masters swimming includes a greater amount of vigorous activity per week than the average person will get from other sports.

Cardiovascular System

When considering the effect that this type of activity has on organ systems, the cardiac system is a good place to start because it is central to providing oxygen and nutrients to the muscles, brain, and other structures of the training athlete. Cardiac and vascular diseases are rapidly on the rise in the United States population. The normal aging process typically results in a decrease in cardiac output (the amount of blood pumped by the heart in a given period), which in turn is affected by heart rate and the volume of the heart. Obviously, the heart has to work harder if the vessels that it is pushing blood into are stiffer. This condition, known as peripheral resistance, increases with aging. The vessels become stiffer either from lipid deposits within the vessel wall or simply because of loss of elasticity of the fibers within the wall. The magic age of decline for the cardiovascular system is usually cited as 60 years of age for men and women, although the starting age is cited as 25 years of age. Does exercise modify this process? Absolutely it does, which supports the observations from the Cooper Clinic.

The cardiovascular system is frequently implicated in a decline in a person's aerobic performance. Three components contribute to aerobic capacity (Tanaka and Seals 2008). The first is exercise economy, which is the efficiency by which an athlete can transfer raw metabolic power to mechanical power, in this case muscular force that can be used to propel the swimmer down the pool. Research has shown that exercise economy typically does not change with age.

The second component to cardiovascular performance is the exercise intensity at which a high fraction of maximum oxygen consumption can be maintained. This point is more commonly referred to as the lactate threshold. A person's lactate threshold may change with aging, but the change is typically not dramatic, and the aerobically training athlete can maintain endurance performance (Robinson et al. 1976; Maffulli, Testa, and Capasso 1994; Evans et al. 1995).

The third component to aerobic performance is maximum oxygen consumption, or $\dot{V}O_2$max, which does seem to show evidence of age-related decline, even in the aerobically training athlete. Multiple factors go into determining $\dot{V}O_2$max, including cardiac output, vessel elasticity, and pulmonary factors. Certainly, aerobic fitness reduces the predicted cardiovascular decline substantially (at least by half) if training is maintained. Limiting the time lost from training and maintaining a consistently high level of training seem to have an effect here (Mountjoy et al. 2010). Consistency matters!

Other issues faced by aging athletes and involving the cardiovascular system include cardiac arrhythmias, the most common of which is atrial fibrillation.

Atrial fibrillation is a condition in which the top chambers of the heart (the atria) lose their regular beating pattern and take on an irregular contraction that does not pump blood effectively. The risk of atrial fibrillation is that cardiac output can decline by more than 10 percent, putting the person at risk for the development of blood clots in the heart, which can break off and travel anywhere in the body. This condition leads to the need for anticoagulation therapy, which frequently is lifelong, or cardiac ablation surgery to correct the arrhythmia. The incidence of atrial fibrillation is inversely proportionate to the exercise that the person is performing on a regular basis. In one study, those who walked 11 blocks weekly had a 22 percent reduction in risk for developing it, whereas walking 60 blocks per week resulted in a 44 percent reduction (Mozaffarian et al. 2008). A fit pump outperforms an unfit one in many ways, and masters swimming can help keep the heart and vascular system healthy. Recent data, however, indicate that as the intensity of the exercise increases with duration, the cardiovascular system undergoes several changes that may actually increase the incidence of atrial fibrillation. Prolonged extremely intense exercise may result in left atrial dilation or remodeling, persistent vagotonia, sympathetic surges, intermittent left atrial hypertension, or chronic inflammation when combined with genetic predisposition, alcohol, caffeine, or psychological stress (Sorokin et al. 2011; Pelliccia et al. 2005). So, people can have too much of a good thing, particularly in the setting of comorbid predispositions.

The forms of exercise that address these cardiovascular changes, whether cardiac output or cardiac arrhythmias, are primarily aerobic in nature, but the addition of resistance training is beneficial. Swimming has some resistance training built into it, because of the water medium through which athletes propel themselves. But the best of both worlds is found in a comprehensive training program that combines resistance training, such as weightlifting, with a swimming program. Resistance training has been shown to decrease blood pressure, decrease heart rate, and improve left ventricular function (a prime component of cardiac output to the system).

Blood vessel elasticity is a prime component of peripheral resistance. The jury is out about whether aerobic training can affect the change in the elastic components of the vessel wall. But a major factor in loss of elasticity is the deposition of lipids in the vessel walls. All cardiac sources point to the problems that most Western societies have with a rise in total cholesterol and triglycerides, which corresponds with the rise in the incidence of obesity, sedentary lifestyle, and insulin resistance. Aerobic training stimulates the production of HDL cholesterol if it is performed up to 40 minutes per day, five days per week. It also stimulates metabolic rate and lowers LDL and VLDL cholesterols. So, whether the deposition of lipids in vessel walls is slowed, stopped, or even reversed, it clearly has an effect on vessel wall stiffness and peripheral resistance.

Musculoskeletal System

The musculoskeletal system is critical to the performance of the masters athlete. Aging brings a decline in the elasticity of the musculoskeletal components.

Sarcopenia refers to the loss of muscle fibers, which are replaced by fibrous tissue and fat. Neither of the replacement cellular types is metabolically as active as muscle fiber. The result of this conversion from active to inactive tissue is a decline in metabolic rate. The effect continues on to broader topics of lessening glucose tolerance, which sets up a state conducive to the expression of diabetes, if that tendency is present. But the data about musculoskeletal decline is generally based on healthy sedentary adults, not masters swimmers (Tanaka et al. 1997, 2000; Tanaka, Monahan, and Seals 2001; Tanaka and Seals 1997, 2003).

From a functional standpoint, musculoskeletal decline results in a decrease in contractile force and rate, meaning that the athlete cannot achieve the same power production and will have difficulty achieving maximum force as quickly as in the past. Microscopically, a change occurs in the ratio of Type II (fast-twitch) fibers to Type I (slow-twitch) fibers from 1:1 to 1:2. A change occurs not only in the number of Type II fibers but also in their cross-sectional dimensions.

The cause of Type II fiber loss is multifactorial, but the first factor listed by all experts is disuse. Disuse contributes to Type II fiber loss, in both volume and number, across studies. The age of onset is somewhat later than that noted for the cardiovascular system, beginning at 35 years of age, and the rate of loss is 1.25 percent per year. The acceleration age is 70 years old. The gender of the athlete does not change the observations. Without disuse, when exercise is moderate, the rate of decline is half that quoted, at least. But the vigorously training athlete

Courtesy of U.S. Masters Swimming www.usms.org. Photographer: Allison Tolpa.

▶ **A swimmer who trains vigorously can slow the muscle decline that comes with age.**

is again a different model (Coggan et al. 1990). With these athletes, little or no change occurs in fiber type or cross-sectional area, giving the dedicated masters athlete a strong edge in avoiding the considerable consequences of declining metabolism (Trappe et al. 1995). This finding represents a huge change from prior impressions. Dedication matters!

Balance

Closely related to the musculoskeletal system are problems associated with balance and falling. Swimming is an ideal lifelong program of exercise for avoiding or delaying balance issues. Falling and balance are affected by a combination of being weaker and having poor muscle feedback (Salzman 2010). Exercising to maintain muscle mass, reactivity, and proprioception can delay this process by at least a decade, providing a tremendous bonus to the aging athlete by allowing more continuous training and reducing the training time lost to injuries. Swimming works on the coordination of muscle firing and performance and aids in the prevention of problems with those functions (Gillespie et al. 2009). Most programs designed to address balance deficits emphasize land-based activity, but swimming certainly assists in the strengthening and coordination that will augment a land-based program.

Joint Health

Rheumatological diseases are most commonly expressed in older athletes. Although rheumatoid arthritis, gout, psoriatic arthritis, and many other types of arthritis require specific therapies, one of the most common types of arthritis in older athletes is osteoarthritis.

Osteoarthritis is a degenerative process involving cartilage. It is not an inflammatory arthritis, but the joint destruction and pain are no less incapacitating. Heredity is always a factor, but the patient's history of performing little impact-related exercise combined with poor aerobic fitness and an elevated weight or body mass index (BMI) all combine to increase the risk of osteoarthritis. Clearly, excellent aerobic fitness and strength training offset the limitations of osteoarthritis but only as long as the program is maintained (Hart et al. 2008). Swimming is uniquely kind to athletes who have osteoarthritis, although swimming stroke modifications may be necessary for the athlete to enjoy the full benefits of training.

Sleep

Sleep and sleep quality are also affected by aging. The normal circadian rhythm changes as a person gets older. Typically, the amount of time spent in deep, restorative sleep declines, and the REM, or dreaming, phase becomes shallower, which results in frequent nighttime awakening.

Several factors seem to have an effect on sleep, which obviously affects quality of life as well as level of alertness. With age the body tends to decrease its production of melatonin, which is the brain chemical that mediates sleep. Aerobic training helps normalize sleep patterns, although it is not clear whether it has a direct effect on melatonin levels. Clarity of thought, coordination, and focus are all affected by quality of sleep, which in turn is affected by aerobic training.

Healing

Finally, a general topic for all systems is recovery, healing, and reserve. Aging has a significant effect on the ability of any organ system to respond to a challenge, such as a simple laceration, surgery, or an illness. Every response is slower and has to be factored in when planning training. Although an athlete may have recovered within a month from a specific surgery two decades ago, a month may not be sufficient for the same recovery now. Older people should plan for that and be pleasantly surprised if recovery is quicker than expected.

Physical Activity and Effects on Aging

Many studies link a sedentary lifestyle to poor health. Cross-sectional studies link screen time, including television viewing and computer use, to obesity, insulin resistance, and diabetes (Owen et al. 2010). These findings should not be surprising because sedentary people will not maintain muscle mass and their basal metabolic rate will decline because they are not doing any aerobic training. Even if the data are adjusted for waist-to-chest ratios and exercise levels (moderate versus vigorous), the results remain the same.

Lack of exercise contributes to a long list of diseases, many associated with aging. The list includes risk of early death, cardiovascular disease, diabetes, dyslipidemia, colon cancer, and breast cancer. Although exercise is recommended to forestall these diseases, a question remains about the importance of ideal BMI as an independent factor (Lee et al. 2010).

Musculoskeletal Challenges for the Active Masters Swimmer

Given the effects that exercise can have on the aging process, we know that the masters swimmer benefits by participation in the sport. But what adjustments need to be made for the masters athlete?

Clearly, the aging process stresses the musculoskeletal system. Elasticity declines, healing capacity and response to injury decline, articular cartilage is unable to repair itself, and repetitive motions can create imbalances and unique stresses. In addition, the supply of oxygen and nutrients involving the cardiovascular and pulmonary systems tends to decline. Creative methods of training must consider these variables, allowing for appropriate recovery, maintenance of stroke technique, and stimulation of an adaptive training response in the setting of decreased reparative capacity. Specific musculoskeletal injuries are worthy of consideration because of their prevalence.

Rotator Cuff Tenosynovitis, Bursitis, or Tear

The shoulder is the most injured joint in swimming, both for competitive (Mountjoy et al. 2010) and recreational athletes. The masters athlete has a greater risk of overuse degenerative changes related to the cuff, which can include a fraying of the cuff or an overuse tear. Standard studies of rotator cuff problems in swimmers are directed to age-group, college, and elite athletes who usually have been pursuing their sport for 10 to 20 years. The masters swimmer has performed millions of rotations over a long training career. The clinical presentation therefore tends to be different for the masters athlete, more often involving a degenerative cuff than the classic acute tear in a healthy joint. The typical presentation in the masters swimmers is consistent with chronic bursitis or tendonitis (tenosynovitis, tendonopathy) followed by a worsening of the symptoms that extends beyond workouts and interferes with sleep. Overhead motions in a flexed position are usually uncomfortable to the athlete, and the combination of complaints leads to a trip to a medical practitioner. Preventative exercises, although important for all swimmers, are particularly relevant for the masters swimmer in helping to maintain strength, address muscular imbalances, and promote the flexibility needed to ensure healthy joints.

After an injury has occurred, the options for therapy are numerous. Regardless of the imaging process used to achieve an accurate diagnosis, not all full-thickness tears need a surgical approach, but some partial-thickness tears do need surgical attention. The management strategy is based on the athlete's response to conservative approaches of core strengthening, scapular strengthening, and linking to the extremity. Primary strengthening of the cuff is critical for success, whether surgery is needed or not, and attention to stroke technique is important when the athlete is released to return to the pool. Although injections into the subacromial bursa may give some temporary relief, multiple injections may weaken the tendonous units, and they have not been found to improve the long-term outlook. NSAID medications can assist temporarily but are poor options for a long-term approach.

Joint Surgery or Replacement

Joint replacements can occur at any age, but they often occur among those of masters swimming age. Knees and hips are the most commonly replaced joints, and swimming is one of the best methods of rehabilitation. As with most situations, the better the muscle tone is around the joint, the easier the recovery will be when the replacement takes place. Thus, someone who swims regularly and is facing joint replacement will benefit from intensifying training in anticipation of the surgery. Intensifying training improves muscle tone, aerobic conditioning, cardiac fitness, weight control (or promotes loss if that is an issue), blood pressure control, and many other variables. The outcome of less disability and an earlier return to work and activities can be impressive. More commonly, an athlete comes into a masters swimming program following joint surgery after being barred from participating in another primary sport, usually running. Going through the learning phases of swimming is more challenging while compensating for the postsurgical joint, replacement or otherwise.

Spinal Stenosis

Spinal stenosis is also more common with aging. It literally means a narrowing of the spinal canal regardless of cause, although most result from cumulative degenerative changes. Bulging discs (herniated or weakened), thickening of the ligament structures, mass effect (cyst or tumor), and slipping of one vertebra on another (spondylolisthesis) are just several of the causes of spinal stenosis. The neural unit that is under pressure will cause pain in tissues innervated by that nerve and possibly muscle atrophy. Water is frequently the only place that the athlete can find relief. The coach must pay strict attention to spinal alignment on the long-axis strokes (freestyle and backstroke) and efficient rolling through the water. Correct stroke technique reinforces the linking and conditioning of the core muscles that in turn support the spine. The coach must also realize that the short-axis strokes (butterfly and breaststroke) may not be possible at all because both have a flexion and extension phase that involves the lumbar spine. Water is frequently the salvation for the athlete who has spinal stenosis, buying time for conservative therapies to take effect if surgery is being delayed or avoided completely. Even easy training will work miracles on the athlete's outlook and coping ability through a frequently long rehabilitation.

Although other musculoskeletal and rheumatological problems are common in the masters athlete, the important focus in many cases is not speed but maintaining independence and aerobic fitness. Few remedies help the athlete who is coping with these physical challenges better than maintaining aerobic fitness and muscle tone in a supportive aquatic environment.

Medications

The listing of the prevalence of disease processes that the aging athlete may be facing brings with it another topic—medications. Medications need to be considered in two major divisions, acute and chronic. When dealing with medication and the masters athlete, the purpose of the medication should be considered. For instance, beta-blockers are common medications used in cardiac medicine to regulate heart rate and blood pressure. Therefore, the athlete who takes this type of medication will not be able to achieve a heart rate or level of exertion that would otherwise be expected. Thus, the anaerobic events (short sprints) will be difficult or impossible to perform. Long aerobic distances will fit in much better. Second, medical practitioners need to be able to look at the effect that a medication may have on athletic performance and training. Many medications compete with the enzyme systems inside the muscle fiber that are involved in refueling the muscle contractile units. The muscle will thus not have the fuel needed to perform. The result will be a quick decline in performance as well as sore muscles.

▶ **Masters swimmers vary in their ability and competitive experience.**

Courtesy of U.S. Masters Swimming www.usms.org. Photographer: Cokie Lepinski.

Two options are available to the athlete. The athlete can be more careful with diet by consuming simple carbohydrate while training to feed the muscle during exercise. In addition to improving the diet, which is always a good option, the athlete needs to consult with the prescribing medical practitioner to see whether an alternative medication would not have the same side effect.

Side effects of medications are typically worst right after the medication is started. Although long-term problems can build up over time the longer a medication is taken, this effect is less common. Therefore, a new medication would likely have a bigger effect on training performance. If a medication will be taken for a brief period for a limited purpose, the athlete may experience only a temporary decline in training. But if a medication is started long term for a chronic condition, the athlete needs to understand how to work around the challenges that the medication may present.

Training the Masters Athlete

Athlete safety is an important place to begin when designing training for the masters athlete. The preceding discussions clearly suggest that developing a fully integrated plan of training is more complex with adults than it is with younger swimmers. A fully integrated program has to take into account training history, which will set the expectations of the athlete for current performances, reasonable or not. The goals of the new masters athlete are equally important to defining a program that will meet the athlete's expectations. The athletic history comes into play here. The medical history is important regarding both past and ongoing medical problems and medications, but the coach should not delve into medical issues unless the athlete has functional problems.

A good preparticipation physical examination is recommended for any athlete starting a masters swimming program. The influence of history, current health, and medications can make the decision to pursue a masters program complex, but this consideration is needed to ascertain whether a swimming program is safe for the athlete without further testing or adjustments in medication (Elsawy and Higgins 2010). The U.S. Department of Health and Human Services in 2008 stated that exercise is safe for those who do not have an underlying medical condition or symptoms suggestive of an underlying condition that has not been evaluated (U.S. Department of Health and Human Services 2008). The American College of Cardiology and the American Heart Association in 2002 suggested that a physician's consultation is wise for men over age 45 and women over age 55 if the exercise being proposed is vigorous (Gibbons et al. 2002). Swimming is clearly defined as a vigorous form of exercise by their standards.

Constructing a Program

After the basics of safety and goal setting are taken care of, the training program can be created. A number of resources provide workout sets and predesigned workouts. Any coach or swimmer can use these examples to help construct a masters swimming program, and this chapter will not re-create that pool of information. Training programs for masters coaches provide certifications for various levels of expertise through United States Masters Swimming. Each level provides enhanced coaching education, which in turn benefits athletes in programs lucky enough to have these motivated coaches.

Nevertheless, this section discusses how a training session should be designed and what it should focus on. This process can be a challenge because adults can come from highly variable backgrounds; some are beginning swimmers who have just finished a program that introduced them to water, others have many years of competitive experience.

As in all levels of sport, the process has to start with teaching. Teaching the most up-to-date concepts of stroke dynamics is more appreciated by masters swimmers than any other group. This aspect is particularly rewarding to the coach. By mixing in some distance training while teaching drills, the coach can give the athlete a sense of accomplishment. Fins and other devices may be necessary to accomplish this goal. Because each athlete has a different base, some will graduate to advanced lanes more quickly than others, but the coach has to be flexible. If she is not, the highly developed athlete will experience frustration by being held back. If the initial instruction emphasizes the importance of stroke technique for speed, efficiency, and reduction of injuries, the athlete can easily be convinced of its importance.

Design of swimming sets requires creativity. The high-yardage repetitive sets seen in many age-group programs are less desirable for masters swimmers because the stresses incurred during the practice become repetitive. Overuse (repetitive) injuries can be more common with masters swimmers in part because of susceptibility, size, forces, and efficiency. Susceptibility is a term worthy of definition here. The joints are older and probably have areas of degenerative changes, and the blood supply and healing capacity are not as good as they are in younger athletes. Both of these variables make the joints more susceptible to overuse injury.

So to get specific, imagine a freestyle-dominated practice that totals 4,100 meters. The component groupings are simple and common:

Warm-up: 1,200 meters

Main set: 1,500 meters

Secondary set: 800 meters

Wrap-up set: 600 meters

How does the coach put this together for masters, keeping in mind the unique physiology of the athlete? The simple answer is to break it up and keep it fun. Fun, fitness, competition, and success are not mutually exclusive. The athlete can have it all. But putting together a warm-up set, 30 × 100 freestyle, and some cool-down does not accomplish all these objectives.

Warm-Up: 1,200 Meters

A number of features must be considered in constructing a warm-up. For example, older athletes are usually stiffer and need to have their heart rates brought up more slowly. The warm-up is an excellent time to combine physical preparation for the workout with instruction. Adults like to learn, so the coach can introduce a topic for the day, which is often technique based, in the warm-up. The coach can teach at every practice and incorporate drills when appropriate.

For example, if the lesson for the day is swimming long and efficiently, the drill to be taught (from among hundreds to choose from) could be any drill that uses a delayed pull until the recovery hand just touches the water. This can be a counted delay drill or a different type to teach the point of moving the recovery arm before moving the pulling arm. Here is the plan:

400 meters easy to loosen up; swimmer's choice of stroke or drills.

4 × 100 meters kicking on back, alternating dolphin and flutter kicks; fire the core to create power and bring in some leg conditioning; fins may be required by some swimmers to complete this set.

8 × 50 meters on an easy interval; on odd 50s, alternate the drill of the day with easy swimming using the principles of the drill; on even 50s, descend by 50 either by time, holding the interval unchanged, or by descending the interval by five seconds for each of the even 50s (swim each one faster than the previous one). This sequence focuses the athlete on using the drill of the day for faster swimming (the last 50 is the fastest one). The coach must emphasize the importance of the technique of the day as the athlete builds to faster swimming.

Main Set: 1,500 Meters

The main set is the longest set of the day. It allows the athlete to build the aerobic base while not losing focus on improved stroke technique. Of course, the tendency is to revert to the old comfortable (but incorrect) stroke. The coach faces a challenge in putting the set together to allow reinforcement of technique while building the aerobic base, which usually means performing short intervals.

5 × 100 meters descending by five seconds per 100 on either a fixed, descending, or ascending interval, depending on the coach's emphasis.

2 × 50 meters of drill 25 and swim 25 on an easy interval; recovery with emphasis on the earlier drill focus of the day's workout helps to maintain technique while extending the education aspect into the main set.

4 × 100 meters descending by five seconds per 100, starting at the second interval from the first task (i.e., dropping only the first or slowest 100).

2 × 50 meters of drill 25 and swim 25 on an easy interval; recovery with emphasis on the earlier drill focus of the day's workout helps to maintain technique while extending the education aspect into the main set.

3 × 100 meters descending by five seconds per 100, starting at the third interval from the original set (i.e., dropping the two slowest 100s).

2 × 50 meters of drill 25 and swim 25 on an easy interval; recovery with emphasis on the earlier drill focus of the day's workout helps to maintain technique while extending the education aspect into the main set.

Secondary Set: 800 Meters

The secondary set allows the athlete to continue to build the aerobic base but in a fashion that changes the repetitive nature of the set and provides joint and muscle recovery. The swimmer can use fins and other training devices, such as paddles or kickboards. The fins and other devices change the forces somewhat and add interest to the practice. Here is the plan:

75 meters kick, swim, kick on a tight interval.

50 meters swim fast using the principles of the day's educational topic; same interval as the 75, which will give plenty of rest.

Repeat six times with an easy 50 meters at the end.

Wrap-Up Set: 600 Meters

This final set can be the most important of the day. It is not junk distance tacked on to the practice and labeled as an easy cool-down. In fact, the term *cool-down* is not used. This set solidifies the teaching point of the day while slowly bringing down the heart rate in an active recovery mode. Here is the plan:

4 × 50 meters descending numbers 1 to 3, with the last one easy; each 50 is faster than the previous one, and the interval should allow no more than 10 seconds of rest.

1 × 100 meters alternating the drill of the day for 25 meters and 25 meters of swimming.

4 × 50 meters ascending numbers 1 to 3, with the last one easy; each 50 is swum slower than the previous one, and the interval allows 10 seconds more rest than the previous interval.

1 × 100 meters alternating the drill of the day for 25 meters and 25 meters of swimming.

The workout uses the physiological goals of training the masters athlete, regardless of age or ability. Learning is a key along with a mix of aerobic and anaerobic and power components. Intervals will change based on the swimmer's ability and level of conditioning. Athletes should be encouraged to train at a level that is challenging but possible. Learning sets are always at a learning pace, not a training pace.

Optimizing Training for Masters

After the training program is in place, additional points need to be considered to help masters get the most out of their training while taking into account the unique physical needs of the adult athlete. Proper hydration of all athletes is critical to performance, but this is more difficult to attain in masters athletes because of the natural decline that occurs in thirst sensation with aging. Coaches need to teach simple methods for monitoring hydration, such as looking at urine color to determine the hydration state, and make sure that hydration is part of every practice.

Aside from hydration, nothing enhances performance and recovery from training like balanced nutrition. Chapter 14 is dedicated to nutrition, and the keys identified there for the high-performance swimmer are applicable as well to masters swimmers. An ideal nutritional plan is to consume a balance of all food groups, pay strict attention to carbohydrate replenishment within 20 to 30 minutes of ending an exercise set, and follow that with a high-quality meal that deemphasizes fats. Balance is key. Because the masters athlete has fewer reserves in the musculoskeletal system, nutrition is more important to maintaining muscle performance.

Strength and flexibility are clearly areas that are difficult to regain completely after they are lost, but athletes of all ages benefit from a well-designed program. Flexibility and strength programs specific to swimmers should focus on stabilization of joints. Stabilization of the shoulder is key, allowing linkage to the core through the scapula to produce power. Strength training should focus on efficient power production by using core strength linked to the arms and legs. This process results in surprising force production and swimming performances. Technique, along with recognizing and overcoming innate weaknesses, is even more important than it is in younger athletes. Flexibility programs should be individualized because each athlete has unique areas of stability and instability.

Without evaluation by a trained professional such as a trainer, coach, or physical therapist, the athlete may destabilize areas of existing hyperflexibility while ignoring areas of the body that are tighter. A well-designed flexibility program is different for every athlete.

Remember that this all results in maintaining muscle mass, power, and the fiber type percentage needed for enhanced performances, either in the pool or in activities of daily living.

Summary

The masters athlete is complex, not simply an older age-group swimmer returning to the past. The health risks and benefits are critical and require understanding by the coach, athlete, and medical practitioner. Some athletes should receive a medical evaluation before they begin a program, particularly if risk factors are known or suspected. The coach has to treat every athlete differently depending on swimming history as well as goals the athlete may have set, realistic or not. The benefits of a well-balanced masters program are substantial. Research indicates that remarkable delays in aging can result from this type of physical activity. Masters coach certification programs reinforce the unique challenges and rewards of working with the aging athlete. Today, masters are achieving incredible swimming performances that are difficult to believe possible, regardless of age.

CHAPTER 23

Female Swimmers

—Jaci L. VanHeest, PhD

The number of girls and women participating in the sport of swimming has grown over the past decade. At the same time, the performances of female athletes have continued to improve across all levels of competition.

Coaches are often tempted to treat and train male and female athletes alike, in and out of the water, but to maximize performance of all athletes, coaches need to know some key gender differences. A number of topics relate to elite female performance, ranging from designing specific training strategies to providing adequate nutritional support to identifying and addressing clinical issues specific to female athletes. Researchers continue to evaluate and study the various factors that affect performance in the female athlete. Even more important, these researchers and practitioners also look to optimizing the long-term health of the female athlete.

This chapter looks specifically at the female athlete and presents information important to the coach who is looking to optimize performance while maintaining health in this group of athletes. This chapter, while presenting a general overview of what makes female swimmers different from the males they may be training with, also focuses on three main topics of debate that relate specifically to the health and performance of the female swimmer:

1. The influence of energy status on sport performance
2. The role of iron status in performance
3. The influence of oral contraceptive use on performance

Coaches, parents, and athletes need to understand each of these issues because all are critical to the optimization of training for competitive female athletes.

Energetics and Performance

Other chapters in this book have described how food fuels performance, whether training or competition, and how proper nutrition is a must to maximize health and performance. Most people try to find the quick and easy way to solve a problem, and swimmers are no different, especially when it comes to nutrition. All swimmers, and female swimmers in particular, face a constant barrage from myriad media influences touting the benefits of a whole host of supplements and diet regimens that will enhance performance and help achieve a certain body image. Coaches and athletes struggle to determine the best methods for fueling the body and achieving a desired body composition while at the same time optimizing performance.

Although chapter 14 outlines in detail how a swimmer should eat and drink to prepare the body for the demands of swimming, a useful restatement here is that the research supports the approach that a diet that is composed predominantly of complex carbohydrate, is relatively low in fat, and contains ample protein will optimize performance in swimmers (Deutz et al., 2000; Hawley and Burke, 1997).

The relationship between energy expenditure (the calories burned in training and activities of daily living) and energy intake (diet or calories consumed) dictates, in large part, the athlete's body weight and overall body composition (distribution and relative amounts of body fat and lean muscle mass). When intake equals expenditure, body weight remains stable. Body weight declines when expenditure outstrips intake, and weight accrues when intake is larger than expenditure (Melby and Hickey 2005). The basic energy equation states the following:

- If energy intake equals energy expenditure, body weight is maintained.
- If energy intake is greater than energy expenditure, an athlete gains weight.
- If energy intake is less than energy expenditure, an athlete loses weight.

These equations are important for the female-specific topics discussed in this chapter that are related to the concept of energy balance. Female athletes often reduce daily caloric consumption for a wide range of reasons (e.g., body image, thinking that thinner equals better performance, and so on), resulting in an overall energy deficit (VanHeest 1996; VanHeest et al. 2014; VanHeest and Mahoney 2007). A prolonged deficit can have long-term implications for both health and performance. Much of the research in this area to date focuses on the energy requirements for the female athlete. Coaches and athletes need to consider not only the total daily calorie needs but also the relationship between energy balance (intake versus expenditure) and body composition.

How much energy is expended by a competitive female swimmer? Knowing this quantity would be useful because it would drive the swimmer's energy consumption needs. Highly trained female swimmers have been reported to expend between 3,000 and 4,500 kilocalories per day during heavy training and between 2,000 and 4,000 kilocalories per day during taper (VanHeest 1996). A study by VanHeest confirmed energy expenditure (EE) data previously reported by Troup (1990) in high-school-aged swimmers. Start-of-season EE reached approximately 3,300 kilocalories per day, midseason training expenditures approached approximately 3,800 kilocalories per day, pretaper EE was about 3,600 kilocalories per day, and end-of-season EE dropped to approximately 2,800 kilocalories per day. Recently, EE was reported to be approximately 2,350 kilocalories per day in collegiate swimmers during taper, supporting previous work (Ousley-Pahnke, Black, and Gretebeck 2001).

Additional research confirms these findings and has shown that energy expenditure varies throughout the season for female swimmers. As one example, Kabasakalis and colleagues (2007) reported dietary intakes (EI) in female Greek swimmers using three-day dietary records over the course of a season. The swimmers consumed on average 2,359.8 kilocalories per day; 46 percent came from carbohydrate (4.4 grams per kilogram of body mass), 36 percent from fat, and approximately 18 percent from protein (1.7 grams per kilogram of body mass). The women did not seem to alter their dietary intake significantly across the season, although a small but insignificant increase in EI was observed between the baseline (nontraining) period, in which the swimmers consumed approximately 1,910 kilocalories per day, and their midseason training, during which caloric intakes rose to over 2,389 kilocalories per day (Kabasakalis et al. 2007). Note that these women were considered to have normal menstrual cycles, based on the menstrual cycle length.

Troup (1990) also found that EI varied in female swimmers depending on the time of the season; midtraining or pretaper EI was about 2,700 kilocalories per day, and end-of-season EI was about 2,400 kilocalories per day. In another study, VanHeest (1996) saw athletes consume 2,200 to 3,700 kilocalories per day during heavy training and 2,000 to 3,500 kilocalories per day during taper. Results from Zietz and coworkers (2009), who looked at EI in average-caliber competitive swimmers (10 to 19 years old), found that consumption was markedly different from that of the elite athletes. The females in this study had EIs ranging as high as 4,411 to 5,258 kilocalories per day across a season, nearly twice that of the more senior elite female swimmers. Moreover, the nonelite athletes consumed a somewhat higher percentage of calories from carbohydrate (50 to 57 percent); the reduced macronutrient was protein (about 13 percent) (Zietz et al. 2009).

The bottom line is that for either elite or subelite swimmers, energy expenditure fluctuates during the season. Females will therefore have to consume more or fewer calories depending on the phase of training. Coaches talk a lot about periodization of training and varying volume and intensity throughout a season. They should also recognize that nutrition, especially as it relates to caloric intake, needs to be periodized to match energy expenditure.

Energy Restriction and the Female Athlete Triad

Chronic dietary restriction has been reported for many years in competitive female athletes. The chronic energy deficit can result in increased risk of developing a condition that has been termed the *female athlete triad*. The female athlete triad is a clustering of three conditions (Nattiv et al. 2007):

- Energy availability: too few calories to support normal physiological function
- Menstrual function: negative changes to the typical menstrual cycle
- Bone mineral density: the amount of various minerals in bone

A position statement issued by the American College of Sports Medicine supports the concept that a spectrum of disorders affects female athletes (Nattiv et al. 2007). The female athlete triad is the result of an athlete's failure to balance adequate caloric consumption with the energy requirements for sport training (Cobb et al. 2003). Female athletes exhibit low energy availability for multiple reasons:

- Pathological eating behaviors
- Attempts to alter body size or composition
- Restrictive eating patterns
- Inability to eat enough calories to match exercise energy expenditure

Low energy availability affects metabolism and endocrine function, resulting in menstrual cycle changes (Cobb et al. 2003; Nattiv et al. 2007). Prevalence of the triad in elite female athletes, in general, across multiple sports is 4.3 percent (Torstveit and Sungot-Borgen 2005). But the prevalence of female athletes presenting with disordered eating (25 to 31 percent) or secondary amenorrhea (3 to 65 percent) is more common (Byrne and McLean 2002; Dusek 2001; Sanborn, Martin, and Wagner 1982; Sungot-Borgen and Torstveit 2004). Note that the female athlete triad spectrum of disorders is consistently linked with chronic energy restriction. Low energy availability has been shown to be highly correlated with reduced swimming performance (VanHeest et al. 2014; VanHeest and Mahoney 2007). Therefore, female swimmers should be educated about proper nutrition and sport fueling early in their careers to ensure that they understand the importance of proper energy intake for both health and performance. Unfortunately, this common sense approach to fueling the body properly is often overcome by the societal expectation of what a female athlete should look like.

Effects of Chronic Energy Deficits

Energy deficits can result in a variety of conditions including weight loss coupled with reductions in lean body mass (i.e., muscle mass) (Dulloo and Girardier

1990; VanHeest and Mahoney 2007). When a female swimmer chronically restricts caloric intake, she will increase both the duration and severity of the energy deficit. The outcome is a loss of muscle mass and in many instances a relative increase in body fat, believe it or not (Benardot 2007; Louis-Sylvestre et al. 2003).

Not uncommonly, coaches suggest that female athletes restrict calories to lose weight and subsequently to perform better in the water. Weight loss is typically not equated with just fat loss. Studies of female runners and gymnasts reported the highest body fatness in athletes who also presented with the largest deficits in energy intake (Deutz et al. 2000). These shifts in lean muscle mass and percent body fat negatively affect health and performance. The negative changes in body composition, specifically the decreased muscle mass, can result in a reduction in overall power and strength.

Chronic energy deficits also can result in reductions in important hormones such as thyroid hormones (VanHeest et al. 2014; VanHeest and Mahoney 2007). Thyroid hormones function to increase cellular activity and aid in the control of metabolism. The thyroid hormones are sensitive to the body's nutrient status; for example, low energy or nutrient availability results in reduced thyroid hormone levels. The decline in thyroid hormones (i.e., triiodothyronine, or T3) has been related to health issues such as decreased bone mass and reductions in sport performance (VanHeest et al. 2014; VanHeest and Mahoney 2007). The negative changes in body composition associated with chronic energy restriction do not support long-term enhancements in sport performance. Coupled with the potential of health-related issues such as the female athlete triad, female swimmers should work to maintain ample fuel supply to meet training and life demands throughout their careers.

Energy deficits also can arise throughout the day as the result of improper timing of nutrient intake. Female athletes often consume most of their daily calories in one large evening meal, typically following their swim workout (Iwao, Mori, and Sato 1996). Benardot (2007) describes this concept as a "backloading of energy intake." Meal patterning, or when meals are consumed relative to training and competition times, has been objectively evaluated in competitive athletes. The relationship between meal patterning or fuel availability and hormone release is critical for body composition and substrate utilization (Atkinson et al. 2008; Fogteloo et al. 2004; Mistlberger and Skene 2005).

Figure 23.1 illustrates a typical eating pattern and energy balance of one elite senior-level female swimmer early in the season (figure 23.1*a*) and again at a point sometime in the middle of the season (figure 23.1*b*). The swimmer consumed between 1,800 and 2,100 kilocalories on the majority of days during the early to midseason period. The swimmer was eating two meals (lunch and dinner) and two snacks for the first three weeks of training. In the middle of the season, she changed her eating pattern by dropping the lunch meal and increasing the total calorie content of her dinner following late-afternoon training. The change in meal patterning resulted in large periods of relative fasting during which the hormones controlling fuel utilization (i.e., insulin) were negatively affected. The swimmer reported excessive fatigue, inability to concentrate, lack of motivation to train, and a decline in performance during this period. When she altered her dietary pattern (by reinstating a lunch meal), her symptoms declined and her performance improved during both training sessions and competition. Athletes need to link dietary intake with energy expenditure throughout the day and week.

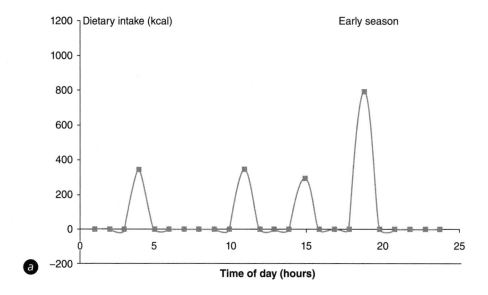

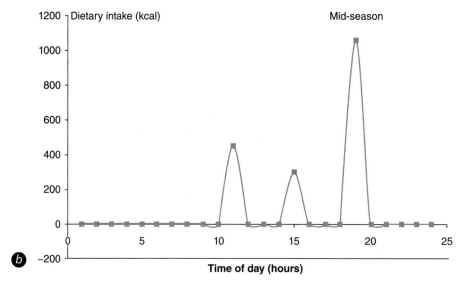

▶ **Figure 23.1**   Example meal pattern of an elite senior female swimmer for two days during the season: (*a*) early season; (*b*) midseason.

Iron Status in Female Swimmers

Reductions in performance coupled with fatigue, lack of motivation to train, and physical decline are other conditions commonly seen in competitive female athletes. Poor iron status can be one of the causes of this chronic fatigue in competitive female swimmers. Iron deficiency is common in the United States (Cook 2005), even in athlete populations. Depending on the study cited, female athletes exhibit iron deficiencies, with and without anemia, at a frequency of 11 to 41 percent (Brownlie et al. 2004; Clement and Asmundson 1982; DiSantolo et al. 2008; Risser and Risser 1990; Sinclair and Hinton 2005; VanHeest and Ratliff 1997, 1998).

Clinical Conditions

One clinical condition frequently seen in athletes is dilutional pseudoanemia. This condition results from an increase in plasma volume coupled with a slight increase or no change in red blood cell mass (erythrocyte), leading to decreased hemoglobin concentration (Shaskey and Green 2000). Ferritin (the storage form of iron in the body) is typically measured to be normal under this condition (VanHeest and Mahoney 2007). Physical activity has been reported to affect red blood cell destruction (hemolysis) in various groups including soldiers, runners, swimmers, and triathletes (Beard and Tobin 2000; Sinclair and Hinton 2005) and may make these groups of athletes more susceptible to dilutional pseudo-anemia. Pseudoanemia has been referred to as a typical response to endurance training. Blood volume increases, while the amount of red blood cells either decreases or remains the same (Rockwell and Hinton 2005). Some researchers suggest that an improvement in sport performance occurs when the athlete exhibits pseudoanemia caused by the increased plasma volume and associated cardiovascular benefits (Rockwell and Hinton 2005; Deakin 2000; Eichner 2001). A second clinical condition seen in this group is exertional hemolysis, a condition in which the physical demand associated with intense training leads to destruction of the body's red blood cells (Shaskey and Green 2000; O'Toole et al. 1988).

Another common problem, especially for female swimmers, is iron deficiency with or without anemia. In iron-deficient anemia, iron stores are depleted and iron supply to body tissues is restricted (Beard and Tobin 2000; Brownlie et al. 2004). Inadequate dietary intake of iron is the most common cause of this condition. The female athlete's diet can also contain compounds such as phytates (from whole grains) or tannins (from tea) that inhibit iron absorption. Female swimmers often restrict their consumption of meat products (often in attempts to reduce fat intake) and consume low amounts of vitamin C. Both practices are known to have a negative effect on the absorption of iron in the body. Coupled with blood loss from menses and a small amount of exertional hemolysis, a female swimmer can quickly become at risk for developing iron deficiencies or anemia.

Athletes with iron deficiency frequently exhibit symptoms such as decreased endurance, elevated heart rate, chronic fatigue, and increased risk of illness (VanHeest and Mahoney 2007; Volpe 2010; Zoller and Vogel 2004). Additional symptoms include irritability, poor appetite, poor concentration, cold intolerance, and increased rate of headaches (VanHeest and Mahoney 2007; Zoller and Vogel 2004). Diagnosis of iron deficiencies or anemia is performed through a blood test. Many of the symptoms overlap symptoms of overtraining, making a definitive diagnosis of iron deficiency or anemia difficult. Therefore, a physician should make the diagnosis of iron deficiency or anemia, although distinguishing pseudoanemia from iron deficiency anemia with a single blood draw may be difficult. Athletes and coaches should consider routine blood screening to monitor for various issues including iron deficiency anemia (Deakin 2000; Rockwell and Hinton 2005).

Hemoglobin, hematocrit, and erythrocyte count in blood samples drawn from national-caliber female swimmers across a 32-week season were found to be significantly lower than in nonathletes (Kabasakalis et al. 2007). In addition, the female athletes showed a decrease in three markers of iron status—hemoglobin, iron stores, and total iron-binding capacity (TIBC)—over the course of the competitive season. The changes were seen even though the athletes doubled their iron intake from 20 milligrams per day to over 40 milligrams per day during the season through the use of iron supplementation at the onset of training (Kabasakalis et al. 2007). Sixty percent of the female swimmers were reported as having ferritin levels below the low end of the reference limits (Kabasakalis et al. 2007). Data from both elite and junior elite American swimmers support these findings; approximately 50 percent of elite female swimmers displayed signs of poor iron status (VanHeest and Ratliff 1997, 1998). Seventy percent were in pre-stage I (ferritin 20 to 50 milligrams per milliliter), 18 percent in stage I, and 12 percent in stage II iron deficiency (high TIBC and low Fe) (Troup 1990).

Treatments

Typically, iron deficiency is treated by increasing dietary iron intake. A sports medicine professional should prescribe iron supplementation regimens or other treatments such as injections.

Ferrous sulfate is the preferred supplement because of its high absorption rate (Kim et al. 2002; Weight, Jacobs, and Noakes 1992; Zoller and Vogel 2004). Drinking a glass of orange juice or consuming 500 milligrams of vitamin C when taking the iron supplement will improve absorption rates. Regardless of treatment (i.e., dietary iron supplementation), consumption of caffeine with the treatment will have the negative result of decreasing iron absorption (Weight, Jacobs, and Noakes 1992). Note that high doses of iron can result in diarrhea, nausea, or constipation (Zoller and Vogel 2004). Gradually increasing the volume of iron intake will help minimize these side effects. Athletes who have normal levels of iron should be cautioned to avoid supplementation. Excess iron or iron overload can lead to serious health risks including death.

The dietary intake of iron in female athletes is often low (Clarkson and Haymes 1995; Kleiner 1995; Hurrell 1997; Zoller and Vogel 2004). The recommended daily allowance (RDA) for iron is 8 milligrams per day for females 9 to 13 years old, 15 milligrams per day for females 14 to 18 years old, and 18 milligrams per day for females 19 to 30 years old (Institute of Medicine 2001). Competitive female athletes tend to control their diets, often reducing fat and meat intake. Kabasakalis and colleagues (2007) reported an average iron intake of 14 milligrams per day from food and 20 milligrams per day from supplements. These dietary values were similar to those reported by Hawley and Williams (1991) for age-group swimmers (iron = 14.4 + 3.9 milligrams per day).

The best dietary sources of iron include lean red meats, legumes, nuts, and fortified cereals. Iron, however, can be found in numerous foods (table 23.1). Consumption of a varied, healthy diet should provide ample iron resources. Dietary restriction and use of various methods to control or reduce body weight can affect iron status in female swimmers.

Table 23.1 Examples of Iron-Containing Foods

MEAT AND MEAT SUBSTITUTES		
Food	**Amount**	**Iron (mg)**
Red meat	3 oz	4
Fish and poultry	3 oz	2–3
Liver	3 oz	8–9
Organ meat	3 oz	7
Tofu	4 oz	2.3
Eggs	1	1
Sunflower seeds	1 oz	2
Cooked dry peas, beans, lentils	1/2 cup	2–3
Peanut butter	1 tablespoon	0.3
Nuts	1/3 cup	0.5–2
JUICES (CANNED)		
Food	**Amount**	**Iron (mg)**
Prune juice	3/4 cup	7.4
Tomato juice	3/4 cup	1.6
FRUITS AND VEGETABLES		
Food	**Amount**	**Iron (mg)**
Watermelon	6 inch by 1/2 inch slice	3
Strawberries	1 cup	1.5
Cooked dark leafy greens (spinach, kale)	1/2 cup	3
Raw dark leafy greens (spinach, kale)	1 cup	2
Raisins, dates, prunes, figs	1/2 cup	3–4

Oral Contraceptive Use

Oral contraceptive use is common in both recreational and elite female athletes, and its use brings with it questions about athlete health and performance in the pool. Typically, oral contraceptives are composed of a combination of estrogen and progesterone-like compounds; the exact composition depends on the varying levels of the two steroid derivatives produced by the various manufacturers.

Besides using them for contraception, athletes may be prescribed oral contraceptives to regulate their menstrual cycles or to treat menstrual cycle issues such as amenorrhea, premenstrual symptoms, and time shifting of cycles.

Athletes often avoid oral contraceptive use because of the reported side effects such as weight gain, fluid retention, and nausea (Frankovich and Lebrun 2000; Constantini, Dubnov, and Lebrun 2005). Lower-dose pills with reduced negative side effects have become more acceptable to female athletes.

The influence of oral ovarian steroids on physical performance has been assessed over the past several decades. To date, the results remain incomplete; both positive and negative outcomes have been reported. For example, some research suggests improvement in muscular strength, power, and endurance when athletes are on oral contraceptives. The research on oral contraceptive use and performance remains equivocal (Frankovich and Lebrun 2000).

The normal female reproductive cycle is a complex relationship among various organs and multiple hormones. Knowing some of the basics will help a coach understand why and how the hormones contained in oral contraceptives can affect performance. Five major hormones are involved in the female reproductive cycle: gonadotropin-releasing hormone (GnRH), follicle-stimulating hormone (FSH), luteinizing hormone (LH), estrogen, and progesterone (Larsen et al. 2003). The hormones are released from the brain and move through the body to the ovaries. They have an effect on bone, muscle, breast tissue, heart tissue, and muscle. The body releases exact amounts of these hormones at specific points in the reproductive cycle (Sherwood 2008).

Overview of Oral Contraceptives

Oral contraceptive pills are available in three major formulations: fixed-dose, combination phasic, and daily progestin. Monophasic pills contain a fixed dose of estrogen and progestin throughout the cycle. Multiphasic pills (i.e., biphasic and triphasic) decrease the total amount of progestin throughout the cycle, mimicking a normal cycle. Injectable progestin-only or combination (estadiol and progestin) drugs are also available. Although many athletes do not consider the type of compounds in their oral contraceptives, the formulations are important to how the pill functions and how it affects metabolism.

Negative side effects such as weight gain, fatigue, headaches, and nausea were common with early types of oral contraceptives (Lebrun et al. 2003). Newer lower-dose drugs have minimized the side effects. These formulations have 30 to 40 percent lower levels of hormones, resulting in significantly reduced side effects. They are therefore more appealing to female athletes (Greenblatt 1985). Insignificant increases in body weight (about one kilogram over six weeks) have been reported in female athletes (Lebrun et al. 2003), and no change in body weight has been reported in female nonathletes (Rosenberg 1998). Remember that the performance of female swimmers may be affected by even a small increase in body weight or a small change in body composition.

Performance Outcomes

Research continues on the effect of oral contraceptives on performance. Results depend on the type of oral contraceptive, the dose, and the type of activity. Outcomes related to substrate or fuel utilization, anaerobic performance, muscle performance and damage, and aerobic performance are presented and discussed in this section. Table 23.2 provides a summary of these factors.

The various compounds found in oral contraceptives have been shown to affect metabolism in multiple ways. Ethinyl estradiol has been shown to decrease amino acids; increase cholesterol (high-density lipoprotein cholesterol, or HDL, the so-called good cholesterol) and triglycerides; and decrease low-density lipoproteins, or LDL (the so-called bad cholesterol) (Dorflinger 1985; Godsland, Crook, and Wynn 1992). Derivatives of 19-nortestosterone have been shown to increase plasma insulin; decrease glucose tolerance and cholesterol, HDL, and triglycerides; and increase LDL cholesterol (Bonen, Haynes, and Graham 1991; Constantini, Dubnov, and Lebrun 2005; Dorflinger 1985; Suh et al. 2003).

Oral contraceptive use appears to have no effect on anaerobic performance. The research assessing oral contraceptives and anaerobic performance is limited. Most studies have shown no effect of oral contraceptives on anaerobic power or capacity. Continued research is essential to understand the relationship in female athletes.

The use of oral contraceptives may protect against muscle damage. Muscle tearing or ultrastructural damage is a common characteristic of physical exertion.

Table 23.2 Potential Positive and Negative Outcomes of Oral Contraceptive Use

Positive outcomes	Negative outcomes
Contraception	Fluid retention
Reduction of dysmenorrhea, cramping, premenstrual symptoms, iron deficiency	Potential weight gain
Improved aerobic economy	Nausea
Carbohydrate sparing	Headache
Bone loss prevention, primarily in females with oligomenorrhea or amenorrhea	Potential cardiovascular problems, including thrombosis
	Decreased aerobic capacity
	Decreased anaerobic performance
	Increased ligament laxity

The role of estradiol, one of the estrogens, on membrane structure has been studied. Although studies of the relationship between oral contraceptive use and muscle damage in athletic women using oral contraceptives remain unclear, women who use oral contraceptives reported lower muscle soreness scores following an exercise routine (Thompson et al. 1997). Additional research suggests a protective role of oral contraceptives on muscle damage (Bar and Amelink 1997; Carter, Dobridge, and Hackney 2001). Overall, estrogens, specifically estradiol, appear to provide a protective influence against muscle damage and muscle soreness following exercise.

Regular oral contraceptive use may decrease $\dot{V}O_2$max, or the body's ability to take in, transport, and use oxygen (De Souza et al. 1990; Bemben et al. 1992; Bemben, Salm, and Salm 1995; Lebrun et al. 1995; Lynch and Nimmo 1998). Early studies reported no difference in performance between oral contraceptive users and nonusers as it relates to $\dot{V}O_2$max (McNeill and Mozingo 1981; Huisveld, Haspers, and Bernink 1983). Triphasic drugs used by moderately active women caused a significant decrease (about 11 percent) in $\dot{V}O_2$max following four weeks of oral contraceptive use (Casazza et al., 2002; Constantini, Dubnov, and Lebrun 2005). Other studies reported a decrease in $\dot{V}O_2$max following a two-month intervention protocol (Lebrun et al. 2003).

Other factors such as heart rate, concentrations of iron or ferritin (the storage form of iron), and hemoglobin (iron-binding protein in red blood cells) are not altered with oral contraceptive use (Mooij et al. 1992). Because these factors did not change, it was unclear why aerobic capacity declined. The sympathetic nervous system is designed to activate the body's resources under stressful conditions through what is often called the fight-or-flight system (Sherwood 2008). Oral contraceptives reduce activation of the sympathetic nervous system, resulting in decreases in aerobic capacity (McMurray, Mottola, and Wolfe 1993).

Summary

Females are participating in the sport of swimming in growing numbers each year. Although swimming provides many health benefits, most coaches and athletes focus on performance outcomes. Research and clinical suggestions continue to aim at optimizing performance in all female swimmers.

Female athletes must work to maintain energy balance during both training and competition. Dietary consumption of iron is essential to optimal performance. Swimmers should be aware of meal patterning by providing fuel throughout the day and avoiding the consumption of one large meal at the end of the day.

Female athletes who intend to use oral contraceptives should consult with their physicians about the type of drug to use. Education is essential for female athletes and coaches who train female swimmers. They should continue to monitor new research findings.

CHAPTER 24

Open Water Swimmers

—Steve Munatones

Swimming faster in the open water involves optimizing and maximizing multiple factors: technique, integration of the sport sciences, training, feedings and nutrition, race tactics, and intangibles such as navigational IQ and tolerance to venomous stings. Compared with the pool, the dynamic environment that swimmers can encounter in open water swimming is incredibly varied. A number of variables can change even within a race. Even the range of venues that people can swim in—oceans, lakes, canals, rivers, reservoirs, fjords—highlights the challenges of open water swimming. Consider some of the dynamic challenges that an open water swimmer can face:

- In ocean races, a variety of marine life may be present—some colorful and beautiful (e.g., tropical fish and sea turtles) and others treacherous and harmful (e.g., sharks and Portuguese man-o-war). Additionally, swells and tides can push swimmers off course or influence race strategies.

- In river and bay swims, changing currents can be tricky and frustrating, requiring the swimmer to invest significant additional effort.

- In point-to-point lake swims, intermediate buoys and turn buoys only occasionally give an accurate indication of the distance left to swim.

- In a competitive race within a large pack, swimmers can become boxed in and limited in what they can do or see, short of stopping or slowing down.

- In a cold-water course, swimmers often need to focus on overcoming the effects of hypothermia. The reverse occurs with hyperthermia in warm water.

- During channel swims, swimmers often have to swim in pitch darkness and try to reach land on a rocky coastline.

Consequently, open water swimmers have to be able to adapt to and handle the unexpected. Preparing for the unknown becomes increasingly important, especially when compared with pool swimming.

To excel and achieve their potential, swimmers must appreciate and plan for six physical parameters, or critical characteristics, of open water swimming (figure 24.1):

1. Distance (short or long)
2. Water condition (smooth or rough)
3. Water type (fresh or salt)
4. Currents (with or against)
5. Temperature (cold or warm)
6. Race type (solo or races)

As with pool swimming, training specificity is important in open water swimming. Although a short-distance freshwater race conducted under smooth conditions in warm water may resemble the tranquil conditions found in a pool, on the opposite end of the spectrum are marathon saltwater swims, which are typically attempted under rough conditions in cold water. Just as preparation for a 50-meter freestyle is vastly different from preparation for a 400-meter IM

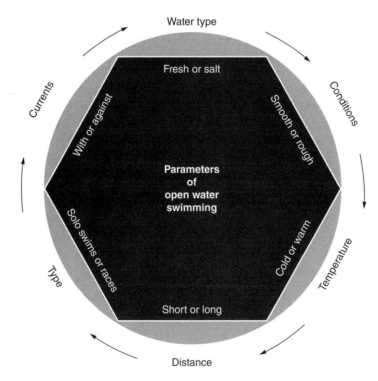

▶ **Figure 24.1** Physical parameters that affect open water swimming.

in the pool, the ways in which an open water swimmer prepares for different types of events differ. Swimming faster in the open water requires swimmers to understand and manage the optimal combination of factors that will prepare them to handle the situations that they may encounter.

Besides these physical parameters of open water swimming, athletes face a number of psychological obstacles not experienced in pool swimming. Again, the dynamic environment provides unique challenges compared with swimming in a pool. Open water swimmers often undergo a unique form of sensory deprivation; they may not know exactly where they are during a race, they may not be able see or hear much around them, and probably most important, they may not know what conditions they will encounter during their swim. As such, educated guesswork; assumptions based on tides, wind, and weather; and gut feel are the tools of experienced open water swimmers rather than the split times and lap counts that are used in the domain of the pool. While pool swimmers focus on their pace, competition, and technique as they push themselves, open water swimmers need to anticipate all of these unknowns, clouded in a haze of uncertainty. As conditions change for the worse, jellyfish stings are felt, or water temperature drops, these changes can wreak havoc with an athlete's psyche.

Although the dynamic and unpredictable nature of open water swimming presents a wide range of challenges, an equal number of practical tools are available to the swimmer to maximize performance. This chapter examines the myriad factors that have a significant effect on performance and describes how swimmers, by understanding these factors, can maximize their performances in the open water.

Distance: Short or Long

Both short and long races provide unique challenges that swimmers must prepare for. Whatever the distance, swimmers need a good navigational IQ to help them get through the course efficiently.

Short Races

In a short open water race, a good warm-up is vital because the race typically will start at an extraordinarily fast pace, ranging anywhere from an all-out running sprint down the beach to a 400-meter pace for the first turn buoy in an in-the-water start. Swimmers generally start fast in these short-distance races to establish a good position early and gain an optimal position approaching the first turn buoy.

To prepare for these short-distance races, swimmers need to withstand a significant and sustained increase in heart rate, similar to what occurs during a 400-meter freestyle. This ability can be improved by repeatedly doing ins-and-outs along the shoreline whereby the swimmer runs into the open water from shore, swims straight out in the water, turns around a buoy or at a specific distance, swims back, dolphins through the shallow water, and then runs back up on shore. Sport-specific improvements also can be achieved by regularly doing deck-ups, a series of repeat swims, performed on a certain interval (e.g., 5 × 100 at 1:20 or 10 × 50 at 0:50), in which swimmers pull themselves out of the water after each repeat. This deck-up set can be followed by a standard long-distance, short-rest interval set (e.g., 5 × 500) to simulate the steady-state, aerobic type of swimming that athletes will experience after the high-intensity start. Ins-and-outs and deck-ups will both create significant heart rate spikes as swimmers change body position from horizontal to vertical and back again.

Another item to factor into preparation for open water swimming, and one that swimmers can specifically train for, is body contact. Physical contact among swimmers is typically more of an issue in a short-distance race than a marathon race, especially at the start, finish, and around the turn buoys. To become accustomed to the physicality experienced in the open water and duplicate it in the pool, several swimmers can swim shoulder to shoulder in one lane during a pool workout. An example set for this training is 12 × 100 meters with three teammates starting together. Each athlete takes the middle position on four of the repeats and then rotates to either the left- or right-side positions for the other repeats.

Long Races

To prepare for marathon races of 10 kilometers or longer, swimmers should regularly perform distance tolerance sessions in which they ultimately build up to swimming distances of at least 60 percent of the expected race distance. If the race is 25 kilometers (15.5 miles), the distance tolerance workouts should gradually be increased until the distance covered in one continuous swim is 15 kilometers. Similarly, if swimmers will be in the water for eight hours on a long swim, the distance tolerance sessions should build up until the athletes are able to swim five hours on their longest nonstop training swims.

Open water swimming nutrition and in-race fueling is another area to address in training. A swimmer's preparation for any swim that will take longer than one hour to complete should include experimenting with various refueling and rehydration flavors, types, and strategies, including practicing with gel packs and water bottles to identify what works best for optimizing performance. Like marathon runners and triathletes, swimmers should rehydrate or refuel frequently during a marathon swim. Athletes should try different flavors and different formulations with occasional solid food or gels to find what the body will tolerate. If an athlete swims in saltwater, keep in mind that any food or drink will likely taste different than it would in a freshwater swim, especially as the swim distance increases. During practice, swimmers should become accustomed to putting gel packs in their swimsuits and then removing and quickly consuming them while treading water. Athletes should do their experimentation during training and should not introduce any new nutrition or hydration practices during a competition.

Navigation

Navigational IQ is a term used to describe a swimmer's ability to swim straight and steady under the dynamically changing or challenging conditions encountered in open bodies of water. This skill is important because whether the race is short or long, swimming faster often depends on the swimmer's ability to swim straight.

A swimmer's ability to swim straight, especially when waves are battering the athlete or race buoys are far apart, is critical to keeping the race distance to a minimum and swimming faster. Swimming in a straight line requires a balanced stroke in which propulsion and drag resistance are produced equally on both sides of the body. Although many coaches and athletes advocate bilateral breathing, which works well for developing a balanced stroke in many swimmers, the ultimate goal is to create symmetry in the arm strokes, kick, and head position. Bilateral breathing can help swimmers become more symmetrical and balanced, but a flaw in the stroke (e.g., a crossover kick or crossing over the centerline with the hand path when breathing to one side or the other) may be the fundamental reason that a swimmer cannot swim straight in the open water.

Often, in the last part of a race, when they are moving the fastest or when they are making a surge, the best swimmers—no matter their age or speed—are able to swim straight without the benefits of lane lines or bilateral breathing. An analysis of their swimming technique shows that they have a symmetrical stroke in which there is little or no crossover kick even if they frequently look up to sight the finish. After each breath, or head lift to sight, the head position is aligned with the spine and the eyes are looking straight down. These athletes also tend to have a remarkably similar pattern of force development with both the left and right hands underwater, which subsequently leads to a symmetric pattern of speed and acceleration. This symmetry helps them swim straight. In addition to being more efficient, being able to swim straight has an additional benefit in that the athletes can swim more economically because they don't need to lift the head to sight as often.

Poor stroke symmetry is associated with various negative effects on swimming speed in the open water. Figure 24.2 presents an overview of the cycle that can ensue from having an unbalanced stroke in the open water. If swimmers can improve their stroke balance and symmetry in the pool, then they will be able to improve speed and navigational IQ in the open water as well.

Developing a balanced stroke and high navigational IQ takes practice, focus, and patience. Few athletes have an innate talent to swim straight even in glassy water, let alone turbulent water. One simple test that can be performed in the open water to confirm whether swimmers have a symmetric stroke is for the swimmers to stand on the shoreline and identify a target (e.g., a buoy, breakwater, pier, pontoon, anchored boat, or lifeguard stand or tall building in the distance) that they will swim toward. The swimmers dive into the water and take 50 to 100 strokes toward the target with their eyes closed. At that point they stop swimming and check to see whether they veered to the left or right of the

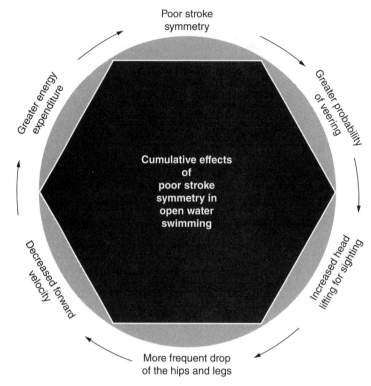

▶ **Figure 24.2** Cumulative effects of poor stroke symmetry in open water swimming.

intended target and by how much. They can repeat this a few times to confirm how far they naturally deviate from the straight-line path. Knowing this information is the first step toward being able to balance the stroke and compensate appropriately during open water races. This test is best performed in calm water first and then later in rough water. Although swimming in smooth water in the morning hours is often more enjoyable, learning to swim straight in the midst of heavy surface chop is invaluable. By learning to swim straighter when the wind is blowing, the current is running, and the line of vision is minimized by surface chop or waves, the swimmer will gain considerable confidence.

Conditions: Smooth or Rough

Water conditions will also affect how a race should be approached. Different swimmers likely will excel under different conditions depending on their strengths and weaknesses. In smooth water where surface chop is virtually nonexistent, few dynamic elements will affect a swimmer's ability to produce forward velocity. But some surface conditions may be beneficial to the swimmer. More likely than not, a rhythmic pattern to the surface chop or swells will allow swimmers to stretch out their stroke and use a lower arm stroke tempo than they need under rough water conditions, or vice versa. Stroke rate may vary, depending on the situation. With that said, research shows that an increased arm stroke turnover is usually the key to swimming faster for most people in the open water. Swimmers need to make sure that they do not get lulled into using a methodical, slower-than-normal stroke rate when competing under glassy, calm conditions if they want to swim faster.

A few words about stroke technique in the open water and the interplay of stroke rate and stroke length are useful here. Swimming velocity is a function of both stroke rate and stroke length, and an athlete can swim faster by increasing one or both variables. Most of the recommendations that characterize good in-pool swimming also pertain to swimming well in the open water, but some differences (e.g., sighting and drafting) introduce variances to the ideal open water swimming technique. In research on swimmers at every level, from Olympic medalists to newcomers, tests show that forward velocity is maximized as a swimmer's hand moves underwater between the breastbone and the belly button. Whether a person is swimming in smooth or rough conditions, this point in the stroke is where the greatest propulsion is generated. Conversely, forward velocity is minimized as the hand enters the water until the catch, the position at which the hand is approximately 25 to 45 degrees under the surface of the water and ready to initiate the pull (see figure 24.3). In most cases, this decrease in forward velocity corresponds to the point in the stroke cycle at which the opposite hand is pushing past the hips as the stroke is finished. A swimmer experiences accelerations and decelerations within each stroke cycle (see figure 24.3). As is the case in pool swimming, the goal in open water swimming should be to reduce the magnitude of these oscillations because swimming is energetically most efficient when traveling at a constant velocity.

If we now imagine that the hand moves 180 degrees from the entry to the catch, then through the pull into the recovery, and finally back to the hand entry, the swimmer's hands and forearms generate propulsion during a relative small percentage of the entire 180-degree range. Although minimizing drag resistance is important, generating propulsion is even more critical to swimming faster in the open water.

Velocity2.3814

▶ **Figure 24.3** Sample forward velocity profile produced when swimming freestyle. Fluctuations in velocity occur as speed decreases during the hand entry and finish and increases when the hand is underneath the body in the power position.

When we observe the swimming styles of world-class and even average open water swimmers at their fastest paces (i.e., at the start and toward the finish) during a race, we find that a higher arm tempo and stroke rate (SR) is an important element to swimming fast. In a review of the 5-kilometer, 10-kilometer, and 25-kilometer open water races at the 2000, 2001, 2003, 2004, 2005, 2007, 2008, and 2009 World Championships, the fastest men generally swam using a stroke rate in excess of 41 stroke cycles per minute (82 individual arm strokes per minute [SPM]). The fastest women generally swam with a stroke rate over 43 cycles per minute (85 SPM) throughout most of their races. In general, swimmers took 5 to 10 strokes per minute fewer in the 25-kilometer races compared with the shorter distances. Peak stroke rates increased to between 45 and 50 cycles per minute as both male and female swimmers reached their maximum speeds during the race. As a means of comparison, the average stroke rates for pool distance swimmers were found to be 41 or 42 stroke cycles per minute for men (1,500-meter swim) and 47 or 48 cycles per minute for women (800-meter swims).

Although most swimmers will not be able to initiate or maintain as high an arm turnover as world-class swimmers do, a faster arm turnover is one good way to swim faster. All swimmers need to learn what their average stroke rates are. They can begin by asking a friend or coach to count the strokes taken during a minute of steady-state swimming in the open water. If the average SR is 70 SPM, then to swim faster the athlete should try to swim at 72 to 75 SPM for as long as possible during an open water workout. When no longer able to hold this pace, the swimmer can reduce the SR to recover and then repeat.

A high-elbow recovery and a high-hand recovery are preferable in situations in which whitecaps or high surface chop exists. Modifying the arm stroke to prevent the arms and hands from being battered about in the turbulence will save energy and minimize frustration. Although swimming with surface chop does not usually cause problems, swimming against surface chop occasionally leads to unintentional swallowing of water. To reduce the chances of swallowing water, the swimmer can slightly modify the head position to breathe farther back in the stroke under the armpit and away from the oncoming waves and surface chop.

Of course, kicking also has an effect on performance. An open water swimmer's legs may often serve as ballast rather than provide propulsion, allowing the swimmer to maintain a more balanced stroke in the swells and surface chop. Although a swimmer may unintentionally do more crossover kicking in turbulent conditions, most of the body should remain in a relatively streamlined position by maintaining a strong core and firm neck position. A swimmer with a strong core, especially when combined with a small-amplitude kick and a shallow sighting technique, is better able to maintain a streamlined body position even while struggling with turbulent surface chop.

Although kicking faster (e.g., by increasing kick tempo from a two-beat kick to a four-beat or six-beat kick) likely will enable a swimmer to go faster in the open water, it also taxes the body physiologically because it uses the larger muscles in the legs, which in turn consume more oxygen. Unlike in pool swimming in which there are turns and changes of direction every lap, kicking faster, especially when done inefficiently in the open water, is a proven way to get winded if an athlete has not trained for this level of sustained effort. A smaller, more compact kick is recommended for open water swimming. Kicking harder (i.e., kicking deeper and more forcefully) can be suboptimal because doing so takes the body out of a streamlined position and exposes more of the body to the dynamic forces that produce drag. Like most skills, however, kicking, and even being able to maintain a higher kick tempo, can be developed. Not long ago athletes believed that maintaining a six-beat kick in the 1,500-meter freestyle would consume too much oxygen and couldn't be done. But by training their bodies to support this level of kicking, many swimmers can now use a six-beat kick in races in which they traditionally relied on a two-beat kick. Clearly, a 1,500-meter pool swim is much different from a 10K marathon swim. The message, however, is that the body can be trained to support a higher kick rate, especially if it is used strategically at specific points in the race.

Body position in open water swimming is critical, just as it is for in-pool swimming. But open water swimming brings huge challenges not seen in the pool, including sighting and drafting. Swimming through whitecaps and against surface chop is not pleasant and is frequently frustrating. Even with great stroke symmetry, swimmers need to lift the head and sight off a buoy or other landmark to stay on course. If we assume that swimmers lift their heads every 25 meters in a 10K race, they will ultimately lift their heads approximately 400 times during the race. Because the head weighs about 10 pounds (4.5 kg), swimmers are partially lifting an additional 4,000 pounds (1,800 kg) that they would not have to lift over the equivalent distance in a pool. Even taking into account the natural buoyancy in the water, which makes the effective lifting of the cumulative 4,000 pounds much lighter, swimmers are still placing a lot more stress on the lower back, neck, and shoulders than they would swimming in a pool. Therefore, having strong core muscles (abdominals and lower back) and maintaining overall body flexibility are both critical to maintaining a proper body line and sighting technique in the open water. Keeping the body as streamlined as possible, even when sighting with increased frequency, will help reduce drag. A strong core can help keep the hips and legs from dropping too much, which is a prime contributor to drag. As rough water pushes, lifts, and drops the body into various positions, a strong core can help keep the body more streamlined by preventing the lower body (hips and legs) and upper body (shoulders) from snaking side to side.

Water: Fresh or Salt

Freshwater is not as dense as saltwater. Because buoyancy is determined by the density of the water, a swimmer will naturally ride higher in saltwater compared with water in lakes, rivers, or reservoirs. Therefore, maintaining body position and streamlining is often easier in the ocean than in freshwater, where the muscles of the core must provide this missing support.

Buoyancy may be the major difference between freshwater and saltwater, but other differences can affect the swimmer as well. Many open water swimmers experience a bloated sensation of their lips, mouth, and tongue when swimming for long durations in the ocean. One recommendation is for the swimmer to wash the mouth periodically with mouthwash after a feeding during a marathon swim to avoid this sensation. Feeling a more normal sensation in the lips, mouth, and tongue on a long swim can help performance.

Psychologically, for some swimmers, competitions in the ocean require a different mentality for them to perform at their best. Experienced ocean swimmers often have a mind-set that minimizes thoughts about risks such as marine life that can frighten some people. The depth and dynamics of the ocean, especially fear of its natural inhabitants, can be problematic for many newcomers. Swimming with friends or parallel to shore is a way to overcome these fears.

Currents: With or Against

Swimming with fast currents and along tidal flows in oceans, bays, and rivers can feel great because swimmers can use this moving water to swim faster than they would in a pool. When large ocean swells, whitecaps, or heavy surface chop is moving in the direction of travel, swimmers can lengthen out the stroke, reduce the kick, railroad (or propel themselves along) with the waves when possible, and conserve energy while still moving quickly. Swimmers should use these elements to their advantage, even if it is riding the wake of a passing boat. This technique is a sign of high navigational IQ. Conversely, swimming against currents and tidal flows either head on or laterally is frustrating. When swimming loop or out-and-back courses, swimmers may face currents, tidal flows, and ocean swells in one direction and then have these same elements in their favor in the other direction.

Temperatures: Cold or Warm

Few things are more difficult to overcome than extreme water temperature, whether too warm or too cold. Both hypothermia (i.e., decreased core body temperature) and hyperthermia (i.e., increased core body temperature) play havoc with the swimmer physiologically, and staying focused is difficult when the body is dramatically cooling or heating.

The feeling of physical discomfort created by sustained immersion in cold water is distinct. The ability to think clearly, enjoy the race, and swim efficiently is severely hampered in cold temperatures. Short of wearing a wetsuit, neoprene cap, and silicone earplugs, the most effective way to prepare for cold water is acclimatization; to swim well in cold water, swimmers must practice in cold water. There are no shortcuts, medicines, or magic solutions. Putting thick coats of lanolin or petroleum jelly on the skin only reduces the initial sting of the cold water; skin lubrication will not retain body heat as a wetsuit will. Acclimatization to cold water takes patience, commitment, and consistency. Swimming in cold water day by day, week by week, and month by month is the only way to develop the ability to swim well for sustained periods in the cold. Consistency and a gradual lengthening of cold-water practices are essential if a swimmer decides to do a cold-water swim. Consistently performing cold-water training for even short periods (i.e., less than 10 minutes) will enable swimmers to increase the time that they can tolerate the cold. In less-than-ideal situations, swimmers should carve out at least 14 to 21 days to adapt to the cold in advance of a race, gradually increasing the amount of time spent in the water over that period.

Being able to swim fast in warm water can also be tricky, but developing that ability is typically much less difficult and time consuming. Holding on to snow cones and putting the feet in an ice bath are some quick ways to lower body temperature before a race. Reducing the kick (e.g., from a four-beat kick to a two-beat kick) may also help minimize heat stress and ultimately allow a swimmer to swim faster. But swimming in warm water does not come without risk. Excessive water temperature can be dangerous, as evidenced by the tragic death in 2010 of open water swimmer Fran Crippen, who was competing in a 10K marathon swim in water temperatures in excess of 87 degrees Fahrenheit (30.6 degrees Celsius). The water temperature likely led to exertional heat illness that ultimately caused his death.

Proper nutrition and hydration are important, whether swimming in warm or cold water. Because of the perception that water is cool, swimmers often do not realize how much they sweat. Therefore, they do not properly hydrate during a training session or race. Swimmers should practice proper nutrition and hydration habits during training. Any dizziness, disorientation, or extreme fatigue should be immediately reported to a coach or teammate.

Type: Solo Swims or Races

Solo swims are entirely different from competitive races. Solo swims are usually long-distance individual efforts that are supported by an escort crew. They can be marathon swims across a channel, a charity swim in a lake, or a multiday stage swim in a river. Besides the mental aspects of a solo swim, swimmers face logistical and financial issues. The swimmer must select pilots and escort boats, carefully study water and weather conditions, decide courses and start times, and organize a support team.

Planning a solo swim requires documenting, discussing, and deciding hundreds of details. One of the important decisions that swimmers make is who will be on the escort boat. Selection of the support team is a critical decision. Is the pilot experienced? Will anyone on the support team get seasick, diverting attention and support from the swimmer? Will the team fully support the swimmer through the night? Are the crew members compatible with each other?

A swimmer does not want to be frustrated, upset, or disappointed by a sick or uncooperative crew member. A swimmer can ill afford avoidable distractions and impediments to success while in the open water.

In assembling the support team and defining responsibilities, the swimmer should appoint one person on the crew to make the final decision to pull the swimmer from the water, if necessary. This person should have the final say if the swimmer's safety is threatened. This person—the pilot, coach, or observer—must be familiar enough with the swimmer to know how hard he can reasonably and safely push himself. By knowing about the athlete's training, personality, and abilities, this person can help the swimmer reach his goal. The person must balance the responsibility of keeping the swimmer safe with the goal of pushing the athlete to realize his full potential.

Competitive Racing

Many open water swimmers train individually, but they race in competitions where they'll be in the water with dozens, if not hundreds, of other athletes. With the addition of the 10K marathon swim to the 2008 Beijing, 2012 London, 2016 Rio, and 2020 Tokyo Olympic Games, the competitiveness of open water swimming at all levels and ages has increased. Athletes are swimming faster than ever before, and their training is becoming more specific to reach their goals. Let's look at the factors that influence open water competition and the way in which swimmers can best prepare to excel in the open water.

To optimize performance in the open water, athletes should base their pool and open water training on the pyramid of open water success. These seven essentials, summarized in figure 24.4, include the optimal training concepts that

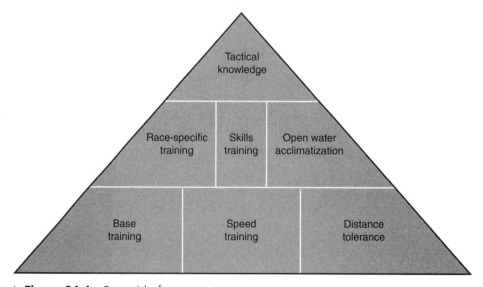

▶ **Figure 24.4** Pyramid of open water success.
Reprinted, by permission, from S. Munatones, 2011, *Open water swimming* (Champaign, IL: Human Kinetics), 102.

can be implemented in preparing for races of all distances. The amount of time that athletes spend on each of the seven essentials depends on the time of year, where they are in their training cycle, the amount of time the swimmers are able to dedicate to training, and the athletes' personal goals and swimming background.

Base training, speed training, and distance tolerance form the base of this open water training philosophy. A good base, or foundation, is essential for an athlete to excel in the open water. These fundamental concepts are rooted in the competitive pool training philosophies that have been used successfully for decades.

Race-specific training, skills training, and open water acclimatization are at the next level. These three fundamentals are less well known among coaches and athletes, but they are specific to open water swimming and equally important to incorporate in a training regimen.

Tactical knowledge is at the apex of the pyramid. Tactical knowledge refers to the knowledge and understanding of what to do in a dynamic environment in which the competitors, weather, and water conditions can change in a moment's notice. To perform well in any open water swim, a swimmer needs to anticipate, adapt, and respond to moves by the competition during the race as well as to changes in the natural environment. Tactical knowledge includes study of everything from the elements (tides, currents, and waves) to the tendencies, strengths, and weaknesses of competitors. A swimmer can obtain and enhance tactical knowledge through observation, study, and race experience.

Developing the Base of Speed and Endurance

Base training helps to establish a solid foundation. Swimmers get in good physical shape by swimming thousands of meters during hundreds of aerobic training sets in the pool. Base training also includes dryland training, specifically stretching and strength training that focus on maintaining overall strength balance throughout the body and building muscular endurance. Even the shortest open water competitive distance is a highly aerobic event. As such, success in open water swimming requires solid aerobic capacity.

Depending on a swimmer's experience, the amount of training time available, and the distance of the swim, base training can take on various forms. Swimmers who need to fit in training around work and family obligations might do 2,000 yards per session several days a week. World-class athletes might swim 10,000 meters per day six days a week.

The quality of training will affect performance on race day. But whether a swimmer is an elite athlete or a casual masters swimmer, the key to developing a training base is consistency. Consistency will help build a solid foundation that will fuel optimal performances. Swimmers who consistently practice by swimming at least a half of the eventual total race distance will likely develop a base that is strong enough to support good performances at competition time. Therefore, an athlete who is aiming to swim a 10K marathon swim should regularly do at least 5K per training session.

Although most of the energy that supplies the working muscles in an open water swim is produced by aerobic metabolism, the anaerobic system is important as well. Speed is needed to produce the final kick to the finish, to counter a move made by a competitor, to cross a strong current, or to break away from the pack. Regular speed training, another cornerstone in swimming, involves developing the anaerobic system by performing short-duration efforts (less than two minutes) at high intensity.

Establishing a Tolerance for Distance

Distance tolerance training helps ensure that a swimmer has the ability to swim the specific race distance on competition day. For shorter distance open water races, swimmers should strive to develop the ability to swim 130 percent of the target race distance. That is, a swimmer who wants to be competitive in a 2.5K race should be able swim at least 3 kilometers straight at a decent pace. If athletes build up to a distance 30 percent longer than the race, they will be prepared to swim well even if the water is colder than expected or the currents are stronger than expected. The extra 30 percent provides the athlete with a buffer to cover the unexpected conditions and intangibles that inevitably occur in open water races.

These distance tolerance guidelines should be modified for marathon and longer distance swims. For swims up to and beyond 25 kilometers (15.5 miles), athletes should build up to at least one swim that is 60 to 80 percent of the expected marathon distance. In most instances, the longest training swim should be done approximately two to four weeks before the date of the competition. In training for an ultramarathon race (e.g., 21-mile [33.8 km] English Channel), swimmers should gradually build up to a six- to eight-hour swim, ideally performed in the water temperature expected at the ultramarathon. Governing bodies set parameters for swimmers to qualify for channel swims. For example, the Channel Piloting and Swimming Federation requires solo swimmers who attempt an English Channel crossing to complete a certified swim of six hours in water under 61 degrees Fahrenheit (16 degrees Celsius) or provide proof of completing an acceptable alternative swim. An athlete who can complete a 15-mile (24.1 km) training swim should be prepared to cross a 21-mile channel, especially if the physical conditioning is partnered with strong psychological preparation and an experienced pilot and support crew.

Simulating Racing Conditions

Coaches often overlook race-specific training. This training component can be used to simulate open water race situations in the pool and can help acclimate a swimmer to open water races in which physical contact, running in and out of the water, drafting, and positioning are part of racing. Some examples of simulated race condition exercises are described here.

Paceline Sets

Paceline sets are drills in the pool in which groups of swimmers (generally three to five) draft off one another, swimming behind the toes of the swimmers in front of them in one lane. In this way, the swimmers use drafting, much like a cycling peloton in the Tour de France. For 100-yard paceline sets, the leader of the group swims 100 yards at a set pace. The other swimmers follow closely behind. After 100 yards, the leader momentarily stops and waits at the side of the lane as the other swimmers continue swimming. The swimmers keep the same order as the new leader takes over and leads the group for the next 100 yards. This pattern is repeated until everyone leads the aquatic peloton for two to four rotations.

If each leader swims at a fairly good pace, the swimmers gain the following advantages:

- Excellent aerobic workout
- Practice drafting on the feet of teammates
- Learning to conserve energy while drafting at a good pace
- Increased awareness of other swimmers and practice at swimming in groups
- Practice in increasing and decreasing pace in the middle of a training set

Pool Open Water (POW) Swims

Even without access to an open water swimming venue, open water racing can be replicated with pool open water (POW) training. POW is an easy-to-implement, educational, and enjoyable introduction to open water swimming that leads to increased confidence and helps acclimate pool swimmers to the open water environment. POW can prepare swimmers for the rigors of swimming in the open water. POW enables a swimmer to practice the following:

- Swimming without lane lines and without following the black lines on the bottom of the pool
- Swimming in a pack of swimmers
- Performing quick turns around buoys in traffic
- Swimming without pushing off the pool walls
- Executing defensive and offensive racing maneuvers and tactics
- Positioning and drafting in various positions
- Dealing with the physicality of swimming in close proximity to other swimmers

POW swimming is typically conducted after removing the lane lines and setting four turn buoys in the corners of the pool near the intersection of the backstroke flags and the outside lane lines. This arrangement creates a rectangular course that is parallel with the perimeter of the pool. If all lane lines cannot be removed because other swimmers are also using the pool, a few lane lines can be removed and two turn buoys can be set near the ends of the pool.

▶ **Figure 24.5** Pool open water (POW) training.

This configuration reduces the footprint necessary to hold a POW workout and provides the same benefits.

After a POW course is set up, swimmers can practice left- and right-shoulder turns around the buoys (see figure 24.5) by alternately practicing in clockwise and counterclockwise directions. The ability to make turns in either direction is important because there are no standard open water courses or turns.

POW swims are useful training tools, but the following guidelines can make these training sessions even more beneficial:

- When a group of swimmers becomes accustomed to POW swimming, add different configurations to the workouts. By doing X- or Z-shaped patterns in the pool, swimmers can become adept in doing any type of turn in the open water (see figure 24.6).

- A triangular course allows swimmers to practice turns at various angles, not only 90-degree and 180-degree turns.

- The coach can use a whistle and issue yellow and red penalty cards in practice to simulate what swimmers might experience in races.

▶ **Figure 24.6** Pool open water training in a Z-pattern.

- Hold some POW sessions in a shallow pool to create more turbulence.
- Practice onshore finishes by doing deck-ups at the end of each set.
- If a large number of swimmers are participating, groups can be set off at different times to maximize the number of people using the course (see figure 24.7). For example, when the first swimmer of group 1 reaches the first turn buoy, the second group can start, enabling more swimmers to swim the course simultaneously.
- To help swimmers become familiar with various positions that they may encounter in races, mix up the positions (e.g., inside or outside, front of the line or drafting, or boxed in) within any given POW set.
- Swimmers need to remain alert for physical contact. Impeding or interfering with teammates is not the goal, but it will happen in POW workouts.

Deck-Ups

Deck-up sets are another race-specific training drill for onshore finishes. In deck-up sets, the swimmers immediately pull themselves out of the pool after every swim and then dive back into the pool to start the next swim. This drill helps swimmers get accustomed to the rapid body position change (from horizontal to vertical) that occurs in an on-the-beach finish.

Developing the Requisite Technical Skills

Skills training teaches the finer technical points of open water swimming, including feedings, sightings, starts, turns, positioning, and navigation, all of which can be simulated in a pool.

Simulating Feedings

If a race is longer than an hour, swimmers should hydrate during the race. Just as runners and triathletes would not compete for more than an hour without hydration, swimmers should hydrate for optimal performance. Athletes should

▶ **Figure 24.7** Starting a POW set.

drink from a water bottle during their pool workouts to practice feedings. They should also practice drinking while treading water in the pool, not while hanging on the wall, to simulate hydrating in open water swims. Alternatively, athletes can practice putting gel packs in their swimsuits and quickly consuming them while swimming in the middle of the pool. Again, proper nutrition should be practiced in training, using the specific products and feeding schedules that the athletes plan to use during competition. Athletes should not try anything new or experiment on the day of a race.

Practicing Navigation

Swimmers can practice navigation and sighting in the pool by lifting their heads and looking forward every fourth lap while doing interval training. They can practice various permutations of this set to make effective sighting second nature. They should try to avoid dropping their hips significantly or lowering their legs when they lift their heads to sight. They should push the water backward, not downward, in the first part of the arm stroke to maintain maximum forward velocity during sighting. Additionally, athletes should incorporate bilateral breathing in their pool training sets, even if they traditionally favor left- or right-side breathing. Breathing on both sides will help to balance their strokes and develop musculature to provide a strength balance throughout the body and around joints like the shoulder. The ability to breathe bilaterally will also enable athletes to check on their competition, sight landmarks and navigational points, and breathe away from oncoming waves in the open water.

Rounding Buoy Turns

Even without turn buoys in a POW set, swimmers can practice turns by swimming to the ends of the black lines on the bottom of the pool. Without touching the wall, swimmers can turn around to head back in the opposite direction to simulate an open water turn. The turn can be accomplished in a variety of ways:

- Swimmers can do a regular flip turn at the end of the black line without touching the wall and build momentum by taking a few quick arm strokes augmented by a strong freestyle or scissors kick.

- Swimmers can perform an open turn at the end of the black line without touching the wall. They can effectively change direction by turning on their sides while performing a crossover arm stroke with the outer arm and a scissors kick.

These no-wall turns simulate open water turns because the athletes have to change direction without the benefit of the pool walls, exactly what they need to do in the open water.

Practicing Starts

Starts can appear chaotic as dozens of swimmers jockey for the same position in the water. For inexperienced competitors, the start can be intimidating, but they can practice and become more comfortable with starting before the actual race. Swimmers can practice open water starts in a pool by swimming shoulder to shoulder with two teammates in the same lane. By experiencing physical contact in practice, the athletes will not get frustrated in a race when unanticipated physical contact occurs.

With practice, swimmers will eventually learn to protect their space and swim defensively, offensively, or aggressively. To maintain position, defensive swimmers protect their space when they get bumped. Offensive swimmers literally move toward and into the space of their competitors to draft or otherwise influence the race by forcing other swimmers to change their race tactics. This action may happen at key points in race, and swimmers may do it purposefully or inadvertently.

Aggressive swimmers intentionally bump or veer into competitors, driving them in a direction that they may not wish to go. Swimmers can swim very close to competitors in open water swimming. In doing so, the other swimmer will likely become uncomfortable and move over slightly, allowing the first swimmer to dictate race tactics and possibly gain a competitive advantage.

Swimmers who prefer to swim offensively or aggressively will bump and make other contact against the torso, feet, legs, arms of competitors (figure 24.8). These swimmers should be careful not to impede the progress of other swimmers, and they should recognize that the more aggressively they swim, the more likely they are to become the recipient of retaliation at some later point in the race.

Expecting the Unexpected

Mishaps occur in open water races. Swimmers may lose their goggles or swim caps. Or they may accidently get petroleum jelly on their hands from brushing up against competitors. Swimmers should practice these situations in the

▶ **Figure 24.8** Swimming defensively and offensively at a FINA World Cup race.

Courtesy of Dr. Jim Miller.

▶ **Figure 24.9** Taping goggles to the swim cap is one way to protect against the unexpected situation of losing goggles in a race.

pool—swim without goggles, swim without a cap, smear petroleum jelly on their hands in a workout—so that they can become adept at handling these situations if they occur in a race. Athletes and coaches should take time to consider what could happen and develop proactive steps to adapt. Preventative steps, such as taping goggles to the swim cap (figure 24.9), can address situations that could pop up in a race.

Acclimating to the Open Water

Open water acclimatization, especially for newcomers, enables swimmers to become familiar with the marine environment. They need to become accustomed to water that can be cold, warm, rough, polluted, or abundant with marine life.

Open water acclimatization should deal with the specific factors that swimmers expect to encounter in a race, including water that is extremely deep, water that is so clear that the swimmer can see everything below, or water that is so dark that the swimmer can see nothing at all. Both total visibility and no visibility can be difficult psychological barriers for some people. A swimmer who is nervous about water conditions should swim with experienced teammates to receive support and help in dealing with those issues. Open water acclimatization also includes swimming into jellyfish, through waves, or amid boat fumes, seaweed, pollution, and flotsam. Some swimmers who experience these situations for the first time in a race may become either frustrated or shocked. Unless the swimmer is hurt or hyperventilating, the best approach is to keep swimming.

Being able to do this, however, requires preparation to deal with the unexpected.

What happens if the swimmer encounters an unforeseen or alarming situation? The focus should be on remaining calm or returning to a state of calm. All the actions listed here can reassure athletes who encounter difficult situations. After the athletes have regained their composure, they should start swimming again.

- Lift the head and look around to see other athletes. Watching others can help relieve stress in an anxious situation.
- Swim closer to shore.
- Switch to breaststroke or backstroke.
- Raise the arms or call over and talk with safety personnel.

Developing Tactical Knowledge

In a sport that is becoming increasingly popular and consequently more competitive, developing tactical knowledge and learning to swim an intelligent race are critically important. This training component is often overlooked. Understanding why packs form, how they form during various points in the race, and why packs take certain shapes during a race will help swimmers elevate their performance.

Because thousands of situations can occur in open water swimming, developing tactical knowledge is an ongoing process that evolves over time. With solid tactical knowledge, a swimmer will better understand what it takes to achieve success in the open water.

Swimmers should be sure to take advantage of the resources available. These days, many races are posted online through video-sharing services such as YouTube. Studying these videos can help swimmers learn the tactics of successful open water swimmers. After every race each athlete should conduct a postrace analysis by thinking about, discussing, and reviewing the performance.

The coach can assist this effort by asking a series of questions using the Socratic method. An experienced open water swimming coach is inquisitive after a race and helps the athlete understand what worked well and what could be improved the next time out. By asking questions, coaches enable their athletes to internalize and understand what they did in a race, both good and bad. By visualizing and becoming aware of things such as who they were swimming with, what their pace was, how they felt, what shape the pack took at various points in the race, and what their positioning was during the race, athletes eventually become more seasoned performers. Open water coaches who question their athletes before and after a race help them understand what they can and should do. The athletes are out there in the open water all alone. Every decision they make in competitive situations—at the start, at the turn buoys, setting up the finish, and during the final sprint—has a direct effect on their performance, placing, and time. Athletes must make these decisions quickly in a dynamic environment. Therefore, coaches can assist their swimmers by questioning them and pushing them to come up with the right answers for themselves in various situations. Sample questions that will help athletes develop this tactical knowledge and become more accountable for their performances are listed here.

Before the race, coaches can ask these questions:

1. Will you use petroleum jelly, lanolin, Trislide, or another product? Do you have rubber gloves to apply the skin lubricant? How many pairs of goggles are you taking to the race?
2. Who is your competition?
3. What is your goal?
4. How did you do last year? Were you satisfied?
5. Who was swimming in front of you?

After the race, coaches can ask about the start:

1. Where were you at the start?
2. Who was next to you?
3. Did you choose that position?
4. What was the pace at the start?
5. How did you feel until the first turn buoy?

Regarding the middle of the race, coaches can ask these questions:

1. Where were you in the middle of the race?
2. Did you purposefully go to this position?
3. Were you boxed in at any point?
4. When did the pace pick up?
5. Who was swimming in front of you?
6. Who was swimming behind you and to your left and right?
7. Are these swimmers faster than you?
8. What was your stroke tempo?

Regarding the turns, coaches can ask these questions:

1. Did you speed up before or after the turn buoys?
2. Did you have the inside position around the turn buoys?
3. Did you get hit? What did you do?
4. How can you avoid being hit around the turns next time?
5. What was your position going into the turns?
6. How did you make the turn?

Coaches can ask these questions about navigation:

1. Did you know where you were going at all times?
2. Was it hard to see anything?

3. Did you take a good line to the finish?

4. Did you feel any ocean swells out there?

5. How often were you lifting your head to sight?

6. Did you see the lead kayak or lead boat?

7. What side were you breathing on? Or did you breathe on both sides?

Regarding the finish, coaches can ask questions like these:

1. When did the sprint begin?

2. Did you catch up to anyone after the sprint began?

3. Were you using your legs the whole time?

4. Did any physical contact occur coming into the finish?

5. Were you satisfied with your finish?

6. How can you train for a better finish?

Although questioning athletes in this way is not exactly the Socratic method used in the academic world, the idea is to help the athlete improve and understand the myriad situations that happen in the open water.

Summary

Some people swim to win, whereas others simply want to finish or improve their times from the previous year. For each type of swimmer, tactical knowledge comprises a different spectrum of information. At its simplest level, tactical knowledge includes only knowledge about the race course. At its highest level, tactical knowledge includes course information, use of the elements, and in-depth knowledge of the strengths, weaknesses, and expected tactics of competitors.

Swimming to win is the ultimate competitive approach. Winning can result in anything from handshakes from the competition to prize money and endorsements. As famed UCLA basketball coach John Wooden stated, "Success is a peace of mind which is a direct result of self-satisfaction in knowing you did your best to become the best you are capable of becoming."

CHAPTER 25

Adaptive Swimmers

—Brendan Burkett, PhD

The foundation for *Science of Swimming Faster* is made up of three main sections: swimming mechanics and technique, aspects of training and competition, and applied sport science and medicine. Within these three sections, many specific topics that discuss attributes that contribute to swimming faster have been addressed. These same three sections and subsequent specific topics form the backbone for the discussions presented in this chapter. In some cases the guidelines set forth are the same regardless of the group of swimmer being considered. For example, the fundamental principles underlying propulsion and drag are the same for able-bodied and adaptive swimmers alike. In other cases, the differences are significant. For example, a swimmer who has a spinal cord injury and spastic muscles may develop a fixed-hip contracture and will have to adopt different techniques to maximize performance. Throughout this chapter, only brief statements will made in cases where the considerations for adaptive swimmers are the same as those for able-bodied swimmers. Otherwise, a more detailed description about the science behind swimming faster in adaptive swimming will be presented.

The highest level of competition for adaptive swimmers with a locomotor disability, a visual impairment, or an intellectual disability is the Paralympic Games. This competition is held every four years, traditionally following the Olympic Games. Paralympic athletes compete in 18 summer sports, and swimming has been part of each Paralympic Games since the inaugural 1960 event in Stoke Mandeville, United Kingdom. Paralympic swimming generally follows the same International Swimming Federation (FINA) rules that are used with able-bodied swimmers, with some essential modifications, such as allowing one-handed touches for swimmers who can extend only one hand out in front.

With that said, specific and unique biological requirements are associated with particular physical disabilities. As a result, an overview of the Paralympic classification system will lend clarity to the subsequent discussion on the science of swimming faster for adaptive swimmers.

Paralympic Swimming Classification System

The original classification system used in swimming was based on a medical model, and athletes competed within five classes of disability:

1. Athletes with an amputation, defined as having at least one major joint in a limb missing (i.e., elbow, wrist, knee, ankle)

2. Athletes with cerebral palsy, defined as having the cerebellar area of the brain affected, which, through palsy, affects the control of movement

3. Athletes with a spinal cord injury or other condition that causes at least a 10 percent loss of function in the lower limbs (e.g., traumatic paraplegia or quadriplegia)

4. Athletes with a visual impairment (i.e., perception of light or hand movement to a visual acuity between 2/60 and 6/60 or a visual field of greater than 5 degrees and less than 20 degrees)

5. Athletes with *les autres*, a French phrase meaning "the others." This group comprises athletes who do not fit within one of the other disability groups but have a permanent physical disability (e.g., one femur shorter than the other, resulting in a significant difference in leg length)

Today, competitions for people with locomotor disabilities are organized under a functional classification system in which swimmers with various physical disabilities compete against each another. Swimmers with physical disabilities compete in one of the following:

- 10 S classes (S1 to S10: for freestyle, backstroke, and butterfly events),
- 10 SB classes (SB1 to SB10: for breaststroke events), and
- 10 SM classes (SM1 to SM10: for individual medley events).

The separate classes distinguish between the distinct arm-dominant freestyle, backstroke, and butterfly strokes; the leg-dominated breaststroke; and the individual medley, which includes all four strokes and therefore warrants its own classification system. Athletes rated as a 10 on the classification scale (e.g., S10, SB10, SM10) have the greatest function. Function gradually decreases (the scope of the disability increases) as the classification moves closer to a 1 rating (S1, SB1, SM1).

Swimmers with visual impairment are divided into three classes—S11, S12, and S13—depending on the level of visual impairment. A person with normal vision can read newsprint at a distance of 100 centimeters, an S13 swimmer needs to be at 10 centimeters to read the same text, an S12 athlete can read the text at a distance of 4 centimeters, and an S11 cannot read the text at all. S11 swimmers are required to wear blackened goggles to level the playing field and ensure that all swimmers have the same level of vision. To ensure that the visually impaired athletes do not run into the wall when swimming, tappers are used during competition. The tappers, positioned on the pool deck at each end of the pool, notify swimmers that they are approaching the wall with a gentle tap using a long rod with a soft bulbous end.

The international swimming community also includes swimming classes for athletes with intellectual disabilities (S14) and hearing impairment (S15). These athletes currently compete outside the Paralympic Games, although for the 2012 London Paralympic Games, swimmers with an intellectual disability competed in a limited number of events. This functional system has been used during the previous five Paralympics Games and is subject to continued evaluation.

The Paralympic swimming classification system places swimmers with varying impairments together in one class. Classification is based on a number of factors, such as muscle strength, movement coordination, joint range of movement, and limb length. In fact, swimming is the only sport that combines the conditions of limb loss, cerebral palsy, spinal cord injury (weakness or paralysis involving any combination of limbs), and other disabilities (such as Dwarfism, major joint restriction conditions) within the same competitive class as well as across classes. Each swimmer must undergo an internationally approved classification procedure that includes medical and swimming evaluations. For more detail on the swimming classification system, go to the International Paralympic Committee website at www.paralympic.org/classification.

From a swimming-specific coaching perspective, the classification system is the method of providing a fair and equitable level of competition for athletes with disabilities. Coaches just need to know that their athletes have classification numbers, just as athletes have weight divisions in sports such as boxing. Our job is to prepare athletes to perform to their maximum potential; their level of classification will not change if we improve their skill level.

Understanding Propulsion and Drag

The same principles of propulsion and drag apply to all swimmers, regardless of ability level, and these principles affect the technique used to achieve optimal performances. One of the fundamentals in swimming is that to swim faster, propulsion must increase, drag must decrease, or a combination of both must occur. When analyzing the swimming mechanics for adaptive swimmers, some variations may be used to generate these net forces. Swimmers with an amputation, cerebral palsy, or spinal cord injury may use different movement patterns because of their disabilities, but the same underlying mechanical principles apply. For example, a swimmer who is a single-leg amputee will have a smaller base of support on the blocks, affecting the swimmer's ability to achieve balance during the start. The natural compensations that the swimmer makes on the blocks can lead to asymmetry on entering the water, which in turn can lead to altered swimming mechanics underwater and when stroking (e.g., altered interarm stroke coordination).

Swimming Mechanics: Swimmers With a Physical Disability

Consider some of the ways that a physical disability can affect stroke technique. A swimmer with a lower-limb amputation, for example, will likely be able to maintain a body line, stroke rate, and stroke length profile similar to those of an able-bodied swimmer. The timing and type of kick used, however, may vary depending on the extent of the disability. Swimmers with a lower-limb amputation tend to use a crossover kick; that is, they kick down on one side in time with the alternate arm stroke and then cross over and kick on the other side to counter that arm stroke. Some swimmers have used the typical one-side-only kicking, but this technique tends to inhibit their longitudinal body roll in the water. The kick rate for the single-lower-limb swimmer is naturally slower than that for a two-legged swimmer. The risk of shoulder injury is also a higher than normal for the lower-limb amputee. This circumstance is attributed to the increased load placed on the shoulder opposite the side with the leg amputation; this shoulder needs to skull the water to maintain balance as well as generate greater underwater force to make up for the lack of the kick that would normally accompany the pull. The lower-limb amputee can use a modified fin during training to unload the shoulder, provide the required overload for the residual stump, and subsequently develop beneficial musculoskeletal symmetry throughout the body.

For swimmers with cerebral palsy, the neuromuscular impairment associated with this disability can influence swimming mechanics, particularly because these athletes often fatigue earlier than able-bodied swimmers do. This fatigue tends to exaggerate any asymmetry between stroke sides, which can lead to increased risk of injury or require the swimmer to adopt novel strategies to generate propulsion.

Similarly, the loss of abdominal control and core stability associated with a spinal cord injury can affect swimming technique, depending on the location of the spinal lesion. The potentially smaller propulsive surface associated with the physical disability or an unbalanced capacity for propulsion when compared with an able-bodied swimmer can influence the swimmer's mechanics.

Swimming Mechanics: Swimmers With a Visual Impairment or Intellectual Disability

Swimmers who have a visual impairment or an intellectual disability generally follow the same swimming mechanics and techniques as able-bodied swimmers because they have the same physical ability. These athletes may use some minor variation in swimming technique in the early stages, such as when they are approaching the end of the swimming pool. In some cases, swimmers may be cautious when approaching the end of the pool because of the difference in visually acuity—they do not want to run into the end of the pool. This issue will diminish with experience. For swimmers with an intellectual disability, this caution about the end of the pool will naturally diminish as their confidence grows. Swimmers with a visual impairment or intellectual disability should be aiming for the able-bodied model of swimming technique.

Freestyle, Backstroke, Breaststroke, and Butterfly Technique

The techniques used when swimming the four strokes are similar for all swimmers because the rules of the sport specifically describe what is required for each stroke. For example, in breaststroke the swimmer's arms and legs must move in a simultaneous movement, in contrast to the alternating movement patterns of backstroke. Therefore, the techniques used for swimming these strokes are typically more similar than different, regardless of disability. Freestyle, as the name suggests, allows swimmers to choose their strokes, and able-bodied swimmers generally choose the front-crawl style. The same selection mostly applies to adaptive swimmers, but as the level of disability increases, some swimmers may select a different stroke in the freestyle event, such as backstroke, which is a popular choice for those who have difficulty rotating to breathe in freestyle.

Technique Considerations for Starts and Turns

The start is an important component of the complete swimming race because it is the section of the race where the swimmer is travelling at the fastest velocity. Typical average velocities for elite male able-bodied swimmers over the first 15 meters of the race are around 3 meters per second, whereas free-swim velocities are about 1.8 to 2 meters per second for elite freestylers. The adaptive swimmer who has a mild or minimal disability can also achieve these velocities. Therefore, regardless of ability level, swimmers need to maximize their velocity at the start and continue this velocity as long as possible into the race.

Some components of the swimming start, such as the underwater phase and break-out stroke, are repeated with every turn that the swimmer makes. Thus, any improvements made to the underwater components of the swimmer's start can apply throughout the race after every swimming turn. Technical modifications to the swim start have been found to reduce swimming race time by 0.10 seconds, and because races have been won and lost by a tenth of this margin, an effective start is critical.

The Swimming Start

The swim start is defined as the distance to the 15-meter mark in the race, which coincides with the break start rope and is the maximum distance a swimmer can travel underwater. According to FINA rules, the same applies to adaptive swimmers. The swim start can be divided into a number of subsections including time components (block, flight, underwater, and free swim) and distance components (entry, underwater, and free swim). In a study of 200-meter starts, 95 percent of the variance in start time was attributed to the underwater phase. Greater entry distance had little relationship with the start time ($r = 0.046$) (Mason and Cossor 2000).

Scientific analysis of the swim start combines the kinematic analysis of segment movements such as rate of arm swing, path of the movement of the head, and the explosive power of the lower limbs. Some work has been done in this area by studying the starts of Olympic swimmers, and similar research is currently being conducted on Paralympic swimmers. Paralympic swimmers who have reduced balance control, such as lower-limb amputations or cerebral palsy, can find balancing on the starting block difficult. Understanding the relationship between balance and propulsion off the blocks requires specific comprehension of the forces generated on the starting block, the positioning of the athlete, and the velocities and accelerations of the human segments as the swimmer leaves the block and enters the water. As discussed in chapter 6, detailed analysis of the start requires the use of specific technology (force plates and underwater video cameras), but many of the techniques described for working with able-bodied swimmers can also be employed in adaptive swim programs.

To understand the swimming start and considerations for adaptive swimmers, comparisons between Olympic and Paralympic swimmers have been done. In a 2010 study by Burkett, Mellifont, and Mason (2010), three specific Paralympic classifications were studied:

- S8, in which swimmers had full use of their arms and trunk with some leg function (can include coordination problems), had double limb loss, or had use of only one arm
- S9, in which the swimmers had severe weakness in one leg only, swam with very slight coordination problems, or had one limb loss
- S10, in which the swimmers had minimal weakness affecting the legs, swam with restriction of hip joint movement, swam with both feet deformed, or had a minor limb loss or loss of part of a limb

Within these classes, three Paralympic disability groups were represented: swimmers with an arm amputation (leg-dominant swimmers), swimmers with a leg amputation (arm-dominant swimmers), and swimmers with hemiplegic cerebral palsy (neuromuscular-impaired swimmers).

Investigating the various disabilities of the Paralympic swimmers enabled the researchers to monitor the influence that some of the variables had on the swimmers' starts. The investigators hypothesized that the different classes of

Paralympic swimmers would execute specific components of the start differently, and this was found to be the case. Here are some of the key results.

The influence of block time is apparent when analyzing swimmers with cerebral palsy, because their inhibited neuromuscular recruitment results in an inefficient link in the kinetic chain. Therefore, they are not able to generate fast block times.

When comparing the start time to 15 meters, a significant difference was found between the Olympic swimmers and three Paralympic classes; the start time progressively increased as the disability level increased. A similar finding was observed in other studies that found distinct changes in swimming performance in the different Paralympic classes (Daly et al. 2001).

The only variable that distinguished start performance between the S9 and S10 classes was underwater velocity. A review of the underwater video footage showed that the S9 swimmers were not able to hold their streamline as effectively as the S10 swimmers. This difference could be attributed to the greater level of disability (such as a greater leg amputation), which naturally affected the swimmers' balance. The result was that the S9 swimmers oscillated more as they corrected their balance, resulting in a less effective streamline position.

The S10 swimmers were able to develop an underwater velocity comparable to that of the Olympic swimmers, both of which were significantly higher than the velocity of the S9 and S8 swimmers. The ability of the S10 swimmers to match the Olympic swimmers in underwater velocity reflects the minimal disability of these swimmers. For example, the arm amputees within the S10 class were missing an arm below the elbow, and the loss of this limb generally affects only the swimmer's arm stroke.

The applied research found that underwater velocity had the greatest influence on the swim start time, so that is an area that the S9 and S8 swimmers need to work on to improve performance. Analysis of the underwater video footage showed that both of these classes of swimmers tended to have a wider streamline profile, which naturally creates increased resistance that consequently reduces underwater velocity. Improved streamlining could help with their underwater technique.

Swimmers with cerebral palsy may require other specific changes, such as interlocking their hands, to prevent the arms from drifting apart underwater and negatively affecting drag when streamlining underwater.

The underwater footage showed that the transition from the underwater phase to the stroke preparation phase appeared appropriate for the S9 and S10 swimmers because they maintained their streamlined body position and started their first underwater arm stroke just before breaking the surface of the water. Kicking was maintained throughout the transition from underwater to the surface.

The entry distances, underwater distances, and free-swim distances all followed a similar pattern; a significant difference was seen between the Olympic swimmers and all Paralympic classes. Although the S10 and S9 swimmers had similar distance relationships, these were significantly different from those of the S8 swimmers.

The Olympic swimmers and the arm amputee swimmers generated essentially the same entry distance. If the Olympic swimmers are used as a benchmark for ultimate performance, then this result indicates that the arm amputee swimmers, whose greatest strength is their legs, may have modified their starts to maximize the entry distance and capitalize on their leg strength.

Olympic swimmers recorded the longest underwater distances. The S10 and S9 swimmers recorded a similar but shorter distance, and the S8 swimmers recorded a significantly shorter distance. The fact that the Olympic swimmers traveled an underwater distance almost double that of the S8 swimmers indicates the difficulty that the S8 swimmers had holding a streamline position because of their neuromuscular or major limb loss of function.

When comparing specific disabilities, the swimmers with a leg amputation or cerebral palsy had shorter underwater distances, although they were not significantly different. Both groups of swimmers have reduced kicking capability because of the loss of a leg or the involuntary muscle spasms that occur in CP, which would interfere with a coordinated leg-kicking action. The result is that the above-water free-swimming phase is more efficient when compared with the kicking-dominant underwater phase.

Because of the diversity in the physical ability of the Paralympic swimmers, the underwater distance traveled depends on the strengths and weaknesses (underwater streamlining and kicking efficiency) of the individual swimmer, although a key requirement for all groups was a smooth transition from underwater to free swimming. Although a difference was found in the absolute distance that the swimmers traveled underwater, in relative terms no difference was seen between the three Paralympic swimming classes, although the entire group of Paralympic swimmers spent significantly less time underwater. This similar proportion of time and distance spent in each phase, regardless of Paralympic class, indicates that the swimmers use a similar swim start technique.

S10 and S9 swimmers generated similar free-swimming profiles that were significantly different from both the Olympic and S8 swimmers. Recalling that the swimmers with minimal disability (S10) were able to generate good underwater velocity, this finding indicates they were not able to transfer this attribute into free swimming. Once underwater, the S10 and Olympic group were able to develop similar underwater velocities, which probably related to their similar ability to place and hold their bodies in a streamline position and then to use two fully functional legs to drive to the surface for the break-out stroke. This skill of obtaining a streamline body position and kicking until the swimmer slows to near race pace has been identified as a characteristic of competitive swim starts.

The transition from underwater to free-swim velocity showed some interesting relationships. The S9 and S8 swimmers transitioned from underwater to free swimming with the least drop in velocity. This observation indicates that these swimmers have determined the appropriate time and distance within their starts to transition from underwater to free swimming, a critical feature identified in other studies (Lyttle et al. 2000). Because the free-swimming velocity is a function of the preceding underwater velocity, the minimum loss during the transition from underwater to free swimming is critical. The aim for the swimmers was a seamless underwater to free-swimming velocity transition. Each athlete may need to be analyzed individually to account for athlete-specific idiosyncrasies, but this research provides important information to guide further investigation. Most important for swimmers and coaches, these components of the start can be modified with training. As with other changes in technique, such as breathing patterns and stroke rates, these elite athletes can apply this new knowledge to help improve their swim start performances.

The Swimming Turn

The swim turn is another important area in understanding the science of swimming faster in adaptive swimming. Research has commonly identified underwater velocity as the only variable that distinguishes elite swim turn performances from others. Underwater video footage demonstrates that swimmers who can hold their streamline more effectively tend to generate faster underwater velocity. Athletes with an amputation are naturally asymmetrical and may find it difficult to maintain balance. They tend to oscillate more as they correct their balance, resulting in a less effective streamline position. A similar scenario applies to swimmers with cerebral palsy.

The ability to produce force for the push-off phase of the turn is also a consideration for the adaptive swimmer. Applying the scientific principles of energy transfer through the kinetic chain suggests that loss of strength, coordination, range of motion, or accuracy of movement force results in inefficient force dissipation from the kinetic chain. The result could be a less efficient turn.

Analysis of the fundamental principles of a swim start and turn demonstrate that there are some elementary differences for the swimmer with a disability compared with the able-bodied swimmer. But the influence of a specific disability on a swimmer's ability to produce an effective start or turn has received comparatively little discussion in the research literature. This is a shortcoming of previous studies because the Paralympic classes are collections of athletes of different abilities and the level of physical function within these classes naturally varies. By considering only the class, and not the disability, some key features of athletic performance are hidden. For example, although a significant difference is seen in the absolute start time between the Olympic swimmers and all three Paralympic classes (S10, S9, and S8), no significant difference is found in start time between the three disability groups of arm amputee, leg amputee, and cerebral palsy. The block times of the S10 and S9 swimmers, as well as the arm and leg amputees, were similar, whereas the cerebral palsy and S8 swimmers had significantly slower block times than all other swim groups. This result highlights the finding that the impaired neuromuscular motor pattern in people with cerebral palsy affects the execution of movement patterns and causes delayed planning of movement.

Effect of Technology on Swimming Technique

In the endeavor to go higher, faster, and longer, athletes have found ways to use technology to enhance performance. Assistive technologies such as wheelchairs and prostheses can clearly help disabled athletes function and recover out of the water, but what technology can be used in the water? As in Olympic swimming, Paralympic athletes are permitted to wear only a swimsuit, goggles, and swim cap; Paralympic athletes are not permitted to use any prostheses or assistive devices while in the water. In some cases, the additional technology required for the adaptive swimmer can be simple. For example, figure 25.1 shows a swimmer with no arms using his teeth to hold on to the towel or rope for the race start. This technology, while not a new device or invention per se, represents an advancement in thinking and creativity that enables the swimmer to execute a better start, thereby enhancing performance.

Technology to Measure Swimming Performance

A number of technical devices have been developed to measure swimming performance. Because the adaptive swimmer requires a more sensitive analysis of the propulsion and drag relationship, this technology is important for advancing the science of swimming faster. One such device is a velocity meter, which can measure the velocity of the swimmer continuously and in real time. This biomechanical measure can provide vital feedback to the athlete and coach about swimming performance. The use of this technology allows informed decisions to be made about any technique modifications for the adaptive swimmer. For example, the swimmer with an arm disability can benefit greatly from this form of analysis because the influence of kicking or stroking with the amputated limb can be objectively quantified.

▶ **Figure 25.1** Swimmer using his teeth to hold on to a towel or rope before the race start.

Another application for the velocity meter is to measure an athlete's ability to maintain a streamline when pushing off from the wall or during the underwater phase of the swimming start. For example, swimmers traditionally maintain an underwater streamline phase as long as possible before gradually rising to the top of the water. The adaptive swimmer may have an impaired ability to hold an effective streamline (arm amputee or cerebral palsy) or an inefficient single-leg kick. The biomechanical measure of instantaneous velocity will enable the optimum underwater time to be determined for the Paralympic athlete. This measure has several other applications, such as monitoring velocity fluctuations within the high-drag strokes such as breaststroke. By quantifying the athlete's velocity, the correlation with other biomechanical measures of stroke rate can be investigated. This will enable the optimum stroke rate of the athlete to be determined. When the swimmer uses a resistive device, or tether, the measure of instantaneous velocity can provide insight into the swimmer's stroke-by-stroke force production and anaerobic power.

Video is another technology that can provide useful feedback on starting, turning, and free-swimming technique. This technology can be used to quantify the arm-stroke timing within the complete swimming stroke, as well as inter- and intraswimmer variability. Using this information, the timing of the swimmer's stroke can be modified, which is particularly important for the adaptive swimmer. For example, the swimmer's stroke may be quantified as a catch-up stroke, in which the hand of the swimmer effectively catches up to the opposite hand at the front of the swimmer's stroke. This technique generally suits swimmers who have a powerful leg kick or a strong, powerful swimming stroke. Adaptive swimmers may need to modify their index of coordination based on the measurement of instantaneous swimming velocity.

Application of Swimming Mechanics and Technique

To develop a swimmer's optimal swim mechanics and swimming technique, the coach and sport scientist first need to watch how the swimmer is moving though the water. An effective way to accomplish this is to use a video camera that provides a hard copy of the swimming, offering features such as slow motion and, more important, providing a time point for comparison. When making changes to a swimmer's mechanics, coaches rely on their fundamental understanding of what is required to move faster through the water—an increase in propulsion and a reduction in resistance. For the swimmer with a disability, a range of techniques may be successful for moving through the water. There is no right or wrong method. The key is to apply the fundamentals of propulsion and resistance.

Recent developments in microtechnology have enabled previously unknown swimming measures to be made, such the swimmer's kick count and kick rate. The kick is typically hidden within the turbulent whitewater of the swimmer, and the kick rate is typically too fast to be measured by the human eye. Small inertial sensors, approximately 25 millimeters long and 8 millimeters thick and weighing less than 20 grams, have been attached to swimmers' legs to measure this new sport science variable. The swimming coach can use this knowledge to design the training program and develop the appropriate swim race strategy.

Energy Systems and Their Application to Swimming

Swimming performance has been extensively studied from the standpoint of energetic characteristics, including lactate production and degradation, oxygen consumption, and heart rate variability. With any athlete, the difference between gold and silver or bronze and fourth can be as small as 0.35 percent, or 0.01 second. Therefore, anything that can make a difference in athletic performance is eagerly sought by Olympic and Paralympic athletes. The role of energy systems for the adaptive swimmer is similar to that for the able-bodied athlete, with a few special considerations, such as thermal regulation. See chapter 8 for more information on the physiology of training, all of which can be applied to work with adaptive swimmers.

Of course, able-bodied and adaptive swimmers differ in some important ways. Thermal regulation can be challenging for Paralympic swimmers, even though they are competing in an aquatic environment. Because thermal regulation is related to surface area and basal metabolism, the adaptive swimmer can be sensitive to small changes in the environmental or water temperature. For example, an athlete with a spinal cord injury tends to have a reduced lower-limb surface area because of the associated muscular atrophy; a similar scenario exists for the amputee who has lost part or all of a limb. This different surface area naturally influences an athlete's thermal regulation. Furthermore, the modified neuromuscular system of some athletes with cerebral palsy has resulted in heightened sensitivity to hot and cold conditions.

The preparations and possible adaptations that needed to be made for the hot and humid environments of the Athens and Beijing Games were major issues for Olympic and Paralympic athletes. As with other applications, the initial sport science approach was to develop generic guidelines and principles for all athletes, but in many cases these standards fell short of addressing the specific needs of Paralympic athletes. From this starting point, however, the Paralympic coach and sport scientist can either adopt the same guidelines or conduct research that will lead them to modify this approach and address the unique characteristics of athletes with disabilities.

Evaluating Performance and Test Sets

Evaluation of a swimming performance is often defined by the fundamental biomechanical parameters of velocity, stroke rate, stroke length, stroke index, active drag, power output, and propelling efficiency. To achieve a certain velocity, the swimmer adopts a specific relationship between stroke rate and stroke length, concomitant with her interlimb coordination.

Kinematic variables can be used to describe and evaluate performance, but the collection and analysis of these data can involve significant effort. The best approach is to use easy and applicable test sets that yield performance-affecting data. Three test sets are presented here: a progressive step test, efficiency golf score, and starts and turns. These test sets have been found to be particularly useful for the adaptive swimmer.

Step Test

A common test set in swimming is the step test, which involves swimming seven 200-meter repeat swims at a controlled pace. For the adaptive swimmer who may not be able to swim this distance, the step test can be modified to reflect shorter distances or fewer repeats such as 6 × 100-meter repeat swims instead of 7 × 200. The step test is designed to train swimmers to develop their sense of pace and to determine their lactate threshold.

The swimmer's personal best 100-meter time plus two seconds is the target for the final swim. The six 100s should be swum at a descending pace:

Swim 1: 100 meters at +25 seconds on 2:00 minutes

Swim 2: 100 meters at +20 seconds on 2:00 minutes

Swim 3: 100 meters at +15 seconds on 2:00 minutes

Swim 4: 100 meters at +10 seconds on 2:00 minutes

Swim 5: 100 meters at +5 seconds on 2:00 minutes

Swim 6: 100 meters at +2 seconds on 2:00 minutes

The swimming variables of stroke rate, distance per stroke, free-swimming velocity, stroke count, turn time, lap time, total time, and lactates should be recorded for each swim. All swims are conducted in the same time interval, so the intensity will progressively increase, as with any test set.

Starting at the personal best time plus 25 seconds, swimmers should try to hold a consistent pace within each 100-meter swim. The first four swims allow the athletes to pace themselves correctly at slower velocities and set themselves up for efficient fifth and sixth swims.

A plot of these data shows how these performance variables change with increasing speed. This information can identify the athlete's lactate threshold and determine whether the athlete's stroke breaks down at any point (e.g., a rapid rise in stroke rate without a change in speed indicates a shorter stroke length).

Recording data from the step test periodically throughout the year makes it possible to track improvement (or deterioration) and identify the most important contributors to performance.

Stroke Efficiency

Another measure of performance is the stroke efficiency test protocol, which is designed to develop a swimmer's efficiency. The test involves swimming 6 × 50-meter efforts at the pace that the swimmer holds during the second 50 meters of a 100-meter race. The swimmer should count the number of strokes taken to swim 50 meters, and the time for the swim should be recorded. These two values (the stroke count and time) are added together to produce a golf handicap score. The aim of the test is to reduce the swimmer's golf handicap over time either by using fewer strokes for the same time or by producing a quicker time while using the same number of strokes.

Starts and Turns

Finally, variables associated with the start and turn, which are measured in the race analysis of the swimmer, can also be tested on a regular basis within training. For example, to measure the swimmer's turn, the swimmer can be positioned at around 20 meters out from the wall and asked to swim in to and out of the wall while executing a turn. Starting from this distance provides the swimmer sufficient time to reach race velocity in to the wall. To measure the turn-in part of the turn, the coach can measure the time from when the swimmer's head crosses the 5-meter backstroke flag mark until the swimmer's feet touch the wall. The time from feet on the wall until the swimmer's head passes the 5-meter window determines the turn-out time. This simple sport science measure enables the effectiveness of the turn to be quantified within a training session and over time. A similar process can be applied to the swimmer's start. Timing measures can be made at 5-, 10-, and 15-meter intervals or as specified by the coach.

Evaluating Progression of Adaptive Swimming

Compared with able-bodied or Olympic swimming, Paralympic swimming has a shorter history of competition; although the first Olympic Games were held in 1896, it wasn't until 1960 that the first Paralympic Games were contested. This difference in evolutionary history has resulted in a fair amount of variance between swimmers, techniques, and tactics, a factor to be considered when evaluating swimming performance.

This difference between Olympic and Paralympic swims is best demonstrated by the variability of swimming performance within and between national and international competitions. In an Olympic year, potential Olympic medal swimmers need to improve their motor skill performance by about 1 percent within competitions and by about 1 percent within the year leading up to the Olympics to keep pace with the competition and give themselves a chance to reach the podium (Pyne, Trewin, and Hopkins 2004). Athletes who are able to obtain an additional enhancement, even one as low as about 0.4 percent between competitions, would substantially increase their chances of a winning a medal.

In a study of Paralympic swimming that involved 15 national and international competitions between 2004 and 2006, 724 official finals times were analyzed for 120 male and 122 female Paralympic swimmers in the 100-meter freestyle event (Fulton et al. 2009). Separate analyses were performed for males and females in each of four Paralympic subgroups: S2 through S4, S5 through S7, S8 through S10 (most through least physically impaired), and S11 through S13 (most through least visually impaired). Mixed modeling of log-transformed times, with adjustment for mean competition times, was used to estimate variability and progression. Within-swimmer race-to-race variability, expressed as a coefficient of variation, ranged from 1.2 percent (male S5–S7) to 3.7 percent (male S2–S4). Swimming performance progressed by about 0.5 percent per year for males and females alike. Typical variation in mean performance time between competitions was about 1 percent after adjustments were made for the ability of the athletes in each competition. The Paralympic Games were the fastest competition. Taking into account this variability, progression, and level of competition, the bottom line is that Paralympic swimmers who want a substantial increase in their medal prospects should aim for an annual improvement of at least 1 to 2 percent, which is higher than the current 1 percent annual improvement expected for Olympic swimmers. In other words, Paralympic swimmers are getting faster at a faster rate, compared with Olympic-caliber swimmers.

Other studies have been conducted over a four-year period to compare the stroking parameters of Paralympic swimmers by analyzing 13 competitions including the Paralympic Games, World Championships, and several national championships (Fulton et al. 2009). In total, 442 races of 100-meter heats (225 performances) and finals (217 performances) were profiled. These studies, which involved collecting race analysis data, showed the following:

- On average, start time correlated best with race time, showing near-perfect correlations for classes S7 ($r = 0.90$), S8 ($r = 0.97$), and S10 ($r = 0.90$). This finding is somewhat in contrast to the findings of Daly et al. (2001) for Atlanta Paralympic heat swims, in which start time was not found to be as important ($r = 0.6$ and lower for classes S7 and above).

- Turn time correlations were very high and consistent for all classes ($r = 0.78$ to 0.89). Finish time correlations were consistently the lowest of the three race times for all classes, showing moderate to high correlations ($r = 0.30$ for class S8 to $r = 0.67$ for class S10). The findings for turning and finished did coincide with results found by Daly et al. 2003.

When comparing the final race time with the stroke parameters for the different Paralympic classes, several relationships were found:

- Small correlations were found between race time and stroke rate in the class S7 and S10 swimmers ($r = -0.05$ to -0.27), indicating that stroke rate may not be as important as stroke length for these swimmers.

- Stroke rate correlations with race time for classes S8 and S9 were high to very high ($r = -0.51$ to -0.78) indicating that high stroke rate may be optimal for these classes. Classes S8 and S9 showed very small correlations for stroke length ($r < -0.13$), and class S9 displayed zero correlation for fourth 25-meter stroke length. These results further highlight the importance of high stroke rate for S8 and S9 swimmers.

- Class S7 showed moderate correlations ($r = -0.42$ to -0.50) and class S10 very high correlations ($r = -0.78$ to -0.88) between race time and stroke length.

- Classes S8 and S9 displayed small correlations ($r = 0.09$ to 0.23) for first- and second-lap stroke count, class S7 showed moderate stroke count correlations ($r = 0.51$ and 0.47), and class S10 showed high stroke count correlations ($r = 0.88$ and 0.84) in relation to final time.

Periodization and Tapering

The principle of providing a suitable overload stimulus followed by appropriate recovery applies to the adaptive swimmer when designing the periodization and seasonal training plan. As with any athlete, careful monitoring is required to ensure that the athlete has suitable recovery between training bouts because inappropriate loading can be detrimental to performance. Note that some athletes with a disability may require a longer recovery period because of the complexity of their musculoskeletal systems. This aspect is discussed with examples in the following section.

Special Considerations for Sprint and Distance Training

Although many of the principles of training for sprint or distance events are similar for able-bodied and adaptive swimmers, in some situations the disability should be considered when developing training (and race strategy) programs. For example, consider swimmers with cerebral palsy. These swimmers generally have two distinct profiles, both of which relate directly to the severity of the disability. For the swimmer with mild cerebral palsy, the swimming stroke initially will be similar to the stroke of an able-bodied athlete. That is, the stroke rate, stroke length, and overall technique will be consistent with what is seen in an able-bodied athlete. After about 30 seconds, however, the technique will deteriorate because of the disability. This phenomenon of deterioration in technique is common in cerebral palsy athletes, whereas for other athletes a change in technique is often related to the level of fitness. For the swimmer with mild cerebral palsy, the level of fitness is not the critical factor in the deterioration of technique; rather it is the consequence of the disability. The mechanism to address this issue is to establish a lower-intensity race strategy in the earlier stages of the race to enable the athlete to counter the effects of fatigue in the later stages of the race. This strategy can be applied to both sprint and distance events.

For swimmers who have a more severe level of cerebral palsy, the ability to control technique can become a challenge. Therefore, the emphasis on strictly following a traditional swimming technique should be reduced. Rather, the athlete and coach need to identify a stroke profile that the athlete can maintain and explore the propulsion and resistance profile further.

Preparing for Competition

The preparation for competition is similar for able-bodied and adaptive swimmers. One consideration is the increased anxiety and pressure that athletes face at an international competition, because this naturally affects all swimmers. Because of their disability, some, but only some, swimmers with cerebral palsy may be more emotional in a stressful situation, such as competing at the World Championships or Paralympic Games. This tension is a function of the athlete's disability, and knowledge of this issue can prepare the coach and support staff to deal with it before it becomes a problem. As with all athletes, there are variations in dealing with and managing stressful situations, and this will vary regardless of disability.

Race Analysis: Evaluating Elite Performances

Swim race analysis identifies the factors that contribute to swim performance. When comparing one athlete's swim with an opponent's, these types of analyses highlight critical performance differences. Sport scientists have used above-water video to conduct competition race analyses at most international swimming events since the 1988 Olympics. Variables that are commonly measured include start, turn, and finish times, as well as 25- and 50-meter segment split times. Using time data and segment distances from competition swimming races, clean swimming speed, stroke rate, and stroke length at various points in a race can be calculated. These measures provide objective insight to the coach and athlete on what is happening within elite swimming performance.

A similar process of race analysis can be applied to adapted swimmers with some variations. For example, for a swimmer who does not have the use of the arms through disease or amputation, the race analysis variable of arm stroke rate is not relevant. Using competition analysis data from all 100-meter freestyle finalists at the Sydney Paralympic Games, Daly et al. (2003) calculated correlations between stroke rate, stroke length, and midpool velocity, as well as for within-race and between-race (heat and finals) changes in these parameters. These were their findings:

- Races were won or lost by better maintaining velocity in the second half of each 50-meter race. Differences in velocity between swimmers were related more to stroke length than stroke rate.

- Within-race velocity changes were more related to changes in stroke rate. Stroke rate changes were also responsible for velocity changes between qualifying heats and finals in the first part of races, whereas stroke length was responsible for better velocity maintenance at the end of races.

Other longitudinally based studies have tracked the performance of individual swimmers from their inaugural international competition as 14-year-olds through their Paralympic and world-record performances four years later (Burkett and Mellifont 2008). This progression provides insight into the differences in skill level and subsequent motor skills in swimming. As seen in table 25.1, the individual swimmer's performance improved 10 percent from her swim in the finals of the 2002 World Championships to the medal performance at the 2004 Paralympic Games. The athlete saw an additional 2.6

Table 25.1 Performance Progression for 100-Meter Freestyle Swim

	Worlds final (2002)	Canada final (2003)	Grand Prix (2004)	Paralympic Athens heat (2004)	Paralympic Athens final (2004)	Commonwealth Games (2006)	Worlds final (2006)
KEY TIMES							
Total time (s)	63.97	62.78	59.64	58.77	58.15	57.41	56.67
Start time (s)	7.81	7.85	7.31	6.70	7.17	6.86	6.89
25 m time (s)	13.94	13.88	13.29	12.60	12.67	12.58	12.57
Finish time (s)	3.42	3.37	3.01	3.48	3.28	3.24	3.11
Start, turns, finish (s)	17.14	17.06	16.00	15.94	15.89	15.40	15.08
Free-swim time (s)	46.83	45.72	43.64	42.83	42.26	42.01	41.59
SPLITS							
50 m (s)	30.50	30.54	29.20	28.53	28.34	28.21	27.87
100 m (s)	63.78	62.63	59.64	58.77	58.15	57.41	56.67
50 M TIMES							
First 50 m	30.51	30.54	29.20	28.53	28.34	28.21	27.87
Second 50 m	33.28	32.09	30.44	30.24	29.81	29.20	28.80
TURNS							
Turn 1 (s)	5.91	5.84	5.68	5.76	5.44	5.30	5.08
STROKE COUNT							
Lap 1	56	58	52	48	52	50	52
Lap 2	64	64	58	56	60	54	56
AVERAGES							
Velocity (m/s)	1.49	1.53	1.60	1.63	1.65	1.65	1.68
Stroke rate (strokes/min)	63.8	65.5	62.7	60.6	64.9	61.4	64.6
Stroke length (m/stroke)	1.43	1.42	1.54	1.63	1.54	1.61	1.57

percent improvement in setting the world record at the 2006 World Championships. More important, these data identify the details that contribute to this performance increase, such as stroke rate and length, segmental velocity, start and turn times, and so forth. The key areas of improvement for this swimmer were improved turn and finish times and better ability to pace the race evenly, knowing that high and stable values of the stroking parameters enable a faster swimming performance.

Examination of the race analysis for swimmers with a visual impairment has found that limitation of visual cues does not influence race strategy, when compared with Olympic swimmers (Burkett, Malone, and Daly 2003). Comparisons made between Olympic and visually impaired 100-meter freestyle swimmers at the Sydney 2000 Games found no significant differences in stroke rate between the Olympic and Paralympic swimmers (table 25.2). Additionally, no significant difference was found between class 12 and 13 visually impaired swimmers. This research shows that for visually impaired swimmers, the ability to see the opposition and race against them may not be as important as employing a suitable race strategy. This finding also indicates that the 100-meter race is relatively simple in that in the long-course event, apparently only one strategy is used by a wide variety of swimmers who nevertheless have sufficient race experience.

Table 25.2 Means and Standard Deviations of Race Variables in Male Olympic and Paralympic Finalists With a Visual Impairment in the 100-Meter Freestyle at the Sydney 2000 Games

	Olympic	S13	S12	S11
Number of subjects	72	13	25	16
Time (s)	48.94 (0.40)	58.81 (1.34)	58.61 (1.06)	63.02 (2.06)
RACE SEGMENT				
1 (15 m–25 m)	2.10 (0.05)*	1.77 (0.07)*	1.74 (0.04)*	1.69 (0.05)*
2 (25 m–42.5 m)	2.02 (0.02)*	1.71 (0.05)*	1.67 (0.02)*	1.60 (0.05)*
3 (57.5 m–75 m)	1.94 (0.03)*	1.65 (0.05)*	1.61 (0.05)*	1.52 (0.05)*
4 (75 m–95 m)	1.85 (0.03)*	1.56 (0.05)*	1.56 (0.04)*	1.43 (0.06)*
STROKE RATE (STROKE/MIN)				
1 (15 m–25 m)	55.55 (3.3)	52.62 (5.23)	53.65 (2.94)	54.68 (6.88)
2 (25 m–42.5 m)	51.47 (3.0)	49.00 (4.68)	49.34 (3.86)	50.51 (6.86)
3 (57.5 m–75 m)	50.80 (2.7)	49.33 (5.89)	47.41 (2.48)	50.06 (6.27)
4 (75 m–95 m)	50.40 (4.0)	47.70 (5.04)	48.68 (4.52)	49.51 (5.69)
STROKE LENGTH (M)				
1 (15 m–25 m)	2.31 (0.11)*	2.02 (0.17)*	1.94 (0.09)*	1.87 (0.22)*
2 (25 m–42.5 m)	2.36 (0.14)*	2.11 (0.18)*	2.03 (0.15)*	1.92 (0.22)*
3 (57.5 m–75 m)	2.29 (0.13)*	2.03 (0.18)*	2.04 (0.16)*	1.84 (0.20)*
4 (75 m–95 m)	2.21 (0.17)*	1.98 (0.17)*	1.93 (0.20)*	1.75 (0.19)*

*Indicates a significant difference (<0.05) between Olympic and Paralympic swimmers.

Nutrition for Swimmers and Performance-Enhancing Drugs

The nutritional demands of able-bodied and adaptive swimmers are similar. The individual athlete needs to be evaluated, and nutritional strategies need to be developed for before, during, and after training and competition to ensure that the nutritional needs of the swimmer are satisfied.

As with able-bodied swimmers, drug testing for illegal performance-enhancing drugs is strictly conducted for adaptive swimmers. They are subject to the same penalties if found guilty of using performance-enhancing drugs. All parties involved (parents, coaches, athletes) need to be aware of the antidoping rules and regulations, especially the procedure to file Therapeutic Use Exemption (TUE) forms. Many adaptive swimmers take prescribed drugs that are medically necessary. In these instances, swimmers are permitted to take the drugs, even if they are on the banned list, as long as the prescribing physician files a TUE with the world and national antidoping agencies.

Swimming Psychology: Merging the Mind and Body

Like Olympic athletes, Paralympians often confront issues related to mental preparation and performance, such as exercise adherence, motivation, and anxiety experienced precompetition or in the middle of a major event. The established process of proactively controlling the athlete's mood state, visualization, and precompetition thought process is of particular importance to the outcome of the sporting performance. In most cases, the Paralympic athlete can apply visualization processes similar to those used by the Olympic athlete, but for athletes with some disabilities, this is not possible. In using visualization techniques, athletes often watch a video of a past performance, usually their best performance, to visualize the perfect race. For athletes with a visual impairment or blindness, this approach is not possible, so they need to use other techniques, such as hearing, or rely on their confidence in the predefined race strategy.

Swimmers with cerebral palsy may also experience some level of intellectual disability in addition to the physical impairments they experience. This condition could restrict their ability to use the power of the mind to modify mood state, concentrate, or have the mental focus to develop and follow a set race plan. Likewise, muscle relaxation techniques that are frequently used to bring the athlete into a desired mood state (e.g., the procedure of systematically contracting and relaxing muscle groups) may need to be modified for the athlete with an amputation. With the loss of limb or a spinal cord injury, the athlete may have limited or no ability to contract and relax systematically. The athlete who has an intellectual disability may have a different response mechanism to the burnout or staleness that is common in athletes following long periods of training and competition.

Swimming Medicine: Swimming Injuries and Prevention

Adaptive swimmers who have visual impairment, intellectual disability, or mild cerebral palsy generally experience swimming-related injuries, such as swimmer's shoulder, at levels similar to those of able-bodied athletes. Injury prevention follows the same principles of ensuring that the musculoskeletal system of the athlete is suitably flexible and stable and that the athlete uses an appropriate swimming technique.

For swimmers with more severe disabilities such as cerebral palsy, amputation, or spinal cord injury, the loss of function within one region can result in overload and compensation and therefore increase injury potential. Avoiding these issues follows the same principles for any swimmer of ensuring that the swimmer's musculoskeletal system is flexible and stable and that the swimmer uses a suitable swimming technique.

Because swimmers with a spinal cord injury rely on a wheelchair for mobility, two key factors must be considered when trying to avoid injury. First, the shoulders should not be overloaded because the athlete typically relies on the shoulders to propel the wheelchair. (A shoulder injury will impair daily mobility as well as swimming performance.) This issue can be addressed by carefully monitoring the athlete's internal and external shoulder range of motion using a regular sport science screening measure. This test will provide valuable feedback on the intensity of both in-water and dryland training regimes. Correct sport science assessment can prevent shoulder injury issues, but the second issue can be more challenging to address.

The second issue relates to the fact that a swimmer may spend the majority of the day in a wheelchair. Because of limited stimulation to the lower limbs, athletes can develop a fixed contracture at the hips; the muscles shorten, resulting in permanent flexion of the hip joint, potentially reaching 90 degrees of flexion. In freestyle, breaststroke, and butterfly strokes, this fixed hip contracture creates an excessive frontal drag profile that significantly affects the swimmer. In the backstroke position, the upright fixed hip position exaggerates body roll and further challenges the limited (or missing) abdominal control that most athletes in this situation experience. Sport science has addressed this issue by having the swimmer use a pull buoy when swimming in the prone position. The floatation of the buoy in the water actively encourages extension of the hip joint. This modification alone will not resolve the situation. Athletes in wheelchairs, regardless of the sport in which they participate, should daily extend the hip joint and stretch the hip flexor muscles to avoid a more permanent fixed contracture. Ultimately, surgical release of the hip capsule may be considered.

Swimming Medicine: Illnesses and General Health

Some athletes require specific medication because of their disabilities. These medications, such as beta-blockers, must be approved by the national and international antidoping agencies. The allowed medications generally relate to the treatment of pressure sores, control of possible neuromuscular spasms, or asthma. As with the wider population, a range of medications is taken to address daily lifestyle requirements, and the adaptive swimmer can have similar requirements.

Equipment such as prostheses and wheelchairs are fundamental in allowing some people with disabilities to carry out the tasks of daily living. Lower-limb amputees rely on the technical attributes of their prosthetic limbs to ambulate, and the specifications of these components have changed considerably in recent years. Of greatest importance are the subtle compensatory factors that come with using prostheses and that can detrimentally influence the swimmer. At first glance, the effect of a lower-limb amputation seems to be confined to the lower limb. But the skeletal image of an amputee identifies several compensatory mechanisms that are employed throughout the body. The amputation alters the orientation of the pelvis, and because the pelvis is connected to the vertebral column, the change in pelvic angle causes scoliosis of the spine (figure 25.2). The altered orientation of the vertebral column then causes the shoulders to change alignment and the orientation of the skull to be altered. Thus, the compensatory mechanisms resulting from the amputation can have far-reaching consequences for the functional ability of the swimmer. This phenomenon highlights the need

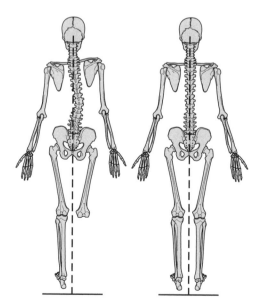

▶ **Figure 25.2** Compensatory mechanisms resulting from a lower-limb amputation.

to address activities outside the pool to provide the best opportunities for the swimmer.

Strength and Conditioning for Performance Enhancement

Biomechanical studies have established that asymmetry is common in the general population and, as expected, is greater in unilateral sports. Studies that investigated functional asymmetry in terms of swimming hand speed and hand path found asymmetric pulling patterns. Because this asymmetry is even higher for the swimmer with an amputation, the task for the coach is to modify or prevent this asymmetry. For instance, an imbalance in muscular strength of the rotator cuff can lead to fatigue, subsequently altering stroke mechanics. That, in turn, can lead to suboptimal performance or put the athlete at a greater risk for developing a shoulder injury. Sport biomechanics studies have also identified subtle changes in body position in the water that can increase either the resistive drag or the propulsive forces of the athlete.

The effect of force symmetry has been identified in front-crawl swimmers, focused particularly on breathing laterality and symmetry of isokinetic forces of shoulder internal rotators. Results showed increased duration of the catch–pull phase of the dominant arm compared with when breathing on the amputated side. Development of greater strength in the dominant arm and unilateral breathing may lead to asymmetry of stroke and force output. More recently, Osborough and colleagues (2009) examined 13 single-arm amputee international-level swimmers for symmetry of arm coordination. All swimmers showed asymmetric coordination between their affected and unaffected arm pulls. This asymmetry did not appear to be affected by an increase in swimming velocity up to a swimmer's maximum. The quickest swimmers possessed more symmetrical coordination between arms, compared with the slower swimmers. This result suggests that pulling both the amputated arm and the intact arm through the water with similar timing might be beneficial for front-crawl swimmers with a single-arm amputation.

Summary

Although adaptive swimmers are taking advantage of many of the sport sciences and methods that able-bodied swimmers are using to improve performance, advances in Paralympic swimming can still be made in a number of areas.

Appropriate and regular feedback from the coach to the athlete is needed to help everyone understand the factors contributing to performance and identify areas where athlete-specific improvements can be made. Race analysis data from competitions and recording basic performance data in training can be helpful here.

There are opportunities to develop disability-specific equipment, particularly for athletes with spinal cord issues and the more severely disabled swimmers, that can help enhance performance within the rules of the sport.

Gaining a more thorough understanding of how and why the human body moves and, as important, the factors that limit or enhance the capacity to move is critical to any sporting performance, especially for athletes with disabilities. What is needed is the application of the tremendous technological developments in various spheres of human endeavor to the challenges faced by Paralympic athletes.

An understandable temptation for researchers is to research only hot topics that are likely to be funded through research grants. Because most people with disabilities are older, the development of assistive devices has naturally focused on this market. Paralympic athletes have created a new, albeit small, market. This new market demand, in the long term, will result in better understanding of the relationships among human biology, the biomedical aspects of disability, the activities to be performed, and the biomechanics of assistive devices. But there is still some way to go because the current market demand for adaptive technology is overwhelmingly biased toward an aged population.

Additionally, authorities must strive to provide an even playing field at both the Olympics and the Paralympics, which includes ensuring equity of access to technology and the use of performance-enhancing substances. Developed countries have access to both the materials and the knowledge behind the technology and therefore can modify the technology to meet their specific requirements. But the situation is more problematic for athletes in developing countries. Future technological developments will have far-reaching effects on Paralympic athletes. Their new assistive anatomy with its higher level of functionality will lead not only to improved efficiency in performing daily tasks but also to more effective performance in the competition arena. If the guidelines that govern the use of novel technology are too restrictive, technological development will be stifled; alternatively, in a free-for-all environment, providing an even playing field for all will be a challenge.

Overall, we have only scratched the surface of what we know about disabled athletes and what works best in helping them maximize their athletic potential. As more coaches and scientists focus on the issues facing Paralympic athletes, including swimmers, we will continue to see improved performance.

References

Chapter 2

Alberty, M., M. Sidney, J. Dekerle, F. Potdevin, J-M. Hespel, and P. Pelayo. 2002. Effects of an exhaustive exercise on upper limb coordination and intracyclic velocity variations in frontcrawl stroke. In *Biomechanics and medicine in swimming IX*, ed. J.C. Chatard, 81–85. St. Etienne, France: University of St. Etienne.

Alberty, M., M. Sidney, P. Pelayo, and H. Toussaint. 2009. Stroking characteristics during time to exhaustion tests. *Medicine and Science in Sports and Exercise* 41 (3): 637–644.

Alberty, M., F. Potdevin, J. Dekerle, P. Pelayo, and M. Sidney. 2011. Effect of stroke rate reduction on swimming technique during paced exercise. *Journal of Strength and Conditioning Research* 25 (2): 392–397.

Arellano, R., P. Brown, J. Cappaert, and R.C. Nelson. 1994. Analysis of 50-, 100-, and 200-m freestyle swimmers at the 1992 Olympic Games. *Journal of Applied Biomechanics* 10 (2): 189–199.

Becker, T., and R. Havriluk. 2006. Bilateral and anterior-posterior muscular imbalances in swimmers. In *Biomechanics and medicine in swimming X*, ed. J.P Vilas-Boas, F. Alves, and A. Marques. *Portuguese Journal of Sport Science* 6 (Suppl. 2): 327–328.

Brukner, P., and K. Khan. 2006. *Clinical sports medicine*. 3rd ed. Australia: McGraw-Hill.

Cappaert, J.M., D.L. Pease, and J.P. Troup. 1995. Three-dimensional analysis of the men's 100-m freestyle during the 1992 Olympic Games. *Journal of Applied Biomechanics* 11 (1): 103–112.

Cappaert, J.M. 1998. Biomechanics of swimming analysed by three-dimensional techniques. In *Biomechanics and medicine in swimming VIII, Proceedings of the VIII International Symposium on Biomechanics and Medicine in Swimming*, ed. K. Keskinen, P. Komi, and A.P. Hollander, 141–145. Jyväskylä, Finland: University of Jyväskylä Press.

Castro, F., F. Minghelli, J. Floss, and A. Guimaraes. 2002. Body roll angles in frontcrawl swimming in different velocities. In *Biomechanics and medicine in swimming IX*, ed. J.C. Chatard, 111–114. St. Etienne, France: University of St. Etienne.

Chollet, D., S. Chalies, and J.C. Chatard. 2000. A new index of coordination for the crawl: Description and usefulness. *International Journal of Sports Medicine* 21:54–59.

Colwin, C. 1969. *Cecil Colwin on swimming*. London: Pelham Books..

Colwin, C. 1977. *Introduction to swimming coaching: Official course content, level one. National Coaching Certification Program*. 2nd ed. Ontario: Canadian Amateur Swimming Association.

Counsilman, J.E. 1973. *The science of swimming*. Englewood Cliffs, NJ: Prentice-Hall.

Costill, D.L., E.W. Maglischo, and A.B. Richardson. 1992. *Swimming*. London: Blackwell Scientific.

Deschodt, V.J., A.H. Rouard, and K.M. Monteil. 1996. Relationships between the three coordinates of the upper limb joints with swimming velocity. In *Biomechanics and medicine in swimming VII, Proceedings of the VII International Symposium on Biomechanics and Medicine in Swimming*, ed. J.P. Troup, A.P. Hollander, D. Strasse, S.W. Trappe, J.M. Cappaert, and T.A. Trappe, 52–58. London: E & FN Spon.

Deschodt, V.J., M.L. Arsac, and A.H. Rouard. 1999. Relative contribution of arms and legs in humans to propulsion in 25-m sprint frontcrawl swimming. *European Journal of Applied Physiology and Occupational Physiology* 80 (3): 192–199.

dos Santos, S. 1998. Relationship among anthropometric characteristics, stroke frequency and stroke length in Brazilian elite swimmers. In *Proceedings of the XVI International Symposium on Biomechanics in Sports*, ed. H.J. Riehle and M. Vieten, 251–254. Konstanz: Konstanz University Press.

Dulcos, F., P. Legreneur, and K. Monteil. 2002. Comparison of front crawl arm lengthening between Olympic Games finalists and French national level swimmers. In *Biomechanics and medicine in swimming IX*, ed. J.C. Chatard, 121–125. St. Etienne, France: University of St. Etienne.

Grace, T. 1985. Muscle imbalance and extremity injury, a perplexing relationship. *Sports Medicine* 2:77–82.

Grimston, S.K., and J.G. Hay. 1986. Relationships among anthropometric and stroking characteristics of college swimmers. *Medicine and Science in Sports and Exercise* 18 (6): 60–68.

Haffner, M., and J.M. Cappaert. 1998. Underwater analysis of the freestyle stroke from three different points in the stroke cycle. In *Biomechanics and medicine in swimming VIII, Proceedings of the VIII International Symposium on Biomechanics and Medicine in Swimming*, ed. K. Keskinen, P. Komi, and A.P. Hollander, 153–157. Jyväskylä, Finland: University of Jyväskylä Press.

Hay, J.G., Q. Lui, and J.G. Andrews. 1993. Body roll and handpath in freestyle swimming: A computer simulation study. *Journal of Applied Biomechanics* 9:227–237.

Kennedy, P., P. Brown, S.N. Chengalur, and R.C. Nelson. 1990. Analysis of male and female Olympic swimmers in the 100-meter events. *International Journal of Sport Biomechanics* 6: 187–197.

Keskinen, K., and P.V. Komi. 1993. Stroking characteristics of front crawl swimming during exercise. *Journal of Applied Biomechanics* 9:219–223.

Laughlin, T., and J. Delves. 1996. *Total immersion*. New York: Fireside.

Lerda, R., and C. Cardelli. 2003. Breathing and propelling in crawl as a function of skill and swim velocity. *International Journal of Sports Medicine* 24:75–80.

Lui, Q., J.G. Hay, and J.G. Andrews. 1993. Body roll and handpath in freestyle swimming: An experimental study. *Journal of Applied Biomechanics* 9:238–253.

Lyttle, A. and M. Keys. 2006. The applications of computational fluid dynamics in human swimming. *Portuguese Journal of Sport Sciences.* 6(2): 233–235.

Maglischo, E.W. 2003. *Swimming fastest: The essential reference on technique, training, and program design.* Champaign, IL: Human Kinetics.

McCabe, C.B. 2008. Effects of 50m and 400m race paces on three-dimensional kinematics and linear kinetics of sprint and distance front crawl swimmers. PhD diss.

McCabe, C.B., S. Psycharakis, and R.H. Sanders. 2011. Kinematic differences between front crawl sprint and distance swimmers at sprint pace. *Journal of Sport Sciences* 29 (2): 115–123.

McCabe, C.B., and R.H. Sanders. 2012. Kinematic differences between front crawl sprint and distance swimmers at a distance pace. *Journal of Sport Sciences* 30 (6): 601–608.

Millet, G.P., D. Chollet, S. Chalies, and J.C. Chatard. 2002. Coordination in frontcrawl in elite triathletes and elite swimmers. *International Journal of Sports Medicine* 23:99–104.

Payton, C.J., and D.R. Mullineaux. 1996. Effect of body roll on hand velocity in freestyle swimming. In *Biomechanics and medicine in swimming VII, Proceedings of the VII International Symposium on Biomechanics and Medicine in Swimming*, ed. J.P. Troup, A.P. Hollander, D. Strasse, S.W. Trappe, J.M. Cappaert, and T.A. Trappe, 59–63. London: E & FN Spon.

Pelayo, P., M. Sidney, T. Kherif, D. Chollet, and C. Tourny. 1996. Stroking characteristics in freestyle swimming and relationships with anthropometric characteristics. *Journal of Applied Biomechanics* 12:197–206.

Pollard, H., and M. Fernandez. 2004. Spinal musculoskeletal injuries associated with swimming: A discussion of technique. *Australian Chiropractic and Osteopathy* 12 (2): 72–80.

Potts, A.D., J.E. Charlton, and H.M. Smith. 2002. Bilateral arm power imbalance in swim bench exercises to exhaustion. *Journal of Sports Science* 20 (12): 975–979.

Sanders, R.H., and S.G. Psycharakis. 2009 Rolling rhythms in front crawl swimming with six-beat kick. *Journal of Biomechanics* 42:273–279.

Seifert, L., L. Boulesteix, and D. Chollet. 2002. Arm coordination of female and male elite swimmers in front crawl. In *Biomechanics and medicine in swimming IX*, ed. J.C. Chatard, 173–178. St. Etienne, France: University of St. Etienne.

Seifert, L., D. Chollet, and B.G. Brady. 2004. Effect of swimming velocity on arm coordination in the front crawl: A dynamic analysis. *Journal of Sports Sciences* 22:651–660.

Seifert, L., L. Boulesteix, and D. Chollet. 2004. Effect of gender on the adaptation of arm coordination in front crawl. *International Journal of Sports Medicine* 25:217–223.

Seifert, L., D. Chollet, and P. Allard. 2005. Arm coordination symmetry and breathing effect in front crawl. *Human Movement Science* 24:234–256.

Seifert, L., D. Chollet, and A. Rouard. 2007. Swimming constraints and arm coordination. *Human Movement Science* 26:68–86.

Seifert, L., H.M. Toussaint, M. Alberty, C. Schnitzler, and D. Chollet. 2010. Arm coordination, power, and swim efficiency in national and regional front-crawl swimmers. *Human Movement Science* 29 (3): 426–439.

Sweetenham, B., and J. Atkinson. 2003. *Championship swim training*. Champaign, IL: Human Kinetics.

Thow, J. 2010. The development and validation of a battery of swimming technique measures associated with strength deficits among competitive front-crawl swimmers. Master's thesis.

Wiegand, K., D. Wuensch, and W. Jaehnig. 1975. The division of swimming strokes into phases, based upon kinematic parameters. In *Swimming II, international series on sports sciences*, ed. J.P. Clarys and L. Lewillie, 161–166. Baltimore: University Park Press.

Wilke, K. 1992. Analysis of sprint swimming: The 50m freestyle. In *Biomechanics and medicine in swimming, swimming science VI*, ed. D. MacLaren, T. Reilly, and A. Lees, 33–46. London: E & F Spon.

Yanai, T. 2001. What causes the body to roll in front-crawl swimming? *Journal of Applied Biomechanics* 17 (1): 28–42.

Chapter 5

Alves, F., Cunha, P., and Gomes-Pereira, J. 1999. Kinematic changes with inspiratory actions in butterfly swimming. In *Swimming science VIII*, ed. K.L. Keskinen, P.V. Komi, and A.P. Hollander, 9–14. Jyväskylä, Finland: University of Jyväskylä.

Hahn, A., and T. Krug. 1992. Application of knowledge gained from the coordination of partial movements in breaststroke and butterfly swimming for the development of technical training. In *Swimming science VI*, ed. D. MacLaren, T. Reilly, and A. Less, 167–171. London: E & FN Spon.

Maglischo, E.W. 2003. *Swimming fastest*. Champaign, IL: Human Kinetics.

Sanders, R.H., J.M. Cappaert, and R.K. Devlin. 1995. Wave characteristics of butterfly swimming. *Journal of Biomechanics* 28 (1): 9–16.

Sanders, R.H. 2007. Rock and roll rhythms in swimming. Geoffrey Dyson Lecture. International Symposium on Biomechanics in Sports. Keynote address. Ouro Preto, Brazil, August, 2007. http://w4.ub.uni-konstanz.de/cpa/issue/current.

Sanders, R.H. 2011. Rhythms in butterfly swimming. In *World book of swimming: From science to performance*, ed. L. Seifert, D. Chollet, and I. Mujika, 191–202. Hauppauge, NY: Nova Science.

Seifert, L., L. Boulesteix, D. Chollet, and J.P. Vilas Boas. 2008. Differences in spatial-temporal parameters and arm-leg coordination in butterfly stroke as a function of race pace, skill, and gender. *Human Movement Science* 27 (1): 96–111.

Seifert, L., D. Chollet, and R. Sanders. 2010. Does breathing disturb arm to leg coordination in butterfly? *International Journal of Sport Medicine* 31:167–173.

Chapter 6

Arellano, R., S. Pardillo, B. De La Fuente, and F. Garcia. 2000. A system to improve the swimming start technique using force recording, timing & kinematic analysis. In *Proceedings of the XVIII Symposium of the International Society of Biomechanics in Sports*, ed. R. Sanders and Y. Hong, 609–613. Hong Kong: University of Hong Kong.

Benjanuvatra, N., A. Lyttle, B.A. Blanksby, and D. Larkin. 2004. Force development profile of the lower limbs in the grab and track start. In *Proceedings of the XXII Symposium of the International Society of Biomechanics in Sports*, ed. M. Lamontagne, D. Gordon, E. Robertson, and H. Sveistrup, 399–402. Ottawa, Canada: University of Ottawa.

Benjanuvatra, N., K. Edmunds, and B. Blanksby. 2007. Jumping ability and swimming grab-start performance in elite and recreational swimmers. *International Journal of Aquatic Research and Education* 1 (3): 231–241.

Blanksby, B.A., D.G. Gathercole, and R.N. Marshall. 1995. Reliability of ground reaction force data and consistency of swimmers in tumble turn analysis. *Journal of Human Movement Studies* 28:193–207.

Blanksby, B.A., D.G. Gathercole, and R.N. Marshall. 1996. Force plate and video analysis of the tumble turn by age-group swimmers. *Journal of Swimming Research* 11:40–45.

Blanksby, B.A., J.R. Simpson, B.C. Elliott, and G.K. McElroy. 1998. Biomechanical factors influencing breaststroke turns by age-group swimmers. *Journal of Applied Biomechanics* 14:180–189.

Blanksby, B., L. Nicholson, and B. Elliott. 2002. Biomechanical analysis of the grab, track and handles starts: An intervention study. *Sports Biomechanics* 1 (1): 11–24.

Blanksby, B.A., S. Skender, B.C. Elliott, G.K. McElroy, and G. Landers. 2004. An analysis of rollover backstroke turns by age-group swimmers. *Sports Biomechanics* 3 (1): 1–14.

Chatard, J., J. Lavoie, B. Bourgoin, and J. Lacour. 1990. The contribution of passive drag as a determinant of swimming performance. *International Journal of Sports Medicine* 11 (2): 367–372.

Clothier, P.J., G.K. McElroy, B.A. Blanksby, and W.R. Payne. 2000. Traditional and modified exits following freestyle tumble turns by skilled swimmers. *South African Journal for Research in Sport, Physical Education and Recreation* 22 (1): 41–55.

Cossor, J., and B. Mason. 2001. Swim start performance at the Sydney 2000 Olympic Games. In *Proceedings of the Applied Swim Sessions of the XIX Symposium on Biomechanics in Sports*, ed. J. Blackwell and R. Sanders, 70–74. San Francisco: University of San Francisco

Cossor, J.M., S.E. Slawson, L.M. Justham, P.P. Conway, and A.A. West. 2010. The development of a component based approach for swim start analysis. In *Proceedings of XI International Symposium in Biomechanics and Medicine in Swimming*, ed. P-L. Kjendlie, R.K. Stallman, and J. Cabri, 59–61. Oslo, Norway: Norwegian School of Sport Sciences.

Costa, L., J. Ribeiro, P. Figueiredo, R.J. Fernandes, D. Marinho, A.J. Silva, A. Rouboa, J.P. Vilas-Boas, and L. Machado. 2010. In *Proceedings of the XI International Symposium in Biomechanics and Medicine in Swimming*, ed. P-L. Kjendlie, R.K. Stallman, and J. Cabri, 62–63. Oslo, Norway: Norwegian School of Sport Sciences.

Counsilman, J., B. Counsilman, T. Nomura, and M. Endo. 1988. Three types of grab starts for competitive swimming. In *Proceedings of the V International Symposium of Biomechanics and Medicine in Swimming*, ed. B. Ungerechts, K. Reischle, and K. Wilkie, 81–91. Champaign, IL: Human Kinetics.

De Jesus, K., P. Figueiredo, P. Goncalves, S.M. Pereira, J.P Vilas-Boas, and R.J. Fernandes. 2010. Biomechanical characterization of the backstroke start in immerged and emerged feet conditions. In *Proceedings of XI International Symposium in Biomechanics and Medicine in Swimming*, ed. P-L. Kjendlie, R.K. Stallman, and J. Cabri, 64–66. Oslo, Norway: Norwegian School of Sport Sciences.

Gambrel, D., D. Blanke, K. Thigpen, and M. Mellion. 1991. A biomechanical comparison of two relay starts in swimming. *Journal of Swimming Research* 7 (2): 5–9.

Goya, T., H. Takagi, and T. Nomura. 1999. Training effects on forces and turning motion during the breaststroke turn. In *Biomechanics and medicine in swimming VIII*, ed. K.L. Keskinen and P.V. Komi, 47–51. Finland: University of Jyväskylä.

Hay, J.G. 1988. The status of research on the biomechanics of swimming. In *Swimming science V*, ed. B.E. Ungerechts, K. Wilke, and K. Reischle, 3–14. Champaign, IL: Human Kinetics.

Hay, J.G. 1992. *The biomechanics of sports techniques.* Sydney: Prentice/Hall International.

Hines, E. 1993. Faster flip turns. *Swim* Jan–Feb: 17–18.

Hohmann, A., U. Fehr, R. Kirsten, and T. Kruger. 2006. EMG-model of the backstroke start technique. *Portuguese Journal of Sport Sciences* 6 (supplement 2): 37–40.

Holthe, M.J., and S.P. McLean. 2001. Kinematic comparison of grab and track starts in swimming. In *Proceedings of the XIX Symposium of the International Society of Biomechanics in Sports*, ed. J.R. Blackwell and R.H. Sanders, 31–34. San Francisco: University of San Francisco.

Honda, K.E., P.J. Sinclair, B.R. Mason, and D.L. Pease. 2010. A biomechanical comparison of elite swimmers' start performance using the traditional track start and the new kick start. In *Proceedings of XI International Symposium in Biomechanics and Medicine in Swimming*, ed. P-L. Kjendlie, R.K. Stallman, and J. Cabri, 94–96. Oslo, Norway: Norwegian School of Sport Sciences.

Hong, L. 1999. The study of start auxiliary training for Chinese elite swimmers. In *XIII FINA World Sports Medicine Congress: Aquatic sports for the new century*, ed. F.H. Fu, E.P. Chien, and P-K. Chung, 73–82. Hong Kong: Hong Kong Association of Sports Medicine and Sport Science.

Hoof, D.L. 2007. Sprinters need faster starts. *American Swimming Magazine* 6:13–19.

Houel, N., M. Elipot, F. Andree, and H. Hellard. 2010. Kinematics analysis of undulatory underwater swimming during a grab start of national level swimmers. In *Proceedings of XI International Symposium in Biomechanics and Medicine in Swimming*, ed. P-L. Kjendlie, R.K. Stallman, and J. Cabri, 97–99. Oslo, Norway: Norwegian School of Sport Sciences.

Hubert, M., G.A. Silvera, E. Freitas, S. Pereira, and H. Roesler. 2006. Speed variation analysis before and after the beginning of the stroke in swimming starts. *Portuguese Journal of Sport Sciences* 6 (supplement 2): 44–45.

Huellhorst, U., B.E. Ungerechts, and K. Willimczik. 1988. Displacement and speed characteristics of the breaststroke turn: A cinematographic analysis. In *International series of sport sciences, volume 18: Swimming science V*, ed. B.E. Ungerechts, K. Reischle, and K. Wilke, 93–96. Champaign, IL: Human Kinetics.

Keys, M., and A. Lyttle. 2010. Computational fluid dynamics: A tool for future swimming technique prescription. In *The impact of technology on sport II*, ed. F. Fuss, A. Subic, and S. Ujihashi, 587–592. London: Taylor and Francis.

Kruger, T., D. Wick, A. Hohmann, M. El-Bahrawi, and A. Koth. 2003. Biomechanics of the grab and track start technique. In *Proceeding of the IX International Symposium on Biomechanics and Medicine in Swimming*, ed. J.C. Chatard, 219–223. Saint-Etienne, France: University of Saint-Etienne.

Kishimoto, T., T. Takeda, S. Sugimoto, S. Tsubakimoto, and H. Takagi. 2010. An analysis of an underwater turn for butterfly and breaststroke. In *Proceedings of XI International Symposium in Biomechanics and Medicine in Swimming*, ed. P-L. Kjendlie, R.K. Stallman, and J. Cabri, 108–109. Oslo, Norway: Norwegian School of Sport Sciences.

Ling, B.H., B.A. Blanksby, B.C. Elliott, and G.K. McElroy. 2004. Force-time characteristics of the butterfly turns by age-group swimmers. *Journal of Human Movement Studies* 47:429–451.

Lyttle, A.D., and M. Keys. 2006. The application of computational fluid dynamics for technique prescription in underwater kicking. *Portuguese Journal of Sport Sciences* 6 (supplement 2): 233–235.

Lyttle, A.D., B.A. Blanksby, B.C. Elliott, and D.G. Lloyd. 1998. The effect of depth and velocity on drag during the streamlined glide. *Journal of Swimming Research* 13:15–22.

Lyttle, A.D., B.A. Blanksby, B.C. Elliott, and D.G. Lloyd. 1999. Investigating kinetics in the freestyle flip turn push-off. *Journal of Applied Biomechanics* 15 (3): 242–252.

Lyttle, A.D., B.A. Blanksby, B.C. Elliott, and D.G. Lloyd. 2000. Net forces during tethered simulation of underwater streamlined gliding and kicking techniques of the freestyle turn. *Journal of Sports Science* 18:801–807.

Maiello, D., A. Sabatini, S. Demarie, F. Sardella, and A. Dal Monte. 1998. Passive drag on and under the water surface. *Journal of Sports Sciences* 16 (5): 420–421.

Marinho, D.A., T.M. Barbosa, N. Mantripragada, J.P. Vilas-Boas, A.H. Rouard, V.R. Mantha, A.I. Rouboa, and A.J. Silva. 2010. The gliding phase in swimming: The effect of water depth. In *Proceedings of XI International Symposium in Biomechanics and Medicine in Swimming,* ed. P-L. Kjendlie, R.K. Stallman, and J. Cabri, 122–123. Oslo, Norway: Norwegian School of Sport Sciences.

Mason, B., A. Alcock, and J. Fowlie. 2007. A kinetic analysis and recommendations for elite swimmers performing the sprint start. In *Proceedings of XXV International Symposium on Biomechanics in Sports,* ed. H.J. Menzel and M.H. Chagas, 385–388. Ouro Preto, Minas Gerais, Brazil: Federal University of Ouro Preto.

McLean, S., M. Holthe, P. Vint, K. Bekkett, and R. Hinrichs. 2000. Addition of an approach to a relay start. *Journal of Applied Biomechanics* 16:342–355.

Miller, M., D. Allen, and R. Pein. 2003. A kinetic and kinematic comparison of the grab and track starts in swimming. In *Proceeding of the IX International Symposium on Biomechanics and Medicine in Swimming,* ed. J.C. Chatard, 231–235. Saint-Etienne, France: University of Saint-Etienne.

Newble, D. 1982. A method of analysing starts and turns in competitive swimming. *Australian Journal of Sports Sciences* 2 (1):11–13.

Nicol, K., and F. Kruger. 1979. Impulse exerted in performing several kinds of swimming turns. In *International series of sport sciences, volume 8; Swimming III,* ed. J. Terauds and E.W. Bedingfield, 222–232. Baltimore: University Park Press.

Pearson, C.T., G.K. McElroy, J.D. Blitvich, A. Subic, and B.A. Blanksby. 1998. A comparison of the swimming start using traditional and modified starting blocks. *Journal of Human Movement Studies* 34:49–66.

Pereira, S., L. Araujo, E. Freitas, R. Gatti, G. Silveira, and H. Roesler. 2006. Biomechanical analysis of the turn in front crawl swimming. *Portuguese Journal of Sport Sciences* 6 (supplement 2): 77–79.

Prins, J.H., and A. Patz. 2006. The influence of tuck index, depth of foot plant and wall contact time on the velocity of push-off in the freestyle flip turn. *Portuguese Journal of Sport Sciences* 6 (supplement 2): 82–85.

Puel, F., J. Morlier, M. Cid, D. Chollet, and P. Hellard. 2010. Biomechanical factors influencing tumble turn performance of elite female swimmers. In *Proceedings of XI International Symposium in Biomechanics and Medicine in Swimming,* ed. P-L. Kjendlie, R.K. Stallman, and J. Cabri, 155–157. Oslo, Norway: Norwegian School of Sport Sciences.

Roig, A. 2010. Evaluation of the gliding capacity of a swimmer. In *Proceedings of XI International Symposium in Biomechanics and Medicine in Swimming,* ed. P-L. Kjendlie, R.K. Stallman, and J. Cabri, 163–165. Oslo, Norway: Norwegian School of Sport Sciences.

Sanders, R. 2003. Do your swimmers kick too soon in turns? *Coaches' InfoService.* International Society of Biomechanics. www.coachesinfo.com/article/114/.

Schnabel, U., and J. Kuchler. 1998. Analysis of the starting phase in competitive swimming. In *Proceedings II of the XVI International Symposium of Biomechanics in Sport,* ed. H.J. Riehle and M.M. Vieten, 247–254. Konstanz, Germany: University of Konstanz.

Slawson, S. 2010. Intelligent user centric components for harsh distributed environments. Unpublished thesis, Loughborough University, UK.

Takahashi, G., A. Yoshida, S. Tsubakimoto, and M Miyashita. 1983. Propulsive forces generated by swimmers during a turning motion. In *International series on sport sciences, volume 14: Proceedings of the IV Symposium of Biomechanics in Swimming,* ed. A.P. Hollander, P.A. Huijing, and G. de Groot, 192–198. Champaign, IL: Human Kinetics.

Takeda, T., H. Ichikawa, S. Tsubakimoto, and T. Nomura. 2008. Effect of take-off angle on start performance in swim start. In *Proceedings of First International Scientific Conference of Aquatic Space Activities,* ed. T. Nomura and B.E. Ungerechts, 374–379. Tsukuba, Japan: University of Tsukuba.

Thorstensson, A., G. Grimby, and J. Karlsson. 1976. Force-velocity relations and fibre composition in human knee extensor muscles. *Journal of Applied Physiology* 40:12–16.

Vilas-Boas, J.P., M.J. Cruz, F. Sousa, F. Conceicao, and J. Carvalho. 2000. Integrated kinematic and dynamic analysis of two track start techniques. In *Proceedings of XVIII International Symposium on Biomechanics in Sports,* ed. R. Sanders and Y. Hong, 113–117. Hong Kong: Chinese University of Hong Kong.

Vilas-Boas, J.P., J. Cruz, F. Sousa, F. Conceicao, R. Fernandes, and J. Carvalho. 2003.

Biomechanical analysis of ventral swimming starts: Comparison of the grab start with two track-start techniques. In *Proceedings of the IX International Symposium on Biomechanics and Medicine in Swimming*, ed. J.C. Chatard, 249–253. Saint-Etienne, France: University of Saint-Etienne.

Vilas-Boas, J.P., K. de Jesus, K.E. de Jesus, P. Figueiredo, S. Pereira, P. Goncalves, L. Machado, and R. Fernandes. 2009. How to start in backstroke considering the new rules? In *Proceedings of XXVII International Symposium on Biomechanics in Sports*, ed. A.J. Harrison, R. Anderson, and I. Kenny, 916. Limerick, Ireland: University of Limerick.

Vint, P.F., R.N. Hinrichs, S.K. Riewald, R.A. Mason, and S.P. McLean. 2009. Effects of handle and block configuration on swim start performance. In *Proceedings of XXVII International Symposium on Biomechanics in Sports*, ed. A.J. Harrison, R. Anderson, and I. Kenny, 102–105. Limerick, Ireland: University of Limerick.

Wada, T., T. Sato, K. Ohishi, T. Tago, T. Izumi, T. Matsumoto, N. Yamamoto, T. Isaka, and Y. Shimoyama. 2010. An analysis of the underwater gliding motion in collegiate competitive swimmers. In *Proceedings of XI International Symposium in Biomechanics and Medicine in Swimming*, ed. P.-L. Kjendlie, R.K. Stallman, and J. Cabri, 185–187. Oslo, Norway: Norwegian School of Sport Sciences.

Walker, J., J. De Lapp, G. Bradford, and J. Cappaert. 1995. A biomechanical analysis of the butterfly turn of age-group swimmers: Three approach characteristics. *Medicine and Science in Sport and Exercise* 27 (supplement, p. S232): abstract 1300.

Welcher, R.L., R.N. Hinrichs, and T.R. George. 1999. An analysis of velocity and time characteristics of three starts in competitive swimming. In *Proceedings of the XVII Congress of the International Society of Biomechanics*, ed. W. Herzog, and A. Jinha, 400. Calgary, Canada: University of Calgary, Department of Kinesiology.

Welshe, A.D., G.J. Wilson, and G.J.C Ettema. 1998. Stretch shorten cycle compared with isometric pre-load: Contributions to enhanced muscular performance. *Journal of Applied Physiology* 84 (1): 97–106.

Wilson, G.J., B.C. Elliott, and G.A. Wood. 1991. The effect on performance of imposing a delay during a stretch-shorten cycle movement. *Medicine and Science in Sport and Exercise* 23:364–370.

Zatsiorsky, V.M., N.Z. Bulgakova, and N.M Chaplinsky. 1979. Biomechanical analysis of starting techniques in swimming. In *Swimming III*, ed. J. Terauds and E.W. Bedingfield, 199–206. Baltimore: University Park Press.

Chapter 7

Barltrop, N.D.P., and A.J. Adams. 1991. *Dynamics of fixed marine structures*. 3rd ed. Oxford, UK: Butterworth-Heinemann.

Bixler, B., and S. Riewald. 2001. Analysis of a swimmer's hand and arm in steady flow conditions using computational fluid dynamics. *Journal of Biomechanics* 35:713–717.

Bixler, B., D. Pease, and F. Fairhurst. 2007. The accuracy of computational fluid dynamics analysis of the passive drag of a male swimmer. *Sports Biomechanics* 6 (1): 81–98.

Hertel, H. 1966. *Structure-form-movement*. New York: Reinhold.

Jager, T. 1999. Personal correspondence.

Keys, M. 2010. Establishing computational fluid dynamics models for swimming technique assessment. Unpublished PhD thesis, University of Western Australia.

Keys, M., and A. Lyttle. 2008. Computational fluid dynamics: A tool for future swimming technique prescription. In *The impact of technology on sport II*, ed. F.K. Fuss, A. Subic, and Ujihashi, 587–592. London: Taylor and Francis Group.

Keys, M., A. Lyttle, L. Cheng, and B.A. Blanksby. 2010. Wave formation as a possible mechanism of propulsion in the freestyle stroke. In *Proceedings of the XI International Symposium on Biomechanics and Medicine in Swimming*, ed. P.L. Kjendlie, R.K. Stallman, and J. Cabri, 48–49. Oslo, Norway: Norwegian School of Sport Sciences.

Lyttle, A., and M. Keys. 2006. The application of computational fluid dynamics for technique prescription in underwater kicking. *Portuguese Journal of Sport Sciences* 6 (supplement 2): 233–235.

Sato, Y., and T. Hino. 2002. Estimation of thrust of swimmer's hand using CFD. *Proceedings of 8th Symposium of Nonlinear and Free-Surface Flows*, 71–75. Hiroshima, Japan: University of Hiroshima.

Versteeg, H.K., and W. Malalasekera. 1995. An introduction to computational fluid dynamics. *The finite volume method*. London: Prentice-Hall.

Von Loebbecke, A., R. Mittal, R. Mark, and J. Hahn. 2009. A computational method for analysis of underwater dolphin kick hydrodynamics in human swimming. *Sports Biomechanics* 8 (1): 60–77.

Chapter 8

Booth, F.W., and K.M. Baldwin. 1996. Muscle plasticity: Energy demand and supply processes. In *Handbook of physiology: Section 12: Exercise: Regulation and integration of multiple systems*, ed. L.B.

Rowell and J.T. Shepard, 1075–1123. Baltimore: American Physiological Society.

Brooks, G.A., T.D. Fahey, and K.M. Baldwin. 2004. *Exercise physiology: Human bioenergetics and its applications.* Boston: McGraw Hill.

Brooks, G.A., and G.A. Gaesser. 1980. End points of lactate and glucose metabolism after exhausting exercise. *Journal of Applied Physiology: Respiratory, Environmental, and Exercise Physiology* 49:1057–1069.

Capelli, C., D.R. Pendergast, and B. Termin. 1998. Energetics of swimming at maximal speeds in humans. *European Journal of Applied Physiology* 78 (5): 385–393.

Costill, D.L., W.J. Fink, and M.L. Pollock. 1976. Muscle fiber composition and enzyme concentrations of elite distance runners. *Medicine and Science in Sports and Exercise* 8:96–100.

Di Prampero, P.E., D.R. Pendergast, D.W. Wislon, and D.W. Rennie. 1974. Energetics of swimming man. *Journal of Applied Physiology* 37:1–5.

Hickson, R.C. 1980. Interference of strength development by simultaneously training for strength and endurance. *European Journal of Applied Physiology* 45:255–263.

Ivy, J., D.L. Costill, P.J. Van Handel, D.A. Essig, and R.W. Lower. 1981. Alteration in the lactate threshold with changes in substrate availability. *International Journal of Sports Medicine* 2 (3): 139–142.

Olbrecht, J. 2000. *The science of winning.* Overijse, Belgium: Self-published.

Stager, J.M., C.L. Brammer, T. Sossong, K. Kojima, D. Spanbauer, K. Grand, and B.V. Wright. 2014. Supplemental recovery nutrition affects swim performance following glycogen depleting exercise. *Medicine and Science in Sports and Exercise* 46 (5): 156.

Stager, J.M., and D.A. Tanner. 2005. *Handbook of sports medicine and science, swimming.* 2nd ed. Malden, MA: Blackwell.

Chapter 9

Bompa, T.O. 1999a. *Periodization training for sports.* Champaign, IL: Human Kinetics.

Bompa, T.O. 1999b. *Periodization: Theory and methodology of training.* 4th ed. Champaign, IL: Human Kinetics.

Brown, L.E. 2001. Nonlinear versus linear periodization models. *Strength and Conditioning Journal* 23 (1): 42–44.

Fevre, M.L., S. Gregory, and Matheny. 2006. Eustress, distress and their interpretation in primary and secondary occupational stress management interventions: Which way first?

Journal of Managerial Psychology 21 (6): 547–565.

Girold, S., P. Calmels, D. Maurin, N. Milhau, and J.C. Chatard. 2006. Assisted and resisted sprint training in swimming. *Journal of Strength and Conditioning Research* 20 (3): 547–554.

Herodek, K., C. Simonovic, and A. Rakovic. 2012. Periodization and strength training cycles. *Activities in Physical Education and Sport* 2 (2): 254–257.

Issurin, V. 2008. Block periodization versus traditional training theory: A review. *Journal of Sports Medicine and Physical Fitness* 48 (1): 65–75.

Issurin, V.B. 2010. New horizons for the methodology and physiology of training periodization. *Sports Medicine* 40 (3): 189–206.

Kell, R.T. 2011. The influence of periodized resistance training on strength changes in men and women. *Journal of Strength and Conditioning Research* 25 (3): 735–744.

Kiely, J. 2012. Periodization paradigms in the 21st century: Evidence-led or tradition-driven? *International Journal of Sports Physiology and Performance* 7:242–250

Matveyev, L.P. 1966. *Periodization of sports training.* Moscow: Fiscultura I Sport.

Plisk, S.S., and M.H. Stone. 2003. Periodization strategies. *Strength and Conditioning Journal* 25 (6): 19–37.

Pyne, D.B., and G. Touretski. 2003. An analysis of training of Olympic swim champion Alexandre Popov. *Australian Swim Coach* 10 (5): 5–14.

Rhea, M.R., and B.L. Alderman. 2004. A meta-analysis of periodized versus non-periodized strength and power training programs. *Research Quarterly for Exercise and Sport* 75 (4): 413–422.

Rice, V.H. 2012. Theories of stress and its relationship to health. In *Handbook of stress, coping, and health: Implications for nursing research, theory, and practice,* ed. V.H. Rice, 22–42. Los Angeles: Sage.

Selye, H. 1974. *Stress without distress.* Philadelphia: Lippincott.

Selye, H. 1976. *The stress of life.* Rev ed. New York: McGraw-Hill.

Sharp, R.L. 1986. Muscle strength and power as related to competitive swimming. *Journal of Swimming Research* 2 (2): 5–10.

Siff, M.C., and Y.V. Verkhoshansky. 1999. *Supertraining.* 4th ed. Denver: Supertraining International.

Stewart, A.M., and W.G. Hopkins. 2000. Seasonal training and performance of competitive swimmers. *Journal of Sports Sciences* 18 (11): 873–884.

Stone, M.H., K.C. Pierce, G.G. Haff, and M. Stone. 1999. Periodization: Effects of manipulating volume and intensity. Part 1. *Strength and Conditioning Journal* 21 (2): 56–62.

Thomas, L., I. Mujika, and T. Busso. 2008. A model study of optimal training reductions during pre-event taper in elite swimmers. *Journal of Sports Sciences* 26 (6): 643–652.

Touretski, G. 2000. Preparation for sprint events. *American Swimming Magazine* 4:4–6.

Vorontsov, A. 2011. Strength and power training in swimming. In *World book of swimming: From science to practice*, ed. L. Seifert, D. Chollett, and I. Mujika, 313–343. New York: Nova Science.

Zatsiorsky, V.M., and W.J. Kraemer. 2006. *The science and practice of strength training*. 2nd ed. Champaign, IL: Human Kinetics.

Chapter 10

Adlercreutz, H., M. Härkönen, K. Kuoppasalmi, H. Näveri, I Huhtaniemi, H. Tikkanen, K. Remes, A. Dessypris, and J. Karvonen. 1986. Effect of training on plasma anabolic and catabolic steroid hormones and their response during physical exercise. *International Journal of Sports Medicine*, 7: 27-28.

Anderson, M.E., W.G. Hopkins, A.D. Roberts, and D.B. Pyne. 2006. Monitoring seasonal and long-term changes in test performance in elite swimmers. *European Journal of Sport Science*, 6: 145-154.

Anderson, M.E., W.G. Hopkins, A.D. Roberts, and D.B. Pyne. 2008. Ability of test measures to predict competitive performance in elite swimmers. *Journal of Sports Science*, 26: 123-130.

Atlaoui, D., M. Duclos, C. Gouarne, L. Lacoste, F. Barale, and J.C. Chatard. 2004. The 24-hr urinary cortisol/cortisone ratio for monitoring training in elite swimmers. *Medicine and Science in Sports and Exercise*, 36: 218-224.

Bannister, E.W. 1991. Modeling elite athletic performance. In *Physiological Testing of the High-Performance Athlete, second edition*, edited by J.D. MacDougall, H.A. Wenger, and H.J. Green. Champaign, IL: Human Kinetics. pp. 403-424.

Banister, E.W., and T.W. Calvert. 1980. Planning for future performance: Implications for long term training. *Canadian Journal of Applied Sport Science*, 5: 170-176.

Banister, E.W., T.W. Calvert, M.V. Savage, and T. Bach. 1975. A systems model of training for athletic performance. *Australian Journal of Sports Medicine*, 7: 57-61.

Banister, E.W., J.B. Carter, and P.C. Zarkadas. 1999. Training theory and taper: Validation in triathlon athletes. *European Journal of Applied Physiology*, 79: 182-191.

Berger, B.G., J.R. Grove, H. Prapavessis, and B.D. Butki. 1997. Relationship of swimming distance, expectancy, and performance to mood states of competitive athletes. *Perceptual and Motor Skills*, 84: 1199-1210.

Bessman, J.D., G.P. Ridgeway, and F.H. Gardner. 1983. Improved classification of anemias by MCV and RDW. *American Journal of Clinical Pathology*, 80: 322-326.

Best, R., and B.R. Walker. 1997. Additional value of measurement of urinary cortisone and unconjugated cortisol metabolites in assessing the activity of 11 beta-hydroxysteroid dehydrogenase in vivo. *Clinical Endocrinology*, 47: 231-236.

Bonifazi, M., F. Sardella, and C. Luppo. 2000. Preparatory versus main competitions: Differences in performances, lactate responses and pre-competition plasma cortisol concentrations in elite male swimmers. *European Journal of Applied Physiology*, 82: 368-373.

Boobis, L. 1987. Metabolic aspects of fatigue during sprinting. In *Exercise: Benefits, Limits and Adaptations*, edited by D. MacLeod, R. Maughan, M. Nimmo, T. Reilly and C. Williams. London: E & FN Spon. pp. 116-143.

Borg, G. 1970. Perceived exertion as an indicator of somatic stress. *Scandinavian Journal of Rehabilitation Medicine*, 2: 92-98.

Borg, G. 1982. Psychophysical bases of perceived exertion. *Medicine and Science in Sports and Exercise*, 14: 377-381.

Borg, G., P. Hassmen, and M. Lagerstrom. 1987. Perceived exertion related to heart rate and blood lactate during arm and leg exercise. *European Journal of Applied Physiology*, 65: 679-685.

Bosquet, L., J. Montpetit, D. Arvisais, and I. Mujika. 2007. Effects of tapering on performance: A meta-analysis. *Medicine and Science in Sports and Exercise*, 39: 1358-1365.

Bothwell, T.H., R.W. Charlton, J.D. Cook, and C.A. Finch. 1979. *Iron metabolism in man*. Oxford: Blackwell Scientific Publications.

Bunt, J.C. 1986. Hormonal alterations due to exercise. *Sports Medicine*, 3: 331-345.

Burke, E.R., H.L. Falsetti, R.D. Feld, G.S. Patton, and C.C. Kennedy. 1982a. Blood testing to determine overtraining in swimmers. *Swim Tech*, 18: 29-33.

Burke, E.R., H.L. Falsetti, R.D. Feld, G.S. Patton, and C.C. Kennedy. 1982b. Creatine kinase levels in competitive swimming during a season of training. *Scandinavian Journal of Sports Science*, 4: 1-4.

Busso, T., H. Benoit, R. Bonnefoy, L. Feasson, and J.R. Lacour. 2002. Effects of training frequency on the dynamics of performance response to a single training bout. *Journal of Applied Physiology*, 92: 572-580.

Busso, T., R. Candau, and J.R. Lacour. 1994. Fatigue and fitness modelled from the effects of training on performance. *European Journal of Applied Physiology,* 69: 50-54.

Busso, T., K. Häkkinen, A. Pakarinen, C. Carasso, J.R. Lacour, P.V. Komi, and H. Kauhanen. 1990. A systems model of training responses and its relationship to hormonal responses in elite weight-lifters. *European Journal of Applied Physiology,* 61: 48-54.

Calvert, T.W., E.W. Banister, M.V. Savage, and T. Bach. 1976. A systems model of the effects of training on physical performance. *IEEE Transactions on Systems, Man, and Cybernetics,* 6: 94-102.

Cavanaugh, D.J., and K.I. Musch. 1989. Arm and leg power of elite swimmers increase after taper as measured by biokinetic variable resistance machines. *Journal of Swim Research,* 5: 7-10.

Chatard, J.C., D. Atlaoui, V. Pichot, C. Gourne, M. Duclos, and Y.C. Guezennec. 2003. Training follow up by questionnaire fatigue, hormones and heart rate variability measurements. *Sci et Sports,* 18: 302-304.

Clement, D.B., and L.L. Sawchuk. 1984. Iron status and sports performance. *Sports Medicine,* 1: 65-74.

Colwin, C. 1995. Mental aspects of the taper. *Swim Tech,* 31: 6-8.

Costill, D.L., D.S. King, R. Thomas, and M. Hargreaves. 1985. Effects of reduced training on muscular power in swimmers. *Physician and Sportsmedicine,* 13: 94-101.

Costill, D.L., R. Thomas, R.A. Roberers, D. Pascoe, C. Lambert, S. Barr, and W.J. Fink. 1991. Adaptations to swimming training: Influence of training volume. *Medicine and Science in Sports and Exercise,* 23: 371-377.

Cumming, D.C., and S.R. Wall. 1985. Non-sex hormone-binding globulin-bound testosterone as a marker for hyperandrogenism. *Journal of Clinical Endocrinology and Metabolism,* 61: 873-876.

D'Acquisto, L.J., M. Bone, S. Takahashi, G. Langhans, A.P. Barzdukas, and J.P. Troup. 1992. Changes in aerobic power and swimming economy as a result of reduced training volume. In *Swimming Science VI.* \D. MacLaren, T. Reilly, A. Less. London: E & FN Spon. pp. 201-205.

Fitz-Clarke, J.R., R.H. Morton, and E.W. Banister. 1991. Optimizing athletic performance by influence curves. *Journal of Applied Physiology,* 71: 1151-1158.

Flynn, M.G., F.X. Pizza, J.B. Boone Jr, F.F. Andres, T.A. Michaud, and J.R. Rodriguez-Zavas. 1994. Indices of training stress during competitive running and swimming seasons. *International Journal of Sports Medicine,* 15: 21-26.

Fry, R.W., A.R. Morton, P. Garcia-Webb, G.P. Crawford, and D. Keast. 1992. Biological responses to overload training in endurance sports. *European Journal of Applied Physiology,* 64: 335-344.

Galbo, H. 1986. The hormonal response to exercise. *Diabetes/Metabolism Reviews,* 1: 385-408

Gledhill, N. 1982. Blood doping and related issues: A brief review. *Medicine and Science in Sports and Exercise,* 14: 183-189.

Gledhill, N. 1985. The influence of altered blood volume and oxygen transport capacity on aerobic performance. *Exercise and Sports Science Review,* 13: 75-94.

Gordon, T., and M.C. Pattullo. 1993. Plasticity of muscle fiber and motor unit types. *Exercise and Sports Science Review,* 21: 331-362.

Haykowsky, M.J., D.J. Smith, L. Malley, S.R. Norris, and E.R. Smith. 1998. Effects of short-term altitude training and tapering on left ventricular morphology in elite swimmers. *Canadian Journal of Cardiology,* 14: 678-681.

Hooper, S.L., and L.T. MacKinnon. 1995. Monitoring overtraining athletes: Recommendations. *Sports Medicine,* 20: 321-327.

Hooper, S.L., L.T. Mackinnon, and E.M. Ginn. 1998. Effects of three tapering techniques on the performance, forces and psychometric measures of competitive swimmers. *European Journal of Applied Physiology,* 78: 258-263.

Hooper, S.L., L.T. Mackinnon, R.D. Gordon, and A.W. Bachmann. 1993. Hormonal responses of elite swimmers to overtraining. *Medicine and Science in Sports and Exercise,* 25: 741-747.

Hooper, S.L., L.T. MacKinnon, and S. Hanrahan. 1997. Mood states as an indication of staleness. *International Journal of Sport Psychology,* 28: 1-12.

Hooper, S.L., L.T. Mackinnon, A. Howard, R.D. Gordon, and A.W. Bachmann. 1995. Markers for monitoring overtraining and recovery. *Medicine and Science in Sports and Exercise,* 27: 106-112.

Hooper, S.L., L.T. Mackinnon, A. Howard. 1999. Physiological and psychometric variables for monitoring recovery during tapering for major competition. *Medicine and Science in Sports and Exercise,* 31: 1205-1210.

Hoppeler, H. 1986. Exercise-induced ultrastructural changes in skeletal muscle. *International Journal of Sports Medicine,* 7: 187-204.

Houmard, J.A. 1991. Impact of reduced training on performance in endurance athletes. *Sports Medicine,* 12: 380-393.

Houmard, J.A., and R.A. Johns. 1994. Effects of taper on swim performance. Practical implications. *Sports Medicine,* 17: 224-232.

Houmard, J.A., B.K. Scott, C.L. Justice, and T.C. Chenier. 1994. The effects of taper on performance in distance runners. *Medicine and Science in Sports and Exercise,* 26: 624-631.

Hultman, E., M. Bergström, L.L. Spriet, and K. Söderlund. 1990. Energy metabolism and fatigue. In *Biochemistry of Exercise VII*, edited by A.W. Taylor, P.D. Gollnick, H.J. Green, C.D. Ianuzzo, E.G. Noble, G. Métivier, and J.R. Sutton. Champaign, IL: Human Kinetics. pp. 73-92.

Johns, R.A., J.A. Houmard, R.W. Kobe, T. Hortobágyi, N.J. Bruno, J.M. Wells, and M.H. Shinebarger. 1992. Effects of taper on swim power, stroke distance and performance. *Medicine and Science in Sports and Exercise*, 24: 1141-1146.

Kaiser, V., G.M.E. Janssen, and J.W.J. Van Wersch. 1989. Effect of training on red blood cell parameters and plasma ferritin: A transverse and a longitudinal approach. *International Journal of Sports Medicine*, 10: S169-S175.

Kannus, P., L. Jòsza, P. Renström, M. Järvtoen, M. Kvist, M. Lento, P. Oja, and I. Vuorl. 1992. The effects of training, immobilization and remobilization on musculoskeletal tissue. 1. Training and immobilization. *Scandinavian Journal of Medicine and Science in Sports*, 2: 100-118.

Karlsson, J., B. Sjodin, I. Jacobs, and P. Kaiser. 1981. Relevance of muscle fibre type to fatigue in short intense and prolonged exercise in man. In *Human Muscle Fatigue: Physiological Mechanisms*, edited by Ciba Foundation Symposium. London: Pitman-Medical. pp. 59-74.

Kenitzer, R.F. Jr. 1998. Optimal taper period in female swimmers. *Journal of Swim Research*, 13: 31-36.

Koziris, L.P., R.C. Hickson, R.T. Chatterton Jr., R.T. Groseth, J.M. Christie, D.G. Goldflies, and T.G. Unterman. 1999. Serum levels of total and free IGF-I and IGFBP-3 are increased and maintained in long-term training. *Journal of Applied Physiology*, 86: 1436-1442.

Kubukeli, Z.N., T.D. Noakes, and S.C. Dennis. 2002. Training techniques to improve endurance exercise performances. *Sports Medicine*, 32: 489-509.

Kuoppasalmi, K., and H. Adlercreutz. 1985. Interaction between catabolic and anabolic steroid hormones in muscular exercise. In *Exercise Endocrinology*. Fotherby K. and S. Pal. Berlin: Walter de Gruyter & Co. pp. 65-98.

Lehmann, M., H.H. Dickhuth, G. Gendrisch, W. Lazar, M. Thum, R. Kaminski, J.F. Aramendi, E. Peterke, W. Wieland, and J. Keul. 1991. Training-overtraining. A prospective, experimental study with experienced middle- and long-distance runners. *International Journal of Sports Medicine*, 12: 444-452.

Lehmann, M., P. Baumgartl, C. Wiesenack, A. Seidel, H. Baumann, S. Fischer, U. Spöri, G. Gendrisch, R. Kaminski, and J. Keul. 1992. Training-overtraining: Influence of a defined increase in training volume vs. training intensity on performance, catecholamines and some metabolic parameters in experienced middle- and long-distance runners. *European Journal of Applied Physiology*, 64: 169-177.

Lehmann, M., C. Foster, and J. Keul. 1993. Overtraining in endurance athletes: A brief review. *Medicine and Science in Sports and Exercise*, 25: 854-862.

Malisoux, L., M. Francaux, and D. Theisen. 2007. What do single-fiber studies tell us about exercise training? *Medicine and Science in Sports and Exercise*, 39: 1051-1060.

Manni, A., W.M. Partridge, and M. Cefalu. 1985. Bioavailability of albumin-bound testosterone. *Journal of Clinical Endocrinology and Metabolism*, 61: 705-710.

McCarthy, D.A., and M.M. Dale. 1988. The leucocytosis of exercise. A review and model. *Sports Medicine*, 6: 333-363.

McNeely, E., and D. Sandler. 2007. Tapering for endurance athletes. *Strength and Conditioning Journal*, 29: 18-24.

Millard, M., C. Zauner, R. Cade, and R. Reese. 1985. Serum CPK levels in male and female world class swimmers during a season of training. *Journal of Swim Research*, 1: 12-16.

Millet, G.P., A. Groslambert, B. Barbier, J.D. Rouillon, and R.B. Candau. 2005. Modelling the relationships between training, anxiety, and fatigue in elite athletes. *International Journal of Sports Medicine*, 26: 492-498.

Morgan, W.P., D.R. Brown, J.S. Raglin, P.J. O'Connor, and K.A. Ellickson. 1987. Psychological monitoring of overtraining and staleness. *British Journal of Sports Medicine*,21: 107-114.

Morgan, W.P., and D.L. Costill. 1987. Psychometric and behavioural changes with overtraining. *USOC Final Grant Report*. Colorado Springs, CO: U.S. Olympic Committee.

Morgan, W.P., D.L. Costill, M.G. Flynn, J.S. Raglin, and P.J. O'Connor. 1988. Mood disturbance following increased training in swimmers. *Medicine and Science in Sports and Exercise*, 20: 408-414.

Morton, R.H. 1991. The quantitative periodization of athletic training: A model study. *Sports Medicine, Training and Rehabilitation*, 3: 19-28.

Morton, R.H., J.R. Fitz-Clarke, and E.W. Banister. 1990. Modeling human performance in running. *Journal of Applied Physiology*, 69: 1171-1177.

Mujika, I. 1998. The influence of training characteristics and tapering on the adaptation in highly trained individuals: A review. *International Journal of Sports Medicine*, 19: 439-446.

Mujika, I., T. Busso, L. Lacoste, F. Barale, A. Geyssant, and J.C. Chatard. 1996a. Modeled responses to training and taper in competitive swimmers. *Medicine and Science in Sports and Exercise*, 28: 251-258.

Mujika, I., J.C. Chatard, T. Busso, A. Geyssant, F. Barale, and L. Lacoste. 1995. Effects of training on performance in competitive swimming. *Canadian Journal of Applied Physiology*, 20: 395-406.

Mujika, I., J.C. Chatard, T. Busso, A. Geyssant, F. Barale, and L. Lacoste. 1996b. Use of swim-training profiles and performance data to enhance training effectiveness. *Journal of Swim Research*, 11: 23-29.

Mujika, I., J.C. Chatard, and A. Geyssant. 1996. Effects of training and taper on blood leucocyte populations in competitive swimmers: Relationships with cortisol and performance. *International Journal of Sports Medicine*, 17: 213-217.

Mujika, I., J.C. Chatard, S. Padilla, C.Y. Guezennec, and A. Geyssant. 1996c. Hormonal responses to training and its tapering off in competitive swimmers: Relationships with performance. *European Journal of Applied Physiology*, 74: 361-366.

Mujika, I., A. Goya, E. Ruiz, A. Grijalba, J. Santisteban, and S. Padilla. 2002a. Physiological and performance responses to a 6-day taper in middle-distance runners: Influence of training frequency. *International Journal of Sports Medicine*, 23: 367-373.

Mujika, I., and S. Padilla. 2000. Detraining: Loss of training-induced physiological and performance adaptations. Part I. Short-term insufficient training stimulus. *Sports Medicine*, 30: 79-87.

Mujika, I., and S. Padilla. 2003. Scientific bases for precompetition tapering strategies. *Medicine and Science in Sports and Exercise*, 35: 1182-1187.

Mujika, I., S. Padilla, A. Geyssant, and J.C. Chatard. 1998. Hematological responses to training and taper in competitive swimmers: Relationships with performance. *Archives of Physiology and Biochemistry*, 105: 379-385.

Mujika, I., S. Padilla, and D. Pyne. 2002b. Swimming performance changes during the final 3 weeks of training leading to the Sydney 2000 Olympic Games. *International Journal of Sports Medicine*, 23: 582-587.

Mujika, I., S. Padilla, D. Pyne, and T. Busso. 2004. Physiological changes associated with the pre-event taper in athletes. *Sports Medicine*, 34: 891-927.

Neary, J.P., T.P. Martin, and H.A. Quinney. 2003. Effects of taper on endurance cycling capacity and single muscle fiber properties. *Medicine and Science in Sports and Exercise*, 35: 1875-1881.

Neary, J.P., T.P. Martin, D.C. Reid, R. Burnham, and H.A. Quinney. 1992. The effects of a reduced exercise duration taper programme on performance and muscle enzymes of endurance cyclists. *European Journal of Applied Physiology*, 65: 30-36.

Neufer, P.D. 1989. The effect of detraining and reduced training on the physiological adaptations to aerobic exercise training. *Sports Medicine*, 8: 302-321.

Noakes, T.D. 2000. Physiological models to understand exercise fatigue and the adaptations that predict or enhance athletic performance. *Scandinavian Journal of Medicine and Science in Sports*, 10: 123-145.

Noble, B.J., and R.J. Robertson. 2000. *Perceived exertion*. Champaign, IL: Human Kinetics.

O'Connor, P.J., W.P. Morgan, J.S. Raglin, C.M. Barksdale, and N.H. Kalin. 1989. Mood state and salivary cortisol levels following overtraining in female swimmers. *Psychoneuroendocrinology*, 14: 303-310.

Papoti, M., L.E Martins, S.A. Cunha, A.M. Zagatto, and C.A. Gobatto. 2007. Effects of taper on swimming force and swimmer performance after an experimental ten-week training program. *Journal of Strength and Conditioning Research*, 21: 538-542.

Pelayo, P., I. Mujika, M. Sidney, and J.C. Chatard. 1996. Blood lactate recovery measurements, training, and performance during a 23-week period of competitive swimming. *European Journal of Applied Physiology*, 74: 107-113.

Pizza, F.X., M.G. Flynn, J.B. Boone, J.R. Rodriquez-Zavas, and F.F. Andres. 1997. Serum haptoglobin and ferritin during a competitive running and swimming season. *International Journal of Sports Medicine*, 18: 233-237.

Prins, J.H., D.A. Lally, K.E. Maes, J. Uno, and G.H. Hartung. 1991. Changes in peak force and work in competitive swimmers during training and taper as tested on a biokinetic swimming bench. In *Aquatic Sports Medicine*, edited by J.M. Cameron. London: Farrand Press. pp. 80-88.

Pyne, D., I. Mujika, and T. Reilly. 2009. Peaking for optimal performance: Research limitations and future directions. *Journal of Sports Science*, 27: 195-202.

Raglin, J.S., D.M. Koceja, and J.M. Stager. 1996. Mood, neuromuscular function, and performance during training in female swimmers. *Medicine and Science in Sports and Exercise*, 28: 372-377.

Raglin, J.S., W.P. Morgan, and P.J. O'Connor. 1991. Changes in mood states during training in female and male college swimmers. *International Journal of Sports Medicine*, 12: 585-589.

Ripol, B. 1993. The psychology of the swimming taper. *Performance Enhancement*, 1: 22-64.

Rushall, B.S., and J.D. Busch. 1980. Hematological responses to training in elite swimmers. *Canadian Journal of Applied Sports Science,* 5: 164-169.

Saltin, B., and P.D. Gollnick. 1983. Skeletal muscle adaptability: Significance for metabolism and performance. In *Handbook of Physiology: Skeletal Muscle,* edited by L.D. Peachey, R.H. Adrian, and S.R. Geiger. Bethesda, MD: American Physiology Society. pp. 555-631.

Selby, G.B., and E.R. Eichner. 1986. Endurance swimming, intravascular hemolysis, anemia, and iron depletion. *American Journal of Medicine,* 81: 791-794.

Shepley, B., J.D. MacDougall, N. Cipriano, J.R. Sutton, M.A. Tarnopolsky, and G. Coates. 1992. Physiological effects of tapering in highly trained athletes. *Journal of Applied Physiology,* 72: 706-711.

Snyder, A.C., A.E. Jeukendrup, M.K Hesselink, H. Kuipers, and C. Foster. 1993. A physiological/psychological indicator of over-reaching during intensive training. *International Journal of Sports Medicine,* 14: 29-32.

Stein, M., S.E. Keller, and S.J. Schleifer. 1985. Stress and immunomodulation: The role of depression and neuroencocrine function. *Journal of Immunology,* 135: 827-833.

Stewart, A.M., and W.G. Hopkins. 1997. Swimmer's compliance with training prescription. *Medicine and Science in Sports and Exercise,* 29:1389-1392.

Stewart, A.M., W.G. Hopkins, and R.H. Sanders. 1997. Enhancement of seasonal training of competitive swimmers. In *Proceedings of the XII FINA World Sports Medicine Congress,* edited by B.O. Eriksson and L. Gullstrand. Goteborg: Chalmers Reproservice. pp. 269-290.

Stewart, A.M., and W.G. Hopkins. 2000. Seasonal training and performance of competitive swimmers. *Journal of Sports Science,* 18: 873-884.

Stewart, A.M., J.P. Shearman, and W.G. Hopkins. 2000. A rational approach to periodization of swim training. *Sw Times,* 77: 23-26.

Stewart, A.M., D. McGowan, and J. Park. 2002. Seasonal manipulation of swim-training loads (intensity & volume) as constraints on competitive performance. Paper presented at the 12th International Commonwealth Sport Conference, Manchester, England.

Tanaka, H., D.L. Costill, R. Thomas, W.J. Fink, and J.J. Widrick. 1993. Dry-land resistance training for competitive swimming. *Medicine and Science in Sports and Exercise,* 25: 952-959.

Taylor, S.R., G.G. Rogers, and H.S. Driver. 1997. Effects of training volume on sleep, psychological, and selected physiological profiles of elite female swimmers. *Medicine and Science in Sports and Exercise,* 29: 688-693.

Tharp, G.D., and M.W. Barnes. 1990. Reduction of saliva immunoglobulin levels by swim training. *European Journal of Applied Physiology,* 60: 61-64.

Thomas, L., and T. Busso. 2005. A theoretical study of taper characteristics to optimise performance. *Medicine and Science in Sports and Exercise,* 37: 1615-1621.

Thomas, L., I. Mujika, and T. Busso. 2008. A model study of optimal training reduction during pre-event taper in elite swimmers. *Journal of Sport Science,* 26: 643-652.

Thomas, L., I. Mujika, and T. Busso. 2009. Computer simulations assessing the potential performance benefit of a final increase in training during pre-event taper. *Journal of Strength and Conditioning Research,* 23: 1729-1736.

Trappe, S., D. Costill, and R. Thomas. 2001. Effect of swim taper on whole muscle and single fiber contractile properties. *Medicine and Science in Sports and Exercise,* 33: 48-56.

Trinity, J.D., M.D. Pahnke, E.C. Resse, and E.F. Coyle. 2006. Maximal mechanical power during a taper in elite swimmers. *Medicine and Science in Sports and Exercise,* 38: 1643-1649.

Van Handel, P.J., A. Katz, J.P. Troup, J.T. Daniels, and P.W. Bradley. 1988. Oxygen consumption and blood lactic acid response to training and taper. In *Swimming Science V,* edited by B.E. Ungerechts, K. Wilke, and K. Reischle. Champaign, IL: Human Kinetics. pp. 269-275.

Viru, A. 1992. Plasma hormones and physical exercise. *International Journal of Sports Medicine,* 13: 201-209.

Walker, J.L., G.J. Heigenhauser, E. Hultman, and L.L. Spriet. 2000. Dietary carbohydrate, muscle glycogen content, and endurance performance in well-trained women. *Journal of Applied Physiology,* 88: 2151-2158.

Watt, B., and R. Grove. 1993. Perceived exertion: Antecedents and applications. *Sports Medicine,* 15: 225-241.

Wittig, A.F., J.A. Houmard, and D.L. Costill. 1989. Psychological effects during reduced training in distance runners. *International Journal of Sports Medicine,* 10: 97-100.

Yamamoto, Y., Y. Mutoh, and M. Miyashita. 1988. Hematological and biochemical indices during the tapering period of competitive swimmers. In *Swimming Science V,* edited by B.E. Ungerechts, K. Wilke, and K. Reischle. Champaign, IL: Human Kinetics. pp. 269-275.

Zarkadas, P.C., J.B. Carter, and E.W. Banister. 1995. Modelling the effect of taper on performance, maximal oxygen uptake, and the anaerobic threshold in endurance triathletes. *Advances in Experimental Medicine and Biology,* 393: 179-186.

Chapter 11

Burke, L. 2000. Preparation for competition. In *Clinical sports nutrition*. 2nd ed. Ed. L. Burke and V. Deakin, 341–368. New South Wales, Australia: McGraw-Hill.

Gould, D., and K. Dieffenbach. 2002. Psychological characteristics and their development in Olympic champions. *Journal of Applied Sport Psychology* 14 (3): 172–204.

Jeffreys, I. 2008. Warm-up and stretching. In *Essentials of strength training and conditioning*. 3rd ed. Ed. T.R. Baechle and R.W. Earle, 295–324. Champaign, IL: Human Kinetics.

Riewald, S.T. 2002. Mental strategies of elite swimmers. Personal communications.

Salo, D., and S.A. Riewald. 2008. *Complete conditioning for swimming*. Champaign, IL: Human Kinetics.

Sokolovas, G. 2003. Lactate clearance after the race. *Coaches Quarterly* 9 (2): 3–7.

Chapter 12

Arellano, R., P. Brown, J. Cappaert, and R. Nelson. 1994. Analysis of 50-, 100-, and 200-m freestyle swimmers at the 1992 Olympic Games. *Journal of Applied Biomechanics* 10 (2): 189–199.

Arellano, R., S. Pardillo, B. De La Fuente, and F. Garcia. 2000. A system to improve the swimming start technique using force recording, timing and kinetic analyses. In *Proceedings of XVIII International Symposium on Biomechanics in Sports*, ed. Y. Hong, 609–613. Hong Kong: Department of Sports Science and Physical Education, Chinese University of Hong Kong.

Arellano, R., J. Cossor, B. Wilson, J. Chatard, S. Riewald, and B. Mason. 2001. Modelling competitive swimming in different strokes and distances upon regression analysis: A study of the female participants of the Sydney 2000 Olympic Games. In *Proceedings of the XIX International Symposium on Biomechanics in Sports*, ed. J.R. Blackwell and R.H. Sanders, 53–56. San Francisco: University of San Francisco, Exercise and Sport Science Department.

Blanksby, B., L. Nicholson, and B. Elliott. 2002. Biomechanical analysis of the grab, track and handle swimming starts: An intervention study. *Sports Biomechanics* 1 (1): 11–24.

Burkett, B., R. Mellifont, and B. Mason. 2010. The influence of swimming start components for selected Olympic and Paralympic swimmers. *Journal of Applied Biomechanics* 26 (2): 134–141.

Cappaert, J., D. Pease, and J. Troup. 1995. Three-dimensional analysis of the men's 100-m freestyle during the 1992 Olympic Games. Analyse tridimensionnelle du 100 metres hommes nage libre lors des jeux olympiques de 1992. *Journal of Applied Biomechanics* 11 (1): 103–112.

Chatard, J., N. Caudal. J. Cossor, and B. Mason. 2001a. Specific strategy for the medallists versus finalists and semifinalists in the men's 200m breaststroke at the Sydney Olympic Games. In *Proceedings of the XIX International Symposium on Biomechanics in Sports*, ed. J.R. Blackwell and R.H. Sanders, 10–13. San Francisco: University of San Francisco, Exercise and Sport Science Department.

Chatard, J., N. Caudal, J. Cossor, and B. Mason. 2001b. Specific strategy for the medallists versus finalists and semifinalists in the women's 200m breaststroke at the Sydney Olympic Games. In *Proceedings of the XIX International Symposium on Biomechanics in Sports*, ed. J.R. Blackwell and R.H. Sanders, 14–17. San Francisco: University of San Francisco, Exercise and Sport Science Department.

Chatard, J., N. Caudal, J. Cossor, and B. Mason. 2001c. Specific strategy for the medallists versus finalists and semifinalists in the women's 200m individual medley at the Sydney Olympic Games. In *Proceedings of the XIX International Symposium on Biomechanics in Sports*, ed. J.R. Blackwell and R.H. Sanders, 18–21. San Francisco: University of San Francisco, Exercise and Sport Science Department.

Chatard, J., S. Girold, J. Cossor, and B. Mason. 2001d. Specific strategy for the medallists versus finalists and semifinalists in the women's 200m backstroke at the Sydney Olympic Games. In *Proceedings of the XIX International Symposium on Biomechanics in Sports*, ed. J.R. Blackwell and R.H. Sanders, 6–9. San Francisco: University of San Francisco, Exercise and Sport Science Department.

Chatard, J., S. Girold, J. Cossor, and B. Mason. 2001e. Specific strategy for the medallists versus finalists and semifinalists in the men's 200m freestyle at the Sydney Olympic Games. In *Proceedings of the XIX International Symposium on Biomechanics in Sports*, ed. J.R. Blackwell and R.H. Sanders, 57–60. San Francisco: University of San Francisco, Exercise and Sport Science Department.

Cossor, J., and B. Mason. 2001. Swim start performances at the Sydney 2000 Olympic Games. In *Proceedings of the XIX International Symposium on Biomechanics in Sports*, ed. J.R. Blackwell and R.H. Sanders, 70–74. San Francisco: University of San Francisco, Exercise and Sport Science Department.

Costa, M.J., D.A. Marinho, V.M. Reis, A.J. Silva, M.C. Marques, J.A. Bragada, and T.M. Barbosa. 2010. Tracking the performance of world-ranked swimmers. *Journal of Sports Science and Medicine* 9:411–417.

Girold, S., J. Chatard, J. Cossor, and B. Mason. 2001. Specific strategy for the medallists versus finalists and semifinalists in the men's 200m backstroke at the Sydney Olympic Games. In *Proceedings of the XIX International Symposium on Biomechanics in Sports,* ed. J.R. Blackwell and R.H. Sanders, 27–30. San Francisco: University of San Francisco, Exercise and Sport Science Department.

Hellard, P., J. Dekerle, M. Avolos, N. Caudal, M. Knopp, and C. Hausswirth. 2008. Kinematic measures and stroke rate variability in elite female 200-m swimmers in the four swimming techniques: Athens 2004 Olympic semi-finalists and French National 2004 Championship semi-finalists. *Journal of Sports Sciences* 26 (1): 35–46.

Ikuta, Y., B. Mason, and J. Cossor. 2001. A comparison of Japanese finalists to other finalists in the 100m swimming races at the Sydney Olympic Games. In *Proceedings of the XIX International Symposium on Biomechanics in Sports,* ed. J.R. Blackwell and R.H. Sanders, 75–78. San Francisco: University of San Francisco, Exercise and Sport Science Department.

Kennedy, P.W., P. Brown, S.N. Changalur, and R.C. Nelson. 1990. Analysis of male and female Olympic swimmers in the 100-meter events. *International Journal of Sport Biomechanics* 6:187–197.

Maglischo, E.W. 2003. *Swimming fastest.* Champaign, IL: Human Kinetics.

Mason, B. 1997. Biomechanical analysis of swimming starts. In *The AIS International Swim Seminar proceedings [Canberra],* 19–23. RWM Publishing for the Australian College of Sports Education. http://articles.sirc.ca/search.cfm?id=480090.

Mason, B., and J. Cossor. 2001. Swim turn performances at the Sydney 2000 Olympic Games. In *Proceedings of the XIX International Symposium on Biomechanics in Sports,* ed. J.R. Blackwell and R.H. Sanders, 70–74. San Francisco: University of San Francisco, Exercise and Sport Science Department.

Pyne, D.B., C.B. Trewin, and W.G. Hopkins. 2004. Progression and variability of competitive performance of Olympic swimmers. *Journal of Sports Sciences* 22 (7): 613.

Riewald, S. 2001. Assessment of the normalized distance per stroke and swimming efficiency in the 2000 Olympic Games. In *Proceedings of the XIX International Symposium on Biomechanics in Sports,* ed. J.R. Blackwell and R.H. Sanders, 43–47. San Francisco: University of San Francisco, Exercise and Sport Science Department.

Trewin, C.B., W.G. Hopkins, and D.B. Pyne. 2004. Relationship between world-ranking and Olym-pic performance of swimmers. *Journal of Sports Sciences* 22 (4): 339.

Wilson, B., B. Mason, J. Cossor, R. Arellano, J. Chatard, and S. Riewald. 2001. Relationships between stroke efficiency measures and free-style swimming performance: An analysis of freestyle swimming events at the Sydney 2000 Olympics. In *Proceedings of the XIX International Symposium on Biomechanics in Sports,* ed. J.R. Blackwell and R.H. Sanders, 79–82. San Francisco: University of San Francisco, Exercise and Sport Science Department.

Chapter 14

Beals, K.A., and A.K. Hill. 2006. The prevalence of disordered eating, menstrual dysfunction and low bone mineral density among US collegiate athletes. *International Journal of Sport Nutrition and Exercise Metabolism* 16 (1): 1–23.

Beelen, M., L.M. Burke, M.J. Gibala, and J.C. van Loon. 2010. Nutritional strategies to promote post-exercise recovery. *International Journal of Sport Nutrition and Exercise Metabolism* 20 (6): 515–532.

Burke, L.M. 2010. Fasting and recovery from exercise. *British Journal of Sports Medicine* 44 (7): 502–508.

Burke, L.M., A.B. Louks, and N. Broad. 2006. Energy and carbohydrate for training and recovery. *Journal of Sports Science* 24:675–685.

Campbell, B., R.B. Kreider, T. Ziegenfuss, P. La Bounty, M. Roberts, D. Burke, J. Landis, H. Lopez, and J. Antonio. 2007. International Society of Sports Nutrition position stand: Protein and exercise. *Journal of the International Society of Sports Nutrition* 26 (4): 8.

Casa, D.J., C.M. Clarkson, and W.O. Roberts. 2005. American College of Sports Medicine round-table on hydration and physician activity: Consensus statements. *Current Sports Medicine Reports* 4:115–127.

Cheuvront, S.N., R. Carter III, and M.N. Sawka. 2003. Fluid balance and endurance exercise performance. *Current Sports Medicine Reports* 2:202–208.

Cox, G.R., E.M. Broad, M.D. Riley, and L.M. Burke. 2002. Body mass changes and voluntary fluid intakes of elite level water polo players and swimmers. *Journal of Science and Medicine in Sport* 5:183–193.

Cox, G.R., S.A. Clark, A.J. Cox, S.L. Halson, M. Hargreaves, J.A. Hawley, N. Jeacocke, R.J. Snow, W.K. Yeo, and L.M. Burke. 2010. Daily training with high carbohydrate availability increases exogenous carbohydrate oxidation during endurance cycling. *Journal of Applied Physiology* 109 (1): 126–134.

Coyle, E., A. Jeukendrup, A. Wagenmakers, and W. Saris. 1997. Fatty acid oxidation is directly regulated by carbohydrate metabolism during exercise. *American Journal of Physiology* 273:E268–E275.

Currell, K., and A.E. Jeukendrup. 2008. Superior endurance performance with ingestion of multiple transportable carbohydrates. *Medicine and Science in Sports and Exercise* 40:275–281.

Duetz, D., D. Benardot, D. Martin, and M. Cody. 2000. Relationship between energy deficits and body composition in elite female gymnasts and runners. *Medicine and Science in Sports and Exercise* 32 (3): 659–668.

Gleeson, M. 2006. Can nutrition limit exercise-induced immunodepression? *Nutrition Reviews* 64 (3): 119–131.

Harris, J., and F. Benedict. 1919. *A biometric study of basal metabolism in man.* Philadelphia: Lippincott.

Haymes, E. 2006. Iron. In *Sports nutrition: vitamins and trace elements,* ed. J. Driskell and I. Wolinsky, 203–216. New York: CRC/Taylor & Francis.

Heaney, S., H. O'Connor, J. Gifford, and G. Naughton. 2010. Comparison of strategies for assessing nutritional adequacy in elite female athletes' dietary intake. *International Journal of Sport Nutrition and Exercise Metabolism* 20 (3): 245–256.

Holick, M.F. 2007. Vitamin D deficiency. *New England Journal of Medicine* 357:266–281.

Jentjens, R., and A. Jeukendrup. 2003. Determinants of post-exercise glycogen synthesis during short-term recovery. *Sports Medicine* 33:117–144.

Jeukendrup, A. 2007. Carbohydrate supplementation during exercise: Does it help? How much is too much? *Gatorade Sports Science Exchange* 20:1–5.

Knez, W.L., and J.M. Peake. 2010. The prevalence of vitamin supplementation in ultraendurance triathletes. *International Journal of Sport Nutrition and Exercise Metabolism* 20 (6): 507–514.

Koopman, R., W.H. Saris, A.J. Wagenmakers, and L.J. van Loon. 2007. Nutritional interventions to promote post-exercise muscle protein synthesis. *Sports Medicine* 37 (10): 895–906.

Maughan, R.J. 2010. Fasting and sport: An introduction. *British Journal of Sports Medicine* 44 (7): 473–475.

Rodriguez, N.R., M.N. DiMarco, and S. Langley. 2009. American College of Sports Medicine, American Dietetic Association and Dietitians of Canada joint position statement: Nutrition and Athletic Performance. *Medicine and Science in Sports and Exercise* 41 (3): 709–731.

Rowlands, D.S., K. Rossler, R.M. Thorp, D.F. Graham, B.W. Timmons, S.R. Stannard, and M.A. Tarnopolsky. 2008. Effect of dietary protein content during recovery from high-intensity cycling on subsequent performance and markers of stress, inflammation, and muscle damage in well-trained men. *Applied Physiology, Nutrition, and Metabolism* 33 (1): 39–51.

Sawka, M.N., L.M. Burke, E.R. Eichner, R.J. Maughan, S.J. Montain, and N.S. Stachenfeld. 2007. American College of Sports Medicine position stand: Exercise and fluid replacement. *Medicine and Science in Sports and Exercise* 39:377–390.

Stellingwerff, T., and M.K. Boit. 2007. Nutritional strategies to optimize training and racing in middle-distance athletes. *Journal of Sports Science* 25 (suppl. 1): S17–S28.

Turcotte, L. 1999. Role of fats in exercise: Types and quality. *Clinics in Sports Medicine* 18:485–498.

Vieth, R., H. Bischoff-Ferrari, B.J. Boucher, B. Dawson-Hughes, C.F. Garland, R.P. Heaney, M.F. Holick, B.W. Hollis, C. Lamberg-Allardt, J.J. McGrath, A.W. Norman, R. Scragg, S.J. Whiting, W.C. Willett, and A. Zittermann. 2007. The urgent need to recommend an intake of vitamin D that is effective. *American Journal of Clinical Nutrition* 85:649–650.

Willis, K.S., N.J. Peterson, and D.E. Larson-Myer. 2008. Should we be concerned about the vitamin D status of athletes? *International Journal of Sport Nutrition and Exercise Metabolism* 18:204–24.

Wilmore, J.H., D.L. Costill, and W.L. Kenney. 2008. *Physiology of sport and exercise.* 4th ed. Champaign, IL: Human Kinetics.

Woolf, K., and M.M. Manore. 2006. B-vitamins and exercise: Does exercise alter requirements? *International Journal of Sport Nutrition and Exercise Metabolism* 16:453–484.

Chapter 15

American College of Sports Medicine. 2013. *ACSM's guidelines for exercise testing and prescription.* 9th ed. Baltimore: Lippincott Williams & Wilkins.

Archer, D.L. 2002. Evidence that ingested nitrate and nitrite are beneficial to health. *Journal of Food Protection* 65:872–875.

Bailey, S.J., J. Fulford, A. Vanhatalo, P.G. Winyard, J.R. Blackwell, F.J. DiMenna, D.P. Wilkerson, N. Benjamin, and A.M. Jones. 2010. Dietary nitrate supplementation enhances muscle contractile efficiency during knee-extensor exercise in humans. *Journal of Applied Physiology (1985)* 109:135–148.

Bailey, S.J., P. Winyard, A. Vanhatalo, J.R. Blackwell, F.J. DiMenna, D.P. Wilkerson, J. Tarr, N. Benjamin, and A.M. Jones. 2009. Dietary nitrate supplementation reduces the O_2 cost of low-intensity exercise and enhances tolerance to high-intensity exercise in humans. *Journal of Applied Physiology (1985)* 107:1144–1155.

Bailey, S.J., P.G. Winyard, A. Vanhatalo, J.R. Black-well, F.J. DiMenna, D.P. Wilkerson, and A.M. Jones. 2010. Acute L-arginine supplementation reduces the O_2 cost of moderate-intensity exercise and enhances high-intensity exercise tolerance. *Journal of Applied Physiology (1985)* 109:1394–1403.

Baylis, A., D. Cameron-Smith, and L.M. Burke. 2001. Inadvertent doping through supplement use by athletes: Assessment and management of the risk in Australia. *International Journal of Sport Nutrition and Exercise Metabolism* 11:365–383.

Billen, A., and L. Dupont. 2008. Exercise induced bronchoconstriction and sports. *Postgraduate Medical Journal* 84:512–517.

Branch, J.D. 2003. Effect of creatine supplementation on body composition and performance: A meta-analysis. *International Journal of Sport Nutrition and Exercise Metabolism* 13:198–226.

Brigham, D.E., J.L. Beard, R.S. Krimmel, and W.L. Kenney. 1993. Changes in iron status during competitive season in female collegiate swimmers. *Nutrition* 9:418–422.

Burke, L.M. 2008. Caffeine and sports performance. *Applied Physiology, Nutrition, and Metabolism* 33:1319–1334.

caffeineinformer. 2014. www.caffeineinformer.com/.

Chung, W., G. Shaw, M.E. Anderson, D.B. Pyne, P.U. Saunders, D.J. Bishop, and L.M. Burke. 2012. Effect of 10 week beta-alanine supplementation on competition and training performance in elite swimmers. *Nutrients* 4:1441–1453.

Cole, K.J., D.L. Costill, R.D. Starling, B.H. Good-paster, S.W. Trappe, and W.J. Fink. 1996. Effect of caffeine ingestion on perception of effort and subsequent work production. *International Journal of Sport Nutrition* 6:14–23.

Collomp, K., S. Ahmaidi, J.C. Chatard, M. Audran, and C. Prefaut. 1992. Benefits of caffeine ingestion on sprint performance in trained and untrained swimmers. *European Journal of Applied Physiology and Occupational Physiology* 64:377–380.

Costill, D.L., G.P. Dalsky, and W.J. Fink. 1978. Effects of caffeine ingestion on metabolism and exercise performance. *Medicine and Science in Sports* 10:155–158.

Dascombe, B.J., M. Karunaratna, J. Cartoon, B. Fergie, and C. Goodman. 2010. Nutritional supplementation habits and perceptions of elite athletes within a state-based sporting institute. *Journal of Science and Medicine in Sport* 13:274–280.

de Groot, P.C., D.H. Thijssen, M. Sanchez, R. Ellenkamp, and M.T. Hopman. 2010. Ischemic preconditioning improves maximal performance in humans. *European Journal of Applied Physiology* 108:141–146.

Derave, W., M.S. Ozdemir, R.C. Harris, A. Pottier, H. Reyngoudt, K. Koppo, J.A. Wise, and E. Achten. 2007. Beta-alanine supplementation augments muscle carnosine content and attenuates fatigue during repeated isokinetic contraction bouts in trained sprinters. *Journal of Applied Physiology (1985)* 103:1736–1743.

Derave, W., and Y. Taes. 2009. Beware of the pickle: Health effects of nitrate intake. *Journal of Applied Physiology (1985)* 107:1677; author reply 8.

de Silva, A., Y. Samarasinghe, D. Senanayake, and P. Lanerolle. 2010. Dietary supplement intake in national-level Sri Lankan athletes. *International Journal of Sport Nutrition and Exercise Metabolism* 20:15–20.

De Souza, M.J., D.K. Lee, J.L. VanHeest, J.L. Scheid, S.L. West, and N.I. Williams. 2007. Severity of energy-related menstrual disturbances increases in proportion to indices of energy conservation in exercising women. *Fertility and Sterility* 88:971–975.

De Souza, M.J., S.L. West, S.A. Jamal, G.A. Hawker, C.M. Gundberg, and N.I. Williams. 2008. The presence of both an energy deficiency and estrogen deficiency exacerbate alterations of bone metabolism in exercising women. *Bone* 43:140–148.

Dhar, R., C.W. Stout, M.S. Link, M.K. Homoud, J. Weinstock, and N.A. Estes III. 2005. Cardiovascular toxicities of performance-enhancing substances in sports. *Mayo Clinic Proceedings* 80:1307–1315.

Durham, N. 2013. *The East German medal machine.* CBC. www.cbc.ca/archives/categories/sports/drugs-in-sports/going-for-dope-canada-and-drugs-in-sport/the-east-german-medal-machine.html.

Froiland, K., W. Koszewski, J. Hingst, and L. Kopecky. 2004. Nutritional supplement use among college athletes and their sources of information. *International Journal of Sport Nutrition and Exercise Metabolism* 14:104–120.

Fuchs, F., Y. Reddy, and F.N. Briggs. 1970. The interaction of cations with the calcium-binding site of troponin. *Biochimica et Biophysica Acta* 221:407–409.

Gibbs, J.C., N.I. Williams, R.J. Mallinson, J.L. Reed, A. Rickard, and M.J. De Souza. 2013. Effect of high dietary restraint on energy availability and menstrual status. *Medicine and Science in Sports and Exercise.* 45: 1790-1797.

Gibbs, J.C., N.I. Williams, J.L. Scheid, R.J. Toombs, and M.J. De Souza. 2011. The association of a high drive for thinness with energy deficiency and severe menstrual disturbances: Confirmation in a large population of exercising women. *International Journal of Sport Nutrition and Exercise Metabolism.* 21: 280-290.

Gilbert, S. 2010. The biological passport. *Hastings Center Report* 40:18–19.

Gropper, S.S., D. Blessing, K. Dunham, J.M. Barksdale. 2006. Iron status of female collegiate athletes involved in different sports. *Biological Trace Element Research* 109:1–14.

Hoch, A.Z., P. Papanek, A. Szabo, M.E. Widlansky, J.E. Schimke, and D.D. Gutterman. 2011. Association between the female athlete triad and endothelial dysfunction in dancers. *Clinical Journal of Sport Medicine* 21:119–125.

Huang, S.H., K. Johnson, and A.L. Pipe. 2006. The use of dietary supplements and medications by Canadian athletes at the Atlanta and Sydney Olympic Games. *Clinical Journal of Sport Medicine* 16:27–33.

Ivy, J.L., D.L. Costill, W.J. Fink, and R.W. Lower. 1979. Influence of caffeine and carbohydrate feedings on endurance performance. *Medicine and Science in Sports* 11:6–11.

Jean-St-Michel, E., C. Manlhiot, J. Li, M. Tropak, M.M. Michelsen, M.R. Schmidt, B.W. McCrindle, G.D. Wells, and A.N. Redington. 2011. Remote preconditioning improves maximal performance in highly trained athletes. *Medicine and Science in Sports and Exercise* 43:1280–1286.

Judkins, C. and P. Prock. 2012. Supplements and inadvertent doping – How big is the risk to athletes. *Medicine Sport Science.* 59: 143–152.

Juhn, M. 2003. Popular sports supplements and ergogenic aids. *Sports Medicine* 33:921–939.

Kindermann, W. 2007. Do inhaled \gb\₂-agonists have an ergogenic potential in non-asthmatic competitive athletes? *Sports Medicine* 37:95–102.

King, D.S., R. Basekerville, Y. Hellsten, D.S. Senchina, L.M. Burke, S.J. Stear, and L.M. Castell. 2012. A-Z of nutritional supplements: Dietary supplements, sports nutrition foods and ergogenic aids for health and performance. *British Journal of Sports Medicine.* 46(9): 689–690.

Kovacs, E.M., J. Stegen, and F. Brouns. 1998. Effect of caffeinated drinks on substrate metabolism, caffeine excretion, and performance. *Journal of Applied Physiology (1985)* 85:709–715.

Larsen, F.J., E. Weitzberg, J.O. Lundberg, and B. Ekblom. 2007. Effects of dietary nitrate on oxygen cost during exercise. *Acta Physiologica (Oxford, England)* 191:59–66.

Larsen, F.J., E. Weitzberg, J.O. Lundberg, and B. Ekblom. 2010. Dietary nitrate reduces maximal oxygen consumption while maintaining work performance in maximal exercise. *Free Radical Biology and Medicine* 48:342–347.

Lindh, A.M., M.C. Peyrebrune, S.A. Ingham, D.M. Bailey, and J.P. Folland. 2008. Sodium bicarbonate improves swimming performance. *International Journal of Sports Medicine* 29:519–523.

Lun, V., K.A. Erdman, T.S. Fung, and R.A. Reimer. 2012. Dietary supplementation practices in Canadian high-performance athletes. *International Journal of Sport Nutrition and Exercise Metabolism* 22:31–37.

MacIntosh, B.R., and B.M. Wright. 1995. Caffeine ingestion and performance of a 1,500-metre swim. *Canadian Journal of Applied Physiology* 20:168–177.

Maravelias, C., A. Dona, M. Stefanidou, and C. Spiliopoulou. 2005. Adverse effects of anabolic steroids in athletes: A constant threat. *Toxicology Letters* 158:167–175.

Maugahn, R.J. 2013. Quality assurance issues in the use of dietary supplements with special reference to protein supplements. *J Nutr.* 143(11): 1843S–1847S.

Maughan, R.J., D.S. King, and T. Lea. 2004. Dietary supplements. *Journal of Sports Science* 22:95–113.

Mero, A.A., K.L. Keskinen, M.T. Malvela, and J.M. Sallinen. 2004. Combined creatine and sodium bicarbonate supplementation enhances interval swimming. *Journal of Strength and Conditional Research* 18:306–310.

Momaya, A., M. Fawal, and R. Estes. 2015. Performance-enhancing substances in sports: A review of the literature. *Sports Medicine.* Epub ahead of print.

Montagnana, M., G. Lippi, M. Franchini, G. Banfi, and G.C. Guidi. 2008. Sudden cardiac death in young athletes. *Internal Medicine* 47:1373–1378.

Nakamaru, Y., and A. Schwartz. 1972. The influence of hydrogen ion concentration on calcium binding and release by skeletal muscle sarcoplasmic reticulum. *Journal of General Physiology* 59:22–32.

Nattiv, A., A.B. Loucks, M.M. Manore, C.F. Sanborn, J. Sundgot-Borgen, and M.P. Warren. 2007. American College of Sports Medicine position stand: The female athlete triad. *Medicine and Science in Sports and Exercise* 39:1867–1882.

Nystad, W., J. Harris, and J.S. Borgen. 2000. Asthma and wheezing among Norwegian elite athletes. *Medicine and Science in Sports and Exercise* 32:266–270.

O'Donnell, E., J.M. Goodman, and P.J. Harvey. 2011. Clinical review: Cardiovascular consequences of ovarian disruption: A focus on functional hypothalamic amenorrhea in physically active women. *Journal of Clinical Endocrinology and Metabolism* 96:3638–3648.

Outram, S. and B. Stewart. 2015. Doping through supplement use: A review of the available empirical data. *International Journal of Sport Nutrition Exercise Metabolism.* 25(1): 54–59.

Paschoal, V.C., and O.M. Amancio. 2004. Nutritional status of Brazilian elite swimmers. *International Journal of Sport Nutrition and Exercise Metabolism* 14:81–94.

Peyrebrune, M.C., K. Stokes, G.M. Hall, and M.E. Nevill. 2005. Effect of creatine supplementation on training for competition in elite swimmers. *Medicine and Science in Sports and Exercise* 37:2140–2147.

Powers, S.K., and E.T. Howley. 2012. *Exercise physiology: Theory and application to fitness and performance.* 8th ed. New York: McGraw Hill.

Przyklenk, K., and P. Whittaker. 2011. Remote ischemic preconditioning: Current knowledge, unresolved questions, and future priorities. *Journal of Cardiovascular Pharmacology and Therapeutics* 16:255–259.

Reed, J.L., J.L. Bowell, B.R. Hill, B.A. Williams, M.J. De Souza, and N.I. Williams. 2011. Exercising women with menstrual disturbances consume low energy dense foods and beverages. *Applied Physiology, Nutrition, and Metabolism* 36:382–394.

Reed, J.L., M.J. De Souza, R.J. Mallinson, J.L. Scheid, and N.I. Williams. 2015. Availability discriminates clinical menstrual status in exercising females. *Journal of the International Society of Sports Nutrition.* 12: 11.

Reed, J.L., M.J. De Souza, and N.I. Williams. 2013. Changes in energy availability across the season in Division I female soccer players. *Journal of Sports Science* 31:314–324.

Rodriguez, N.R., N.M. Di Marco, and S. Langley. 2009. American College of Sports Medicine position stand: Nutrition and athletic performance. *Medicine and Science in Sports and Exercise* 41:709–731.

Rundell, K.W., and D.M. Jenkinson. 2002. Exercise-induced bronchospasm in the elite athlete. *Sports Medicine* 32:583–600.

Sajber, D., J. Rodek, Y. Escalante, D. Olujic, and D. Sekulic. 2013. Sport nutrition and doping factors in swimming: Parallel analysis among athletes and coaches. *Collegium Antropologicum* 37 (suppl. 2): 179–186.

Sawka, M.N., M.J. Joyner, D.S. Miles, R.J. Robertson, L.L. Spriet, and A.J. Young. 1996. American College of Sports Medicine position stand: The use of blood doping as an ergogenic aid. *Medicine and Science in Sports and Exercise* 28:i–viii.

Silva, A.J., V. Machado Reis, L. Guidetti, F. Bessone Alves, P. Mota, J. Freitas, and C. Baldari. 2007. Effect of creatine on swimming velocity, body composition and hydrodynamic variables. *Journal of Sports Medicine and Physical Fitness* 47:58–64.

Slater, G., B. Tan, and K.C. Teh. 2003. Dietary supplementation practices of Singaporean athletes. *International Journal of Sport Nutrition and Exercise Metabolism* 13:320–332.

Sottas, P.E., N. Robinson, O. Rabin, and M. Saugy. 2011. The athlete biological passport. *Clinical Chemistry* 57:969–976.

Tesch, P., B. Sjodin, A. Thorstensson, and J. Karlsson. 1978. Muscle fatigue and its relation to lactate accumulation and LDH activity in man. *Acta Physiologica Scandinavica* 103:413–420.

Thompson, J., M. Manore, and J. Sheeshka. 2005. *Nutrition: A functional approach.* 2nd Canadian ed. Toronto, Ontario: Pearson.

Vanhatalo, A., S.J. Bailey, J.R. Blackwell, F.J. DiMenna, T.G. Pavey, D.P. Wilkerson, N. Benjamin, P.G. Winyard, and A.M. Jones. 2010. Acute and chronic effects of dietary nitrate supplementation on blood pressure and the physiological responses to moderate-intensity and incremental exercise. *American Journal of Physiology. Regulatory, Integrative and Comparative Physiology* 299:R1121–R1131.

Vanheest, J.L., C.D. Rodgers, C.E. Mahoney, and M.J. De Souza. 2014. Ovarian suppression impairs sport performance in junior elite female swimmers. *Medicine and Science in Sports and Exercise* 46:156–166.

Volpe, S.L. 2007. Micronutrient requirements for athletes. *Clinics in Sports Medicine* 26:119–130.

Wolfarth, B., J.C. Wuestenfeld, and W. Kindermann. 2010. Ergogenic effects of inhaled beta2-agonists in non-asthmatic athletes. *Endocrinology and Metabolism Clinics of North America* 39:75–87, ix.

World Anti-Doping Agency. 2005. Gene doping. *Play True* 1:2–12.

World Anti-Doping Agency. 2009. World anti-doping code. Montreal, QC.

World Anti-Doping Agency. 2013. Athlete biological passport. www.wada-ama.org/en/Science-Medicine/Athlete-Biological-Passport/.

World Anti-Doping Agency. 2014. Gene doping. www.wada-ama.org/en/Science-Medicine/Science-topics/Gene-Doping/.

Zenic, N., M. Peric, N.G. Zubcevic, Z. Ostojic, and L. Ostojic. 2010. Comparative analysis of substance use in ballet, dance sport, and synchronized swimming: Results of a longitudinal study. *Medical Problems of Performing Artists* 25:75–81.

Chapter 16

Atkinson, J. 1958. Towards experimental analysis of human motivation in terms of motives, expectancies, and incentives. In *Motives in fantasy, action and society,* ed. J. Atkinson, 288–305. Princeton, NJ; Von Nostrand.

Duran, G. 1981. There's a S.M.A.R.T. way to write management goals and objectives. *Management Review* 70(11).

Goodhart, D. 1986. The effects of positive and negative thinking on performance in an achievement situation. *Journal of Personality and Social Psychology* 51:117–124.

Gould, D., R. Eckland, and S. Jackson. 1992. 1988 U.S. Olympic wrestling excellence: Thoughts and affect occurring during competition. *Sport Psychologist* 6:383–402.

Hardy, L., and J. Fazey. 1987. The inverted U hypothesis: A catastrophe for sport psychology? Paper presented at the annual conference of the North American Society for the Psychology of Sport and Physical Activity. June 1987.

Hardy, L., and G. Parfitt. 1991. Catastrophic model of anxiety and performance. *British Journal of Psychology* 82:163–178.

Hardy, L., K. Gammage, and C. Hall. 2001. A description of athlete self-talk. *Sport Psychologist* 15:306–318.

Lewin, K., T. Dembo, L. Testinger, and P. Sears. 1944. Level of aspiration. In *Personality and the behavior disorders*. Vol. 1. Ed. J. Hunt. New York: Ronald Press.

Locke, E. 1967. Performance goals as determinants of performance and boredom. *Journal of Applied Psychology* 51 (12): 120–130.

Locke, E., and G. Latham. 2002. Building a practically useful theory of goal setting and motivation. *American Psychologist* 57 (9): 705–717.

Newton, I. 1729. *Mathematical principles of natural philosophy*. Trans. John Machin. University of California Press (1960).

Ryan, T.A. 1970. *Intentional behavior*. New York: Ronald Press

Van Raalte, J., B. Brewer, P. Rivera, and A. Petitpas. 1994. The relationship between observable self-talk and competitive junior tennis players' match performance. *Journal of Sport and Exercise Psychology* 16:400–415.

Weinberg, R., J. Smith, S. Jackson, and D. Gould. 1984. Effects of association, dissociation, and self-talk strategies on endurance performance. *Canadian Journal of Applied Sport Sciences* 9:25–32.

Yerkes, R., and J. Dodson. 1908. The relationship of strength of stimulus to rapidity of habit formation. *Journal of Comparative Neurology and Psychology* 18:459–482.

Chapter 17

Balyi, I., and C. Williams. 2010. *Coaching the young developing performer: Tracking physical growth and development to inform coaching programmes*. Leeds, UK: Coachwise.

Baker, J., and J. Côté. 2006. Shifting training requirements during athlete development: Deliberate practice, deliberate play and other sport involvement in the acquisition of sport expertise. In *Essential processes for attaining peak performance*, ed. D. Hackfort and G. Tenenbaum, 92–109. Oxford: Meyer & Meyer Sport.

Baxter-Jones, A.D.G. 1995. Growth and development of young athletes: Should competition levels be age related? *Sports Medicine* 20 (2): 59–64.

Baxter-Jones, A.D.G., and L.B. Sherar. 2007. Growth and maturation. In *Paediatric Exercise Physiology*, ed. N. Armstrong. London: Elsevier.

Beunen, G. 2001. Physical growth, maturation and exercise. In *Kinanthropometry and exercise physiology laboratory manual: Tests, procedures and data. Volume 1 Anthropometry*, ed. R. Eston and T. Reilly, 73–100. New York: Routledge.

Beunen, G., and R. Malina. 2008. Growth and biological maturation: Relevance to athletic performance. In *The young athlete—the encyclopedia of sports medicine*, ed. H. Hebestreit and O. Bar-Or, 3–17. Malden, MA: Blackwell.

Bloom, B. 1985. *Developing talent in young people*. New York: Ballantine Books.

Bompa, T.O. 2000. *Total training for young champions*. Champaign, IL: Human Kinetics.

Bruner, M.W., M.A. Eys, and J. Turnnidge. 2013. Peer and group influences in youth sport. In *Conditions of children's talent development in sport*, ed. J. Côté and R. Lidor, 85–98. Morgantown, WV: Fitness Information Technology, West Virginia University.

Cassidy, T., R. Jones, and P. Potrac. 2004. *Understanding sports coaching: The social, cultural and pedagogical foundations of coaching practice*. London: Routledge.

Côté, J., M.W. Bruner, K. Erickson, L. Strachan, and J. Fraser-Thomas. 2010. Athlete development and coaching. In *Sport coaching: Professionalism and practice*, ed. J. Lyle and C. Cushion, 63–83. Oxford, UK: Elsevier.

Côté, J., and R. Lidor. 2013. Early talent development in sport: A multifaceted approach. In *Conditions of children's talent development in sport*, ed. J. Côté & R. Lidor, 1–8. Morgantown, WV: Fitness Information Technology, West Virginia University.

Eklund, R.C., and D. Gould. 2008. Emotional stress and anxiety in the child and adolescent athlete. In *The young athlete: The encyclopedia of sports medicine*, ed. H. Hebestreit and O. Bar-Or, 319–334. Malden, MA: Blackwell Publishing.

Edgar, S., and P. O'Donoghue. 2005. Season of birth distribution of elite tennis players. *Journal of Sports Sciences* 23 (10): 1013–1020.

Hambrick, D.Z., F.L. Oswald, E.M. Altmann, F.G. Meinz, F. Gobet, and G. Campitellli. 2013. Deliberate practice: Is that all it takes to become an expert? *Intelligence* 45:34–45.

Herman-Giddens, M.E., J. Steffes, D. Harris, E. Slora, M. Hussey, S.A. Dowshen, R. Wasserman, J.R. Serwint, L. Smitherman, and E.O. Reiter. 2012. Secondary sexual characteristics in boys: Data from the pediatric research in office settings network. *Pediatrics* 130 (5): e1058–e1068.

MacNamara, Á., A. Button, and D. Collins. 2010. The role of psychological characteristics in facilitating the pathway to elite performance. Part 2: Examining environmental and stage related differences in skills and behaviours. *Sport Psychologist* 24 (1): 74–96.

Malina, R., and G. Beunen. 2008. Growth and maturation: Methods of monitoring. In *The young athlete: The encyclopedia of sports medicine*, ed. H. Hebestreit and O. Bar-Or, 430–442. Malden, MA: Blackwell.

Malina, R.M., C. Bouchard, and O. Bar-Or. 2004. *Growth, maturation and physical activity.* UK: Human Kinetics.

Martindale, R.J.J., and P. Mortimer. 2011. Talent development environments: Key considerations for effective practice. In *Performance psychology: A practitioners guide*, ed. D. Collins, A. Button, and H. Richards, 65–84. Oxford: Elsevier.

Morris, J.G., and M.E. Nevill. 2006. *A sporting chance. Enhancing opportunities for high-level sporting performance: Influence of "relative age."* Produced for Sport Nation, Institute of Youth Sport, Loughborough University, UK.

Musch, J., and S. Grondin. 2001. Unequal competition as an impediment to personal development: A review of the relative age effect. *Developmental Review* 21 (2): 147–167.

Pankhurst, A.E., and D. Collins. 2013. Talent identification and development: The need for coherence between research, system and process. *Quest* 65 (1): 83–97.

Rogol, A.D. 2008. Delayed puberty in girls and primary and secondary amenorrhea. In *The young athlete: The encyclopedia of sports medicine*, ed. H. Hebestreit and O. Bar-Or, 227–242. Malden, MA: Blackwell.

Weiss, M.R., J.A. Bhalla, and M.S. Price. 2008. Developing positive self-perceptions through youth sport participation. In *The young athlete: The encyclopedia of sports medicine*, ed. H. Hebestreit and O. Bar-Or, 302–318. Malden, MA: Blackwell.

Willams, C.A. 2007. Exercise and environmental conditions. In *Paediatric exercise physiology*, ed. N. Armstrong, 235–273. London: Elsevier.

Chapter 18

Bak, K., and P. Fauno. 1997. Clinical findings in competitive swimmers. *American Journal of Sports Medicine* 25 (2): 254–260.

Bedi, A., and S.A. Rodeo. 2009. Os acromiale as a cause for shoulder pain in a competitive swimmer: A case report. *Sports Health* 1 (2): 121–124.

Brushoj, C., K. Bak, H.V. Johannsen, and P. Fauno. 2007. Swimmers' painful shoulder arthroscopic findings and return rate to sports. *Scandinavian Journal of Medicine and Science in Sports* 17:373–377.

Echlin, P.S., and J.E. Michaelson. 2006. Adolescent butterfly swimmer with bilateral subluxing sternoclavicular joints. *British Journal of Sports Medicine* 40 (4): e12.

Fraxino de Almeida, D., and R.D. Meyer. 2007. True neurogenic thoracic outlet syndrome in a competitive swimmer. *Arquivos de Neuro-psiquiatria* 65 (4-B): 1245–1248.

Gregory, P.L., A.C. Biswas, and M.E. Batt. 2002. Musculoskeletal problems of the chest wall in athletes. *Sports Medicine* 32:235–250.

Heinlein, S.A., and A.J. Cosgarea. 2010. Biomechanical consideration in the competitive swimmer's shoulder. *Sports Health* 2 (6): 519–25.

Jobe, F.W., R. S. Kvitne, and C.E. Giangarra. 1989. Shoulder pain in the overhand or throwing athlete. The relationship of anterior instability and rotator cuff impingement. *Orthopedic Reviews* 18 (9): 963–975.

Kaneoka, K., K. Shimizu, M. Hangai, T. Okuwaki, N. Mamizuka, M. Sakane, and N. Ochiai. 2007. Lumbar intervertebral disk degeneration in elite competitive swimmers: A case control study. *American Journal of Sports Medicine* 35 (8): 1341–1345.

Katayama, N., T. Ishikawa, K. Kaneoka, Y. Mutoh, M. Ariyoshi, and M. Sonoda. 2000. Traumas and overuse injuries in elite swimmers. *Japanese Journal of Orthopedic Sports Medicine* 20:34–41.

Katirji, B., and R.W. Hardy. 1995. Classic neurogenic thoracic outlet syndrome in a competitive swimmer: A true scalenus anticus syndrome. *Muscle & Nerve* 18:229–233.

Kennedy, J.C., and R. Hawkins. 1974. Swimmers shoulder. *Physician Sports Medicine* 2 (4): 34–38.

Kennedy, J., R. Hawkins, and W. Krissof. 1978. Orthopaedic manifestations of swimming. *American Journal of Sports Medicine* 6:309–322.

McMaster, W.C., A. Roberts, and T. Stoddard. 1998. A correlation between shoulder laxity and interfering pain in competitive swimmers. *American Journal of Sports Medicine* 26 (1): 83–86.

Nyska, M., N. Constantini, M. Cale-Benzoor, Z. Back, G. Kahn, and G. Mann. 2000. Spondylolysis as a cause of low back pain in swimmers. *International Journal of Sports Medicine* 21:375–379.

Pink, M.M., and J.E. Tibone. 2000. The painful shoulder in the swimming athlete. *Orthopedic Clinics of North America* 31 (2): 247–261.

Richardson, A.B. 1999. Thoracic outlet syndrome in aquatic athletes. *Clinics in Sports Medicine* 18 (2): 361–378.

Richardson, A.B., F.W. Jobe, and H.R. Collins. 1980. The shoulder in competitive swimming. *American Journal of Sports Medicine* 8 (3): 159–163.

Rodeo, S.A. 1999. Knee pain in competitive swimming. *Clinics in Sports Medicine* 18 (2): 379–387.

Rodeo, S.A. 2004. Swimming. In *The shoulder and the overhead athlete*, ed. S.G. Krishnan, R.J. Hawkins, and R.F. Warren. Philadelphia: Lippincott, Williams, and Wilkins.

Rovere, G., and A. Nichols. 1985. Frequency, associated factors, and treatment of breaststroker's knee in competitive swimming. *American Journal of Sports Medicine* 13:99–104.

Sanders, R.J., and N.M. Rao. 2007. Pectoralis minor obstruction of the axillary vein: Report of six patients. *Journal of Vascular Surgery* 45 (6): 1206–1211.

Sein, M.L., J. Walton, J. Linklater, R. Appleyard, B. Kirkbride, D. Kuah, and G.A. Murrell. 2010. Shoulder pain in elite swimmers: Primarily due to swim-volume-induced supraspinatus tendinopathy. *British Journal of Sports Medicine* 44:105–113.

Schenk, T.J., and J.J. Brems. 1998. Multidirectional instability of the shoulder: Pathophysiology, diagnosis, and management. *Journal of the American Academy of Orthopedic Surgeons* 6:65–72.

Seiler, J.G., K.E. Hammond, S.H. Payne, and R. Ivy. 2011. Bilateral exertional compartment syndrome of the forearm: Evaluation and endoscopic treatment in an elite swimmer. *Journal of Surgical Orthopaedic Advances* 20 (2): 126–131.

Taimela, S., U.M. Kujala, and S. Orava. 1995. Two consecutive rib stress fractures in a female competitive swimmer. *Clinical Journal of Sport Medicine* 5 (4): 254–256.

Udermann, B.E., D.G. Cavanaugh, M.H. Gibson, S.T. Doberstein, J.M. Mayer, and S.R. Murray. 2005. Slipping rib syndrome in a collegiate swimmer: A case report. *Journal of Athletic Training* 40 (2): 120–122.

Vogel, C.M., and J.E. Jensen. 1985. "Effort" thrombosis of the subclavian vein in a competitive swimmer. *American Journal of Sports Medicine* 13 (4): 269–272.

Zemek, M.J., and D.J. Magee. 1996. Comparison of glenohumeral joint laxity in elite and recreational swimmers. *Clinical Journal of Sport Medicine* 6 (1): 40–47.

Chapter 19

American Psychiatric Association. 2000. American Psychiatric Association Task Force on DSM-IV. *Diagnostic and statistical manual of mental disorders: DSM-IV-TR*. 4th ed., 538–595. Washington DC: American Psychiatric Association.

Beals, K. 2003. Eating disorder and menstrual dysfunction screening, education and treatment program: Survey results from NCAA Division 1 Schools. *Physician and Sport Medicine* 31:33–38.

Beck, K. 2000. Infectious diseases in sports. *Medicine and Science in Sports and Exercise* 32:431–438.

Bennell, K., G. Matheson, W. Meeuwisse, and P. Brukner. 1999. Risk factors for stress fractures. *Sports Medicine* 28 (2): 91–122.

Brackenridge, C. 2008. Coach swimmer interaction: Traps, pitfalls and how to avoid them. Sixteenth FINA World Sports Medicine Congress. *Journal of Sport Science* 26:1–3.

Carter, J., D. Steward, and C. Fairburn. 2001. Eating disorder examination questionnaire: Norms for young adolescent girls. *Behaviour Research and Therapy* 39:625–632.

Corrado, D., C. Basso, A. Pavei, P. Michieli, M. Schiavon, and G. Thiene. 2006. Trends in sudden cardiovascular death in young competitive athletes after implementation of a preparticipation screening program. *Journal of the American Medical Association* 296 (13): 1593–1601.

Cotton, A., C. Ball, and P. Robinson. 2003. Four simple questions can help screen for eating disorders. *Journal of General Internal Medicine* 18:53–56.

Drinkwater, B., S. Nilson, C. Ott, and H. Chestnut. 1986. Bone mineral density after resumption of menses in amenorrheic athletes. *Journal of the American Medical Association* 256:380–382.

Fallon, K. 2004. Utility of hematological and iron-related screening in elite athletes. *Clinical Journal of Sport Medicine* 14:145–152.

Fitch, K.D., M. Sue–Chu, S.D. Anderson, L.P. Boulet, R.J. Hancox, D.C. McKenzie, V. Backer, K.W. Rundell, J.M. Alonso, P. Kippelen, J.M. Cummiskey, A. Garnier, and A. Ljungqvist. 2008. Asthma and the elite athlete: Summary of the International Olympic Committee's Consensus Conference, Lausanne, Switzerland, January 22–24, 2008. *Journal of Allergy and Clinical Immunology* 122 (2): 254–260.

Garner, D. 2004. *Eating disorder inventory-3 (EDI-3)*. Lutz, FL: Psychological Assessment Resources.

Helenius, I, P. Rytilä, S. Sarna, A. Lumme, M. Helenius, V. Remes, and T. Haahtela. 2002. Effect of continuing or finishing high-level sports on airway inflammation, bronchial hyperresponsiveness, and asthma: A 5-year prospective follow-up study of 42 highly trained swimmers. *Journal of Allergy and Clinical Immunology* 109 (6): 962–968.

International Olympic Committee. 2005. *IOC consensus statement on the female athlete triad.* www.olympic.org/content/news/media-resources/manual-news/1999-2009/2005/11/09/ioc-consensus-statement-on-the-female-athlete-triad/.

International Olympic Committee. 2008. IOC consensus statement on sexual harassment and abuse in sport. Understanding and preventing sexual harassment and abuse in sport: Implications for the sport psychology profession. *International Journal of Sport and Exercise Psychology* 6 (4): 442–449.

International Olympic Committee. 2010. *Nutrition for athletes: A practical guide to eating for health and performance.* International Olympic Committee.

Junge, A., L. Engebretsen, M.L. Mountjoy, J.M. Alonso, P.A. Renström, M.J. Aubry, and J. Dvorak. 2009. Sports injuries during the Summer Olympic Games 2008. *American Journal of Sports Medicine* 37 (11): 2165–2172.

Kohrt, W.M., S.A. Bloomfield, K.D. Little, M.E. Nelson, and V.R. Yingling. 2004. American College of Sports Medicine position stand: Physical activity and bone health. *Medicine and Science in Sports and Exercise* 36 (11): 1985–1996.

Luck, A.J., J.F. Morgan, F. Reid, A. O'Brien, J. Brunton, C. Price, L, Perry, and J.H. Lacey. 2002. The SCOFF questionnaire and clinical interview for eating disorders in general practice: Comparative study. *British Medical Journal* 325 (7367): 755–756.

Ljungqvist, A., P.J. Jenoure, L. Engebretsen, J.M. Alonso, R. Bahr, A.F. Clough, G. de Bondt, J. Dvorak, R. Maloley, G. Matheson, W. Meeuwisse, E.J. Meijboom, M. Mountjoy, A. Pelliccia, M. Schwellnus, D. Sprumont, P. Schamasch, J.B. Gautheir, and C. Dubi. 2009. The International Olympic Committee (IOC) consensus statement on periodic health evaluation of elite athletes, March 2009. *Clinical Journal of Sport Medicine* 19 (5): 347–365.

Meeusen, R., M. Duclos, C. Foster, A. Fry, M. Gleeson, D. Nieman, J. Raglin, G. Rietjens, J. Steinacker, and A. Urhausen. 2013. Prevention, diagnosis and treatment of the overtraining syndrome: Joint consensus statement of the European College of Sport Science and the American College of Sports Medicine. *Medicine and Science in Sports and Exercise* 45 (1): 186–205.

Mountjoy, M. 2008. Weight control strategies of Olympic athletes striving for leanness: What can be done to make sport a safer environment? *Clinical Journal of Sport Medicine* 17 (1): 2–4.

Mountjoy, M., N. Armstrong, L. Bizzini, C. Blimkie, J. Evans, D. Gerrard, J. Hangen, K. Knoll, L. Micheli, P. Sangenis, and W. van Mechelen. 2008. IOC consensus statement: Training the elite child athlete. *British Journal of Sports Medicine* 42 (3): 163–164.

Mountjoy, M., A. Junge, J.M. Alonso, L. Engebretsen, I. Dragan, D. Gerrard, M. Kouidri, E. Leubs, F. Moradi Shahpar, and J. Dvorak. 2010a. Injury prevention in elite international sport: Are we missing an important performance parameter in surveillance? *Clinical Journal of Sport Medicine* 20 (3): 223–224.

Mountjoy, M., A. Junge, J.M. Alonso, L. Engebretsen, I. Dragan, D. Gerrard, M. Kouidri, E. Leubs, F.M. Shahpar, and J. Dvorak. 2010b. Sports injuries and illnesses in the 2009 FINA World Aquatic Championships (Aquatics). *British Journal of Sports Medicine* 44 (7): 522–527.

Nattiv, A., A.B. Loucks, M.M. Manore, C.F. Sanborn, J. Sundgot-Borgen, and M.P. Warren. 2007. American College of Sports Medicine position stand: The female athlete triad. *Medicine and Science in Sport and Exercise* 39 (10): 1867–1882.

Peeling, P., B. Dawson, C. Goodman, G. Landers, and D. Trinder. 2008. Athletic induced iron deficiency: New insights into the role of inflammation, cytokines and hormones. *European Journal of Applied Physiology* 103 (4): 381–391.

Pipe, A., B. Corrigan, and M. Mountjoy. 2005. The use of medications, supplements and ergogenic aids by elite competitors at the 2003 World FINA Swim Championships. *Clinical Journal of Sport Medicine* 15 (5): 394.

Rumall, J., and C. Lebrun. 2004. Preparticipation physical examination: Selected issues for the female athlete. *Clinical Journal of Sport Medicine* 14 (3): 153–160.

Sanborn, C.F., M. Horea, B.J. Siemers, and K.I. Dieringer. 2000. Disordered eating and the female athlete triad. *Clinics in Sports Medicine* 19 (2): 199–213.

Spence, L., W.J. Brown, D.B. Pyne, M.D. Nissen, T.P. Sloots, J.G. McCormack, A.S. Locke, and P.A. Fricker. 2007. Incidence, etiology, and symptomatology of upper respiratory illness in elite athletes. *Medicine and Science in Sport and Exercise* 39 (4): 577–586.

Sundgot-Borgen, J., and M.K. Torstveit. 2004. Prevalence of eating disorders in elite athletes is higher than in the general population. *Clinical Journal of Sport Medicine* 14 (1): 25–32.

Thompson, R., and R. Sherman. 2010. *Eating disorders in sport.* New York: Routledge/Taylor & Francis.

Torstveit, M.K., and J. Sundgot-Borgen. 2005. Bone mineral density in athletes. *British Journal of Sports Medicine* 39:282–287.

van Mechelen, W., H. Hlobil, and H.C. Kemper. 1992. Incidence, severity, aetiology and prevention of sports injuries. A review of concepts. *Sports Medicine* 14:82–99.

World Anti-Doping Agency. 2015. *World anti-doping code.* www.wada-ama.org/en/World-Anti-Doping-Program/Sports-and-Anti-Doping-Organizations/The-Code/.

World Anti-Doping Agency. 2013. *The 2014 prohibited list international standard.* http://www.wada-ama.org/en/World-Anti-Doping-Program/Sports-and-Anti-Doping-Organizations/International-Standards/Prohibited-List/.

Yager, J. 2007. Assessment and determination of initial treatment approaches for patients with eating disorders. In *Clinical Manual of Eating Disorders,* ed. J. Yager and P. Powers, 31–77. Arlington, VT: American Psychiatric.

Chapter 20

Baechle, T.R., and R.W. Earle. 2008. *Essentials of strength training and conditioning.* 3rd ed. Champaign, IL: Human Kinetics.

Bak, K. 2010. The practical management of swimmer's painful shoulder: Etiology, diagnosis, and treatment. *Clinical Journal of Sport Medicine* 20 (5): 386–390.

Bardzukas, A., S. Spry, J.M. Cappaert, and J.P. Troup. 1992. Developmental changes in muscle size and power of elite age group swimmers. In *Swimming science VI,* ed. D. McLaren, T. Reilly, and A. Lees, 359–364. London: E&FN Spon.

Blanksby, B., and J. Gregor. 1981. Anthropometric, strength, and physiological changes in male and female swimmers with progressive resistance training. *Australian Journal of Sport Science* 1:3–6.

Bulgakova, N., A. Vorontsov, and T. Fomichenko. 1990. Improving the technical preparedness of young swimmers by using strength training. *Soviet Sports Review* 25:102–104.

Cossor, J., B. Blanksby, and B. Elliot. 1999. The influence of plyometric training on the freestyle tumble turn. *Journal of Science and Medicine in Sport* 2:106–116.

Costill, D. 1999. Training adaptations for optimal performance. In *Biomechanics and medicine in swimming VIII,* ed. K.L. Keskinen, P.V. Komi, and A.P. Hollander, 381–390. Jyväskylä, Finland: University of Jyväskylä.

Council on Sports Medicine and Fitness. 2008. Strength training by children and adolescents. *Pediatrics* 121:835–840.

Faigenbaum, A.D. 2012. Youth strength training: Facts and fallacies. www.acsm.org/access-public-information/articles/2012/01/13/youth-strength-training-facts-and-fallacies.

Faigenbaum, A.D., W.J. Kraemer, J.R. Cameron, I.J. Blimkie, L.J. Micheli, M. Nitka, and T.W. Rowland. 2009. Youth resistance training: Updated position statement paper from the National Strength and Conditioning Association. *Journal of Strength and Conditioning Research* 23 (suppl. 5): S60–S79.

Faigenbaum, A.D., and L.J. Micheli. 2013. *ACSM current comment: Youth resistance training.* www.acsm.org/docs/current-comments/youth-strengthtraining.pdf.

Garrido, N., D.A. Marinho, T.M. Barbosa, A.M. Costa, A.J. Silva, J.A. Perez-Turpin, and M.C. Marques. 2010. Relationships between dry land strength, power variables and short sprint performances in young competitive swimmers. *Journal of Human Sport and Exercise* 5 (11): 240–249.

Girold, S., P. Calmels, D. Maurin, N. Milhau, and J.C. Chatard. 2006. Assisted and resisted sprint training in swimming. *Journal of Strength and Conditioning Research* 20 (3): 547–554.

Girold, S., D. Maurin, B. Gugue, J.C. Chatard, and G. Millet. 2007. Effects of dry-land vs. resisted- and assisted-sprint exercises on swimming sprint performances. *Journal of Strength and Conditioning Research* 21 (2): 599–605.

Kibler, W.B. 1998. The role of the scapula in athletic shoulder function. *American Journal of Sports Medicine* 26 (2): 325–337.

Kibler, W.B., J. Press, and A. Sciascia. 2006. The role of core stability in athletic function. *Sports Medicine* 36:189–198.

Kondraske, G.V. 2008. Establishing the relationship between basic subsystem performance capacities and performance in functional tasks. Poster presented at the 2008 Annual Meeting of the National Center for Human Performance. Houston, TX.

Kraemer, W.J., and S.J. Fleck. 2005. *Strength training for young athletes.* 2nd ed. Champaign, IL: Human Kinetics.

Maglischo, E.W., C.W. Maglischo, D.J. Zier, and T.R. Santos. 1995. The effect of sprint-resisted swimming on stroke mechanics. *Journal of Swimming Research* 1:27–33.

McLeod, I. 2010. *Swimming anatomy.* Champaign, IL: Human Kinetics.

McMaster, W.C. 1999. Shoulder injuries in competitive swimmers. *Clinics in Sports Medicine* 18 (2): 349–359.

Miyashita, M., and H. Kanehisa. 1983. Effects of isokinetic, isotonic and swim training on swimming performance. In *Biomechanics and medicine in swimming,* ed. A.P. Hollander, P.A.

Huijing, and G. deGroot, 329–334. Champaign, IL: Human Kinetics.

Rodeo, S.A. 2004. Swimming. In *The shoulder and the overhead athlete*, ed. S.G. Krishnan, R.J. Hawkins, and R.F. Warren, 349–362. Philadelphia: Lippincott, Williams and Wilkins.

Salo, D., and S.A. Riewald. 2008. *Complete conditioning for swimming*. Champaign, IL: Human Kinetics.

Scovazzo, M.L., A. Browne, M. Pink, F.W. Jobe, and J. Kerrigan. 1991. The painful shoulder during freestyle swimming: An electromyographic cinematographic analysis of twelve muscles. *American Journal of Sports Medicine* 19 (6): 577–582.

Sharp, R.L. 1986. Muscle strength and power as related to competitive swimming. *Journal of Swimming Research* 2 (2): 5–10.

Sharp, R.L., D.L. Costill, and D.S. King. 1983. Power characteristics of swimmers at the 1982 US Senior National Long Course Swimming Championships. Research report. Colorado Springs, CO: American Swimming Coaches Association.

Sharp, R.L., J.P. Troup, and D.L. Costill. 1982. Relationship between power and sprint freestyle swimming. *Medicine and Science in Sports and Exercise* 14:53–56.

Siff, M.C., and Y.V. Verkhoshansky. 1999. *Supertraining*. 4th ed. Denver, CO: Supertraining International.

Spiegelman, T. 2006. Identifying and assessing glenohumeral internal-rotation deficit. *Athletic Therapy Today* 11 (3): 23–25.

Tanaka, H., and T. Swensen. 1998. Impact of resistance training on endurance performance. A new form of cross training? *Sports Medicine* 25:191–200.

Torres, R.R., and J.L. Gomes. 2009. Measurement of glenohumeral internal rotation in asymptomatic tennis players and swimmers. *American Journal of Sports Medicine* 37 (5): 1017–1023.

Toussaint, H.M., and K. Vervoorn. 1990. Effects of high resistance training in water for competitive swimmers. *International Journal of Sports Medicine* 11:228–233.

USA Swimming Task Force on Injury Prevention. 2002. Shoulder injury prevention: A series of exercises for the un-injured swimmer. *USA Swimming's Coaches Quarterly* 8 (4): 1–20.

Vorontsov, A. 2011. Strength and power training in swimming. In *World book of swimming: From science to practice*, ed. L. Seifert, D. Chollett, and I. Mujika, 313–343. New York: Nova Science.

Zatsiorsky, V.M., and W.J. Kraemer. 2006. *The science and practice of strength training*. 2nd ed. Champaign, IL: Human Kinetics.

Chapter 21

Aiking, H., M.B. van Acker, R.J. Scholten, J.F. Feenstra, and H.A. Valkenburg. 1994. Swimming pool chlorination: A health hazard? *Toxicology Letters* 72 (1–3): 375–380.

American Academy of Pediatrics, Committee on Sports Medicine and Fitness. 2000. Intensive training and sports specialization in young athletes. *Pediatrics* 106:154–157.

Bak, K. 2010. The practical management of swimmer's painful shoulder: Etiology, diagnosis, and treatment. *Clinical Journal of Sport Medicine* 20 (5): 386–390.

Blimkie, C.J., S. Rice, C.E. Webber, J. Martin, D. Levy, and C.L. Gordon. 1996. Effects of resistance training on bone mineral content and density in adolescent females. *Canadian Journal of Physiology and Pharmacology* 74:1025–33.

Cammann, K., and K. Hubner. 1995. Trihalomethane concentrations in swimmers' and bath attendants' blood and urine after swimming or working in indoor swimming pools. *Archives of Environmental Health* 50 (1): 61–65.

Chan, G.M. 1991. Dietary calcium and bone mineral status of children and adolescents. *American Journal of Diseases of Children* 145:631–634.

Drobnic, F., A. Freixa, P. Casan, J. Sanchis, and X. Guardino. 1996. Assessment of chlorine exposure in swimmers during training. *Medicine and Science in Sports and Exercise* 28 (2): 271–274.

Duchateau, J., and K. Hainaut. 1984. Isometric or dynamic training: Differential effects on mechanical properties of a human muscle. *Journal of Applied Physiology: Respiratory, Environmental and Exercise Physiology* 56 (2): 296–301.

Faigenbaum, A., W. Kraemer, C.J. Blimkie, I. Jeffreys, L. Micheli, M. Nitka, and T.W. Rowland. 2009. Youth resistance training: Updated position statement paper from the National Strength and Conditioning Association. *Journal of Strength and Conditioning Research* 23 (5 suppl.): S60–S79.

French, S.A., J.A. Fulkerson, and M. Story. 2000. Increasing weight-bearing physical activity and calcium intake for bone mass growth in children and adolescents: A review of intervention trials. *Preventive Medicine* 31 (6): 722–731.

Geithner, C., M. Thomis, B. Vanden Eynde, H.H. Maes, R.J. Loos, M. Peeters, A.L. Claessens, R. Vlietinck, R.M. Malina, and G.P. Beunen. 2004. Growth in peak aerobic power during adolescence. *Medicine and Science in Sports and Exercise* 36 (9): 1616–1624.

Golden, N.H. 2002. A review of the female athlete triad (amenorrhea, osteoporosis and disordered eating). *International Journal of Adolescent Medi-*

cine and Health 14 (1): 9–18.

Helenius, I.J., P. Rytila, T. Metso, T. Haahtela, P. Venge, and H.O. Tikkanen. 1998. Respiratory symptoms, bronchial responsiveness, and cellular characteristics of induced sputum in elite swimmers. *Allergy* 53 (4): 346–352.

Kanders, B., D.W. Dempster, and R. Lindsay. 1998. Interaction of calcium nutrition and physical activity on bone mass in young women. *Journal of Bone Mineral Research* 3: 145–149.

Kohrt, W.M., S.A. Bloomfield, K.D. Little, M.E. Nelson, and V.R. Yingling. 2004. American college of sports medicine position stand: Physical activity and bone health. *Medicine and Science in Sports and Exercise* 36 (11): 1985–1996.

Lloyd, T., M.B. Andon, N. Rollings, J.K. Martel, J.R. Landis, L.M. Demers, D.F. Eggli, K. Kieselhorst, and H.E. Kulin. 1993. Calcium supplementation and bone mineral density in adolescent girls. *Journal of the American Medical Association* 270:841–844.

Malina, R. 2010. Early sport specialization: Roots, effectiveness, risks. *Current Sports Medicine Reports* 9 (6): 364–371.

McMaster, W.C., and J. Troup. 1993. A survey of interfering shoulder pain in United States competitive swimmers. *American Journal of Sports Medicine* 21 (1): 67–70.

Metzl, J.D., and C. Shookhoff. 2002. *The young athlete: A sports doctor's complete guide for parents.* New York: Hachette Book Group.

Nattiv, A., A. Loucks, M. Manore, C. Sanborn, J. Sundgot Borgen, and M. Warren. 2007. American College of Sports Medicine position stand: The female athlete triad. *Medicine and Science in Sports and Exercise* 39 (10): 1867–1882.

Nichols, D.L., C.F. Sanborn, and A.M. Love. 2001. Resistance training and bone mineral density in adolescent females. *Journal of Pediatrics* 139:494–500.

Nowson, C.A., R.M. Green, J.L. Hopper, A.J. Sherwin, D. Young, B. Kaymakci, C.S. Guest, M. Smid, R.G. Larkins, and J.D. Wark. 1997. A co-twin study of the effect of calcium supplementation on bone density during adolescence. *Osteoporosis International* 7:219–225.

Pettersson, U., P. Nordstrom, H. Alfredson, K. Henriksson-Larsen, and R. Lorentzon. 2000. Effect of high impact activity on bone mass and size in adolescent females: A comparative study between two different types of sports. *Calcified Tissue International* 67 (3): 207–214.

Reiff, D.B., N.B. Choudry, N.B. Pride, and P.W. Ind. 1989. The effect of prolonged submaximal warm-up exercise on exercise-induced asthma. *American Review of Respiratory Disease* 139:479–484.

Rizzoli, R., M.L. Bianchi, M. Garabedian, H.A.

McKay, and L.A. Moreno. 2010. Maximizing bone mineral mass gain during growth for the prevention of fractures in the adolescents and the elderly. *Bone* 46 (2): 294–305.

Silva, C., T.B.L. Goldberg, A. Teixeira, and J. Dalmas. 2011. The impact of different types of physical activity on total and regional bone mineral density in young Brazilian athletes. *Journal of Sports Sciences* 29 (3): 227–234.

Sinha, T., and A.K. David. 2003. Recognition and management of exercise-induced bronchospasm. *American Family Physician* 67 (4): 769–774.

USA Swimming. 2010. Organizing the wet side. www.usaswimming.org/ViewMiscArticle.aspx?TabId=1781&Alias=Rainbow&Lang=en&mid=7897&ItemId=5088.

Valovich McLeod, T., L. Decoster, K. Loud, L. Micheli, J.T. Parker, M. Sandrey, and C. White. 2011. National Athletic Trainers Association position statement: Prevention of pediatric overuse injuries. *Journal of Athletic Training* 46 (2): 206–220.

Wade, G.N., J.E. Schneider, and H.Y. Li. 1996. Control of fertility by metabolic cues. *American Journal of Physiology* 270:E1–E19.

Whalen, R.T., and D.R. Carter. 1988. Influence of physical activity on the regulation of bone density. *Journal of Biomechanics* 21:825–837.

Williams, A., M.P. Schwellnus, and T. Noakes. 2004. Increased concentration of chlorine in swimming pool water causes exercise-induced bronchoconstriction (EIB). *Medicine and Science in Sports and Exercise* 36 (5): supplement abstract 2046.

Witzke, K.A., and C.M. Snow. 2000. Effects of plyometric jump training on bone mass in adolescent girls. *Medicine and Science in Sports and Exercise* 32 (6): 1051–1057.

Chapter 22

American College of Sports Medicine. 1978. Position stand on the recommended quantity and quality of exercise for developing and maintaining fitness in healthy adults. *Medicine and Science in Sports and Exercise* 10:vii–x.

Coggan, A.R., R.J. Spina, M.A. Rogers, D.S. King, M. Brown, P.M. Nemeth, and J.O. Holloszy. 1990. Histochemical and enzymatic characteristics of skeletal muscle in master athletes. *Journal of Applied Physiology* 68:1896–1901.

Elsawy, B., and K. Higgins. 2010. Physical activity guidelines for older adults. *American Family Physician* 81 (1): 55–59.

Evans, S.L., K.P. Davy, E.T. Stevenson, and D.R. Seals. 1995. Physiological determinants of 10-km performance in highly trained female runners of different ages. *Journal of Applied Physiology* 78:1931–1941.

Gibbons, R.J., G.J. Balady, J.T. Bricker, B.R. Chaitman, G.F. Fletcher, V.F. Froelicher, D.B. Mark, B.D. McCallister, A.N. Mooss, M.G. O'Reilly, W.L. Winters Jr., R.J. Gibbons, E.M. Antman, J.S. Alpert, D.P. Faxon, V. Fuster, G. Gregoratos, L.F. Hiratzka, A.K. Jacobs, R.O. Russell, and S.C. Smith Jr. 2002. ACC/AHA 2002 guideline update for exercise testing, summary article: A report of the American College of Cardiology/ American Heart Association Task Force on Practice Guidelines (Committee to Update the 1997 Exercise Testing Guidelines). *Circulation* 106 (14): 1883–1892.

Gillespie, L.D., M.C. Robertson, W.J. Gillespie, S.E. Lamb, S. Gates, R.G. Cumming, and B.H. Howe. 2009. Interventions for preventing falls in older people living in the community. *Cochrane Database System Review* 2:CD007146.

Hart, L.E., D.A. Haaland, D.A. Bariubeau, I.M. Mukovozov, and T.F. Sablijic. 2008. The relationship between exercise and osteoarthritis in the elderly. *Clinical Journal of Sports Medicine* 18:508–521.

Institute of Medicine of the National Academies of Science. 2002. *Dietary reference intakes for energy, carbohydrate, fiber, fat, fatty acids, cholesterol, protein and amino acids (macronutrients)*, 880–935. Washington DC: National Academy Press.

Lee, I.M., L. Djousse, H.D. Sesso, L. Wang, and J.E. Buring. 2010. Physical activity and weight gain prevention. *Journal of the American Medical Association* 303:1173–1179.

Maffulli, N., V. Testa, and G. Capasso. 1994. Anaerobic threshold determination in master endurance runners. *Journal of Sports Medicine and Physical Fitness* 34:242–249.

Mountjoy, M., A. Junge, J.M. Alonso, L. Engebretsen, I. Dragan, D. Gerrard, M. Kouidri, E. Luebs, S.F. Moradi, and J. Dvorak. 2010. Sport injuries and illnesses in the 2009 FINA World Aquatic Championships. *British Journal of Sports Medicine* 44:522–527.

Mozaffarian, D., C.D. Furberg, B.M. Psaty, and D. Siscovick. 2008. Physical activity and incidence of atrial fibrillation in older adults: The cardiovascular health study. *Circulation* 118 (8): 800–807.

Owen, N., G.N. Healy, C.E. Matthews, and D.W. Dunstan. 2010. Too much sitting: The population health science of sedentary behavior. *Exercise and Sport Sciences Reviews* 38 (3): 105–113.

Pelliccia, A., B.J. Maron, F.M. Di Paolo, A. Biffi, F.M. Quattrini, C. Pisicchio, A. Roselli, S. Caselli, and F. Culasso. 2005. Prevalence and clinical significance of left atrial remodeling in competitive athletes. *Journal of the American College of Cardiology* 46 (4): 690–696.

Robinson, S., D.B. Dill, R.D. Robinson, S.P. Tzankoff, and J.A. Wagner. 1976. Physiological aging of champion runners. *Journal of Applied Physiology* 41:46–51.

Salzman, B. 2010. Gait and balance disorder in older adults. *American Family Physician* 82 (1): 61–68.

Sorokin, A.V., C.G. Araujo, S. Zweibel, and P.D. Thompson. 2011. Atrial fibrillation in endurance-trained athletes. *British Journal of Sports Medicine* 45 (3): 185–188.

Tanaka, H., C.A. DeSouza, P.P. Jones, E.T. Stevenson, K.P. Davy, and D.R. Seals. 1997. Greater rate of decline in maximal aerobic capacity with age in physically active vs. sedentary healthy women. *Journal of Applied Physiology* 83:1947–1953.

Tanaka, H., F.A. Dinenno, K.D. Monahan, C.M. Clevenger, C.A. DeSouza, and D.R. Seals. 2000. Aging, habitual exercise, and dynamic arterial compliance. *Circulation* 102:1270–1275.

Tanaka, H., K.D. Monahan, and D.R. Seals. 2001. Age-predicted maximal heart rate revisited. *Journal of the American College of Cardiology* 37:153–156.

Tanaka, H., and D.R. Seals. 1997. Age and gender interactions in physiological functional capacity: Insight from swimming performance. *Journal of Applied Physiology* 82:846–851.

Tanaka, H., and D.R. Seals. 2003. Dynamic exercise performance in masters athletes: Insight into the effects of primary human aging on physiological functional capacity. *Journal of Applied Physiology* 95:2152–2162.

Tanaka, H., and D. Seals. 2008. Endurance exercise performance in masters athletes: Age-associated changes & underlying physiological mechanisms. *Journal of Physiology* 586 (pt.1):55–63.

Trappe, S.W., D.L. Costill, W.J. Fink, and D.R. Pearson. 1995. Skeletal muscle characteristics among distance runners: A 20-year follow-up study. *Journal of Applied Physiology* 78:823–829.

U.S. Department of Health and Human Services. 1996. *Physical activity and health: A report of the surgeon general*. Atlanta, GA: U.S. Department of Health and Human Services.

U.S. Department of Health and Human Services. 2008. *2008 physical activity guidelines for Americans*. www.health.gov/paguidelines/report/default.aspx.

Whitten, P. 2010. Do swimmers live longer? *USMS Swimmer* 6 (3): 34–36.

Chapter 23

Atkinson, G., S. Fullick, C. Grindey, D. MacLaren, and J. Waterhouse. 2008. Exercise, energy balance and the shift worker. *Sports Medicine* 38 (8): 671–685.

Bar, P.R., and G.J. Amelink. 1997. Protection against muscle damage exerted by oestrogen: Hormonal or antioxidant action? *Biochemical Society Transactions* 25:50–54.

Beard, J., and B. Tobin. 2000. Iron status and exercise. *American Journal of Clinical Nutrition* 72 (2): 594S–597S.

Bemben, D.A., R.A. Boileau, J.M. Bahr, R.A. Nelson, and J.E. Misner. 1992. Effects of oral contraceptives on hormonal and metabolic responses during exercise. *Medicine and Science in Sports and Exercise* 24:434–441.

Bemben, D.A., P.C. Salm, and A.J. Salm. 1995. Ventilatory and blood lactate responses to maximal treadmill exercise during the menstrual cycle. *Journal of Sports Medicine and Physical Fitness* 35:257–262.

Benardot, D. 2007. Timing of energy and fluid intake: New concepts for weight control and hydration. *ACSM's Health & Fitness Journal* 11 (4): 13–19.

Bonen, A., F.J. Haynes, and T.E. Graham. 1991. Substrate and hormonal responses to exercise in women using oral contraceptives. *Journal of Applied Physiology* 70:1917–1927.

Brownlie, T., V. Utermohlen, P.S. Hinton, and J.D. Haas. 2004. Tissue iron deficiency without anemia impairs adaptation in endurance capacity after aerobic training in previously untrained women. *American Journal of Clinical Nutrition* 79:437–443.

Byrne, S., and N. McLean. 2002. Elite athletes: Effects of the pressure to be thin. *Journal of Science and Medicine in Sport* 5:80–94.

Casazza, G.A., S.H. Suh, B.F. Miller, F.M. Navazio, and G.A. Brooks. 2002. Effects of oral contraceptives on peak exercise capacity. *Journal of Applied Physiology* 93:1698–1702.

Carter, A., J. Dobridge, and A.C. Hackney. 2001. Influence of estrogen on markers of muscle tissue damage following eccentric exercise. *Fiziologiia Cheloveka* 27:133–137.

Clarkson, P., and E.M. Haymes. 1995. Exercise and mineral status of athletes: Calcium, magnesium, phosphorus, and iron. *Medicine and Science in Sports and Exercise* 27:831–843.

Clement, D.B., and R.C. Asmundson. 1982. Nutritional intake and hematological parameters in endurance runners. *Physician Sports Medicine* 10:37–43.

Cobb, K.L., L.K. Bachrada, G. Greendale, R. Marcus, R.M. Neer, J. Nieves, M.F. Sowers, B.W. Brown Jr., G. Gopalakrishman, C. Luetters, H.K. Tanver, B. Ward, and J.L. Kelsey. 2003. Disordered eating, menstrual irregularity, and bone mineral density in female runners. *Medicine Science in Sport and Exercise* 35 (5): 711–719.

Constantini, N.W., G. Dubnov, and C.M. Lebrun. 2005. The menstrual cycle and sport performance. *Clinics in Sport Medicine* 24:e51–e82.

Cook, J.D. 2005. Diagnosis and management of iron-deficiency anaemia. *Best Practice & Research Clinical Haematology* 18 (2): 319–332.

Deakin, V. 2000. Iron depletion in athletes. In *Clinical sports nutrition*. 2nd ed. Ed. L. Burke and V. Deakin, 273–305. Roseville, NSW, Australia: McGraw-Hill Australia.

De Souza, M.J., M.S. Maguire, K.R. Rubin, and C.M. Maresh. 1990. Effects of menstrual phase and amenorrhea on exercise performance in runners. *Medicine and Science in Sports and Exercise* 22 (5): 575–580.

Deutz, B., D. Benardot, D. Martin, and M. Cody. 2000. Relationship between energy deficits and body composition in elite female gymnasts and runners. *Medicine and Science in Sports and Exercise* 32 (3): 659–668.

DiSantolo, M., G. Stel, G. Banfi, F. Gonano, and S. Cauci. 2008. Anemia and iron status in young fertile non-professional female athletes. *European Journal Applied Physiology* 102:703–709.

Dorflinger, L. 1985. Relative potency of progestins used in oral contraceptives. *Contraception* 3 (6): 557–570.

Dulloo, A.G., and C. Girardier. 1990. Adaptive changes in energy expenditure during refeeding following low-calorie intake: Evidence for a specific metabolic component favoring fat storage. *American Journal of Clinical Nutrition* 52:415–420.

Dusek, T. 2001. Influence of high intensity training on menstrual cycle disorders in athletes. *Croatian Medical Journal* 42:79–82.

Eichner, E.R. 2001. Fatigue of anemia. *Nutrition Reviews* 59 (1): S1–S12.

Fogteloo, A.J., H. Pijl, F. Roelfsema, M. Frolich, and A.E. Meinders. 2004. Impact of meal time and frequency on the twenty-four-hour leptin rhythm. *Hormone Research* 62 (2): 71–78.

Frankovich, R.J., and C. Lebrun. 2000. Menstrual cycle, contraception, and performance. *Clinics in Sports Medicine* 19 (2): 251–271.

Godsland, I.F., D. Crook, and V. Wynn. 1992. Clinical and metabolic considerations of long-term oral contraceptive use. *American Journal of Obstetrics and Gynecology* 166:1955–1964.

Greenblaat, R.B. 1985. Oral contraceptives: The state of the art. *Clinical Therapeutics* 8:6–27.

Hawley J.A., and L.M. Burke. 1997. Effect of meal frequency and timing on physical performance. *British Journal of Nutrition* 77:S91–S103.

Hawley, J.A., and M.M. Williams. 1991. Dietary intakes of age-group swimmers. *British Journal of Sports Medicine* 25 (3): 154–158.

Huisveld, I.A., J.E.H. Haspers, and M.J. Bernink. 1983. The effect of oral contraceptives and exercise on hemostatic and fibrinolytic mechanisms in trained women. *International Journal of Sports Medicine* 4:97–103.

Hurrell, R.F. 1997. Bioavailability of iron. *European Journal of Clinical Nutrition* 51:S4–S8.

Institute of Medicine. 2001. *Dietary reference intakes: Applications in dietary assessment.* Washington DC: National Academy Press.

Iwao, S., K. Mori, and Y. Sato. 1996. Effects of meal frequency on body composition during weight control in boxers. *Scandinavian Journal of Medicine & Science in Sports* 6 (5): 265–272.

Kabasakalis, A., K. Kalitsis, G. Tsalis, and V. Mougios. 2007. Imbalanced nutrition of top-level swimmers. *International Journal Sports Medicine* 28:780–785.

Kim, S.H., H.Y.P. Kim, W.K. Kim, and O.J. Park. 2002. Nutritional status, iron-deficiency-related indices, and immunity in female athletes. *Nutrition* 18 (1): 86–90.

Kleiner, S.M. 1995. The role of meat in an athlete's diet: Its effect on key macro- and micronutrients. *Sports Science Exchange* 8:1–8.

Larsen, P.R. H.M. Kronenberg, S. Melmed, and K.S. Polonsky. 2003. *Williams textbook of endocrinology.* Philadelphia: Saunders.

Lebrun, C.M., D.C. McKenzie, J.C. Prior, and J.E. Taunton. 1995. Effects of menstrual cycle phase on athletic performance. *Medicine and Science in Sports and Exercise* 27:437–444.

Lebrun, C.M., M.A. Petit, D.C. McKenzie, J.E. Taunton, and J.C. Prior. 2003. Decreased maximal aerobic capacity with use of a triphasic oral contraceptive in highly active women: A randomized controlled trial. *British Journal of Sports Medicine* 37:315–320.

Louis-Sylvestre, J., A. Lluch, F. Neant, and J.E. Blundell. 2003. Highlighting the positive impact of increasing feeding frequency on metabolism and weight management. *Forum Nutrition* 56:126–128.

Lynch, N.J. and M.A. Nimmo. 1998. Effects of menstrual cycle and oral contraceptive use on intermittent exercise. *European Journal of Applied Physiology* 78:565–572.

McMurray, R.G., M.F. Mottola, and L.A. Wolfe. 1993. Recent advances in understanding maternal and fetal responses to exercise. *Medicine and Science in Sports and Exercise* 25:1305–1321.

McNeill, A.W., and E. Mozingo. 1981. Changes in the metabolic cost of standardized work associated with the use of an oral contraceptive. *Journal of Sports Medicine* 21:238–244.

Melby, C.M., and M. Hickey. 2005. Energy balance and body weight regulation. *Sports Science Exchange* 18:2.

Mistlberger, R.E., and D.J. Skene. 2005. Nonphotic entrainment in humans? *Journal of Biological Rhythms* 20 (4): 339–352.

Mooij, P.N.M., C.M.G. Thomas, W.H. Doesburg, and T.K.A.B. Eskes. 1992. The effects of oral contraceptives and multivitamin supplementation on serum ferritin and hematological parameters. *International Journal of Clinical Pharmacology and Therapeutics* 30:57–62.

Nattiv, A., A.B. Loucks, M.M. Manore, C.F. Sanborn, J. Sungot-Borgen, and M.P. Warren. 2007. American College of Sports Medicine position stand: The female athlete triad. *Medicine and Science in Sports and Exercise* 39 (10): 1867–1882.

O'Toole, M.L., W.D.B. Hiller, M.S. Roalstad, and P.S. Douglas. 1988. Haemolysis during triathlon races: Its relation to distance. *Medicine and Science in Sports and Exercise* 3:272–275.

Ousley-Pahnke, L., D.R. Black, and R.J. Gretebeck, 2001. Dietary intake and energy expenditure of female collegiate swimmers during decreased training prior to competition. *Journal of the American Dietetics Association* 101 (3): 351–353.

Risser, W.L., and J.M. Risser. 1990. Iron deficiency in adolescents and young adults. *Physician Sports Medicine* 18:87–101.

Rockwell, M., and P. Hinton. 2005. Understanding iron. *Training and Conditioning* 15 (8):19–25.

Rosenberg, M. 1998. Weight change with oral contraceptive use and during the menstrual cycle. *Contraception* 58:45–49.

Sanborn, C.F., B.J. Martin, and W.W. Wagner Jr. 1982. Is athletic amenorrhea specific to runners? *American Journal of Obstetrics and Gynecology* 143:859–861.

Shaskey, D.J., and G.A. Green. 2000. Sports haematology. *Sports Medicine* 29:27–38.

Sherwood, L. 2008. *Human physiology: From cells to systems.* 8th ed. Belmont, CA: Cengage Learning.

Sinclair, L.M. and P.S. Hinton. 2005. Prevalence of iron deficiency with and without anemia in recreationally active men and women. *Journal of the American Dietetic Association* 105:975–978.

Suh, S.H., G.A. Cassazza, M.A. Horning, B.F. Miller, and G.A. Brooks. 2003. Effects of oral contraceptives on glucose flux and substrate oxidation rates during rest and exercise. *Journal of Applied Physiology* 94:285–294.

Sungot-Borgen, J., and M.K. Torstveit. 2004. Prevalence of eating disorders in elite athletes is higher than in the general population. *Clinical Journal of Sports Medicine* 14:25–32.

Thompson, H.S., J.P. Hyatt, M.J. DeSouza, and P.M. Clarkson. 1997. The effects of oral contraceptives on delayed onset muscle soreness following exercise. *Contraception* 56:59–65.

Torstveit, M.K., and J. Sungot-Borgen. 2005. The female athlete triad exists in both elite athletes and controls. *Medicine and Science in Sports and Exercise* 37:1449–1459.

Troup, J.P. 1990. *International Center for Aquatic Research annual: Studies by the International Center for Aquatic Research 1989–1990.* Colorado Springs, CO: United States Swimming Press.

VanHeest, J.L. 1996. Energy expenditure of elite female swimmers during heavy training and taper. In *Biomechanics and medicine in swimming VII,* ed. J.P. Troup, A.P. Hollander, D. Strasse, S.W. Trappe, J.M. Cappaert, and T.A. Trappe, 241–246. London: E & FN Spon.

VanHeest, J.L., C.D. Rodgers, C.E. Mahoney, and M.J. DeSouza. 2014. Ovarian suppression impairs sport performance in junior elite female swimmers. *Medicine and Science in Sports and Exercise* 48:156–166.

VanHeest, J.L., and C.E. Mahoney. 2007. Female athletes: Factors impacting successful performance. *Current Sports Medicine Reports* 6:190–194.

VanHeest, J.L., and K. Ratliff. 1997. Incidence of poor iron status in national caliber swimmers. *Medicine and Science in Sports and Exercise* 29 (5): 217.

VanHeest, J.L., and K. Ratliff. 1998. Hematological and hormonal changes in elite female swimmers. *Medicine and Science in Sports and Exercise* 30 (5): 173.

Volpe, S.L. 2010. Iron and enhanced performance in adolescents. *American Journal of Lifestyle Medicine* 4:457–461.

Weight, L.M, P. Jacobs, and T.D. Noakes. 1992. Dietary iron deficiency and sports anemia. *British Journal of Sports Nutrition* 68:253–260.

Zietz, B., S. Schnabl, M. Nerlich, J. Schoelmerich, and A. Schaeffler. 2009. Nutritional composition of different training stages in young female athletes (swimming) and association with leptin, IGF-1 and estradiol. *Experimental Clinical Endocrinology and Diabetes* 117:283–288.

Zoller, H., and W. Vogel. 2004. Iron supplementation in athletes: First do no harm. *Nutrition* 20 (7–8): 615–619.

Chapter 25

Burkett, B., L. Malone, and D. Daly. 2003. 100m race strategy comparison between Olympic and visually impaired Paralympic swimmers. *Journal of Science and Medicine in Sport,* 6 (4, supplement 1): 80.

Burkett, B., and R. Mellifont. 2008. Sport science and coaching in Paralympic swimming. *International Journal of Sports Science & Coaching* 3 (1): 105–112.

Burkett, B., R. Mellifont, and B. Mason. 2010. The influence of swimming start components for selected Olympic and Paralympic swimmers. *Journal of Applied Biomechanics* 26 (2): 134–141.

Daly, D., S. Djobova, L. Malone, Y. Vanlandewijck, and R. Steadward. 2003. Swimming speed patterns and stroking variables in the Paralympic 100-m freestyle. *Adapted Physical Activity Quarterly* 20 (3): 260–278.

Daly, D., L. Malone, D. Smith, Y. Vanlandewijck, and R. Steadward. 2001. The contribution of starting, turning, and finishing to total race performance in male Paralympic swimmers. *Adapted Physical Activity Quarterly* 18 (3): 316–333.

Fulton, S., D. Pyne, W. Hopkins, and B. Burkett. 2009. Variability and progression in competitive performance of Paralympic swimmers. *Journal of Sports Sciences* 27 (5): 535–539.

Lyttle, A.D., B.A. Blanksby, B.C. Elliott, and D.G. Lloyd. 2000. Net forces during tethered simulation of underwater streamlined gliding and kicking techniques of the freestyle turn. *Journal of Sports Sciences* 18 (10): 801–807.

Mason, B., and J. Cossor. 2000. What can we learn from competition analysis? *Proceedings of XVIII International Symposium on Biomechanics in Sports,* ed. Y. Hong, R. Saunders, and D. Johns. Hong Kong: Department of Sports Science and Physical Education, Chinese University of Hong Kong.

Osborough, C.D., C.J. Payton, and D.J. Daly. 2009. Relationships between the front crawl stroke parameters of competitive unilateral arm amputee swimmers, with selected anthropometric characteristics. *Journal of Applied Biomechanics* 25 (4): 304–312.

Pyne, D.B., C.B. Trewin, and W. Hopkins. 2004. Progression and variability of competitive performance of Olympic swimmers. *Journal of Sports Sciences* 22:613–620.

Index

Note: The italicized *f* and *t* following page numbers refer to figures and tables, respectively.

About the Editors

Scott Riewald, PhD, is the U.S. Olympic Committee's winter sport high-performance director. He works closely with eight winter sport national governing bodies to coordinate sport science and medical services for their athletes. He has served as the biomechanics director for USA Swimming at the U.S. Olympic Training Center in Colorado Springs. In this role, he was part of an international biomechanics research team at the Sydney 2000 Olympic Games and provided education and services to many of the nation's top swimmers. He has given presentations to athletes and coaches about using science to positively affect performance. Riewald has also been involved in cutting-edge research in evaluating new technologies and swim performance, and he has worked as the sport science director for the United States Tennis Association in Key Biscayne, Florida.

As an undergraduate at Boston University, Riewald was a competitive swimmer and still holds several school and conference records. He was named a GTE Academic All-American his senior year and was later inducted into Boston University's Athletic Hall of Fame. After earning an undergraduate degree in biomedical engineering, he competed in triathlons and coached a masters swimming team. He earned his MS and PhD in biomedical engineering from Northwestern University. Riewald is a certified strength and conditioning specialist (CSCS) and a certified personal trainer. He is coauthor of *Complete Conditioning for Swimming* (Human Kinetics, 2008).

Riewald and his wife, Suzie, live in Colorado Springs, Colorado, with their two children, Maddox and Callie.

Scott A. Rodeo, MD, is a clinician-scientist at the Hospital for Special Surgery in New York City, where he also serves as co-chief of the Sports Medicine and Shoulder Service. His specialty includes treating sport injuries to the knee, shoulder, ankle, and elbow. He also is a professor of orthopedic surgery at Weill Cornell Medical College and co-director of the Tissue Engineering, Regeneration, and Repair Program at the Hospital for Special Surgery. He served as team physician for the 2004, 2008, and 2012 U.S. Olympic swimming teams and is currently the associate team physician for the New York Giants football team. He has been involved with USA Swimming, serving as a chair of their Sports Medicine and Science Committee. Rodeo is also a former competitive swimmer and provides medical support for local swimming programs.

About the Contributors

Dr. James Bauman has been the sport psychologist for University of Virginia athletics since 2011. Previously, he was the sport psychologist at the University of Washington (2009 to 2011), the U.S. Olympic Committee (1999 to 2009), and Washington State University (1991 to 1999). He has provided psychological and high-performance services to collegiate, professional, and Olympic athletes for more than 24 years. He has worked with Olympic athletes and coaches at the 2000 Sydney, 2002 Salt Lake City, 2004 Athens, 2006 Torino, 2008 Beijing, and 2012 London Olympic Games as well as multiple Olympic Trials, World  University Games, Pan American Games, World Cups, and World Championships. He created and developed a working relationship between the Chula Vista Olympic Training Center and the Navy Special Warfare Center in San Diego. He has been the consulting sport psychologist for USA Swimming since 2004 and continues to work with swimmers preparing for the 2016 Rio Olympics. Dr. Bauman has an undergraduate degree in prephysical therapy, a master's degree in education, and a doctorate in psychology. He is a licensed psychologist in Washington, California, and Virginia. Finally, he is a husband and father of four children who have grown into amazing young adults.

 **Brian Blanksby, PhD,** has taught and coached swimming in Australia and the U.S. He has also taught functional anatomy and biomechanics at the University of Western Australia (UWA). While there, Blanksby developed an aquatics program and was head of school for 16 years. He has written more than 250 research and professional papers and books on exercise and sport science—mainly the aquatics area.

Charlene Boudreau spent 17 years in Colorado Springs, Colorado, developing and leading USA Swimming's nutrition education and sports medicine programs. She lectured at numerous national camps and conferences and provided on-site support to athletes and coaches at more than 25 national and international pool and open water championship events and three Olympic Trials. Boudreau created USA Swimming's national blood chemistry testing program and *Nutrition Tracker*, and she went on to serve as the director of sports medicine for U.S. Figure Skating. In 2009 Boudreau was appointed associate director of the sport management program at the University of Colorado in Colorado Springs and was later named executive director of the Partnership for Clean Competition, an antidoping research group founded by the U.S. Olympic Committee, the National Football League, Major League Baseball, and the U.S. Anti-Doping Agency. Boudreau holds advanced degrees in nutrition and exercise science and an MBA in marketing and service management. She is an avid cyclist and finisher of three Ironman triathlons, two 24-Hours of Adrenalin World MTB Championships, and dozens of half and full marathons, including Pikes Peak Ascent and Pikes Peak Marathon. Boudreau currently lectures full-time in the F.C. Manning School of Business at Acadia University in Nova Scotia.

Professor Brendan Burkett (OAM) is a professional engineer, professor in biomechanics, and a Paralympic swimming champion. He competed at four Paralympic Games, winning several medals. Burkett lead the Australian team into the open ceremony at the Sydney 2000 Games. The combination of engineering and human movement qualifications along with sporting experience has given Burkett a solid understanding of biomechanics. Because of his focus on sports technology for people with a disability, Burkett is recognized as the Professional Engineer of the Year by the

Australian Institution of Engineers and part of the Prime Minister's 2020 Summit. His sporting achievements include being an inductee in the Swimming Queensland Hall of Fame and being listed as one of Queensland Q150 sporting legends.

Dr. Morgan A. Busko is currently an internal medicine resident at NYU Langone Medical Center. She obtained her medical degree from NYU School of Medicine in 2014. Busko is a three-time finisher of the Hawaii Ironman World Championship, placing second and third in her age group in 2011 and 2014. She ran track and cross-country for Duke University before taking up swimming and biking on her way to becoming an elite triathlete. Busko has a love for being active and helping others maximize their athlete potential. She has invested her time in research on sports physiology, musculoskeletal injuries, and heat stroke.

Liang Cheng, PhD, received his BE from Tsinghua University in 1983 and his PhD from Dalian University of Technology, China in 1990. He joined the University of Western Australia (UWA) in 1992 as a research associate and has been a Winthrop professor in civil engineering since 2006. Cheng's research areas cover vortex-induced vibrations of offshore structures, sediment transports, flow/structure/seabed interactions, and computational fluid dynamics (CFD) modeling of various industrial flows. Cheng has published widely in his career—about 200 publications—and has won a number of government and industrial awards for his research contributions to the offshore oil and gas industry.

Dr. Jodi Cossor has been performing in the area of swimming biomechanics since 1997, when she began working under the leadership of Dr. Bruce Mason at the Australian Institute of Sport. After five years supporting the Australian swimming team, Cossor moved to the United Kingdom to lead the biomechanical support to British swimming and manage the sports science and medicine team between 2004 and 2008. In 2013, she began working for High Performance Sport New Zealand to assist Swimming New Zealand and the Paralympic swimmers in their preparation for the Rio Olympic and Paralympic Games in 2016. The focus of her postgraduate research has been in the areas of swimming starts, turns, and competition analysis. Cossor has provided race analysis for Australia, Great Britain, and New Zealand at the World Championships, Pan Pacific Championships, European Championships, Commonwealth Games, and Olympic Games since 1998. Over the past five years, she has also helped to update and design race analysis software.

Dr. Courtney Dawson is an orthopaedic surgeon specializing in the care and treatment of sports medicine, knee, and shoulder injuries. She grew up in California and attended UCLA where she was a student athletic trainer before moving to the Pennsylvania State University for medical school. Once she decided to pursue a career in orthopaedic surgery, Dawson went to Boston to complete her residency  training in the Harvard Combined Orthopaedic Surgery Residency Program. Following residency, she spent a year in New York at the Hospital for Special Surgery where she completed a fellowship in Sports Medicine and Shoulder Surgery. During her time in New York, Dawson served as assistant team physician for the New York Mets baseball club and St. Peter's College. She also served as an orthopaedic consultant for the U.S. Open Tennis Championships. Dawson has worked with high school athletes through both the Boston and New York City public school systems.

Her special interests include the treatment of shoulder and knee pain, including rotator cuff pathology and instability, the treatment of early arthritis, fracture care, and sports medicine injuries in athletes of all ages. She is especially interested in the specialized care of the female athlete. Dawson currently serves as a clinical instructor at Harvard Medical School and is an orthopaedic surgeon with the VA Boston Healthcare System.

Kirk Grand graduated from Ohio State University with a degree in evolutionary biology. He then completed his master's degree at Indiana University while studying at the Counsilman Center for the Science of Swimming. While pursuing his degree he was the head senior coach for the Counsilman Center Swim Team and the head boy's swimming coach at Bloomington South High School. He was voted the Indiana State Coach of the year in 2012. Kirk is pursuing his PhD in psychophysiology and is a volunteer assistant for the men's and women's swim team at Auburn University.

Koji Honda completed his BAppSci (exercise and sport science) at the University of Sydney in 2005. He has spent over 10 years providing sport science support to swimmers and coaches; this has included five years working at the Australian Institute of Sport in Swimming Biomechanics, where he also completed his Masters at the University of Sydney. Honda is currently completing a PhD in swimming biomechanics through the University of Western Australia and the Western Australian Institute of Sport, using computational fluid dynamics to evaluate the freestyle swimming stroke.

Sean Hutchison was a 2008 U.S. Olympic team swim coach and two-time Order of IKKOS recipient, an honor that the U.S. Olympic Committee bestows on coaches whose athletes win Olympic medals. Sean is founder of the Aquatic Management Group and current director and former head coach of KING Aquatic Club, which has become a national  powerhouse in swimming. Sean's most recent entrepreneurial endeavor is as CEO and founder of Ikkos, a patent-pending, proven, brain-based movement learning system to help people master movements both athletically and in health care settings.

Matt Keys, PhD, completed his BEng and PhD at the University of Western Australia. He has over 17 years of experience in the offshore oil and gas and offshore renewable sectors, using advanced techniques such as finite element analysis, computational fluid dynamics, and fluid/structure interaction to solve some of the industries more complex problems. As well as being an Australian national finalist in freestyle, Keys has worked with the Western Australian Institute of Sport and the University of Western Australia since 2004 to develop a full-body freestyle simulation of world-class swimmers, using the latest computational fluid dynamics technologies.

Andrew Lyttle, PhD, is a senior sports biochemist at the Western Australian Institute of Sport. Since completing his PhD in swimming biomechanics at the University of Western Australia in 1999, Lyttle has been at the forefront of biomechanics applies and basic research of elite swimmers in Australia. He has been widely published in various peer-reviewed scientific journals and presented the research at numerous international conference on sports biomechanics.

Russell Mark has worked for USA Swimming since 2002, studying countless hours of film and discussing technique with the best coaches and swimmers in the world. With this knowledge, he has worked directly to help the USA national team, including the 2004, 2008, and 2012 Olympic teams, given hundreds of lectures on swimming technique, and contributed to many books and research articles. While swimming at the University of Virginia, Mark graduated with a degree in aerospace engineering. He then pursued a career in engineering, briefly doing work in Pratt & Whitney's experimental military jet engine programs. This unlikely career path has served Mark well in the swimming world. He has used his knowledge in physics, fluid dynamics, and engineering to identify and advise what makes the fastest swimmers.

Dr. Carla B. McCabe is a sports biomechanist at Ulster University and is a member of the Sports and Exercise Sciences Research Institute (SESRI). Her main research areas are aquatics and sports performance. McCabe lectured in biomechanics at the University of Edinburgh from 2011 to 2014, and she formed part of the Human Performance Sciences research team. McCabe was awarded her PhD at the University of Edinburgh in 2008. She was a key member of the Centre of Aquatic Research  and Education (CARE) team. Her work at CARE entailed innovative aquatic research in addition to performance analysis servicing for elite swimmers, international teams, and recreational swimmers. Her interest in aquatic research stemmed from a rich competitive swimming background. This directed McCabe to study sport and exercise sciences (BSc) at the University of Limerick, where she obtained a first class honors and awarded highest achiever at graduation in 2003.

Jordan D. Metzl, MD, is a sports medicine physician at Hospital for Special Surgery, America's premier orthopedic hospital in New York City, New York. Rated as being among New York's top sports medicine doctors by *New York* magazine, Metzl takes care of athletic patients of all ages. He also lectures and teaches extensively both nationally and internationally. Widely published in medical literature, Metzl's research interests include the treatment and prevention of running-related injury, the effectiveness of preventative wellness programs, and the prevention of youth sport injury. The author of bestselling titles, *The Exercise Cure, The Athlete's Book of Home Remedies,* and *Running Strong,* Metzl is the medical columnist for *Triathlete* magazine. He appears in media and print, including the *Today Show, National Public Radio,* and the *New York Times,* discussing fitness and health. Metzl created the Ironstrength Workout featured on RunnersWorld.com, which he teachers throughout the country. He is a 32-time marathon runner and 12-time Ironman finisher.

James W. Miller, MD, FAAFP, practices Family Practice and Sports Medicine in Midlothian, Virginia in private practice he founded in 1994. He also trains medical students as an associate clinical professor at the University of Virginia and Virginia Commonwealth University. He has traveled extensively since 1998 as the national team physician for USA Swimming. He is the chair for the Sports Medicine Task Force for USA Swimming and sits on the International Relations Committee. Miller is a member of the FINA Sports Medicine Committee and serves as the co-editor of sports medicine for the *FINA Aquatic World Magazine.* He was the chair of the FINA World Sports Medicine Congress in 2004 and has lectured at subsequent congresses. He has been a presenter at the IOC World Conference for Prevention of Illness and Injury in Sports in 2011 and 2014 as well as the International Prevention Conference preceding the IOC involvement in 2008. Miller has served as the president of United States Masters Swimming from 2001 to 2005, and he currently sits on the USMS Board of Directors. While still competing in Masters swimming, Miller remains active in coaching Masters swimmers as a Level V masters coach.

Margo Mountjoy, MD, CCFP, FCFP, FACSM, Dip Sport Med, received her medical education and her family medicine training at McMaster University. She obtained her sports medicine specialty degree in Ottawa, Canada in 1990. Mountjoy has worked as a community sports medicine physician in the Health and Performance Centre at the University of Guelph since 1988 where she focused her practice on promoting elite athlete care and physical activity in the general population. In addition, Mountjoy has acted as the national team physician for Synchro Canada for 20 years as well as for the National Endurance Training Centre Athletes (middle- and long-distance track athletes) and the national triathlon and wrestling team training centers. Mountjoy is an assistant clinical professor in the faculty of Family Medicine in the Michael G. DeGroote School of Medicine, McMaster University, where she teaches sports medicine. She is also the director of student and resident affairs. Mountjoy is a member of the FINA Executive Board and holds the portfolio of Sports Medicine. She is also a member of the ASOIF Medical Consultative Group and the IOC Medical Commission Games Group. Mountjoy sits on the TUE committees of the IOC, WADA, and CCES as well as the USADA and IRB anti-doping review boards. Her areas of research focus on elite athlete health and safety.

Iñigo Mujika earned a PhD in Biology of Muscular Exercise at the University of Saint-Etienne, France, and a PhD in Physical Activity and Sport Sciences at the University of the Basque Country. He is also a level III swimming and triathlon coach and coaches world-class triathletes. Mujika's main research interests are in the field of applied sport science and include training methods and recovery from exercise, tapering, detraining, and overtraining. He has also performed extensive research on the physiological aspects associated with sports performance in professional cycling, swimming, running, rowing, tennis, soccer, and water polo. Mujika received research fellowships in Australia, France, and South Africa; published over 100 articles in peer-reviewed journals, 5 books, and 30 book chapters; and has given 260 lectures and communications in international conferences and meetings. He was the senior physiologist at the Australian Institute of Sport and team selector for Triathlon Australia in 2003 and 2004. In 2005, Mujika was the physiologist and trainer for the Euskaltel Euskadi professional cycling team, and from 2006 and 2008, he was head of research and development for the Athletic Club Bilbao. From 2009 to 2013, Mujika was director of physiology and training at Araba Sport Clinic. He was physiologist of the Spanish Swimming Federation in the lead-up to the 2012 London Olympics and head of physiology and training at Euskaltel Euskadi World Tour Cycling Team in 2013. He is now an associate professor at the University of the Basque Country, associate researcher at Finis Terrae University in Chile, and associate editor for the *International Journal of Sports Physiology and Performance*.

Steve Munatones is a nine-time USA Swimming national open water swimming team coach and manager. He is currently the editor-in-chief of *Daily News of Open Water Swimming* and created Oceans Seven, the World Open Water Swimming Association, Openwaterpedia, the WOWSA Awards, *Open Water Swimming Almanac*, *Open Water Swimming* magazine, and the Swimming Is Medicine program. He is also vice president and chief administrator for the International Marathon Swimming Hall of Fame and an honor swimmer in the same organization. He authored the textbook *Open Water Swimming* and has written on open water swimming for *Swimming World* magazine since the 1980s. He is the open water swimming consultant for the *Guinness Book of World Records* and a KAATSU training master instructor. A former water polo player and professional marathon swimmer from Harvard University, he lives in Huntington Beach, California, with his wife and four children.

Dr. Anne Pankhurst is currently a consultant to the United States Tennis Associations Player Development and to the Professional Teachers Registry, as well as several other sports organizations and tennis academies in different nations around the world. She is a qualified physical education teacher and holds an advanced diploma (Exercise Physiology and Biomechanics) and a BA in Developmental Geography from universities in the UK. In addition, she hold a post-graduate diploma in higher education (Sports coaching and Coach Education) from De Montfort University. She recently obtained her PhD, researching the coherence of practices in talent identification and development in young athletes. Pankhurst was director of coach education for the Lawn Tennis Association in the UK for 10 years before becoming manager of coaching education for three years with the USTA in 2006. In 2000, she received the UK Award for Services to Coach Education. Pankhurst's principle interest is good practice for children in sport. She is the author of a number of books and articles on the development of children in sport and has presented on this topic to many seminars and conferences around the world.

Dr. Andrew L. Pipe graduated from Queen's University in 1974. He is chief of the Division of Prevention and Rehabilitation at the University of Ottawa Heart Institute and is a professor in the faculty of medicine at the University of Ottawa. He is currently involved in clinical research assessing new approaches to smoking cessation, strategies designed to facilitate exercise adoption, and novel initiatives to prevent cardiovascular disease. Besides his clinical responsibilities, Pipe has been extensively involved in sport and sports medicine for many years. He served

as a physician at 10 Olympic Games and has been the team physician for Canada's national men's basketball team and national women's soccer team. An associate editor of the *Clinical Journal of Sport Medicine,* he served as chair of the Canadian Centre for Ethics in Sport, Canada's national antidoping organization. He is currently the chair of FINA's Doping Control Review Board and the chair of the WADA Prohibited List Expert Group. Pipe is the recipient of the International Olympic Committee's Award for Sport, Health and Wellbeing and honorary degrees from Queen's University (LLD), Brock University (DSc), and University of Guelph (DSc). In 2002 he was named to the Order of Canada.

Dr. Jennifer L. Reed is currently an associate scientist in the Division of Prevention and Rehabilitation at the University of Ottawa Heart Institute and part-time professor in the faculty of health sciences at the University of Ottawa. She earned a doctorate in kinesiology with a specialization in exercise physiology from Pennsylvania State University in 2012 and a master of education in coaching studies from the University of Victoria in 2007. Dr. Reed is one of Canada's leading exercise physiologists. Her research interests include the role of exercise in cardiovascular

disease prevention and rehabilitation, sports science, and women's health. She is the recipient of the Jan & Ian Craig Cardiac Prevention and Rehabilitation Endowed Fellowship from the University of Ottawa Heart Institute and was awarded the Harold F. Martin Graduate Assistant Outstanding Teaching Award from Pennsylvania State University in 2011. Dr. Reed has been extensively involved in sport for many years. She is NCCP certified and a former competitive swimming coach at the Saanich Commonwealth Place and University of Victoria with Pacific Coast Swimming in Victoria, British Columbia, Canada.

Ross H. Sanders has been a professor and head of exercise and sport science at the University of Sydney in the faculty of health sciences since 2013. His research interests bridge biomechanics and motor control with particular emphasis on aquatic sports. In 2001 he established the Centre for Aquatics Research and Education at the University of Edinburgh. He has supervised eight PhD students specializing in research of aquatic activities.

J.M. Stager received his PhD in Physiology from the Medical Science Program at IU in 1980 and then spent four years as a post-doctoral fellow within the College of Veterinary and Biomedical Sciences at Colorado State University in Ft Collins, Colorado. He was recruited back to Indiana in 1984 to lead the Exercise Physiology program and has been at IU ever since where he currently holds the titles of director of the Counsilman Center for the Science of Swimming, director of the H H Morris Human Performance Laboratories, and professor of Kinesiology at IUB. He runs an active research laboratory and graduate program directed toward the health, safety, and physiology related to swimming and to swimmers of all ages. He has authored and co-authored more than 100 peer reviewed research articles and has made numerous national and international research presentations primarily related to issues pertaining specifically to competitive swimming.

Andrew M. Stewart has an extensive competitive, coaching, scientific, and administrative background in high-performance sport. This background includes representing Scotland at junior level in both swimming and rugby; coaching international swimmers in Scotland and New Zealand; earning a BPhEd/BEd (Hons) from the Scottish School of Physical Education (1986) and a PhD from the University of Otago (1996); and serving as director of the Scottish Institute of Sports Medicine and Sport Science (1997-2000) and general manager of High Performance Sport at Millennium

Institute of Sport and Health, New Zealand (High Performance Sport New Zealand). Stewart also has a vast support history with athletes of different sporting backgrounds around the globe. His service includes head exercise physiologist and chair of Sports Science & Medicine of Great Britain Swimming (1997-2001); an invited research fellow at the United States of America Olympic Training Centre (1992); head exercise physiologist of the New Zealand Swimming Academy (1990-1996); chair of New Zealand Federation of Sports Medicine (Otago) (1994-1995); and conditioning consultant to the Otago Rugby Football Union (1993). Stewart has a renowned international reputation in high-performance sport management and sport science, with over 200 outputs in journal articles, books, Internet publications, conference presentations, and seminars on topics mostly related to training, periodization, tapering, and overtraining and overreaching with national and international athletes from a range of sports but mostly swimming, water polo, rugby union, Australian football, cycling, and tennis. He is currently a professor of Sport and Exercise Science and the director of Research Training in the College of Sport and Exercise Science and the Institute of Sport, Exercise and Active Living (ISEAL), at Victoria University, Melbourne.

Jonathon Stickford, PhD, is a post-doctoral fellow at the Southwest Texas Medical Center in Dallas Texas. He received his PhD in Human Performance from Indiana University. He earned his master's degree in Exercise Physiology from the Department of Kinesiology at Indiana University. He has recently accepted a faculty position at Appalachian State University in Boone, North Carolina.

Jaci L. VanHeest, PhD, is an associate professor of Kinesiology and Educational Psychology and a university teaching fellow at the University of Connecticut. She graduated from Michigan State University in 1993 with a PhD in exercise endocrinology. VanHeest trained as a post-doctoral fellow at the University of Cincinnati in the area of protein chemistry (the Department of Physiology and Biophysics in 1993) and at the University of Colorado Health Sciences Center in the area of body weight regulation (Department of Pediatrics in 1996). She began her tenure at UCONN in 1998, following her work as the director of physiology for USA Swimming at the Olympic Training Center. Her research specialization is in the area of endocrine control of body weight and metabolism.

Timothy Wei is the Richard L. McNeel Professor and dean of engineering at the University of Nebraska, Lincoln. He holds a BS from Cornell, an MS from Lehigh, both in mechanical engineering, and a PhD in aerospace engineering from Michigan. Tim has been on the engineering faculty at Rutgers, RPI, and Nebraska. He is a fellow of ASME, APS, and IMechE. Tim's research interests lie in coupling fundamental fluid dynamics experiments with critically important technologies. One of his favorite projects has been making flow measurements around elite swimmers through a collaboration with the U.S. Olympic swimming movement.

Randall L. Wilber, PhD, is a senior sport physiologist at the U.S. Olympic Training Center in Colorado Springs. In that position, he works closely with Team USA athletes and coaches in the areas of altitude training, heat/humidity acclimatization, blood chemistry analysis, overtraining, international air travel (jet lag), and exercise-induced asthma. In 22 years at the USOC, Wilber has been privileged to work with Olympic and World Champions Michael Phelps (swimming), Missy Franklin (swimming), Allison  Schmitt (swimming), Tyler Clary (swimming), Kristin Armstrong (cycling), Mari Holden (cycling), Alison Dunlap (cycling), Barb Lindquist (triathlon), Sheila Taormina (triathlon), Jenny Simpson (track), Apolo Ohno (speedskating), Derek Parra (speedskating), Joey Cheek (speedskating), Christine Witty (speedskating), Johnny Spillane (Nordic ski) Bill Demong (Nordic ski), and Todd Lodwick (Nordic ski), as well as other notable Olympic medalists Meb Keflezighi (track), Galen Rupp (track), Leo Manzano (track), Shalane Flanagan (track), and Deena Kastor (track). Wilber has been a staff member of Team USA at three Olympics (Athens 2004, Beijing 2008, London 2012); four Winter Olympics (Salt Lake City 2002, Torino 2006, Vancouver 2010, Sochi 2014); two Pan American Games (Santo Domingo 2003, Rio de Janeiro 2007); and multiple World Championships. In addition, he serves as a consultant to the U.S. Navy SEALs on issues related to combat performance at high altitude.

In the area of scholarship, Wilber has authored more than 25 papers in peer-reviewed scientific journals and has written several book chapters in the areas of sports medicine and sport science. He has authored the book Altitude Training and Athletic Performance (Human Kinetics 2004) and co-authored